THE L.M. MONTGOMERY READER

Volume 2: A Critical Heritage

Cover art from the Canadian Children's Favourites edition of
L.M. Montgomery's *A Tangled Web* (1972); used by permission
of McClelland and Stewart

THE
L.M. MONTGOMERY
READER

Volume 2: A Critical Heritage

Edited by Benjamin Lefebvre

UNIVERSITY OF TORONTO PRESS
Toronto Buffalo London

© University of Toronto Press 2014
Toronto Buffalo London
www.utppublishing.com
Printed in Canada

ISBN 978-1-4426-4492-2 (cloth)

Printed on acid-free, 100% post-consumer recycled paper
with vegetable-based inks.

Library and Archives Canada Cataloguing in Publication

The L.M. Montgomery reader / edited by Benjamin Lefebvre.

Includes bibliographical references and indexes.
Contents: v. 2. A critical heritage.
ISBN 978-1-4426-4492-2 (v. 2 : bound)

1. Montgomery, L.M. (Lucy Maud), 1874–1942 – Criticism and interpretation.
I. Lefebvre, Benjamin, 1977–, editor of compilation.
II. Title: A critical heritage.

PS8526.O55Z63538 2014   C813'.52   C2013-905295-X

University of Toronto Press acknowledges the financial assistance to its publishing
program of the Canada Council for the Arts and the Ontario Arts Council.

This book has been published with the help of a grant from the
Canadian Federation for the Humanities and Social Sciences, through the
Awards to Scholarly Publications Program, using funds provided by the
Social Sciences and Humanities Research Council of Canada.

University of Toronto Press acknowledges the financial support of the
Government of Canada through the Canada Book Fund for its publishing activities.

"L.M. Montgomery" is a trademark of Heirs of L.M. Montgomery Inc.
"Anne of Green Gables" is a trademark of the
Anne of Green Gables Licensing Authority Inc.

Every effort has been made to secure permissions for the material reproduced in
this book. Any errors or omissions brought to our attention will be
corrected in subsequent editions of the book.

Contents

Contents

Contents

Acknowledgments

This second volume of *The L.M. Montgomery Reader* is indebted to a number of colleagues and friends whose assistance and encouragement over several years of research are greatly appreciated. I am grateful to Rita Bode, Vanessa Brown, Cecily Devereux, Kelly Norah Drukker, Elizabeth Rollins Epperly, Melanie Fishbane, Carole Gerson, Andrea McKenzie, Mary Henley Rubio, Cynthia Soulliere, Margaret Steffler, and Lorraine York, as well as to two anonymous referees for their advice and feedback and to the authors, periodicals, and publishers who granted me permission to reprint the material included in this volume. I am also grateful to the staff at several university libraries, including Guelph, Laurier, McMaster, Prince Edward Island, and Winnipeg.

At University of Toronto Press, I am grateful to Siobhan McMenemy for her expertise and collegiality, and to· Frances Mundy and Ani Deyirmenjian for their work throughout the volume's production stages. I gratefully acknowledge the Macdonald Stewart Foundation for supporting the Visiting Scholar position at the L.M. Montgomery Institute, University of Prince Edward Island, which I held between 2009 and 2011, and the 2013 Marie Tremaine Fellowship awarded by the Bibliographical Society of Canada / La Société bibliographique du Canada.

My special thanks are for my partner, Jacob Letkemann, for all his support throughout this project; my siblings, Melanie Lefebvre and Jeremy Lefebvre; my siblings-in-law, Éric Lemay and Julie Trépanier; and my five nieces and my nephew. I dedicate this volume to my mother, Claire Pelland Lefebvre, whose integrity and high ideals inspire us all.

Abbreviations

The following abbreviations refer to sources attributed to L.M. Montgomery:

AA   *Anne of Avonlea*. 1909. Toronto: Seal Books, 1996.

AfGG   *After Green Gables: L.M. Montgomery's Letters to Ephraim Weber, 1916–1941*. Edited by Hildi Froese Tiessen and Paul Gerard Tiessen. Toronto: University of Toronto Press, 2006.

AGG   *Anne of Green Gables*. 1908. Toronto: Seal Books, 1996.

AHD   *Anne's House of Dreams*. 1917. Toronto: Seal Books, 1996.

AIn   *Anne of Ingleside*. 1939. Toronto: Seal Books, 1996.

AIs   *Anne of the Island*. 1915. Toronto: Seal Books, 1996.

AP   *The Alpine Path: The Story of My Career*. 1917. Don Mills, ON: Fitzhenry and Whiteside, n.d.

AWP   *Anne of Windy Poplars*. 1936. Toronto: Seal Books, 1996.

BC   *The Blue Castle*. 1926. Toronto: Seal Books, 1988.

BQ   *The Blythes Are Quoted*. Edited by Benjamin Lefebvre. Toronto: Viking Canada, 2009.

CA   *Chronicles of Avonlea*. 1912. Toronto: Seal Books, 1993.

CJLMM, 1   *The Complete Journals of L.M. Montgomery: The PEI Years, 1889–1900*. Edited by Mary Henley Rubio and Elizabeth Hillman Waterston. Don Mills, ON: Oxford University Press, 2012.

Abbreviations

EC	*Emily Climbs*. 1925. Toronto: Seal Books, 1998.
ENM	*Emily of New Moon*. 1923. Toronto: Seal Books, 1998.
EQ	*Emily's Quest*. 1927. Toronto: Seal Books, 1998.
GGL	*The Green Gables Letters from L.M. Montgomery to Ephraim Weber, 1905–1909*. Edited by Wilfrid Eggleston. 1960. Ottawa: Borealis Press, 1981.
GR	*The Golden Road*. 1913. Toronto: Seal Books, 1987.
JLH	*Jane of Lantern Hill*. 1937. Toronto: Seal Books, 1993.
MDMM	*My Dear Mr. M: Letters to G.B. MacMillan from L.M. Montgomery*. Edited by Francis W.P. Bolger and Elizabeth R. Epperly. 1980. Toronto: Oxford University Press, 1992.
MM	*Magic for Marigold*. 1929. Toronto: Seal Books, 1988.
MP	*Mistress Pat*. 1935. Toronto: Seal Books, 1988.
PSB	*Pat of Silver Bush*. 1933. Toronto: Seal Books, 1988.
RI	*Rilla of Ingleside*. 1921. Edited by Benjamin Lefebvre and Andrea McKenzie. Toronto: Viking Canada, 2010.
RV	*Rainbow Valley*. 1919. Toronto: Seal Books, 1996.
SG	*The Story Girl*. 1911. Toronto: Seal Books, 1987.
SJLMM	*The Selected Journals of L.M. Montgomery*, Volume 1: *1889–1910*; Volume 2: *1910–1921*; Volume 3: *1921–1929*; Volume 4: *1929–1935*; Volume 5: *1935–1942*. Edited by Mary Rubio and Elizabeth Waterston. Toronto: Oxford University Press, 1985, 1987, 1992, 1998, 2004.
SR	"Scrapbook of Reviews from Around the World Which L.M. Montgomery's Clipping Service Sent to Her, 1910–1935." L.M. Montgomery Collection, University of Guelph archives.
UJ	Unpublished journals (ten handwritten ledgers), 1889–1942. L.M. Montgomery Collection, Archival and Special Collections, University of Guelph archives.
TW	*A Tangled Web*. 1931. Toronto: Seal Books, 1989.

THE L.M. MONTGOMERY READER

Volume 2: A Critical Heritage

Introduction: A Critical Heritage

BENJAMIN LEFEBVRE

In 2008, the centenary of the publication of *Anne of Green Gables* led to a worldwide celebration of the novel itself, the global reach of its title character, and by extension the literary and cultural legacies of its author, L.M. Montgomery (1874–1942). Several new editions of the novel appeared, in hardcover and in paperback, for adults and for children, including a Modern Library Classics edition introduced by prominent children's literature scholar Jack Zipes and a Penguin Canada hardcover gift edition that was published as part of an extensive "100 Years of Anne" marketing campaign. These editions were joined by several attempts to extend, analyze, and complicate a work of fiction whose popularity had shown no signs of waning in one hundred years. A major biography, several academic studies, two prequels, an annotated facsimile of selected pages from Montgomery's scrapbooks, countless newspaper and magazine articles, and exhibits and conferences all contributed to our collective understanding of novel, character, and author throughout this centenary year. Moreover, a *Globe and Mail* article by Kate Macdonald Butler, one of Montgomery's granddaughters, provided a missing puzzle piece about the author of *Anne*, disclosing publicly for the first time the family's belief that Montgomery's death in 1942 had been a suicide.[1] Throughout 2008, it seemed that Anne – and to a lesser extent Montgomery – was everywhere.

Compared to this massive celebration of the centenary of *Anne of Green Gables* in 2008, the celebration of the centenary of Montgomery's birth in 1974 was decidedly low-key. Two volumes of rediscovered work appeared that year, the first posthumous Montgomery texts since Wilfrid Eggleston's *The Green Gables Letters from L.M. Montgomery to Ephraim Weber, 1905–1909* appeared in 1960: the collection of short stories *The Road to Yesterday* (McGraw–Hill Ryerson), an abridgement of a book-length typescript discovered in Montgomery's papers by Stuart Macdonald (1915–1982), by then her sole surviving son, and *The Alpine Path: The Story of My Career* (Fitzhenry and Whiteside), a reprint of a 25,000-word memoir first serialized in the Toronto magazine *Everywoman's World* in 1917. But neither text makes any reference to the centenary of Montgomery's birth in its prefatory material, and although the unsigned preface to *The Alpine Path* boasts that the volume contains "the most complete source of information about the childhood and early struggles of this accomplished and well-loved Canadian writer," neither book was particularly well received.[2] As well, Francis W.P. Bolger published that year *The Years Before "Anne"* (Prince Edward Island Heritage Foundation), a first and detailed account of Montgomery's writing career prior to the publication of her breakout first novel, drawing on Montgomery's scrapbooks to provide never-before-seen early letters and publications that would lead to *Anne of Green Gables*. Although they were not linked to any kind of organized commemoration of Montgomery, these volumes of rediscovered fiction and non-fiction were a welcome influx of new materials on Canada's most enduringly popular author and began a pattern of rediscovery and reassessment that continues to this day.

By the centenary of her birth in 1974, Montgomery's critical and popular reputation was caught in a fairly odd conundrum: although a number of her novels continued to sell in sufficient numbers to remain in print in Canada, the US, the UK, and Australia, relatively little seems to have been widely known about Montgomery herself during this period. Except for *The Green Gables Letters* and Hilda M. Ridley's biography *The Story of L.M. Montgomery* (1956), the known biographical details consisted mainly of those that Montgomery herself had circulated throughout her career as a best-selling author. As I show in Volume 1 of *The L.M. Montgomery Reader*, subtitled *A Life in Print*, Montgomery went to great lengths to restrict the number of private details – about her age, her birth, her romantic relationships – that were released to the public, preferring for the most part to keep the focus squarely on what she deemed to be the most salient part of her celebrity: her work. That strategy worked only too well: in a 1975 contribution to *Atlantis: A Women's Studies Journal*, Carrie Fredericks wrote that "it has always seemed remarkable to me that the creator of so popular a character as the intelligent, imaginative and accident-prone Anne Shirley ... should herself remain such a mystery to her audience." When writing an article on the centenary of Montgomery's birth in the *Winnipeg Free Press*, Tom Saunders relied exclusively on Eggleston's and Ridley's books for information about the author, ignoring the newly available material in *The Years Before "Anne"* and *The Alpine Path*, but his article ended up having more to do with the writing, publication, and reception of *Anne of Green Gables* than with Montgomery herself – indeed, it appeared under the title "Anne's Author."[3]

Volume 1 of *The L.M. Montgomery Reader* ends with two tribute articles in *The Dalhousie Review* by Ephraim Weber, one of Montgomery's two long-standing correspondents, from 1942 and 1944, and with one of the earliest Anne afterlives – namely, a magazine story based on the first screen version of *Anne of Green Gables*. This second volume, subtitled *A Critical Heritage*, extends this major reassessment of Montgomery's critical reputation from the years since her death to the present day. It does so, first, by discussing the major trends, shifts, and turning points in her reception by academic critics and popular readers, and second, by including a selection of twenty items from the interdisciplinary field of L.M. Montgomery Studies from 1966 to 2012. In selecting materials for this volume, I have opted to include items in full rather than offer a more comprehensive book of excerpts; I have also attempted to provide representative samples of a wide range of primary texts and approaches. Given that several monographs and essay collections focusing exclusively on Montgomery have become important resources for both academic researchers and trade readers, often overshadowing contributions made elsewhere, this volume favours materials that first appeared in academic and non-academic periodicals (particularly ones that have not yet become part of major digital repositories) or in books that encompass a wider range of texts, genres, and authors. I hope this volume will give both experienced and novice Montgomery readers and scholars a solid overview of the critical conversation that has been generated collaboratively since her death in 1942. This ongoing consideration on the part of academic critics and literary journalists traced throughout these two volumes occurred in tandem with marketing strategies throughout and beyond Montgomery's lifetime in the form of reviews and ads in periodicals devoted to the support of the book industry, a facet of her reception history that is the focus of Volume 3 of *The L.M. Montgomery Reader*, subtitled *A Legacy in Review*.

Benjamin Lefebvre

"Not Great Literature"

As I show in the introduction to Volume 1 of *The L.M. Montgomery Reader*, although there certainly were times when Montgomery's work received positive treatment in her lifetime, academic and middlebrow criticism during this period was dominated by men: academics (J.D. Logan, Archibald MacMechan, V.B. Rhodenizer), book review editors (William Arthur Deacon), anthologists (John W. Garvin), and critics (Lorne Pierce, Donald G. French, E.J. Hathaway, Lionel Stevenson). The fact that men controlled the field well into the twentieth century had a marked effect on the creation of a canon of Canadian literature within the walls of the ivory tower. As Carole Gerson notes in her contribution to *Canadian Canons: Essays in Literary Value* (1991), "from approximately 1918 to 1940, the canon of English-language Canadian literature was particularly arbitrary and malleable, governed less by cultural consensus than by the whims and agendas of certain individuals in positions of power." The one consistent pattern throughout this period, she notes further, was that "the position of women writers reached a particularly low ebb." Montgomery may have been mentioned in five of the six foundational studies of Canadian literature published in the 1920s, but relatively little ink was spilled for her or her female contemporaries, who included Isabella Valancy Crawford (1850–1887), Sara Jeannette Duncan (1861–1922), Nellie L. McClung (1873–1951), and Pauline Johnson (1861–1913), compared to the prominent and detailed treatment of the work of Charles G.D. Roberts (1860–1943), Archibald Lampman (1862–1899), Bliss Carman (1861–1929), Duncan Campbell Scott (1862–1947), and W.H. Drummond (1854–1907).[4] Given that the exclusion of female authors from the canon of Canadian literature was fairly systematic, Montgomery's critical decline had less to do with the quality or content of her books than with the fact that they had been written by a woman.

Nor did Montgomery's continued popularity with both adults and children endear her to academics who, like MacMechan in the 1920s, were yearning for a robust Canadian *literature*. In *On Canadian Poetry* (1943), E.K. Brown devoted his initial chapter to "The Problem of a Canadian Literature," portions of which were reprinted in A.J.M. Smith's influential anthology *Masks of Fiction* (1961). Keen to impose an unmistakable hierarchy between "Canadian books" and "Canadian literature," he damned all Canadian novelists who were able to earn a living by their pen, including Gilbert Parker (1862–1932), Mazo de la Roche (1879–1961),

Stephen Leacock (1869–1944), and Morley Callaghan (1903–1990). According to Brown, Montgomery and her contemporaries Ralph Connor (1860–1937) and Robert Service (1874–1958) were all "more or less aggressively unliterary; and their only significance for our inquiry is the proof they offered that for the author who was satisfied to truckle to mediocre taste, living in Canada and writing about Canadian subjects, was perfectly compatible with making an abundant living by one's pen."[5] I am not convinced that this comment actually qualifies as an evaluation of Montgomery's work, for Brown not only refused to look at it in any detail, but he also seemed to be damning her simply because she managed to make a living from her writing without leaving Canada. Moreover, Montgomery was one of only two women whom he included in his list of "popular" authors, and his list of Canadian poets was also startlingly male-heavy: a year after Aida B. McAnn opined that Montgomery's *The Watchman and Other Poems* "reveals the power of a mature mind, rich in wisdom and sympathetic understanding," Brown declared flatly that Crawford was "the only Canadian woman poet of real importance in the last century" and devoted entire chapters to the three poets whom he deemed to be "The Masters" – Lampman, Scott, and E.J. Pratt (1862–1964).[6] This boys' club of Canadian poetry continued in Desmond Pacey's *Ten Canadian Poets* (1958), which included not necessarily "the best poets in Canada" but "the ones ... who have most interested me": Roberts, Carman, Lampman, Scott, Pratt, and Smith, joined by Charles Sangster (1822–1893), F.R. Scott (1899–1985), A.M. Klein (1909–1972), and Earle Birney (1904–1995). This androcentric pattern occurred in tandem with a trend involving Canadian literary critics that Gabriella Åhmansson defines as "a strong critical ambivalence, even a disdain, towards their own literature," which Åhmansson, writing from the perspective of a Swedish scholar, finds puzzling.[7]

Far more ambivalent were the comments of Arthur L. Phelps in his book *Canadian Writers* (1951), which sought to "be friendly and positive without denial of literary standards," according to his preface. He began by echoing the most negative criticism of Montgomery's work, suggesting that "no critic" would believe that she (along with Connor, Service, and de la Roche) had "made a serious contribution to literature," that "by the standards of discriminating literary criticism none of these writers is important," and that their popularity all over the world, in English and in translation, was evidence that Canadians "export only sentimentality and mediocrity." As though trying to justify including such work in his book, he then added that this kind of "soft reading ... has its public and it performs a function for that public." Yet as part of his "confession" that he enjoyed *Anne of Green Gables* when he actually read it, despite finding it "unpretentious to the point of being naive," his conclusion was so tentative that Elizabeth Epperly later referred to it as "a whimsical apology for his own inability to dismiss what his strict literary judgment tells him is popular and inferior":

> Of course the Montgomery popularity has been, in the main, popularity with young girls and their amiable ordinary parents. L.M. Montgomery is a category story teller. She writes girls' stories. Anne of Green Gables is a girl in whom every girl can see a good deal of herself. But what if as well, those of us, male and female, who are not girls, can see in Anne something of that precious commodity, universal girlhood, made into such engaging flesh-and-blood reality that we laugh or weep and are tender with solicitude over the bright vulnerability of happy youth? What if L.M. Montgomery has given to all of us an enduring symbol in Anne? That might put L.M. Montgomery at least among the respectable story tellers.

Phelps ended his chapter by recommending that, "just for fun," readers should "get a copy of *Anne of Green Gables* by L.M. Montgomery and read it," even though, given his analysis of her work, this recommendation could hardly be seen as persuasive. Indeed, for Åhmansson, Phelps's comments are an indication of the ways in which "a critic can become a prisoner of his own critical principles when trying to deal fairly or objectively with a writer whose popularity is undisputable but somehow embarrassing to the literary establishment," given that, "although he defends Montgomery on one level, to him she is no writer at all."[8] Still, it is worth emphasizing that Montgomery was the only woman among the fourteen authors profiled in his book, which also examined the work of Callaghan, Frederick Philip Grove (1879–1948), Leacock, Hugh MacLennan (1907–1990), and W.O. Mitchell (1914–1998).

Yet the dominant sound bite about Montgomery that would recur in the second wave of Canadian literature surveys of the 1960s did not originate in Brown's *On Canadian Poetry* but in Clara Thomas's 1946 book *Canadian Novelists 1920–1945*. In her brief entry on "Lucy Maude [*sic*] Montgomery Macdonald," Thomas summarized Montgomery's life in three paragraphs before adding a brief evaluation of her work that likened her to Louisa May Alcott (1832–1888): "Her first success was in the writing of books for teen-age girls," she claimed, whereas the later books *The Blue Castle* and *A Tangled Web*, "primarily for adults," were "romantic, improbable, whimsical stories, more complex than most of Miss Montgomery's novels."[9] Here we see two patterns that would be repeated for decades to come: the barely perceptible shift from V.B. Rhodenizer's term "stories *of* children" in *A Handbook of Canadian Literature* (1930) to Thomas's "books *for* teen-age girls" in 1946, as well as the reliance on *Anne of Green Gables* to generalize about her entire body of work and the mention of two "less successful" books for adults to note an exception to the pattern. This critical stance is repeated in Sylvestre, Conron, and Klinck's *Canadian Writers / Écrivains canadiens* (1964), in Story's *The Oxford Companion to Canadian History and Literature* (1967), and in Rhodenizer's *Canadian Literature in English* (1965). For his part, however, Rhodenizer linked Montgomery to Duncan and McClung, claiming that these "three women novelists [are] remembered for their humor as well as for their other literary merits," and refusing to fall into the trap that would consider fiction for young people as necessarily inferior: "The excellence of the others as juvenile fiction is shown by the fact that they can be enjoyed by professors and statesmen as well as by teen-age girls."[10]

Throughout these scholarly debates, however, the popularity of Montgomery's work – and of *Anne of Green Gables* in particular – never waned: in 1951, the same year as the publication of Phelps's book, a short biographical sketch appeared in Helen Palk's *The Book of Canadian Achievement*, and a *Maclean's* article by Ian Sclanders offered a glowing (and, at times, excessively sentimental) tribute to Anne and her author, even claiming that "[Montgomery] herself was Anne of Green Gables."[11] Ridley's biography *The Story of L.M. Montgomery*, which Rhodenizer called "a welcome study of an internationally known Canadian novelist," now seems rather superficial, given that Ridley had no access to Montgomery's letters or journals, but it received positive media attention in periodicals such as *Canadian Author & Bookman*, *The Globe and Mail*, and the *Times Literary Supplement*.[12] And in Alice Payne Hackett's *70 Years of Best Sellers 1895–1965* (1967), *Anne of Green Gables* appeared twenty-fourth on the list of best-selling juvenile books during that seventy-year period, with an estimated 812,000 copies sold.[13] Moreover, two booklets published in the 1960s revealed another source of commentary: heritage organizations committed to preserving Montgomery's legacy. *Lucy Maud Montgomery: "The Island's Lady of Stories"* (1963), compiled by the Women's Institute of Springfield, PEI, includes a detailed biographical sketch as well as three of Montgomery's poems and her essay "Prince Edward Island," first published in 1939 and included in Volume 1 of *The L.M. Montgomery Reader*. As well, *L.M. Montgomery as Mrs. Ewan Macdonald of the Leaskdale Manse 1911–1926*, published in 1965, contains a detailed essay by Margaret H. Mustard that offers a loving tribute to Montgomery and her family from the perspective of their former neighbours and parishioners. Extracts from Montgomery's work also appeared in at least three major collections during this period: "Anne's Company Gets Drunk," portions of a chapter in *Anne of Green Gables*, in Will R. Bird's *Atlantic Anthology* (1959); "Calling a Minister," an extract from *Rainbow Valley*, in William Toye's *A Book of Canada* (1962), part of the Collins National Anthologies series published in Great Britain; and "Anne Says Her Prayers," a chapter from *Anne of Green Gables*, in *A Century of Canadian Literature / Un siècle de littérature canadienne* (1967), accompanied by a telling biographical note: "Few Canadian writers have ever been so affectionately regarded outside of their own country as L.M. Montgomery. Her childhood classic *Anne of Green Gables* has remained a best seller for over fifty years."[14]

In the midst of this overwhelmingly male debate about the literary worth and cultural value of Montgomery's work, the first MA thesis devoted to that work, "The Literary Art of L.M. Montgomery," was successfully defended at the Université de Montréal in 1961. Its author was not only a woman but a Roman Catholic nun, Gertrude McLaughlin (1913–1988), who wrote the thesis under the name Sister M. Joanne of Christ. In contrast to surveys that relied on generalizations about *Anne of Green Gables* to make grand pronouncements about Montgomery's entire body of work, McLaughlin's thesis looked at all of her books in detail. Divided into six chapters – "Biographical Sketch," "Style and Technique," "Setting," "Themes and Plots," "Characters," and "Value as Juvenile Literature" – it concluded that Montgomery's work deserves "a permanent place in the heritage of Canadian children":

In her creations she has presented characters who can make Canada and the Canadian child known at home and abroad. As Switzerland has its Heidi, Holland its Hans Brinker, France its Sophie, Scotland its Margaret Ogilvie, the United States its March sisters, and England a whole bevy of children, so Canada has its Anne, a truly Canadian child in an authentic Canadian background. Anne, however, transcends the limits of time and space. She possesses a universal quality which can bring joy to readers unfamiliar with her background ... [Montgomery] was the pioneer writer of Canadian stories for girls. She helped make them aware of the beauty of their country, the nobility of its people, the wealth of opportunity open to each of them. She awakened in them a pride of origin, a pride of achievement, and a pride of land and people.[15]

Given that this kind of detailed study of Montgomery's work had never been undertaken before, McLaughlin's thesis is a stellar achievement, and while to my knowledge it has not been referenced in subsequent scholarship, it should now be acknowledged as an important milestone in the field.

Along with Rhodenizer's *Canadian Literature in English*, the first edition of Carl F. Klinck's *Literary History of Canada: Canadian Literature in English*, also published in 1965, was the next major contribution to Canadian literature criticism. In Klinck's volume, an uneasy tension between perceptions of Montgomery as a writer for adults and as a writer for children appeared in competing chapters. Although Gordon Roper, S. Ross Beharriell, and Rupert Schieder acknowledged in "Writers of Fiction 1880–1920" that *Anne of Green Gables* "turned out to have an appeal far beyond the local and juvenile level," they added that her later work "never came close to the standard or the popularity of the early Anne books." Their comment on *The Green Gables Letters* anticipated a future fascination with Montgomery's life writing while denigrating her fiction further: "Miss Montgomery's letters reveal an intellectual depth and a speculative mind which is seldom evidenced in her fiction, where her successes are largely to be found in her description of the Prince Edward Island scene, and in her sensitive creation of an imaginative little girl, Anne of Green Gables." Marjorie McDowell's chapter on "Children's Books," by contrast, was far more enthusiastic:

The highest survival value, among books of this period, is probably possessed by the "Anne" and "Emily" stories of Lucy Maud Montgomery ... Intensely regional, her stories manoeuvre their episodes on a flowing tide of description. Idiosyncratic characters are rendered in loving detail; Scottish tradition, Calvinistic influence, and rural habits of individualism all play their parts. Domestic incident, handled with whimsical humour and gentle idealism, holds the reader's attention ... Young readers, moreover, falling under the spell of the early books, read on into later, weaker variants of this theme of girlhood growing into womanhood, without losing their affection for this lovely world. All told, the corpus of L.M. Montgomery's work represents a real, if modest, triumph in the history of Canadian letters and her place in the record is assured.[16]

The final word on Montgomery in Klinck's edited volume, however, appeared in the frequently republished conclusion to *Literary History of Canada* by Northrop Frye (1912–1991), who was either unaware of or indifferent to the baggage surrounding Montgomery's texts when he included *Anne of Green Gables* along with Leacock's *Sunshine Sketches of a Little Town* (1912), Louis Hémon's *Maria Chapdelaine* (1913), and Mitchell's *Jake and the Kid* (1961) in a list of texts that fit the parameters of what he called the "pastoral myth," which he claimed was "associated with childhood, or with some earlier social condition ... that can be identified with childhood" and that offered "the vision of the social ideal." *Anne of Green Gables* is old-fashioned and escapist, according to Frye, but even so, the connotations of this pastoral myth are healthy, worthwhile, and satisfying because these texts offer "nostalgia for a world of peace and protection, with a spontaneous response to the nature around it, with a leisure and composure not to be found today."[17]

Ultimately *Literary History of Canada* seemed unable to offer a consensus about the audience of Montgomery's books or their literary merit. Yet the two most damning treatments of Montgomery's work during the middle decades of the twentieth century actually contradicted each other in terms of intended audience. In *Creative Writing in Canada* (1952), by Desmond Pacey, neutral comments about Montgomery's popularity and her reliance on the forms of the regional idyll were followed by blistering comments about *Anne of Green Gables*, which he saw as "a children's classic, and it would be silly to apply adult critical standards to it." Although he then attempted to backtrack slightly – "The tone throughout is that of pleasant whimsy, the didacticism is, for the most part, implicit and unobtrusive, and the sentimentalism a little less cloying than is usual in books of its type" – he concluded that the novel "had all the features of the kind of escape literature which a materialistic and vulgar generation craved." *The Blue Castle*, on the other hand, "had all the weaknesses of the Anne books and none of their redeeming charm."[18] Later, in *The Republic of Childhood* (1967), a foundational study of Canadian literature for children, Sheila Egoff suggested in her comments that Montgomery's novels simply did not work as children's literature either:

To denigrate the literary qualities of *Anne of Green Gables* is as useless an exercise as carping about the architecture of the National

War Memorial ... Mrs. Montgomery belongs to that breed of writers who give themselves away in their second and succeeding books. Of Anne, we are inclined to say, "Her I can accept," but the increasingly sentimental dishonesty of the succeeding books tends to destroy the first. Only the most avid Anne fans will refuse to admit that the appealing qualities of the first book are soon dissipated. It is sad but true that the Anne books continue to evoke great nostalgia from many adults to whom much vastly superior modern Canadian writing is unknown.[19]

After half a century of ambiguity regarding whether Montgomery's fiction was intended for adults or for children, Pacey and Egoff seemed to be indicating that *Anne of Green Gables* – and by extension all of Montgomery's books – no longer worked in either category: unworthy of "adult critical standards," marred by their "dishonesty" as children's books, and dismissed by both commentators after the most superficial reading. Taken together, all of these mid-century evaluations, most of which focused solely on *Anne of Green Gables* to determine the successes and failures of Montgomery's entire output, set the stage for more detailed and more nuanced readings of Montgomery's body of work.

What makes Elizabeth Waterston's 1966 chapter on Montgomery in *The Clear Spirit: Twenty Canadian Women and Their Times* so deserving of recognition as a foundational study in the field of Montgomery Studies is that, instead of generalizing about Montgomery's entire library in a short survey, she had the luxury of a full-length chapter to devote space to each of Montgomery's novels in turn, using the forms of life writing available at the time to the best advantage. Although the volume in which the chapter appeared had the explicit agenda of recovering and celebrating the achievements of Canadian women, Waterston was neither gratuitous in her praise nor overly negative in her criticism; she attempted to strike a balance that would open up the discussion rather than provide definitive answers. Waterston's work, the lead chapter in this volume, paved the way for a broader recovery and reassessment of Canadian women writers, one that would begin in earnest in the 1970s and that continues to the present day.

At the end of the 1960s, Pacey published a collection of his own critical essays from the preceding three decades. These show that, in his own way, he had gradually learned to appreciate Montgomery: after dismissing her "lack of realism" in 1945 and placing her in a list of authors of her period who were not "serious artist[s]" in 1951, he finally included her work in a list of "outstanding examples" of the regional idyll in 1965.[20] As well, Helen FitzPatrick's article "Anne's First Sixty Years" appeared in the Spring 1969 issue of *Canadian Author & Bookman and Canadian Poetry*. It purported to tell the story of "Canada's favorite girl" – at least the version of the story that could emerge out of the primary and archival sources that were available then. Narrating the story of Montgomery's childhood, education, early publications, and rise to fame thanks to a best-selling first novel, FitzPatrick quoted liberally from *The Green Gables Letters* and from a letter she had received from Stuart Macdonald that provided a snapshot of the life of a busy woman:

[My mother] was capable of prodigious industry and worked very hard, as a minister's wife is expected to take the lead in innumerable activities. She did her writing early in the morning and reading late at night. As long as I can remember she slept five hours at night – occasionally six. She read and reread all the classics, current books, magazines and newspapers, and ate up one or two detective novels daily. At the same time she maintained a voluminous correspondence, writing by hand every fan letter reply; and kept a detailed diary for over 55 years. She was also in great demand as a speaker at many meetings over most of the country.

In the end, however, FitzPatrick claimed that Montgomery had been "remarkably humble about her talents," again quoting Stuart Macdonald: "[My mother] was the first to admit that her writings were not great literature. She said they did not spring to life through any inspiration, but were the result of constant observation, note-taking, phrase-making and hard work."[21]

Perhaps, then, the biggest obstacle to the recovery of Montgomery's work as worthwhile Canadian literature originated with Montgomery herself – or rather with her ingrained notion that women should be self-effacing and not take themselves too seriously in public, an attitude that was foundational to her public persona and that permeates many of the items included in Volume 1 of *The L.M. Montgomery Reader*. After all, as Åhmansson suggests, "No writer who denies her own creative impulse and who wrote 'ostensibly for girls' could hope to be defined as a true artist."[22] For Montgomery's legacy to be remembered in a different way, the field of Canadian literature would need to broaden beyond the mid-twentieth-century boys' club and to challenge the hierarchy between Canadian "books" and Canadian "literature." It took the publication of

Montgomery's journals to make critics and readers start to take her work more seriously, for that is when they finally saw that, privately, she had done so all along.[23] In 1970, the publication of Montgomery's journals was still fifteen years in the future; in the meantime, a number of additional contributions to the field would help to turn the tide.

The Woman behind the Legend

By the end of the 1960s, Montgomery criticism was limited to a few magazine articles and to descriptive, contradictory, or derogatory mentions in exhaustive treatments of Canadian literature and children's literature in North America. Within the scholarly community, the recuperative work that started with Waterston's chapter in *The Clear Spirit* continued into the early 1970s, a decade that, as Gerson notes, was marked by "the rise of second-wave feminism and its challenge to traditional masculine cultural and literary canons."[24] In 1971, the same year that Brown's comment about Montgomery's work being "more or less aggressively unliterary" was reprinted in Eli Mandel's anthology *Contexts of Canadian Criticism*, Waterston's chapter was cited prominently in Sandra Gwyn's report *Women in the Arts in Canada*, one of several "Studies of the Royal Commission on the Status of Women in Canada." As well, Montgomery's work was referenced briefly but fairly positively in a number of sources published in the first half of this decade, notwithstanding Kent Thompson's comment, in the introduction to his anthology *Stories from Atlantic Canada* (1973), that he could find "no writer to represent Prince Edward Island. Obviously I do not take Lucy Maud Montgomery as seriously as the tourist bureau does." In *Survival: A Thematic Guide to Canadian Literature* (1972), Margaret Atwood made a passing reference to "the wizened spinster Marilla in *Anne of Green Gables*" in her list of "powerful, negative old women in Canadian fiction." In *Survey: A Short History of Canadian Literature* (1973), whose cover depicts five portraits of Canadian authors (including one of Montgomery), Waterston referred to *Anne of Green Gables* as the "first of a long series of gentle, imaginative stories set against the red roads, white sands, and proud, though threadbare, people of 'The Island,'" adding that "Montgomery's Island became part of the adolescent dream-world, a magic-island world of imaginative freedom," a statement that anticipated the focus of her more recent book-length study *Magic Island: The Fictions of L.M. Montgomery* (2008).[25]

As well, in "Women in Canadian Literature," an article published in *Canadian Literature* in 1974, Isobel McKenna noted that "Anne learns to blend her independence with the conventionality of her time and place," and, moreover, that "women in Montgomery's books still belong to the rural society that dominates them, but they feel fortunate in comparison to preceding generations." Also that year, John Robert Colombo included twelve quotations from Montgomery's fiction and letters in *Colombo's Canadian Quotations*. A quarter of a century after profiling "Macdonald, Lucy Maude [*sic*] Montgomery" in *Canadian Novelists 1920–1945*, Clara Thomas included a short chapter on Montgomery and Anne in her book *Our Nature – Our Voices: A Guidebook to English-Canadian Literature* (1972). Although she continued to misspell Montgomery's name ("Maude") – something that, for Gerson, "suggests her lack of status" – Thomas revealed in her comments an appreciation for the universal appeal of Montgomery's female protagonists: "the young heroines of most of her books were remarkably alike in their essential natures, and their adventures and testings all mark every girl's journey from childhood to womanhood and from innocence to experience." In contrast to this positive treatment, however, a revised edition of *Encyclopedia Canadiana* (1972) noted that, in addition to her books for children, Montgomery "also published a volume of verse ... and attempted adult fiction, but with mediocre success."[26]

Given that the aim of most of these texts was to survey an entire literary field, even a brief mention of Montgomery's work can be interpreted as a sign of her perceived cultural and critical value. But what these items from the first half of the 1970s all had in common, besides the fact that they discussed the work without the author, was that they placed that work – *Anne of Green Gables* specifically – within the conventions of a form of criticism, first popularized by Northrop Frye, that emphasized "characteristic thematic patterns and models of nationality or collective identity."[27] The first shift to this approach can be found in a 1974 *Globe and Mail* interview with Stuart Macdonald, in which he discussed Montgomery's journals publicly for the first time and announced his intention to edit them himself once he had retired from his career as a well-respected gynecologist and obstetrician. As journalist Jo Carson declared in the article's lead, "When the real story of Lucy Maud Montgomery is told, it will be in her own words. And there are plenty of them." According to the article, publication of the "estimated ... one million words" in the form of ten handwritten journals was planned for 1976, but, according to Macdonald, the project would "not go beyond 1933 'because mother says some unkind things about people who are still living.'" Reminiscing about his time at home, Macdonald revealed that smoking had not been permitted in his parents' house. "Mother never had an ashtray in her home. She never thought about having one, and she didn't make things easy for the people who smoked when they came to the house. They ended up putting ashes in their pant cuffs." As for the continued appeal of Prince Edward Island tourist destinations related to *Anne of Green Gables*, the article concluded:

> Her son feels that his mother would enjoy her on-going international popularity, but the way Prince Edward Island has exploited her as a tourist attraction would have given her pain.
>
> "They've got a thing across the road, near where she is buried, called Madam Tussaud's wax museum.
>
> "During one of those centennial openings I attend in sort of re-flected glory, I was taken on a tour of this place. There was this thing crouched in a corner and I asked 'what the hell's that?' Someone said 'that's your mother.'
>
> "I couldn't help thinking that this wax thing looked like the third witch in Macbeth. I know I was thinking this when I stood at my mother's grave when I felt the slight tremor."[28]

The publication of Montgomery's journals in the 1980s would steer the field of Montgomery studies in the direction of biographical approaches, whereby biographical and autobiographical materials are used to frame analyses of primary texts, sometimes in the quest of "authorial intent." That approach would still later be joined by additional critical paradigms from comparative literature, critical and literary theory, book history, feminist criticism, life writing, and cultural studies. As the field developed, one of the challenges would come to involve determining the categories for situating and discussing her fiction: as Canadian literature, children's literature, popular fiction, *bildungsroman*, Atlantic literature and culture, or women's writing. Rather emphatically in Montgomery's case, the line between Canadian literature and children's literature would continue to divide critics, given persisting notions that the study of Canadian literature for children requires entirely different approaches and methods than those applied to "real" Canadian literature.[29] As well, the contin-ued popularity of her work would, in the following decades, in many ways hinder rather than help the reclaiming of Montgomery as an author worthy of academic study, not only in terms of how her work was re-ceived by readers, but also in terms of how it was marketed and packaged to a diverse audience within Canada and beyond.

So, while the centenary of Montgomery's birth provoked a rather luke-warm reaction in 1974, the interview with Macdonald published that Oc-tober ended up paving the way for a noticeable shift the following year in academic and popular circles alike. Rae Macdonald included a discussion of *Anne of Green Gables* in her PhD dissertation, "The Regional Novel in Canada, 1880–1925," which she defended at Dalhousie University. Scholarship on Montgomery's work received a significant boost when Waterston and three of her colleagues at the University of Guelph – Mary Rubio, John R. Sorfleet, and Glenys Stow – founded the academic jour-nal *Canadian Children's Literature*, publishing its first issue in spring 1975 and a special "L.M. Montgomery Issue" that autumn. The latter issue, republished in book form as *L.M. Montgomery: An Assessment* in 1976, included Sorfleet's introduction and a reprint of Waterston's 1966 chapter, as well as new articles by Rubio, Gillian Thomas, Ann S. Cowan, Muriel A. Whitaker, Jane Cowan Fredeman, and Jean Little on a num-ber of topics, including satire, fantasy, depictions of childhood, and the development of Canadian writers. The shift from the criticism published earlier in the 1970s was twofold: these articles offered sustained readings of Montgomery's texts as opposed to brief mentions, and nearly all of them studied this work not as an example of a broader genre or national literature but in isolation from other authors. The exception, Rubio's article "Satire, Realism, and Imagination in *Anne of Green Gables*," compared Montgomery not to texts by a fellow Canadian author but to those by an American author whose early enthusiasm for *Anne of Green Gables* had been used as a marketing tool for her work – Mark Twain.

This issue of *Canadian Children's Literature* provided, in Sorfleet's words, "a fitting commemorative tribute to L.M. Montgomery and to the child, woman, and author that she was." The same journal (which became officially bilingual in 1983, adding the French title *Lit-térature canadienne pour la jeunesse*) would eventually publish more than one hundred articles, editorials, and reviews about Montgomery between the mid-1980s and its final issue in 2008.[30] As Gerson notes, many of the items published in *CCL/LCJ* "do not treat [Montgomery] as an author of juvenile fiction."[31] Indeed, much of the scholarship that fol-lowed – even in journals that declared their focus to be on children's litera-ture – made little concerted effort to place Montgomery's texts within the conventions of children's literature and its assumptions about narrative, ideology, and readership. This disjunction is curious, given that, the same year that *CCL/LCJ* published its initial Montgomery issue, Robert W. Read noted in *Canadian Author & Bookman* that Montgomery's writing, "apart from some of the *Anne* books, has a drastically diminished appeal for contemporary children." Indeed, Antonia Allen, writing in *Saturday Night* magazine in 1973, called recent editions of *The Blue Castle* and *A Tangled Web* "sociological goldmines": "Here is WASP Canada early this century with all its pomp, religious bigotry, and nasty self-righteousness hanging out." As Allen remarked, "There is a real joy in reading L.M. Montgomery as an adult."[32]

In the trade market as well, 1975 proved to be a milestone year for L.M. Montgomery, even more than it was for *Anne of Green Gables.* Canada Post issued a commemorative stamp that depicted Anne Shirley as a child but placed the words "Lucy Maud Montgomery" above "Anne of Green Gables / Anne de Green Gables"; it reportedly had a print run of twenty-seven million,[33] and samples are still available at selected tourist shops in Prince Edward Island today. Sixteen never-before-seen photographs were published in *The Canadian Magazine* as "Lucy Maud's Album," with prefatory comments by Patricia Holtz. Adrian Waller's article "Lucy Maud of Green Gables" appeared in the December issue of the Canadian *Reader's Digest*, and while it is remarkably similar to Sclanders's *Maclean's Magazine* article from 1951, what is especially noteworthy about this article is how determinedly it ignored all the new biographical details that had become public that year, in Mollie Gillen's biography *The Wheel of Things* (Fitzhenry and Whiteside) and in Terence Macartney-Filgate's ninety-minute CBC documentary *Lucy Maud Montgomery: The Road to Green Gables.* Both relied on similar but unrelated sources that had not yet been made available for public consumption: Gillen on Montgomery's correspondence with her Scottish pen pal George Boyd MacMillan and Macartney-Filgate on Montgomery's journals, which he used by arrangement with Stuart Macdonald. Although Gillen had already published a shorter version of her biography as "Maud Montgomery: The Girl Who Wrote Green Gables" in *Chatelaine* in July 1973, the book's contents were as much a surprise to reviewers as were those of the documentary. Commenting in the *Lethbridge Herald* on the gap between the public and private Montgomerys in her review of Gillen's book, Elspeth Walker noted that "perhaps [Montgomery's] apparent reticence to expose her precious privacy ought to have been given more kindly consideration before this biographical intrusion was made into her life." Ann S. Cowan, reviewing Gillen's book in *The Canadian Historical Review*, took a different tack, calling it "a thought-provoking study of a complex woman, the perception of whose life and work has been too long obscured by the legend of L.M. Montgomery."[34] As for *The Road to Green*

Gables, Jed Stuart of the *Winnipeg Free Press* hailed Macartney-Filgate's documentary as a "remarkable film biography" in which "the author's outwardly conforming mask is peeled away" to reveal "a person who, while outwardly calm, seethed inwardly with passions and frustrations." As he noted further, "the recent discovery of the author's personal diaries was a major event in the history of Canadian letters."[35]

Armed with these templates for more substantial discussions of Montgomery's work and with new, concrete knowledge of the "complex woman" behind the legend, scholars in the second half of the 1970s continued to find new ways to discuss Montgomery's fiction. In 1976, the same year that *Colombo's Canadian References* mentioned *Anne of Green Gables* as "a lively, warm novel for young girls" that was followed by "seven less-successful sequels," Frances M. Frazer included Montgomery, "the most solidly-talented prolific writer the Island has produced," in her *Canadian Literature* article on "Island Writers"; in an article published in *The Dalhousie Review,* Lesley Willis discussed nostalgia and fairy-tale elements in *Anne of Green Gables*; and Verna Reid examined *Anne of Green Gables* alongside Mordecai Richler's then-recent *Jacob Two-Two Meets the Hooded Fang* in *The English Quarterly.* Bolger also gave a lecture on Montgomery at the Belfast Historical Society in Prince Edward Island in November 1976, a transcription of which was published in *The Island Magazine* the following year. In 1977, George Woodcock declared *Anne of Green Gables,* "with its haunting evocation of rustic Prince Edward Island," to be an example of a "local-color" book that "was so well done that it survived its time by the sheer appeal of the idyllic atmosphere it created," whereas Jane Burns, discussing Anne Shirley and Emily Byrd Starr in the feminist journal *Room of One's Own,* noted that "if Lucy Maud Montgomery were alive today, her remarks about the role of women would be prefaced by that contradictory phrase, 'I'm not a women's libber, but ... '" That same year, Susan Elizabeth Jones at the University of Windsor and Leslie Goddard Scanlon at Carleton University each defended an MA thesis specifically on Montgomery's fiction, the first since 1961, whereas Janet E. Baker mentioned Montgomery in her PhD dissertation on Archibald MacMechan. Finally, in 1979, Jacqueline Berke included Anne Shirley in a discussion of "the self-sufficient heroine in popular girls' fiction"; Catherine Sheldrick Ross compared Montgomery's depiction of "the old-time heroine" with that of Sara Jeannette Duncan, Margaret Laurence, Margaret Atwood, and Alice Munro; Mary Vipond demonstrated the popularity of Montgomery's fiction in terms of its placement on Canadian best-seller lists until 1918; E. Blanche Norcross included a chapter on "Maud Montgomery" in her book *Pioneers Every One: Canadian Women of Achievement*; and the women's studies journal *Atlantis* reprinted Montgomery's 1896 article "A Girl's Place at Dalhousie College."[36] This range of contributions is especially remarkable given Margaret Steffler's recent observation that Montgomery's critical reputation by 1980 was still under the shadow of critics such as Brown and Deacon, who had denigrated her work decades earlier, and given Rubio's report that her first application for funding to support the editing of Montgomery's journals was turned down in 1980–81 because "several assessors were hostile to spending any money whatsoever on Montgomery."[37]

At the same time, Montgomery's books remained very much in print throughout the 1970s, even without popular television adaptations to renew interest in them, as would be the case in the two decades to follow.[38] In Canada, Montgomery's seven pre-1916 novels, originally published by L.C. Page and Company, had been reprinted in hardcover by the Ryerson Press (later McGraw–Hill Ryerson) starting in 1942 and would continue in that format until the late 1980s; *Further Chronicles of Avonlea*, an unauthorized collection of short stories that Montgomery had fought for eight years to be taken off the market, was added to this set in 1954. As early as 1970, the first three Anne books were also available from this publisher as mass market paperbacks, often as part of a "Triple Treat" boxed set featuring images from *Anne of Green Gables: The Musical*, which has been performed at the Confederation Centre of the Arts in Charlottetown since 1965 and which toured London in 1969 and Osaka, Japan, in 1970.[39] The sales success of *The Road to Yesterday* in 1974 led to two further posthumous Montgomery texts with McGraw–Hill Ryerson in the years that followed: *The Doctor's Sweetheart and Other Stories* (1979), a sample of fourteen short stories originally published in periodicals between 1899 and 1935 and edited by Catherine McLay, and *My Dear Mr. M: Letters to G.B. MacMillan from L.M. Montgomery* (1980), edited by Francis W.P. Bolger and Elizabeth R. Epperly (Ridley's 1956 biography was also reprinted by this firm sometime in the late 1970s). Fourteen of Montgomery's remaining sixteen books originally published in Canada by McClelland and Stewart were reissued as colourful trade paperbacks as part of the firm's "Canadian Children's Favourites" umbrella series beginning in 1972. The name of this series perplexed Helen Porter, whose review of the "Favourites" editions of *The Blue Castle* and *A Tangled Web* appears in this volume. Perhaps in response to her outrage that even these "adult" Montgomery texts were deemed to be children's literature, the series was renamed "Canadian Favourites" by 1973 and continued until at least the mid-1980s.

In the United States and Britain, only *Anne of Green Gables* and some of its sequels were still being reprinted by 1970. New York publisher Grosset and Dunlap, which had published cheaper reprints of Montgomery's Page books as far back as 1908, that year released new hardcover editions of the Anne books – excluding *Rainbow Valley* and *Rilla of Ingleside* but including *Chronicles of Avonlea* and *Further Chronicles of Avonlea*, each with the tag "An Anne of Green Gables Book" on the cover – and kept them available in that format throughout the decade. In the UK, Harrap Books continued to reprint the Anne books, the two Chronicles volumes, and *Emily of New Moon*, as well as *The Doctor's Sweetheart* and Gillen's biography, until the end of the decade, while various imprints of Penguin Books had reissued the Anne, Chronicles, and Emily books as mass market paperbacks from the mid-1960s onward, although only *Anne of Green Gables* and its first two sequels remain in that format today. According to the compilers of *Lucy Maud Montgomery: A Preliminary Bibliography* (1986), Montgomery's remaining novels were no longer being reprinted outside Canada by 1970, and indeed had fallen out of print gradually from the late 1930s onward.[40]

In 1976, while Grosset and Dunlap continued to publish eight Anne texts in hardcover in the United States, Bantam Books of New York reissued *Anne of Green Gables*, *Anne of Avonlea*, and *Anne of the Island* as mass market paperbacks. The reprinting of these three editions by Toronto-based Seal Books in 1981 led to two publishing decisions that have influenced an entire generation of Montgomery readers: the creation of a numbered "Anne of Green Gables Series" and a standard set of editions of all of Montgomery's books. The former occurred by 1983, two years after *Anne of Windy Poplars*, *Anne's House of Dreams*, and *Anne of Ingleside* were added to the Bantam–Seal list in both countries (*Rainbow Valley* and *Rilla of Ingleside*, as books 7 and 8, were also published in this format in the United States in 1985 but not in Canada until 1987). The latter occurred gradually across the 1980s as further Montgomery texts were added in this format in Canada: *Emily of New Moon* and its two sequels in 1983, *Kilmeny of the Orchard*, *The Story Girl*, *Chronicles of Avonlea*, *The Golden Road*, and *Further Chronicles of Avonlea* in 1987, *The Blue Castle*, *Magic for Marigold*, *A Tangled Web*, *Pat of Silver Bush*, *Mistress Pat*, and *Jane of Lantern Hill* in 1988, followed by *The Road to Yesterday* and *The Doctor's Sweetheart* in 1993.[41] Many readers (including this one) have criticized the Seal editions for their poor paper and print quality, for pastel colour schemes and cover images that seem to brand Montgomery visually as a romance novelist, and for numerous typographical errors and unacknowledged deletions,[42] yet these editions also need to be credited with keeping Montgomery's fiction available in affordable editions since the 1980s. Although some of the Anne novels, especially *Anne of Green Gables*, have also appeared in a number of trade paperback and hardcover editions (as well as critical editions and abridgements for younger readers), the vast majority of Montgomery's books were available exclusively from Seal Books for more than a quarter of a century.

In terms of scholarship, the topics and texts that were part of the discussion likewise continued to broaden throughout the 1980s. Although Montgomery was omitted from major multivolume projects such as Lecker and David's *The Annotated Bibliography of Canada's Major Authors* (1979–94) and Lecker, David, and Quigley's *Canadian Writers and Their Works* – both "Fiction Series" (1983–95) and "Poetry Series" (1988–96) – references to Montgomery and to *Anne of Green Gables* began to appear with greater frequency in standard reference books and surveys, such as Joseph Jones and Johanna Jones's *Canadian Fiction* (1981), James Vinson's *Twentieth-Century Romance and Gothic Writers* (1982), Helen Hoy's *Modern English-Canadian Prose: A Guide to Information Sources* (1983), William Toye's *The Oxford Companion to Canadian Literature* (1983), Humphrey Carpenter and Mari Prichard's *The Oxford Companion to Children's Literature* (1984), David Stouck's *Major Canadian Authors* (1984), Anita Moss and Jon C. Stott's *The Family of Stories* (1986), Linnea Hendrickson's *Children's Literature: A Guide to the Criticism* (1987), Albert Moritz and Theresa Moritz's *The Oxford Illustrated Literary Guide to Canada* (1987), Judith Saltman's *Modern Canadian Children's Books* (1987), Jane M. Bingham's *Writers for Children: Critical Studies of Major Authors Since the Seventeenth Century* (1988), Jon C. Stott and Raymond E. Jones's *Canadian Books for Children: A Guide to Authors and Illustrators* (1988), Eugene Benson and L.W. Conolly's *The Oxford Companion to Canadian Theatre* (1989), and W.H. New's *Canadian Writers, 1890–1920* (1990).[43] As well, many of the earliest scholarly contributions on Montgomery, along with early reviews of some of her books in North American newspapers, were reprinted or excerpted in the eighth volume of the multivolume encyclopedia *Children's Literature Review* (1985), edited by Gerard J. Senick. While the inclusion of Montgomery in major book-length studies of Canadian literature during the 1920s and later signalled a tacit acknowledgment of her literary worth, not until the 1980s did these mentions become so numerous and so detailed.

Anne of Green Gables also received favourable treatment in Mary Cadogan and Patricia Craig's *You're a Brick, Angela! The Girls' Story 1839–1985* (1986), in which the authors praised Montgomery's "skill as a story-teller" but lamented the fact that "the book noticeably deteriorates" once Anne becomes a quieter, more introverted adolescent. Commenting directly on Montgomery's stated surprise (in a letter to Ephraim Weber) that *Anne of Green Gables* appealed to a wider range of readers than the schoolgirls for whom it was supposedly intended – at least in this telling – Cadogan and Craig made a crucial point about the artificial boundary between children's literature and adult literature: "Logically, after the first half of *Anne of Green Gables*, it can, or should, please no one: the child reader cannot identify with a heroine for whom growing up has meant that the zest is taken out of her; the adult is irritated by the falsity of the sentiment. Possibly its greatest appeal has been to grown-up people who wish to remember only the least disturbing elements of their own childhood."[44] The question of audience continued to be debated in several additional sources throughout this decade: John Moss noted in *A Reader's Guide to the Canadian Novel* (1981) that "Montgomery wrote many other works for young readers" besides *Anne of Green Gables*, but he added that "some would say even her adult writing is more suitable for young readers." Conversely, André Gagnon and Ann Gagnon in their bilingual guide *Canadian Books for Young People / Livres canadiens pour la jeunesse* (1988) designated the audience for all of Montgomery's books as "older, young adult," except for *The Alpine Path* and *The Doctor's Sweetheart and Other Stories*, both of which were specifically "young adult."[45]

As had been the case with *Literary History of Canada* in 1965, the most glaring contradiction during the 1980s in terms of Montgomery's critical reputation and target audience occurred in the same book, this time in William Toye's *The Oxford Companion to Canadian Literature* (1983). In her entry on "Children's Literature in English," Egoff commented that while "Anne sounded an original and refreshing note" in *Anne of Green Gables*, this novel was followed by "many books of sticky sweetness that are best forgotten." In contrast to her scathing comments on Montgomery's work in *The Republic of Childhood*, however, Egoff nevertheless added that "even these contain effective lyrical passages on the natural beauty of Prince Edward Island" and called Montgomery's

Emily books "outstanding examples of realistic domestic novels for the young ... Montgomery had a sharp ear for dialogue; and though her books are not strongly plotted, she manages to keep reader interest to the very end. True to her period, and to the canons of children's literature of the time, Montgomery was a moralist; but unlike most of her contemporaries, she was not doctrinaire." George L. Parker struck a different note in his entry on *Anne of Green Gables*, which he called an "enduring children's classic [and] perhaps the best-selling book by a Canadian author," yet he did not actually treat the novel as a work for children in his discussion: "One of the first portraits in Canadian fiction of the artist as a young girl, Anne's transformation from ugly duckling to comely maiden leads to a compromise between the private world of her imagination and the genteel, practical world around her ... Generations of women have applauded Anne's determination to succeed on her own terms in a man's world and yet retain her identity."[46]

Indeed, one of the most recurring contradictions in Montgomery's critical reputation is that while some commentators insisted on seeing her work as part of children's literature, they also tended to see it as more successful and more appealing to readers outside this genre. In some cases, such a label seemed arbitrary and illogical, such as David Stouck's reference to *Anne of Green Gables* as "a regional idyll that has become a children's classic," without any consideration of how such a shift could have happened, or the question was raised and never settled, such as in John Robert Sorfleet's entry on Montgomery in *Twentieth-Century Children's Writers* (1978): "At times, L.M. Montgomery's work challenges conventional opinion about what makes a children's book. Is it a child or adolescent protagonist? ... Is it comparatively innocuous subject matter?" Pointing out that her work breaks both of these conventions, Sorfleet added that in her fiction "Montgomery deals with the psychological realities and conflicts of childhood and adolescence" – even though such realities and conflicts can be found just as often in texts about children and adolescents but not written for child or adolescent readers.[47] Frequently, when critics discussed *Anne of Green Gables* (and by extension the remainder of Montgomery's book-length fiction) as a work for children, they interpreted it either as a flawed example of the genre or as a book that was *so successful* as a book for children that it appealed to adults as well – rarely did these reference books offer detailed treatment of her work as a legitimate example of children's literature. In addition to these contributions in reference books, however, article-length scholarship would increase throughout the 1980s, particularly after the coincidental creation of two types of supplementary texts, which led to an increased but also a more complex audience.

Turning Point: Life Writing Meets Network Television

The biggest shift by far in Montgomery's critical reception and reputation occurred in late 1985, when the publication of the first volume of *The Selected Journals of L.M. Montgomery* (Oxford University Press), edited by Rubio and Waterston, preceded by only a month the Canadian Broadcasting Corporation premiere of Kevin Sullivan's television miniseries *Anne of Green Gables*, a project produced by Sullivan Films in partnership with the CBC, the Public Broadcasting Service, the ZDF network (in what was then West Germany), and Telefilm Canada. As Gerson notes, these two projects together – both of which would have several followups over the years – "had a huge effect on Montgomery's subsequent status by engaging audiences in two different realms: young viewers and mature readers." Not only did the regular broadcast of television texts associated with Montgomery's name maintain (and arguably increase) an already sizeable readership, but "the journals' timely intersection with the interest of second-wave feminists in women's self-representation has enhanced their reception by academics involved in the emergence of life-writing as a scholarly field."[48] In spite of their popularity of many of these productions, numerous academics have criticized them for inevitably recentring the story of *Anne of Green Gables* on opposite-sex romance and for downplaying geographic and historical specificity in order to become more palatable to a worldwide audience.[49] Nevertheless, these productions – which include not only *Anne of Green Gables* and three television sequels released in 1987, 2000, and 2008, but also the telefilm *Lantern Hill* (Sullivan Entertainment, 1990) and the episodic series *Road to Avonlea* (Sullivan Entertainment, 1990–96) and *Emily of New Moon* (Salter Street Films/CINAR Productions, 1998–99, 2002–3), as well as *Anne of Green Gables: The Animated Series* (Sullivan Animation, 2000–1) – exported alternate Montgomery universes to viewers all over the world, and *Road to Avonlea* became one of the most successful long-form series in the history of Canadian television, despite (or perhaps because of) the financial and creative involvement of the Disney Channel, which aired the series in the United States as *Avonlea*. It also spawned twenty-nine "storybooks" based on episodes from the first three seasons and was nominated for numerous Gemini, Emmy, and CableAce Awards.[50] Sullivan Entertainment now sells a wide range of books, DVDs, soundtracks, posters, collectables, lifestyle products, and even props from its productions on its Shop at Sullivan website.

The premiere of the first *Anne of Green Gables* miniseries in 1985 precipitated a French Canadian translation of the novel in 1986, following earlier French-language translations *Anne ou les illusions heureuses* (Anne of the Happy Illusions), published in Geneva in 1925, and the abridged translation *Anne et le bonheur* (Anne and Happiness), published in Paris in 1964. Henri-Dominique Paratte's translation, *Anne ... La Maison aux pignons verts* (Anne: The House of the Green Gables) was published jointly by Ragweed Press (Charlottetown) and Éditions Québec–Amérique (Montreal), and Paratte's title was also used for the French translations of Sullivan's miniseries and of the Japanese anime *Akage no An* (1979). In her review of Paratte's translation in *The Atlantic Provinces Book Review*, Martine Jacquot noted that Paratte "has written the story in a more modern language rather than strictly translated it," adding that "*Anne* reads well in modern French and manages at the same time to keep the atmosphere of the beginning of the century."[51] This French-Canadian edition occurred rather late in the history of Montgomery translations, which, as Gerson has noted, started with Northern European languages within Montgomery's own lifetime before becoming more global after the Second World War, with a "fresh spate of translations follow[ing] international sales of the Sullivan films."[52]

In contrast to popular adaptations and translations, however, the publication of a compelling, multivolume life narrative had a remarkable effect on Montgomery scholarship, given that, as Irene Gammel has observed, "many scholars today read her novels ... through the lens of the journals."[53] It is worth noting, though, that the use of life writing to provide biographical, historical, or cultural context to Montgomery's fiction actually predated the publication of the *Selected Journals*: five of the six original articles in the "L.M. Montgomery Issue" of *CCL/LCJ* published in 1975 drew on *The Alpine Path* or *The Green Gables Letters* or both, and Thomas E. Tausky's article on the Emily books and T.D. MacLulich's article on *Anne of Green Gables* as an example of the regional idyll, both originally published in 1983 and the latter reprinted in this volume, made excellent use of published and unpublished letters by Montgomery to MacMillan and Weber. The trend was amplified by Rubio and Waterston themselves, both of whom were understandably keen to draw readers' attention to Montgomery's life writing in their scholarship on her fiction. In two book chapters published even before the release of the first volume of *Selected Journals*, for instance, Rubio noted that these journals grant readers "the opportunity to enter Montgomery's inner life" and to "show how many elements in *Anne* have their origin in the psyche and actual experiences of the child, Maud Montgomery."[54] Rubio and Waterston relied on the journals prominently in their afterwords to reissues of six early Montgomery books by the New American Library between 1987 and 1991. Also, in Rubio's 1994 collection of essays *Harvesting Thistles: The Textual Garden of L.M. Montgomery; Essays on Her Novels and Journals*, nearly all of the contributors drew on Montgomery's journals to inform their interpretations of her fiction. Thanks to all of these efforts, scholarship on Montgomery's fiction has been greatly enriched by the historical, biographical, and cultural contexts this resource provides. More and more scholars and readers have since discovered, as has Epperly, that the *Selected Journals* "mark Montgomery as a compelling writer in yet another genre."[55]

In the popular press, the journals transformed public perceptions of Montgomery almost immediately; examples of this include David Weale's "'No Scope for Imagination': Another Side of Anne of Green Gables" in a 1986 issue of *The Island Magazine* and Mark Abley's "The Girl She Never Was" in a 1987 issue of *Saturday Night*. Although initially surprising to the general public, the tone and voice found in the *Selected Journals* have altered significantly the way Montgomery is written about in the media: unlike in the 1970s, when the details of her life were largely unknown, the publication of her life writing in the 1980s caused the biographical to assume a significantly different relationship to her work. And in some cases, Montgomery's life writing led to reconsiderations' of her fiction: Egoff, one of the harshest critics of Montgomery's books as children's literature, revealed in her posthumously published memoir *Once upon a Time: My Life with Children's Books* (2005) how her thinking about Montgomery and her work had evolved: "I greatly enjoyed Lucy Maud's journals, and I have grown to respect her as a person and as a writer. I had not realized what a stylist Montgomery was until I became immersed in her journals, where her real passions and understanding are revealed ... I also discovered, when rereading Montgomery, that she excelled in her portrayal of adult characters. She did not hide their foibles or their dark sides from her youthful readers."[56]

A major consequence of readers' fascination with Montgomery's journals, of course, was that it shifted the focus away from *Anne of Green Gables* and toward L.M. Montgomery. Indeed, between the late 1980s and the late 1990s Canadians had access to several non-*Anne* texts that were linked to Montgomery's name – besides the *Selected Journals* and several popular television adaptations, there were also John Ferns and Kevin McCabe's 1987 volume *The Poetry of Lucy Maud Montgomery* and Rea Wilmshurst's eight edited collections of rediscovered short stories from across Montgomery's career, beginning with *Akin to Anne: Tales of Other Orphans* in 1988 (Wilmshurst's account of discovering the short stories and compiling these volumes, originally an afterword to two later collections, appears in this volume). Major contributions to the field of Montgomery Studies in the 1990s did include two books focusing exclusively on Montgomery's best-known novel: Mavis Reimer's collection of reprinted articles *Such a Simple Little Tale: Critical Responses to L.M. Montgomery's* Anne of Green Gables (1992) and Waterston's short book-length study *Kindling Spirit: L.M. Montgomery's* Anne of Green Gables (1993), the latter part of the Canadian Fiction Studies series published by ECW Press. But these studies were joined by several more that encompassed Montgomery's larger body of work: Ruth Weber Russell, D.W. Russell, and Rea Wilmshurst's *Lucy Maud Montgomery: A Preliminary Bibliography* (1986), which remains an unparalleled account of Montgomery's publishing history in book and periodical form; Hanna Schwarz-Eisler's *L.M. Montgomery: A Popular Canadian Writer for Children* (1991), which considers qualitative characteristics and themes as well as the treatment of religion and the quest for identity in Montgomery's work; Elizabeth Rollins Epperly's monograph *The Fragrance of Sweet-Grass: L.M. Montgomery's Heroines and the Pursuit of Romance* (1992), which studies Montgomery's subversive transformation of the romance genre as it pertains to her compelling female protagonists; Genevieve Wiggins's book-length contribution on Montgomery to the Twayne's World Authors Series (1992), which suggests that Montgomery, in fact, believed in the generic conventions that required her protagonists to prioritize marriage and domesticity over all other interests; and four self-published studies by Sylvia DuVernet, which have remained undervalued resources in the field: *L.M. Montgomery and the Mystique of Muskoka* (1988), *Theosophic Thoughts Concerning L.M. Montgomery* (1988), *L.M. Montgomery on the Red Road to Reconstruction: A Survey of Her Novels* (1993), and *The Meaning of Men and the Boys in the Anne Books* (1998).[57]

Several sets of additional resources pertaining to L.M. Montgomery appeared during this period: new biographies by Jacqueline Langille (1992), Harry Bruce (1992), Catherine M. Andronik (1993), and Rubio and Waterston (1995); fan periodicals such as *Kindred Spirits* (1990–2012), *The Avonlea Traditions Chronicle* (1991–99), *The Shining Scroll* (1992–), and *The Road to L.M. Montgomery* (1995–2003), all of which contain a medley of articles, interviews, information about new books and adaptations, reprinted materials, profiles of actors, letters, photos from lookalike contests, and puzzles; and supplementary texts such as Francis W.P. Bolger, Wayne Barrett, and Anne MacKay's *Spirit of Place: Lucy Maud Montgomery and Prince Edward Island* (1982), Kate Macdonald's *The Anne of Green Gables Cookbook* (1985), Eric Wilson's novel *The Green Gables Detectives: A Liz Austen Mystery* (1987), Shelley Tanaka's *The Anne of Green Gables Diary* (1987), Carolyn Strom Collins and Christina Wyss Eriksson's *The Anne of Green Gables Treasury* (1991) and two follow-ups, Elaine Crawford and Kelly Crawford's *Aunt Maud's Recipe Book: From the Kitchen of L.M. Montgomery* (1996), Nancy Rootland's *Anne's World, Maud's World: The Sacred Sites of L.M. Montgomery* (1996), Lynn Manuel's picture book *Lucy Maud and the Cavendish Cat* (1997), Jack Hutton and Linda Jackson-Hutton's non-fiction book *Lucy Maud Montgomery and Bala: A Love Story of the North Woods* (1998), and Mary Frances Coady's novel for middle readers *Lucy Maud and Me* (1999). The diversity of all these texts, in terms of both content and readership, indicates that by the 1990s there was room for all approaches and for all readers in the Montgomery community. Meanwhile, in a clear sign that Montgomery had been embraced by the canon of Canadian literature, four Montgomery titles were added to the prestigious New Canadian Library series by McClelland and Stewart, with afterwords by prominent contemporary authors: *Emily of New Moon* (Alice Munro), *Emily Climbs* (Jane Urquhart), and *Emily's Quest* (P.K. Page) in 1989, followed by *Anne of Green Gables* (Margaret Atwood) in 1992.

In addition to all these new resources, what has had the greatest impact on Montgomery scholarship is the launch, in 1993, of the L.M. Montgomery Institute at the University of Prince Edward Island. Spearheaded by Elizabeth Rollins Epperly, its founding chair, the LMMI has supported visual exhibits, hosted a "Kindred Spirits" listserv, produced a CD-ROM (*The Bend in the Road: An Invitation to the World and Work of L.M. Montgomery*, released in 2000), produced a research website (*Picturing a Canadian Life: L.M. Montgomery's Personal Scrapbooks and Book Covers*, launched in 2002), and organized learning opportunities for PEI schoolchildren. Most significantly in terms of building and nurturing an international community of scholars, the LMMI hosts biennial conferences on Montgomery, a unique occurrence in Canadian literary studies. Each conference has been organized around a particular theme, thus helping steer scholarly inquiry into Montgomery's work in a number of directions. Since an initial symposium on "L.M. Montgomery and Her Works" in 1994, the LMMI has hosted conferences on Montgomery and Canadian culture (1996), the literature of small islands (1998), popular culture (2000), life writing (2002), interior and exterior landscapes (2004), conflict (2006), *Anne of Green Gables* and "the Idea of Classic" (2008), the matter of nature (2010), cultural memory (2012), and war (2014). These conferences have also laid the groundwork for a number of collections of essays, journal issues, and conference proceedings: Gammel and Epperly's *L.M. Montgomery and Canadian Culture* (1999); Laurie Brinklow, Frank Ledwell, and Jane Ledwell's *Message in a Bottle: The Literature of Small Islands* (2000); Gammel's *Making Avonlea: L.M. Montgomery and Popular Culture* (2002) and *The Intimate Life of L.M. Montgomery* (2005); "L.M. Montgomery's Interior/Exterior Landscapes," a special 2005 issue of the Australian journal *CREArTA*, edited by Rosemary Ross Johnston; Jean Mitchell's *Storm and Dissonance: L.M. Montgomery and Conflict* (2008); and Ledwell and Mitchell's *Anne Around the World: L.M. Montgomery and Her Classic* (2013), which was launched at the twentieth-anniversary celebration of the Institute in June 2013. In 1998, also with the aim of nurturing scholarly community, Jason Nolan, Yuka Kajihara, and I launched the LMM-L, an L.M. Montgomery listserv restricted to researchers (university-affiliated or not) who are active in the field. It became the basis for a Web 2.0 resource under my direction: the L.M. Montgomery Research Group, launched in 2006 and relaunched in 2014 as L.M. Montgomery Online, in order to support and extend several book-length studies (including this one) and to facilitate scholarly research.

Whether they treated her life writing as a lens through which to read her fiction, or whether they examined her fiction or her life writing separately, scholars approaching Montgomery's work in the final two decades of the twentieth century relied on a range of approaches and methods to probe a number of topics. Under the rubric of gender, scholars discussed Montgomery's writing in terms of feminist theory and practice, motherhood, female friendship, trauma, work (including teaching and writing), modernism (by Irene Gammel in this volume), gossip as social regulator and social performance (by Diane Tye in this volume), women writers and artists (by Carole Gerson in this volume), and male sexuality.[58] Scholars were also interested in creating links between Montgomery and nineteenth- and twentieth-century American, British, and Australian children's literature and girls' books, either to the conventions of the overall genres in terms of characters and plots or to specific authors such as Gene Stratton-Porter, Lewis Carroll, Louisa May Alcott, Ethel Turner, and Kate Douglas Wiggin.[59] In the matter of genre criticism, critics during this period examined conventions and structures – in terms of the regional idyll (by T.D. MacLulich in this volume), folklore, poetry, and romance – as well as symbols and countertexts, strategies of resistance (by Mary Rubio and Laura M. Robinson in this volume), character studies (by Rosamond Bailey in this volume), setting, and recurring character motifs such as orphans and twins.[60] Although scholarship specifically on Montgomery's life writing and private papers was only beginning during this period, this included foundational studies of Montgomery's writing processes in her journals and manuscripts (by Helen M. Buss and Elizabeth Epperly in this volume).[61]

Scholars also pursued Montgomery's work in connection with wider textual and cultural contexts, such as connections to earlier and later texts and genres, Prince Edward Island history and religious culture, reader response, her depiction of the First World War (by Owen Dudley Edwards in this volume), the popularity of her books around the world (particularly in Sweden, Poland, and Japan), and extensions to her work in the form of merchandise, spin-off books, tourist sites, and online communities.[62] Montgomery's work became a focus of four PhD dissertations during this period: Gordon Philip Turner's "The Protagonists' Initiatory Experiences in the Canadian Bildungsroman: 1908–1971," defended at the University of British Columbia in 1979; Christina Dorothy Neutze's "Colonial Children: The Fictional Worlds of L.M. Montgomery, Isabel Maud Peacocke, and Ethel Turner," defended at the University of Auckland (New Zealand) in 1981; Gabriella Åhmansson's *A Life and Its Mirrors: A Feminist Reading of L.M. Montgomery's Fiction*, defended at Uppsala University (Sweden) in 1991 and published there the same year; and Laura Mae Robinson's "Educating the Reader: Negotiation in Nineteenth-Century Popular Girls' Stories," defended at Queen's University in 1998. Moreover, students undertaking theses for MA degrees in Canada, Italy, Finland, Poland, and Germany broached topics such as characterization, romance, tourism, humour, language, faith, international reception, and the interplay between fiction and life writing and made connections to authors such as Marshall Saunders, Nellie L. McClung, Ralph Waldo Emerson, Alice Munro, Margaret Laurence, and Stephen Leacock.[63]

At the same time, proof of the multiplicity of possible avenues of investigation can be found most clearly in two unlikely late twentieth-century additions to the conversation. A discussion of Anne Shirley's career as a schoolteacher in *Anne of Avonlea* appeared in Edward Anthony's book-length study *Thy Rod and Staff: New Light on the Flagellatory Impulse* (1996), in which he discussed extracts describing Anne's initial resistance to corporal punishment in the classroom and her reliance on such tactics in a fit of anger against an unruly male student. For Anthony, the extracts in question "contain many of the elements most valued in flagellatory erotica," and the scene in which Anne strikes her student with a pointer – Montgomery's narrator is discreet enough not to specify which part of the body is stricken – "contains an even stronger *frisson*, for it offers the spectacle of an attractive sixteen-year-old girl" – whom he also calls "a teenage sadist" – "administering corporal punishment to a twelve-year-old boy in front of a mixed class, to a point where he weeps, if only a little."[64] And in an essay on Montgomery's fiction on a website called "Balaam's Ass," in which numerous Bible verses are scattered every-where, Mary Van Nattan explained that "the Lord brought some disturb-ing things to [her] attention" during her reading of Montgomery's books, including the posthumous volume of short stories *Among the Shadows: Tales from the Darker Side* (1990). Van Nattan vilified Montgomery's books for featuring "strong-willed" heroines "who do not need a man *too* much" and for including mentions of witches, ghosts, and extra-sensory perception (which "shows that she had a very sick heart and mind"), then declared that Montgomery's feelings of entrapment in her marriage were evidence of her "resisting the order that God has set up in His word." She concluded that "Montgomery had a real talent for writ-ing, making her books very powerful tools for her father the devil." And, echoing a point made by earlier critics about Montgomery's books being flawed or anomalous examples of children's literature, she added, "These books will soil children's minds."[65]

L.M. Montgomery Studies into the Twenty-First Century

By the end of the 1990s, it seemed as though Montgomery had finally "arrived" as far as scholarly legitimacy and popular endurance were con-cerned. Arlene Perly Rae's volume *Everybody's Favourites: Canadians Talk about Books That Changed Their Lives*, published in 1997, con-tained an entire chapter on *Emily of New Moon* and its sequels, the only texts to be featured so prominently, with seven short essays by authors such as Alice Munro, Kit Pearson, Budge Wilson, and Jane Urquhart. In October of that year, *Quill and Quire* announced that *Anne of Green Gables* had been named "the best Canadian kids book[] of all time," even though the article noted that some panelists – including Sheila Egoff – had overlooked it entirely on their lists of contenders. In July 1999, a *Globe and Mail* poll billed Montgomery the fifth most influential Canadian in the arts, the first woman to appear on the list. Six months later, in an online poll by the CBC on "Great Canadian Writers," she was voted the top Canadian writer of the twentieth century, ahead of Farley Mowat, Margaret Laurence, Marshall McLuhan, and Margaret Atwood.[66] Chapters on Montgomery and Anne appeared in *Mondo Canuck: A Canadian Pop Culture Odyssey* (1996) and *Called to Witness: Profiles of Canadian Presbyterians* (1999).[67] *The Annotated Anne of Green Gables*, an oversized hardcover edited by Wendy E. Barry, Margaret Anne Doody, and Mary E. Doody Jones, complete with an exhaustive introduction and numerous appendices covering everything from literary allusions to flower names, had been published by Oxford University Press in 1997 and would be followed by several more critical editions of *Anne of Green Gables*, including a Broadview edition (2004) edited by Cecily Devereux, a Norton edition (2007) edited by Rubio and Waterston, and even a Focus on the Family edition (1999) that "silently updated [the text] for easier reading" and featured paratexts by Joe Wheeler.[68] The publication of two major collections of essays in 1999 likewise demonstrated the varied audience for Montgomery materials: *The Lucy Maud Montgomery Album* (Fitzhenry and Whiteside), compiled by Kevin McCabe and edited by Alexandra Heilbron, a coffee table book featuring over one hundred essays covering virtually every aspect of Montgomery's life, work, publishing history, and cultural legacy, and *L.M. Montgomery and Canadian Culture* (University of Toronto Press), edited by Irene Gammel and Elizabeth Epperly, a scholarly volume in which the contributors discussed both Montgomery's writing and its cultural context, with topics including education, technology, publishing practices, cultural heritage, transnational adaptation, xenophobia and community, war, and feminism. Both books received high praise from reviewers, but they clearly targeted and engaged with remarkably divergent audiences of readers.[69]

Moreover, since the end of the 1990s, a number of additional primary texts by Montgomery have appeared: the fourth and fifth volumes of *The Selected Journals of L.M. Montgomery* (1998, 2004), edited by Rubio and Waterston; the picture book *The Way to Slumbertown* (2005), illustrated by Rachel Bédard; *After Green Gables: L.M. Montgomery's Letters to Ephraim Weber, 1916–1941* (2006), edited by Hildi Froese Tiessen and Paul Gerard Tiessen; my edition of Montgomery's rediscovered final book, *The Blythes Are Quoted* (2009); a booklet consisting of a facsimile of Montgomery's long-lost serial "Una of the Garden" (2010) prepared by Donna J. Campbell and Simon Lloyd and published by the L.M. Montgomery Institute; as well as a restored and annotated edition of *Rilla of Ingleside* (2010), which I edited in collaboration with Andrea McKenzie. These new texts have appeared in tandem with an increasing number of trade editions, abridgments, and supplements, such as Marion Hoffmann's *Anne of Green Gables Puzzle Book* (2007).

So far in the twenty-first century, scholarship on L.M. Montgomery has taken a wide range of forms and approaches, particularly in studies published in 2008 to coincide with the worldwide centenary celebration of *Anne of Green Gables*. Oxford University Press published Elizabeth Waterston's book-length study *Magic Island: The Fictions of L.M. Montgomery* as a companion volume to Mary Henley Rubio's biography *Lucy Maud Montgomery: The Gift of Wings* (Doubleday Canada); Penguin Canada released Elizabeth Rollins Epperly's *Imagining Anne: The Island Scrapbooks of L.M. Montgomery* as part of its "100 Years of Anne" campaign; and Key Porter Books published both Irene Gammel's study *Looking for Anne: How Lucy Maud Montgomery Dreamed Up a Literary Classic* and Kevin Sullivan's novelization *Anne of Green Gables: A New Beginning*, both of which sought – in vastly different ways – to unearth the origins of this beloved character. Five book-length studies published since 2000 demonstrate the diversity of both field and audience: Deirdre Kessler's coffee table book *Green Gables: Lucy Maud Montgomery's Favourite Places* (2001, reissued 2010); Alexandra Heilbron's book of interviews *Remembering Lucy Maud Montgomery* (2001); Deborah Quaile's trade study *L.M. Montgomery: The Norval Years, 1926–1935* (2006); Elizabeth Rollins Epperly's academic study *Through Lover's Lane: L.M. Montgomery's Photography and Visual Imagination* (2007); and Jane Urquhart's biography *L.M. Montgomery* (2009), part of the prestigious Extraordinary Canadians series. Several collections of essays published in addition to books related to the L.M. Montgomery Institute conferences show this range of approaches, albeit as part of a renewed emphasis on Montgomery's best-known novel: a 2008 issue of *Canadian Children's Literature / Littérature canadienne pour la jeunesse*, introduced by Perry Nodelman; Holly Blackford's volume *100 Years of Anne with an "e": The Centennial Study of* Anne of Green Gables (2009); a 2010 issue of *The Lion and the Unicorn* on *Anne of Green Gables*, introduced by Michelle Ann Abate; and Gammel's and my volume *Anne's World: A New Century of Anne of Green Gables* (2010). Also appearing during this period are a number of new biographies for young readers by Elizabeth MacLeod, Janet Lunn, Stan Sauerwein, Marylou Morano Kjelle, Anne Dublin, and Alexandra Wallner.

As well, detailed treatment of Montgomery and her work has appeared in broader book-length studies published since 2000, by Clarence Karr, Alan MacEachern, Theodore F. Sheckels, John Seelye, Faye Hammill, Lorraine York, Carole Gerson, and Mary McDonald-Rissanen. Chapters specifically on Montgomery have appeared in collections of essays such as *Working in Women's Archives* (2001), *Interfaces: Women, Autobiography, Image, Performance* (2002), *Windows and Words: A Look at Canadian Children's Literature in English* (2003), *Home-Work: Postcolonialism, Pedagogy, and Canadian Literature* (2004), *Turning the Page: Children's Literature in Performance and the Media* (2006), *A Narrative Compass: Stories That Guide Women's Lives* (2009), *The Oxford Handbook of Children's Literature* (2011), *The Nation in Children's Literature* (2013), and *Textual Transformations in Children's Literature* (2013).[70] By placing Montgomery alongside her peers and contemporaries, these books complement academic titles focused specifically on her work by expanding the reach of Montgomery scholarship and providing her work with much needed historical and cultural context.

Recent scholarship devoted to Montgomery has revisited and expanded past conversations about print culture, tourism, links to American and British children's fiction (by Monique Dull and Jennifer H. Litster in this volume), gender and motherhood (by Cecily Devereux in this volume), translation and international reception (by Emily Aoife Somers in this volume), adaptation and afterlives, modernism, trauma, and war (by Andrea McKenzie in this volume). It has also initiated new discussions about feminist theology, the uncanny, repetition and variation in multivolume fiction, literary celebrity, class conflict, sexuality and performance, copyright and trademark law, archives (by Vanessa Brown and me in this volume), physical and mental health, domesticity, fashion, branding, disability, and ecofeminism.[71] Doctoral students during these years have also found new avenues of analysis for Montgomery's fiction and life writing: constructions of self and religious identity, theories of childhood, print culture and archives, tourism and mythmaking, the orphan figure, war, dance, and Scottish heritage.[72] Trade articles have continued to appear on a regular basis, not only about Montgomery and Anne but sometimes about the communities that her work creates (by Cynthia Brouse in this volume). As well, in addition to international conferences held at the University of Prince Edward Island, scholars from all around the world gathered at "L.M. Montgomery – Writer of the World" at Uppsala University (Sweden) in August 2009, which coincided with the one-hundredth anniversary of the first translation of *Anne of Green Gables*, and at "Lucy Maud Montgomery at Home in Leaskdale: A Centennial Celebration," in Leaskdale, Ontario, in October 2011, which coincided with the one-hundredth anniversary of Montgomery's arrival in Ontario as a minister's wife.

Moreover, since the beginning of the twenty-first century, discussions of Montgomery as an important and influential writer have continued to crop up in unexpected places, including a SparkNotes study guide for *Anne of Green Gables* in 2002. As well, Mona Holmlund and Gail Youngberg's *Inspiring Women: A Celebration of Herstory* (2003) includes profiles of twelve women writers who remain popular and influential in the twenty-first century, beginning with the reminder that "the late 20th century stars of Canadian literature are almost all women." Montgomery appears first in this section, which also profiles Martha Ostenso, Gabrielle Roy, Anne Hébert, Alice Munro, Margaret Laurence, Joy Kogawa, Margaret Atwood, and Carol Shields. In her contribution to *The Cambridge Companion to Canadian Literature* (2004) devoted to the ongoing tension between "the story of a nation and the stories written by its citizens," specifically to the role of comedy in this national literature, Magdalene Redekop includes Montgomery in a "catalog of comic writers" alongside Robert Kroetsch, Stephen Leacock, Robertson Davies, Mordecai Richler, Thomas King, and several others. In Elizabeth MacLeod's *The Kids Book of Great Canadians* (2004), Montgomery, the author of numerous "wonderful children's books," leads the section devoted to "The Arts," preceding the likes of Oscar Peterson, Céline Dion, Emily Carr, Cornelius Krieghoff, and the Group of Seven.[73]

In recent years we also have seen another trend – namely, of Anne without Montgomery. There have been numerous abridgments of *Anne of Green Gables*, *Anne of Avonlea*, *The Story Girl*, and *Emily of New Moon* over the years (the earliest, condensed and abridged by Mary W. Cushing and D.C. Williams, appeared in 1961), but the centenary of *Anne of Green Gables* in 2008 witnessed two major extensions to the Green Gables story. Budge Wilson's prequel *Before Green Gables*, authorized by Montgomery's heirs, narrates the married life of Anne's parents, her mother's pregnancy, and Anne's life with two foster families and in an orphanage until the moment she disembarks from the train at Bright River Station in expectation of Matthew Cuthbert. Published simultaneously in Canada, the United States, and the United Kingdom in February 2008, it was followed by paperback editions, audio books, and translations into numerous languages; it even inspired a Japanese *anime* series, *Kon'nichiwa Anne: Before Green Gables*, which aired in 2009. Unrelated to this novel is Kevin Sullivan's telefilm *Anne of Green Gables: A New Beginning*, which alternates between a fifty-something Anne and the child Anne prior to her arrival at Green Gables, and aired on Canadian television in December 2008, a month after its publication in book form. While *Before Green Gables* remains reasonably faithful to the clues given by Anne in Montgomery's books about her past, *A New Beginning* invents an alternate scenario in which young Anne feels compelled to lie about being an orphan because of her father's role in her mother's accidental death. Further transformations have occurred in several books published since then. In 2009, D.J. Foster of Alabama published *Lucy Maud Montgomery's* Anne of Green Gables *for the 21st Century*, in which "long paragraphs, lengthy descriptive passages, and rambling dialogue ... have been revised to fit modern tastes," apparently with the goal of "opening up this classic to a new generation";[74] and in 2010, Sullivan Entertainment's Davenport Press published four novelizations based on episodes of *Anne of Green Gables: The Animated Series*, beginning with Kevin Sullivan and Elizabeth Morgan's *Anne's New Home*.

The character of Anne and even the novel itself have become central motifs in several recent books: Montgomery's novel is read in a mother–daughter book club in Heather Vogel Frederick's *Much Ado about Anne* (2008); Caroline Stellings's *The Contest* (2009) tells the story of a young girl who is determined to win an Anne of Green Gables lookalike contest even though, due to her Aboriginal heritage (of which she is most proud), physically she looks nothing like Anne; Erin Blakemore devotes a chapter to Anne and "Happiness" in her book *The Heroine's Bookshelf: Life Lessons, from Jane Austen to Laura Ingalls Wilder* (2010); and Catherine McKenzie's novel *Arranged* (2011) features as protagonist a woman who was named Anne Blythe by her mother after Montgomery's character (as was Anne's brother, Gilbert). Additional transformations have proved to be quite imaginative, to say the least: L.A. Swart's *Anne of Green Gremlins: Pixie Slayer* (2010) rewrites Montgomery's story to include "an invasion of deadly pixies"; and in Nanci Adderley's *Kate Visits Green Gables* (2011), "the fates ha[ve] intervened and whisked make believe Kate" – Catherine, Duchess of Cambridge, to be exact – "to a different time, in a parallel universe to live the misadventures of her red-haired counter-part, Anne" – in other words, a near-perfect reproduction of the full text of *Anne of Green Gables* in which "Kate Gold" replaces Anne Shirley and "William Spencer" replaces "Gilbert Blythe."[75]

Montgomery herself has been reimagined by creative writers, such as Sara Peters, whose poem "Your Life as Lucy Maud Montgomery" appears in her collection *1996* (2013); and Montgomery's life, as revealed in her journals, has been staged in a number of fascinating plays, including Don Hannah's *The Wooden Hill* (1994), Anne Kathleen McLaughlin's *Maud of Cavendish* (2004), and Leo Marchildon and Adam-Michael James's *The Nine Lives of L.M. Montgomery* (2008).

There have also been a number of books whose covers depict red-headed protagonists but whose contents are otherwise unrelated to Montgomery's narrative worlds: Allan Gould's satirical non-fiction text *Anne of Green Gables vs. G.I. Joe: Friendly Fire between Canada and the U.S.* (2003), M. Carol Coffey's young adult novel *Zoe Lucky and the Green Gables' Mystery* (2009), and Herb Wyile's monograph *Anne of Tim Hortons: Globalization and the Reshaping of Atlantic-Canadian Literature* (2011). Whether seen as loving tributes or as blatant attempts to cash in on the continued popularity of Montgomery's characters, these follow-ups are nevertheless of interest as examples of how recent authors have interpreted or reinterpreted these compelling characters and narratives. None of these "new" Anne texts has come close to eclipsing Montgomery's own novel, however: the Seal edition of *Anne of Green Gables* made the Canadian best-seller list three times in the first half of 2012, indicating that there continues to be a sizeable audience for Montgomery's work – a novel published more than a century ago remains far more in demand than any attempt to update or reinvent it.[76]

Conclusion: The Future of Montgomery Studies

In June 2012, a familiar collision occurred between life writing and popular culture, between academic and mainstream audiences, echoing the events of late 1985: just as the Toronto production company Breakthrough Entertainment announced its plans to produce a new, ongoing television series based on *Anne of Green Gables* and its sequels, Oxford University Press released Rubio and Waterston's *The Complete Journals of L.M. Montgomery: The PEI Years, 1889–1900*, with a second volume, covering the years 1901 to 1911, appearing in March 2013. Once again, these two projects promised to bring together Montgomery's diverse audience: of readers and viewers, of adults and children, of academics and non-academics alike. Unlike in 1974, when Montgomery was completely overshadowed by the renown of Anne during the centenary year of her birth, they also encompass the current dual fascination with

Montgomery and with Anne. And in October 2013, Penguin Canada announced that it had acquired a YA novel by Melanie J. Fishbane fictionalizing Montgomery's life as an adolescent. The novel, set for publication in 2015 with the support of Montgomery's heirs, promises further collisions between fact and fiction while at the same time attempting to attract new readers to Montgomery's own story.

Moreover, the publication of this present volume occurs in the midst of a major Montgomery renaissance in the field of trade publishing. In Canada, the Seal Books editions are in the process of being phased out by Random House of Canada, to be replaced by a new set of hardcover and trade paperback editions under its Tundra Books imprint, beginning with the Anne and Emily books in fall 2014. In the United States, Illinois publisher Sourcebooks reissued, in spring 2014, fifteen Montgomery titles as trade paperbacks,[77] whereas Aladdin Books, an imprint of Simon and Schuster, reissued *Anne of Green Gables, Anne of Avonlea, Anne of the Island*, and *Anne's House of Dreams* as both jacketed hardcovers and trade paperbacks. In the United Kingdom, where the copyright to Montgomery's novels expired in 2013, new editions are in the process of appearing with a range of publishers: *The Blue Castle* and *A Tangled Web* with Hesperus Press, *Anne of Green Gables* and *Anne of Avonlea* with Vintage Books, and *The Story Girl, The Golden Road, Rilla of Ingleside, Emily of New Moon* and its sequels, and *Jane of Lantern Hill* with Virago Books. Not only do these new editions offer the opportunity to remarket Montgomery's texts to new readers – most of the non-Anne novels have not been available in the United Kingdom for several decades – but they also, and crucially, demonstrate a continued attempt to rebrand Montgomery visually in terms of cover art and book design.

All of this demonstrates that interest in L.M. Montgomery – her life, her work, her legacy – shows no signs of slowing down in the twenty-first century. Indeed, as Richard J. Lane writes concerning *Anne of Green Gables* in *The Routledge Concise History of Canadian Literature* (2011), "While for some readers reading this novel is like eating too many pancakes with maple syrup, it is also extremely seductive, and seductively transparent. The reality is that the text is far more complex than first appears."[78] As this volume shows, what has emerged since Montgomery's death is a consensus that her fiction and her own personal legacy continue to appeal and to prove complex to readers and viewers all around the world. The range of topics, approaches, and combinations indicates that scholarship on Montgomery is hardly dwindling – in fact, in many ways it has only just begun.

NOTES

1 See Butler, "The Heartbreaking Truth about Anne's Creator."
2 Preface to *AP*, 6. The reception of these two volumes is discussed in the epilogue to Volume 3 of *The L.M. Montgomery Reader*.
3 Fredericks, review of *The Wheel of Things*, 129–30; Saunders, "Anne's Author."
4 Gerson, "The Canon between the Wars," 47, 205–6n7. The five texts in question – J.D. Logan and Donald G. French's *Highways of Canadian Literature*, Archibald MacMechan's *The Headwaters of Canadian Literature*, Lionel Stevenson's *Appraisals of Canadian Literature*, William Arthur Deacon's *Poteen: A Pot-Pourri of Canadian Essays*, and Lorne Pierce's *An Outline of Canadian Literature (French and English)* – are all discussed in the introduction to Volume 1 of *The L.M. Montgomery Reader*.
5 Brown, *On Canadian Poetry*, 5, 4.
6 McAnn, "Life and Works of L.M. Montgomery," 21; Brown, *On Canadian Poetry*, 42.
7 Pacey, *Ten Canadian Poets*, vii; Åhmansson, *A Life and Its Mirrors*, 7.
8 Phelps, *Canadian Writers*, v, 85–86, 87, 88, 89, 93; Epperly, "L.M. Montgomery," 178; Åhmansson, *A Life and Its Mirrors*, 20, 23.
9 C. Thomas, *Canadian Novelists 1920–1945*, 83–84.
10 Rhodenizer, *A Handbook of Canadian Literature*, 102; Sylvestre, Conron, and Klinck, *Canadian Writers / Écrivains canadiens*, 111; Story, *The Oxford Companion*, 534; Rhodenizer, *Canadian Literature in English*, 975, 418.
11 Palk, *The Book of Canadian Achievement*, 146–49; Sclanders, "Lucy of Green Gables," 36.
12 Rhodenizer, *Canadian Literature in English*, 1024; Wales, review of *The Story of L.M. Montgomery*; *The Globe and Mail*, "The Power to Enchant"; *The Times Literary Supplement*, "Lives That Led to Fame."
13 Hackett, *70 Years of Best Sellers*, 73.
14 Montgomery, "Anne Says Her Prayers," 83.
15 G. McLaughlin, "The Literary Art of L.M. Montgomery," 107–8.
16 Roper, Beharriell, and Schieder, "Writers of Fiction 1880–1920," 331; McDowell, "Children's Books," 626–27.
17 Frye, Conclusion, 840.
18 Pacey, *Creative Writing in Canada*, 106; see also 89, 91.
19 Egoff, *The Republic of Childhood*, 252.
20 Pacey, *Essays in Canadian Criticism 1938–1968*, 24, 67, 239.
21 FitzPatrick, "Anne's First Sixty Years," 7, 13.

22 Åhmansson, *A Life and Its Mirrors*, 48. The phrase "ostensibly for girls" appears in Montgomery's initial description of *Anne of Green Gables* prior to its publication, in Montgomery to Weber, 2 May 1907, in *GGL*, 51.

23 One aspect of Montgomery's career that the *Selected Journals* revealed was the extent to which Montgomery struggled as an author even after the publication of *Anne of Green Gables*: as she revealed in a 1910 journal entry about the difficulties she faced living with her aging grandmother in Cavendish, "Many times I am at my wits' end between the chains which bind me on all sides and the numerous calls and claims which my literary success has brought forth. My life was hard enough before I became 'a celebrity.' My success, instead of making it easier, has made it twice as hard by doubling the worries and mortifications which attend my circumstances here. I am well off and tolerably famous – but the conditions of my life are not even physically comfortable and I am beset with difficulties on every side" (Montgomery, 21 September 1910, in *SJLMM*, 2: 17–18). These difficulties only intensified after her grandmother's death, at which point she left Prince Edward Island for a life as a minister's wife in rural Ontario, where church duties and motherhood left her with even less time to write. "I have written it from sheer love of it and revised it painstakingly," she claimed concerning *The Story Girl*, the last novel she wrote in PEI before her marriage, whereas her next novel, its sequel *The Golden Road*, was an entirely different experience: "I have not enjoyed writing it. I have had to write it at high pressure, all the time nervously expecting some interruption" (Montgomery, 29 November 1910, in *SJLMM*, 2: 20; Montgomery, 21 May 1913, in *SJLMM*, 2: 119).

24 Gerson, "*Anne of Green Gables*," 20.

25 Brown, *On Canadian Poetry*, 5; Thompson, Introduction, xv; Atwood, *Survival*, 205; Waterston, *Survey*, 102, 147.

26 McKenna, "Women in Canadian Literature," 73; Colombo, *Colombo's Canadian Quotations*, 427–28; Gerson, "*Anne of Green Gables*," 20; C. Thomas, *Our Nature – Our Voices*, 77; *Encyclopedia Canadiana*, s.v. "Montgomery, Lucy Maud," 134.

27 Greene, "Criticism and Theory," 258.

28 Carson, "Million Words in 10-Volume Diary," W4. According to Mary Rubio, it was Elizabeth Waterston who first learned of Montgomery's journals when she interviewed Macdonald for her chapter in *The Clear Spirit*. Due to his inexperience with scholarly editing and his failing health, he later arranged for the ledgers to be sold to the University of Guelph archives and left to Rubio's editorial discretion how best to prepare them for publication (M.H. Rubio, "Why L.M. Montgomery's Journals," 474–77).

29 In this respect, Montgomery is not unique even within the field of Canadian literature: as Michael Greene notes in *Encyclopedia of Literature in Canada* (2002) when introducing the "literary contexts that influence how we read and understand" primary texts, "Margaret Laurence's *The Diviners* can be placed in the contexts of 20th-century Canadian fiction, Canadian Prairie writing, the regional novel, women's writing, Laurence's 'Manawaka' books, postwar fiction, or the künstlerroman" (Greene, "Criticism and Theory," 249). In Montgomery's case, questions of genre are an additional form of literary context, particularly as far as the conventions of children's literature are concerned.

30 Sorfleet, Introduction, 6–7. *CCL/LCJ* continued as a quarterly journal at the University of Guelph until the end of 2004, publishing 116 issues, including three more devoted specifically to Montgomery: "L.M. Montgomery and Popular Culture" (Fall–Winter 1998), "L.M. Montgomery and Popular Culture II" (Fall 2000), and finally "Reassessments of L.M. Montgomery" (Spring–Summer 2004), which I edited. It then moved to the University of Winnipeg, where a new editorial team published eight semi-annual issues, including one with new Montgomery content in fall 2008. See Lefebvre, "Editorial"; Nodelman, "Editorial." Since 2009, the journal has continued with a revised mandate as *Jeunesse: Young People, Texts, Cultures*. For a 1980 profile of the journal, see Chambers, "Kids' Stuff."

31 Gerson, "*Anne of Green Gables*," 26.

32 Read, "Writing for Children in Canada," 9; Allen, "Not for Grandmas," 34.

33 Heilbron, "Canada's Commemorative Stamps," 463.

34 Walker, review of *The Wheel of Things*, 5; Cowan, review of *The Wheel of Things*, 513. In her review in *Canadian Literature*, Frances Frazer added that the weakness of the biography stemmed from "the fact that Gillen was not at liberty to quote freely from Montgomery's diaries, which repose in the protective custody of the author's son, Dr. Stuart MacDonald [*sic*]." She added, however, that "Gillen does make some notable additions to our knowledge of L.M. Montgomery" by quoting from her correspondence with MacMillan (Frazer, "Not the Whole Story," 106, 107). A shorter version of Gillen's biography, entitled *Lucy Maud Montgomery*, appeared as part of Fitzhenry and Whiteside's The Canadians series in 1978. See also Gillen, "The Rescue of the Montgomery–MacMillan Letters."

35 Stuart, "'Nearer to God in Lover's Lane,'" 44; see also M.H. Rubio, "Uncertainties Surrounding the Death of L.M. Montgomery," 52. Macartney-Filgate's documentary dramatizes sections from *Anne of Green Gables*

and key events depicted in Montgomery's journals, including her passionate yet unconsummated love affair with Herman Leard. Some of its casting choices are also noteworthy: Patricia Hamilton, who would play Mrs. Rachel Lynde in a number of Sullivan Entertainment productions from 1985 on, plays Mrs. Lynde in this production as well, and Jackie Burroughs, who would play series lead Hetty King in Sullivan Entertainment's *Road to Avonlea* (1990–96), is the narrative voice of Montgomery's journals, a role she would reprise in Barbara Doran's documentary *The Many Mauds* (1996), part of the *Life and Times* biography series that also aired on the CBC.

36 Colombo, *Colombo's Canadian References*, 346; Frazer, "Island Writers," 76; Willis, "The Bogus Ugly Duckling"; Reid, "From Anne of G.G."; Bolger, "Lucy Maud's Island"; Woodcock, "Possessing the Land," 76; Burns, "Anne and Emily," 37; S.E. Jones, "Recurring Patterns"; Scanlon, "Alternatives"; Baker, "Archibald MacMechan"; Berke, "'Mother I Can Do It Myself!'"; Ross, "Calling Back the Ghost"; Vipond, "Best Sellers in English Canada, 1899–1918"; Norcross, *Pioneers Every One*, 77–87; Montgomery, "A Girl's Place at Dalhousie College"; ellipsis in original. Woodcock's chapter also appeared in Woodcock, *The World of Canadian Writing*, 18–19. See also Vipond, "Best Sellers in English Canada: 1919–1928."

37 Steffler, "Anne in a 'Globalized' World," 152; M.H. Rubio, "'A Dusting Off,'" 52. Brown's and Deacon's comments are discussed at length in the introduction to Volume 1 of *The L.M. Montgomery Reader*.

38 In the United Kingdom, *Anne of Green Gables* was dramatized as a five-part BBC miniseries in 1972, followed in 1975 by the six-part *Anne of Avonlea*, which dramatized parts of Montgomery's *Anne of Avonlea* and *Anne of the Island*; tie-in editions of all Anne novels were subsequently published in the UK. Neither miniseries ever aired in North America, although *Anne of Avonlea* was released on Region 1 DVD in 2006.

39 See Campbell and Harron, "*Anne of Green Gables*"; Harron, *Anne of Green Gables*.

40 *The Road to Yesterday* was republished by Angus and Robertson, in England and Australia, in 1975. I also have in my personal collection a large print edition of *Emily of New Moon* published in the United Kingdom in 1980. For more on Montgomery's publishing history until the mid-1980s, see Russell, Russell, and Wilmshurst, *Lucy Maud Montgomery*, 1–58.

41 The Bantam editions were released on a slightly different timetable in the United States, with *Kilmeny of the Orchard*, *The Story Girl*, *Chronicles of Avonlea*, *The Golden Road*, *Further Chronicles of Avonlea*, *Magic for*

Marigold, *A Tangled Web*, and *Jane of Lantern Hill* not released in that country until 1989. Many of these editions remain in print to this day, now published by Laurel-Leaf Books, a YA imprint of Random House Children's Books.

42 The Seal edition of *Rilla of Ingleside* reprinted a 1976 edition by the American Reprint Company that had silently deleted 4,530 words from Montgomery's text (Lefebvre and McKenzie, "A Note on the Text"), and as I indicate in an annotation in Mary Rubio's chapter "Subverting the Trite" in this volume, the sentence "One pays for it in bondage of some kind or other" is absent from the Seal edition of *Emily of New Moon*.

43 See, in particular, Jones and Jones, *Canadian Fiction*, 45, 56, 120; Cadogan, "Montgomery, L(ucy) M(aud)"; Hoy, *Modern English-Canadian Prose*, 328–35; Parker, "*Anne of Green Gables* (1908)"; Parker, "Montgomery, L.M. (1874–1942)"; Carpenter and Prichard, *The Oxford Companion to Children's Literature*, 25–26, 356; Stouck, *Major Canadian Authors*, 45, 289; Moss and Stott, *The Family of Stories*, 646–47; Hendrickson, *Children's Literature*, 198–99; Moritz and Moritz, *The Oxford Illustrated Literary Guide*, 20–21, 33–34, 36–39, 119, 127, 133, 175, 200; Saltman, *Modern Canadian Children's Books*, 9, 58, 127; Stott, "L.M. Montgomery (1874–1942)"; Stott and Jones, *Canadian Books for Children*, 124–28; M.H. Rubio, "*Anne of Green Gables*"; Frazer, "Lucy Maud Montgomery."

44 Cadogan and Craig, *You're a Brick, Angela!* 95, 96, 99.

45 J. Moss, *A Reader's Guide to the Canadian Novel*, 344; Gagnon and Gagnon, *Canadian Books for Young People*, 51–52, 67.

46 Egoff, "Children's Literature in English," 118–19; Parker, "*Anne of Green Gables* (1908)," 14.

47 Stouck, *Major Canadian Authors*, 289; Sorfleet, "Montgomery, L(ucy) M(aud)," 906. This paradox echoes a statement made in Sylvestre, Conron, and Klinck's reference book *Canadian Writers / Écrivains canadiens*, in which they referred to *Anne of Green Gables* as "a story for girls in early adolescence" that is "popular with an adult as well as a young reading public" (111).

48 Gerson, "Seven Milestones," 27, 28.

49 Scholars who have examined these screen adaptations include Susan Drain ("'Too Much Love-Making'"), Trinna S. Frever, Philippa Gates and Stacy Gillis, Christopher Gittings, Eleanor Hersey, Patsy Aspasia Kotsopoulos ("Avonlea as Main Street USA?"), Benjamin Lefebvre ("*Road to Avonlea*"; "Stand by Your Man"), and Wendy Roy. See also Cole, *Here's Looking at Us*, 190–91, 234–36.

50 See the titles by Dennis Adair and Janet Rosenstock, Heather Conkie, Amy
    Jo Cooper, Gail Hamilton, Marlene Matthews, Fiona McHugh, and Linda
    Zwicker. These books were preceded by *The Avonlea Album* (1991), a
    book of photographs and captions edited by McHugh, who developed the
    series and who wrote *The Anne of Green Gables Storybook* (1987) based
    on the Sullivan miniseries.

51 Jacquot, "Anne of Green Gables," 33.

52 Gerson, "Seven Milstones," 24. The Québec–Amérique translations consist
    of the eight Anne books, the two Chronicles volumes, *Kilmeny of the Or-
    chard*, *The Story Girl*, *The Golden Road*, *Magic for Marigold*, *A Tangled
    Web*, four of Rea Wilmshurst's collections of rediscovered short stories,
    and a biography by Harry Bruce. *Emily of New Moon* and its sequels
    were published in French translation by Éditions Pierre Tisseyre begin-
    ning in 1983, whereas *The Blue Castle*, *Pat of Silver Bush*, *Mistress Pat*,
    and *Jane of Lantern Hill* were published in French translation by Éditions
    Flammarion. While the bulk of these editions remain in print today, little
    information about Montgomery's life has been made available in French,
    let alone scholarship on her work. See Russell, "L.M. Montgomery";
    Lefebvre, "Présentation."

53 Gammel, "Introduction: Reconsidering Anne's World," 8.

54 M.H. Rubio, "L.M. Montgomery: Where Does," 109; M.H. Rubio, "*Anne
    of Green Gables*: The Architect," 71.

55 Epperly, "L.M. Montgomery," 180.

56 Egoff with Sutton, *Once upon a Time*, 10. For a discussion of reviews of
    Montgomery's journals and other posthumous texts, see the epilogue in
    Volume 3 of *The L.M. Montgomery Reader*.

57 As coincidence would have it, and as evidence of a rather small scholarly
    community, Epperly and Wiggins ended up reviewing each other's books.
    In *CCL/LCJ*, Epperly praised Wiggins's volume as "a good, solid piece of
    work" that is "often shrewd and enjoyable," but she faulted Wiggins's ten-
    dency to see Montgomery as an author who was always willing to capitu-
    late to public taste (Epperly, "A Successful Montgomery," 38, 39). In *The
    American Review of Canadian Studies*, Wiggins singled out Epperly's focus
    on romance and discussion of Montgomery's literary allusions, concluding
    that "Epperly's discerning treatment of the heroines should prove of inter-
    est not only to Montgomery devotees but to any reader interested in social
    history and particularly in attitudes toward women reflected in popular
    fiction" (Wiggins, review of *The Fragrance of Sweet-Grass*, 462).

58 See work by T.D. MacLulich ("L.M. Montgomery's Portraits"), Nancy
    Huse, Janet Weiss-Townsend, Temma F. Berg, Charlene E. Gates, Susan

Drain ("Feminine Convention and Female Identity"), Gabriella Åhmansson ("The Survival of the Artist"), Marie Campbell, Denyse Yeast, Patricia Kelly Santelmann, Jennie Rubio, Shirley Foster and Judy Simons, K.L. Poe, G.A. Woods, Kate Lawson ("Adolescence and the Trauma"), as well as my article "Walter's Closet."

59　These critics include Perry Nodelman ("Progressive Utopia"), Shirley Wright, Anne Scott MacLeod, T.D. MacLulich ("L.M. Montgomery"), Gillian Avery ("'Remarkable and Winning'"), Constance Classen, Clara Thomas ("Anne Shirley's American Cousin"), Eve Kornfeld and Susan Jackson, Brenda Niall, and Robin McGrath.

60　Consider contributions by Elizabeth R. Epperly ("L.M. Montgomery's *Anne's House of Dreams*"), Kevin McCabe ("Lucy Maud Montgomery"), John Ferns, Marilyn Solt, Susan Drain ("Community and the Individual"), Ian Menzies, Theodore F. Sheckels ("In Search of Structures"), and Elizabeth Waterston ("Orphans, Twins, and L.M. Montgomery").

61　See work by Epperly ("Approaching the Montgomery Manuscripts") and Margaret Turner. See also Paul Tiessen and Hildi Froese Tiessen's early article on Ephraim Weber, published in 1993.

62　In all these topics, see work by Gabriella Åhmansson ("'Mayflowers Grow in Sweden Too'"), Douglas Baldwin, J.M. Bumsted, Virginia Careless, Donna Coates, Lorna Drew, Julie Fenwick, Angela E. Hubler, Rosemary Ross Johnston, Yuka Katsura, Jeanette Lynes, Jason Nolan and his colleagues, Catherine Sheldrick Ross ("Readers Reading L.M. Montgomery"), Shelagh J. Squire, Judy Stoffman, Denise Thomson, Diane Tye ("Multiple Meanings Called Cavendish"), Barbara Wachowicz, Gavin White ("L.M. Montgomery and the French"; "The Religious Thought"), Rea Wilmshurst ("L.M. Montgomery's Use"), and Alan R. Young.

63　For a list of MA theses pertaining to Montgomery, see the L.M. Montgomery Online website at http://lmmonline.org.

64　Anthony, *Thy Rod and Staff*, 89–90. I am grateful to Jennifer H. Litster for bringing this book to my attention.

65　Van Nattan's essay is undated, but I have in my personal archive a print-out of her Web page dated February 2000; it was still online in August 2013. For the biblical significance of the term "Balaam's Ass," see Numbers 22 in the Judeo-Christian Bible. Mary Van Nattan, "L.M. Montgomery," *Balaam's Ass*, http://www.balaams-ass.com/journal/-homemake/lmmont.htm.

66　Oppel, "The Best Canadian Kids Books," 16, 15; *The Globe and Mail*, "The Ten Most Influential Canadians." The CBC poll and its results are no longer online.

67 See Pevere and Dymond, *Mondo Canuck*, 12–15; Waterston, "L.M. Montgomery (1884 [*sic*]–1942)."

68 While both the texts and the paratexts of the Oxford, Broadview, and Norton editions have been cited frequently since their respective publications, the Focus on the Family *Anne* has rarely, if ever, been even mentioned in subsequent scholarship.

69 As well, an odd collision between academia, the mainstream media, and the general public made L.M. Montgomery and *Anne of Green Gables* front-page news again in May 2000, when a conference paper by Laura M. Robinson on lesbian desire and compulsory heterosexuality in Montgomery's Anne books was misrepresented in an article in the *Edmonton Journal* that claimed that Robinson had declared that Anne "was" a lesbian. The story spiralled in media outlets from around the world for several weeks. An expansion of that paper, entitled "Bosom Friends," was published in *Canadian Literature* in 2004 to far less furor. For analyses of the media frenzy, see L.M. Robinson, "'Big Gay Anne'"; L.M. Robinson, "'"Outrageously Sexual" Anne'"; and Devereux, "Anatomy of a 'National Icon.'" See also White, "Falling Out of the Haystack."

70 See chapters by Mary Henley Rubio ("'A Dusting Off'"), Irene Gammel ("Mirror Looks"), Cecily Devereux ("'Not One of Those Dreadful New Women'"), Jennifer Henderson, Margaret Mackey, Elizabeth Ebony Thomas, Catherine Posey, Mavis Reimer ("A Daughter of the House"), Danielle Russell, Andrea McKenzie ("Patterns, Power, and Paradox"), Emily Somers, and Maria Nikolajeva.

71 This scholarship includes work by Yoshiko Akamatsu, Danièle Allard, Poushali Bhadury, Mary Beth Cavert, Gabrielle Ceraldi, Alison Matthews David and Kimberly Wahl, Clare Fawcett and Patricia Cormack, Ashley Cowger, Janis Dawson, Cecily Devereux ("'Not a "Usual" Property'"), Hilary Emmett, Janice Fiamengo ("' ... The Refuge of My Sick Spirit ... '"), Irene Gammel ("Embodied Landscape Aesthetics"), Anne Golden, Marah Gubar, Monika B. Hilder, Colin Hill, Kylee-Anne Hingston, Nancy Holmes, Ann F. Howey, Helen Hoy ("'Too Heedless and Impulsive'"), Yuko Izawa, Christine Trimingham Jack, Rosemary Ross Johnston ("Landscape as Palimpsest"), Caroline E. Jones, Clarence Karr ("Addicted to Reading"), Kate Lawson ("The Victorian Sickroom"), Benjamin Lefebvre ("Pigsties and Sunsets"; "'That Abominable War!'"; "What's in a Name?"), Jenn Macquarrie, Kathleen A. Miller, Perry Nodelman ("Rereading *Anne of Green Gables*"), D. Jason Nolan and Joel Weiss, E. Holly Pike ("'Tempest in a Teapot'"), Mavis Reimer ("The Child of Nature"), Laura M. Robinson ("'Sex Matters'"), Rosemary Rowe, Dawn Sardella-Ayres,

Andrea Slane, Katharine Slater, Jackie E. Stallcup, Amy Tector, Christa Zeller Thomas, Robyn Weaver, and Kate Wood.

72　See doctoral dissertations by Shauna Joanne McCabe, Jennifer H. Litster, Danièle Allard, Patsy Aspasia Kotsopoulos, Lin Haire-Sargeant, Andre Narbonne, Kathleen Patchell, and Emily S. Woster.

73　Mehlinger, *Anne of Green Gables*; Holmlund and Youngberg, *Inspiring Women*, 226; Redekop, "Canadian Literary Criticism," 264; MacLeod, *The Kids Book of Great Canadians*, 32.

74　D.J. Foster, *Lucy Maud Montgomery's*, back cover.

75　Adderley, *Kate Visits Green Gables*, n.pag. In *Kate Charms Avonlea*, Anne's pupil Paul Irving is transformed into Harry Spencer. Two additional sequels appeared in 2013, in ebook format only: *Kate's Prince Charming* and *Kate's Castle*.

76　Katie Gowrie, "Booknet Bestsellers: Canadian Fiction," *Quill and Quire*, 3 July 2012, http://www.quillandquire.com/blog/index.php/2012/07/03/booknet-bestsellers-canadian-fiction-6; Natalie Samson, "Booknet Bestsellers: Canadian Fiction," *Quill and Quire*, 14 May 2012, http://www.quillandquire.com/blog/index.php/2012/05/14/booknet-bestsellers-canadian-fiction-4; Sue Carter Flinn, "Booknet Bestsellers: Canadian Fiction," *Quill and Quire*, 26 March 2012, http://www.quillandquire.com/blog/index.php/2012/03/26/booknet-bestsellers-canadian-fiction-2.

77　The Sourcebooks editions consist of the eleven novels still protected by copyright in the United States – *Emily of New Moon, Emily Climbs, The Blue Castle, Emily's Quest, Magic for Marigold, A Tangled Web, Pat of Silver Bush, Mistress Pat, Anne of Windy Poplars, Jane of Lantern Hill*, and *Anne of Ingleside* – as well as *Anne of Green Gables, Anne of Avonlea, Anne of the Island*, and *Anne's House of Dreams*, which are in the public domain in all territories.

78　Lane, *The Routledge Concise History*, 69. Elsewhere in this text, Lane refers to *Rilla of Ingleside* as one of the two "strongest feminist narratives" of the First World War in Canada, alongside Francis Marion Beynon's *Aleta Day* (ibid., 82).

A Note on the Text

This edition reproduces twenty items published in journals, magazines, and scholarly books in Canada, the United States, and the Netherlands over a forty-six-year period. While I have retained the conventions of spelling, hyphenation, and usage of the original publications, for ease of reading I have silently corrected obvious mechanical errors and standardized the capitalization of titles and subheads. I have also silently corrected errors in the publication dates of L.M. Montgomery's books and misspellings of real and fictional surnames such as Barry, Lavendar, Macdonald, Macneill, Stacy, Stuart, and Stirling.

All in-text citations in the original publications have been moved to endnotes and refer to a standard set of Montgomery's primary texts. Although I have silently corrected and emended quotations from her work to reflect the text in these editions, I have refrained from making excessive editorial interventions. When a source that was unpublished at the time of the original publication has since been published, I have added an updated citation in square brackets, and in some instances, when citations were not provided in the original publication, I added these (along with occasional editorial notes) also within square brackets. My goal throughout has been to create a standard form of presentation while maintaining the practices of these items in their original form.

The bibliography is limited to sources cited in the text. For a more exhaustive bibliography of editions, abridgements, adaptations, supplementary texts, and contributions to Montgomery scholarship, see the L.M. Montgomery Online website at http://lmmonline.org.

1

Lucy Maud Montgomery 1874–1942

—— 1966 ——

ELIZABETH WATERSTON

This volume of *The L.M. Montgomery Reader* begins with a chapter that, as Mary Henley Rubio has noted, was "the first substantial scholarly article taking [Montgomery's] books seriously."[1] This chapter by Elizabeth Waterston, then an Associate Professor of English at the University of Guelph and later co-editor, with Rubio, of seven volumes of Montgomery's journals published between 1985 and 2013, appeared in *The Clear Spirit: Twenty Canadian Women and Their Times*, a project edited by Mary Quayle Innis, undertaken by the Canadian Federation of University Women in honour of Canada's centenary, and published by University of Toronto Press in 1966. Waterston had no access to L.M. Montgomery's journals in her research for this chapter, but she made good use of the sources that were available to her then: a volume of Montgomery's letters to Weber, published as *The Green Gables Letters* in 1960, as well as the magazine copy of "The Alpine Path." As Vida Peene, "chairman" of the CFUW editorial committee, explained in her foreword to the volume, "this book may show what women could do before academic doors opened to them and also how their own freedom was gradually won."[2] The volume includes fifteen chapters, profiling such prominent women as Pauline Johnson, Agnes Macphail (1890–1954), the "Five Persons from Alberta," Emily Carr (1871–1945), and Mazo de la Roche. Although Innis, in her introduction to the volume, notes that the chapters "display the very real struggle of able and forceful women against very real obstacles," the volume celebrates achievement instead of dwelling on adversity: "Twenty women stand forth, vividly alive. Holding hands, they would draw together not just the century of Canada's political existence but the whole span of her history."[3] In spite of this celebration, Waterston was later advised by a senior colleague not to bother with Montgomery as a topic of worthwhile study.[4] She ignored this advice and has continued to play an instrumental role in keeping the fire of Montgomery criticism going ever since. Besides co-editing volumes of Montgomery's journals and a Norton Critical Edition of *Anne of Green Gables* with Rubio, she has published several book-length studies, including *Kindling Spirit: L.M. Montgomery's* Anne of Green Gables (1993) and *Magic Island: The Fictions of L.M. Montgomery* (2008).

She was born on a beautiful island. Her mother died when she was very young. Her father left her with an old lady and an old man, in an apple-orchard, by the sea. When she grew up, she was put under a vow, never to leave the old people. But a young man loved her, and after ten years of waiting he carried her off, away from the island.

This is the language of fairy-tale. It seems to be the first way to tell the story of Lucy Maud Montgomery. Girls following her biography in H.M. Ridley's *Life of L.M. Montgomery* may feel they are reading another romance in the sequence of "Anne" and "Emily" and "Pat" and "Story Girl" books.[5]

Many women *have* lived "fabulous" lives. But in L.M. Montgomery's case the real miracle is that she could exploit her experience in an enduring art-form. She universalized her story; she recreated it against vivid regional settings; she structured it into mythical patterns. She retold the legends she had lived, in haunting and memorable style.

She used her life materials in a way that brought her personal fame, and brought her country's literature a popular international recognition. Literary critics throughout the Western world saw at once the values she had achieved. If subsequent sophisticated criticism agreed to laugh at or to by-pass the creator of "Anne," critics today are less ready to be patronizing.

We find in her life, her letters, her journals, the story of an important craftsman, a professional writer fighting to clarify and improve the conditions of an artist's work. And in her novels we find a subtle and illuminating use of archetypal patterns, particularly of the recurring myths of girlhood.

If we re-examine her life story and look at her books as in part an unconscious supplement to the biography, we come close to watching the miracle of the creative imagination.

Born in 1874, in a North Shore village on Prince Edward Island, Lucy Maud Montgomery was brought as a baby from Clifton to Cavendish, to her mother's family. Her grandmother Macneill gave her a home when her young mother, Clara Woolner Macneill Montgomery, died, twenty-one months after Lucy Maud's birth. Her father, Hugh John Montgomery, left the Island to strike out for the West, and settled in Prince Albert.

Lucy Maud Montgomery's memories of childhood were very intense. She could recall "spots of time"[6] from her third year on. She was a bright, quick child: when she started school she moved eagerly through the old P.E.I. "readers," with their characteristic Maritime blend of New England and British writers. Years later she would place on the title-pages of her books verses from that same range of great Romantic and Victorian writers of America and Britain: Whittier, Emerson, Longfellow, Oliver Wendell Holmes; and Tennyson, Byron, Cowper, and Burns.

Life was dominated by the grandparents' notions of how a little girl should dress and behave. She was a solitary child, creating imaginary friends, and living in the book-worlds of Bunyan and Scott and Thackeray. Slowly and sensitively she realized the beauty of her native setting: the apple-orchard slopes of the Macneill farm; the red-earth, tree-lined road winding past pond and woods to the village of Cavendish; the blueberry barrens; and the circling, sounding sea.

She responded; and she wrote. She phrased her impressions of the world around her in the formal and already old-fashioned diction of Thomson's *Seasons*. She liked, later, to tell the story of showing her earliest lines to her family – who complained, "It doesn't rhyme!" But one point of the story is that although she defended the "blankness" of her verse, she was willing to re-work it, producing soon reams of rhyme. It was a first, characteristic effort to adjust to critical suggestions. From the beginning it was not just self-expression that she wanted – it was recognition. She wanted to write; but she also wanted to be read. She sent off her first manuscript, hopefully, when she was eleven, to an American magazine, *The Household*. It was returned, but she tried again, this time for a Canadian publication. It would be four years before her first appearance in print, but those years were characterized by an amazing persistence. Composing, copying, mailing, continued in the face of total lack of interest – this would not be in the scope of most twelve-year-old, thirteen-year-old, fourteen-year-old lives.

The first heartening acceptance came for a verse-narrative, reworking a P.E.I. legend, sent to the Charlottetown *Patriot*. This was in the winter of 1889–90, and the manuscript was sent from the far West, for

Lucy Maud had now moved out to Prince Albert to join her father. From Prince Albert, while she was in high school, she sent other poems and sketches to Montreal, to Charlottetown, and to New York.

The reunion with her father was brief. He had remarried, and although she enjoyed the company of her step-brother and step-sisters,[7] the adolescent girl did not fit comfortably into the new home. The year, so productive of immediate literary work, never seemed "usable" later: she by-passed it when she was exploiting other events of her girlhood and assigning bits of her own experience to her fictional heroines.

Meanwhile, the young Islander trailed back to Cavendish to finish school and to write entrance examinations for Prince of Wales College. In 1893 she moved to Charlottetown to attend the College (where courses covered the final two years of high school and the first two of university). Her one-year course qualified her for a teacher's licence. In this same year she had her first "pay" for literary work: two subscriptions to the magazine that accepted her poem, "Only a Violet." It was an American magazine.

L.M. Montgomery (as she now signed her manuscripts) continued to write and submit stories and poems to Canadian and American magazines, after she had taken her teacher's licence and begun to work at Bideford School. Most of the manuscripts came back, but enough were accepted (though without any monetary reward) to make the young author decide to get further training in the field of literature. She went to Halifax in 1895, enrolled at Dalhousie College, and took a course in English literature from Archibald MacMechan, himself a poet and short story writer. The alternative for an Islander would be McGill – many of the characters in her stories go to the Montreal university; but L.M. Montgomery's formal education was all in the Maritimes. During her year in Halifax she earned her first money for writings: five dollars from *Golden Days* in Philadelphia; five dollars from the *Halifax Evening Mail*; twelve dollars from the Philadelphia *Youth's Companion*. She was also placing more and more work with the Sunday School papers, enough to encourage her ambition for a career as a writer.

In 1896, back on Prince Edward Island, school-teaching left little time or energy for composition. But for many months she worked at her writing each morning from six to seven, by lamplight, sitting on her feet to keep warm in the old farmhouse where she was boarding.

She resigned her teaching job two years later to return to Cavendish. The death of her grandfather Macneill in 1898 left her grandmother alone. L.M. Montgomery decided to see if she could make a living by her writing, eked out by the money her grandmother made as local postmistress. Lucy Maud was twenty-two years old; she was selling enough to cover board and clothing; she was improving her work. "I never expect to be famous," she wrote. "I merely want to have a recognized place among good workers in my chosen profession."[8] In the year after her grandfather's death, in double dedication to family and career, she promised her grandmother to stay and work at home.

Briefly, she interrupted her Island life when she accepted a job on the Halifax *Daily Echo* in November, 1901. She moved into a Halifax boarding-house, and for almost a year wrote a weekly gossip column, edited a page of "society letters," proof-read, answered the phone, and did free "write-ups" of the advertisers' goods. She was learning to work under pressure, to produce for a given audience. Meantime she could submit manuscripts to other publications, with a growing percentage of acceptances. She was sending to more sophisticated journals now: *Ainslie's, The Delineator, The Smart Set*, published in the eastern States.

The young author acquired "pen-pals" among other young people aspiring to literary success. She began an interesting correspondence, for instance, with Ephraim Weber, a Kitchener man who had gone homesteading in Alberta, but shared her literary ambitions and frustrations: "We'll be dead long before Canadian literature will be a bread-and-butter affair."[9] By June, 1902, she was writing all her friends to tell them she was going home to the Island, hoping for more free time for writing.

Settled again in Cavendish, she was beginning a long courtship with a young Presbyterian minister, the Reverend Ewan Macdonald, a fine-looking man a few years older than she, and product of the same kind of schooling and family. She worked hard at her sketches and stories, mailing them to a great variety of magazines: *Canadian Magazine, McClure's*, the *Family Herald, Current Literature*, the Boston *National, Sunday School Times*, the Battle Creek *Pilgrim, Modern Women*, New York *Gunton's, Lippincott's*. Her letters are filled with indefatigable zest, and eager interest in the possibilities for publication. She was reading *Trilby, Dr. Jekyll and Mr. Hyde, The Story of an African Farm*, the poetry of Markham, catching up on contemporary best-sellers. She was puzzling over matters of faith, the possibility of psychic experience, the mystery of pain, evolution, the divinity of Christ, eagerly discussing, exploring, opening her mind to any new trend of thought. She was simultaneously re-exploring the Bible, Gibbon's *Decline and Fall of the Roman Empire*, and Emerson. The best way to catch a notion of her work at this time is to read *Further Chronicles of Avonlea*, published much later, but consisting mostly of stories written in her early twenties, "pot-boilers" as she herself scornfully dubbed them, but intriguing in their range of interests.

She could report making $591.85 in 1904. Ideas for stories and poems came fast, caught into notebook jottings, set aside till a mood or a market suggested a way of "working up." She could pass along practical advice: "*To work at once, stick to it*, write something *every day*, even if you burn it up after writing it."[10]

In 1904, she re-read a note-book entry: "Elderly couple apply to orphan asylum for a boy. By a mistake a girl is sent them." Although her first intention was to work this notion into a short story for a Sunday School paper, she found the character "grew on her" so much that the work expanded to book length. She worked on it for eighteen months, keeping other writing on the go at the same time. The manuscript was mailed out hopefully to a publisher, and rejected. Mailed again, three more times, to other possible publishers, including Macmillan. Rejected again – and finally stowed away by the author in discouragement.

Meanwhile she had placed another story, *Kilmeny of the Orchard*, in serial form, with an American magazine, and other stories with the Chicago *Blue Book*, New York *Watson's*, Chicago *Rural Magazine*. She made about $800 in 1906, but by dint of unremitting writing. She rarely left Cavendish; her grandmother was now eighty-two, and the younger woman had almost all the housework to do. She was reading less, and an odd mixture: the Book of Job, Upton Sinclair's "hideous" *The Jungle*, Lewis Carroll's *Alice through the Looking Glass*.[11]

Then spring came, and wonderful news. The manuscript of *Anne of Green Gables*, which she had dug out, re-worked, and sent off to one more publisher, was accepted. "I am blatantly pleased and proud and happy," she said, "and I shan't make any pretence of not being so."[12]

The L.C. Page Company of Boston, "her" publisher, was not a major house, but they did handle Bliss Carman, Charles G.D. Roberts, and other writers well known to Maritime readers. They offered 10 per cent royalties (nine cents on a wholesale price of ninety cents), plus a flat sum for dramatic rights, and bound her to give them first refusal of all her books for the next five years. Pitman's of London would hold the English rights. On the whole, acceptable terms, and certainly a glorious realization of the long, long dream of having a full-length book published.

In June, 1908, the first copy of *Anne of Green Gables* arrived from the publishers, attractively bound, in good clear print on good firm paper – a format that would stand up to the readings and re-readings that awaited it when it reached the hundreds of thousands of its young audience.

The book instantly appealed to an incredibly large market, and one not limited to girls. It brought floods of letters to its author, including a note from Bliss Carman, and one from Mark Twain. The proud author thrilled to Mark Twain's comment: in Anne she had created "the dearest, and most lovable child in fiction since the immortal Alice."[13] *Anne of Green Gables* went into four editions in three months, and rolled on from there into one printing after another.

The terms of the publishers' contract did not include any sliding scale of royalties for this run-away best-seller. If the author wanted to cash in on the "Anne-mania" she must get to work on a sequel. The publishers insisted that she should write "like mad" to meet the demand. She settled into a new routine: two hours of writing, one of transcribing onto the typewriter – thinking out plot and dialogue as she worked around the house. She was less than happy with her new book. It didn't "grow"; she had to "build" it.[14] She blocked it all out in her mind before writing it. "All the incidents have happened [and] I have only to write about them now."[15]

Meanwhile she house-cleaned, sewed, gardened, played the organ for the church choir. The Reverend Ewan Macdonald was still hovering near, trying to persuade her to marry him. He found adamant refusal for a number of reasons: her grandmother, her writing commitments, her career, her new book – reasonable barriers multiplied. There were still serious puzzles in her religious thinking also: "I call myself a Christian, but oh!"[16]

In November, 1908, she sent off the manuscript of *Anne of Avonlea*. She was feeling tired, head-achey, nervous, worn out by the publicity surrounding "that detestable *Anne*." "Petty flings of malice and spite" followed local readings of the book. She was brooding over "certain worries and troubles that have been ever present in my life for the past six years [i.e., since 1902]. They are caused by people and circumstances over which I have no control, so I am quite helpless in regard to them and when I get run-down I take a too morbid view of them." A favourite aunt died in 1909. That year she refused an invitation to speak at a World's Congress of Women in Toronto: "couldn't get away."[17]

But in the fall of 1909 she started a new book – beginning by composing the first sentence and the last paragraph. *The Story Girl* she considered "away ahead of *Anne* from a literary point of view."[18] She enjoyed writing this tale of a golden summer, a gathering on the Island of a family group, focused and dramatized by the story-telling skill of the one gifted cousin. Writing this nostalgic book about the few "opulent months" gave the author great pleasure.[19] It occupied her most of 1910. While it was in the making her publishers brought out *Kilmeny of the Orchard* (1910), a re-working of a story previously published serially.

The Story Girl was published in May, 1911. The year had already brought a major change in L.M. Montgomery's life. Her grandmother died, at the age of eighty-seven, thirteen years after the grandfather's death and the restraining promise to stay on. Lucy Maud Montgomery now felt free to marry, in July, 1911, Ewan Macdonald, and to set out on a wedding trip to England and Scotland. Like the teen-age trip to her father in Prince Albert, this long voyage never seemed usable to the author. There are no references in any of her later books to the sights and experiences of this long-dreamt-of tour. She returned to Canada, not to Prince Edward Island, but to Leaskdale, Ontario, where Mr. Macdonald had accepted a call.

When she left the Island, L.M. Montgomery had produced four works of unequal value. *Kilmeny of the Orchard* is fervid in style, melodramatic in plot. It followed a contemporary fad for books about psychosomatic impairment. Kilmeny's dumbness is not unlike the hysterical crippling of the child in *The Secret Garden* (1911), and her pathos is linked with that of "Freckles" in Gene Stratton-Porter's novel (1904), her violin-playing with that of *The Girl of the Limberlost* (1912). *Trilby* contributes something to the tone. But L.M. Montgomery set her plot of impediment released by love in an Island setting. Kilmeny in her magic trance is guarded by an old aunt and uncle and a gypsy boy, in the best Gothic tradition, but her Eden is a clearly realized orchard, with "real toads"[20] – and an indoor world of antimacassars.

In *Anne of Green Gables*, the world of dour propriety is assaulted by the daemonic force of a red-headed child brought miraculously from "off the Island." This book seems almost untouched by timely fashions in "girls' stories." It opens its casements into timeless myths of youth and growth and the quest for identity. Every incident in it is at the same time vivid and deeply suggestive: Anne comes down a long lane with Matthew, to the old farm where angular Marilla sits between a west window flooded by sunlight and an east window framing a cherry tree in bloom but "greened over by a tangle of vines."[21] Anne dyes her red hair green. She is given first a brown dress by Matthew, then a green one by Marilla. Anne makes her "kindred spirit," Diana, drunk, just before she herself walks a ridge-pole, and breaks an ankle. Midway through the book she breaks a slate over Gilbert's head, then must work out her resentment of him and accept his "friendship" as the book ends. Psychologists today would interpret the story symbolically; they would suggest that reading such a story probably helps young girls accept imaginatively the processes of growing up and edging toward adult physical passion. For the millions of girls who have "identified" with Anne, these deep patterns *may* work in some such subconscious way; but the book satisfies also in its romantic pantheism, its regional humour, and its fresh sense of the excitement of language. L.M. Montgomery knew more than the psychologists about the dreams and the anxieties of adolescent girls: her childhood loneliness, her early power of expression and her suspended maturing had kept open the channel to "lost time."

A glance at *Anne of Avonlea* shows a decrease of power. Anne, "half-past sixteen,"[22] putting in a year of teaching, is a "Sleeping Beauty." All action rises from minor characters. They interest, because they represent types that will recur: a cranky old man from New Brunswick; a pair of ill-matched twins; a gifted, poetic "Yankee" boy; a long-waiting spinster. L.M. Montgomery was not yet ready for a real study of late adolescence. Anne's romance builds no suspense. (There are good regional bits still, such as Mrs. Lynde's view of a neighbour: "a slack-twisted creature who washes her dishes sitting down."[23])

The Story Girl might seem at first reading equally episodic. But the book begins on a May morning on the road to an orchard-farm, and runs rhythmically to November, when "the sharp tops of the spruces" stand "against the silvery sky."[24] It presents three mysteries: that of the old "witch," Peg Bowen; that of the secret chamber of the "Awkward Man"; and that of the family "blue chest," heritage of broken romance. The "Story-Girl," Sara, motherless, gifted, differs from Anne in that her father exists though in the background. (Anne, we remember, dreamt of being called "Cordelia," like Lear's loving daughter.) And Sara's circle can meet with the grown-up world of adults, occasionally, but happily, at twilight, in the orchard. The boy who tells the story knows himself to be only temporarily on "the Island." The identification of island with orchard and spring with youth is tactfully handled and effective. All these things give organic unity to *The Story Girl*. They justify L.M. Montgomery's own fondness for the book.

She had now left Cavendish and the routines of her old home. The new life would have its new routines: running the manse, helping with parish work, women's groups, choirs, Sunday school. New duties would be added, a year later, with motherhood. Like most women-writers of her generation she had always had at least two lives: that of producing artist and that of conscientious house-keeper. The "woman's world" was hers by no choice of her own. What woman in 1912, in a small provincial town, could expect to resign from this sphere? The artist's world was a different matter. There was nothing automatic in the intense determination that freed a couple of hours a day for writing and revising, and kept the imagination active in undeviating devotion to a régime of steady craftsmanship. L.M. Montgomery had inherited some special talent, and had grown up in a gossipy community where anecdotes were valued, and a good raconteur much admired; she had worked at her craft in hope of money and a career. But now the real mystery appears: what force, what drive, what aspirations powered the undeviating drive on through the long string of successful books, one every other year, from the year of her marriage till the year before her death? Not only for the royalty money, welcome as that was in a small-town manse, but for other rewards, she found time to detach herself from the "real" world of Leaskdale, to continue the tales of the other "reality," the remembered island of adolescence.

Chronicles of Avonlea was published in 1912. In this set of Island stories Anne Shirley appears very briefly, and rarely as a moving force. These tales of proud poverty, of loneliness, of frustrated courtships are interesting experiments in point of view. Romance and sensibility are filtered through the practical viewpoint of matter-of-fact narrators, the unpoetic neighbours who watch poignant events. "Sentiment and humor" (as L.M. Montgomery says of one of the *Chronicles* characters) "wage an equal contest."[25]

The Golden Road (1913) is an elegy on childhood. It completes the seasonal cycle of *The Story Girl*, running from December through the riches of summer to "sere" autumn in the orchard setting. Most mysteries of the earlier book find rather prosaic fulfilment: a bride for the Awkward Man, a visit to church for the Witch. The "Story-Girl," Sara, tells a new cycle of tales: Indian and classical legends, and local folk tales, while her sad alternate, Sara Ray, suffers new repressions. The children's rituals and fears are convincing and funny. But the family disperses as the book ends, and a sadness tinges the story.

Perhaps the elegiac mood reflected the author's entry into a new phase of life. Her first son, Chester Cameron, was born in 1912. A second infant, Hugh, born in 1914, lived only for a day.[26] In 1915 the birth of Ewan Stuart completed the Macdonalds' family.

By this time, war had broken out, and the manse was touched by the tension in all Canadian life. L.M. Montgomery turned once again to the story of Anne, to satisfy "all the girls all over the world who [had] wanted more."[27] It was a relief to escape to girlhood and romance and the friendships and escapades of student days, "pre-war."

Anne of the Island (1915) takes Anne away to the mainland and to maturity. Anne is at college, involved in the love-stories of her friends, and in a delusive romance with "Royal Gardner." Gilbert lurks near, offering apples. Anne rejects his first offer of love, in a very real moment of tension and fear. The reconciliation at the close is autumnal and subdued. The whole book is perfectly adapted to its audience of adolescent girls, in its timidity, its repressions, and its lyric romanticism and idealism. The book is "real" too in the gentle growth of Anne's friendships with other girls as she comes nearer to a sense of her own identity. The moving climax to this development occurs when a "Mainland" friend takes her to "Bolingbroke," her birthplace, where she feels "not an orphan any longer."[28]

The major weakness in plot is the ending, when Anne's "spell" is broken, and she accepts her love for Gilbert, because of a melodramatic sudden illness and miraculous cure. But such a resolution is acceptable in myth; and once again L.M. Montgomery had released mythic energies in the story she had created. She had prepared for such a supervenience of miracle by the recurring use of symbolic settings, suggestive of Eden. The tone of the closing is wistful, perfect for its insecure audience, and its saddened time.

Emotions stirred by the war had led L.M. Montgomery to a revived activity in poetry. In 1916 she brought out *The Watchman and Other Poems*, dedicated to the Canadian soldiers who had died in the war. The title poem is a meditative monologue on the first Easter, in a manner reminiscent of Browning. The other poems, lyrics of sea, of hills and woods (rather heavily fraught with dryads and dingles and fisher-folk and moonrise) are mostly reprints from a surprisingly long list of magazines, *Youth's Companion*, *Forward*, *Maclean's Magazine*, *East and West* – and fifteen others, all markets for occasional poems. These are Edwardian, water-colour descriptions:

> Elusive shadows linger shyly here
>   And wood-flowers blow, like pale, sweet spirit-bloom,
> And white, slim birches whisper, mirrored clear
>   In the pool's lucent gloom.[29]

This volume marks an important change. It was published by the Canadian firm of McClelland, Goodchild and Stewart in 1916, and by Stokes of New York in 1917. Constable's of London issued an English edition in 1920. The old connection with the Page Company of Boston was broken. The galling sense that she had had less than a fair return for the best-selling *Anne of Green Gables* had irked L.M. Montgomery throughout the five-year period when she was bound to give Page's the first refusal of her new books. Now she moved happily into an arrangement that involved a reputable Canadian publisher along with American and British affiliates. (English rights were later transferred from Constable's to Hodder and Stoughton.)

In the next six years, the new publishers brought out *Anne's House of Dreams* (1917), *Rainbow Valley* (1919), and *Rilla of Ingleside* (1921). All three are shadowed by war. The focus moves from Anne to her family. Even in *Anne's House of Dreams* Anne and Gilbert have become unreal, and their friends seem phoney and sentimental. Owen Ford speaking:

"The rose is the flower of love – the world has acclaimed it so for centuries. The pink roses are love hopeful and expectant – the white roses are love dead or forsaken – but the red roses – ah, Leslie, what are the red roses?"

"Love triumphant," said Leslie in a low voice.[30]

Not low enough, say we – but the author seems unable to suppress this false strain. The real vitality in the book lies in the middle-aged, gossipy ladies, Susan and Miss Cornelia.

The gossip continues in *Rainbow Valley*, easing the shadow of world catastrophe into the small talk of neighbours and pets. Anne's young family are joined by the motherless brood at the nearby manse. Her own children are shadowy, and she herself is reduced to some cliché gestures ("hands clasped before her") and "tag" descriptions ("shining grey eyes").[31] A newcomer joins the range of types: Mary Vance, an orphan, but a brassy, skinny, pale-eyed, pugnacious one. The widowed minister, dreamily abstracted from his children's needs, is firmly realized also. And how L.M. Montgomery must have enjoyed "naming" the children of this Presbyterian minister: Jeremy and Carlyle, turbulent Faith and gentle Una![32]

The play of names in *Rilla of Ingleside* is thought-provoking too. It is Walter, named after Anne's father, who is killed – the father dies again, in a sense. Marilla's namesake adopts a war-baby, Jims, while Jem, given up as dead, lives again at the end. Nan and Di, the twins, are "off-stage" most of the time although the notion of twins still seems to press on L.M. Montgomery's fancy.

The book makes an interesting contrast with *Anne of the Island*. Anne's daughter waits through a four-year period for her romance, just as the mother had done, but the inhibition is imposed from without, by war. In a little experiment with first-person point-of-view, Rilla recounts her waiting in her journal – a preview of the major method of the Emily Books which will come soon.

These three "Anne" books were brought out by the new publisher in a format similar to the earlier volumes. Their sales were excellent.

Trouble flared in 1920 when the former publisher, Page's of Boston, brought out a collection of early pieces, which had appeared years before as magazine sketches, under the title *Further Chronicles of Avonlea*. Their reasoning seems to have been that the author had owed them "refusal" on these stories. L.M. Montgomery indignantly protested against "piracy," and decided to sue for invasion of her rights. The suit dragged on for about nine years, wearying, sometimes embarrassing and humiliating, always irritating and distracting. This battle over the publishers' "right" to the book was important for professional writers. It stirred furious discussion in authors' associations, and spot-lighted the need for business acumen and a readiness to fight for due rewards. It revived all the old tensions over copyright and piracy which had so long plagued Canadian writers.

Of the book itself, L.M. Montgomery spoke slightingly. But there are at least two aspects worth notice. First, a number of ghost stories in the late Kipling manner reflect the author's interest in psychic phenomena and her ability to blend new ideas about extra-sensory perceptions with the old patterns of folk tale. Second, the "Western" sketch, "Tannis of the Flats," set in Prince Albert, and reminiscent of Bret Harte and Owen Wister, catches attention as a single use of that alien setting experienced briefly when Lucy Maud Montgomery visited her father in the 1880s.[33]

The furore about her lawsuit increased her status among Canadian writers. She was in demand as a speaker at literary societies, and was still bombarded with letters and questions about her methods of working and the "originals" of Anne and of Green Gables.

In 1921 she had the rather unhappy experience of seeing a silent movie based on her book, but distorting many elements in it. Her old contract with the Page Company gave her no royalties for "screen rights," and she had no control over the revision of the story for movie purposes. She particularly objected to the school-room scenes, in which the Stars and Stripes flew bravely over the P.E.I. school-house.[34]

Perhaps the tension over rights to the products of her imagination, combined with this public focus on its processes, led L.M. Montgomery to a new subject. She went back again to the memory of her own girlhood, and began the story of a girl living between the world of fact and the world of words. "Emily" is a character whose joy and release consist of writing – first a letter journal to her dead father, then a set of sketches in her "Jimmy-books" (note-books offered by a sympathetic old cousin) and finally tales and poems, proffered to publishers.

The theme of a writer's ambition had been a sub-current in early "Anne" books. Now it becomes a major strand. In the three "Emily" books (*Emily of New Moon, Emily Climbs,* and *Emily's Quest*), chapters of Emily's journals reflect and intensify the third-person narrative sequence.

Emily of New Moon (1923) is an intriguing book even without this looking-glass effect. In it L.M. Montgomery moves powerfully into a mythical tale of girlhood. Names of people and places half-reveal and half-disguise the undercurrents of meaning and emotion. The little girl named Emily Byrd Starr comes from Maywood to the New Moon farm of her mother's people (the mother was named Juliet). Her false friend is Rhoda (rodent?), her true friend is Ilse (ipse?). Her first teacher is Miss Brownell (who destroys imagination), her second Mr. Carpenter (who, obviously, builds). Midway through the book a priest encourages her to "keep on" writing; but at Wyther Grange she meets a man *named* Priest – Dean Priest at that – the crippled "Jarback," her own dead father's friend, who brings her to life again, at the cost of possessing her soul. None of this is obtrusive, but it adds a dimension of interest to the surface story. That story is an intriguing though unpretentious version of Wordsworth's *Prelude*, a careful recreation of those "spots of time" in which the creative imagination is nurtured. It clarifies the directions of a growing child's fantasy-life. The story is climaxed by a mysterious vision in which Emily's mind, in delirium, fuses three bits of memory, and prophetically "sees" a hidden truth (the "real" story of Ilse's lost mother). This prophetic second sight restores Ilse to her estranged father, by clearing the dead mother's reputation. It is an effective fable of art. It is also a good solution of the double plot, a fusion of Emily's "real" life among her friends and her life as poetic creator.

Having opened the doors of memory so far, L.M. Montgomery pushed them wider – perilously wider – in her sequel. *Emily Climbs* (1925) recreates the tone of a teen-aged girl's view of life: her sense of being misunderstood and repressed, her obsessive interest in her own identity. Emily has gone to "Shrewsbury" to the town where shrewish Aunt Ruth waits to curb, censor and belittle her. Yet in spite of never being understood Emily manages to enjoy, innocently, most forbidden pleasures. This fantasy of adolescence is a precursor of *Catcher in the Rye, A Separate Peace* and the whole fashionable swarm of such books. It expresses the romance and dreaminess of adolescence, as well as the arrogance, self-pity and inhibitions we have been taught ruefully to recognize. The material is awkwardly handled: the structure and style seem to have some of the clumsiness and unsureness of the adolescent. But the book is a pioneering entry into a difficult and important area.

It is no accident that L.M. Montgomery's first mature attempt at an adult novel came as an interruption of the "Emily" series. *The Blue Castle* (1926) was an effort to "climb" past the stereotypes of girls' books.

In 1925 the permanence of her appeal was marked by the beginning of a re-issue of her work in a "uniform edition" (Harrap, 1925–1935).[35] Her family life had made a welcome shift, from Leaskdale in the rather remote Uxbridge area, to the larger town of Norval, near Toronto, and in the centre of the earlier settled regions of western-central Ontario. Here Mr. Macdonald hoped for an easing of his duties, since his health was not good. The Macdonalds' sons were now boys of thirteen and ten. Perhaps the vigorous reality of their lives suggested a vivid alternative to the retrospective dreams of remembered childhood.

The Blue Castle is energetic and tough. It is an amazingly blunt story of a frustrated woman's attempt to find a real life in defiance of family tabus and conventions. It has a Cinderella plot, but the settings and characters mark a definite break from cliché. The story begins with a pompous family dinner party, which may echo Galsworthy but which certainly precedes *Jalna* (1927). It moves to "the verge of up back,"[36] to the derelict home of a drunken no-good, and from there to a roaring barndance brawl at Chidley's Corners. Exactly half-way through, Valancy (what a nice name for an independent Canadian heroine!) accepts joyfully the fact of her love for the mystery man from Muskoka, and moves with him to an enchanted island. In the second half of the book the author piles up improbable plot twists with jaunty unconcern, without losing the sardonic realism of her portraits of the family group left behind in "civilization." Valancy's Dionysian revolt is blurred a little by the third plot thread – her devotion to the romantic nature-writings of "John Foster." But as one young reader says, "You can skip the John Foster stuff," and keep a book with real vitality: a fairy-tale set to a jazz tempo.

The reviewers were not impressed. Professor Desmond Pacey some years later summarized the contemporary reaction: "all the weaknesses of the Anne books and none of their redeeming charm."[37] L.M. Montgomery had an over-developed sensitivity to reviews. She had an old habit of quoting reams of critical comments to her friends, to her correspondents, to lecture audiences. Good or bad, she found reviews very important. In *The Blue Castle*, reviewers had missed the special quality she was aiming for, or had not found it impressive.

In 1927, *Emily's Quest* marked the author's retreat from her experimental venture. This is another "girls' book," in magazine style. The familiar characters are re-assembled, re-aligned, and finally sorted out into romantic pairs. "Jarback Priest," after threatening to become a distinct person, diminishes and fades as conventional poetic romance takes over. The book makes an interesting pair with *The Blue Castle*, so different in tone.

In 1929 another gifted fantasy-child was added to the established pattern, in *Magic for Marigold*.

Then came one more attempt to break the mold. *A Tangled Web* (1931) is an effort at mosaic method in plotting a story for grown-ups. *Aunt Becky Began It* was the English title of this novel – Aunt Becky being the old-witch character who dangles a family treasure before the Dark–Penhallow clan, and sets its members to weaving a number of webs in hope of the heirloom. This folk-tale motif of treasure and hag-guardian has recurred in almost every one of L.M. Montgomery's novels. The novel "up-dates" the Island girls, now lipsticked, silk-stockinged, bobbed, and given to small swearings. The author offers a cheap "come-on" in the opening paragraph when she implies that we will learn how Big Sam Dark "learned to appreciate the beauty of the unclothed female form."[38] But in spite of this minor naughtiness the stories are still the conventional tales of "Avonlea," not really lifted into any newly mature vision.

The author had now an impressive list of still-popular books to her credit. A new generation was "growing up on Anne," and the production of new books had settled to a rhythm of one novel every alternate year. A new movie version of *Anne of Green Gables* was in the making (to be released in 1934). A number of tours of Canada, east (every summer) and west, had shown the author how universally popular her books continued to be, and how strong the demand for "more about the Island."

During these years at Norval she added two more to her list of seventeen books: *Pat of Silver Bush* (1933) and *Mistress Pat* (1935). "Pat" is a convincing child, in her deep attachment to her home and her dread of change and chance. "Old Judy Plum," the Irish housekeeper who watches the child's initiation into maturity, becomes wearisome in her stage-Irish mannerisms, but she delighted (and still delights) young readers. Dialect humour holds its appeal for children.

L.M. Montgomery's own "children" were now young men ready for university. Perhaps the give-and-take of their boyhood life together was now far enough distanced in the author's memory to have become accessible for re-creation. Such a theory of the way her imagination worked, at a distance in time from experienced fact, might account for the new strength in the "Pat" books of studies of family life. Brother-and-sister relations, not well handled or handled with false sentimentality in *Rainbow Valley* and *Rilla of Ingleside*, are better managed now, with new variety and a sometimes rueful realism.

Before leaving Norval, L.M. Montgomery found time also to collaborate on a compilation of lives of *Courageous Women* (1934). The list of women includes Pauline Johnson, Marshall Saunders, Madame Albani, and Catharine Parr Traill, along with non-Canadian "heroines" such as Joan of Arc, Florence Nightingale and Helen Keller. The collaborators were Mabel Burns McKinley and Marian Keith (Mrs. Donald MacGregor). Mrs. MacGregor had been a treasured friend since 1911, the year both young women, newly established authors and newly married brides of ministers, had met at a Toronto reception given by the Women's Press Club. It was a friendship that perhaps exerted unfortunate pressures on L.M. Montgomery to conform to the conventions of romantic escapist fiction of the moral uplift sort.

The Macdonald family moved to Toronto in 1935 when Mr. Macdonald retired from the active ministry. Life centred around the activities of the two university students, Chester in law and Stuart in medicine. The Women's Press Club, the Canadian Authors' Association, and other groups of professional and amateur artists absorbed time and energy. So did the business of arrangements with publishers, and the still voluminous correspondence with friends, relations and readers. She was herself an omnivorous reader of classics, mystery stories, best sellers, magazines – anything and everything.

In this year of flattering official recognition, 1935, L.M. Montgomery appeared on the King's Silver Jubilee List as an officer in the Order of the British Empire. She was also elected Fellow of the Royal Society of Arts and Letters.[39] The Institut des Lettres et des Arts of France made her a member, and later awarded her a silver medal for literary style.

She set to work again in her new home on Riverside Drive in Toronto, to rebuild the pattern of plotting, writing, and revising, all dove-tailed into the daily chores of housekeeping. Two last "Anne" books were to be written: *Anne of Windy Poplars* (1936) and *Anne of Ingleside* (1939). These stories are concocted to "fill in the gaps" in Anne's story: the years she spent in waiting for Gilbert to finish his medical course (*Windy Poplars*) and the years when her children were small (*Ingleside*). Both books have a warmed-over flavour. The people are "characters" revived from earlier models. Neither book has distinction in structure. The slang is an odd mixture of phrases of the 1930s and the remembered cadences of the 1900–1910 period. Even "Susan" has lost her gossipy vigour. Anne's children are quaint and cute and not very believable.

But there remained one further flame of creativity. One last girl would be added to the roll-call of convincing heroines. *Jane of Lantern Hill* (1937) begins in Toronto. It is a Toronto of dreary grey mansions and more dismal filling-stations, family dinners, and ashy back-yards. But Jane goes every summer from this Toronto to join her father, on Prince Edward Island. Eventually she draws her golden mother with her, back to the Island. This small and poignant version of Orpheus and Eurydice ends in pastoral reunion and fulfilment. It is equally vivid in its Island paradise, where Jane keeps house for her father, and in its Toronto hell, where Jane quakes before Grandmother (who calls her "Victoria"). If, as Professor Northrop Frye says, literature is "two dreams, a wish-fulfilment dream and an anxiety dream, that are focussed together, like a pair of glasses, and become a fully conscious vision,"[40] this last book stakes a claim as literature. Not just "children's literature," either, for both Jane's anxiety and her dream are successful metaphors of adult psychic realities. Jane's island paradise is deeply meaningful and satisfying; and not only for children.

L.M. Montgomery was increasingly conscious of her role as myth-maker. She talked mystically about "the Island" as a place of the soul. Asked to contribute an article on P.E.I. to a memorial volume on Canada, designed for presentation by the Canadian Pacific Railway to King George and Queen Elizabeth, L.M. Montgomery sidestepped the expected conventions of travel-book descriptions. She wrote of the Island's beauty, its reality, its peace; the feeling it gave, in "dimming landscape ... and long, white-sand beach and murmuring ocean ... homestead lights and the old fields tilled by dead and gone generations who loved them," of being "home."[41]

By 1939, the life of L.M. Montgomery was far from paradisal. Her health was no longer good, and her spirits very depressed. She was deeply distressed by the coming of war. Her husband's ill health was a great worry. She was in correspondence with the Ryerson Press, which planned a Canadian edition of her earlier works. Ryerson had been agents for the old Page Company of Boston; now they were bringing the early books out again in Canada. There would be no change in the royalty arrangements. The whole business revived L.M. Montgomery's resentment over what she considered the exploitation of her efforts by the publishers. Two movie versions of *Anne* had been made, and two three-act plays based on *Anne* appeared in 1937, one by Alice Chadwicke, one by Wilbur Braun.[42] Both, issued by French in New York, brought no returns to L.M. Montgomery, for she had sold all "rights" to dramatic versions for a lump sum back in 1907. She brooded also over the "piracy" suits she had suffered through in the twenties. Illness and depression grew together. She wrote to a correspondent who had paid her a tribute in 1940, "It always gives me pleasure to hear that [my books] have given a little help or enjoyment to my readers. Certainly in the kind of world that this has become we need all the help we can get."

L.M. Montgomery died April 24, 1942. She was buried in Cavendish, in

> the loveliness
> Of cool, far hill, and long remembered shore,
> Finding in it a sweet forgetfulness
> Of all that hurt before.[43]

Her husband died a year later. In Prince Edward Island, a stone monument has been erected at the entrance to Cavendish National Park, and the old "Green Gables" house, near L.M. Montgomery's childhood home, stands as a shrine to her memory and a recognition of the continuing reality of "Anne."

Her death brought a wave of retrospective articles, mostly nostalgic. Her old correspondent, Ephraim Weber, prepared two articles for the *Dalhousie Review*, "L.M. Montgomery as a Letter Writer," October, 1942, and "L.M. Montgomery's 'Anne,'" April, 1944.[44] They remained the major serious contribution to knowledge of the author for many years. Subsequent critics of Canadian literature – such as Arthur Phelps, in *Canadian Writers* (1951), and Desmond Pacey, in *Creative Writing in*

Canada (1952), were patronizing and casual. They spoke of her naïve plotting, her whimsy, her sentiment. Hilda M. Ridley's biography, *The Story of L.M. Montgomery* (1956), blurred some details, and over-emphasized the childhood background of the author. Wilfrid Eggleston in his graceful edition (1960) of *The Green Gables Letters (From L.M. Montgomery to Ephraim Weber, 1905–1909)*, has done much to restore our sense of the wisdom and wit of this "lively and attractive personality."[45]

Her established audience – girls between ten and fourteen – continues to read and love the L.M. Montgomery books. But she may also lay increasing claim to our attention as adult critics. The books have an intensity because they *were* written as "children's books." The same kind of sesame that unlocked Lewis Carroll's inhibitions and let him write the classic of fantasy and repression that we now see in *Alice* – that same magic releasing power seems to have operated with the Canadian, late-Victorian, provincial spinster. Writing "for children," she could re-enact the rituals of childhood. Recreating her own remembered yearnings and anxieties, she could create a myth of the hesitant desires and worries of the virginal years.

Modern psychology explains some of the hidden power of L.M. Montgomery's books, especially for adolescent girls. Most teen-aged girls find it hard to get along with their mothers, the psychologists say, yet not daring consciously to dislike the mother, they are torn by mixed emotions of admiration, rivalry, dependence, hostility, all operating at a subconscious level. The heroines of L.M. Montgomery have no mothers. They do have aunts and grandmothers (who can safely be hated). Indeed, they usually have a range of aunts, some restrictive, some permissive. The adolescent reader can discriminate ambivalent feelings by loving one aunt (mother-substitute), while hating another. Also, in adolescence there is a normal intensity of feeling for the father, a feeling that must be outgrown or re-directed, but that is very powerful in the transitional stage between family relations and extra-familial ones, and correlated with the transition from homosexual to heterosexual devotion. In most of L.M. Montgomery's books, the father, safely distanced by death, stirs deep feelings of attachment (usually disapproved of by the aunts or grandmothers).

Other tenets of the psychologists who study adolescence can similarly be illustrated from the Montgomery books. "Girls may feel unconscious jealousy of boys":[46] in the novels girls replace boys, as Anne replaced the asked-for boy orphan, as Valancy replaced her mother's desired son. Many times, also, names are used to suggest a crossing of boundaries: "Peter" in "The Quarantine" is a girl; "Bev," the boy-narrator in the Story Girl series, has an ambivalent name, as have "Phil," "Jo," Jamesina, Pat, and a long list of others. The theory would be that reading such tales gives young girls an outlet for their fantasies of changing sex. Another tenet: "The adolescent longs for yet dreads the coming of physical passion." No doubt this accounts for the pleasure girls find in reading the long, long sequence of tales in which consummation of a romance is suspended, usually by some illogical tabu. Item: "The ending of virginity may be symbolically accepted in dreams, as a prelude to reality." Re-reading the L.M. Montgomery books with even a reserved acceptance of Freudian symbolism would surprise most of us! Once again, the theory is that such gentle, sublimated acceptance into the young reader's consciousness can be a healthy form of gradual adjustment. Such a Freudian re-reading, besides increasing our interest in the "Anne" and "Emily" books, may lead to a revaluation of *The Blue Castle*, where many of the suppressed themes are directly stated.

The basic assumption in this revaluation is that L.M. Montgomery was probably not conscious of the forces she was releasing. She was, however, honest enough to use the patterns her memory suggested. Furthermore, she was a good enough craftsman to lift the stories from the level of clinical confession to that of archetypal statement.

We may guess, also, that this author was increasingly conscious of the basic equation she had established, almost by chance, in her first successful novel. "The Island" is adolescence. And adolescence, that time of intense dreaming, of romantic yearning and disturbing hostility, remains as a part of every consciousness. Encircled by the mature sands of logic, pragmatism, utilitarianism and conformity, the island of youth exists for us and in us still. Perhaps art can be the channel by which we rediscover the island. L.M. Montgomery's world of poetry, virginity, and pantheism still opens for the adult reader the way back to his own world of young realization: he "wakes, to dream again."[47]

This brings us to the final claim of L.M. Montgomery on our attention and respect. She is the novelist for the bookish child, the word-conscious child to whom she gives reassurance about a sense of the magic of "naming." She knows that words are her tool, and have been so ever since as a child, by naming, she made her own Island in time.[48]

NOTES

1 [Rubio, *Lucy Maud Montgomery*, 4.]

2 [Peene, Foreword, v.]

3 [Innis, Introduction, xii.]

4 [Rubio, *Lucy Maud Montgomery*, 4–5.]

5 [Hilda M. Ridley's biography *The Story of L.M. Montgomery* was published in Canada by the Ryerson Press and in England by George G. Harrap, both in 1956.]

6 [A phrase used in *The Prelude*, by William Wordsworth.]

7 [Montgomery's half-sister Kate was a toddler when Montgomery arrived in Prince Albert in August 1890; her half-brother Bruce was born in January 1891. Her half-siblings Ila and Carl were born after she left Saskatchewan.]

8 [*AP*, 64. Here, Montgomery quotes a journal entry dated 21 March 1901. In the published *Selected Journals*, however, the first sentence reads "I never expect to be famous – I don't want to be, really, often as I've dreamed of it" (*SJLMM*, 1: 258).]

9 [Weber to Montgomery, date unknown, quoted in Eggleston, "General Introduction," 16.]

10 [Montgomery to Weber, 8 April 1906, in *GGL*, 38.]

11 [Montgomery to Weber, 8 October 1906, in *GGL*, 47.]

12 [Montgomery to Weber, 2 May 1907, in *GGL*, 51.]

13 [This misquotation appears in Montgomery to Weber, 22 December 1908, in *GGL*, 80.]

14 [See Montgomery to Weber, 10 September 1908, in *GGL*, 74.]

15 [Montgomery to Weber, 10 November 1907, in *GGL*, 59.]

16 [See Montgomery to Weber, 5 April 1908, in *GGL*, 67.]

17 [Montgomery to Weber, 22 December 1908, in *GGL*, 77, 79; Montgomery to Weber, 28 March 1909, in *GGL*, 84–85. See also Montgomery to Weber, 2 September 1909, in *GGL*, 90. The aunt in question was Mary Lawson, to whom Montgomery dedicated *The Golden Road*.]

18 [Montgomery to Weber, 2 September 1909, in *GGL*, 92.]

19 [*SG*, 258.]

20 [Properly, "imaginary gardens with real toads / in them." From "Poetry" (1916), by Marianne Moore (1887–1972), American poet.]

21 [*AGG*, 4.]

22 [*AA*, 1.]

23 [See *AA*, 8.]

24 [*SG*, 258.]

25 [See *CA*, 183.]

26 [According to Montgomery's journals, her second son was in fact born dead (Montgomery, 30 August 1914, in *SJLMM*, 2: 151).]

27 [Montgomery dedicated *Anne of the Island* "to all the girls all over the world who have 'wanted more' about ANNE" (*AIs*, n.pag.).]

28 [*AIs*, 147.]

29 [From "The Wood Pool," originally published in *Christian Endeavor World* in 1913 and reprinted in *The Watchman and Other Poems*.]

30 [*AHD*, 213.]

31 [See *RV*, 2, 122.]

32 [Jerry Meredith's full name is, in fact, Gerald.]

33 [Montgomery lived with her father and his new family in Saskatchewan from August 1890 to August 1891.]

34 [See Montgomery's 1935 essay "Is This My Anne" in Volume 1 of *The L.M. Montgomery Reader*.]

35 [This uniform edition was published in Britain only. In North America, Montgomery's books would not be published by a single imprint until Bantam-Seal began issuing her books as mass market paperbacks throughout the 1980s.]

36 [*BC*, 114.]

37 [Pacey, *Creative Writing in Canada*, 106.]

38 [*TW*, 1.]

39 [She was made a Fellow of the Royal Society of Arts and Letters in 1923 (see Montgomery, 28 January 1923, in *SJLMM*, 3: 111).]

40 [Frye, *The Educated Imagination*, 43.]

41 [See Montgomery's essay "Prince Edward Island" in Volume 1 of *The L.M. Montgomery Reader*.]

42 [Alice Chadwicke was in fact the *nom de plume* of Wilbur Braun (1894–1968), American playwright. This play version of *Anne of Green Gables* was followed by *Anne of Avonlea* (1940), by "Jeanette Carlisle," pseudonym of James Reach (1910–1970), American playwright.]

43 [From "Night" (1935), a poem by L.M. Montgomery that was reprinted in *The Blythes Are Quoted*.]

44 [Both of Weber's articles appear in Volume 1 of *The L.M. Montgomery Reader*.]

45 [Eggleston, "General Introduction," 2.]

46 [Included in the bibliography of the original publication of this chapter is Rolf E. Muuss's *Theories of Adolescence*.]

47 [Properly, "when I waked, / I cried to dream again." From *The Tempest* (1610–11), by William Shakespeare.]

48 [The original publication includes a bibliography that lists ten sources. In addition to those cited here, see "Montgomery, Lucy Maude"; Phelps, *Canadian Writers*, 85–93; and Sclanders, "Lucy of Green Gables."]

2

The Fair World of L.M. Montgomery

—— 1973 ——

HELEN PORTER

In this short piece, originally published in *Journal of Canadian Fiction* as a review of new editions of *The Blue Castle* and *A Tangled Web*, Newfoundland author Helen Porter reflects on her reading as a child and on her rereading as an adult of some of L.M. Montgomery's works. In particular, she takes issue with the decision by McClelland and Stewart to reissue Montgomery's post-1916 novels as part of the "Canadian Children's Favourites" umbrella series the year before – even their cover image of Montgomery's "adult" novel *A Tangled Web* depicts a young girl sitting under a tree (see the frontispiece to this volume) – expressing her doubts that current young people would find these two particular novels appealing. As Porter's comments reveal, very little information about Montgomery's life was widely known in the early 1970s, with only *The Green Gables Letters* available as a supplementary text. Although Mollie Gillen's *Chatelaine* article "Maud Montgomery: The Girl Who Wrote Green Gables" appeared the same year as Porter's article, it was only once Gillen's book-length biography *The Wheel of Things* was published in 1975 that Montgomery's life became part of the broader conversation. Perhaps in agreement with Porter's comments about the inappropriate label "Children's Favourites" for Montgomery's work, McClelland and Stewart soon dropped the term "Children's" from the series title and continued to reprint Montgomery's novels as "Canadian Favourites."

My children have fun about something that I admitted to them recently. We had been discussing Bertrand Russell's statement that we must start with the premise that the cosmos is not fair. "How old were you when you found out the world wasn't fair, Mom?" one of them asked, with an invisible wink at the others. "Oh, when I was about twenty-five," I told them. And the teasing began.

I've been re-reading some of L.M. Montgomery lately, specifically *A Tangled Web* and *The Blue Castle*, and I've concluded now that it was my heavy reliance on her books in my young days that resulted in my long-standing "all things work together for good" philosophy. In the Montgomery books, people died at the right time, and though I shed buckets of tears over each death I would have had the stories no other way. Ruby Gillis (*Anne of the Island*), after a few dark nights of the soul, nevertheless died with a smile on her face; Mr. Carpenter (*Emily's Quest*) passed out in the happy expectation of soon knowing "everything there is to know"; and Captain Jim (*Anne's House of Dreams*) gently closed his eyes just as he finished reading "The Life Book of Captain Jim" as written by Owen Ford. Anne's son Walter (*Rilla of Ingleside*), who feared death during most of his life, nevertheless wrote a letter to his sister on the night before his last battle, proving beyond a shadow of a doubt that he was quite prepared to die.[1] There is even humour in some of the Montgomery deaths. A minor character in one of the books, quite a young woman, quips on her death bed that she's glad she'll be dead before fall house-cleaning time, and Judy Plum, the old Irish housekeeper in the Pat books, actually died laughing![2] With a few exceptions, notably the death of Bets in *Pat of Silver Bush*, the deaths were "fair" and so, in most cases, was life.

"Canadian Children's Favourites." Who in the name of the Lord put that name on this new series of Montgomery books? Fine for the Anne series, I suppose, and for most of Pat and Emily, but *A Tangled Web* and *The Blue Castle* are anything but children's books. I believe the author intended them as adult books and I don't think children would enjoy them at all. Some teenagers probably would, and young adults, but I'd say it's the older adults who would like them most of all. I still found, on re-reading, that they had the power to hold my attention and that, once begun, I couldn't stop reading them until I was finished. I suppose I'm more of a realist than I was when I first read them years ago (I no longer believe that everything is fair) but I still enjoyed them more than I ever would have believed possible, especially *A Tangled Web*. I can only repeat that it's doing the books a great disservice to call them Children's Favourites.

The Blue Castle was first published in 1926 and *A Tangled Web* in 1931, much later than the original Anne books. Manners and mores had changed then, not perhaps so much as in the real world but more than the period between the publication dates suggests. *Anne of Green Gables*, though written in 1907–08, is set in the late nineteenth century, while *A Tangled Web* and *The Blue Castle* are set much closer to the time of writing. It's important to remember too, I think, that *Web* and *Castle* were written when Lucy Maud Montgomery, who did not marry until she was thirty-seven and who bore her first child at thirty-eight, was living in Ontario with her minister-husband and their children, while the early Anne books were done when she was something of a housebound single woman taking care of her grandmother in Cavendish, Prince Edward Island. The difference in her lifestyle shows, sometimes for good and sometimes for ill.

As I said before, I liked *A Tangled Web* much better than *The Blue Castle*, although I think my feelings were the exact opposite when I first read the two books in the late nineteen-forties. *Castle* very definitely has a heroine, although for the first several pages Valancy Stirling appears to be more of an anti-heroine. But this is soon changed and the poor, pale, weak-spirited twenty-nine year old is transformed into a warm, attractive, strong-willed woman, all through one of the most amazing coincidences I've ever found in any book. At forty-three I find this a little hard to take but when I was in my teens it was just my cup of tea. I doubt, though, if today's teenagers would agree with me. I don't think they're so taken with Cinderella stories as I was. But perhaps I'm being unfair. *The Blue Castle* is very, very far from being an Emilie Loring or a Grace Livingston Hill. The minor characters, like the minor characters in most of the Montgomery books, are simply terrific and even Valancy has her moments. I do maintain, though, that for me anyhow, *The Blue Castle* is the least memorable of all the Montgomery books.

As I read about Valancy, especially in the first part of the book, I found myself thinking of some of Margaret Laurence's characters. In many ways Rachel of *A Jest of God* appears to be a direct descendant of Valancy. Both young women live in small Canadian towns, both are browbeaten by petulant, autocratic mothers, both are fatherless, both are anxious about their health and neither has ever had a love affair. Rachel's dreams, however, both day and night ones, are much more earthy and physical than Valancy's, whose fantasies never seem to go beyond the kissing stage, and indeed take a long time to get to that point. Rachel's are most explicit. But of course Canadian women writers (and Canadian writers generally) have changed a great deal since 1926 and so have books in general. What kind of books would L.M. Montgomery be turning out, I wonder, if she were writing today? A strong undercurrent of sensuality runs through *Castle* and *Web*, and some of her other books as well, but apart from the temper of the times and her own natural reticence, Miss Montgomery probably felt it would be out of place for a Presbyterian minister's wife to be frank about sexual matters, and about some other matters as well. I believe she cared a great deal about the fitness of things and I was rather shocked the first time I read *The Green Gables Letters* (edited by Wilfrid Eggleston) to find her admitting to her pen-friend Ephraim Weber that she could not accept the divinity of Jesus Christ. This from a woman who was a regular churchgoer and parish worker and who taught a Sunday-school class all her life. She was very far from being a hypocrite but she kept her doubts to herself and did her duty as she saw it.

The last part of the previous sentence would have made L.M. shudder for it's just the type of sententious statement that brought out the devil in her, and in many of her characters. Just look at this lovely little bit from *A Tangled Web* where Aunt Becky is holding her famous levee at which she has promised to tell her relatives, the Darks and the Penhallows, what will become of the much-coveted old Dark jug. Sharp-tongued and malicious at eighty-five, she takes pleasure in digging up the very fact about each of her visitors that he or she would like forgotten. To Mrs. Toynbee Dark she says:

> " ... By the way, while I think of it, will you tell me something? I've always wanted to know and I'll never have another chance. Which of your three husbands did you like best ... ? Come now, make a clean breast of it." ...
>
> "I had a deep affection for all my partners," [Mrs. Toynbee] said.
>
> Aunt Becky wagged her head.
>
> "Why didn't you say 'deceased' partners? You were thinking it, you know."[3]

And, just a couple of pages earlier, there's an absolutely delicious part where she frightens the whole clan out of its wits by reading her own self-composed obituary:

"'*No gloom was cast over the communities of Indian Spring, Three Hills, Rose River or Bay Silver when it became known that Mrs. Theodore Dark – Aunt Becky as she was generally called, less from affection than habit – had died ... at the age of eighty-five.*'

"You notice," said Aunt Becky, interrupting herself, "that I say *died*. I shall not pass away or pass out or pay my debt to nature or depart this life or join the great majority or be summoned to my long home. I intend simply and solely to die.

"'*Everybody concerned felt that it was high time the old lady did die ... There was therefore neither sense, reason nor profit in pretending gloom or grief ... She had a hard man to please in Theodore Dark, but she made him quite as good a wife as he deserved. She was a good neighbour as neighbours go and did not quarrel more than anybody else in the clan. She had a knack of taking the wind out of people's sails that did not make for popularity. She seldom suffered in silence. Her temper was about the average ... and did not sweeten as she grew older. She always behaved herself decently, although many a time it would have been a relief to be indecent ... She longed for freedom, as all women do, but had sense enough to understand that real freedom is impossible in this kind of a world, the lucky people being those who can choose their masters ... In short, she was an average person who had lived as long as anybody should live.*'"[4]

The obituary caused the sensation she had hoped for, and after reading it she settled back to enjoy herself. It's mainly for this kind of writing that I've always loved L.M. Montgomery and will continue to do so, even if her love bits are like something that never was on land or sea. And you see, just as I've been saying, even Aunt Becky's death will be "fair": "An average person who had lived as long as anybody should live."

The levee ends, and the Darks and Penhallows are still no wiser about who will get the heirloom they all want. Aunt Becky has arranged it so that they must wait over a year to find out and the reader gets the idea that she'll be chuckling in her grave (for of course she must die soon since she has said she would) over the strange turn of events that comes out of this arrangement. A dozen or more stories are mingled in *A Tangled Web*, and mingled with a master touch. With a few exceptions, such as the unbearably romantic tales of Thora and Murray and Joscelyn and Hugh, they are interesting, unusual and, in many cases, truly funny. The reader might yawn at yet another reference to the lovely placid Thora and the stormy-eyed Murray who loved her from afar (until the jug put things right, of course), and to Joscelyn's theatrical flight from Hugh on their wedding night, but he'll want more of Big Sam and Little Sam's falling out over the naked hussy, the strangely comic romance of Penny and Margaret (and Margaret's final, *fair* happiness), and Donna's sudden discovery that she's not finished with love after all. I can't make too much of the minor characters. As in all the Montgomery books, they're real people, looked at with a clear eye, perhaps occasionally a bit overdrawn but unforgettable just the same. Such people as Drowned John, the Moon Man, the two Sams, Uncle Pippin, Brian Dark, Dandy and all the others – one would like to meet them today. Perhaps we do, and don't know it.

Some of the minor characters in *The Blue Castle* are memorable too, in spite of the triteness of the main story, which, as I've hinted before, is the tale of a colourless young spinster who, when she believes she has only a year to live, decides to do exactly as she wants in the time she has left. Valancy's romance with Barney Snaith is unbelievable from start to finish but the aching longing of a doormat daughter for a life of her own and some colour in her drab days rings true enough. I could never understand, even when I read the book as a dreamy young girl, what Valancy saw in Barney, but perhaps someone so starved for romance is not difficult to please. I liked his father, though, and again, as on previous readings, I loved the story of the dust piles and Valancy's new-moon wish "that I may have *one* little dust-pile before I die."[5] Whimsy and humour are present in *The Blue Castle* but at times they are almost completely overpowered by sentimental mush. The author keeps telling us how lovable Barney is, and he must be, for Valancy is aquiver throughout almost the entire last half of the book, but we never really see Barney as a person. He remains the shadowy dream-lover of Valancy's and (Lucy Maud's?) imagination, and is a pale character indeed beside the likes of Uncle Benjamin, with his endless riddles, and Roaring Abel, that strange combination of philosopher, theologian and drunk.

In *A Tangled Web* the Darks and Penhallows are bathed in a warm light, but Valancy's relatives are shown in a very cold one. Indeed I believe the most bitterness I've seen in any of the Montgomery books, with the possible exception of *Emily's Quest*, comes across in *The Blue Castle*. In one of L.M. Montgomery's letters to Ephraim Weber she comments on the jealousy and total misunderstanding, on the part of some of her acquaintances, that greeted her success as a writer. Perhaps this was an introduction to bitterness for her.

Still, one cannot blame Valancy for rebelling, and I suppose her family's treatment of her is not too far-fetched when one remembers the kind of life many small-town girls had at that time.

"Have you got your flannel petticoat on?" asked Mrs. Frederick [Valancy's mother].
"No." [Valancy is twenty-nine.]
" ... I really do not understand you. Do you want to catch your death of cold *again*?"[6]

And then, further along, after Valancy had left home: "Mrs. Frederick wept. It would really have been so much easier to bear if Valancy had died. She could have worn mourning then."[7]

Quite early in the book we discover that Valancy is not allowed to read novels but, after some persuasion by the librarian, her mother permits her to read the "nature books" of John Foster (who later turns out to be – but no fair, I won't tell you) though Mrs. Frederick is not happy about it, "for it was only too evident that [Valancy] enjoyed them too much. It was permissible, even laudable, to read to improve your mind and your religion, but a book that was enjoyable was dangerous."[8] Surely Valancy had a right to be bitter if anyone ever did.

In spite of her sweetness and light image, I believe L.M. Montgomery must have been a very earthy woman, in the best sense of the word. I think this side of her personality (and it is evident of many of her books) has been neglected. I remember Anne's fascination with trees and all growing things, the moonlight dance of the child Pat – naked and unashamed – that so shocked her aunts, the helpless love of all her heroines for beautiful things, the anguished cry of one of her characters that "*Things* last so much longer than people," Emily's mysterious "flash" (which I am not going to pretend was really an orgasm – I'm not *that* Freud-ridden). Lucy Maud evidently really *enjoyed* the physical world and, in most cases, the people in it. In spite of her occasional sentimentality and her unreal love affairs she is a much, much better writer than she is usually considered to be today. I don't think it would do young writers any harm at all if they gave her books more than a casual reading. And you know, it probably didn't hurt me very much to believe, until I was twenty-five or so, that the world was fair. I've known for a long time now that it's not, and I haven't been able to do a thing about it.

NOTES

1 [See *AIs*, 108; *EQ*, 23–24; *AHD*, 219–20; *RI*, 244–46.]
2 [*RV*, 102; *MP*, 264.]
3 [*TW*, 49–50.]
4 [*TW*, 46–48.]
5 [*BC*, 71.]
6 [*BC*, 19–20.]
7 [*BC*, 101–2.]
8 [*BC*, 8.]

3

Anne of Green Gables and the Regional Idyll

—— 1983 ——

T.D. MacLULICH

This article, published in *The Dalhousie Review* in 1983, is the first of three articles on Montgomery by Thomas Donald (Don) MacLulich,[1] who that year also published a book-length study on Hugh MacLennan for Twayne's World Authors Series. Part of the significance of this article is its emphasis on placing *Anne of Green Gables* in the context of Canadian literary forms of the late nineteenth and early twentieth centuries. Calling *Anne of Green Gables* "Canada's most conspicuous contribution to the world's literary culture," he suggests that part of the book's continued appeal stems from the form of the regional idyll, a term that he ascribes to Desmond Pacey, and argues for the importance of taking seriously regional and rural fiction. He would return to this discussion of *Anne of Green Gables* in his book *Between Europe and America: The Canadian Tradition in Fiction* (1988). T.D. MacLulich died in 2004.

In early May of 1907 L.M. Montgomery had some heady news for her literary pen-friend Ephraim Weber. She was going to have a book published! "I am blatantly pleased and proud and happy," she announced, "and I shan't make any pretence of not being so." Nonetheless, she modestly warned: "Don't stick up your ears now, imagining that the great Canadian novel has been written at last. Nothing of the sort. It is merely a juvenilish story, ostensibly for girls." But she quickly added: "I am not without hope that grown-ups may like it a little."[2] Indeed, the grown-ups did like her book. Soon after its publication, Montgomery commented on the respectful treatment that *Anne of Green Gables* had received from most of its reviewers: "I am surprised that they seem to take the book so seriously – as if it were meant for grown-up readers and not merely for girls." And she boasted that Mark Twain had written to her describing Anne as "the dearest, and most lovable child in fiction since the immortal Alice."[3]

It is natural enough that young readers should like Montgomery's story of a high-spirited girl who gets into amusing scrapes but always wins adults over to her side in the end. Anne's appeal to adult readers may be harder to explain. Those who have not encountered *Anne of Green Gables* since childhood may remember the book just as a series of striking episodes: Anne's outrageous apology to Mrs. Rachel Lynde; Anne making Diana drunk; Anne cracking her slate over Gilbert Blythe's head; Anne's discomfort over her green hair; and so on. But Montgomery's novel is a good deal more than just a chain of linked comic scenes. In fact, *Anne of Green Gables* deserves to be acknowledged not just as a children's classic but as an essential part of the Canadian tradition in fiction. It has claims on our attention that rest both on its intrinsic merits and on its place in our literary history.

Wilfrid Eggleston rightly calls the post-publication history of Montgomery's novel "one of the most impressive success stories of Canadian authorship."[4] So successful has the book been that its central character has entered the mythology of North American popular culture. Anne has been turned into the heroine of two American movies and has starred in a British television series; a musical version of her story has become the centrepiece of an annual festival aimed at promoting the Prince Edward Island tourism industry; and Montgomery's childhood home has been transformed into a shrine for visitors seeking a reminder of the innocence and security of their own lost childhoods.

Such popular adulation is by no means a guarantee of literary merit. The opinions of critics – in contrast, say, to the opinions of politicians – are not coerced by the results of questionnaires, Gallup polls, or general elections. Nonetheless, critics may do well to take note of the enormous number of readers – adults as well as children – who have confessed their pleasure in Montgomery's book. The enduring popularity of Montgomery's best-known creation suggests that her writing has the capacity to evoke a strong and abiding emotional response in many readers. In fact, *Anne of Green Gables* is probably the best-loved and most widely read of all Canadian novels.

Surely Montgomery's accomplishment ought to earn her a secure place in any study of the development of English-Canadian letters. Yet it remains a fact that most critics outside the children's literature fraternity have felt uncomfortable when dealing with her work. The plain truth is that Montgomery's book has committed what comes close to being the unpardonable literary sin – *Anne of Green Gables* has attained a vulgar commercial success without first securing academic approval as "serious" art. Comments by E.K. Brown and Desmond Pacey illustrate the habitual academic uneasiness with Montgomery's work. Brown lists Montgomery among those turn-of-the-century authors who "were all more or less aggressively unliterary" and were "satisfied to truckle to mediocre taste." Pacey writes sternly of *Anne of Green Gables*, "it would be silly to apply adult critical standards to it," and he dismisses the book with patronizing compliments for its tone of "pleasant whimsy" and for sentimentalism that is "a little less cloying than is usual in books of its type."[5]

There is a syllogism implicit in these pronouncements. Major premise: Children's literature is different from, and inferior to, adult or serious literature. Minor premise: *Anne of Green Gables* is known to be a children's book. Conclusion: *Anne of Green Gables* should not be treated as a serious work of literature. Given the prevalence of this attitude, it is hardly surprising that Montgomery is not mentioned in the major studies of the Canadian literary tradition published by D.G. Jones, Margaret Atwood, Ronald Sutherland, and John Moss. The encyclopaedic *Literary History of Canada* does consider Montgomery, but makes no distinction between her books and the work of many other turn-of-the-century writers of popular fiction. However, if *Anne of Green Gables* is Canada's most conspicuous contribution to the world's literary culture, perhaps it is time our critics gave Montgomery's work a more careful scrutiny. Admittedly, even the most sympathetic review of Montgomery's output cannot conceal the weakness of most of her fiction. But a study of her works does show that her best book holds its own with other works that are presently acknowledged as milestones in the development of our fiction.

I think it is generally agreed that the two most accomplished works of fiction dating from the turn-of-the-century era are Sara Jeannette Duncan's *The Imperialist* and Stephen Leacock's *Sunshine Sketches of a Little Town*. Some commentators rank Leacock's *Arcadian Adventures with the Idle Rich*, the urban companion piece to *Sunshine Sketches*, at the same level of achievement. A few people might wish to put in a word for Duncan Campbell Scott's *In the Village of Viger* or Ralph Connor's *The Man from Glengarry*, although the latter book loses much of its intensity in its second half, after Ranald departs from the Glengarry settlement whose Scottish traditions Connor describes in such affectionate detail.

All of the books just mentioned, with the exception of *Arcadian Adventures*, are closely related to the sub-genre that predominated in Canadian fiction immediately prior to the First World War. The form Desmond Pacey calls the regional idyll[6] was the Canadian version of the local colour and kailyard fiction that was popular in America and Britain just before the turn of the century. The regional idyll recreated a simple rural world, usually a heightened version of the author's childhood environment. Readers could join the author on a sentimental journey into the immediate past of their own country. The resulting blend of sentiment and nostalgia offered readers a welcome temporary escape from a world grown increasingly urban and industrial. Prominent among the writers of this sort of fiction are clergymen such as Robert Knowles and moralizing ladies such as Marian Keith and Nellie McClung. Typical examples are Knowles' *St. Cuthbert's*, Keith's *Duncan Polite*, and McClung's *Sowing Seeds in Danny*.

Neither *The Imperialist* nor *Sunshine Sketches* is a typical example of the regional idyll, but Duncan and Leacock nonetheless show a well-developed awareness of the conventions of the form. They deliberately create variations on the form's usual themes, so that their books become critiques of the values expressed in orthodox regional idylls. *Anne of Green Gables*, like the books by Knowles, Keith, and McClung just mentioned and like the books by Scott and Connor mentioned previously, is a thoroughly conventional regional idyll, almost a definitive example of the form. The strength of Montgomery's book comes from her skillful but straightforward use of the literary conventions her age gave her to work with, not from her witty innovations on familiar themes.

The importance of the regional idyll in the development of Canadian fiction has never been adequately acknowledged. Our critics have tended until recently to agree with E.K. Brown's assessment of regionalism as "another force which tells against the immediate growth of a national literature."[7] Today we are far more ready to look with approval on "regional" art, seeing it as an authentic expression of a particular culture's traditions and attitudes. However, we still tend to view the era of the regional idyll as simply an embarrassing phase that Canadian writing has outgrown. Rather, we need to recognize the pre-War vogue of the regional idyll as one more instance of the slow response to international literary developments that has characterized our literary past.

We need to remember that, for a new nation, the stages of cultural history may take on a significance that differs from their significance in the cultural history of the parent state, or even in the cultural history of an older neighbouring state. In the history of British fiction and probably of American fiction as well, the rise of the regional idyll must be considered a relatively minor event, important chiefly as an incident in the history of popular taste. In Canada, however, the literary tradition was still relatively undeveloped in the later years of the nineteenth century. The appearance of the regional idyll had a major effect on our embryonic literary tradition, marking an important step towards the use of local settings and local themes as the basis for literature.

Before the emergence of the regional idyll, the most significant form in Canadian fiction had been the historical romance. Earlier in the nineteenth century, Major John Richardson had taken a significant step towards the assimilation of native materials into fiction when he blended the influences of Scott and Cooper in several stories of love, adventure, and warfare set in the North American forest, above all in his best tale *Wacousta*. William Kirby relied heavily on Scott – and not at all on Cooper – when in 1877 he published *The Golden Dog*. Kirby wanted to show that Canadian history could furnish the materials for a monumental novel, which would lend dignity to the new nation. But Kirby felt compelled to set his story in what was, for Canada, the distant past. Specifically, he set *The Golden Dog* in pre-Conquest French Canada, whose history had recently been popularized by the publication of the first volumes of Parkman's history of the *ancien régime* in North America. That is, Kirby shied away from using his own immediate time and place as the source material for his art.

Unlike Kirby and unlike Kirby's more popular successor Sir Gilbert Parker, the authors of regional idylls looked to their own experiences to furnish the subjects of their books. There is still a historical aspect to most regional idylls, but usually the authors are looking back to their own childhood, not to an historical era outside their own experience. Despite the sentimentality of most of their books, the authors of regional idylls helped to create a sense that their new nation did have a cultural identity of its own. The self-conscious and sophisticated exploration of the past in search of collective and personal myths, as happens in Margaret Laurence's *The Diviners* and Margaret Atwood's *Surfacing*, is a more recent development in our fiction. But the emphasis on acknowledging a Canadian ancestry that is so prominent in recent fiction continues the process of self-scrutiny that was begun by the writers of the turn-of-the-century regional idylls.

One early writer of a Canadian regional idyll, Adeline M. Teskey, reported that her book *Where the Sugar Maple Grows* originated in response to her reading of Ian MacLaren's *Beside the Bonnie Briar Bush*. After reading MacLaren's book, she realized "I know just as interesting people in Canada."[8] Montgomery apparently experienced a moment of insight similar to Teskey's, for she projected a similar idea into her fiction on several occasions. In *Anne of Green Gables*, for example, Montgomery first tells how Anne organizes a "story club," whose members must every week compose a far-fetched tale of love or murder, in which, as Anne says, "All the good people are rewarded and all the bad ones are suitably punished." As Anne grows up, however, the story club is disbanded, and Anne's implausible story-telling is disciplined. Her new teacher, says Anne, has curbed her pretentious vocabulary and "won't let us write anything but what might happen in Avonlea in our own lives."[9]

Although Montgomery was not among the first authors to write regional idylls set in Canada, her fiction did affirm to the world at large that Canadian materials could be used as the basis for art. As a child, Montgomery invented tales of sentiment or piety, perhaps modelled on the polite fiction she read in *Godey's Lady's Book*, in which "villains and villainesses were all neatly labelled and you were sure of your ground."One of her finest early efforts was a lugubrious saga titled "My Graves," which detailed the sufferings of a Methodist minister's wife as she buried a child in every one of her husband's postings on a journey that took her from Newfoundland to British Columbia.[10] As she grew older, Montgomery learned that fiction could be built around the ordinary doings of the people of her native island, and in her twenty novels she created a pastoral image of Prince Edward Island that endures to the present day.

In other words, Montgomery quite deliberately attempted to do what the major figures of the next generation of Canadian writers have been praised for accomplishing, the making of serious literature out of materials that are unmistakenly and unashamedly Canadian. If she did not fully succeed in attaining her artistic goals, she nonetheless helped to chart a path for her successors. Her discovery that fiction could be written about her own Prince Edward Island and its people anticipates similar discoveries of the artistic potential of their native place that were made by later writers such as Hugh MacLennan and Margaret Laurence.

There are also important strands of thematic continuity extending from Montgomery's work to later books that are recognized as Canadian classics. In particular, *Anne of Green Gables* presents a benign version of the generational conflict that is central to books such as MacLennan's *Each Man's Son* and several of Margaret Laurence's novels.

Montgomery surrounds Anne with older members of the same sort of puritanical and emotionally reticent society that MacLennan and Laurence depict in much bleaker terms, and that is still conspicuous in more recent works such as Rudy Wiebe's *Peace Shall Destroy Many*, Percy Janes' *House of Hate*, and Harold Horwood's *Tomorrow Will Be Sunday*.

Montgomery's novel stands, in fact, at the head of a tradition that has given rise to some of the most memorable works of Canadian fiction. Many of the central works of the Canadian tradition, such as Sinclair Ross's *As for Me and My House*, MacLennan's *Each Man's Son*, Ernest Buckler's *The Mountain and the Valley*, Laurence's *A Bird in the House* and *The Stone Angel*, and even Robertson Davies' *Fifth Business*, are lineal descendents of the regional idyll. These books examine the darker side of life in rural, church-centred communities that bear many resemblances to the Prince Edward Island communities Montgomery depicts so sunnily in *Anne of Green Gables* and in her other fiction. Moreover, books such as W.O. Mitchell's *Jake and the Kid* and *Who Has Seen the Wind*, and more recently Alden Nowlan's *Various Persons Named Kevin O'Brien* and Dennis T. Patrick Sears' *The Lark in the Clear Air* show the continuing vitality of the form.

The term regional idyll usually has dismissive connotations in critical usage, implying both sentimentality and lack of skill on the part of the author who is stigmatized as producing one. This adverse judgment is not entirely a fair reaction to Montgomery's best book. Certainly *Anne of Green Gables* tells a sentimental story: Montgomery creates an outcast child who happily acquires the secure home and the loving guardians she feared she had lost forever when her parents died. But great novels – Dickens' *Great Expectations* is one example – have been built around similar and equally sentimental themes. The strength of Montgomery's novel comes from the originality and piquancy of many of the separate incidents, and from the psychological insight she displays in constructing her characters and her story.

Anne of Green Gables is built on compassionate understanding of human emotional needs. Although Montgomery does not look into the darker recesses of human nature, she reveals herself to be an astute observer of the petty quarrels and everyday joys that make up the texture of life in a relatively untroubled community. She displays a flair for revealing the humorous side of everyday incidents, and her dialogue shows a good ear for vigorous colloquial turns of phrase. Her plotting is simple but serviceable: although her control slips a bit in the loosely connected middle chapters, the novel does move to a satisfactory conclusion.

Young readers undoubtedly experience the novel mainly from Anne's perspective. They identify with Anne, and take vicarious comfort in the fulfillment of Anne's desire for parents who will love her for herself, and will not view her simply as a household drudge. Some young readers, however, may not appreciate the irony contained in Anne's more extravagant speeches, in which Montgomery both exposes Anne's immaturity and satirizes the excesses of the romantic popular fiction of her day. Adult readers of Montgomery's book will also pay considerable attention to the characters around Anne, and will relish the satirical viewpoint animating some of Montgomery's portraits.

The best example of Montgomery's skill as a satirist is the superbly rendered opening vignette of Mrs. Rachel Lynde, who embodies the restrictive standards of Avonlea, Montgomery's fictionalized version of her home community. Avonlea is governed by well-understood social conventions, and Mrs. Rachel acts as a self-appointed guardian of communal standards. Montgomery tells us what to expect from Mrs. Rachel when she describes the small stream that flows so sedately past Mrs. Rachel's door. As Montgomery archly puts it, "not even a brook could run past Mrs. Rachel Lynde's door without due regard for decency and decorum." Indeed, decency and decorum are Mrs. Rachel's consuming passions. Everyone in the community, says Montgomery, knew "that Mrs. Rachel was sitting at her window, keeping a sharp eye on everything that passed, from brooks and children up, and that if she noticed anything odd or out of place she would never rest until she had ferreted out the whys and wherefores thereof." Mrs. Rachel is herself a perfect embodiment of the domestic industry and circumscribed virtue that pass for perfection in Avonlea: "She was a notable housewife; her work was always done and well done; she 'ran' the Sewing Circle, helped run the Sunday-school, and was the strongest prop of the Church Aid Society and Foreign Missions Auxiliary." Moreover, Mrs. Rachel's household exemplifies the superior moral authority held by women in this community. Her husband, Thomas Lynde, is described as "a meek little man whom Avonlea people called 'Rachel Lynde's husband.'"[11]

When Mrs. Rachel sees Matthew Cuthbert taking an unexplained buggy ride, we glimpse her prying mind at work. She reasons: "he wore a white collar and his best suit of clothes, which was plain proof that he was going out of Avonlea; and he had the buggy and the sorrel mare, which betokened that he was going a considerable distance." But try as she may, Mrs. Rachel cannot fathom the purpose of Matthew's errand. She reflects to herself, "if he'd run out of turnip seed he wouldn't dress up and take the buggy to go for more; he wasn't driving fast enough to be going for the doctor. Yet something must have happened since last night to start him off." She concludes, in language that reveals her officious personality, "I'm clean puzzled, that's what, and I won't know a minute's peace of mind or conscience until I know what has taken Matthew Cuthbert out of Avonlea today."[12] This is exactly right. There is a colloquial informality, combined with self-dramatization, that captures Mrs. Rachel's self-righteous conception of herself. This is exactly how a woman such as Mrs. Rachel Lynde *would* talk to herself.

Among the strongest features of the book are the portraits of Matthew and Marilla Cuthbert, whose constricted lives are opened out by their contact with the vivacious Anne. Matthew Cuthbert "was the shyest man alive and hated to have to go among strangers or to any place where he might have to talk." He takes refuge in farm work from the trials that even ordinary social life imposes on his retiring nature. Marilla Cuthbert distrusts anything that smacks of frivolity or self-indulgence. She has severely disciplined the lighter side of her nature, in conformity with her belief that the world is "meant to be taken seriously." As a result, "She looked like a woman of narrow experience and rigid conscience, which she was." But Montgomery adds, "there was a saving something about her mouth which, if it had been ever so slightly developed, might have been considered indicative of a sense of humor."[13]

Into the drab lives of this pair comes the irrepressible Anne. Anne's unflagging vitality and enthusiasm may be overdone by Montgomery, but they do present an effective image of the adult's remembered picture of childhood as a time of uncompromised joy. Anne is not quite a real child, but she embodies the essence of childhood, seen as a time of innocence before knowledge of failure or limitation sours the child's outlook. And Anne's appetite for life is contagious. Her quick response to natural beauty, her spontaneity, and her intensity of feeling are healthy correctives to the inhibited, cramped existence of the Cuthberts. Matthew soon finds that he "kind of liked her chatter," and Marilla quickly finds herself defending Anne against criticism voiced by Mrs. Rachel. "But we must make allowances for her," Marilla insists. "She's never been taught what is right. And you *were* too hard on her, Rachel." Under Anne's influence, Marilla rediscovers her sense of humour, and Matthew starts to take notice of the world around him. As Mrs. Rachel remarks: "That man is waking up after being asleep for over sixty years."[14]

Matthew and Marilla, in their different ways, break out of the shell of restraint they have imposed on themselves. Above all, they eventually learn to express their feelings. Matthew takes Anne's part when it comes to letting her participate in the community's social life, alongside her peers. He favours letting her go to the Debating Club's Christmas concert, when Marilla feels such gatherings are the height of frivolous dissipation; and he can understand the importance of puffed sleeves, the lack of which has painfully marked Anne off from her school companions. Just before his fatal heart attack, Matthew tells Anne: "Well now, I guess it wasn't a boy that took the Avery scholarship, was it? It was a girl – my girl – my girl that I'm proud of." And Marilla, under the shock of Matthew's death, overcomes her reluctance to voice her private feelings: "I've been kind of strict and harsh with you maybe – but you mustn't think I didn't love you as well as Matthew did, for all that. I want to tell you now when I can ... I love you as dear as if you were my own flesh and blood and you've been my joy and comfort ever since you came to Green Gables."[15]

Anne too is changed by the life she finds at Green Gables. When Anne first arrives she is described as "a lonely, heart-hungry, friendless child."[16] She has spent most of her young life, since being orphaned, as a household drudge in the homes of families who gave her no real affection, no feeling of being wanted for herself. To escape from a consciousness of her drab existence, Anne has developed a rich fantasy life, based largely on the inflated clichés of phrase and action that she finds in popular sentimental fiction. Her absorption in this fictional world has given her speech a precocious fluency, yet she remains a child with a child's need for affection. When she is first told that Matthew and Marilla had expected a boy rather than a girl, she exclaims: "Nobody ever did want me. I might have known it was all too beautiful to last. I might have known nobody really did want me. Oh, what shall I do? I'm going to burst into tears!" Anne's language may be sentimental and stilted, but her feeling of rejection is plainly conveyed. Matthew is right to describe her as "one of the sort you can do anything with if you only get her to love you."[17] Emotion is the keynote of Anne's nature. She has an unused reserve of strong feelings that can be released by any sign that she is liked for herself.

From the first time we meet her, Anne is portrayed as different from the usual "Avonlea type of well-bred little girl." These well-trained young ladies, as Matthew has noticed, have a way "of sidling past him timidly, with sidewise glances, as if they expected him to gobble them up at a mouthful if they ventured to say a word."[18] That is, these girls defer to their elders in an obsequious way that seems to point at something approaching a climate of fear. Certainly, children are not expected to assert themselves before adults. Anne, however, confronts adults squarely, especially when they presume that their "adult" status entitles them to patronize her, or ignore her feelings.

Young readers simply enjoy Anne's rebellions against grown-up authority. Adult readers, however, will have a subtler appreciation of Montgomery's sharp eye for exposing the injustices that adults can inflict upon children, wittingly or unwittingly. She knows that adult condescension can grievously offend a child's tender sense of selfhood, and she remembers how an unfeeling remark, passed in a child's hearing, can leave a deep emotional wound. In short, she knows the many ways in which adults infringe on the individuality of children. Anne refuses to submit quietly to such treatment, and her rebellious moments arouse Marilla's sympathy, for Marilla can remember how she herself had once "heard one aunt say of her to another, 'What a pity she is such a dark, homely little thing.' Marilla was every day of fifty before the sting had gone out of that memory."[19]

Adults are also drawn to Anne in her role as truth-teller, the naive child-observer who dares to puncture adult pretentiousness. Anne says of the mean-spirited Mrs. Blewett: "She looks exactly like a – like a gimlet." She tells Mrs. Rachel Lynde: "How dare you say I'm freckled and redheaded? You are a rude, impolite, unfeeling woman!" Anne's directness and naivety also enable her to voice some of Montgomery's own reservations about the more formal and rigid aspects of Avonlea's religious practices. When Marilla is aghast that Anne knows no prayers, Anne asks: "Why must people kneel down to pray? If I really wanted to pray I'll tell you what I'd do. I'd go out into a great big field all alone or into the deep, deep woods, and I'd look up into the sky – up – up – up – into that lovely blue sky that looks as if there was no end to its blueness. And then I'd just *feel* a prayer." Soon afterwards, Anne excuses herself for daydreaming during Mr. Bell's prayer by saying: "He was talking to God and didn't seem to be very much interested in it, either." In this speech, and elsewhere in the novel, Anne expresses feelings of rebellion that Marilla has never dared to let herself fully acknowledge: "some of the things Anne had said, especially about the minister's sermons and Mr. Bell's prayers, were what she herself had really thought deep down in her heart for years, but had never given expression to. It almost seemed to her that those secret, unuttered, critical thoughts had suddenly taken visible and accusing shape and form in the person of this outspoken morsel of neglected humanity."[20] In other words, Anne represents everything that Marilla has kept suppressed within herself, greatly to her cost.

Of course, there are weaknesses in Montgomery's portrayal of Anne, and defenders of "serious" fiction will undoubtedly be happy to point them out. One basic difficulty in Montgomery's conception of Anne arises from a discrepancy between Anne's ebullient personality and her unhappy childhood. Anne ought to be emotionally scarred to a much greater extent than she is. Her disposition is unrelievedly sunny, and she expresses no bitterness against those who have deprived her of a normal childhood, refused her emotional warmth, and turned her into an unpaid servant. When Anne is allowed to remain with the Cuthberts, she fits into life at Green Gables with unlikely smoothness. She never rebels against Marilla's disciplinary measures, nor is she ever willfully disobedient. In short, Montgomery's vision of Anne's nature is entirely too roseate for complete plausibility.

But Montgomery does not portray Anne as entirely perfect. Most obviously, Anne is prone to excessive self-dramatization, and is overly fond of imagining herself in the role of a long-suffering romantic heroine. In consequence, one of the unifying themes of *Anne of Green Gables* concerns the disciplining of Anne's hyperactive imagination. What she learns involves more than simply managing not to daydream while she is mixing a cake. She must learn not to confuse fantasy with reality, as she does, for example, in the affairs of the Haunted Wood. She must learn that thoughtless indulgence in fantasy may even become dangerous, as it does when she almost drowns during a disastrous reenactment of an episode taken from Tennyson's *Idylls of the King*.

Anne has presumably developed her tendency to fantasize as a compensation for the poverty of her early circumstances. As she grows more secure at Green Gables, and becomes assured of Matthew and Marilla's affection, she needs her imaginative world less and less. Instead, her imaginative faculties are channelled into her school-work. She vies with Gilbert Blythe for academic honours in the provincial Entrance examinations, thereby gaining self-confidence, and she continues the competition during her year at Queen's College. With the aid of the scholarship she gains for her work at Queen's, she forms a plan to cultivate her intellectual abilities further by pursuing university studies at Redmond College. In the end, however, she gives all of this up in favour of a life of service to Marilla.

Concerning the conclusion of her first novel, Montgomery once wrote: "If I had the book to write over again I would spare Matthew for several years. But when I wrote it I thought he must die, that there might be a necessity for self-sacrifice on Anne's part."[21] Fortunately, Montgomery's second thoughts came to her only long after the book had been committed to print. Matthew's death, combined with the failing eyesight that makes Marilla unable to carry on alone at Green Gables, does make a satisfying conclusion to Anne's story. Anne is chastened and matured by her first encounter with what Montgomery calls the "cold, sanctifying touch" of sorrow. And then, after Anne has decided to remain at Green Gables, we are told that she "had looked her duty courageously in the face and found it a friend – as duty ever is when we meet it frankly."[22] But the true significance of Montgomery's conclusion does not reside in the religious moral she appends to her story. Rather, the conclusion is appropriate because it completes Anne's emotional education in the meaning of having a home. She learns that membership in a family brings duties as well as pleasure.

Anne of Green Gables was published during a period described by Desmond Pacey as "without doubt the age of brass" succeeding the "golden age" of the Confederation Poets and their contemporaries.[23] Once I was prepared to agree, but I am no longer entirely convinced that this judgment holds good. It is based on comparing pre-War fiction with a highly selective version of subsequent literary history. Pacey, and most other academic critics of Canadian fiction, have looked for instances of novelty and rebellion on the part of our writers. They have singled out for praise the authors who introduced new modes such as naturalism or symbolism and new themes such as personal alienation into Canadian letters. In other words, the academic critics have assigned a special value to the rather belated and tentative outcroppings of Modernism that begin to appear in Canadian writing during the twenties and thirties.

Our critics, then, have usually judged our literature entirely by the canons of Modernism. Yet, despite the critics' earnest attempts to unearth a significant early avant garde movement, the mainstream of Canadian fiction has remained remarkably conservative both in technique and in philosophy. Is it possible that our academic critics have let their preference for Modernism influence their judgments unduly? They have been trained to value works in which an individual rebels against social forces. Perhaps they have also been conditioned to undervalue works in which the individual is not seriously at odds with the community. They may not have learned to appreciate works, such as Montgomery's, that celebrate communal solidarity.

Montgomery accepted most of the values that prevailed in her time, and by the end of her novel the narrative voice has endorsed the fundamental values held by the residents of Avonlea. In consequence, Montgomery is a more typical representative of her era than are Duncan and Leacock, who deliberately adopt an ironic, at times satiric, perspective towards the societies they portray. The pervasive irony of the narrator's voice is probably the feature that modern readers find most attractive in both *The Imperialist* and *Sunshine Sketches*. Montgomery's straightforwardness and simplicity have little appeal for many of today's readers. Yet to neglect Montgomery's book is to disavow an important part of our literary past. In a doom-shadowed age, Montgomery's sunny outlook may no longer be fashionable. Nonetheless, we owe it to her, and to ourselves as well, to acknowledge the validity of her accomplishment.

NOTES

1 [The remaining two articles were published in 1985. See MacLulich, "L.M. Montgomery"; MacLulich, "L.M. Montgomery's Portraits."]
2 Montgomery to Weber, 2 May 1907, in *GGL*, 51.
3 Montgomery to MacMillan, 31 August 1908, in *MDMM*, 39; Montgomery to Weber, 22 December 1908, in *GGL*, 80.
4 Eggleston, "General Introduction," 2.
5 Brown, "The Problem of a Canadian Literature," 41; Pacey, *Creative Writing in Canada* (rev. ed.), 106.
6 Ibid., 91, 102–3, 196–97.
7 Brown, "The Problem of a Canadian Literature," 51.
8 Quoted in Logan and French, *Highways of Canadian Literature*, 299.
9 *AGG*, 210–11, 255.
10 *AP*, 48, 57.
11 *AGG*, 1, 2.
12 *AGG*, 2, 3.
13 *AGG*, 2–3, 4, 5.
14 *AGG*, 15, 65–66, 200.
15 *AGG*, 292, 296.
16 *AGG*, 29.
17 *AGG*, 24, 48.
18 *AGG*, 15.
19 *AGG*, 68.
20 *AGG*, 47, 65, 50–51, 81, 83.
21 *AP*, 75.
22 *AGG*, 292, 301.
23 Pacey, *Creative Writing in Canada* (rev. ed.), 89.

4

Little Orphan Mary: Anne's Hoydenish Double

— 1989 —

ROSAMOND BAILEY

In this character study, Rosamond Bailey directs our attention to one of L.M. Montgomery's most fascinating child characters, Mary Vance, who takes over the narrative of Montgomery's 1919 novel *Rainbow Valley*. Although Bailey agrees with past scholars as Gillian Thomas that Anne Shirley Blythe becomes a far less dynamic character as she grows older, she also notes that the inclusion of Mary as "a bold, battered version of Anne Shirley" injects a much-needed form of realism that even *Anne of Green Gables* lacked.

L.M. Montgomery's *Rainbow Valley* – a novel without a protagonist – contains a strong anti-heroine in the ragged waif Mary Vance, who not only dominates much of the book but also represents a bold, battered version of Anne Shirley.

Rainbow Valley is supposedly about "Anne's children growing up,"[1] their mother being little more than a background figure. Yet the story is really about the Meredith family: in particular, the efforts of the manse children to protect their father from parish criticism. At first, the impulsive and quick-tempered Faith Meredith, who is continually getting into scrapes, seems intended as a successor to the Green Gables heroine. "Just like me. I'm going to like your Faith," Anne Blythe remarks.[2] As the book progresses, however, Faith's timid sister Una becomes increasingly important, acting on several occasions with the desperate courage known only to the very shy. Elizabeth Waterston notes that in comparison with "the motherless brood at the nearby manse" the young Blythes are "shadowy."[3] The sole exception here is the bookish Walter, who briefly abandons the realm of literature to defend his mother and Faith with his fists. In structuring *Rainbow Valley* around the adventures and misadventures of a group of children, Montgomery looks back to *The Story Girl* and its sequel *The Golden Road*. Like the Story Girl's cousins, the young Merediths and Blythes find themselves enthralled by a child with strange tales to tell (though Mary Vance and Sara Stanley have very little else in common). Perhaps the author realized that something was needed to inject vigour into the anticlimactic first meeting between the Blythe and Meredith children. The newcomers are accepted immediately into the Rainbow Valley circle, sharing a sacramental meal of dry bread and fried fish. "When the last trout had vanished, the manse children and the Ingleside children were sworn friends and allies. They had always known each other and always would. The race of Joseph recognized its own."[4] Such absolute harmony among eight children is admirable, but it makes dull reading. Fortunately, Montgomery was inspired to introduce an additional outsider: the half-starved runaway who, once discovered in the old barn, proceeds to occupy the next four chapters.

Now the centre of an admiring and horrified group, Mary recounts her ill-treatment at the hands of Mrs. Wiley: "She's an awful woman ... She worked me to death and wouldn't give me half enough to eat, and she used to larrup me 'most every day ... She licked me Wednesday night with a stick ... 'cause I let the cow kick over a pail of milk. How'd I know the darn old cow was going to kick?" She reveals her confused theology:

"Hell? What's that?"

"Why, it's where the devil lives," said Jerry. "You've heard of him – you spoke about him."

"Oh, yes, but I didn't know he lived anywhere. I thought he just roamed around. Mr. Wiley used to mention hell when he was alive. He was always telling folks to go there. I thought it was some place over in New Brunswick where he come from."

And on a later occasion she vents her rage at the overdressed lisping Rilla Blythe: "You think you're something, don't you, all dressed up like a doll! Look at me. My dress is all rags and *I* don't care! I'd rather be ragged than a doll baby. Go home and tell them to put you in a glass case. Look at me – look at me – look at me!"[5] In an effort to shift this colourful interloper and return to her central characters, Montgomery gets Mary out of the manse and into the home of Miss Cornelia. Yet even after having been cleansed, clothed, fine-tooth-combed, and set to learning the catechism, Mary persists in reappearing to disturb the serenity of Rainbow Valley. In her new role as self-appointed critic of her former playmates, she acts as catalyst for much of the subsequent action of the book.

No matter how hard the manse children try to avoid disgracing their father before his congregation, they generally make matters worse. Mary, echoing the officious Miss Cornelia, provides a constant and maddening refrain: "The talk is something terrible. I expect it's ruined your father in this congregation. He'll never be able to live it down, poor man ... You ought to be ashamed of yourselves."[6] The Merediths never consider that the situation might be exaggerated by Mary, that accomplished teller of tall stories.

For example, it is Mary who breaks the news that Faith and Una have acted scandalously in staying home from church on Sunday in order to clean house. Faith is accordingly inspired to explain the mistake – in church: "'It was all Elder Baxter's fault' – sensation in Baxter's pew – 'because he went and changed the prayer-meeting to Wednesday night and then we thought Thursday was Friday and so on till we thought Saturday was Sunday ... And then we thought we'd clean house on Monday and stop old cats from talking about how dirty the manse was – '"[7] Again, Mary brings word that the well-off and influential Mrs. Davis has left the church. Summoning her courage, Faith confronts the fearsome Norman Douglas to request that he attend church and pay towards her father's salary. He turns on her in fury: "If you wasn't such a kid I'd teach you to interfere in what doesn't concern you. When I want parsons or pill-dosers I'll send for them." But Norman is not to get off scot-free: Montgomery turns the situation around. Her temper aroused, Faith retaliates with a vigour worthy of Anne: "I am not afraid of you. You are a rude, unjust, tyrannical, disagreeable old man. Susan says you are sure to go to hell, and I was sorry for you, but I am not now. Your wife never had a new hat for ten years – no wonder she died ... Father has a picture of the devil in a book in his study, and I mean to go home and write your name under it."[8] Faith's winning-over of Norman, who admires her "spunk," provides temporary relief from the ever-present fear that the Rev. Meredith will lose his church. Mary Vance, however, keeps reappearing with further accounts of the manse children's dreadful behaviour (such as holding a praying competition in the Methodist graveyard). The Merediths are eventually goaded into forming a Good-Conduct Club – from which Mary is to be excluded: "We agree to punish ourselves for bad conduct, and always to stop before we do anything, no matter what, and ask ourselves if it is likely to hurt dad in any way, and anyone who shirks is to be cast out of the club and never allowed to play with the rest of us in Rainbow Valley again."[9]

Heretofore the efforts of the manse children to defend their father have had relatively harmless – and comic – results. On two occasions, however, the stern judgments handed down by the Good-Conduct Club result in near-tragedy. The delicate Una collapses during a fast day endured by the children as punishment for having sung "Polly Wolly Doodle" in the graveyard during a Methodist prayer-meeting. A short time later, Carl nearly dies of pneumonia following an all-night vigil "on Mr. Hezekiah Pollock's tombstone."[10] By running from what he thought was a ghost, Carl has acted like a coward and thereby brought disgrace upon the family. Mary Vance has been indirectly responsible for this incident: it was her vivid account of Henry Warren's ghost that caused Carl and his sisters to run screaming from the supposed apparition.

Mary's lurid imagination has also caused trouble in another quarter. Local speculation concerning the possible remarriage of the Rev. Meredith leads Mary to warn her friends: "It'll be awful if you get a stepmother ... the worst of stepmothers is, they always set your father against you."[11] Una in particular becomes terrified at the prospect of her father's marrying Rosemary West, especially since Mary seems unable to leave the subject alone. "Mary has told me blood-curdling things about [stepmothers]. She says she knew of one who whipped her husband's little girls on their bare shoulders till they bled, and then shut them up in a cold, dark coal cellar all night. She says they're *all* aching to do things like that."[12] At the end of the book, the reconciliation of John Meredith and Rosemary West is made to depend ultimately on Una's overcoming her fears and facing the woman who (according to Mary) is a potential Wicked Stepmother.[13] Rosemary is quick to dismiss Mary as "a silly little girl who doesn't know very much."[14] Nevertheless this silly little girl has figured prominently in the novel, despite the author's efforts to keep her in her place. In contrast, Anne Blythe (the nominal heroine) is almost completely passive. It is Mary who fulfills, however imperfectly, the role that Mrs. Blythe supposedly adopts: sympathetic friend and champion of the Meredith family.

At the beginning we discover Anne, upon hearing of these motherless newcomers, "beginning to mother them already in her heart." We never actually see her with these children; we must take on trust Faith's averral that Mrs. Blythe "always understands – she never laughs at us."[15] What we do witness, on the other hand, is Mary Vance immediately taking over the disordered manse household, cleaning and mending and tidying, even chasing the poor minister out of his study. We see Mary informing the Meredith children of their disgraceful behaviour, in the lofty tone of someone four times their age. Blunt, tactless, and eminently practical, Mary Vance is the one who actually "mothers" the manse family. Even allowing for her love of exaggeration, there is considerable truth in her warnings, which come as a shock to the children. Apparently Anne Blythe, who disdains to repeat gossip, has never thought to caution her protégés about the dangers of antagonizing the "old cats" in the congregation. Anne defends the children in private, soothing the agitated Miss Cornelia, who rushes to Ingleside after every fresh scandal to wail "What *is* to be done?" As though tired of this constant refrain, Anne eventually asserts herself, announcing that she would like to speak out in defense of the Merediths before the community. Saying she would "*like* to*" is as far as she goes.[16] Mary Vance, on the other hand, does not hesitate to lock horns with the formidable Mrs. Davis: "Mrs. Elliott [Miss Cornelia] says she never saw the like of me for sticking up for my friends. I was real sassy to Mrs. Alec Davis about you and Mrs. Elliott combed me down for it afterwards. The fair Cornelia has a tongue of her own and no mistake. But she was pleased underneath for all, 'cause she hates old Kitty Alec and she's real fond of you. *I* can see through folks."[17] Mary's defense naturally counts for little – who will heed a nobody of an orphan? But at least she is not afraid to "stick up for her friends," while the more socially prominent Mrs. Dr. Blythe remains silent. The once lively Anne, as Elizabeth Waterston points out, has been "reduced to some cliché gestures."[18] Gillian Thomas suggests that Anne's reticence as a matron stems from the realization that she "must behave appropriately for her role as 'Mrs. Dr.'"; but total passivity scarcely seems appropriate in a woman who has achieved such status.[19] Anne Blythe is curiously reluctant to express any opinions at all; it is almost as though she still feels herself the friendless orphan on probation before the community. As we have seen, Mary Vance – who is actually in this position – has no such qualms at first. As the story progresses we find the shadows of the prison-house of respectability beginning to close about her. "I simply feel that I can't associate with you any longer," she tells Faith unhappily. (Faith has disgraced herself by appearing at church without stockings.) "It ain't that I don't want to ... [but] I'm in a respectable place and trying to be a lady." Compare Anne's rueful "we must be conventional or die, after we reach what is supposed to be a dignified age."[20]

Mary Vance, whether or not intended as a substitute for Mrs. Blythe, is presented as the exact opposite of that more famous orphan Anne Shirley. That both children come from Hopetown Orphanage[21] seems a coincidence meant to heighten the subsequent contrasts. Anne twice remarks that she too was once a "homeless little orphan"; Miss Cornelia on one occasion retorts, "I don't think this Mary-creature is or ever will be much like you."[22] Elizabeth Waterston recognizes Mary as a different breed of orphan – "a brassy, skinny, pale-eyed, pugnacious one."[23] There are, however, many surprising similarities between these children, and even the contrasts often suggest Mary as an inverted double for the Green Gables heroine: a rough, street-wise Anne.

Mary's initial description seems to set her apart from her predecessor. Anne is discovered more or less respectably outfitted for her journey and calmly awaiting Matthew at the station; Mary, wearing nothing except a ragged dress, is found cowering in a hayloft. Her "lank, thick, tow-coloured hair and very odd eyes – 'white eyes'" are an unattractive contrast to Anne's red braids and large green-gray eyes.[24] Note, however, that both children have braided hair; both are garbed in dresses "much too short and tight"[25] – the typical hand-me-down wear of an orphan; both are equally skinny. Anne is eleven, Mary approximately twelve. Anne has a striking and expressive countenance; Mary's face is "wizened," unchildlike.[26] Drain the colour from Anne's hair and eyes, and (more important) eradicate from her face the hope and innocence and love of life – and what might be left? Mary Vance.

Mary, despite her pale colouring, is far from insipid. Fortified by a square meal, she reverts to her "natural vivacity,"[27] dominating her rescuers almost at once. She is slangy, ungrammatical, near-profane; she is boastful and bossy among the other children; she is impudent to adults. Montgomery has gone to great lengths to create in this bold orphan the antithesis of the well-spoken and (usually) well-mannered Anne. Not that the Green Gables heroine is shy or withdrawn; she has a spirited nature of her own, a tongue and temper as quick as Mary's. Both heredity and environment appear to be responsible for making one child a hellion, the other a lady. The author supplies Mary with parents far different from those of Anne:

"I was two years in the asylum. I was put there when I was six. My ma had hung herself and my pa had cut his throat."

"Holy cats! Why?" said Jerry.

"Booze," said Mary laconically.[28]

In the same matter-of-fact way she adds that her parents used to beat her. More extreme opposites for those tragic lovers Walter and Bertha Shirley, who cherished their infant daughter, would be hard to imagine. Again, the child-battering Mrs. Wiley seems intended as a contrast to Anne's former guardians, who overworked and neglected her but stopped short of active ill-treatment. Or at least we assume so: Anne, normally so talkative, is reticent about her early life. "I know they meant to be just as good and kind as possible," she tells Marilla. "And when people mean to be good to you, you don't mind very much when they're not quite – always." We hear, almost in passing, of Mrs. Thomas's telling Anne that she was "desperately wicked"; of Mr. Thomas's habit of smashing things when he was "slightly intoxicated."[29] Anne escapes the memories of drunken rages or verbal abuse by retreating into her fantasy-world; Mary, lacking such inner resources, boasts of her traumatic childhood. "She divined that the manse children were pitying her for her many stripes and she did not want pity. She wanted to be envied."[30]

Given her long history of abuse, Mary's tough and belligerent exterior is believable. What is unrealistic, by comparison, is Anne's educated vocabulary and ladylike deportment. A child reared first by a scrubwoman with an alcoholic husband and then by a large backwoods family might be expected to turn out speaking, if not behaving, more like Mary Vance than Anne Shirley. The latter has actually had less formal education than her counterpart: four months in the orphanage as against Mary's two years, plus an even more sketchy attendance at public school. And neither the Thomas nor Hammond household seems to have contained books.[31] The explanation for this striking contrast in behaviour between the two orphans lies in the wide social gulf established by Montgomery. Jean Little points out that Anne, "although definitely an orphan, is discovered to have sprung from genteel stock. By their relatives shall ye know them."[32] Contrast Anne's polite opening speech, "I suppose you are Mr. Matthew Cuthbert of Green Gables?" with Mary's wail of "I hain't had a thing to eat since Thursday morning, 'cept a little water from the brook out there."[33] That "hain't" immediately suggests Mary's social level. Her ancestors may have had pretensions – such as the rich grandfather who was a "rascal" – but they exist now only in her overloaded name, her sole legacy: "Mary Martha Lucilla Moore Ball Vance." Mary would doubtless scorn Anne's plain, single Christian name which the owner herself must embellish "with an *e*."[34] A genteel background presumably accounts also for Anne's quickly acquired love of literature. Mary's domestic talents again place her on a lower plane: she seems actually to relish doing servants' work.

Regardless of their origins, both Anne and Mary find that to be an orphan is to be at a social disadvantage. The myth of the Wicked Orphan who poisons wells and sets farms afire (one of Mrs. Lynde's favourite topics) is given a comic application in *Anne of Green Gables*: Anne not only gets Diana drunk but also offers the minister's wife a cake flavoured with liniment.[35] In *Rainbow Valley* the community of Glen St. Mary is suspicious of "home children." "You know yourself what that poor little creature the Jim Flaggs' had, taught and told the Flagg children," Miss Cornelia warns the Rev. Meredith.[36] But Mary, another such poor little creature, is surprisingly restrained in her speech: "If you knew some of the words I *could* say if I liked you wouldn't make such a fuss over darn."[37] Gossip is her downfall; the ill effects of her wagging tongue have already been pointed out. (We may recall, in this connection, that Anne Shirley is reprimanded by Marilla for bringing home tales about the schoolmaster and Prissy Andrews.) Unwanted at first, both children are eventually accepted into the homes of strong-minded, spinsterish women.[38] Miss Cornelia, who retains her maiden title, is a former old maid who married an old bachelor (see *Anne's House of Dreams*). Her mild, long-suffering husband Marshall echoes Matthew in encouraging the adoption of the orphan. Mary, however, goes into no Anne-like raptures at the prospect. Unable to visualize a home in which she might be wanted or even loved, she is content to know that she will not be beaten. Miss Cornelia admits, "I've no fault to find with Mary ... she's clean and respectful – though there's more in her than *I* can fathom. She's a sly puss."[39] Mary is shrewd enough to learn almost overnight the best way of getting along with her new guardian – how different from the impulsive, blundering Anne! The relationship between Mary and Miss Cornelia reflects a mutual, if grudging, respect, rather than the genuine affection that develops between Anne and Marilla.

Indeed, Miss Cornelia seems the nearest thing to a "kindred spirit" that Mary encounters. "We was made for each other ... She's pizen neat, but so am I, and so we agree fine."[40] Among her contemporaries Mary seeks no bosom friend; she prefers to be at the centre of the group, bossing, bragging, telling her horrific yarns. Oddly enough, only the introverts Walter Blythe and Una Meredith have any real influence over her. And even Una, once her confidante, is eventually provoked into resentful envy over the new velvet cap and squirrel muff that Mary flaunts. Fine feathers, for Mary, seem more important than friendship. On the very day she is rescued she turns on Faith for having made an unwise remark about the ragged dress: "When I grow up I'm going to have a blue sating dress. Your own clothes don't look so stylish."[41] She chases Rilla Blythe – with dried codfish – simply for being better attired (although the author admits there was some provocation, Rilla being all too aware of her finery). Anne Shirley is also capable of rage over slurs on her appearance – witness the famous attacks upon Mrs. Lynde and Gilbert – and she has her own vanities: she longs for raven-black hair and fashionable puffed sleeves. Yet behind this attitude is a strong desire to be loved. She is convinced that no one wants an ugly child: "If I was very beautiful and had nut-brown hair would you keep me?"[42] Having acquired her stylish clothes, she does not show them off quite as Mary does. Mary, whose emotional development has been stunted by ten years of abuse, craves status: she must feel superior even to her friends. Would Anne, in the same circumstances, still be capable of putting affection first – or would she, too, settle for good clothes and respectability as her highest goals?

It is hardly surprising that both Anne and Mary, neglected upon earth, should place little confidence in a loving Deity. Hopetown Orphanage has provided some religious instruction: Anne can recite the catechism flawlessly, while Mary has learnt "an old rhyme" to repeat at bedtime. Anne, however, has never said any prayers: "Mrs. Thomas told me that God made my hair red *on purpose*, and I've never cared about Him since." Mary is more tolerant: "Mind you, I haven't got anything against God, Una. I'm willing to give Him a chance. But, honest, I think He's an awful lot like your father – just absent-minded and never taking any notice of a body most of the time, but sometimes waking up all of a sudent and being awful good and kind and sensible."[43] The good ladies Marilla and Cornelia endeavour to overcome the ignorance of these little near-heathens by conventional methods: Anne is given the Lord's Prayer to learn, Mary the Shorter Catechism. Neither orphan is thereby transformed into a pious child of the Elsie Dinsmore variety. Instead, we find Anne moved to "irreverent" delight over a picture of Christ blessing little children: "I was just imagining ... I was the little girl in the blue dress, standing off by herself in the corner as if she didn't belong to anybody, like me."[44] Once she finds she is to remain at Green Gables, she finds it easy to pray. On the other hand, Mary – despite the kind efforts of the Rev. Meredith – remains dubious. She even speculates that it might be wise to ask the devil not to tempt her, thereby unconsciously paraphrasing part of the Lord's Prayer. Her subsequent model behaviour at Miss Cornelia's appears, as previously suggested, to be due to expediency rather than religious conversion.

Finally, Mary – although created as Anne's opposite – is by no means lacking in imagination. We find her moved almost to tears by Walter's prophecy of the Piper who will one day lead the boys away to war; we find her terrified at the prospect of going to hell because of her lies. She entertains the Rainbow Valley children with accounts of ghosts and superstitions and cruel stepmothers, much after the manner of Riley's Little Orphant Annie.[45] The young Anne also enjoys Gothic horrors: her misadventure in the Haunted Wood has its parallel in the incident of Henry Warren's ghost, which Mary herself claims to have seen. Mary's imaginings are almost invariably morbid: we find no Snow Queens, no dryads, no Lady Cordelias. Like Anne, she enjoys self-dramatization, but rather than playing romantic heroines like Elaine the Lily Maid, she draws from her own history, presenting herself as the victim of Mrs. Wiley (that real-life Wicked Witch). Mary might be accused of exaggeration here, were it not that she bears actual bruises. For she is less careful of the truth than is Anne (whose constant refrain of "I'll imagine" as a preface to every fantasy becomes somewhat tedious after the first few chapters). Mary swears to have witnessed apparitions "all in white with skellington hands and heads" and actually to have met the Wandering Jew.[46] The Merediths are charitable about these yarns. Nevertheless Mary has told actual untruths, thereby committing one of the worst childhood sins in the Montgomery canon. She is given some excuse: she lied to avoid further ill-treatment from the Wileys. (She is not a malicious troublemaker like Emily's false friend Rhoda in *Emily of New Moon*, or Nan's playmate Dovie in *Anne of Ingleside*.) Once informed of her wickedness, Mary repents. She continues, however, to confuse fiction with falsehood, calling Walter's readings "in'resting lies."[47] There are some indications here that she might develop some appreciation of literature, given the opportunity. She will never, of course, be permitted by the author to reach Anne's cultural level. Mary belongs to a lower order, spiritually as well as socially.

Mary Vance is one of Montgomery's best comic characters. Considerable insight is shown as well in this portrait of a child warped both emotionally and intellectually by a brutal environment. Yet the author seems never to have considered that psychological abuse might have been just as harmful for Anne, destroying the capacity for affection and the rich imaginative vision that make her what she is. Matthew and Marilla might well have been confronted with a Mary Vance: but that is a story L.M. Montgomery never wrote.

NOTES

1 Gillen, *The Wheel of Things*, 78.
2 *RV*, 8.
3 [See Elizabeth Waterston's chapter "Lucy Maud Montgomery 1874–1942," in this volume.]
4 *RV*, 26.
5 *RV*, 31, 34, 46.
6 *RV*, 74.
7 *RV*, 79, 80.
8 *RV*, 114–15.
9 *RV*, 163.
10 [*RV*, 202.]
11 *RV*, 66.
12 *RV*, 165.
13 One can only speculate on the extent to which Mary's condemnation of stepmothers reflects Maud Montgomery's own feelings about her father's second wife. Note that a stepmother's worst sin is not to beat her stepchildren but to separate them from their father's affections.
14 *RV*, 220.
15 *RV*, 8, 137.
16 [*RV*, 180, 183.]
17 *RV*, 160.
18 [See Waterston's "Lucy Maud Montgomery 1874–1942."]
19 Thomas, "The Decline of Anne," 28. Frances Frazer's review of *The Road to Yesterday* contains a pertinent comment: "a kind of goddess, with Susan Baker as her priestess, Anne dwells apart" (Frazer, "Scarcely an End," 91).
20 *RV*, 174, 175, 183.
21 Note the change in spelling: "Hopeton" in *Anne of Green Gables*, "Hopetown" in *Rainbow Valley*.
22 *RV*, 62.
23 [See Waterston's "Lucy Maud Montgomery 1874–1942."]
24 *RV*, 29.
25 [*RV*, 30; see also *AGG*, 11.]
26 [*RV*, 30.]
27 [*RV*, 31.]
28 *RV*, 33.
29 *AGG*, 41[, 54, 58].
30 *RV*, 33.

31 Anne informs Marilla that Mrs. Thomas used her bookcase to store pre-
     serves, while Mrs. Hammond had no bookcase at all (*AGG*, 58).
32 Little, "But What about Jane?" 74.
33 *AGG*, 11; *RV*, 30.
34 [*RV*, 64, 33; *AGG*, 25.]
35 After "intoxicating" Diana, Anne redeems herself by saving the life of
     Diana's little sister. A parallel incident occurs in *Rilla of Ingleside*: Mary
     Vance saves little Jims, who is also dying of croup.
36 *RV*, 58.
37 *RV*, 44.
38 It never appears to occur to Anne Blythe to admit a home child into the
     sacred circle of Ingleside; she sees no reason to do as she was once done by.
39 *RV*, 84.
40 *RV*, 131.
41 *RV*, 35.
42 *AGG*, 25.
43 [*RV*, 38;] *AGG*, 50; *RV*, 64.
44 *AGG*, 56.
45 See James Whitcomb Riley's "Little Orphant Annie," lines 5–12:
           An' all us other childern, [*sic*] when the supper-things is done,
           We set around the kitchen fire an' has the mostest fun
           A-list'nin' to the witch-tales 'at Annie tells about,
           An' the Gobble-uns 'at gits you
                Ef you
                   Don't
                     Watch
                       Out!
46 [*RV*, 42, 54.]
47 [*RV*, 54.]

5

Subverting the Trite:
L.M. Montgomery's "Room of Her Own"

—— 1992 ——

MARY RUBIO

In this article, published in *Canadian Children's Literature / Littérature canadienne pour la jeunesse*, Mary Rubio draws a number of parallels between Montgomery and her female contemporaries, particularly Virginia Woolf, who struggled to find "rooms of their own" in the house of fiction, in order to contextualize her discussion of Montgomery as a "cleverly political writer." Rubio, co-editor of seven volumes of Montgomery's journals and author of the biography *Lucy Maud Montgomery: The Gift of Wings* (2008), outlines nine strategies that Montgomery uses in her books to subvert the conventions of domestic fiction, focusing in particular on *Emily of New Moon* (1923), *Emily Climbs* (1925), *The Blue Castle* (1926), and *Emily's Quest* (1927).

"Woe to the poor mortal who has not even one small room to call her own."
                                        – L.M. Montgomery, journal entry, May 1, 1899[1]

"But you may say, we asked you to speak about women and fiction – what has that got to do with a room of one's own?"
                                        – Virginia Woolf, *A Room of One's Own*, 1929[2]

Both L.M. Montgomery and Virginia Woolf, almost exact contemporaries, experienced many of the same impediments to female authorship, and each succeeded in very different ways in spite of these. Montgomery lived from 1874 to 1942, Virginia Woolf from 1882 to 1941. Despite the enormous difference in their access to culture – Montgomery was raised in a small farming community on Prince Edward Island and Woolf was raised in an extremely literate household in cultured London – there are a number of similarities between their work, lives and temperaments. Both came from intense, energetic families who were socially prominent in their individual spheres. Both left voluminous journals and letters which provide a rich background for understanding their literary production. And both have been a powerful force in the empowerment of women in the 20th century.

Montgomery and Woolf have left a record of major depressive episodes which reveal either inherently fragile nervous systems or incredibly stressed lives, depending on one's interpretative stance. Both lost their mothers at an early age – Montgomery at 21 months and Woolf at 13 years. Both were very sensitive, and as children suffered from hostility and instability in their patriarchal environment – Maud from the abusive outbursts of temper of her grandfather and nearby uncle, Virginia from sexual abuse by her brothers. Both Montgomery and Woolf exhibited labile emotions, with wide mood swings, and both sought an explanatory concept for this in their ancestry – each saw herself derived from an ascetic, Puritan lineage on one side and a volatile, passionate lineage on the other side. Both married relatively late – Montgomery in 1911 at 35, Woolf in 1912 at 30; Montgomery to a man whose mental instability imprisoned her in shame and loneliness, and Woolf to a man whose assiduous control of her life, though apparently well-meaning, was a kind of custodial imprisonment. Both Montgomery and Woolf brooded on their childhood traumas and inscribed their concern with the welfare of children into their art; each wrote powerfully of the inner lives of women and children. Not only did each resent the fact that she had been denied the same education that bright young men in her family had been given, but each also resented the fact that women were given little psychological and physical space in which to grow and write. As a result, both wrote about the importance of a woman having a metaphorical "room of her own."

At the time that these women began writing, the cards were stacked against women who wanted a literary career. It was difficult for most women to compete with better-educated men in the writing of novels, and when women did write, their books were rarely taken as seriously. Creative literature shows us who we are, and what issues are important in our lives. Women were shut out of an experiential creative realm that validated their existence and challenged oppressive attitudes. What both Montgomery and Woolf recognized was that it is necessary for women writers to have equal opportunity to create fictional worlds from women's perspectives – to create, so to speak, rooms of their own. The medium (and style) through which Montgomery and Woolf spoke may have been radically different, but their message was much the same.

Cultural anthropologists and feminist historians of the last quarter century have thoroughly examined the patriarchal nature of our culture: they have exposed the way it has placed the male sex at its centre and designated the female sex as marginal and less important. Literary historians like Elaine Showalter (*A Literature of Their Own*) have documented the fact that the intellectual climate engendered by the patriarchal system in the 19th century made women feel anxious about authorship. Because public discourse was a male domain, women who wrote sought ways to avoid censure: some prefaced their works with apologies pleading necessity to earn a respectable living; others, like the Brontës, used androgynous or male pseudonyms; and most women kept a low literary profile because they wrote in non-canonical forms. Some 19th century female authors like Jane Austen have been dismissed by male academics well into this century. "George Eliot" (Mary Ann Evans) was a rare female writer in that she managed to be taken seriously in her own time, but she did this partly by breaking out of traditional female gender roles in her own personal life. Her situation was unusual and complicated. She railed as much as male critics about "silly scribbling women" which was, at the least, sensible protection against being thought to be one of them.

A second wave of feminists has also begun to see how the previously ignored 19th century women writers who wrote *popular* fiction, as distinct from the male writers of "canonized" *serious* literature, managed to challenge the ideologies that informed and shaped their culture despite the restrictions imposed by the genres within which they worked. Women produced a huge number of "popular" romances from the 18th century onward, but these were considered ephemeral literature – not worthy of notice beside the novels written by male literary greats. We are only learning now, through the studies of feminist literary theorists, that these women writers in fact did a great deal to question the validity of their male-centred culture and its patriarchal values even though they wrote in genres judged "inferior." One excellent book of the past decade is Rachel Blau DuPlessis's *Writing beyond the Ending: Narrative Strategies of Twentieth-Century Women Writers*.[3] She outlines the ways that modern women writers present fictions that confront and challenge the prevailing ideologies. Her comments about the way that 20th century women writers choose and execute their literary discourses are in many cases applicable to earlier novels as well and certainly to L.M. Montgomery:

> narrative may function on a small scale the way that ideology functions on a large scale – as a "system of representations by which we imagine the world as it is." To compose a work is to negotiate with these questions: What stories can be told? How can plots be resolved? What is felt to be narratable by both literary and social conventions? Indeed, these are issues very acute to ... feminist critics and women writers, with their sense of the untold story, the other side of a well-known tale, the elements of women's existence that have never been revealed.[4]

My focus in this paper is on the way Montgomery both works within the traditional literary genre of domestic romance and yet circumvents its restrictive conventions when she critiques her society; how she decides to incorporate elements of women's experience that were not usually dealt with in fiction for women and children in her era; how she makes it safe for herself to tell tales and say things which are outside the pale of acceptable female public discourse. In the semi-autobiographical *Emily* trilogy, for instance, she focuses on how a young woman who wants to become a writer learns to negotiate with a patriarchal society which discourages female selfhood and individuality, denying her "a room of her own." The three *Emily* books and *The Blue Castle* incorporate much of Montgomery's inner life, though the details are fictional. The books were all published between 1923 and 1927, and form a very important progressive sequence, with the order of publication being *Emily of New Moon* (1923), *Emily Climbs* (1925), *The Blue Castle* (1926), and *Emily's Quest* (1927).

One of the sources of the extraordinary appeal of Montgomery's books in her own time and ours lies in the fact that she was able to reinforce all the prevailing ideologies which her conventional readers expected while at the same time embedding a counter-text of rebellion for those who were clever enough to read between the lines. And in many cases, I expect, this countertext entered young minds subliminally, there to grow as the child grew until it became a discernible, compelling discourse on women's rights. For instance, a book called *The Girl Within*, by the Harvard-trained psychologist Emily Hancock (Random House,

1989), deals with the question of how girls establish their identity. Emily Hancock cites Montgomery's *Emily of New Moon* as a book which had much impact on her personal life.[5] In their "Afterwords" to the recent New Canadian Library editions of *Emily of New Moon* and *Emily Climbs* Alice Munro and Jane Urquhart respectively talk about the way in which Montgomery's "Emily" provided a model of female authorship for them. Alice Munro makes further comments about the L.M. Montgomery books in interviews with Catherine Ross and with Tim Struthers. Because Munro is certainly acclaimed as one of Canada's very best writers, we take especial notice when she states that "the three Emily books ... were all *very* important to me." She continues, "I think *Emily of New Moon* is by *far* her [Montgomery's] best book ... In many ways there's great psychological truth in it, and it's also a very powerful book"; when asked if there are features of Montgomery's fictional world that connected Montgomery's world with rural Ontario, Munro replies: "Oh, very much so. In the family structure, I think ... A connection with the sort of people she was dealing with, the old aunts and the grandmothers, the female power figures ... a sense of injustice and strangeness in family life and of mystery in people that was familiar to me."[6]

Montgomery's *Emily* books have obviously encouraged much female authorship. Another of the Canadian women who writes with such deep insight into the lives of women in small communities is Margaret Laurence who mentions her own youthful acquaintance with Montgomery's writing in her last book, *Dance on the Earth: A Memoir*. Margaret Atwood, the Canadian author who probably has the highest international profile, notes more than a passing familiarity with Montgomery also. In an interview in Götenberg, Sweden, in August 1990, Atwood was asked a few questions by an audience after a radio interview. One of the first questioners began with the rather breath-taking assertion that "There are two Canadian authors, you, and the other is Lucy Maud Montgomery ... " and proceeded to ask if there was a connection between her and L.M. Montgomery. Atwood replied that "we all read *Anne of Green Gables* as children" and then explained that she had read it again together with her daughter, with both of them crying over Matthew's death. She added that when she was young, "they" had been told "there was no Canadian literature" and that "that book [*Anne of Green Gables*] and other books ... were not really literature, but," she added, "they *are*." She also told how it had been pointed out to her, and she hadn't thought of it consciously before, "that the alterego, best-friend/worst enemy/shadow-reflection/mirror-figure of Elaine in *Cat's Eye* is named Cordelia which is also the name [in *Anne*]." She summed it all up by stating that "Obviously *Anne of Green Gables* is a subcutaneous archetypal memory ... "[7] A few of the other writers who have mentioned Montgomery's influence on them are Astrid Lindgren of Sweden,[8] Rosemary Sutcliff of England and Jean Little of Canada.[9] Another highly regarded Canadian writer, Carol Shields, has said, "My mother loved *Anne of Green Gables*. She couldn't wait till we were old enough to read it ... I suppose that *Anne* was a model to just millions of girls who weren't ever able to act out the kind of battles that she had."[10]

One of the battles Anne and Emily had was to be taken seriously. Being a female was a handicap in this enterprise. Not far into *Emily of New Moon* (1923), the child "Emily" is told that she is of little importance in the scale of things: this is very true, for orphaned girls at the turn of the century in North America were particularly low on the social totem pole. When Emily is told, "You ought to be thankful to get a home anywhere. Remember you're not of much importance," Montgomery's Emily replies proudly: "I am important to myself."[11] That retort was astonishing for its era, and many a little girl must have been amazed at Emily's audacity, while tucking away the comment as an empowering idea: *girls* can be important!

It is the fact that Montgomery was able to employ "narrative strategies that express critical dissent from the dominant narrative pattern"[12] which has kept her books *au courant* as society changed. Because of Montgomery's strategic position between the end of Victorianism and the growth of Modernism, her subcutaneous "counter-texts" of rebellion have given her an important role in helping young women – and young female writers – formulate a healthy sense of female self.

Since the recent opening of the canon to women writers, two major books on Montgomery's works have already been written: a recent doctoral dissertation on Montgomery by Gabriella Åhmansson is available from the University of Uppsala, Sweden, in book form as *A Life and Its Mirrors: A Feminist Reading of L.M. Montgomery's Fiction (Volume I: An Introduction to Lucy Maud Montgomery and Anne Shirley)*.[13] In Canada Elizabeth Epperly's *The Fragrance of Sweet-Grass: L.M. Montgomery's Heroines and the Pursuit of Romance* will be available this year. The newer branches of cross-disciplinary criticism which look at all literary and textual production as a phase of wider human culture have given new impetus to the study of popular and powerful writers like Montgomery. The University of Guelph Archives holds L.M. Montgomery's "Clipping Book" into which she compiled reviews which came to her from a clipping service, starting in 1910. It shows that her books were reviewed all over the English-speaking world as soon as they appeared, and the reviews were almost always favourable.

Now that foreign academics have started writing doctoral and M.A. dissertations on Montgomery, and a flood of articles has started appearing in American journals, Canadians recognize that in Montgomery they have a truly unique figure who has embedded her imprint on generations of readers worldwide. Sometimes this imprinting is at an unconscious level. When Colleen McCullough's 1987 novel, *The Ladies of Missalonghi*, was published, enraged L.M. Montgomery fans from the USA, Britain, and Australia wrote letters of protest to McCullough's publisher and to other representatives of the L.M. Montgomery Estate saying that it bore too many similarities for their taste to Montgomery's *The Blue Castle*. One Canadian newspaper, the Kingston *Whig–Standard*,[14] did a feature article on the similarity, and immediately the media in Britain, Australia, and the United States fell upon the story, turning it into a minor international incident. After a long silence, out of reach of reporters on an island, McCullough stated tersely through her publisher that she had read *The Blue Castle* "as a child and loved it," as she had loved all of L.M. Montgomery's books.[15]

Thus, Montgomery's world-wide impact has been both cultural and economic, and some preliminary studies have already been done to assess her influence. A substantial, thoroughly researched dissertation by Krystyna Sobkowska entitled "The Reception of the *Anne of Green Gables* Series by Lucy Maud Montgomery in Poland" was completed at the University of Lodz, Poland, in 1982/3. Unfortunately, attempts to research the Montgomery publishing history in North America have been hampered by the destruction of many of the McClelland & Stewart publishing records, as well as those of the L.C. Page Company, which was acquired by Farrar, Straus, and Giroux in the 1950s. Another approach to establishing an author's reach is by citing references to her work by readers and other writers who have been influenced by her. A further dimension of Montgomery's influence is seen in the way that she has affected tourism and inspired "spinoff" industries. For instance, *CCL* issue #34 (1984) looks at the way the Japanese have made an industry out of "Anne."[16] In 1991 15,000 Japanese tourists came to Prince Edward Island to see the landscape Montgomery made famous. Tourism, thanks to Montgomery's books, has become one of the Island's biggest industries, with over 750,000 people visiting tiny PEI in 1991.[17] This infusion of tourists started in 1909, the year after *Anne*'s publication. Last year Japan developed part of a Japanese island into a multi-million-dollar themepark, part of which is devoted to Montgomery, with reconstructions of Cavendish in it.[18]

Not too long after Elizabeth Waterston and I published the first volume of *The Selected Journals of L.M. Montgomery*, we began to realize how geographically diverse was the interest in her. Calls and letters asking when the next volume would be ready came from all over: the United States, England, Australia, Scotland, Germany, Sweden and other places. Several Montgomery fans urged us to hurry because they were too old to last much longer and couldn't, as one caller put it, bear to die without reading the rest of the journals. One fan's husband wrote that his wife had cancer, and he begged us to let them know what happened since his wife might not survive to read about the subsequent unfolding of Montgomery's life. Many spoke of the joy they had in finding "another book" by Montgomery after a lifetime of rereading her other published books and thinking there were no more. In 1984, Dr. Waterston and I, along with Mrs. Ruth Macdonald, the widow of Montgomery's son Stuart, travelled to Poland to see theatrical productions of Montgomery's *Anne of Green Gables* and *The Blue Castle* in Warsaw and Cracow, and we were astonished at the deep attachment people had to her books in that country. Clearly L.M. Montgomery was far more than Canadians had taken her to be, a mere author of successful "children's" books: she was a writer of international influence who had changed lives and affected the ways that people thought. Despite the array of forces discouraging female authorship in her era, she had in fact created a small room of her own in the great house of fiction. In that room, she had been holding forth for nearly 100 years, drawing in a steady stream of readers from around the globe, and they had kept her writings alive.

L.M. Montgomery can make some unique claims to fame. Most of the writers from earlier eras who are still in print are so by virtue of their books having become "canonized" texts that are assigned to college and university students, a process which creates an academic "life-support" system. Otherwise, both popular and serious writers of any era tend to fade away: popular writers because public tastes and concerns change and "serious" writers because their audience, small to begin with, wanes. Montgomery's first claim is that she is one of the few writers who has left a large corpus of work – 22 works of fiction in her case – which have survived for nearly a century *without* being in that "canonized" group of texts with artificially inflated sales.[19] Montgomery's loyal readers, which include librarians and elementary school teachers, have kept her books in print; some, like *Anne of Green Gables*, have consistently maintained enormous sales.

Secondly, she is one of the few writers who retain their readers throughout a full life cycle: when her young readers grow up, many keep re-reading her books, often finding new levels of meaning at different stages of their lives. We have met or heard from scores of readers past retirement age who tell us that they reread their favourite Montgomery books every year.

Third, Montgomery is a writer who has had a strangely diverse appeal to thousands of people from widely different cultures, nationalities, and geographical locations. Her books are so rich that they have provided whatever a cultural subgroup of readers needed: for women writers all over the world they have pointed the way to female authorship; for ordinary people, especially women, in countries as widely divergent as the United States and Japan, they have provided personal empowerment; and for nations like Poland they have furnished a subversive political agenda. It is very difficult to think of any other single writer – male or female – who can make all of these three claims. It is to our shame that we have only begun to document the extent of her influence nearly half a century after her death.

The next question to ask is, "what gives her books such far-ranging and powerful appeal?" I attempt only a preliminary and partial outlining of the techniques which Montgomery uses to subvert the triteness of genre in which she works so that her books confront issues of wide cultural significance. Working in a very restrictive genre, the domestic romance, she presented a surface reinforcement of all the prevailing ideologies which her early 20th century audience demanded: beliefs, for instance, that women's place was in the home and that they should confine their activities to the domestic sphere; that they should be subservient to men; that female heroines should be sexless, refined "ladies" of spiritual purity who conformed to society's expectations; that any "bad" girls should be punished with bad fortune or death; that the ideal closure for a "good" young girl's story must be marriage. Montgomery's society and readership were patriarchal, whether we look at the largely Presbyterian Prince Edward Island about which she wrote or at the multi-denominational world-wide readership which devoured her novels.

Yet though Montgomery has been long dismissed by those who set the literary canons as someone who wrote only sentimental, escapist, rosy-coloured fictions, scholars of the last decade have been uncovering ways in which other writers like her offer elements of protest and resistance within highly "orthodox" plots. In *Anne's House of Dreams* (1917), for instance, Montgomery works up the frame story of Anne and Gilbert's idealized love, confirming all the expectations about marriage her conventional readers held, but she subverts this narrative frame with a nightmare version of marriage. The real story within the frame story is the horrifying tale of Leslie Moore (note: initials "LM"), a mysterious, refined, intelligent, and passionate woman yoked by marriage to a crazy man – a "big, handsome fellow, with a little ugly soul"[20] who had been abusive, alcoholic and destructive until an accident mercifully rendered him mindless through amnesia. Children read the story on one level; adult women may read it on another. Montgomery knows how to reach both audiences. And she knows whereof she writes: she herself presents the illusion to the public that she has a marriage as idyllic as Anne and Gilbert's is in *Anne's House of Dreams*, but the truth is that as she writes she is beginning to experience the horror of being locked into a marriage that is far worse than dead. Montgomery knew a lot about passionate and intelligent women being married to men who were not their equals; her own husband, albeit a kindly man, shared nothing of her intellectual life and slipped by degrees into a frightening mental illness. Of her own situation she writes in her private journals, "A man who is physically ill is still the same man: but a man in Ewan's case is *not* ... An altogether different personality is there – and a personality which is repulsive and abhorrent to me. And yet to this personality I must be a wife. It is horrible – it is indecent ... I feel degraded and unclean."[21] Yet, as an author she incorporates an alternate story of an unsatisfactory marriage in such a way that its subversive and disturbing quality is not terribly apparent, at least to adults who would otherwise censor the book and keep it from children.

This is achieved several ways: the marriage of Leslie Moore is not presented as a marriage that could actually happen to anyone. The circumstances that surround her "husband's" loss of his mental faculties were simply too unusual: it's in the realm of the "fabulous," rather like a fairy story. Montgomery's use of the oral narrative style of storytelling distances material which is not "proper" discourse for a domestic novel for women and children. Montgomery very successfully blends realistic material and serious subjects into the materials of entertaining, gossipy oral narrative.

Although Montgomery's books almost always end on a happy note, her characters often suffer great emotional distress. The cruelty they encounter is real: her narratives contain a virtual compendium of the forms of psychological abuse which real women and children have been subjected to. But Montgomery is clever, and like her revered Emily Dickinson, she tells things "slant." Nor does she consciously write to the same audience as Virginia Woolf does. Yet many of their themes are similar. Louise DeSalvo's *Virginia Woolf: The Impact of Childhood Sexual Abuse on Her Life and Work* argues that Woolf has so many closely drawn adolescents because she was concerned with children's welfare. Woolf's childhood, like Montgomery's, had lacked stability and safeness, but for different reasons. Montgomery suffered, for instance, because of the unpredictable, irritable, and occasionally explosive nature of her grandfather, a primary care-giver who made her own personal world unstable and unsafe.

Woolf writes out of a cultured, literary tradition for a sophisticated audience. Montgomery writes out of the vernacular, oral tradition transplanted from Scotland into the red, verdant soil of isolated Prince Edward Island life and she writes for an all-encompassing popular audience. She surely describes herself perfectly when she writes of her alter ego, "Emily of New Moon" in *Emily's Quest*: "She belonged by right divine to the Ancient and Noble Order of Story-tellers. Born thousands of years earlier she would have sat in the circle around the fires of the tribe and enchanted her listeners. Born in the foremost files of time she must reach her audience through many artificial mediums."[22]

Montgomery's artificial medium is chiefly the domestic romance. It serves her well, so long as she does not aim to write in an innovative form to impress the male canon-setters. *The Blue Castle* (1926), for instance, is a tidy little romance about an aging spinster (of 29) who finds a perfect mate after many trials and tribulations. The age of 29 appears to have been crucial. For instance, Virginia Woolf wrote in her own journal of June 8, 1911, "To be 29 and unmarried – to be a failure – childless – insane too, no writer."[23] The Montgomery novel winds up with the expected conventional ending of marriage. But Montgomery manages to circumvent the restrictions of the genre and to show, before her ending, how badly society treated women who were unable to "get a man." Montgomery's own rage rises perilously close to the surface, but she camouflages it with humour. Furthermore, she presents a subversive model of womanhood: her heroine Valancy rebels against the clan which uses her so badly. Her rebellion, which would have been untenable in reality for a respectable woman living in the real PEI community of Montgomery's youth, would have been punished with death in a conventional domestic novel of her era; instead, Montgomery rewards her heroine with marriage to a man who is both a millionaire and a sensitive creative writer. On a small domestic stage humanity's greatest struggle is enacted: that of the powerless against the powerful. Linda K. Christian-Smith states in *Becoming a Woman through Romance* that contemporary popular fiction and romances also often express ways for females to resist "patterns of domination."[24] The struggle in romance like Montgomery's is seen most often when women offer resistance to patriarchy or when children defy adult behaviour which damages them. Montgomery makes subjects that are still taboo today (like child abuse) acceptable through the use of humour and the oral tradition, both of which distance the otherwise unacceptable material.

Thus, when Montgomery dramatizes the struggle between those who control and those who are controlled, she usually depicts those who suffer as children or young women. Those who control are invariably adults, but they are not exclusively males. Instead, they are sometimes forceful females who have assumed or have been granted a position of power in the patriarchal social structure. The patriarchal society in which Montgomery grew up provided her with wonderful material for fiction. And the beautiful landscape of Prince Edward Island creates a strikingly ironic background: her depiction of the flawed human world becomes more dramatic when juxtaposed against the idyllic natural world. Likewise, her use of irony and sarcasm in dialogue fairly sparkles because of its contrast with the purple prose she employs to describe the settled beauty of the nature she loves.

"Authority" is manifested in various guises in a patriarchal culture, but it operates to keep women in the place tradition demands they occupy. Montgomery finds her own ways of criticizing a social system which puts women down. She says what is socially acceptable about male-female relationships, but she embeds a counter-message of numerous underlying dissonances. The disruptive and subversive elements serve to energize her texts; these elements also prevent her novels from portraying only the sentimental view of life that so many other contemporary domestic romances did. Nothing enraged Montgomery more than being called "sentimental," a term frequently used to dismiss women's writing, sometimes justifiably, of course. She defended herself against this charge. In her diary entry of January 27, 1922, she makes a clear distinction between "sentimentality" and "sentiment":

Today I had a nice letter from Sir Ernest Hodder Williams (of Hodder and Stoughton) and some English reviews of *Rilla*. All were kind but one which sneered at my "sentiment." The attitude of some English critics towards anything that savors of sentiment amuses me. It is to them as the proverbial red rag to a bull. They are very silly. Can't they see that civilization is founded on and held together by sentiment. Passion is transient and quite as often destructive as not. Sentiment remains and binds. Perhaps what they really mean is sentimentality, which *is* an abominable thing. But my books are not sentimental. I have always tried in them to register normal and ordinary emotions – not merely passionate or unique episodes.[25]

Because her critics confused the materials she processed within her novels with the literary form (romance) she processed it into, they confused the "sentiment" in her novels with the "sentimentality" of the form. Montgomery's work has either been ignored or denigrated by male critics who dismissed it as sentimental,[26] confusing her medium with her message, if they in fact read her books which most of them probably did not.[27] Female academics have until recently been too intimidated to give scholarly attention to Montgomery, for work on a female writer deemed unimportant would be dismissed at annual Promotion and Tenure time.[28] The fact that gifted women writers with the unquestioned international stature of an Alice Munro have spoken with respect for Montgomery's works has helped make it safe for others to admit a serious interest in her works.

Montgomery may have suffered from lack of academic attention, but her readers were a loyal bunch, mothers passing along their love of her to their daughters. And as soon as feminist criticism made it respectable to look at writers like her, Montgomery has quickly become seen as an influential writer. She has validated female experience, given voice to female emotion, and helped remove women from imprisonment within silence and pain. Her techniques for circumventing the sentimentality which is inherent in formulaic prescriptions of domestic romance are many, varied, and obviously effective.

First, by working within a genre marketed primarily for a general audience consisting mostly of women and older children, Montgomery kept a low profile with her subversive comments, most of which are about patriarchal society. Various feminist historians, like Rachel DuPlessis and Sidonie Smith, have noted that most women of the 19th and early 20th century wrote in the "safe" genres of autobiography or romance; they also wrote for juveniles.[29] It was an enforced choice for various economic and social reasons, but, given that fact, these types of writing were outside the literary preserve of serious male writing, and hence did not come under the scrutiny of highbrow critics: women's writing was simply considered beneath serious notice. When Montgomery has Emily state in *Emily Climbs* that "I have made up my mind that I will never marry. I shall be *wedded to my art*,"[30] Emily is making a second revolutionary statement for a girl of her era (after the one asserting that she was important to herself, if to no one else). Male authors had the right to consider themselves professionals who were producing "art," but 19th and early 20th women who wrote generally had to pretend that they wrote as an avocation or hobby, to get necessary income, or to educate the young. If they did take themselves seriously, they did not dare assert this publicly. George Eliot was an exception, but her situation was very unusual and complicated.

We can see Montgomery still operating under these strictures in 1917, when, already a world-famous author due to *Anne of Green Gables* (1908) and six more books, she began a series of biographical sketches on herself: "When the Editor of *Everywoman's World* asked me to write 'The Story of My Career,' I smiled with a little touch of incredulous amusement. My career? *Had* I a career? Was not – should not – a 'career' be something splendid ... ?"[31] She explains that she's so in the habit of obliging editors that she will write the requested piece. A male author of equal fame would have felt no need to begin his sketch in such a self-effacing way – he would have considered his writing a profession and his success proof of its excellence. But women authors were not expected to take themselves too seriously, or to toot their own horns too loudly.

However, Montgomery probably did take herself more seriously as the result of this assignment, for shortly afterwards, on August 24, 1920, she wrote, "I want to create a new heroine now – she is already in embryo in my mind."[32] Her trilogy about "Emily," the little girl who aspired to be a writer, was published between 1923 and 1927. In the *Emily* books, Montgomery details all the impediments to a woman's authorship: "interruption, blockage, censorship, derision, self-hatred, and ... repression," factors which DuPlessis says have plagued 20th century female authors.[33] Most women authors, 19th or early 20th century, have experienced these, but often without being consciously aware of the problems as being endemic to all other women writers. Thus, the *Emily* novels must have been eye-opening books for many struggling and would-be female authors.[34]

Two years after the last *Emily* book, Virginia Woolf wrote her famous *A Room of One's Own* (1929) to explain how hard it was for a woman to become an author. Montgomery's books were marketed in Britain, of course, where they were widely reviewed and read by people from all walks of life. Even the Prime Minister of England, Stanley Baldwin, read them. In 1927, the year of the publication of Montgomery's third *Emily* book, for instance, Prime Minister Baldwin wrote to Montgomery: "Dear Mrs. Macdonald:– I do not know whether I shall be so fortunate during a hurried visit to Canada but it would give me keen pleasure to have an opportunity of shaking your hand and thanking you for the pleasure your books have given me ... "[35] It is intriguing to wonder if Virginia Woolf might also have picked up Montgomery's *Emily* trilogy and mused over the fictional representation of all the obstacles to female authorship which Montgomery lays out so clearly. Bishop's *A Virginia Woolf Chronology* lists many books which Woolf read, and Montgomery's books are not among these. Montgomery had a high profile in Britain, however, and was reviewed quite favourably by major British papers like the London *Times*, *Punch*, the *TLS*. It is, of course, certain that Woolf did read many books that she did not record, just as Montgomery herself did.[36]

In 1923 Montgomery was the first Canadian woman to be made a Fellow of the Royal Society of Arts in Great Britain. Her increasing visibility in the UK is shown by Prime Minister Baldwin's attention in summer 1927. It is possible that in June 1927, when Woolf went on a binge reading "trash," Montgomery's books may have been among these books, for Montgomery was considered a popular writer, not a writer of highbrow literature. In October 1928 Woolf gave the lectures at Girton which became, in 1929, *A Room of One's Own*. We also do not know if Montgomery ever read Woolf. I think it unlikely for in 1929 Montgomery's life was very hectic, and she was more often rereading old favourites for comfort instead of books on the "cutting edge" of literary Modernism. Whether they read each other's books or not, Montgomery's *Emily* books have been read by young writers all over the world, and Woolf's *A Room of One's Own* by older writers, particularly women, and critics. Both have been immensely influential.

For instance, Lady Wilson, wife of Harold Wilson, Prime Minister of England, wrote a Preface for the *Emily* books in which she gave an eloquent account of her own affection for them: when she was 11 she had been ill for a year and one of her father's parishioners had given her a copy of *Emily of New Moon*. She had read and reread it until she knew parts of it by heart. Then, later, when she recovered and went away to school, she "reread the book and realised that it must be set in Canada, and it was with a shock of delight that, looking at the map, I found Prince Edward Island. I decided to write to L.M. Montgomery, telling her of my liking for the book, of my own aspirations to write, and also to explain that I could 'see wallpaper small in the air!'" She received a long letter, circa 1931–2, which said: "I'm glad you like 'Emily,' because she is my own favourite. She is purely a creature of my imagination but a good deal of my own inner life in childhood and girlhood went into her." She also mentioned that many people were under the impression, wrongly, that her "books are only for children." Lady Wilson finishes her Preface by adding that she is glad to have read *Emily*, for "Although I first read the book as a child I should not describe it as primarily a children's book, and certainly the two sequels are for adults. L.M. Montgomery meant the book to be read – as it is – by people of all ages, but possibly one cannot appreciate the character delineation until one is adult." Then she concludes, "I sat down one day to write this preface: two hours later I was still reading the book, not a word written. Not many books of our earlier years could be re-read with such pleasure."[37]

Both Montgomery and Woolf read many of the same books when they were young: both were obviously much influenced by a common text: *Jane Eyre*. As Showalter notes, Brontë empowered later women writers to engage in "self-exploration" and create a "separatist literature of inner space":

Psychologically rather than socially focused, this literature sought refuge from the harsh realities and vicious practices of the male world. Its favourite symbol, the enclosed and secret room, had been a potent image in women's novels since *Jane Eyre* ... In children's books, such as Mrs. Molesworth's *The Tapestry Room* (1879) and Dinah Craik's *The Little Lame Prince* (1886), women writers had explored and extended these fantasies of enclosure. After 1900, in dozens of novels from Frances Hodgson Burnett's *The Secret Garden* (1911) to May Sinclair's *The Tree of Heaven* (1917), the secret room, the attic hideaway, the suffragette cell came to stand for a separate world, a flight from men and from adult sexuality.[38]

Undeniably, Montgomery was an architect of "safe spaces": for Stanley Baldwin, living in a country which had just undergone the Great War, she probably created an idyllic haven in Green Gables' domesticity and the Avonlea setting. For women she created a space in which they could be domestic and yet discuss the inadequacy of that world, looking for "bends around the road" where there might be escape and empowerment. Women were locked into domesticity, and both Montgomery and Woolf explore ways in which it confined females. Women's rights were a growing concern to women everywhere. Female achievement in the Great War had given impetus to their empowerment, but much still lay ahead. For example, it was not until 1929, the year of Woolf's *A Room of One's Own*, that the British Privy Council reversed the famous 1928 "Persons Case" decision of the Supreme Court of Canada – which had declared that women were not "persons" and were therefore not entitled to hold public office as Canadian senators.

In using the traditional domestic romance, Montgomery herself found a safe space in which to write. She could give sharp critical digs to a social system prejudiced against women. The very use of the domestic romance leads her audience to expect her to confirm all its conventions, and when she does this – at least on the surface – no warning lights flash that she may be planning subversive forays en route: expressing her own frustration with the way the males (her maternal grandfather and her mother's brothers) had treated her personally, she speaks out the only way she could – in fiction. In the *Emily* trilogy, for instance, much is made of the fact that Emily cannot have a "room of her own," her dead mother's empty room, a space of freedom and self-hood. Montgomery tells stories about women and children, and uses hackneyed plots, but she treats the subject of power within the context of women and children's lives in a patriarchal society.

This deviousness was necessary because many women readers would have been quite disturbed by a frontal attack on the social system which they took for granted, or on the institution of marriage; but they were not averse to seeing oppressive patriarchal power structures satirized. In their social world, conservative women condemned their more articulate Suffragette sisters while yet envying their freedom. Montgomery's small subversions make tidy "surgical strikes" without threatening to topple the overall system. A perfect example of indirect attack can be seen in "The Strike at Putney," one of Montgomery's some 500 short stories.[39] Here women disrupt the male power structure; eventually the men who run the church admit that they were unfair in refusing to let a woman speaker use the church pulpit for an address, and subsequently the women return happily to their subordinate roles in the old power structure. Montgomery has shown her readers, however, that pompous, authoritarian men are helpless when women go on strike to assert their rights.

A **second** strategy Montgomery uses is to sugarcoat all of her subversive elements with humour. When Montgomery devotees explain today their affection for Montgomery, many cite this sense of humour. Her writing abounds with situational humour, verbal wit, and ironic and comic juxtapositions. She cleanses the souls of her readers by making them laugh. A nasty patriarch impaled by humour's hook ceases to threaten. Much of her humour arises because of the patriarchal structure of society. Here is a sample taken from a short story in *The Chronicles of Avonlea* (1912). The speaker is a woman of middle age who is being courted by an old beau, and she grumbles to another woman: "I don't want to be married. Do you remember that story Anne Shirley used to tell long ago of the pupil who wanted to be a widow because 'if you were married your husband bossed you and if you weren't married people called you an old maid?' Well, that is precisely my opinion. I'd like to be a widow. Then I'd have the freedom of the unmarried, with the kudos of the married. I could eat my cake and have it, too. Oh, to be a widow!"[40] By using such humour to present the subordinate position of women after marriage, Montgomery avoids sounding like a crusading suffragette. However, something else is operating here, too, that makes her jibes against patriarchy unobjectionable to conventional readers: the careful distancing of the voice of L.M. Montgomery behind that of the person who supposedly makes the actual subversive statement. The above anecdote we are told originated with a child of indeterminate social status, was heard by the proper Anne Shirley who remembered it and passed it throughout the female community where it was then overheard by our maiden lady; finally Montgomery's narrator repeats it for us in the story. No one takes responsibility for the statement or judges it. It's a safe comment, partly because it is presented in the layering of storyteller's anecdote.

Indeed, one of the characteristics that distinguishes Montgomery's writing is its "oral" quality. Montgomery had been raised in a family of gifted storytellers. Local gossip and clan history were very quickly elevated to polished oral narrative. Montgomery embeds secondary fictions throughout her surface narrative to create a distinctively layered structure which replicates the oral gossip of female gatherings. As readers we *love* hearing the risqué and unseemly things which get repeated, but such comments do not taint Montgomery herself since they are so far removed from her narrative voice. A minister's wife, as Montgomery was, could not be too careful in her choice of subjects, but she manages to bring into the sphere of literary discourse an amazing array of rather shocking statements.

A **third** strategy is that of having characters of "no importance" make the subversive comments. In the *Anne* series, Anne as a child makes outrageous comments and in this lies much of her personality. The minute Anne grows up and becomes the dignified wife, "Mrs. Dr. Gilbert Blythe," Montgomery sanitizes her thoughts and tongue and has her peppery, subversive comments delivered by people with less social standing in the community. Susan Baker, her cook, can express opinions that a proper, married Anne cannot. So can an unmarried eccentric like Miss Cornelia. Other unruly, motherless children like the Merediths are created for the same reason. It has been frequently claimed by critics that Montgomery's later *Anne* novels are not as good as the first; though this may appear true on the surface, for "Anne" loses her tartness, the novels do not lose their bite. We should note that Anne is simply no longer the focal character; she is only a device to hang the series together on. Montgomery keeps the later novels sparkling by devising a series of characters who can say or do what Anne cannot.[41]

This leads us to Montgomery's **fourth** strategy, her narrative method. Montgomery's plots – and there sometimes are no plots *per se* – are usually unoriginal, if not hackneyed. They depend heavily on unrealistic coincidence which is, of course, not uncommon in the romance genre. But plot is not important for her: her focus is on character, thoughts, feelings, and ideas. Since women in Montgomery's society were not expected even to *have* relevant independent thoughts, it was hard for fictional ones to create the action which propelled the novel. Women in Montgomery's later novels don't *cause* events to happen so much as *react* to what has happened, and then *discuss* it. For instance, in *Anne's House of Dreams* Gilbert decides when and where they will move, etc.; the novel consists mostly of the rest of the characters talking about what has happened, is happening, or will happen in the community.

In a patriarchy, a woman's personal power lay largely in what she could manoeuvre by using language (flattery, nagging, or subtly manipulating her husband); women's public power lay in their being able to censure through community gossip. Patricia Meyer Spacks' *Gossip* gives an extended discussion of the function of gossip in women's lives and novels. Men may have controlled the law, but women could wreak havoc through the innuendoes of gossip. It was not only a source of entertainment but also it was a form of social control. In Montgomery's novels, people lived in fear of what others would say, as Montgomery herself did in her real life. In her novels, this female gossiping frequently produces a relatively non-linear plot progression, a pattern which Annis Pratt sees as typical for women writers.[42] In the Emily books it is not the surface events that are important: it is what Emily feels and thinks as she tries to accommodate her desire to be a writer to society's expectations that she marry and subordinate herself to a husband, not to art. Emily's feelings are complex and often rebellious, and although the narrative structure of the book is vaguely chronological, her thought processes consist of a mental looping back and forth, not of a straightforward chronological advancing of events. The book is not the story of how Emily chooses a husband; it is the story of what she thinks along the way to her inevitable fate.

A **fifth** strategy, used primarily in the *Emily* books, is for Montgomery to intrude directly as narrator into the story and discredit the sanctity of traditional plot and genre conventions. For example, in *Emily of New Moon*, the narrator says, "This does not point [to] any particular moral, of course; in a proper yarn Emily should either have been found out and punished for disobedience or been driven by an uneasy conscience to confess; but I am sorry – or ought to be – to have to state that Emily's conscience never worried her about the matter at all."[43]

An intrusive narrator who tells us that she disapproves of the conventions of the novel's formulae and that her heroine does not behave according to these is a rather bold disjunctive element in a 1920s domestic novel. Montgomery accomplishes a great deal with such a comment. She strikes up a personal, intimate relationship with the readers who feel they are the narrator's accomplice in the crime of flaunting convention. Montgomery and her readers know that wayward women and girls are fated to be punished in fictions about them, but another level of suspense is achieved through the suggestion that Emily may get away with unusual adventures. To approve of being "naughty," but only as Montgomery's accomplice, is very safe and appealing to a convention-bound reader.

In the oral tradition, establishing closeness between the narrator and the narratee is important. I have noticed that one of the most uniform elements among Montgomery's fans is their feeling of closeness to her. People who write us about her books and journals think of the author behind her works as a personal friend. There are many reasons why different people respond to her fiction, but they are all alike in feeling her a "kindred spirit" whose actual human presence lies in her writing – she is not seen as a distant, disembodied author. Here, in *Emily*, Montgomery is simply telling her readers that their approval of Emily's rebellious feelings is fine. She makes her readers her accomplices, part of the inner female circle, as she hints that she, the author, chafes at the restrictive conventions of the genre. Just as a postmodern writer of our time might do, Montgomery creates a secondary and self-reflexive discourse on the act of writing: she examines the fact that the "happy endings" of women's domestic romances are no more cliched than the convention of the "tragic ending" in serious male fiction. She has a lot more to say about the conventions of the "realistic" novel, too. As Emily's mentor Mr. Carpenter lies dying, he says: "No use trying to please – critics. Live under your own hat. Don't be – led away – by those howls about realism. Remember – pine woods are just as real as – pigsties – and a darn sight pleasanter to be in. You'll get there – sometime – you have the root – of the matter – in you. And don't – tell the world – everything. That's what's the – matter – with our – literature. Lost the charm of mystery – and reserve." In Montgomery's journals she cites Morley Callaghan as the epitome of male realism become predictably tedious; he sees only pigsties and "latrines" and "insists blatantly that you see nothing else also. If you insist on seeing sky and river and pine you are a 'sentimentalist' and the truth is not in you."[44]

Closely related to the foregoing technique of narratorial intervention is her **sixth** device of having "respectable" characters within her novel verbally affirm the prevailing ideology of the society after her narrator and other less respectable characters have undercut it. This becomes complicated: (1) the genre sets up the expectations that the author will follow the standard conventions (2) the narrator or non-proper characters inside the novel subvert the conventions (3) then "respectable" characters like Anne reassure the readers that the conventional sentiments are correct.

For instance, in *Anne's House of Dreams* the primary "subversive" character in the novel is Miss Cornelia, an avid "man-hater" who is forever saying, "Isn't it just like a man?" in condemnation, rightly or wrongly. She's highly eccentric, but as the country saying goes, she does quite often "hit the nail on the head." A full-fledged war between the sexes erupts when Dr. Gilbert Blythe suggests that Leslie Moore's husband be given a newly developed brain operation in hopes it might restore him to his rightful senses. Dick Moore is better as he is, with no mind, the women argue, than restored to his former hateful self. The men argue for the operation on the basis of reason and the women vigorously oppose it on the basis of emotion. To everyone's surprise, the operation is successful, and the newly conscious "Dick" tells them he is not in fact the Dick Moore they think he is. All the women eat humble pie, and Montgomery has Anne say, "Oh, Gilbert, you were right – so right. I can see that clearly enough now – and I'm so ashamed of myself – and will you ever really forgive me?"[45] The undiscriminating reader in the 1920s would feel reassured when Montgomery confirmed the prevailing ideology that women should always accept their husband's judgement as better than their own; however, Montgomery has made it perfectly clear that the operation could have been a disaster just as easily as a success, and it was chance, not moral strength, that made Gilbert right. And somehow the last word comes from the irascible Miss Cornelia, who snorts that Leslie Moore has sacrificed "the best years of her life to nursing a man who hadn't any claim on her! Oh, drat the men! No matter what they do, it's the wrong thing. And no matter who they are, it's somebody they shouldn't be. They do exasperate me."[46] Thus, Dr. Gilbert Blythe's male superiority seems less certain after Montgomery pointedly reinforces first Anne's belief in it and then Miss Cornelia's disbelief.

Montgomery's journals show that no matter what her thoughts were she comported herself as a highly conservative woman, not as a rabble-rousing women's rights firebrand. When Emily wrote in her diary that "it is a tradition of New Moon that its women should be equal to any situation and always be graceful and dignified,"[47] she was voicing Montgomery's own personal credo. Montgomery simultaneously admired suffragettes and looked askance at them. It is only honest to say that she was ambivalent about many of the social conventions she criticized. For instance, she thought she should obey her husband and accept his decisions even when she did not agree; she apparently maintained this belief even when he sank into irrationality with his mental problems. However, even though she let him make the decisions, people who remember them, and knew the family dynamics, say that the force of her opinion, even if unexpressed, was so strong that he could not fail to take it into account in making up his own mind. However, as her husband receded deeper into mental illness, she took over more of the decision-making process although she always attempted to make him feel the final word had been his.

The training she had had as a child continued to influence her to conform to social norms, but her reason told her that it was wrong for an intelligent woman to have to accept her husband's every decision as superior. It is her conscious mind that so deftly exposes the irrationality of the myth of male superiority in her writing while Miss Cornelia, like a funny subconscious, has the last word.

A **seventh** subversive strategy is a curious one. Montgomery often presents her most overbearing authority figures in women's clothing. In fact, there aren't many convincingly realistic men in Montgomery's narratives, and the ones who are there are often minor or shadowy characters. On the other hand, there are two types of very realistic women: the submissive, feminine types and the authoritarian mannish types who mimic the male prerogative to rule. Her fiction often presents two sisters who live together: one rules and the other submits. Such is the case in the *Emily* books, and we are told explicitly several times that Aunt Elizabeth Murray, who is the tall, angular authority figure, is made in the image of her formidable father, Archibald Murray. Aunt Elizabeth bosses little Emily about, making her life miserable through her authoritarian ways. Aunt Elizabeth's autocratic behaviour would have been unnoteworthy in a man of the time, but it looms unnatural and unacceptable in a woman. The reader can see how grotesque the behaviour is precisely because a woman enacts it. As a foil for mannish Aunt Elizabeth, Montgomery gives us Aunt Laura who is gentle, sympathetic and feminine. Montgomery can present what she considers objectionable authoritarian male characteristics with impunity because she disguises them in the female form of Elizabeth Murray, chip off the block of old Archibald Murray.

An **eighth** strategy is to embed allusions and references to other authors and books – often subversive – throughout the text; if the reader knows the other works, these comment indirectly on the action within Montgomery's story. For instance, Montgomery read, reread, and was deeply moved by Olive Schreiner's *The Story of an African Farm* (1883), a novel which, between 1883 and 1900, sold over 100,000 copies and upset most of the orthodoxies of its Victorian age.[48] Montgomery's reference to it in *Emily's Quest* bears curiously on what happens to one of the important characters, the impossibly jealous and neurotic Mrs. Kent, whose husband had left her years earlier. We wonder if Montgomery may have intended to suggest that Mrs. Kent's whole life might have been less miserable had she had only opened Schreiner's book after it was returned to her among her dead husband's effects. It contained a letter from her husband forgiving her for what appears to have been her possessive, manipulative behaviour. We can conjecture that when *he* read Schreiner, he may have developed new sympathy for women and then have been able to forgive his wife, for one of Schreiner's main aims in this novel was to show how badly men treated women.

A subtle but perceptible intertextual discourse also operates between Montgomery's *Emily* books and other women-authored narratives which also deal with the way a woman can get on in a world which sees her as worthless unless she obtains a man and becomes his property. All her life

Montgomery had been fascinated by the Brontë sisters. Her allusions to *Jane Eyre* figure large in the *Emily* books. When this trilogy was written in the 1920s, Montgomery had barely escaped marriage to one self-absorbed man, Edwin Simpson, and she had been yoked in her marriage for over a decade to a minister whose mental illness brought on another destructive kind of turning inward. It is no accident that elements of the similarly self-absorbed minister St. John Rivers appear in Emily's lovers, particularly Dean Priest. In fact, Montgomery wants to make sure that we don't miss the connections between her book and Brontë's. For instance, when Dean first saves Emily from falling into the ocean, he claims her life as his. Significantly, she fell only because she had reached over a dangerous cliff to pick a beautiful wild aster. Dean remarks: "'your life belongs to me henceforth. Since I saved it it's mine. Never forget that.' Emily felt an odd sensation of rebellion. She didn't fancy the idea of her life belonging to anybody but herself."

Dean sees this and says jokingly, "one pays a penalty when one reaches out for something beyond the ordinary. One pays for it in bondage of some kind or other. Take your wonderful aster home and keep it as long as you can. It has cost you your freedom."

Montgomery as narrator tells us that, "He was laughing – he was only joking, of course – yet Emily felt as if a cobweb fetter had been flung round her. Yielding to a sudden impulse she flung the big aster on the ground and set her foot on it." Dean "stooped and picked up the broken aster. Emily's heel had met it squarely and it was badly crushed. But he put it away that night between the leaves of an old volume of *Jane Eyre*."[49] This reference makes clear that Dean, like the would-be master of "Jane Eyre," wants to take his little wild flower and press her between the leaves of his own life. There would be no room for a woman's growth, either in marriage to Brontë's Rivers or to Montgomery's Priest.

Maud Montgomery had been a bookish child and young woman who lived vicariously and intensely in the fictional worlds she read about. It is not surprising, therefore, that the febrile language in *Jane Eyre* echoes faintly through Montgomery's description of her own wedding day in her journal:

> sitting there by my husband's side ... I felt a sudden horrible inrush of *rebellion* and *despair*. I *wanted to be free*! I felt like a prisoner – a hopeless prisoner. Something in me – something wild and free and untamed – something that Ewan had not tamed – could never tame – something that did not acknowledge him as master – rose up in one

frantic protest against the fetters which bound me. At that moment if I could have torn the wedding ring from my finger and so freed myself I would have done it! But it was too late – and the realization that it was too late fell over me like a black cloud of wretchedness. I sat at that gay bridal feast, in my white veil and orange blossoms, beside the man I had married – and I was as unhappy as I had ever been in my life.[50]

Montgomery's words in her journal depict how a gifted and imaginative female artist of her era must have felt when she entered into a traditional marriage. By the time of her marriage Montgomery had become a world-famous author with a large private income, and she knew she was marrying a stodgy man who was well educated in theology but who had no wider intellectual interests: he was kind and not unintelligent, but otherwise unexceptional. When she sat down a decade later and penned her story of little Emily, she remembered all her own decisions and the hardships she had gone through to become and remain a writer. On July 20, 1922, she wrote in her journals, "I packed Emily [of New Moon] off on her journey to the portals of the world – dear little 'Emily' whom I love far better than I ever loved 'Anne.' I felt as if I were sending part of myself." On August 29, 1923, after Emily begins getting good reviews, she admits in her journal, "'Emily's' inner life was my own, though outwardly most of the events and incidents were fictitious."[51]

It is instructive, in this context, to note the journal comments that she makes about her husband at the time she is writing Emily. On March 25, 1922, she writes:

Whenever we have been anywhere that an allusion was made to my literary success Ewan has invariably greeted it with a little jibe or deprecating joke … Ewan's attitude to women – though I believe he is quite unconscious of this himself – is that of the mediaeval mind. A woman is a thing of no importance intellectually – the plaything and servant of man – and couldn't possibly do anything that would be worthy of a real tribute … Ewan has never had any real sympathy with or intelligent interest in my literary work and has always seemed either incredulous or resentful when anyone has attributed to me any importance on the score of it.[52]

Thus, we can see that in writing her own story into Emily's, Montgomery is affirming the importance of her own individuality as a writing female.

As well, the perceptive adult reader can see that not only is *Jane Eyre* a presence in Montgomery's *Emily* series, but the character of Jane Eyre is a presence in Montgomery's own mind. Brontë's character gave young Maud a model of female independence which took root and grew in both Montgomery and "Emily." Jane's language shaped Montgomery's, and Jane's struggle to develop and affirm her personal worth informed Montgomery's personal conception of female possibility and strength. Intertextuality is both literary and personal.

We now come to Montgomery's **ninth** strategy. She writes the expected "happy endings" which reassure her readers, but she even undercuts these in some of her novels. Montgomery's happy endings do not necessarily betoken sentimentality. She knew too well how to introduce hidden agendas – "discourses of rebellion" under the "discourses of submission." Montgomery does this not only with the controlling structure of her novels but also with the specific motif of the happy ending of marriage to which her heroine must submit.

Rachel DuPlessis notes in *Writing beyond the Ending* that in a patriarchal society a female artist's *bildung* is antithetical to marriage. Marriage requires self-sacrifice and submission, whereas becoming a writer-artist demands self-assertion. In fact, marriage usually becomes a barrier to female achievement for any ambitious and gifted woman in a patriarchal society. This is very noticeable in the conclusion of the *Emily* series, a trilogy which makes up a Künstlerroman.

Emily Byrd Starr, the sensitive and artistic little girl whose beloved father is dying, is left to be raised by her dead mother's clan, the Murrays, a threesome consisting of the two sisters, Aunt Elizabeth, Aunt Laura, and "simple" Cousin Jimmy. Cousin Jimmy is dominated by the authoritarian and aggressive Elizabeth, but he is in fact far from simple: he gives Emily the needed paper on which to write and he softens Emily's painful encounters with Aunt Elizabeth by his commonsensical advice. The Murrays are proud of their "traditions," but Aunt Elizabeth is so inimical to an imaginative life, and most specifically to creative endeavour, that she makes Emily promise to give up writing stories in exchange for permission to go to school.

In the first two *Emily* books, Emily runs the whole gamut of barriers to female artistic achievement. She is belittled, ridiculed, bullied, forbidden to write, even forbidden to think, mostly by Aunt Elizabeth. Predictably, she seeks an escape. As soon as she is old enough, she accepts an unfortunate engagement to Dean Priest[53] who offers Emily enormous wealth and his all-consuming passion; *all* he asks is that she pour the passion she has for writing into loving him, and that she forget her writing completely, *forever*. Dean tricks Emily into believing that she cannot write because he is jealous of her love for her writing. He demotes her to a sex-object by telling her, "You can do more with those eyes – that smile – than you can ever do with your pen." Later he says of her first unpublished novel which she gives him to read, "It's a pretty little story, Emily. Pretty and flimsy and ephemeral as a rose-tinted cloud. Cobwebs – only cobwebs. The whole conception is too far-fetched. Fairy tales are out of the fashion. And this one of yours makes overmuch of a demand on the credulity of the reader. And your characters are only puppets. How could you write a real story? You've never *lived*." Only after she breaks her engagement with him, does he tell her the truth: "You remember that book of yours? You asked me to tell you the truth about what I thought of it? I didn't. I lied. It is a good piece of work – very good. Oh, some faults in it of course – a bit emotional – a bit overstrained. You still need pruning – restraint. But it is good. It is out of the ordinary both in conception and development. It has charm and your characters *do* live. Natural, human, delightful. There, you know what I think of it now."[54] For all his deception, however, Dean has helped her mature and come to some degree of self-understanding; yet, he embodies the worst features of both the early Rochester and St. John Rivers, the suitors in *Jane Eyre*. Marriage and men threaten Emily even more than mannish Aunt Elizabeth did. Aunt Elizabeth only stiffened Emily's resolve; Dean destroyed her courage.

At the end of the *Emily* trilogy, Emily will of course have to find a man who can be her master; she will have to settle down to focusing on him and their marriage and not on her own art. The happy ending will restore the social order where women and children are in their proper place. If Montgomery is going to satisfy her readers, her young heroines must come around and do what their culture demands of them: get married to promising young men rather than strike out on their own. In the genre of the domestic romance, the closure of marriage rewarded good girls. The closure of marriage was both Montgomery's and Emily's fate. However, it is clear that Montgomery does not believe that a woman's wedding day is always the dreamy ideal ending of "romance." By the time that she was writing her *Emily* series, she could see what a mistake she had made in her own marriage.

Although Montgomery had read feminist texts in the 1890s, she had been thoroughly indoctrinated during her childhood with the "Angel in the House" ideology – that a woman's place was in the home and that her duty was to be cheerful and long-suffering.[55] She noted in her October

15, 1908, journal entry that a reviewer praised *Anne of Green Gables* because it "radiates happiness and optimism." She continued: "Thank God, I can keep the shadows of my life out of my work. I would not wish to darken any other life – I want instead to be a messenger of optimism and sunshine."[56] There was a connection between her role as a woman in being cheerful and her role as an author in putting cheerful "endings" onto her books, as the romance required. But by the time that she was writing *Emily* in the 1920s her own experience in marriage, and her observation of other marriages, made it very clear to her that marriage and a woman's subservience in it did not always lead to happiness. In the last section of *Emily's Quest* we see her using two techniques to undercut her "happy ending."

First, she embeds a metafictional discourse on happy endings in the actual text. In Chapter 17 a self-important male author proposes to Emily who herself is already a published and best-selling author. His proposal concludes with the gushy endearment that he will teach her "never to write happy endings – never ... I will teach you the beauty and artistry of sorrow and incompleteness. Ah, what a pupil you will be! What bliss to teach such a pupil! I kiss your hand." Emily punctures his pompous proposal with the statement that he "*must* be crazy" and boots him out, giving him the real-life jolt of a beautifully tragic ending for his would-be romance.[57] The scene is very comic and reflects a bitter clash in the real world between women like Montgomery who were patronized for writing romances and male writers who wrote only realism, following the dictates of the then-trendy literary Modernism.

Montgomery's second trick for undercutting the unpalatable closure is to shift into farce and make the wedding ceremony in *Emily's Quest* so ridiculous that all semblance of the earlier seriousness in the novel is lost. A cultural historian might say that Montgomery's own era should have found the marriage of Emily very satisfactory: Teddy has become a distinguished artist and he has been made even more respectable by being offered an art-school vice-principalship in Montreal. I cannot accept that Montgomery herself saw the ending as idyllic, however, for the trilogy's tone shifts rapidly. The first two Emily books were firmly grounded in PEI society, circa 1890, with local colour and vivid characterization. The conversations between characters were tart and plausible, and the events believable. Yet, the last Emily book slides into a comedic mode. Its dénouement is more than unbelievable coincidence – it is pure slapstick, with shifts in romantic partners, as in Shakespeare's *A Midsummer Night's Dream* – a play that Montgomery had loved as a young student, by the way. Just as Emily's best friend Ilse is on the point of marrying Teddy Kent, long a suitor of Emily, Ilse jumps out the window, slides down the roof in her silk wedding dress, and vanishes into the distance, leaving a room of gaping wedding guests and a surprised bridegroom behind. This ending is so ridiculous and so fast-paced that the seriousness of the situation is completely trivialized. The marriage vows are put into a farcical context. Lest the reader miss the shift of tone, Montgomery has the jilted groom speak of his intended having "'left [him] at the altar' according to the very formula of Bertha M. Clay," a formulaic and now forgotten writer.[58] No further apologies are given, but Montgomery has made it very clear that she is not responsible for such a trite ending. The trite is identified with this dollop of slapstick and hence subverted. By alerting the readers to the fact that she does not take the ending of her novel seriously, Montgomery suggests that they should not either. When Emily finally accepts the jilted Teddy, no idyllic atmosphere is restored. In fact, the tone is almost elegiac against the backdrop of a dark hill and a sunset, as Teddy and Emily prepare to move into their grey house which, significantly, has always been called "The Disappointed House." Montgomery tells the reader that the "grey house ... was to be disappointed no longer,"[59] but the reader knows that Emily's creativity will sink into grey domesticity within. The vivacious outspoken Emily-heroine with the accomplished and witty pen is dead, and the trilogy can end: she is no longer interesting or full of promise as a writer. She is ready to be a supportive wife whose husband's profession comes first.

It is important to note that writing her fictions normally provided Montgomery with a soul-satisfying escape from the tensions in her real life, but writing *Emily's Quest* seems to have been a trial, not a joy. In fact, and not surprisingly, she suffered unusual blockage before she began it, and had to write another novel which unblocked her first. It must have been a grim day for her when she sat down to begin *Emily's Quest*. First she had to domesticate Emily. This meant that Emily had to give up her ambitions to write. Dean Priest had to persuade her that because she had no talent she should give up her writing for marriage. That was the first step. He succeeded in convincing her to destroy the manuscript of her first book. Then came step two. Emily tripped over a sewing basket at the top of the stairs, tumbled down, and landed with a pair of scissors piercing her foot. Scissors, a symbol of woman's domesticity, appropriately gave her blood poisoning. She had to spend her winter in bed recuperating. Her "rest-cure" sounds rather like those proscribed by the real life Dr. Weir-Mitchell who was the apparent model for

Charlotte Perkins Gilman's famous feminist story "The Yellow Wallpaper."[60] Montgomery's imagery makes *her* opinion of Emily's choice quite clear.

Not only did it go against the Montgomery grain to submit Emily to a formulaic happy-wedding ending. It was painful for Montgomery to make her feisty little alter-ego into a creature of bland domesticity. Certainly, the self-assertive Emily of the first two books would not have been a suitably selfless wife, an "Angel in the House."[61] Montgomery's beloved Emily was already – as she herself had been – a successful author when it came time to marry her into oblivion and to end the book. It would hardly do for Emily to feel as she, Maud Montgomery, had at her own wedding. Thus, Teddy Kent, Emily's intended, had to subsume Emily's role as the artist figure.

She knew from personal experience that no creative female would want to give up writing when it was her income, her means of self-expression, and her very identity. So she tried to suggest that Emily's uniqueness would live in Teddy's art: he would take his inspiration from Emily's face and its "elusive mystery." If Emily had not been an artist in her own right, this might have been acceptable, but since she was, it was problematical to reduce her to an object, a beautiful human face, which a male artist could turn into something timeless, a pictorial icon. Elevating Teddy's painting over Emily's writing is simply not satisfactory, and it was little wonder that Montgomery had a hard time finishing off the final book. On June 30, 1926, she wrote grimly: "I began work – again – on *Emily III.* I wonder if I shall *ever* get that book done!" On October 13, 1926, she breathed a sigh of relief: "Yesterday morning I actually finished writing *Emily's Quest.* Of course I have to revise it yet but it is such a relief to feel it is off my mind at last. I've never had such a time writing a book. Thank heaven it is the last of the Emily series."[62]

In the third Emily book, after numerous other proposals, Emily manages to marry a childhood friend, Teddy Kent, an artist of growing fame. Of the choices Emily has, Teddy is the only serious contender.[63] The only problem with him is that he is totally absorbed in himself and his own art. Although he puts Emily's haunting face into every picture that he paints, it is not clear that he ever sees the real Emily, though Montgomery makes various attempts to redeem him as a suitable groom. Just as Montgomery's husband was absorbed by the demons in his mental illness at the time she was writing this series, Teddy is absorbed by his own creative life. Many young girls reading the *Emily* trilogy today have told me that they feel vaguely unhappy with the way the novel concludes, though it is idyllic on the surface.[64] Their uneasiness comes from the implication that Emily's creativity will be eclipsed in marriage.

Finally, we come to a very complicated technique which is perhaps less a conscious strategy than a telling sequence. The order in which Montgomery's *Emily* books are written reveals how complex the creative processes become when Montgomery had to pack her material into an inappropriate genre.

We recall that the first *Emily* book was published in 1923, the second in 1925, the third in 1927. It is extremely significant, then, that in 1926 – after the first two *Emily* books and before the third – Montgomery stopped to write *The Blue Castle*. I think that Montgomery had simply poured too much of her own psychic energy into Emily's successful assaults on the patriarchal culture which sought to marginalize women and especially female artists. She hated to face the inevitability of leading Emily to the sacrificial altar of marriage. Emily was posited in the first two books as fighting for her artistic life and wanting to be taken seriously as a writer. Emily's world had been all against her; and in spite of this she had achieved a legitimate existence as an artist-figure, a writer of note. Now, literary convention demanded that Emily's self-development be effaced, with her literally reduced to being an inspiring female "face" in a male artist's repertoire. Montgomery did not want to kill Emily's spirit. But this is what the genre dictated, and what her publisher and readership expected. She had no alternatives.

Thus, *The Blue Castle* comes next instead of *Emily's Quest*. What is *in* this book which interrupts Emily's tale, and permits Montgomery to forestall Emily's inevitable fate of marginalization and effacement? Tucking *The Blue Castle* in before the third Emily book, Montgomery blows off the steam that had been gathering as she faced the unhappy prospect of marrying off Emily. *The Blue Castle* becomes part of the *Emily* series: the foursome forms a critique of patriarchal society.

The Blue Castle is an unadulterated and bitter assault on the patriarchal system of Montgomery's era, one which oppressed women psychologically and economically. In *The Blue Castle*, Montgomery sublimates the anger she feels towards her own maternal uncles and her maternal grandfather. The first part of *The Blue Castle* shows the heroine, Valancy Stirling, oppressed by an entire clan, men and wives alike, because she has failed to catch a husband. The reader hears every vicious comment that is made to her. Her relatives belittle her, chastise her, shame her. Montgomery downplays the bite of her satire, as she often does, through the use of humour, but the reader ascertains that the author of this book was one very angry woman when she wrote those wickedly funny lines. In no other book does Montgomery's anger come through so clearly.

The second phase of the plot shows Valancy doing the worst things she can do, as far as her clan is concerned. She asserts herself and leaves; she commits the scandalous act of nursing a dying girl who gave birth out of wedlock;[65] she proposes to a man of unknown and doubtful character and marries him. As long as Valancy had been among them, the clan could enjoy pecking at her wounds, but after she escapes they are without their victim.

The first part of the novel reads as sharp social satire, and it seems that Montgomery might herself be moving to the realistic novel which was then in vogue. Suddenly, Montgomery changes the tone of the novel, and shifts back to the easy flow of romance. Valancy marries, is thoroughly and completely happy in her marriage, and she spends all of her time in domestic bliss. It's rather startling to have the tone and genre change so suddenly. To satirize marriage and patriarchy and then dump one's heroine into a marriage seems odd, to say the least. However, there are some references to the Bluebeard legend, and the reader does begin to wonder what Valancy's husband keeps in the room he will not allow her to enter. Perhaps this wayward Valancy will end up dead, as indeed she should, since she has flaunted social convention.

Finally, in the last 30 pages, so many improbable coincidences and surprises occur that even the most gullible reader knows that Montgomery is playing games. This novel which began as an angry and biting satire of a patriarchal society ends up as a spoof on romance. Or perhaps it is a joke on the reader who demands romance, for the man Valancy has married turns out to be a writer of books which are remarkably like Montgomery's own. He writes purple passages about nature and he espouses "female" values like sensitivity and nurturing. He is as gentle as the patriarchal uncles and their accommodating wives were overbearing. If Emily's Aunt Elizabeth was a man in woman's clothing, Valancy's husband is a woman in man's clothing. It's Montgomery's transvestite trick again, her playing with the gender stereotypes of her era. Among other things, Valancy's husband has rejected the values of his father, a wealthy entrepreneur and businessman: the world of power, money, and of "real" men. But since he will still inherit his father's millions, Valancy's grasping, materialistic clan is delighted and they make utter fools of themselves in turning about-face. Thus, Montgomery gives her publishers and readers their happy ending of marriage, but she undercuts the stereotypical image of masculinity as much as she can when she devises her hero. It's not unlike Charlotte Brontë's alteration of Rochester into a different kind of man at the end of *Jane Eyre*. Montgomery emasculates her man, too, into a sensitive person with the values that her patriarchal society would restrict to sentimental women.

In *The Blue Castle* other disjunctive elements are used: Valancy gets married in green, with an unkempt groom who has agreed to marry her out of pity. In the end, romantic love does release Valancy, as Montgomery herself believed it should, if one only found and married the right partner. But the ending has complex undertones, as does the entire novel.

Thus, when Montgomery began the novel in a realistic mode, but shifted to the unbelievable coincidences of romance, she created subversions which eroded the trajectory of romance, while conforming to it outwardly. Her discourses are not only the obvious ones put into the characters' mouths, but they are of a more subtle order – between the conventions of realism and those of domestic romance. She satisfies her readers and has her revenge at the same time.

It is likely that Montgomery dispelled some of her own pent-up anger in the actual act of writing out *The Blue Castle*. When her lampooning of the uncles threatened to become too virulent, Montgomery softened her attack with humour, effectively telling the readers that she did not mean what she was saying. And she reverted to her genre of domestic romance partway through the novel. Montgomery was cautious and conventional as a minister's wife and too much in need of money, as well, to risk sustained vicious satire. She did not want to alienate her readers or her publishers. But she was too angry to completely repress her feelings. We glimpse these in *The Blue Castle*. Hence, its power. Many, many Montgomery fans say it is their favourite book. So does, perhaps, the entire nation of Poland which voted the play based on it as the most popular musical stage play in Poland in 1990.

At the beginning of this article, I spoke about Montgomery's books having a political dimension in Poland.[66] I only began to feel *The Blue Castle*'s power when I viewed it on the stage in Poland in 1984, when Russian communism still oppressed the Polish nation, and Lech Walesa's Solidarity was pitted against the official government. This musical had its Cracow premiere in 1982, and has continued playing continuously as one of Poland's most successful stage plays since then. It had an especial bite because of its production in historical Poland. The Polish *Blue Castle* took on the aura of allegory when it pitted the powerful clan against the powerless Valancy. On stage, Valancy seemed to symbolize the Polish nation as she sang hopelessly of her "blue castle" where she could have freedom from the overbearing, restrictive, destructive clan which policed her actions and thoughts. Her voice and the music became a disembodied longing for freedom from centuries of oppression all massed into and represented by her horrible clan. The play had a subtext which the Polish nation well understood, having lived in the crossroads of Europe under the heels of invaders for centuries. Polish theatre had been long accustomed to speaking its politically dangerous frustrations and anger through theatrical subtexts, and Montgomery's *The Blue Castle* provided the perfect vehicle. How could their censors object to this harmless fiction about 19th century Scots in Canada? It was just a sentimental love story, at least on the surface! I shall never forget the atmosphere in the Cracow theatre when Valancy freed herself from the clan, became self-determining, and sang of her freedom: it was as if – for the moment, at least – the people in the audience dared hope that they, too, might eventually achieve what Valancy had achieved – freedom from oppression. The atmosphere was charged with energy as the glorious and triumphant music swelled and rolled over the audience.

Those of us who saw the production were quite surprised that Montgomery's book had become part of a subversive political agenda in Poland and that she was such a cult figure there. Her books were in such short supply that whenever the publishers acquired enough paper to print more, they then sold through the Polish underground. It was even more surprising to learn that the government had tried (unsuccessfully) to block Montgomery's books after World War II.[67] Montgomery – the woman Canadians thought wrote only *sentimental fictions for children*? I recall Montgomery's words in *Emily's Quest*: "she [Emily] must reach her audience through many artificial mediums." The political conditions of 1980's Poland do not operate in Canada. Nevertheless, an attack on authoritarianism appeals to children and women who have felt oppressed: all can see their own enemy in Montgomery's story if they choose to.

Thus, we can see how Montgomery's various methods provide a critique of the values of her patriarchal society. In these books, she turns her closures into farce. She uses the hackneyed plots of romance, but her stories push against these formal constraints. Her allusions, references, images, and comments threaten again and again to disrupt the trajectory of romance – if in no other way than by sending the reader off into a search for significant intertextualities. The energy in her books comes partly from these collisions between genre and subject. Thus, her narratology is far more sophisticated than appears on the surface. When Montgomery begins her *Emily* novels with a realistic heroine whose

"Bildung" into a female-artist figure is incompatible with her inevitable fate (marriage), she challenges her culture's views about women. Montgomery plays the literary and social games of her society with superb finesse, producing novels that conform on one level to the expected conventions while at the same time skilfully subverting the triteness of the domestic romance.

She may have written, as she tells us, in an "artificial medium," but behind it we find that L.M. Montgomery is a cleverly political writer who used the material of women's domestic lives to question their inferior status in a patriarchal culture. She stole by stealth into the august house of fiction where 19th century female writers like Jane Austen and Charlotte Brontë had already staked out claims to small attic rooms while the male literary giants like Henry James and Thackeray held forth in the pretentious drawing rooms below. Entering this house in the early part of the 20th century, Montgomery found her own small room, decorated it simply, and established herself in it. She remained unobtrusive as she wrote easily and prolifically within the traditional genres of romance, camouflaging her subtle agenda of empowerment with humour and with the unpretentious language of the oral storyteller. Next door to her was Virginia Woolf, painfully toiling to find significant new forms, but writing out of many of the same concerns. What the serious male writers in the drawing rooms did not notice – they were too busy fulsomely discussing each other's books – was that much of their audience was slipping upstairs to listen to the tales of the scribbling women. These women were quietly creating a literature of their own.

NOTES

This article (excluding the Woolf material) was first given in March 1988 as an informal lecture at the University of Ottawa. An adaptation of one part of it was delivered as a formal conference paper at the International Research Society for Children's Literature in Salamanca, Spain, in September 1989.

1 [Montgomery, 1 May 1899, in *SJLMM*, 1: 237.]
2 [Woolf, *A Room of One's Own*, 3.]
3 Chapter 6, "To 'Bear My Mother's Name': *Künstlerromane* by Women Writers," provides theoretical material that can be related to Montgomery's *Emily* trilogy.
4 DuPlessis, *Writing beyond the Ending*, 3.
5 Hancock, *The Girl Within*, 220–26.

6 Munro, "The Real Material," 18–19 [see also Munro, "An Interview"].

7 Atwood, radio interview.

8 Cott, "The Astonishment of Being," 57–58.

9 Little, "A Long-Distance Friendship," 23.

10 Shields, "Interview with Carol Shields," 9. Carol Shields was raised in Oak Park, Illinois, so her mother's comment reflects an American view.

11 [ENM, 20–21].

12 DuPlessis, *Writing beyond the Ending*, 3.

13 A full-page article on Montgomery's reception in Sweden can be found in Lönnroth, "Halva himlens frihetshjaltinna." The release of the Åhmansson book on Montgomery occasioned this full-page article in Sweden's foremost newspaper.

14 Newspapers and radio/television stations around the world gave coverage to the story. See newspaper accounts in Hills, "Thorn Birds Colleen"; *The Gazette*, "Is McCullough Novel"; Garvie, "A Tale of Two Books"; Kirchhoff, "Echoes of Montgomery." Radio Melbourne gave the controversy a thorough airing, as did stations in the United States and Canada. In February 1988 an Australian TV crew came to PEI to explore similarities between McCullough's book and Montgomery's for "Sixty Minutes," a current affairs program in Australia, and in Canada it was covered by CBC Television's "Fifth Estate."

15 Her statement to her publishers, Harper and Row (New York), made an excellent point which applies to many writers: "A creative writer is the sum total of what he or she absorbs from their earliest years. It goes without saying ∴.. that there are moments in any creative career when the subconscious resonates with buried data and out comes something new, but owing part of itself to what has gone before, whether in one's own life, or the lives of others, real or imagined." A copy of McCullough's statement to her publishers is in my own archive.

16 [Katsura, "Red-Haired Anne in Japan."]

17 Tom Reddin, fax to the author, 29 February 1992.

18 For accounts of this, see Patricia Orwen's article "Kindred Spirits" and Kate Taylor's "Anne of Hokkaido."

19 Virginia Woolf's fiction is in the group with artificially stimulated sales because her books are on university courses.

20 [AHD, 73.]

21 Montgomery, 1 November 1921 [in *SJLMM*, 3: 24].

22 *EQ*, 2.

23 Bishop, *A Virginia Woolf Chronology*, 22.

24 Christian-Smith, *Becoming a Woman*, 9.

25 Montgomery, 27 January 1922 [in *SJLMM*, 3: 37].

26 Montgomery's journals recount how scholars like Prof. Pelham Edgar scorned her work during her Toronto years. Åhmansson's book gives a very good analysis of the critical reception of Montgomery's work.

27 When *The Selected Journals of L.M. Montgomery* were published, it was only one lone male reviewer who said that the "Introduction" should not have taken for granted that readers would actually know the Montgomery novels. Female reviewers of course did know them.

28 Elizabeth Waterston was the first scholar to give serious critical attention to Montgomery's work in a book entitled *The Clear Spirit: Twenty Canadian Women and Their Times*. This ground-breaking book was the Centennial Project of the Canadian Federation of University Women in 1966. But in 1966, well-meaning older male colleagues tried to dissuade her from wasting her time on Montgomery.

29 See Elaine Showalter's *A Literature of Their Own* for an extended account of this [see also Smith, *A Poetics of Women's Autobiography*].

30 [*EC*, 6.]

31 *AP*, 9.

32 Montgomery, 24 August 1920 [in *SJLMM*, 2: 390].

33 DuPlessis, *Writing beyond the Ending*, 103.

34 And not only women authors of an earlier age. A contemporary Canadian playwright has mentioned to me that the *Emily* books were important to him because they showed one could get rejections and still be successful.

35 Quoted in Montgomery, 14 July 1927 [in *SJLMM*, 3: 342].

36 Bishop lists about 1,500 books that Virginia Woolf refers to during her lifetime from all sources in his *Chronology*. Montgomery records the titles of approximately 500 books which she read between 1889 and 1942 in her journals, and she almost always discusses them. But she mentions having several thousand books at one time, and her son said she often read a book a day, even when busy. There is no comprehensive list of books she read compiled from other sources, but Rea Wilmshurst has been compiling a list of all the books alluded to (by name or by a quote taken from it). A checklist of books referred to in the *Anne* books appears in *CCL* #56 [Wilmshurst, "L.M. Montgomery's Use"]. Both Woolf and Montgomery were compulsive readers, but Woolf had access to outré books that Montgomery did not.

37 [Lady Wilson, Foreword, vi–vii, ix, x.]

38 Showalter, *A Literature of Their Own*, 33.

39 This story, adapted into a witty stage play by Charlottetown playwright Jane Wilson in 1990, played at the Charlottetown Festival mainstage.

40 [*CA*, 174–75.]

41 For an explication of this, see [Rosemary Bailey's article "Little Orphan Mary," earlier in this volume.]

42 A. Pratt, *Archetypal Patterns*, 11.

43 *ENM*, 133–34.

44 [*EQ*, 24;] Montgomery, 30 December 1928 [in *SJLMM*, 3: 387].

45 *AHD*, 180.

46 *AHD*, 183.

47 *EC*, 9.

48 Pierpont, "A Woman's Place."

49 *ENM*, 271, 272. [Editor's note: Rubio's original publication quoted the Canadian Children's Favourites edition of *Emily of New Moon*. The sentence "One pays for it in bondage of some kind or other" is absent from the Seal edition of this book, quoted here.]

50 Montgomery, 28 January 1912 [in *SJLMM*, 2: 68].

51 Montgomery, 20 July 1922 [in *SJLMM*, 3: 61]; Montgomery, 29 August 1923 [in *SJLMM*, 3: 147].

52 Montgomery, 25 March 1922 [in *SJLMM*, 3: 48].

53 Showalter would undoubtedly put "Jarback" Priest in her second group of women's men, the "collateral descendants of Scott's dark heroes and Byron's Corsair, but direct descendants of Edward Fairfax Rochester." She talks about how *Jane Eyre*'s influence became international, and these types of heroes appeared everywhere, showing their family resemblance to his predecessors: they are "not conventionally handsome, and often downright ugly; they have piercing eyes; they are brusque and cynical in speech, impetuous in action. Thrilling the heroine with their rebellion and power, they simultaneously appeal to her reforming energies." They can be at once "sardonic, sarcastic, satanic, and seraphic" (Showalter, *A Literature of Their Own*, 139, 140).

54 *EQ*, 31, 51–52, 97.

55 In fact, when she was interviewed in Boston, during a visit to her publisher in 1910, she was quoted as saying: "I am a quiet, plain sort of person and while I believe a woman, if intelligent, should be allowed to vote, I would have no use for suffrage myself. I have no aspirations to become a politician. I believe a woman's place is in the home" (Montgomery, Red Scrapbook, 1 [11]) [see "Says Woman's Place Is Home," in Volume 1 of *The L.M. Montgomery Reader*]. She probably believed this, at least in part, though the fact that she was pressed to make a public statement for a newspaper would have made her more conservative. By the mid-twenties, when she was writing the *Emily* trilogy, she has come to see how confining

this ideology can be when a woman marries the wrong man in the wrong occupation.

56 Montgomery, 15 October 1908, in *SJLMM*, 1: 339.

57 *EQ*, 135.

58 [*EQ*, 227.] In her diary entry of August 24, 1896, Montgomery is at Park Corner, everyone is away, and it is raining, and she says, "I have read everything that is readable in the house, including several 'shilling shockings' by Bertha M. Clay and others of that ilk, so you may realize to what straits I am reduced" [Montgomery, 24 August 1896, in *CJLMM*, 1: 327].

59 [*EQ*, 228].

60 See an account of this in Showalter, *A Literature of Their Own*, 274.

61 Showalter traces the development of this ideal of Victorian womanhood: "a Perfect Lady, an Angel in the House, contentedly submissive to men, but strong in her inner purity and religiosity, queen in her own realm of the House" (ibid., 14).

62 Montgomery, 30 June 1926 [in *SJLMM*, 3: 298]; Montgomery, 13 October 1926 [in *SJLMM*, 3: 310].

63 Perry Miller did not have enough social status to deserve a Murray of "New Moon," although he had many positive merits.

64 A clipping in Montgomery's "Clipping Book" states: "L.M. Montgomery, whose charming story of love in an elysian Canadian summer 'Blue Castle' has just been published by Stokes, writes that she is busy now on the third Emily book and a 'dreadful time I am having, too, with all her beaux. Her love affairs won't run straight. Then, too, I'm bombarded with letters from girls who implore me to let her marry Dean, not Teddy. But she is set on Teddy herself so what am I to do? One letter recently was quite unique. All previous letters have implored me to write "more about Emily, no matter whom she marries," but the writer of this begged me not to write another Emily book because she felt sure if I did she would marry Teddy and she (the writer) couldn't bear it'" (SR, 268). Note: Montgomery blames the final marriage to Teddy on Emily, who is a product of her culture. She as author does not defend it.

65 This feature resulted in *The Blue Castle* being subject to censorship after it was published. Several older women have told me that they were not allowed to read it.

66 An article in issue #46 of *CCL* presents many reasons why the Polish nation has taken a particular liking to Montgomery's works and *The Blue Castle* in particular. This article, written by Barbara Wachowicz, the Polish writer who adapted Montgomery's book into a musical stage play, was published in 1987, before the long, dark "Stalinist night" was

over and Communism collapsed. Her article stresses positive elements of Montgomery – her love of home, beauty, friendship, etc. – and skirts over any possible political innuendos [see Wachowicz, "L.M. Montgomery"].

67 There is an account of this in the Polish M.A. thesis mentioned earlier, and Barbara Wachowicz's article covers it, too.

6

Women's Oral Narrative Traditions as Depicted in Lucy Maud Montgomery's Fiction, 1918–1939

—— 1993 ——

DIANE TYE

In this essay, which first appeared in the collection *Myth and Milieu: Atlantic Literature and Culture 1918–1939*, Diane Tye places Montgomery's later fiction within the field of women's folklore in order to consider the function of oral narrative in all its forms: gossip, domestic narratives, tall tales, family lore, and community legends. Tye, who teaches in the Department of Folklore at Memorial University of Newfoundland and is the author of *Baking as Biography: A Life Story in Recipes* (2010), is particularly committed to taking seriously the function of talk as a form of social cohesion within women's rural communities in Atlantic Canada.

In her fictional depiction of life in late 19th- and early 20th-century rural Prince Edward Island, Lucy Maud Montgomery drew heavily on her knowledge of women's oral narrative traditions.[1] Montgomery's writing confirms Jean M. Humez's belief that "if we overcome our fear of violating one of the ultimate academic taboos – that against using literature to study life – and agree to treat fictional representations of women's verbal arts with some delicacy and care, we open up an enormously rich body of source material for the study of female talk traditions."[2] Particularly because we are unable to explore directly the experiences of earlier women relying on usual methodology – such as observation, participant observation, and personal interviews – the insights Montgomery offers into the networks, contexts, genres, and meanings of oral narrative are important. The following reading presents Montgomery's full-length fiction published between the wars – focusing on the "Anne" and "Emily" series – as one exploration of women's talk in rural Prince Edward Island.

L.M. Montgomery's fiction depicts a gendered world of talk where rules of appropriateness governing the creation and exchange of oral narrative are further dictated by factors including age and status. Young people develop their own narratives away from adult scrutiny, for ideally children and adolescents do not verbally challenge the authority of their elders either by questioning or interrupting and are often excluded from the narrative exchange of older family and community members. In the Anne series, the Blythe children and their companions tell stories and have uninterrupted conversation as they play in Rainbow Valley, and, in the Emily trilogy, Emily Starr and her friends seek privacy in groves, valleys, and other natural refuges. However, the narrative networks of children and adolescents may be connected to those of their elders by a messenger who has overheard an adult conversation or otherwise tapped an adult narrative resource, or conversely who reports to an adult a story shared by the children.

As part of their maturation process, young women are taught who are appropriate companions and confidantes. Emily is discouraged from interacting too regularly with the hired hand from Stovepipe town[3] while Anne Blythe worries over her daughter's friendship with Jenny from the lower status Penny family. She shares her anxiety with housekeeper Susan Baker: "Oh, Susan, I don't want her to feel that anyone is 'beneath' her. But we must draw the line somewhere."[4] In other words, kin influences the formation of childhood friendship groups, and most children bonded through friendship descend from families of similar status.

However, children and adolescents are free to develop narrative networks that cross gender lines. In the rural community of New Moon, Emily Starr's circle of friends includes males, just as young friendship circles in the Anne series are mixed. In rural settings, some young female characters claim to look to young males for sympathetic, intelligent and interesting talk. For example, in *Rilla of Ingleside*, Rilla feels that her brother Walter understands her better than anyone else.[5] This apparently equalitarian rapport breaks down when examined closely, for Walter Blythe relies more heavily on his sisters for emotional support than they on him, and Emily Starr is very aware of the comforting role she plays in Dean Priest's life.[6] Nonetheless, the freedom of rural adolescents to enjoy mixed gender friendships contrasts with the mores of a more urban setting, as Emily discovers when she attends school in the town of Shrewsbury. There her interactions with male friends are restricted by both her aunt and school authorities.[7]

By adulthood, narrative networks in the novels are strictly divided along gender lines. In the Anne books, Gilbert Blythe makes several comments that indicate he neither understands nor appreciates female talk:

> "So the Ladies' Aid is going to have their quilting at Ingleside," said the doctor. "Bring out all your lordly dishes, Susan, and provide several brooms to sweep up the fragments of reputations afterwards."
>
> Susan smiled wanly, as a woman tolerant of a man's lack of all understanding of vital things ... [8]

Female narrative exchange is foreign to Gilbert and while he is in the room for some female conversations, his presence is not necessary to the talk. In fact, his arrival may bring an end to a female conversation in progress. In *Anne of Ingleside*, her neighbour, Miss Cornelia, rises to go home when Gilbert enters the room.[9]

According to the picture painted by Montgomery, women of rural Prince Edward Island during this time period most often talked among themselves in small groups comprised of kin or neighbours. The most frequent adult female narrative network in the Anne books published between the wars consists of Anne Blythe, the housekeeper Susan and the neighbour Miss Cornelia. The three women gather regularly, and while status differences make themselves clear in many of the exchanges (enunciated through Susan's use of dialect and Anne's use of grammatically correct English, for example), the visits demonstrate that for the purpose of narrative, gender sometimes supersedes differences in age and status in binding this adult group closely together.

Most often, female characters meet for talk in their own or neighbours' homes. Often the women talk as they work. Susan and Anne exchange stories as they carry out their domestic routine, but rarely does Montgomery set their work or talk in the kitchen. In the Anne series, only the domestic help, Susan Baker and Rebecca Dew, retreat to the kitchen at night to stick their feet in the oven and enjoy a storytelling session.[10] Rather, the work around which women's talk is organized is done in the living room or more commonly on the verandah. When more than two or three women gather, their work may relate to that of associations such as the Red Cross, or communal events such as quilting. When women visit each other singly in the afternoons and early evenings, they usually work independently on needlework projects. It is possible that Montgomery's choice of more formal rooms of the home instead of the kitchen as a place for talk reflects her own experience as a minister's wife being entertained by her husband's parishioners.[11] Alternatively, the setting may relate to Anne's elevated status as a doctor's wife or it may reflect a growing tendency for the aspiring middle class to entertain neighbours and extended family on a more formal basis.

Women's social experience creates a context for their speech that is different from that of their male counterparts.[12] In Montgomery's books, women do not have access to such public space forums for high performance male storytelling as the general store in the evenings, the blacksmith shop, the carpenter's shop or the fish stores. Miss Cornelia often visits Anne and Susan in the early evening when her husband spends time socializing with men at the store. While the advent of the First World War opens the general store to women as a narrative resource – no longer do women rely solely on men to bring them reports of public space interactions but gather new narratives themselves while on shopping trips[13] – it never offers women a performance venue. At the close of the novels, Susan – demonstrating women's increasing reliance on the telephone to keep abreast of news and exchange narratives – phones the store for war and community news rather than visiting herself.[14]

Most of women's narratives take place within conversation and therefore follow conversational dictates. This is not to say, however, that there are no experts within women's narrative networks. Montgomery introduces several "information specialists,"[15] such as Miss Cornelia, who demonstrate an impressive knowledge of past and current community events and personalities in their narratives. A few women in the books are described as superb oral storytellers and they offer masterful, usually uninterrupted narrative performances. Emma Pollock skilfully tells the Red Cross quilting party a narrative of Abner Cromwell who, although reported dead, was still very much alive. In *Rainbow Valley* Ellen West's narrative abilities are valued by her friends and family. Rev. John Meredith enjoys her "pleasant, deep, rumbly voice" and the "hearty laugh with which she always ended up some jolly and well-told story."[16] Yet, without access to male-dominated public space forums, such as the store during the evenings, even women who have a knack for storytelling are without an audience. Thus, Ellen West must share some of her feelings and narratives with her cat and Emily Starr must turn her narrative talents to a written forum.

Most of the oral narratives shared among women exhibit what folklorist Hugh Jansen terms a low performance level[17] and are pieced together by more than one person, collectively developing what Susan J. Kalčik terms the "kernel story."[18] As a result, traditional genres of oral narrative are not very useful in analyzing the women's narratives depicted in Montgomery's novels. As Marta Weigle notes, traditional male-centred narrative typology overlooks the low-performance conversational genres in favour of the high-performance genres such as the tall tale, or märchen.[19] While a few men and at least one elderly woman engage in a jocular teasing that might be termed "tall talk,"[20] it does not represent an important genre in the books, nor are such narratives portrayed favourably. The vast majority of women's oral narrative appearing in Montgomery's texts falls under the formal classification of anecdote or personal experience narrative. Even basic distinctions between third person anecdote or legend and first person experience narrative blur, however, as women in the novels interpret individual or family behaviour in a narrative or related narrative sequence by combining personal experience with community knowledge gained from others' reported experience, dite, proverb or local legend.

A unifying characteristic running through much of the women's narrative is a focus on the local. Women rely heavily on the local scene for their subject matter with the vast majority of narratives centring on lives of local residents and their families. Even when the stories incorporate material from the outside world – such as the many narratives and conversations shared about developing events of the First World War in *Rilla of Ingleside* – part of the interpretation inherent in the narrative relates world events to village events. Women's stories reflect what Montgomery writes in *Emily's Quest* is the material of "story weaving ... in all ages and all places[.] Births, deaths, marriages, scandals – these are the only really interesting things in the world."[21]

The narratives that are most important to Montgomery's female characters constitute what anthropologists such as Susan Harding define as gossip. Based on her exploration of women's verbal culture in a Spanish village, Harding understands gossip to be "the collection, circulation and analysis of certain portions of the village script."[22] Within this loosely defined category of "informal communication,"[23] the single criterion is that outlined by John Robinson in his exploration of personal experience narrative – the story must have a point.[24] Mrs. Anthony Mitchell who visits Anne is critiqued when her narratives stretch on endlessly without making a point.[25] Additionally, in most cases – especially when more than two or three women are present – meaning should have social as well as personal value. In *Anne of Ingleside* Mrs. Donald Reese is depicted as an ineffectual and uninteresting narrator when she continually interjects anecdotes about her daughter into the conversation when they are unrelated and inappropriate.[26]

While Montgomery explores some of the elements of gossip that contribute to its popular dismissal as idle, destructive talk, she demonstrates an appreciation of gossip in its earlier meaning, relating to women's private culture.[27] L.M. Montgomery communicates the ambivalent nature of gossip for women as she presents what Daniel Segal and Richard Handler would describe as its "multiple realities."[28] Gossip may be entertaining and create intimacy; gossip may also be restrictive and destructive.

Women in Montgomery's novels clearly enjoy gossip. In *Anne of Windy Poplars*, Anne lures cantankerous old Mrs. Gibson onto her verandah with the attractive promise that they will "sit there and criticize everybody who passes,"[29] and when living in Glen St. Mary's, Anne looks forward to Miss Cornelia's visits and the opportunity for narrative exchange that accompanies them. In *Anne of Windy Poplars*, Miss Valentine Courtaloe sympathetically recounts the story of her Aunt Cecilia who upon finding out that she had only hours to live, delighted in ending her life with a gossip session.[30] It is not an enjoyment men in the books always appreciate, as Gilbert demonstrates when he warns Susan that she had better "supply brooms to help sweep up broken reputations" when Ingleside is host to a quilting party.

Part of gossip's value for women lies in the opportunity it offers to share emotional burdens. Anne finds comfort in sharing with Cornelia personal experience narratives concerning Gilbert's difficult Aunt Mary Maria who becomes a lingering house guest. Cornelia affirms Anne's impatience with the aunt by sharing her interpretation of Mary Maria and validates Anne's frustration with Gilbert's lack of understanding of his aunt's disruptive presence. This is not a topic Anne feels free to discuss with her husband, or with Susan, the housekeeper. In this instance her status as mistress of the house and member of the extended family prevents her from looking to Susan for consolation. Rather she turns to another member of her female network and one of the community's gossip experts to express impatience with the visiting aunt.

The emotional support women receive from narrative exchange is clear in *Rilla of Ingleside* as the women of the Blythe household (Anne,

Susan, and Gertrude Oliver, the teacher who boards with them) compare personal experience narratives that help them cope with events of the war. In these narrative exchanges they recount dreams, share experiences and trade advice on how to cope with the stress each of them feels. The talk constitutes what Patricia Meyer Spacks labels "healing talk"[31] that soothes, offers sympathy and possible coping strategies, and affirms the validity of both the emotion and the overall female perspective.

The integrative function of female narrative exchange is an important one. Women may use narratives to demonstrate their alliance with others in the conversation. Collectively they piece together a story and develop an acceptable interpretation of events or behaviour. As well, many of the stories women relate affirm one's membership in a particular family and/or in the community at large. Young women are taught about the status of their family directly but much of their understanding of what it means to belong to a particular family derives from the many family history narratives they are told. Emily Starr is constantly related stories about her ancestors by older relatives. The result is that, soon after her arrival in her aunts' home, Emily has an appreciation of "the Murray women" who have come before her and she thinks she knows what Murray women would or would not do. The family narratives aid her assimilation into the new household.

Women also rely on narratives to help their integration into the overall community. When Anne returns to Ingleside after a visit outside the community, she eagerly looks forward to hearing "all the juicy tidbits of gossip and news, everyone contributing something."[32] Through the exchange of gossip exploring others' activities and motivations the women get in touch with what people in the family and in the community are doing and feeling. Montgomery mirrors this methodology in her writing as she relies heavily on conversation and anecdote in her character development.

Through their intimate knowledge of family and community, the women in Montgomery's novels fashion the history of people and places close to them. In a real sense this is a woman's history that concentrates on the more immediate fabric of everyday life and in large part consists of anecdotes that crystallize an individual's character or role in the community. It is also an ever-changing history as new anecdotes are added to the existing community store that may support, embellish or contradict those already circulated. The women's interpretation may at times be harsh, but there is always opportunity for renegotiation for individual community members. Their narratives help comprise what anthropologist John

Szwed refers to as the "tally sheet" that exists for each member of a small community and is continually being updated and reassessed.[33]

As the women rework the present and the past, they weave a master narrative of the community and its residents. In the course of narrative development, as two or more women craft a story, participants have the opportunity to affect others' interpretation of what happened and why. Through their versions of events and personalities they potentially influence personal and community identity. Because of this ability to affect opinion, women's knowledge of family and community narratives is recognized as a source of power. To know is to be able to control. The Pringles, who offer Anne in *Anne of Windy Poplars* resistance when she assumes the role of principal, become her allies when she learns what they consider to be an unsavoury aspect of their family past.[34] So concerned are they that she will exploit this knowledge and allow it to enter into the public domain that they form an alliance with her to prevent the possibility.

Many of the narratives, like the one concerning a member of the elite Pringle family, not only re-evaluate an individual's character, but renegotiate that person's or family's status. The narratives have the ability to level social rank and create new bonds.[35] As a result, the women's narratives are respected by community members and can act as a form of social control. Women in Montgomery's work often demonstrate an appreciation for the power of "talk" and will assess the potential of their behaviour as impetus for gossip before acting. For example, in *Rainbow Valley* Rosemary West considers the speculation she will generate when she visits the manse with a gift for the widowed minister's daughter.[36] Women's knowledge of family and community narratives may allow them some indirect control over people's actions and community affairs that they are unable to exercise directly through channels such as politics.[37]

Montgomery demonstrates an appreciation of the importance of women's narrative exchange – women's gossip – to the fabric of the communities she writes about. Gossip mediates between the individual and the family and between the individual and the community, fixing one's place in the network of kin and neighbours. The "multiple realities" Montgomery presents are not all positive, however. As shown in the example of Rosemary West and her decision to visit the minister, just as a woman has the power to influence the actions of others through narrative, so they have control over her. Women in Montgomery's novels of this period do not always curtail their activities to avert the possibility of becoming the subject of talk – Rosemary does make the visit – but they frequently express an awareness of and respect for the power of women's gossip.

Montgomery's fictional world provides ample illustration of the destructive side of women's oral narrative exchange. In *Emily of New Moon*, Ilse's father treats her with disinterest because she reminds him of his wife who, community gossip says, ran off with another man many years earlier. In the course of the novel, as Emily helps discover the truth that Ilse's mother did not abandon her husband and child but died when she fell in an open well, the father shows a new commitment to his daughter. In *Jane of Lantern Hill*, Jane's parents are separated because of female relatives' destructive and interfering talk. When individuals – sometimes males outside of female narrative networks – are not appreciative of the power of women's talk, they may be harmed by it. Narratives can divide families, church congregations, and communities, and they can be personally hurtful to individuals.

Many examples of the harmful nature of gossip arise when the rules governing its exchange are broken. Based on the novels, one learns that gossip is shared within the course of conversation and is linked thematically with topics immediately preceding and following the narrative. The subject should not be present nor should anyone whose alliance with the subject is close enough to mean that his or her membership in a family or friendship is challenged. Thus, Emily's pride is damaged when she overhears two neighbours evaluating her character and behaviour and the neighbours are embarrassed when they discover that she has heard their appraisal.[38] Moreover, much gossip is viewed as inappropriate – perhaps too emotionally powerful – for children to hear. Emily is emotionally distraught when she learns the community interpretation of what happened to Ilse's mother and for a while can think of nothing else.[39] There should also be no one present who will report the narrative to the subject later. In *Rainbow Valley*, Mary Vance's reports of community gossip to the Meredith children resulted in emotional distress and even more socially inappropriate behaviour. Finally, when individuals get caught up in the pleasure of the telling and fashion narratives around fabricated incidents and information, people are hurt. Mary Vance upsets the other children with her exaggerated stories of community events and her fabricated accounts of supernatural happenings.[40] Gossip should have a truthful base and part of young women's informal education consists of learning to distinguish the false from the truthful, the invented from the real.

Montgomery paints vivid pictures of the narrowness of the world of women's narrative. Some female characters yearn for a greater narrative resource. Aunt Chatty of *Anne of Windy Poplars* longs for the expanded repertoire of her sister Kate, who sailed with her sea captain husband.[41] And Emily Starr envies Dean Priest for the travel adventures he is able to recount. Both Rosemary and Ellen West welcome John Meredith's visits and the opportunities they bring for them to talk about matters of the wider world:

> Rosemary thought the Glen minister was by no means as shy and tongue-tied as he had been represented. He seemed to find no difficulty in talking easily and freely. Glen housewives would have been amazed had they heard him. But then so many Glen housewives talked only gossip and the price of eggs, and John Meredith was not interested in either. He talked to Rosemary of books and music and wide-world doings and something of his own history, and found that she could understand and respond.[42]

Rosemary's sister Ellen is even more interested in discussing politics and topics associated with the public sphere. Relegated by patriarchy to the domestic realm, some women clearly feel confined by its limitations.

Restricted to the private sphere and aware of the active narrative networks of women, some of Montgomery's female characters feel they have no privacy. Even in the liminal places where most women's talk is staged – such as the verandah – privacy may be violated and the women overheard. In the Red Cross quilting party hosted on Anne's verandah, little Walter hides under the table and listens to the proceedings. There is a constant need for what Erving Goffman terms "impression management."[43] Homes, dress, and conversation are all vigilantly managed to create a favourable outward impression without suggesting that any of it is staged. Susan and Anne prepare for members of the Red Cross by cleaning, baking, and decorating the verandah with flowers. Details right down to vases and tablecloths are attended to with care.[44]

Most of Montgomery's main female characters, such as Anne and Emily, are left alone to create and manage this front. Anne has Susan and Gilbert, and Emily has the help of her mother's siblings, but they cannot always be counted on. Both Emily and Anne strongly feel the lack of close female kin to support and defend them.[45] Montgomery's primary female characters lack the mother and sisters that historians indicate were essential to women in the 19th century. In her study of women's emotional networks, Smith-Rosenberg suggests an "inner core of kin" was integral to the female world in the 19th century. She comments, "Such women, whether friends or relatives, assumed an emotional centrality in each other's lives."[46]

Female friends are present in Montgomery's novels and women profess loyalty and affection for them. Yet, they do not always help form strong enough alliances to guard against community misinterpretation. Alone and usually young, they may not have the power base associated with family. In *Jane of Lantern Hill*, Jane's close friend, Jody, is an orphan, without any support system of her own. In depicting close female friendships, Montgomery provides frustratingly few details, often allowing the reader to question the depth of feeling the character professes. For example, few of Jane and Jody's conversations are reported and, while Anne keeps in lifelong contact with her childhood friend Diana, there are no detailed accounts of their narrative exchanges. One wonders about the closeness of this latter friendship as Montgomery presents two very different women when they meet as adults in *Anne of Ingleside*. Additionally, false friends are a recurring theme throughout Montgomery's novels and many young female protagonists are hurt and betrayed by other young women whom they considered to be true friends.

Diaries and letters written by Maritime women from this time period support the primacy of close kin and female friends to women's narrative networks. Without these connections and without this support, some women in Montgomery's novels remain largely alone to defend themselves against gossip generated about them and to argue for their interpretation of any event. For these women – like Anne and Emily – talk is seldom safe. They guard against being misunderstood (as they inevitably are) and against being betrayed.

Through her creation of Anne and Emily, Montgomery offers several strategies for influencing one's own assessment on the community "tally sheet." Primary among these is the option of silence. Emily frequently chooses not to speak her thoughts and Anne is invariably depicted as holding back. Their lives are characterized by restraint and silence, broken infrequently by outbursts of true feeling which may either alleviate a conflict or create one. There is always risk involved in speaking one's mind.

Silence is a successful strategy but a difficult one to manage. While Anne holds herself back, Miss Cornelia informs her that other women hold themselves back in her presence.[47] As folklorist Debora Kodish indicates, restraint can be unsuccessful if one gives the impression that one considers oneself above the exchange, that one is resisting the levelling and binding process that gossip represents.[48]

Diane Tye

Silence is perhaps easier to maintain when one has other outlets. Montgomery shows females who are skilled storytellers extending beyond the networks of oral narrative for expression. Jane talks to her "secret moon"[49] and she, like most of Montgomery's young female protagonists, keeps a diary. Writing provides an important outlet for Anne and Emily who express themselves in character descriptions, poetry, novels and short stories, essays and, on occasion, even in obituaries. Emily, in particular, writes out her feelings when she feels unable to express them orally.

Through her creation of a largely female world that is both enriched and constricted by its narrative subjects and forms, Montgomery offers a variety of interpretations of the role narrative played in the lives of Maritime women. Unlike social science explorations of gossip that too often present it only as a form of social control, Montgomery does not create a single vision. Rather, her presentation is multi-stranded. Narrative exchange with the social opportunity and entertainment it affords are important to the women in her novels. The reader is shown how family and community history allows them an area of expertise and an opportunity to exercise influence. Yet, this network leaves one open to others' interpretations. Those women without the support of close female kin are especially vulnerable in this process and may be forced to resort to a number of strategies, including silence, in order to manage their impression. Just like the emergent quality of oral narrative that Montgomery demonstrates such an understanding of (each narrative has life breathed into it in a specific context by a particular set of people that will never be repeated in exactly the same way again), so she creates the emergent functional quality of gossip. It may have multiple meanings. Gossip may enhance status or diminish it, but Montgomery demonstrates that how one interprets the functions of women's oral narratives depends in large part on how one defines power.[50]

NOTES

1 While Montgomery's writing is yet to be recognized as a source for exploring aspects of women's culture, some folklorists have appreciated its rich portrayal of folk traditions. For example, see Coldwell, "Folklore as Fiction." Montgomery noted her reliance on traditional culture in *The Alpine Path*.
2 Humez, "'We Got Our History Lesson,'" 129.
3 *ENM*, 152–53.

4 *AIn*, 164.

5 *RI*, 20.

6 Significantly most of the young men to whom female characters turn for narrative exchange speak with what might be termed the feminine voice. In the Anne series, Walter is teased by others for writing poetry and being a "sissy," while in the Emily books, both of Emily's male confidantes, Dean – or "Jarback" as he is referred to within the community – and Cousin Jimmy, have disabilities.

7 *EC*, 105.

8 *AIn*, 194.

9 *AIn*, 159.

10 *AIn*, 57.

11 In Volume 2 of her *Selected Journals*, L.M. Montgomery describes many of her visits as a minister's wife. During visits to parishioners, she would often work on needlework projects.

12 Ruth Borker makes this point as well (Borker, "Anthropology," 32–33; see also Harding, "Women and Words," 301).

13 *RI*, 125. Susan Baker returns from a shopping trip to the store with news.

14 *RI*, 289–90. Susan Baker attempts to call the store for news.

15 John Szwed coins the term "information specialist" (Szwed, "Gossip, Drinking and Social Control," 435).

16 *AIn*, 200–1; *RV*, 144.

17 See Jansen, "Classifying Performance," in which he distinguishes levels of "performance" in verbal art. For example, a folktale has cues, including a formulaic opening – "Once upon a time" – that signals audience members that they are to be entertained. A single narrator tells the tale, bringing it alive with various narrative devices, including facial expressions, gestures and imitated dialogue. The "high" performance level here may contrast to that of an anecdote or legend, told without artistic embellishment and pieced together by two or more people within the confines of a larger conversation.

18 Kalčik, "' … Like Ann's Gynecologist,'" 3.

19 See Weigle, "Women as Verbal Artists."

20 For example, see *AIn*, 25.

21 *EQ*, 2.

22 Harding, "Women and Words," 301.

23 Paine, "What Is Gossip About?" 278.

24 See J.A. Robinson, "Personal Narratives Reconsidered."

25 *AIn*, 115–21.

26 *AIn*, 198. For a discussion of rules governing the exchange of gossip, see Abrahams, "A Performance-Centred Approach to Gossip."

27　The *Oxford English Dictionary* indicates that "Gossip" descends from the Old English "godsibb," meaning one who has contracted spiritual affinity with another by acting as a sponsor at a baptism. It also referred to a special acquaintance or friend, especially one of those female friends invited to be part of "shared, secret activity at a woman's lying in."

28　See Handler and Segal, *Jane Austen.*

29　[*AWP*, 95.]

30　*AWP*, 45.

31　Spacks, "In Praise of Gossip," 25.

32　*AIn*, 15.

33　Szwed, "Gossip, Drinking and Social Control," 435.

34　*AWP*, 55.

35　Debora Kodish explores this element of gossip (see Kodish, "Moving towards the Everyday," 100).

36　*RV*, 140.

37　Richard Bauman notes that verbal artists are both admired and feared for their artistic skill and the potential power they hold to subvert and transform the status quo. Bauman observes that often individuals marginal to formal power structures are attracted by verbal performance's inherent potential to bring about change (Bauman, *Verbal Art as Performance*, 45).

38　*EC*, 68.

39　*ENM*, 260.

40　For an example of Mary Vance's tales, see *RV*, 195–96.

41　*AWP*, 15.

42　*RV*, 89–90.

43　Goffman, *The Presentation of Self;* see also Szwed, "Gossip, Drinking and Social Control," 435.

44　*AIn*, 194. Much of Montgomery's drama and humour is based on the levelling that occurs when flaws are exposed in elite and/or pompous community members or when apparent flaws in a central female character are clarified and proved innocent.

45　Lack of close, supportive female kin is central to much of Montgomery's writing. In *Jane of Lantern Hill*, where there is a mother figure, she is presented as ineffectual and unable to protect her daughter against a critical and overbearing grandmother. Rather, Jane is forced to emotionally care for and support her mother.

46　Smith-Rosenberg, "The Female World," 13.

47　*AIn*, 210.

48　Kodish, "Moving towards the Everyday," 100.

49　See *JLH*, 22.

50　See Borker, "Anthropology," 40.

7

L.M. Montgomery's *Rilla of Ingleside*: Intention, Inclusion, Implosion

—— 1994 ——

OWEN DUDLEY EDWARDS

This chapter, reprinted from Mary Henley Rubio's collection *Harvesting Thistles: The Textual Garden of L.M. Montgomery; Essays on Her Novels and Journals*, reconsiders the cultural significance of *Rilla of Ingleside* by placing it in concert not only with Montgomery's journals but also with non-Canadian authors such as Tolstoi, Joyce, and Browning. Owen Dudley Edwards, a Reader in Commonwealth and American History at the University of Edinburgh (now retired), is the author of numerous books and the editor of several critical editions of work by Sir Arthur Conan Doyle and Oscar Wilde. He also contributed (in collaboration with Jennifer H. Litster) a chapter to *L.M. Montgomery and Canadian Culture* (1999). In his most recent book, *British Children's Fiction in the Second World War* (2008), he refers to *Rilla of Ingleside* as a book that "may well be the best children's novel to emerge from the First World War."[1]

Rilla of Ingleside is L.M. Montgomery's *War and Peace*: Anne's poet son Walter is its Prince Andrew meeting a soldier's death with idealism remolded in war's cauldron, and his youngest sister Rilla its Peter/Pierre before whose eyes the home front of an entire nation seems to pass. To say that Montgomery is no Tolstoi is irrelevant snobbiness: neither is anyone else. And if Montgomery's Canada is no Russia, the societies are comparable in their vastness, their diffuseness, their centrifugal forces, the youth of their expansion, the antiquity of some of their traditions, the alienation of their intellectuals. Montgomery set *Rilla* in her native Prince Edward Island with all the other Anne books (save in part

Anne of the Island): but she wrote it in Leaskdale, Ontario, whence it derived some of its data, from time to time echoing the records and reactions in her journals.

Montgomery's celebration of Canadian participation in support of the United Kingdom's cause in World War I may seem far removed from Tolstoi's pacifism, yet it may not be as far as it seems. Montgomery is no philosopher of history akin to Tolstoi, yet her focus on Susan Baker, the maid-of-all-work, seems unconsciously to answer Tolstoi's demand for the kind of sources historians should seek. And in one respect Montgomery has the advantage of Tolstoi in historians' eyes: he was writing from fifty years' distance the greatest historical novel ever written, whereas she wrote her version of 1914–18 between 11 March 1919 and 24 August 1920.

Montgomery's keen observation, social perceptions, community cartography, delicious irony, catalysis in comedy, infectious pathos make her works admirably serviceable to the historian with the sense to use her.[2] In earlier writings before *Rilla* she had recorded much that was particular to Prince Edward Island, to Canadians, to Presbyterians, to Scots, and to village culture in general. But *Rilla* is much more specific, and much more inescapable. To Sandra Gwyn in *Tapestry of War: A Private View of Canadians in the Great War*, "Though sentimental and jingoistic, it is in some ways her most interesting book, virtually the only Canadian work of fiction to describe everyday life on the home front from direct experience."[3] It is a work of much more scientific precision, much greater control over source-material and its deployment; at the same time it loses some of the P.E.I. context in its valuable but silent dependence on Ontario experience.

Mary Rubio calls *Rilla* "underrated."[4] Her own publication (with Elizabeth Waterston) of the *Journals* covering the Great War and *Rilla*'s subsequent creation has for the first time put the book into its historical context, to the great enhancement of its scholarly appeal. Other scholars such as Elizabeth Rollins Epperly (*The Fragrance of Sweet-Grass*) have made important appraisals of its critical stature. Montgomery would not have been surprised at its long sojourn in the cold. "I don't suppose it will be much of a success, for the public are said to be sick of anything connected with the war," she noted on 3 September 1921, on receiving published copies. "But at least I did my best to reflect the life we lived in Canada during those four years ... It is the first one I have written with a purpose."[5] But she "had expected" the shortfall of 2000–3000 in its sales as against those of "the other books."[6]

On 30 December 1928, Montgomery reacted angrily to an anti-war critic in her *Journals*: "I wrote *Rilla* not to 'glorify war' but to glorify the courage and patriotism and self-sacrifice it evoked. War is a hellish thing and some day it may be done away with – though human nature being what it is that day is far distant. But universal peace *may* come and *may* be a good thing. But there will no longer be any great literature or great art. Either these things are given by the high gods as a compensation – or else they are growths that have to be fertilized with blood."[7] She gave her final verdict in her journals on 13 July 1936 after re-reading *Rilla*: "I have decided it is the best book I ever wrote."[8] The rest of this essay will address three questions: What did Montgomery want put into *Rilla of Ingleside*? What did she agree to put into it? What went into it in spite of herself?

Intention: What Did She Want Put into *Rilla*?

Montgomery had been at work on *Anne of the Island* since 1 September 1913 and had been writing it since 18 April 1914, when World War I broke out; she finished it on 20 November 1914. *Anne's House of Dreams* she began on 16 June 1916 and finished on 5 October; *Rainbow Valley* took her from 19 January 1917 to 26 December 1918. Elizabeth Rollins Epperly points out that the last is a celebration of the youth "who were to mature into the soldiers and the workers of the war" and thus another "response to war"[9] – and the "Piper" vision of Walter and its proclamation at the book's end by Jem formally assert as much. But in another sense all the books written during the war have been war books. Montgomery is variously celebrating intellectual ambition, old tradition, democratic and hierarchical social patterns, the value of convention and the rebellions it induces, and so forth: and Canada is to be seen as fighting for all of these things. Jem will be wounded and Walter will die for the Canada whose ideals are represented both by their mother's acquisition of a university degree and by Mrs. Rachel Lynde's disapproval of higher education. Montgomery, like her master Sir Walter Scott, believed passionately in cultural conservation.

But the main unifying business of Montgomery's earlier wartime novels is to prepare the way for the theme of Death in *Rilla of Ingleside*, particularly for the sacrifice of Walter. Death ("Kindertotenliede") is a famous staple of Victorian fiction, headed by Little Nell in Dickens's *The Old Curiosity Shop*, Little Eva in Harriet Beecher Stowe's *Uncle Tom's Cabin*, and Beth in Louisa May Alcott's *Good Wives*. Montgomery is conscious of these traditions, but has no use for them for their own sake; having begun the war with the agony of the still-birth of her son Hugh (13 August 1914) she saw no reason either to shield her child readers from the existence of Death or to wallow in it. Death to her wartime readers, child or adult, was a fact, and she invited them to face it with a sympathetic but not schmaltzy eye. We see Ruby Gillis dying in *Anne of the Island*, learn of Kenneth West's horrific death as an eight-year-old under the eyes of his sister Leslie (Moore) in *Anne's House of Dreams*, and witness the birth and death of Anne's first baby Joyce.

So *Rilla of Ingleside* readers knew what was ahead of them. But its opening abrupt announcement of the death of Marilla Cuthbert symbolises a death of "Avonlea" as far as the book and Anne's family are concerned: we learn that Billy Andrews, Anne's first proposal (via his sister Jane), has a son who enlists, and that Jack or Jock, a son (hitherto unknown to us) of Diana, is severely wounded wherefore Anne visits her. Nothing more is heard from Avonlea. It is an almost savage sacrifice to ask of readers. All we are left with is our own fantasies (mine being of Anthony Pye drinking Ernest Hemingway under the table). The book breathes a wind of death from the battlefront, but little is said of specific casualties. Nor does this depart from realism. Death pervades the book, because we know we are waiting for one death, in which Canada's 50,000 dead will be subsumed. Walter is a Christlike sacrifice and in Walter they die.

Montgomery had doomed Walter from long before his first appearance in *Rainbow Valley*. In one of Rilla's few precursors in war fiction for girls, Martha Finley's *Elsie's Womanhood* (1875), the likeable Walter Dinsmore hesitates to enlist for the Confederacy, is called a coward by his loathsome brother and mother, decides after three days to join up, takes a brief emblematic farewell of his home, is killed at Shiloh and has previously contrived that a last letter will posthumously reach his sympathetic half-niece Elsie.

Montgomery restricts sibling rivalry to Jem's confession to Rilla after his return: "Afraid! I was afraid scores of times – sick with fear, – I who used to laugh at Walter when he was frightened. Do you know, Walter was *never* frightened after he got to the front. *Realities* never scared him – only his imagination could do that. His colonel told me that Walter was the bravest man in the regiment. Rilla, I never *realized* that Walter was dead till I came back home. You don't know how I miss him now – you folks here have got used to it in a sense – but it's all fresh to me."[10] Thereby Montgomery records a vital, and neglected, factor in the destructive reappraisals by ex-combatants: they knew less of the effects of war than did those on the home front, and its total impact on them was postponed, often much longer. She also showed much more awareness of the varieties of courage and fear than her fellow-votaries of the war effort. And it is this delicately-graded analysis the historian requires, rather than simple classification that X was for war and Y against it (where much of the general critical debate seems to end up).

But Walter is also namesake to Anne's father Walter Shirley, an evident salute to Walter Scott, father of romanticism as a form of literary manipulation. *Rob Roy* was one of the three novels in the house where she grew up "and I pored over them until I knew whole chapters by heart."[11] Its heroine is Di Vernon, whence Diana Barry. In *Anne of the Island* Anne writes her first story, "Averil's Atonement," and Diana, permitted to name the little hired boy, chooses "Robert Ray." Later Anne remarks: "I must have *one* pathetic scene in it ... I might let *Robert Ray* be injured in an accident and have a death scene."[12]

Diana vetoes this (at the cost of any significance for Robert Ray in the story) but it seems a clear revelation that after the outbreak of war and the death of her son Hugh, Montgomery had determined on a plot with the death of a character linked to Scott. Once we meet Walter in *Rainbow Valley* we are promptly told "he was secretly hard at work on an epic, strikingly resembling 'Marmion' in some things, if not in others" (which, given Marmion's sex-life, is unusually ribald for Montgomery).[13] Scott seems omnipresent in *Rilla*: when Jem enlists, Rilla writes in her diary:

> "'He goes to do what I had done
> Had Douglas' daughter been his son,'"

and was sure she meant it. If she were a boy of course she would go, too! She hadn't the least doubt of that.

This is promptly counterpointed by Walter's self-reproach "I – I should have been a girl."[14]

Walter is the hero of *Rilla of Ingleside* (with Rilla and Susan as its heroines), but the whole book is intended as a refutation of his transient thesis of courage as a male monopoly, and his own courage in facing the horror of war implies a feminine quality superior to unthinking masculinity.

Walter wrote that some one had sent him an envelope containing a white feather.

"I deserved it, Rilla. I felt that I ought to put it on and wear it – proclaiming myself to all Redmond the coward I know I am. The boys of my year are going – going. Every day two or three of them join up. Some days I *almost* make up my mind to do it – and then I see myself thrusting a bayonet through another man – some woman's husband or sweetheart or son – perhaps the father of little children – I see myself lying alone torn and mangled, burning with thirst on a cold, wet field, surrounded by dead and dying men – and I know I *never* can. I can't face even the thought of it. How could I face the reality? There are times when I wish I had never been born. Life has always seemed such a beautiful thing to me – I wanted to make it more beautiful – and now it is a hideous thing."[15]

Montgomery had always testified to the alienation of the imaginative or the creative from society: not necessarily painfully, and frequently with some of the laughs, credit and sympathy going to the anti-imaginative side (seen in Susan with her anti-poetry biases). But here she looks much more directly at alienation in wartime before the general pattern of poets' disillusionment. Walter is no Rupert Brooke or Charles Peguy or Patrick Pearse to rush to martyrdom; his real-life counterparts are figures of whom Montgomery surely had no notion, like Wilfrid Owen and Isaac Rosenberg. Like Walter, neither enlisted until 1915, and both were killed in action.

The parallels with Owen are at times striking: the bayonet passage, for instance, seems to anticipate Owen's "Strange Meeting." Walter's own war poem, "The Piper," obviously echoes John McCrae's "In Flanders Fields" in impact and reputation: Montgomery had met the Guelph doctor before he took service as a medical officer in France (where he died of pneumonia on 27 January 1918). McCrae's poem first appeared on 6 December 1915, and Walter's around the same time, with similar results:

The poem was a short, poignant little thing. In a month it had carried Walter's name to every corner of the globe. Everywhere it was copied – in metropolitan dailies and little village weeklies, in profound reviews and "agony columns," in Red Cross appeals and Government recruiting propaganda. Mothers and sisters wept over it, young lads thrilled to it, the whole great heart of humanity caught it up as an epitome of all the pain and hope and pity and purpose of the mighty conflict, crystallized in three brief immortal verses. A Canadian lad in the Flanders trenches had written the one great poem of the war.[16]

Why the unknown Canadian doctor should have eclipsed Housman and Hardy, Kipling and Newbolt, Brooke newly dead and Sassoon/Owen/Rosenberg/Blunden yet to come is another matter: in a sense it might seem his Canadian origin immunised him from the subtler disillusionment or the metropolitan sophistication eroding the force of British bards. British poetry had its revenge when Paul Fussell, in his magisterial and nearly (but not quite) definitive study of World War I poets, savaged "In Flanders Fields" for culminating in "a propaganda argument ... words like vicious and stupid would not seem to go too far ... against a negotiated peace";[17] and he contrasts it with the beauty and integrity of Rosenberg's "Break of Day in the Trenches" from mid-1916, which Fussell salutes as the best single poem of the war. Fussell is himself vulnerable to a charge of cheapening his just praise of Rosenberg by this preliminary hatchet-work. But McCrae, little though he knew Montgomery, admirably represented her sentiments in her journal and those she ascribed to Susan Baker. At the close of *Rilla* there is a strong suggestion Walter's poem has the McCrae text:

" ... We have won the victory – but oh, what a price we have paid!"
"Not too high a price for freedom," said Gertrude softly. "Do you think it was, Rilla?"
"No," said Rilla, under her breath. She was seeing a little white cross on a battlefield of France. "No – not if those of us who live will show ourselves worthy of it – if we 'keep faith.'"
"We *will* keep faith," said Gertrude. She rose suddenly. A silence fell around the table, and in the silence Gertrude repeated Walter's famous poem "The Piper."[18]

But while the intention here is to make the reader – at least the reader of 1920 – think of "In Flanders Fields," Montgomery is surely without the propaganda-intent which Fussell deplores, since the war is over. Montgomery, if not McCrae, gave the later lines of "In Flanders Fields" a purpose beyond war, the nobler end of consolidating war sacrifice into a lasting peace. Future advocates of world order such as the diplomatic historian Thomas A. Bailey (in *Woodrow Wilson and the Great Betrayal*) would use the poem in the same way.

Similarly, while the use of Walter in the novel suggests cunning deployment of pacifism to strengthen war propaganda, as John Buchan did so smoothly with Launcelot Wake in *Mr. Standfast* (1919), it was only armistice that prevented the latter book counting in the world war. *Rilla*, not started until 1919, used Walter to explain that Canadian soldiers had not been bloodcrazed fanatics. Montgomery was as credulous respecting German atrocities after the war as during it, but even so, as Mary Rubio said, it "shows the force that propaganda and war media play in the formation of people's attitudes."[19] Among other ways it did so in recording the cruelty of people's attitudes to the initially non-combatant Walter.

Rilla's own great achievement is to assert the hunger for life perpetually struggling to assert itself in the omnipresence of death. Most soldiers' songs, and even soldiers' sexual escapades, assert as much: they want to counterbalance their own imminent deaths by willing themselves a posterity ("In Flanders Fields" does this, in a way). Rilla's adoption of little Jims is a home-front version of this, as well as a recognition that Montgomery in fact considers the evacuee problem, and argues that it can only be solved by the growth of love for the new community-consciousness engendered by war. She also shows, in Rilla's misadventures over wartime concerts, how new priorities and old hostilities reassert and alter themselves under war's demands. All of this is handled with optimism, but with realism: Rilla begins the war as a selfish, self-pitying little teenage emptyhead, and she gains stature with the challenge she faces. Yet the war also transforms Anne into a largely useless neurasthenic, Gilbert into a pedantic, cynical, nit-picking sadist: while his sons try to score off the Germans, he tries to score off the maidservant, Susan Baker, who is worth a hundred of him. "Anne's will be a slow, happy, and peaceful obsolescence" prophesied the *London Times Literary Supplement* on 27 May 1920 in a review of *Rainbow Valley*.[20] The magnitude of its error is the symbol of revolution which war brought and to which *Rilla* attests.

Inclusion: What Did She Agree to Put into It?

Montgomery consented to her own inclusion of data beyond her intentions, but how consciously she did so we may never know. Did she realize how far she was recording Canada's self-discovery as a nation?

Rilla's own role as symbol of Canada's discovery of her powers of self-sufficiency was an obvious consequence of Montgomery's own recent motherhood of three children, loss of one, and (on 25 January 1919) her witness to the death of Frede Campbell, her cousin and closest friend. Her husband's post-war psychological collapse underlined the principle of feminine self-reliance and assertion of leadership, thematic in the Anne stories since Montgomery wrote the first three words of *Anne of Green Gables*: "Mrs. Rachel Lynde."[21] Mrs. Lynde's death is one of the many unspoken presumptions in the Avonlea holocaust darkening *Rilla* (even though she surely greeted eternity with the highly appropriate theological observation "that's what"); but in Rilla's case the usual feminine assertiveness is thrown into relief by the male relegation to the supposed female preserves of carping and vituperation. Sometimes this may appear desirable, as in Norman Douglas's manhandling of "Whiskers-on-the-Moon" for publicly uttering pacifist prayer. But it is Susan who turns confrontation into eradication by pursuing the pacifist-turned-suitor from the house with a "huge, smoking," iron dye-pot.[22] Men do determine some significant events in the earlier books, if only by constructive and positive criticism (Matthew, Mr. Harrison, Gilbert, Captain Jim, Owen Ford). In *Rilla*, apart from Gilbert's decree that Rilla must care for Jims (in itself an abdication), men remaining in P.E.I. are largely useless. The most visible one is Walter, who proclaims his own uselessness. Rilla – the adroit use of whose journal makes her Montgomery's own observant wartime voice recreated from her own journals – is "young Canadian woman." Susan is "mature Canadian woman," all the more that her moment of apotheosis in Gilbert's belated attempt at homage can only achieve the banality "from first to last of this business you have been a brick!"[23] Language is vital in *Rilla*, and male inadequacy within it symbolises the wealth of female deployment of it – headed, of course, by the author's deployment of language.

But Susan is also Canada herself. The women are the country, other than the embattled youth overseas. As such, the chosen representative, quite significantly, is elderly, maternal (without necessarily being a child-bearing mother), unattractive, working-class, resourceful, self-reliant. Montgomery seems to have grown much more fiercely democratic in her attitudes during the war. On 10 December 1916 she told her journal: "And Lloyd George is Premier of England – the ruler of the British Empire. It took the Roumanian crisis to bring that about. Nothing less could have put the foot of the Welsh lawyer on the neck of the aristocrats of England."[24] And in *Rilla* aristocracy is the enemy, as shown in the sneering, paternalistic dog named "Sir Wilfrid Laurier" which belongs to the equally offensive Whiskers-on-the-Moon. It was personally a grief to Montgomery to find herself politically opposed to her old idol, but the dog's dialogue with Little Dog Monday, who waits throughout the war for Jem at the railway station (a derivation from Odysseus's faithful Argos in Homer), offers Canada the choice of (a presumably American-style) lap-dog or one which represents self-chosen patriotic sacrifice:

> Sir Wilfrid remarked condescendingly,
> "Why do you haunt this old shed when you might lie on the hearthrug at Ingleside and live on the fat of the land? Is it a pose? Or a fixed idea?"
> Whereat Dog Monday, laconically:–
> "I have a tryst to keep."[25]

(Ironically, the antecedent is by an American, Alan Seeger, who had died in 1916 fighting for France, and who wrote, "I have a rendezvous with Death," the second most famous World War I poem.) The authoritarianism of Whiskers-on-the-Moon is specifically male chauvinist, first dictating that his daughter shall not even see her sweetheart when he volunteers (a neat, propagandistic reversal of the classic literary pattern whereby Father forbids his daughter to see her non-combatant suitor), and finally seeking Susan's hand in marriage to enslave her in his service. Canada's acceptance of war is hence portrayed as self-liberation in feminine terms.

Susan's centrality to *Rilla* is above all as spokesperson for the real sentiments of Canada, and her voice serves as its own democratic declaration: she is very marginal in *Anne's House of Dreams*, and even in *Rainbow Valley* much of the humour is at her expense, enabling Anne to be quizzical and worldly-wise towards Susan, portrayed as having some Philistine qualities. With Anne largely off-stage in *Rilla*, Susan comes into her own: there is almost a suggestion that Anne fails the war test and Susan supremely rises to it. Anti-Americanism is nothing new for the Anne books, but again it is Susan who levels the charge of selfish elitism against Woodrow Wilson: "'And I also see that Woodrow Wilson is going to write another note. I wonder,' concluded Susan, with the bitter irony she had of late begun to use when referring to the poor president, 'if that man's schoolmaster is alive.'"[26] Canadian hostility to American neutrality thus becomes for Montgomery the insistence that the USA is not to be granted the primacy in democratic sentiment. Susan is a brilliant vehicle by which to make the point: the author may have been amused to notice that American reviewers of *Rilla* were condescending towards Susan (no doubt in retaliation for her sentiments to the USA) whereas some British found themselves democratised by her into self-identification.

But Canada's normally negative non-British, non-American stance becomes positive with its stress that participation in the war is Canada's choice, and thereby Canada's declaration of psychological independence: "'*I* knew this war was coming,' said Mrs. Norman triumphantly. '*I* saw it coming right along. *I* could have told all those stupid Englishmen what was ahead of them.'" The criticism of Britain is war's liberation of Canadian sentiment, all the more when myths of British invincibility crumble:

> perhaps they all shared subconsciously in Susan's belief that "the thin grey line" was unbreakable, even by the victorious rush of Germany's ready millions. At any rate, when the terrible day came – the first of many terrible days – with the news that the British army was driven back they stared at each other in blank dismay.
> "It – it can't be true," gasped Nan, taking a brief refuge in temporary incredulity ...
> "'A broken, a beaten, but not a demoralized, army,'" muttered the doctor, from a London dispatch. "Can it be England's army of which such a thing is said?"[27]

And so, it becomes Canada's war, with Susan and her employers internationalising themselves to understand it. This is Montgomery's own testimony of her personal reactions, amazed, like Susan, at her own absorption in Greek court politics: "Not a move on the great chess board of king or bishop or pawn escaped Susan, who had once read only Glen St. Mary notes. 'There was a time,' she said sorrowfully, 'when I did not care what happened outside of P.E. Island, and now a king cannot have a toothache in Russia or China but it worries me. It may be broadening to the mind, as the doctor said, but it is very painful to the feelings.'"[28] And nations, like other children, are born in pain.

Implosion: What Went into the Novel in Spite of Herself?

What did Montgomery attestify in *Rilla* against her own will? We must respect the author's intention, but historians at least – if not literary critics – must audit what they find in the author's holdings, however unwanted or unwittingly acquired. She would have been horrified to learn that Rilla's final "Yeth" to her inexplicably tardy swain Kenneth Ford, with whose proposal the book ends,[29] would be matched in the ending to James Joyce's *Ulysses*, published a few months after *Rilla of Ingleside*. Nor was it mere coincidence. In each case the end is affirmation of love, creativity, and harvest after a man's long voyage home. Joyce and Montgomery had each sought their Homeric antecedent, Montgomery finding hers in the Argos-incident where, for once, Joyce had gleaned little. The significance of "Yeth" and "yes I said yes I will Yes" – one monolithic, the other ending the longest sentence in literature – stands as hope of humanity's future after war, clearly in Montgomery's case but – as she helps us to see – implicitly in Joyce's also.

Rilla of Ingleside is far less comfortable in its support of the war on at least one level than its critics have imagined. However entertaining Norman Douglas's abuse of and Susan's dye-kettle attack on Whiskers-on-the-Moon, the persecution of Walter before he enlists is very ugly, and it suggests a social sickness beneath the pro-war patriotism. A much sicker symptom surfaces when little Bruce Meredith murders his beloved pet kitten to persuade God to bring Jem back alive. This is a powerful passage, and if Walter's story can leave readers in tears, the kitten story seems deliberately designed to make them ill: "It oughtn't to take longer'n a week, mother. Oh, mother, Stripey was such a nice little cat. He purred so pretty. Don't you think God *ought* to like him enough to let us have Jem?"[30] But whatever Montgomery's intention, her effect here is subversive. She shows that with the impact of war, God has been transformed in children's eyes into the Carthaginian Moloch, to whom children were sacrificed for military gain.

More directly intended, but no less questioning to conventional propaganda, is *Rilla*'s revelation of despondent and even despairing moods. And the book makes a savage attack on Canadian smugness: "'Good news!' said Miss Oliver bitterly. 'I wonder if the women whose men have been killed for it will call it good news. Just because our own men are not on that part of the front we are rejoicing as if the victory had cost no lives.'"[31]

Finally, it may be that the most subversive thing in *Rilla of Ingleside* is the subject of Walter's famous poem, "The Piper." The Piper firmly originates in Browning's poem: we learn early in *Rainbow Valley* that "best of all he [Walter] loved the stories of the Pied Piper and the San Greal [*sic*]." A Galahad identity and a Grail quest are appropriate for Walter, but Montgomery wisely takes them no farther. But the passage develops the Piper image: "'Some day,' said Walter dreamily, looking afar into the sky, 'the Pied Piper will come over the hill up there and down Rainbow

Valley, piping merrily and sweetly. And I will follow him – follow him down to the shore – down to the sea – away from you all. I don't think I'll want to go – Jem will want to go – it will be such an adventure – but I won't. Only I'll *have* to – the music will call and call and call me until I *must* follow.'"[32] This is simply good psychology disguised as vision, such as a creative writer like Montgomery well knew. But as the two novels progress, fancy is taken to have been a vision. *Rainbow Valley* concludes:

> He began to speak dreamily, partly because he wanted to thrill his companions a little, partly because something apart from him seemed to be speaking through his lips.
>
> "The Piper is coming nearer," he said, "he is nearer than he was that evening I saw him before. His long, shadowy cloak is blowing around him. He pipes – he pipes – and we must follow – Jem and Carl and Jerry and I – round and round the world. Listen – listen – can't you hear his wild music?"[33]

But what is the implication of Browning's "The Pied Piper of Hamelin" if we attach it to the Canadian cause in World War I? An older generation of rulers, perhaps in Britain, have refused to meet their obligations because of their own corruption and self-indulgence. A war machine has obliterated enemies; uncontrolled, it demands its price, failing which it lures away the youth of Canada on completely false grounds, transporting them to a remote land. The propaganda ("the war to end war" / "making the world a safe for democracy" / etc.) has a horrible ring in retrospect of the following lines in Browning's poem:

> For he led us, he said, to a joyous land,
> Joining the town and just at hand,
> Where waters gushed and fruit-trees grew,
> And flowers put forth a fairer hue,
> And everything was strange and new;
> The sparrows were brighter than peacocks here,
> And their dogs outran our fallow deer,
> And honey-bees had lost their stings,
> And horses were born with eagles' wings ... [34]

The Browning passage casts its shadow on what Walter later writes in *Rilla of Ingleside*, giving a terrible ambiguity to the central image of the Piper:

"Rilla, I saw the Piper coming down the Valley with a shadowy host behind him. The others thought I was only pretending – but I *saw* him for just one moment. And, Rilla, last night I saw him again. I was doing sentry-go and I saw him marching across No-man's-land from our trenches to the German trenches – the same tall shadowy form, piping weirdly, – and behind him followed boys in khaki. Rilla, I tell you I *saw* him – it was no fancy – no illusion. I *heard* his music, and then – he was *gone*. But I *had* seen him – and I knew what it meant – I knew that I was among those who followed him.

"Rilla, the Piper will pipe me 'west' [to death] tomorrow. I feel sure of this ... "[35]

Thus, on one level, Walter is a boy following the Canadian wartime ideal of blood-sacrifice. But on another level, he is a boy lured to his death by a lying Piper.[36]

NOTES

1 [Edwards, *British Children's Fiction*, 185.]
2 I am grateful to all my students at the University of Edinburgh for their aid in analyzing *Rilla of Ingleside* as a course document in "North American Literature and Society," as well as to my late mother, and to my sisters and daughters, for preliminary dissection of Montgomery. I am also greatly indebted to Jennifer Litster, who is preparing a doctoral thesis on Montgomery under my supervision and who kindly offered me comments on this paper, and to Mary Rubio, an endlessly resourceful benefactor.
3 Gwyn, *Tapestry of War*, 165.
4 M.H. Rubio, "Lucy Maud Montgomery," [40].
5 Montgomery, 3 September 1921 [in *SJLMM*, 3: 17].
6 Montgomery, 28 February 1922 [in *SJLMM*, 3: 43].
7 Montgomery, 30 December 1928, in *SJLMM*, 3: 387–88.
8 Montgomery, 13 July 1936 [in *SJLMM*, 5: 80].
9 Epperly, *The Fragrance of Sweet-Grass*, [95].
10 *RI*, [347].
11 *AP*, 49.
12 *AIs*, [87].
13 [*RV*, 18.]
14 *RI*, [57, 61].
15 *RI*, [106–7].

16 *RI*, [215].
17 Fussell, *The Great War*, 250.
18 *RI*, [338].
19 M.H. Rubio, "Lucy Maud Montgomery," [40].
20 [This review appears in Volume 3 of *The L.M. Montgomery Reader*.]
21 [*AGG*, 1.]
22 [*RI*, 276.]
23 [*RI*, 314.]
24 Montgomery, 10 December 1916, in *SJLMM*, 2: 197.
25 *RI*, [209].
26 *RI*, [121].
27 *RI*, [64, 78].
28 *RI*, [189].
29 [*RI*, 350.]
30 *RI*, [331].
31 *RI*, [182].
32 *RV*, [54, 55].
33 *RV*, [224].
34 [Browning, *Robert Browning's Poetry*, 81.]
35 *RI*, [245].
36 [In addition to the texts cited here, the original version of this chapter lists the following works consulted in the bibliography: Buitenhuis, *The Great War of Words*; Cadogan and Craig, *Women and Children First*; Cohen, *Journey to the Trenches*; Fussell, *The Bloody Game*; McCrae, "*In Flanders Fields*"; Owen, *Collected Poems of Wilfrid Owen*; Parsons, *Men Who March Away*.]

8

Decoding L.M. Montgomery's Journals/ Encoding a Critical Practice for Women's Private Literature

—— 1994 ——

HELEN M. BUSS

Helen M. Buss, now Professor Emerita of English at the University of Calgary, published this article in *Essays on Canadian Writing* shortly after the release of her book-length study *Mapping Our Selves: Canadian Women's Autobiography in English* (1993). She describes self-consciously her own reading practice of Montgomery's *Selected Journals*, of which three volumes had by then been released, focusing specifically on the narrative of Montgomery's intense entanglements with two men that she never intended to marry and on the generic tropes that she appears to rely on in telling the tale even while writing in a diary, which Buss calls a place "of improvisation, experimentation, and collation." Buss's later books include the co-edited collection (with Marlene Kadar) *Working in Women's Archives: Women's Private Literature and Archival Documents* (2001), which includes a chapter on Montgomery's journals by Mary Henley Rubio, and the book-length study *Repossessing the World: Reading Memoirs by Contemporary Women* (2002).

> The unconscious of the work (*not*, it must be insisted, of the author) is constructed in the moment of its entry into literary form, in the gap between the ideological project and the specifically literary form.
>
> – Catherine Belsey[1]

In seeking a "critical practice" rich enough for reading L.M. Montgomery's diaries/journals, my efforts are complicated by four challenges: the problem of expressing a female gendered subjectivity in a male tradition of humanist and poststructuralist ideas of the autobiographical subject; the marginal place of private literature outside the literary canon and its critical practices; the exclusion of the text's writer as a human subject in current critical discourse (that parenthetical individual whom Belsey is careful to distance from her practice); and last, but certainly not least, my own construction as a critical reader.

Sidonie Smith speaks to the first challenge when, in *A Poetics of Women's Autobiography*, she traces the repeated silencing of the female in the history of the West's philosophical/linguistic symbol systems from Aristotle to Lacan and describes how the continuing characterization of woman as Aquinas's "misbegotten man" enforces an "injunction against woman's legitimate claim to public discourse and the power it commands[, which] has profound ramifications for her engagement in literary self-representation." To mediate this oppression in language, to "situate woman's *bios*, her *autē*, her *graphia*," it is necessary to uncover "her reading between the lines of that story," of the misbegotten-man narrative that constructs all women in our culture.[2] Smith is concerned only with public autobiographies by women, and, while she suggests important strategies, my transfer of her critical practice to private writings demands that I do considerable "reading between the lines" myself, of the kind that involves overcoming the second challenge that I encounter as a reader of women's diaries: that is, I cannot effectively carry out the reading of private literature with the critical practices that I have learned in reading the discourses constructed for public consumption as "literary" texts.

To meet this challenge, I need a critical practice that overcomes the profound split that our culture and literary tradition have made between public and private genres. I am discontent, though not in disagreement, with deconstructive methodologies developed from and for public texts because these practices have as their aim the dismantling of an ideological apparatus rather than the construction of an oppressed subjectivity. As well, as a reader of texts meant for public consumption during the life of the writer, the first discovery I make, with chagrin, is that a first reading of many diaries, as Margo Culley warns, "may mean nothing to the reader." In order to make meaning, I must engage in an activity "akin to putting together pieces of a puzzle – remembering clues and supplying the missing pieces, linking details apparently unrelated in the diarist's mind, and decoding 'encoded' materials."[3] Culley's quoted reference to "encoded" materials alludes to the theoretical strategies that some critics of private literature use, strategies that go under the name "speech act theory." These strategies are part of an attempt to connect the more interactive world of speech and the less directly interactive public world of writing, from which all speakers who are also readers learn at least part of their ability in language. Traditional critical practice separates the world of improvisational daily speech and the literary construction of language. Speech act theory allows for reading strategies based on their integration. As Sandy Petrey observes in *Speech Acts and Literary Theory*, "This socialized criticism can address two principal topics, the status of literature in general and the status of the separate utterances making up a given text."[4] Although Petrey is concerned with removing literary texts from their privileged aesthetic status and considering them as similar to all linguistic performance (a project held in common with ideologically based theorists), speech act theory can help the critic to read the diary, which seems to emerge in part from the private, daily world of improvisational speech, as literary text while developing a critical practice that accounts for the previously unreadable "utterances" of this literary genre.

Petrey acknowledges the work of Richard Ohmann and Mary Louise Pratt in the development of the link between speech act theory and literary texts. It is Pratt's work on the place of the "hearer" that especially serves my reading needs. Pratt emphasizes the reader's "active" role: communication is a cooperative venture in which the hearer, "in decoding the speaker's utterance, will make all the deductions and inferences necessary" so that communication takes place. If the hearer did not supply all sorts of codes of reference, then we would all take a long time to say anything at all, for "The coherence of any conversation, text, or extended utterance almost invariably depends a great deal on implicatures." Pratt describes hearers as supplying all sorts of implicature for the success of the speech act, especially causal and chronological sequence, but obviously also ideological viewpoints, cultural assumptions, and contextual elements. When she transfers speech act theory to literature, the "hearer" becomes the reader and "implicature" becomes the codes of reference that the "active" reader brings to the text. She asserts that

> There are enormous advantages to talking about literature in this way, ... for literary works, like all our communicative activities, are context-dependent. Literature itself is a speech context. And as with any utterance, the way people produce and understand literary works depends enormously on unspoken, culturally-shared

knowledge of the rules, conventions, and expectations that are in play when language is used in that context.[5]

Ironically, the reason that students of the diary form find speech act theory's terms – such as "encoding," "decoding," and "implicature" – so useful is because literary readers need to become more conscious of their "unspoken" rules, the shared conventions and expectations shaped by public literary discourses: they must come to know new modes of implicature in order to meet new generic needs. As Petrey observes,

> We react to a given sentence – "There was a knock at the door" will do – in distinct ways that vary with genre. Knocks on doors aren't the same in detective stories, horror fiction, Harlequin romances, and hard-core pornography, and this spectrum of generic distinctions is directly comparable to the spectrum of illocutionary [the social force of utterances] distinctions available for a non-literary utterance … "There was a knock at the door" puzzles, frightens, thrills, or titillates not in itself but through its generic matrix. In literary as in non-literary discourse, communal procedures are paramount.[6]

Petrey's reference to the difference that genre makes to illocutionary force is salutary. My experience in reading diaries is that this genre invites my "active" involvement, and I must bring with me, yet be able to discard at any moment, all the possible generic assumptions that I have learned as a literary reader. Indeed, a knock on the door in a diary may need implicatures from all the above-named genres, because diaries, as places of improvisation, experimentation, and collation, make use of all the discourses that a writer knows. In addition, because women's diaries are often written not in the recesses of sacred studies but at kitchen tables, on back porches, or in shared bedrooms, knocks on doors can have more than thrills or titillation in store. Montgomery wrote in all these places, and, when she did retreat, she was frequently interrupted. (Her young son once beat on the door until in frustration she decided that it was less interrupting to have it open.) Thus, in journals and in diaries, the knock on the door has a real-life illocutionary meaning that speech act theory can help me to account for, not just in terms of social action in the life of the diarist but also in terms of the writing moment. If the diarist is describing a knock on the door in the moment of relating it to me, her reader, then she is refusing to get up and answer it. A woman's encoding of the concurrence of knock and writing, aided by my decoding with the appropriate implicatures, may make manifest the ways in which female subjectivity must read "between the lines" of the story that the tradition of the "misbegotten man" has written for us.

Speech act theory provides another facilitating strategy that much current literary theory refuses: a means to consider the writer as a human subject in a more nuanced way than in critical practice that emphasizes the author as a function of the text. In this way, speech act theory speaks to my third and fourth difficulties as a reader of diaries. Part of my project as a feminist is to take account of the human subjects who wrote diaries, to be part of what Domna Stanton calls "a global and essential therapeutic purpose: to constitute the female subject."[7] Critical practices in literary studies teach me to "insist" on the separation of writer and narrator, whereas diaries encourage the conflation of the two. Speech act theory helps me to observe the development of the human subject as writer through the strategies of the narrator. In this regard, speech act theory helps me by allowing me to take into account the active involvement of speakers or, what speech act theorists call, in both oral storytelling and writing acts, "narrators." For example, speech act theorists describe four kinds of narrators who are "*knowingly*" disobedient to rules of communal practice, speakers who "*violate* a maxim," "*opt out*" of rules, "*clash*" with rules of evidence, and "*flout* a maxim."[8] Even the use of a term such as "decoding" in reference to reading texts assumes that an "encoding" has occurred. The possibility of the writer's complicity in my reading is one that I do not wish to exclude. It will be part of the critical practice that I now wish to construct for the fullest possible reading of particular sections of Montgomery's journals.

In constructing my critical consideration of these journals, I want to explore the possible ways that women encode in their personal writings. I agree with Suzanne L. Bunkers when she speaks of the "selective use of speech and silence" as a central strategy in the encoding process.[9] In private writings in the era when Montgomery wrote, a woman practised "self-editing and self-censoring as a means of encoding messages" while maintaining a conventional perception of self in the text. Encoding "means the transmission of the writer's message in an oblique rather than in a direct manner. For a woman writing in a diary or journal, encoding can take a variety of syntactic or semantic forms, including indirection, contradiction, deviation, and silences."[10] For example, a woman can express dissatisfaction yet insist that she is content; she can use sentence fragments, neologisms, or repeated silences on taboo subjects that are nevertheless indirectly present in her writing; and she can be frustratingly (for the reader) circumspect on emotionally charged issues. These strategies are similar to those that Mary Rubio points to in Montgomery's fiction, strategies showing that Montgomery can play "the literary and social games of her society with superb finesse" while subverting those games.[11]

While Bunkers's analysis of women's diaries and Rubio's analysis of Montgomery's fiction seem to indicate that women such as Montgomery may be fully conscious of their strategies (the very word *strategies* implies this), I think that at least part of the encoding phenomenon is an act occurring at the linguistic level, as Julia Kristeva describes such a process. She speaks of a semiotic genotext, which breaks through the realist representation or "spectacle" of a traditional novelistic text and reveals a "rhetoric," or a lived experience, that might be quite at odds with the surface conventions in the text.[12] It would seem that by referring to the semiotic genotext I am abandoning my stated intention of including the female subjectivity – Montgomery – in my reading strategy. That is not my intention. The advantage of adding a Kristevan dimension to my reading is that I can limit the need to deal with authorial intention while emphasizing a reading that foregrounds my active input as reader.

While wanting to avoid having constantly to posit an intentional argument, much of *The Selected Journals of L.M. Montgomery* makes me think that, while the text constructs a rhetoric at the linguistic level that contradicts its "spectacle," the writer of that text is complicit with my reading. Thus, I wish to take a position between authorial and readerly authorities. I wish to avoid the binaries of a traditional literary reading for intentionality and a reading that, while in theory locating authority in the linguistic level of text, in practice locates it in the critical reader of the text. As a feminist continuously dancing through minefields of patriarchal binaries, I find this literary one the most troublesome, and speech act theory, with its assumptions of encodings and decodings through the methodology of implicature (thus avoiding a one-to-one relationship between encoding and decoding), is a helpful stance. I am most comfortable with the idea of an unwritten, unspoken womanly pact between me and the writer. As Julia Watson puts it, "the reader's task is in part to discover what Philippe Lejeune has termed 'the autobiographical pact,' here situated in a female difference that asks to be decoded."[13] This pact allows me to undertake a feminist strategy in reading women's texts, an "intersubjective" strategy that Patrocinio Schweickart describes:

On the one hand, reading is necessarily subjective. On the other hand, it must not be wholly so. One must respect the autonomy of the text. The reader is a visitor and, as such, must observe the necessary courtesies. She must avoid unwarranted intrusions – she must be careful not to appropriate what belongs to her host, not to impose herself on the other woman. Furthermore, reading is at once an intersubjective encounter and something less than that ... The text is a screen, an inanimate object. Its subjectivity is only a projection of the subjectivity of the reader.[14]

Schweickart advises the feminist reader intent on the "recuperation" of women's texts from a phallocentric tradition and language to practise a dialectic of reading in which she, knowing that the author's subjectivity is "threatened by the author's absence," makes an effort to refer constantly to a "duality of contexts," the "context of writing" and the "context of reading."[15] This dialectic adds a measure of ethical responsibility to the Kristevan power that the reader has and to the licence that speech act theory gives me regarding implicature, an ethics that I think is a necessary part of a feminist reading.

The kind of interactive decoding process that I have just described is open to all sorts of problems in practice. And it speaks especially to the fourth difficulty that I mentioned at the beginning of this discussion: my own construction as a critical reader. In undertaking an active, self-conscious, decoding practice in the reading of women's private literature, I am attempting to unlearn my entire literary training. Brought up as I was on classical realism, interpellated in my later education by every reading stance from New Criticism through archetypalism to deconstruction, I want to deconstruct my education while holding on to whatever canniness as a reader my education has given me. I am doing this in an academic world in which the critic typically addresses her audience in the assured tones of arrival. Critics rarely confess to having just learned what they are practising, when in fact that is what we are all doing if we are not repeating ourselves. As well, we hardly ever confess to having practised more naïve strategies than we do now. Add to this confessional reluctance my affirmation of a feminist ideological agenda that believes in all the correct theories of women's exclusion from patriarchal language and culture while insisting on the imperative need to rescue women's culture and tradition from the past and give them as matrimony to other women. Matrimony is not, in its ancient meaning, a marriage contract but an inheritance of power and tradition that, like patrimony, is handed down in a culture, descending from mothers to daughters (surrogate and actual). These reading agendas affect the codes of reference, the implicatures, that I bring to texts. As well, as a trained literary reader, I may well stumble over more than one skeleton as I attempt to come out of the closet of my literary education.

Let me confess one of the skeletons that I came across on my first close reading of six entries in volume one of the *Selected Journals*, entries from pages 186 to 221, covering the time period from "Wednesday Night, June 30, 1897" to "Saturday, Oct. 8, 1898." In the six long entries in this section, Montgomery describes the course of her engagement to Edwin Simpson and her love affair with Herman Leard. In my first reading of these entries, I sought a decoding of the psychic implications embedded in the descriptions and images that Montgomery uses, a reading that would reveal her attitude toward sexuality, which she could not directly speak in her Victorian language. In Belsey's words, I sought the "unconscious of the work," which constructs itself in the moment when the ideological project – in this case, the expression of a woman in love (the belief in falling in love being a stubborn tenet in our culture) – enters into the literary form. I found a strange similarity of image in the descriptions of the supposedly very different relationships, one with a man who physically repulses Montgomery, the other with a man to whom she is intensely attracted. Both descriptions are filled with parallel images of self-disintegration, self-effacement, and a morbid terror of possession.

I had no problem in finding proof for this reading. Montgomery introduces herself by saying: "The girl who wrote on June 3rd is as dead as if the sod were heaped over her – dead past the possibility of any resurrection"; "*everything*," she states, "seems hopelessly changed. *I* am not Maud Montgomery at all." She describes her growing dislike of Simpson as a "*physical repulsion*," his touch an "icy horror. I shrank from his embrace and kiss. I was literally terrified at the repulsion which quivered in every nerve of me at his touch. It seemed as if something that had been dormant in me all my life had suddenly wakened and shook me with a passion of revolt against my shackles."[16]

Certainly the intensity of the language would indicate the significant psychic material that I sought. I assumed the significance and seriousness of Montgomery's language despite the fact that my literary education encouraged me to discount such intensity in women's descriptions of their emotional lives as inappropriate, melodramatic, overwrought, and aesthetically naïve. What is assessed by literary standards as sentimental or melodramatic is often a very accurate representation, not so much of the degree of emotional value that patriarchal culture places on particular states of being, but of how much value women caught in the intertwined cultural and personal imperatives of patriarchy place on their own psychic and emotional states.

For example, a nineteenth-century woman's characterization of what she feels during sexual arousal will seem overextended only by those who do not have to worry on a personal level that sexual arousal defines the self out of a particular category of human (i.e., woman and sexually aroused human being, states that cannot be linked). Nor do such human subjects (i.e., men and some twentieth-century women) have to worry that on both a societal and a personal level sexual arousal could mean becoming pregnant and economically enslaved. In this regard, it is interesting that Montgomery's revulsion grows when she discovers that Simpson intends to become a Baptist minister and that, as his wife, she will have to be rebaptized by immersion in water. This image of self-effacement gives Montgomery many a sleepless night and makes for a number of the passages that literary critics might well dismiss as "purple prose." Thus, reading at the linguistic level of the text, where Kristeva advises that a different "rhetoric" may be found than in the realist "spectacle," reading with respect for the narrator as a developing human subjectivity, and reading with a feminist implicature, I discover a difference in women's uses of literary language.

One would expect that the relationship with Leard, which seemed to have helped Montgomery release herself from her perceived bondage to the Simpson engagement, would speak of a different passion, a different rhetoric. In fact, she introduces this relationship in very similar terms to the Simpson debacle, first in the sense of a dramatic change in subjectivity: "Sometimes I ask myself if the pale, sad-eyed woman I see in my glass can really be the merry girl of olden days or if she be some altogether new creature, born of sorrow and baptized of suffering, who is the sister and companion of regret and hopeless longing." The feeling that arises when Leard first caresses her is "like a *spell* the mysterious, irresistible *influence* which Herman Leard exercised over me from that date – an attraction I could neither escape nor overcome and against which all the resolution and will power in the world didn't weigh a feather's weight. It was indescribable and overwhelming."[17] The beloved's embrace is a power over her, a "*spell*." While his kiss sends "flame through every vein and fibre of my being," it is not a flame that the writer delights in but one that is a "wild, passionate, unreasoning love that dominated my entire being and possessed me like a flame – a love I could neither quell nor control – a love that in its intensity seemed little short of absolute madness."[18] Even after the first few episodes of stolen caresses and kisses, made more intense by the constant danger of interruption and discovery in the small house that the lovers share with the Leard family (even the bedroom into which Leard creeps to find Montgomery is one that she shares with his sister), the images with which she figures her love do not become less painful. Although they share a "dreamy, rapturous silence," she feels even "as I write" a "wild, sick, *horrible* longing" to feel his "magnetic pressure."[19] When she comes close to sexual intercourse, she terms it "the fatal rapture of the hour my resolution was forgotten. Nevertheless in calmer moments it came back to me and I struggled like a drowning man."[20] The image of drowning recalls her distaste for baptism by immersion. For present-day readers, her characterization of sexual arousal as enslavement may seem like a quaint, nineteenth-century prudery. However, if one's culture teaches that sexual arousal is not something that one is supposed to have, and indeed if that arousal will lead to a quite literal enslavement in the modest, unliterary life of a farmwife, then the use of such prose is an accurate reflection of one's psychic state and cannot be dismissed as mere self-dramatization of the melodramatic kind.

For readers of the three published volumes, my psychological decoding of images at the linguistic level of the text, images that speak to a fear of sexual involvement as debilitating, will make sense in terms of the Montgomery who all her life both wanted intensely personal relationships and found those with men to be the most limiting of her freedom of self-expression. That she is largely silent about her physical relationship with her husband would support my reading, as would the tenor of unhappiness that pervades her representation of their relationship. However, when I finished my reading of the six entries considered here and was only able to make the rather obvious conclusion that, for creative women of Montgomery's time, sexual intimacy, desired or not, was dangerous to their private and public existence as persons, I was profoundly dissatisfied with my reading act. I felt that I had not been true to my autobiographical reading pact with the writer. I had "imposed on my host," as Schweickart might put it, had showed too little respect for the text as a place that I might use – not as a barrier to be penetrated in search of a subjectivity that Montgomery herself could not construct, but as a filtrating screen through which her encoding could become the subject of my decoding. In short, I needed to give fuller attention to the "context of writing" as well as the "context of reading"; I needed another layer of implicature to bring to my conversation with Montgomery.

The moment that I made that confession, after my initial reading, which I have just characterized, I realized that the literary skeletons I had stumbled over were my assumptions that women's private literature is primarily valuable as the place where we can gain special access to the psychological construction of the writer and that traditional literary conventions have no purchase in such relatively unartificed texts. As I realized the limitation of my psychological reading, I realized as well that a corrective to too great an emphasis on psychological readings of private literature lay in another part of my literary closet. Another skeleton in my closet is my genre education. I have never really moved beyond expecting certain conventions to be well used in certain generic contexts, and I always find the term "genre blending," as applied to postmodern literature, a bit flip and sometimes a cover for the amateurish use of older generic conventions. In reviewing my reading expectations in this way, I realized that my consciousness of the encoding/decoding activity of speech act theory was making me more conscious of the nature of my own assumed decoding practices. This realization led almost immediately to the insight that there was no point in getting rid of my reading skeletons: they were mine after all and had taught me what I knew. What I needed to do was to bring them out of the closet, clothe them (flesh them) and arrange them (contextualize them) in this new consciousness of myself as a decoder.

As I resolved to do this, I immediately found another skeleton, one so suddenly obvious to me that I wondered how I could not have noticed it. I had assumed a certain naïveté, even in a practised writer, because of the use of the diary format. Then, eureka-like, I saw that only a reader assuming a writerly naïveté far greater than Montgomery's could fail to see that in these six passages – with their narrative compactness, their dramatically intense and stereotypically literary language of romance, their careful characterization, and their constant metatextual references to the writing act – is a sophisticated use of that most dominant of nineteenth-century literary conventions: the two-suitors convention. Here lay the possibility of a decoding practice that would draw on the common ideological interpellation of both the encoder and the decoder: Montgomery and I were both raised on romance: we both learned early, through the literature of domestic prose romance, the stereotypical ways of placing men at the centre of our self-development. Working through our mutual knowledge of romance conventions, but as an active decoder of Montgomery's encoded use of those conventions in the personal diary, bringing to it the cultural implicatures of a feminist deconstructive theory informed by speech act theory's respect for the communal nature of utterance, I could further nuance my critical practice.

To overcome the debilitating effects of one's reading history, and to theorize a different reading strategy, one has first to historicize that practice. Hence, I reviewed critical and theoretical literature on the development of the conventions of the female novel – particularly of the romance variety – in English. I gave attention to texts from Annis Pratt's *Archetypal Patterns in Women's Fiction* through Mary Poovey's *The Proper Lady and the Woman Writer* to Laurie Langbauer's *Women and Romance*. After some explorations through texts especially concerned with popular culture – Tania Modleski's *Loving with a Vengeance* and Linda Christian-Smith's *Becoming a Woman through Romance* – I finally found what I was looking for in Jean E. Kennard's 1978 study *Victims of Convention*. Unlike Elaine Showalter's 1977 study *A Literature of Their Own*, which does not quite recognize the continuing victimhood waiting for female characters and their writers in the mere convention of imaging a woman's development through her choice of men, Kennard's study centres on this important literary fact, showing us how, from Jane Austen to Erica Jong, we keep getting ourselves reappropriated into patriarchal linguistic and cultural practices by that same old convention of the two suitors. This writing history certainly demonstrates Belsey's point: an "unconscious" constructs itself from that which cannot be expressed when "ideological project" meets "literary form." Part of the ideological project of these uses of the convention of mirroring women's self-development through the males whom they choose was just that, self-development. However, the novelistic forms in which they worked offered no literary convention for its expression.

Kennard points out that we need to make a "clear distinction between fictional formula and historical or social truth," to get over our "tendency to treat literature, particularly the novel, as mimetic in the simplest way, as the documentation, more or less accurate, of certain human experiences."[21] I would add that the need is even greater when we are dealing with a woman's journals based on her lived experiences. We must not expect Montgomery's *Selected Journals* to operate without the use – and, I would suggest, the very sophisticated and subversive use – of literary conventions. Literary conventions are part of what Schweickart calls the "context of writing," and, given Montgomery's considerable interests as a professional, money-making writer, we cannot ignore such conventions even though the form of the personal journal might lead us to seek the kind of psychological decoding that my first reading indicates. Kennard's exploration of the two-suitors convention can act intertextually with the psychological reading to enrich a feminist decoding practice.

Kennard describes in detail the tropes of victimhood waiting for female writers who show a "heroine's personality and development ... through comparison with two male characters," a comparison in which "Maturity is seen to consist of adjusting oneself to the real world which is synonymous with becoming like the right suitor" and/or marrying him.[22] Of course, the greatest trap is found in the ending of such a novel, in which the conventional ending of marriage conflates the heroine's self-development with her role as wife. From George Eliot's *Middlemarch* to Doris Lessing's *The Summer Before the Dark*, women get subsumed into less than adequate husbandly containers. The only way out, from Emily Brontë's *Wuthering Heights* to Virginia Woolf's *The Voyage Out*, is for the heroine to die. Kennard, while noting that more contemporary novelists such as Margaret Laurence and Gail Godwin attempt to resist the convention, concludes that it is poets such as Adrienne Rich who are self-consciously attempting to free us from this oldest of novelistic conventions. Kennard's book, published in 1978, could not take into account the part that women's private literature and its related theory, both now undergoing a publishing explosion, might play, along with the poets, in releasing us from this convention.

Rereading the same six entries in Montgomery's journals with this new set of implicatures in mind, I would like to indicate how a decoding of Montgomery's use of the literary convention of the two suitors works. One way that we can unravel the code of the two-suitors convention is to observe the ways in which Montgomery uses and changes the convention at the level of plot and character. As well, I can be alert to how the poetic (in a Kristevan sense) language of the section works to deconstruct the surface message of this level. An awareness of the effects of Montgomery's life circumstances (such as two significant family deaths and the change of schools) that surround and interrupt the text can also inform the reading. Finally, tracing the continuing interruption of the two-suitors convention with another narrative, the almost unspoken text of Montgomery's development as a writer during this period, can lead to an understanding of her subversive use of the two-suitors convention.

This last is the factor that interests me the most and that I would like to foreground in my reading, partially because, as a reader of the *Selected Journals*, I am aware that Montgomery had considerable difficulty reconciling her public career with her perception of herself as a very private nineteenth-century woman. In the second volume, she observes about her writing career, by then well established: "Hitherto my literary success has brought me some money, some pleasant letters and an increase of worries and secret mortifications. I had experienced only the seamy side of fame. But now I was to see the other side [on a visit to Boston and the Pages' publishing house]. I was to find everything made easy and pleasant for me. It was very delightful – but of course it was only a dream!"[23] A woman who feels so ambiguous about her lifework must, from the beginning, have a difficult time expressing how essential it is to her self-definition. Thus, I am involved in reading against the grain of the text – looking in the other end of the telescope so to speak – to discover what Montgomery is working out for herself through her literary experimentation with the two-suitors convention, of which she nevertheless cannot speak openly if she is to preserve that perceived self of the proper Victorian lady who would no more admit to having career ambitions than a proper young middle-class woman of today would admit to having none.

As is her habit in her journals, Montgomery, in these six entries, constantly refers to her need to write things "out." In these sections, she begins with that typical nineteenth-century female apology for her expressive inability, the one made just before the writer splendidly articulates some subtle experience: "I do not know if I can write down a lucid account of the events and motives that have led me to this." She then observes, "I had almost concluded that it was not in me to love as *some* people seem to do in real life and *all* in novels,"[24] alerting us to both the lived and the literary plots of her account. Later in the entries she speaks of "a good dose of confession," and she promises that she is "going to write it all down from beginning to end. I suppose this is foolish – but I think it will help me to 'write it out.' It always does."[25] Her references to the writing act draw my attention not only to her different use of the two-suitors convention but also to the references in these entries to writing in general, hers and others'. For example, it is an exchange of letters that finally allows Montgomery to tell Simpson that she cannot marry him, the words that she could never say to his face. And it is only when she lets herself behave very badly and write out to him the full measure of her dislike that he finally releases her from their engagement. Her references to the two suitors' spoken texts are interesting in this regard. One of Simpson's most repulsive qualities, in Montgomery's estimation, is his facile use of words to draw attention to himself, a habit, incidentally, that keeps him from noting any subtle clues to his fiancée's frame of mind. Leard, on the other hand, is characterized as almost totally silent. His wooing is a subtle combination of caresses, kisses, silences, and sighs, which almost succeed in their aim until he finally speaks: "at last Herman whispered a single sentence in my ear – a request whose veiled meaning it was impossible to misunderstand!" From then on, the girl whose "fatal rapture" had almost won has the will to "recoil" from the "insidious temptation of silent caresses."[26] By my reading of these journal entries, once a conventional male script is in place, a man's braggadocio, a man's whispered desire, Montgomery is in charge of her own emotions, her own self-definitions; she is in the territory that she knows best: words.

My suggestion that writing is essential to Montgomery's self-integrity is borne out by several short, casual references in the six entries to her nascent writing success, references that now seem to me very strategically placed in terms of her self-development during this crisis period, which I will describe as the two-suitors interval. The first reference occurs in the 7 October 1897 entry and comes after Montgomery has realized the folly of her engagement and (reading with hindsight now) after she has begun her affair with Leard, though not confessed it in the text. She has just finished a detailed account of her religious beliefs and the ways in which she has resisted the most extreme doctrines of organized religions, doctrines that have "drop[ped] away like an outgrown husk." She observes in a brief, seemingly unrelated paragraph: "I have written a good deal this summer and had a few acceptances. Had a poem taken by *Munsey*. The latter is quite an encouragement as it is a good magazine." She immediately changes the subject, going on at length about Hattie Gordon's letters and the nostalgia of school days. The reference to her creative summer and publishing success comes at the end of an entry that she begins by saying that she "*could not* write" for the whole summer.[27] Of course, it is the diary that she cannot write, which I believe was the most necessary writing for Montgomery, which made the public writing possible yet worked to disguise its importance.

Her second comment on her career occurs in the 22 January 1898 entry, right after she has promised a full confession of her breakup with Simpson and just before she gives her first hints of her affair with Leard. She states: "Somehow or other, during all this unhappy time I have worn a mask of outward gayety and kept up with my usual pursuits. I have written a good deal and met with some success, having had several acceptances – and of course plenty of rejections." The observation shows that she now thinks of herself as a professional, writing being "my usual pursuits" and "rejections" being, "of course," part of the profession. It is interesting to note that she again turns immediately to girlhood friends: "Whom do you think was married in September?" she asks,[28] as if even a glancing reference to her career must be smothered in a correctly female preoccupation with real-life marriage and its characters and scripts. But her realization of her increasingly rewarded talent also immediately precedes the details of her confession of her physical intimacy with Leard, details that are not the proper content of a young girl's writing. Once again, an empowerment and a disguise of that empowerment concurrently take place.

The third and longest reference to writing appears in the very long 8 April 1898 entry, after Montgomery overcomes her fear of honesty and reports that she has written the difficult letter to Simpson; after she describes her affair with Leard, admitting that it was almost consummated; and, significantly I think, after she records her grandfather's death and uses it to write a detailed reconstruction of her mother's death. I say significantly because the two deaths are important markers of her realization of her place in life. Her grandfather's death put her in a very difficult position because his will left the farm, on which she had to live to care for her grandmother, to Montgomery's uncle, the appropriate patriarchal heir, who then spent some effort to remove the women from the house even though the will gave Montgomery's grandmother the right to occupy it until her death. As female caretaker, Montgomery was given no patrimony, nor did she expect any. However, that she juxtaposes her grandfather's death with a description of the long-ago death of her mother, and symbolically the loss of any empowering maternal relationship, indicates that Montgomery had a growing awareness of her position as a female orphan in patriarchy, as a woman without any maternal legacy of power or any patriarchal inheritance: in short, a woman without matrimony or patrimony.

Such a woman must seek empowerment at a linguistic level, and, even though the passage that contains self-empowerment is immediately preceded by a typical attempt to downplay its importance, I find that it contains Montgomery's empowerment as a writer. She begins with this caution: "It seems very much of an anti-climax after all these confessions to write of other and lesser matters. But all things are mingled in this life – the most insignificant follow on the heels of the most tragic ... And so it is only in keeping with this that I turn from these passionate memories to other and lesser things."[29] Now that the nineteenth-century lady teacher has made the correct dismissal of the importance of her talent and accomplishments, constructed the correct realist "spectacle" of woman as only concerned with others, she can tell us the following: "I have had some successes in literature – several acceptances, some of them in new places. My work is a great comfort to me in these sad days. I forget all my griefs and perplexities while I am absorbed in it. *I am very ambitious* – perhaps too ambitious. Herman told me that once – he seemed to hate my ambition – perhaps he felt the truth that it was the real barrier between us. *But at least it is all I have to live for now and I may as well hunt it down.*"[30] A "writing out" indeed occurs in these six entries, not just the writing out of emotions to relieve the pressure of her power-less place in patriarchy, but also her writing herself *out* of an imprisoning ideology by which femaleness and creative writing are mutually exclusive categories. Although Montgomery continued to be ambiguous about her achievements as a writer all her life, what comes *out* of these six journal entries is, by my reading, her birth as a writer, a new subjectivity that she has conceived in the rigour of her emotional intercourse with two suitors. She is saved from them finally by engaging in that most difficult of acts, which all writers must finally accomplish, the displacement of the most significant energy of the libido into the act of writing, which happens when the writer realizes that writing is what "I have to live for now" and decides to pursue that empowerment with the intensity of a "hunt."

Two facts confirm the appropriateness of my decoding in this re-gard. This reference to writing is followed not by references to old girl-friends' letters or marriages but to an exploration of the insufficiencies of the novel as a genre, and the next entry contains a final reference to Montgomery's own writing, ending with these images of the loss and gain involved in the birth of a new version of the self: "I suppose it would be hard if all I have gone through didn't bring me some compensation. Sometimes I think it has taught me to see *too* clearly – I might be happier if my delusions and illusions were left to me. But yet – one would think blindness could never be considered a beatific state, and possibly when I get over the blinking and shrinking of new vision and accustomed to the fierce white light of reality I may feel as comfortable as of yore in my soothing twilight."[31] Although Belsey correctly speaks to the "uncon-scious" of the text existing in the "gap" between ideology and literary form, she does not directly address the idea that writers can realize a new consciousness in this act of writing (Belsey is more concerned with readers), especially in the act of private writing, in which the inhibitions caused by the thought of an immediate audience are not a hindrance. The imaginative and subversive use of the two-suitors convention has been the vehicle by which Montgomery, through the rhetoric of her text, has written herself into this "new vision" and constructed her subjectivity differently than it had been shaped. The diary format has helped her transformation. It is a revisionary, improvisational form in which a writer can practise her full range of literary conventions in manners not encouraged by public formats, and an "unconscious" can be constructed that the text shares, at least partially, with the writer, who can find in the private text a tenable, if secret, place to begin the subversion of her enslavement in ideology. L.M. Montgomery had great need of such a place.

It is Nancy K. Miller, in *Subject to Change*, who articulates for me the best metaphor of the kind of active feminist reading strategies that I have been attempting to describe and illustrate. She speaks of the mythical figure of Arachne, the spider artist, who began as a weaver of texts, whose tapestry, whose text, is "first discredited, then detached from the cultural record, and finally ignored." Miller advises various strategies in reading against the grain of the phallocentric inscriptions that cover the woman's text in order to construct our own feminist reading, our "arachnology," "a critical positioning which reads *against* the weave of indifferentiation to discover the embodiment in writing of a gendered subjectivity; to recover within representation the emblems of its construction."[32] This is what I have tried to gesture toward in this abbreviated reading of Montgomery's *Selected Journals*, and I would like to finish by asserting her complicity with me in this reading. In such an assertion, I am attempting to remove from my critical practice the silence that literary deconstruction (as advocated by Belsey) puts between reader and writer, a distance that effectively, whether it was meant to or not, empowers the reader at the expense of the writer, that seeks the "unconscious" of a text, the voice that public language cannot speak, yet silences the encoder of that other text, that other voice. Felicity A. Nussbaum's formulation of the diary format as used by eighteenth-century English writers (especially female writers) speaks to Montgomery's use of the form in late-nineteenth-century Canada: "it does not ... escape the familiar ways of making meaning in a given historical moment," but it does work "to articulate modes of discourse that may disrupt and endanger authorized representations of reality in their alternative discourses of self and subject. As such, it poses tentative textual solutions to unresolvable contradictions."[33]

When I was first struggling through the phallic overlay of the two-suitors convention in these six entries in order to find Montgomery's subversive use of that convention to construct the threads of another tapestry, another rhetoric, I found parenthetical reference to another woman's autobiographical writing, that of Olive Schreiner. Montgomery, pondering her own cultural definitions as a correct little Christian girl, observes: "Last winter I read for the first time 'The Story of An African Farm.' The writer was describing just such experiences of childhood. When I came to the sentence, 'We conscientiously put the cracked coffee cup for ourselves at breakfast' I leaned back and laughed. It was as if I had unexpectedly seen my own face peering out at me from a mirror. So this Boer girl, living thousands of miles away in South Africa, had had exactly the same experience as mine!"[34] Here, if I could have seen it in my first reading, was the key to my reading strategy: Montgomery engaged in her own reading "arachnology," her own decoding of another woman's encoded subjectivity, Montgomery allowing another woman's text to inform her own living and writing. I like her figuring herself as leaning back and laughing. That was exactly my reaction when I discovered her subversive use of the two-suitors convention and began the pleasurable construction of this text.

NOTES

1 Belsey, *Critical Practice*, 107–8.
2 Smith, *A Poetics of Women's Autobiography*, 28, 20. For a fuller exposition of Smith's poetics and other theoretical texts concerning women's autobiographical writing, see chapter 1 of my *Mapping Our Selves: Canadian Women's Autobiography in English*.
3 Culley, Introduction, 21.
4 Petrey, *Speech Acts and Literary Theory*, 70.
5 M.L. Pratt, *Toward a Speech Act Theory*, 154, 155, 86.
6 Petrey, *Speech Acts and Literary Theory*, 76.
7 Stanton, "Autogynography," 14.
8 M.L. Pratt, *Toward a Speech Act Theory*, 159.
9 Bunkers, "Midwestern Diaries and Journals," 191.
10 Ibid., 194.
11 [See Mary Rubio's "Subverting the Trite" earlier in this volume.]
12 Kristeva, *Desire in Language*, 89.
13 Watson, "Shadowed Presence," 182.
14 Schweickart, "Reading Ourselves," 131.
15 Ibid., 131, 135.
16 Montgomery, 30 June 1897, in *SJLMM*, 1: 186, 189.

17 Montgomery, 8 April 1898, in *SJLMM*, 1: 204, 209.

18 Montgomery, 8 April 1898, in *SJLMM*, 1: 209, 210.

19 Montgomery, 8 April 1898, in *SJLMM*, 1: 211.

20 Montgomery, 8 April 1898, in *SJLMM*, 1: 214.

21 Kennard, *Victims of Convention*, 10.

22 Ibid., 11, 12.

23 Montgomery, 29 November 1910, in *SJLMM*, 2: 23.

24 Montgomery, 30 June 1897, in *SJLMM*, 1: 187.

25 Montgomery, 22 January 1898, in *SJLMM*, 1: 201; Montgomery, 8 April 1898, in *SJLMM*, 1: 208.

26 Montgomery, 8 April 1898, in *SJLMM*, 1: 215, 214, 215.

27 Montgomery, 7 October 1897, in *SJLMM*, 1: 197, 195.

28 Montgomery, 22 January 1898, in *SJLMM*, 1: 203.

29 Montgomery, 8 April 1898, in *SJLMM*, 1: 220.

30 Montgomery, 8 April 1898, in *SJLMM*, 1: 220; emphasis added.

31 Montgomery, 8 October 1898, in *SJLMM*, 1: 225.

32 N.K. Miller, *Subject to Change*, 78, 80.

33 Nussbaum, *The Autobiographical Subject*, 29.

34 Montgomery, 7 October 1897, in *SJLMM*, 1: 197.

9

"Fitted to Earn Her Own Living": Figures of the New Woman in the Writing of L.M. Montgomery

—— 1995 ——

CAROLE GERSON

In this essay, the first of two in this volume that originally appeared in Hilary Thompson's collection *Children's Voices in Atlantic Literature and Culture: Essays on Childhood*, Carole Gerson historicizes the "new woman" figure as a way to contextualize Montgomery's stated disinterest in women's suffrage and her depiction of a specific kind of feminism and independence in her fiction. A professor of English at Simon Fraser University, Gerson has since contributed several additional articles and chapters on Montgomery's literary history – in *L.M. Montgomery and Canadian Culture* (1999), *Making Avonlea: L.M. Montgomery and Popular Culture* (2002), *Storm and Dissonance: L.M. Montgomery and Conflict* (2008), and *Anne's World: A New Century of Anne of Green Gables* (2010) – and has included Montgomery in her recent book *Canadian Women in Print 1750–1918* (2010).

In November, 1933, L.M. Montgomery wrote in her journal:

> In an old book today I came across the phrase "the new woman" – and smiled. It is so dead now – nobody would know what you meant if you used it. Yet it was a world-wide slogan in the 90's – and meant a woman who wanted "equal rights" and dared to think she ought to vote. To some it was a dreadful epithet; to others a boast. And now the new woman and the old woman are gone and the eternal woman remains – not much changed in reality and not, I am afraid, any happier.[1]

Although Montgomery omits the title of the book that inspired these comments, this passage confirms how the identity of the New Woman of the 1890s received recognition and definition through literary and textual representation.[2] During the first wave of feminism, advocates of women's rights and their often savage detractors used the public media of journalism, fiction, poetry, cartoons and theatre to test or to demolish many possibilities of social change. Popular images of the New Woman tended to focus on the more external aspects of her challenges to the Victorian doctrine of separate spheres: "Bicycles, Bangs and Bloomers," to cite the title of Patricia Marks' recent book on the image of the New Woman in the popular press. Cartoons and illustrations depicting dress reform, smoking, drinking, bicycling (indicating personal mobility) and the latch key (indicating personal independence) both signal the significance of these individual issues and encode the deeper social threats textually expressed in the plays of Ibsen and in an abundance of fiction, most of it by now-forgotten authors.

Rural Prince Edward Island occasioned few of the dramatic challenges to conventional decorum that inspired the cartoons from *Punch* and other periodicals reproduced in Marks' book. Many of the explicit material symbols of the New Woman's quest for independence failed to interest Montgomery. According to her journal, the first time she saw women smoking in public in Canada was at the 1923 Toronto convention of the Canadian Authors' Association, a spectacle she deemed *"ugly."*[3] Young Emily of New Moon defiantly cuts her hair in a "bang" (thereby fulfilling Montgomery's own thwarted childhood desire)[4] without any conscious notion of acting in the name of women's rights. Dress reform per se is never an issue: in *Rilla of Ingleside* some women don overalls for wartime harvest work, and later in *Mistress Pat* Suzanne Kirk rather strikingly wears knickerbockers. Montgomery was eager to win the right to vote, yet in her journal entry of March 4, 1917, recording the decision of the Ontario government to extend the ballot to women who were sisters, wives, widows, or mothers of men on active service, she doubts whether women's suffrage "will make as much change in things as its advocates hope or its opponents fear."[5] For the women in *Rilla*, obtaining the vote is among the less significant outcomes of the Great War; Montgomery might well have shared the opinion of Miss Cornelia that "when the men realise they've got the world into a mess they can't get it out of, they'll be glad to give us the vote, and shoulder their troubles over on us."[6]

Nonetheless, while latchkeys were unimportant in rural communities where doors were not always locked, and few people in

Montgomery's real or fictional world seem to have ridden bicycles,[7] the absence of these symbols in her work does not indicate a lack of concern with some of the major issues articulated by the New Women of the 1890s. A 1921 retrospective journal passage describes her childhood fantasy of being "Lady Trevanion," a famous novelist "and a member of the British House of Commons to boot"; another, from 1925, mentions a book she once planned to write called "'How We Ran the Farm' ... an amusing story about two girls who, by some twist of circumstances, were left with a P.E. Island farm on their hands and determined to show all and sundry that they could run it."[8] Although Montgomery never takes up the direct arguments for sexual freedom embodied in representations of "women who did," to cite the title of Grant Allen's provocative 1895 novel, her sympathetic representation of a dying unwed mother in *The Blue Castle* (1926) caused several vigilant parents to forbid their daughters to read it.[9] As both Mary Rubio and Jennie Rubio have argued, many of Montgomery's books contain implicit criticisms of the Victorian institution of marriage.[10] More explicitly articulated are the issues emanating directly from her own life that will be discussed in this essay: the desire for higher education for women, women's need for economic self-sufficiency, and the cultural valorization of women writers and women's writing. In 1924, Montgomery recorded having told a reporter who requested her opinion of the present-day girl "that I thought the present day girl exactly like the girl of yesterday – the only difference being that the girls of today *did* what we of yesterday *wanted* to."[11]

It is difficult to determine Montgomery's acquaintance with Ibsen or the more than 100 New Woman novels written in English between 1883 and 1900.[12] A voracious and omnivorous reader, in her journals she recorded and commented upon an incomplete and eclectic selection of titles. Authors of particular biographical interest included the Brontës and Eliot: *The Mill on the Floss*, a precursor to the later New Woman novel, was her "favorite among George Eliot's books."[13] Within her own fiction, most citations and allusions refer to mainstream canonical or popular authors and texts (the Bible, Shakespeare, Tennyson, Burns, Whittier, Wordsworth).[14] Her access to other work was often limited; for example she didn't read *The Diary of Marie Bashkirtseff* (1885) until June of 1924: "This book came out when I was a young girl and made a tremendous sensation. It was discussed in all the reviews. I longed to read it but books like that never penetrated to Cavendish and I could not afford to buy it."[15]

Two New Woman novels that did penetrate to rural Prince Edward Island during the winter of 1897, when Montgomery was 22, were Lucy Lane Clifford's *Love Letters of a Worldly Woman* (1891), a moving affirmation of female sexuality and psychological strength, and Olive Schreiner's *The Story of an African Farm* (1883), a book to which Montgomery would return many times.[16] In 1900, she wrote in her journal: "At the outbreak of the Transvaal war I re-read 'The Story of An African Farm.' It is one of my favorites. It is speculative, analytical, rather pessimistic, iconoclastic, daring – and *very* unconventional. But it is powerful and original and fearless, and contains some exquisite ideas. It is like a tonic, bitter but bracing. Also, many people call it a dangerous book. Perhaps it is so, for an unformed mind – but there is more of truth than pleasantness in many of its incisive utterances."[17] Now valued as the first new woman novel,[18] Schreiner's book addresses the woman question with a vehement and penetrating analysis of the social construction of gender. Schreiner herself went on to become a leading theorist of first-wave feminism, one of her key issues (elaborated in *Woman and Labor*, 1911) being the need of (middle-class) women for meaningful education and work.

Taken up in other major texts like George Gissing's novel *The Odd Women* (1893) and later in Virginia Woolf's extended essay, *A Room of One's Own* (1929) (neither of which Montgomery records having read), the theme of women's desire for education, economic independence, and recognition of the value of their work runs steadily through most of Montgomery's fiction. As a student, she wrote a Commencement essay on Portia commending the "magnificent intellect" of Shakespeare's heroine, and a newspaper article, "A Girl's Place at Dalhousie," firmly justifying the right of women to a university education.[19] In her creative work, despite writing in the genre of romance rather than the social realism characteristic of most New Woman fiction, Montgomery seldom lost sight of the advances being made by women of her generation. When the issue of Anne Shirley's education and destiny arises, Marilla declares (in the quotation that gives this essay its title), "I believe in a girl being fitted to earn her own living whether she ever has to or not." Later, in *Anne of Avonlea*, it is Marilla who pushes Anne to pursue the university education she had been prepared to relinquish.[20] Montgomery herself knew a good deal about earning her own living as a teacher and later as an author: her surviving account books show that she not only tracked every penny of her earnings from her writing, but also kept a keen eye on the commodity value of her work, calculating each year the average prices obtained for stories and poems.[21]

In both the fictional world of Montgomery's stories and the historical reality of Victorian and Edwardian Canada, teaching school until
marriage was the most respectable way for a middle-class young woman
to support herself.[22] To do so was scarcely revolutionary; important in
Montgomery's fictional depiction of school teaching is her insistence on
taking Anne beyond the one year of basic training required for a teaching certificate, to give her the BA which qualifies her to be a high school
principal. This had remained beyond Montgomery's own reach, a matter
of bitter, ongoing regret.[23]

Virginia Woolf's description (in *A Room of One's Own*) of being un-
ceremoniously ejected by an Oxbridge beadle has iconized the difficulties
experienced by British women who sought to enter the male bastion of the
university. Yet Anne's decision to attend Redmond (i.e., Dalhousie) during the early 1890s, thus distinguishing herself as "the first Avonlea girl
who has ever gone to college," twitches only a few eyebrows.[24] There
are, I think, two ways to account for this. First of all, by creating both
her major heroines, Anne Shirley and Emily Byrd Starr, as orphans,
Montgomery implicitly frees them from overbearing patriarchal interfer-
ence. Instead of being defiant, their determination to support themselves
can be represented as laudable even while transgressing some of their
community's traditional gender boundaries (Anne's university education, Emily's writing career), thereby allowing them to chart new paths
without appearing to threaten the patriarchal order. Secondly, women
advanced into higher education relatively easily and rapidly in Maritime
Canada, where Mount Allison, a Methodist institution, became the first
university in the British Empire to grant a Bachelor's degree to a woman
when Annie Lockhart Hughes received the BSc in 1875. Of the six Canadian universities that had awarded degrees to women by 1885, three
(Mount Allison, Acadia [Baptist], and Dalhousie [non-sectarian]) were
in the provinces of Nova Scotia and New Brunswick.[25] However, degree
graduates represent only a small portion of the women who attended university during the last two decades of the nineteenth century. The number
who attended occasional classes or, like Montgomery herself, were able
to enroll for only one or two years, vastly outnumbered those who completed degrees. For example, Dalhousie admitted its first woman student
in 1881 (as did Toronto), and by 1900 had been attended by 392 co-eds,
only about one quarter of whom fulfilled degree programs.[26]

Montgomery's own limited one-year experience of Dalhousie (1895–
96) weakens her depiction of Anne's actual studies in *Anne of the Island*,
and her fiction does not abound with educated women. Yet on several

occasions she goes out of her way to insert advanced women into the frames of her romances. Peripheral to the plots of the stories but not marginal to their meaning, these characters serve as contextualizing figures, reminding attentive readers that in the non-fictional world, women's lives and work were expanding beyond conventional domesticity. *Kilmeny of the Orchard* (1910), one of Montgomery's most formulaic romances, opens with reference to women's recent gains in higher education, the number of female graduates at Queenslea having increased ten-fold over the past 10 years, from two to 20, with women achieving top honours in mathematics and philosophy – seldom viewed as feminine areas of achievement. In *The Golden Road* (1913), the children are inspired to create their own monthly newspaper by the example of Aunt Jane, who "helped edit a paper when she was at Queen's Academy."[27] *Magic for Marigold* (1927) is framed by the presence of Dr. Marigold, the woman physician who saves the life of the young heroine. Although Dr. Marigold seems to give up her professional practice after her marriage, she reappears regularly as a source of wise, authoritative advice; moreover, the replication of her name in that of the book's heroine keeps her achievement constantly in view. Other women's work includes Faith Meredith's stint as a VAD during the Great War (*Rilla of Ingleside*) and Nora Nelson's talk of studying nursing (*Anne of Windy Poplars*). Nursing, however, is too advanced a career for an obstinate father in *A Tangled Web* (1931) and, in the same book, arouses the suspicions of an old sailor who feels that "a trained nurse ... knew too much about her own and other people's insides to be really charming."[28] Music (performance or teaching) is represented as valid work in several stories in *Chronicles of Avonlea* as well as being the occupation of Rosemary West in *Rainbow Valley*.

An engaging collection of self-empowering women appears in Montgomery's scattered magazine stories recently gathered by Rea Wilmshurst in *Against the Odds: Tales of Achievement* (1993). During the first decade of this century, Montgomery produced a cluster of tales which, like those written during the same period by American feminist Charlotte Perkins Gilman, are "exercises in problem-solving,"[29] encouraging women to take advantage of their own undervalued skills and resources. Devising ways to extract college tuition fees from a reluctant rich uncle ("A Patent Medicine Testimonial") or prove her skill as a serious reporter ("A Substitute Journalist"), Montgomery's young women acquire self-reliance and self-esteem. Some stories teach women to recognize and exploit the commodity value of their traditional domestic skills –

also a recurring theme in Gilman's stories ("The Genesis of the Doughnut Club," "Lillian's Business Venture"). In "The Strike at Putney," however, the lesson is for the men, who discover their previously unacknowledged dependence upon their wives when the women withdraw all their services in protest against an edict forbidding a woman to address a meeting in the local church. This resourcefulness culminates in Valancy Stirling of *The Blue Castle* (1926), whose belief that she has only a short time to live inspires her to refuse fear, abandon her psychologically abusive family, and propose marriage to the man of her choice.

In 1934, Montgomery participated in an explicitly didactic effort with her contribution to *Courageous Women*, co-authored with Marian Keith '(Mary Esther McGregor) and Mabel Burns McKinley. Published without a preface identifying its intentions and the occasion of its production, the book is not mentioned in Montgomery's journals. Pitched at young female readers, this volume contains sketches of 21 historically or locally significant women, 15 of them Canadian, and many noted as "firsts" in their field or as founders of social organizations. Included are predictable figures like Joan of Arc, Laura Secord, Queen Victoria, Marshall Saunders, and Pauline Johnson, as well as less famous women like Ada May Courtice, founder of the Home and School Club movement in Ontario, Margaret Polson Murray, founder of the IODE, and northern missionary nurse Anna J. Gaudin.[30]

The New Woman of the 1890s not only broke into the masculine domains of higher education and professional careers, but also resisted male domination by resisting marriage. Lyndall, the heroine of Olive Schreiner's *Story of an African Farm*, commits the ultimate transgression of refusing to marry the father of her child. In Montgomery's fiction, in contrast, even happily independent single women (Miss Cornelia of *Anne's House of Dreams*, Miss Lavendar of *Anne of Avonlea*, Ellen West of *Rainbow Valley*), eventually succumb, in line with Ann Ardis's image of the "boomerang" ending of the New Women novels that conclude with their transgressive heroines safely recaptured at the altar.[31] The only exceptions appear in working-class domestics like the Blythes' Susan Baker and Judy Plum of the Pat books, whose spinsterhood is required to sustain the comfort of their middle-class employers. Miss Lavendar's query – "what is the use of being an independent old maid if you can't be silly when you want to, and when it doesn't hurt anybody?"[32] – is answered by Montgomery's deployment of romantic conventions that require old maids to regret their lost chances to marry, careers to be a prelude to marriage, and marriage to be the inescapable destiny of nearly all women. Thus it is important to consider her exceptions and points of resistance.

Unmarried women, like Pat of Silver Bush and Emily's aunts, may be in danger of losing their beloved homes because property is inherited through the men in their families (replicating the plight of Montgomery's widowed grandmother); property is therefore Emily's first major purchase with her earnings from her writing. Margaret Penhallow of *A Tangled Web* succinctly voices the social value attributed to marriage: "If you were married you were somebody. If not, you were nobody."[33] Nonetheless, fortuitous circumstances allow Margaret to achieve her goal of living in her own home and adopting a child without having to acquire a husband as well. Several of Montgomery's adolescent girls abhor the notion of marriage. Twelve-year-old Felicity of *The Story Girl* is a precociously capable cook and housekeeper, yet when teased by her brother that "You girls are always thinking about weddings and getting married," she responds indignantly, "We ain't ... I am *never* going to get married. I think it is just horrid, so there!"[34] The resistance of Emily, who knows of no happy marriages other than that of her deceased parents, is more sustained. Planning to be "*wedded to [her] art*,"[35] she is quite discomforted by Great-Aunt Nancy's objectification of her physical features in terms of her sexual attractiveness to potential husbands: "Your ankles will do more for you than your brains ever will."[36]

The era of the New Woman was also the era of Havelock Ellis and public discussion of homosexuality. The ventures of New Women into domains hitherto reserved for men were sometimes attributed to sexual "inversion" (to use Ellis's term), a fear of lesbianism being one component of the backlash against advanced women.[37] Most of the women whom Montgomery describes as unfeminine are eventually tamed and married off, such as Ellen West, whose voice carries "a suggestion of masculinity," and Miss Cornelia who says, "I don't hate [men]. They aren't worth it. I just sort of despise them."[38] However, in a late book, *Anne of Windy Poplars* (1936), there appears an exception in Anne's fellow teacher, embittered Katherine Brooke, who has "almost a man's voice" and declares that she hates men. She eventually escapes from dead-end teaching and is last seen still unmarried and happily working as "private secretary to a globe-trotting M.P."[39] While Anne expresses no overt notion that Katherine might represent an alternative sexuality, Montgomery was herself less innocent; her journal account of her rejection of the attentions of a persistent young woman reveals that at the time of writing this book she was familiar with the word "Lesbian" and its meaning.[40]

Katherine's job is self-evidently incompatible with marriage; other women may take jobs when widowed or deserted, such as lecturer Merle Henderson and sales agent Mrs. Tillytuck both in *Mistress Pat*. In Montgomery's oeuvre, the only respectable work that a woman can carry into her marriage is writing: reduced to a hobby for Anne but later a dedicated career for Emily.

In *Anne's House of Dreams*, which recounts Anne's first years of marriage, her self-deprecation as a writer is presented with considerable slyness on Montgomery's part. Anne continually downplays the value of her work, telling Paul Irving, her former pupil who has become a poet: "I can write pretty, fanciful little sketches that children love and editors send welcome cheques for. But I can do nothing big. My only chance for earthly immortality is a corner in your Memoirs." This opinion is shared by Captain Jim, who "thought women were delightful creatures, who ought to have the vote, and everything else they wanted, bless their hearts; but he did not believe they could write." With Anne's encouragement, Captain Jim gives his "life-book" to Owen Ford, "a 'real writing man'" who transforms it into "a great Canadian novel."[41] Yet throughout *Anne's House of Dreams*, Captain Jim is reading a woman-authored serial romance that captivates his attention, however much he denigrates the author and the genre. Refusing the stereotype of the frivolous woman reader, Montgomery here (and again in Uncle Horace of *Mistress Pat*[42]) rehabilitates sentimental romance by presenting male addicts to the genre. Furthermore, Montgomery's subplot – which frees Leslie Moore from the man believed to be her abusive first husband and concludes with a happy second marriage – validates the work of authors like Anne who write "for the people who still believe in fairyland." The binary complement of reality, fairyland signals its opposite; as young Emily declares: "I shall always end *my* stories happily. I don't care whether it's 'true to life' or not. It's true to life as it *should be* and that's a better truth than the other."[43] Montgomery's readers know that, in real life, the other truth prevails, as demonstrated by the many child and female victims of abuse inhabiting the margins of her stories. Women like Leslie Moore usually remain chained to their abusive spouses, a truth demonstrated in this novel by the thoroughly improbable sequence of events that must be concocted to allow the fictional character to escape, and more explicitly in *Anne of Ingleside* when the sister-in-law and wife of cruel Peter Kirk finally speak up at his funeral.

In Sara Jeannette Duncan's New Woman novel, *A Daughter of Today* (1894), Elfrida Bell exclaims, "Fancy being the author of babies when one could be the author of books!"[44] Montgomery managed to accomplish both, the lateness of her marriage reducing the number of babies and increasing the number of books. But beyond scattered references to Anne's occasional publications she does not project her own successful combination of literary and domestic activity onto any of her major characters (consistent with Ann Ardis's ironic observation that new woman authors rarely share their own success with their characters).[45] Mrs. Charlotte E. Morgan, the obviously married novelist greatly admired by Anne in *Anne of Avonlea*, serves more as an occasion for several of Anne's misadventures than as a model to emulate. However, while Emily's story terminates with her marriage, the three Emily books amply document the choices, difficulties, and determination of a young woman writer of Montgomery's own era and origins as she progresses from newspaper writing to popular periodicals, to the production of real books. As with the many earlier New Woman novels that, in Lyn Pykett's words, make "writing women and women's writing their subjects," the Emily books, "by foregrounding the figure of the woman writer ... foreground the problems of their own production." Pykett points out that the figure of the woman writer or artist in New Woman fiction "is repeatedly used as a way of figuring the lack of fit between women's desire, the socially prescribed norms of the woman's lot, and the actuality of women's lives."[46]

An orphan, Emily is raised in a female household by a pair of maiden aunts who both empower her by their example of competence and authority, and oppress her by their social conservatism and disapproval of imaginative indulgence. Stern, puritanical Aunt Elizabeth eventually concedes, "I don't mind your writing – now. You seem to be able to earn a living by it in a very ladylike way."[47] Scrupulously honest, she proves less obstructive than Emily's possessive suitor, Dean Priest, whose very name embodies the institutional oppression of women. Lacking female mentors, Emily seeks guidance from male authority figures like Father Cassidy, Mr. Carpenter (her teacher), and Dean Priest. Obsessively jealous of Emily's talent, Priest betrays her by lying about the quality of her first full-length manuscript, which she consequently destroys. This bitter representation of the abuse of cultural power reaches far beyond this particular novel, and back to Olive Schreiner's analysis of the disempowerment of women by prevailing cultural norms. In all her published work, Montgomery refers only once to Schreiner's *Story of an African Farm*: in *Emily's Quest*, nearly one hundred pages after Emily learns of Priest's treachery, a letter that would have reconciled the parents of Teddy Kent (Emily's eventual husband) is found unopened in an old copy of the book Montgomery calls *The South African Farm*. This passing reference to Schreiner has less to do with the rather clichéd story of the Trents than with Emily's quest for value and identity, as she is the only one of Montgomery's characters to actually read the book. While we do not receive Emily's direct response, we may infer the book's significance, for of all Montgomery's characters it is Emily who most closely resembles Schreiner's Lyndall, as she consistently pits herself against her culture's narrow construction of woman to forge her literary career.

To do so requires the kind of negotiation and compromise that Lyndall refuses. In order to conclude with Emily living happily ever after in Prince Edward Island with Teddy Kent, Montgomery shows her seriously considering and then rejecting the example of Janet Royal, very much a New Woman, whose literary career as an unmarried, well-paid journalist in New York City was the goal of many ambitious young Canadian women around the turn of the century.[48] It was not, however, a situation about which Montgomery had first-hand knowledge. Her resolution – to keep Emily at home because she requires PEI for her art – represents an ingenious compromise, both acknowledging the attractiveness of Janet Royal's example, and remaining faithful to her own experience.

Montgomery's images of women's potential for independence and success, presented fictionally in Emily and non-fictionally in her own career, remain with her readers. Alice Munro, Margaret Laurence, Margaret Atwood, and Jane Urquhart have all spoken of the importance of Montgomery's example as a successful Canadian woman author.[49] Despite Montgomery's historical marginalization in the Canadian literary canon, many of the millions of girls who have read her work have absorbed a similar message of responsible self-empowerment. In the words of young Marigold's great-grandmother, "Do anything you want to, Marigold – as long as you can go to your looking-glass afterwards and look yourself in the face."[50]

NOTES

I would like to thank Professor Mary Rubio of the English Department at the University of Guelph for sharing some of her research materials on L.M. Montgomery; and both Dr. Rubio and Nancy Sadek, Head of Archival and Special Collections at the University of Guelph Library, for facilitating my access to Montgomery's unpublished journals.

1 Montgomery, 25 November 1933, in UJ, 8: 499 [see also *SJLMM*, 4: 233]. I have noticed only one appearance of the term "new woman" in Montgomery's fiction: in *Anne of Windy Poplars* (written shortly after the cited journal entry), confused young Hazel Marr claims, "I'm not a bit ambitious ... I'm not one of those dreadful new women. *My* highest ambition was to be a happy wife and make a happy home for my husband" (*AWP*, 187; ellipsis in original). More frequent references appear in Montgomery's journals; in the entry for 4 April 1899, she ironically mentions "the newest of 'new' women" (Montgomery, 4 April 1899, in *SJLMM*, 1: 236).

2 Ardis, *New Women, New Novels*, 12–13.

3 Montgomery, 30 April 1923, in *SJLMM*, 3: 128; emphasis in original. In *Mistress Pat*, Judy Plum is afraid that Rae will learn to smoke if she attends the University of Guelph (*MP*, 167).

4 Montgomery, 27 January 1911, in *SJLMM*, 2: 41.

5 Montgomery, 4 March 1917, in *SJLMM*, 2: 211.

6 *AHD*, 93.

7 For Montgomery, the bicycle occasionally served as a vehicle for taunting an elderly aunt: "Very conservative indeed was old Aunt Caroline. Anything new her soul abhorred. *Hymns* were antichrist, and *bicycles*, heaven preserve us, were part of the direct equipment of the Prince of Darkness. I used to take an unholy delight in telling her I was going to get one, although I really hadn't any idea of so doing. I couldn't afford one, worse luck! It *was* such fun to see her horror. She couldn't have looked more aghast if I had told her I was going to appear out in trousers" (Montgomery, 31 December 1898, in *SJLMM*, 1: 229).

8 Montgomery, 29 December 1921, in *SJLMM*, 3: 32; Montgomery, 16 July 1925, in *SJLMM*, 3: 239.

9 [See Mary Rubio's "Subverting the Trite," earlier in this volume.] Sympathetic treatment of an unwed mother appears again in the story "A Commonplace Woman," published posthumously in *The Road to Yesterday*.

10 [See Mary Rubio's "Subverting the Trite," earlier in this volume;] J. Rubio, "'Strewn with Dead Bodies.'"

11 Montgomery, 23 November 1924, in *SJLMM*, 3: 208. [See also "Thinks Modern Flapper Will Be Strict Mother," in Volume 1 of *The L.M. Montgomery Reader*.]

12 Ardis, *New Women, New Novels*, 4.

13 Montgomery, 12 December 1923, in *SJLMM*, 3: 152.

14 See Wilmshurst, "L.M. Montgomery's Use." In 1921 Montgomery read but didn't comment on Edith Wharton's *House of Mirth* (1905) (Montgomery, 16 January 1921, in *SJLMM*, 2: 397).

15 Montgomery, 6 June 1924, in *SJLMM*, 3: 187.

16 Montgomery, 31 January 1920, in *SJLMM*, 2: 370; Montgomery, 29 October 1925, in *SJLMM*, 3: 258.

17 Montgomery, 14 January 1900, in *SJLMM*, 1: 248.

18 Ardis, *New Women, New Novels*, 10.

19 Bolger, *The Years Before "Anne,"* 142, 161–68.

20 *AGG*, 242; *AA*, 228–29.

21 See Montgomery's Book Price Record Book, held at the University of Guelph archives.

22 In 1894, Montgomery recorded her dismay that one of her cousins had gone to work as a domestic servant in Boston: "If she wanted to earn her living [her parents] were quite able to afford to educate or train her to some occupation which would not have involved a loss of social caste" (Montgomery, 4 September 1894, in *SJLMM*, 1: 119).

23 Montgomery, 1 March 1919, in *SJLMM*, 2: 308.

24 *AIs*, 12–13. It is difficult to date Anne's university years. Working backward from the ages of her children in relation to World War I, Rilla, her youngest, is born around 1900 and Jem, her eldest, around 1893. This would put Anne's marriage at 1891, when she is 25, and her graduation five years previously at 1886, thus enrolling her in one of Dalhousie's first classes of women students. On the other hand, Montgomery attended Dalhousie for one year, 1895–96, after several years of striving to get there. Elizabeth Epperly notes that the manuscript of *Anne of the Island* shows that Montgomery considered establishing a firm date for this phase of Anne's life, and then gave up (Epperly, "Approaching the Montgomery Manuscripts," 76).

25 Ronish, "Sweet Girl Graduates."

26 Fingard, "College, Career, and Community," 27.

27 *GR*, 2.

28 *TW*, 39.

29 Schwartz, Introduction, xxiv. "The Yellow Wallpaper," Gilman's earlier, best-known story, is very different in both style and content from these later stories.

30 [Montgomery's three chapters in *Courageous Women* are included in Volume 1 of *The L.M. Montgomery Reader*.]

31 Ardis, *New Women, New Novels*, 140–55.

32 *AA*, 188.

33 *TW*, 16.

34 *SG*, 133.

35 *EC*, 6.

36 *ENM*, 257.
37 Smith-Rosenberg, *Disorderly Conduct*, 245–96; Showalter, *Sexual Anarchy*.
38 *RV*, 91; *AHD*, 48.
39 *AWP*, 29, 255.
40 Montgomery, 7 February 1933 [in *SJLMM*, 4: 215–16].
41 *AHD*, 15, 142, 136.
42 *MP*, 134.
43 *AIn*, 264; *EC*, 222–23. In a similar fashion, the plot of *Emily's Quest* ends up following the formulas of romantic author Bertha M. Clay (see *EQ*, 227).
44 Duncan, *A Daughter of Today*, 157.
45 Ardis, *New Women*, 148.
46 Pykett, *The "Improper" Feminine*, 177.
47 *EQ*, 49.
48 For Montgomery's excitement about her newspaper work in 1901–2, see Montgomery, 13 November 1901, in *SJLMM*, 1: 264–65; Montgomery, 14 November 1901, in *SJLMM*, 1: 265–68. For the larger context, see Gerson, "Canadian Women Writers."
49 [See Mary Rubio's "Subverting the Trite" earlier in this volume.]
50 *MM*, 74.

10

"Pruned Down and Branched Out": Embracing Contradiction in *Anne of Green Gables*

—— 1995 ——

LAURA M. ROBINSON

This paper, published while the author was still a PhD candidate at Queen's University, also in *Children's Voices in Atlantic Literature and Culture*, brings together contradictions in past scholarship on *Anne of Green Gables*, which concludes that Anne is either a feminist or an anti-feminist figure, noting the ways in which Anne's negotiation of the dominant ideologies of Avonlea becomes a "survival manual[] for the next generation of women readers." Laura M. Robinson, now an Associate Professor of English at the Royal Military College of Canada, has continued her research on Montgomery, sexuality, friendship, and community, most notably in her chapter in *L.M. Montgomery and Canadian Culture* (1999) and her journal articles "Bosom Friends: Lesbian Desire in L.M. Montgomery's Anne Books" and "'Sex Matters': L.M. Montgomery, Friendship, and Sexuality."

"There's such a lot of different Annes in me. I sometimes think that is why I'm such a troublesome person. If I was just the one Anne it would be ever so much more comfortable, but then it wouldn't be half so interesting."[1] As Anne notes in the above quotation, her character is multiple, complex and not easy to reconcile. That is, of course, one of the reasons readers love *Anne of Green Gables*; they enjoy watching Anne learn to successfully balance the different parts of her personality. Critics have been relatively unsuccessful at doing just that, more often than not focusing their attentions on one aspect of Anne's character over another. Some critics, like T.D. MacLulich, Elizabeth Epperly, and

E. Holly Pike, focus on Anne's ultimate conformity and conclude that *Anne of Green Gables* ultimately upholds the domestic *status quo*. Other critics, like Temma Berg and Janet Weiss-Townsend, by granting more weight to Anne's subversions and rebellions, suggest that she is a feminist figure.[2] That these two interpretations are possible attests to the irreconcilable tensions in this novel, but neither perspective fully represents the many-faceted Anne. Critics must work to integrate these two positions as Denyse Yeast, Susan Drain, and Mary Rubio successfully have, not by amalgamating them but by holding them in dialogue with one another.[3] *Anne of Green Gables* represents conflicting ideological movements – one stressing conformity for the heroine and one allowing agency – without resolving or reconciling them. Anne, herself, seems to recognize her ability to negotiate the two forces of agency and conformity when she reassures her adopted mother Marilla that she has not changed; she is only "pruned down and branched out."[4] Anne embraces the contradictory ideology facing her with a zeal that critics could learn from.

In *Feminist Criticism and Social Change*, Judith Newton and Deborah Rosenfelt call for a kind of criticism that demonstrates a "capacity to embrace contradiction." Dialectical criticism, they write, establishes "a way of seeing that prompts us to locate in the same situation the forces of oppression and the seeds of resistance; to construct women in a given moment in history simultaneously as victims and as agents."[5] But how does a heroine make sense of herself if she is constructed as both a victim and an agent? Franco Moretti in his study on the *Bildungsroman* has claimed that the structure of this genre is "intrinsically contradictory." The protagonist must either synthesize "the conflict between the ideal of self-determination and the equally imperious demands of socialization" or compromise.[6] In *Anne of Green Gables*, and girls' stories like it, another strategy for dealing with the fundamental contradiction facing young women manifests itself. The character of Anne establishes a sense of identity for herself that is multiple and fluid yet still comprehensible through her negotiation of the conflicting ideological movements of conformity and agency.

This negotiation is a powerful position for feminists to recognize and explore as it shows a capacity to embrace contradiction without trying to reconcile it as Moretti suggests with synthesis, or without giving in as his category of compromise implies. Keeping contradictions intact can be a powerhold for women and feminists as it opens more than one space where identity can be constructed at once. Negotiating the contradictions is like having cake *and* eating it: Anne can be, for example, both subversive and conformist, accepted and unacceptable. She can be both pruned down and branched out. To be a negotiator means having a foot in both camps, understanding both perspectives, being able to function in both roles. A fundamental irony underlies negotiation, as well, as the negotiator can destabilize both ways of being: readers can never be sure whether the character is sincere in her subversiveness or in her conformity. When a woman wants to achieve an amount of autonomy, yet her society or community perceives that autonomy as potentially threatening, she can only negotiate: give in a bit here, to get a bit there. Negotiation is active and slippery. Montgomery's novel also potentially teaches young, and old, readers how to do what Anne does: Montgomery introduces generations of women to the effectiveness of negotiation. Anne's precarious negotiation of the conflicting ideological movements is revealed in the image of the brook, in Anne's self-sacrifice and in Montgomery's narrative technique.

Before examining the text in detail, I would like to discuss the potential didacticism of this and other children's novels. Many readers and critics assume that children's literature is didactic because it is for children. I would argue, instead, that all literature has a didactic function because literature constructs and disseminates ideology. For theorist Louis Althusser, "ideology represents the imaginary relationship of individuals to their real conditions of existence": ideology is the way we represent ourselves to ourselves. Althusser claims that, along with schools, religion, law and so on, culture is an Ideological State Apparatus operating to indoctrinate individuals as good citizens. He sees ideology as ultimately operating in favour of the state by continually reproducing the means of production. Ideological State Apparatuses in concert are, he claims, "dominated by a single score, occasionally disturbed by contradictions."[7] While Althusser sees the contradictions inherent in ideology, he does not pursue this avenue of study to the extent I would like to. If the ideology we as citizens function within is ultimately contradictory, then we must constantly be attempting to reconcile or negotiate the differing messages we receive. Just as Anne does.

Moreover, the ideology produced in texts potentially teaches individuals new kinds of subjectivity, new ways of making sense of themselves and their position in the world. Althusser has suggested that individuals become subjects by freely accepting ideology. Just as Anne identifies with Tennyson's Elaine, other romance heroines, and all the ideological implications connected to these figures, so too might a reader recognize and identify with Anne. Teresa de Lauretis indicates that there are two senses of the word subject: "subject-ed to social constraint and yet subject in the active sense of maker as well as user of culture, intent on self-definition and self-determination."[8] Anne, for example, is both encouraged to conform and able to establish her own distinct sense of self. Readers, through their identification with Anne, might find a subject position from which to make sense of their own material conditions of existence. Ultimately, *Anne of Green Gables* is doubly didactic: not only does Anne create and accept her subject position through a learning process, but the reader learns of a subject position she may potentially use to make sense of herself in the world: the reader has been presented with a potential ideological roadmap. Significantly, Montgomery constructs Anne at the end of the novel literally as a teacher.

Anne Shirley's negotiation of the conflicting ideological movements of conformity and agency forms her subjectivity. The recurring image of the brook that runs close to Green Gables and through Avonlea mirrors the "pruned down and branched out" development of Anne. By the end of the novel, Anne, like the brook in the first line, has conformed to Avonlea standards of propriety represented by Mrs. Lynde. This brook "was reputed to be an intricate, headlong brook in its earlier course through those woods, with dark secrets of pool and cascade; but by the time it reached Lynde's Hollow it was a quiet, well-conducted little stream, for not even a brook could run past Mrs. Rachel Lynde's door without due regard for decency and decorum." Elizabeth Epperly has pointed out the importance of this brook as a symbol for what will happen to Anne: she will grow from a headlong and untamed child into a civilized and acceptable young lady. But the brook, which appears again and again in the novel, takes on an even greater significance than Epperly gives it credit for: while Anne, like the brook, learns to be quiet and well-conducted, she also learns what she can get away with. Anne hints at another interpretation of the brook on her first morning in Green Gables: "I can hear the brook laughing all the way up here. Have you ever noticed what cheerful things brooks are? They're always laughing. Even in wintertime I've heard them under the ice."[9] The brook, like Anne, is always laughing, even when its environment – either wintertime or Avonlea propriety – causes it to grow a superficial layer to mask this laughter. That the brook's and Anne's expression is laughter rather than murmuring or babbling, words also associated with brooks, indicates the response Montgomery looks for in the reader: we as readers are not to take Anne's conformity too seriously. While Anne's hiding her emotions under the surface can be seen as repression, so too can the initial emotional make-up of both Anne and the brook: both are always laughing, no other response seems possible. Arguably, if Anne can only laugh and act cheerfully, she begins the novel more repressed about her emotions than she ends it.[10]

Anne certainly does seem to learn to cloak her emotions like the brook. As the novel progresses she begins to talk less and takes on a more demure demeanour as Epperly and others have pointed out.[11] Anne's conformity fully manifests itself in the chapter entitled "Where the Brook and River Meet," which outlines Anne's physical and mental growth alongside Marilla's sense of loss and regret at losing her adopted child. When Marilla confronts Anne about her new-found quietness, Anne replies, "It's nicer to think dear, pretty thoughts and keep them in one's heart, like treasures. I don't like to have them laughed at or wondered over." The narrator suggests that "perhaps she thought all the more and dreamed as much as ever, but she certainly talked less."[12] Anne recognizes that she must keep secret her deep pools and cascades, but she still has them nonetheless. She has learned to conform on the surface. But laughter is always still possible underneath.

Anne's negotiation lies in her apparent conformity which conceals but does not erase her "improper" thoughts and desires. She actively finds outlets for emotions other than laughter: her gothic-style writing makes her cry "like a child" while writing it; she pretends to be Tennyson's lily maid, a heartbroken woman who dies because she wants what she cannot have; and she publicly recites "The Maiden's Vow" which she labels "pathetic," saying "I'd rather make people cry than laugh."[13] She learns where it is acceptable to vent a full range of emotions. While she seems to have conformed and become increasingly repressed, she has, in fact, more fully developed expression for her emotional responses to the world around her.

Anne's self-sacrifice also reveals the conflicting ideological movements between conformity and agency. The penultimate moment that some critics decry as Anne's capitulation comes when Anne relinquishes her four year scholarship to Redmond to stay home with Marilla at Green Gables. Anne's sacrifice of her desires represents what Segal suggests is the staple of girls' stories: "the appeal of many favourite girls' books heroines rested on their resistance to the confines of the feminine role, but nearly all capitulate in the end."[14] Superficially Anne appears to have given in to community pressure – not only is she more demure but she will not go away to school. She has conformed to the domestic ideal.

Yet the sacrifice can also be seen as representing active agency for Anne. In her essay "Community and the Individual in *Anne of Green*

Gables," Susan Drain suggests that the process of adjustment in the novel is mutual and does not imply conformity only on the part of the child. Anne must actively take on the responsibility of belonging in order to truly have her home. Her self-sacrifice in Drain's view, then, is "a commitment which confirms belonging."[15] In addition to this affirmation of Anne's place in the Avonlea social fabric, a sense of power manifests itself for Anne in the "sacrifice" as well: Green Gables can only be kept if Anne stays to look after things. She takes on a parental role of looking after the almost blind Marilla and overseeing the maintenance of Green Gables.

Furthermore, as Gabriella Åhmansson points out, the real sacrifice is not made by Anne but by Gilbert.[16] He gives up Avonlea school for Anne. He is not motivated to do this by friendship as they have hardly been civil to each other in four years. Rachel Lynde explains: "Real self-sacrificing, too, for he'll have his board to pay at White Sands, and everybody knows he's got to earn his own way through college." Gilbert's sacrifice is a gloss on Anne's: he gains relatively little by it, where Anne keeps Green Gables and Marilla and her sense of home. Moreover, where Anne appears to have made a sacrifice in giving up school, she does not, in fact, give up her schooling. She plans to take Redmond courses by correspondence "right here at Green Gables." There is no capitulation to Mrs. Lynde's notion that women don't need an education.[17] And while Anne can also finally forge a friendship with Gilbert, she does not, as is typical of girls' stories, capitulate to marriage pressures. She has negotiated the contradictory ideological pressures of conformity and agency: even if she's a little pruned down and limited because of social pressures, she ends the novel having done what she wants to do.

The ideological conflict between passive conformity and active agency also presents itself in Montgomery's narrative technique. Critics have almost always recognized the multiple forms at play in the construction of *Anne of Green Gables*. Theodore Sheckels recaps the different genres and forms this novel employs: orphan tale, female *Bildungsroman*, *Kunstlerroman*, regional idyll, female utopia, community novel, and subverted romance. That a wide variety of critics, as Sheckels points out, label this novel in such a wide variety of often contradictory genres attests to its multiplicity. Most critics – Santelmann, Keefer, MacLulich and Ross, for example – have recognized a fundamental narrative conflict in *Anne of Green Gables*, whether between the romantic and domestic, the idyllic and non-idyllic, the ideal and real, or the romantic and real.[18]

What is most important to my study is the fact that the text's subversion, represented by a subtext like romance, hailed by critics like

Mary Rubio,[19] does not cancel out or diminish the ideological thrust represented by the dominant genre, nor does the dominant form prevail over the playful subtext as Epperly suggests. Both narrative strains and their respective ideological messages remain in constant dialogue with one another. The realism in this novel presents the dominant ideological message. The romantic mode clears a space where Anne can find her own agency: Anne uses the romantic discourse she has learned through her extensive reading to deal with her often harsh existence, portrayed by Montgomery through realism. This text teaches more than what Carol Gay describes as "a life lived without imagination is not worth living."[20] It shows the reader that while conformity is necessary, space can be located for one's agency. For Anne, negotiating her everyday life with romantic fantasy is the route to survival.

Realism is dominant when Anne's control over her circumstances is severely limited. When confronted with the reality of being handed over to Mrs. Blewett and a life of hard work and lack of love, Anne does not cloak herself in the language of romance. When Mrs. Blewett demands her name, she gets a very real response: "'Anne Shirley,' faltered the shrinking child, not daring to make any stipulations regarding the spelling thereof."[21] Anne can see that with Mrs. Blewett there can be no opportunity for negotiation.

On the other hand, when Anne is negotiating for some kind of control, whether it will be later checked or not, the romantic mode is dominant. When Marilla asks Anne for her name, for example, Anne immerses herself in the stuff of romance: "'Will you please call me Cordelia?' she said eagerly." She relents when Marilla pushes for her real name, "'Anne Shirley,' reluctantly faltered forth.the owner of that name, 'but oh, please do call me Cordelia. It can't matter much to you what you call me if I'm only going to be here a little while, can it? And Anne is such an unromantic name.'"[22] The conversation continues until Marilla agrees to spell Anne with an "e." Sadly, this romantic whim on Anne's part shows how desperately she wishes to be someone else – a Cordelia, the much-loved daughter of King Lear. More importantly, Anne is making a bid for control over who she is, what people call her and how she is perceived. The whole novel is testament to the fact that she is successful in getting Anne spelled with an "e."

Anne's recounting of her imagined childhood friends combines the romantic and realistic modes. In her oppressive childhood homes where conformity is her only option, she clings to a secret discourse of romance for a measure of agency. These imaginary and romanticized friends help her to establish a sense of identity for herself based on self-worth and intimacy, obviously lacking in her everyday life. Since she creates the friends, she is also in control of the relationship. Anne tells Marilla about one friend: "When I lived with Mrs. Thomas she had a bookcase in her sitting room with glass doors. There weren't any books in it; Mrs. Thomas kept her best china and her preserves there – when she had any preserves to keep. One of the doors was broken. Mr. Thomas smashed it one night when he was slightly intoxicated. But the other was whole and I used to pretend that my reflection in it was another little girl who lived in it. I called her Katie Maurice, and we were very intimate." The language and mode describing the Thomases' homestead is one of realism: the lack of preserves, the broken bookcase, the intoxicated and abusive husband. Realism is not the dominant mode in Anne's usual discourse and the reader, like Marilla earlier, has to be "shrewd enough to read between the lines of Anne's history and divine the truth."[23] The romantic mode dominates the entire section that follows this passage. Anne has managed to gain an element of control and a sense of self-worth through her imagined female friend, but this does not obscure the fact that she is in a situation where she is powerless.

Romance and realism also combine in Anne's perception of her room at Green Gables. The descriptions of the room and its oppressiveness for Anne are presented by Montgomery with realism which Anne transcends by using the discourse of romance. The initial description of the room conveys the harsh environment Anne finds herself in:

> The whitewashed walls were so painfully bare and staring that she thought they must ache over their own bareness. The floor was bare, too, except for a round braided mat in the middle such as Anne had never seen before. In one corner was the bed, a high, old-fashioned one, with four dark, low-turned posts. In the other corner was the aforesaid three-cornered table adorned with a fat, red velvet pincushion hard enough to turn the point of the most adventurous pin. Above it hung a little six by eight mirror. Midway between table and bed was the window, with an icy white muslin frill over it, and opposite it was the washstand. The whole apartment was of a rigidity not to be described in words, but which sent a shiver to the very marrow of Anne's bones.[24]

While the dominant mode here is realism, showing Anne's oppressive environment, romantic discourse also infiltrates the text. Anne thinks the walls must ache and she shivers as the heroine of a gothic romance might.

Anne does manage to turn the oppressiveness of her room around with romantic discourse when Marilla bans her to it as punishment. Keefer isolates these and similar incidents as moments where the non-idyllic glares out from the idyllic mode.[25] But the reader can also see how Anne negotiates with the non-idyllic by using romance. The first of these incidents occurs when Anne has lost her temper with Mrs. Lynde. She is sent to her room until she agrees to apologize. After her adopted parent Matthew convinces her not to stay in her room like a martyr, the apology is overdone to the point of parody. Anne is "rapt and radiant" to Marilla's consternation until she reaches Mrs. Lynde's side: "Then the radiance vanished. Mournful penitence appeared on every feature. Before a word was spoken Anne suddenly went down on her knees before the astonished Mrs. Rachel and held out her hands beseechingly." The apology that follows is melodramatic and humorous but most disturbing is the fact that "Anne was actually enjoying her valley of humiliation – was reveling in the thoroughness of her abasement."[26] She applies the discourse of romance she has learned from her reading to distance herself from the oppressive injustice of her circumstance – being locked up until she apologizes to someone who called her ugly – and thus can turn it to a kind of pleasure. Other examples abound in her confession to Marilla, her imagining the room to be grand, and so on. But both the real and the romantic co-exist in these incidents: Anne uses romantic discourse to negotiate her often unjust everyday circumstances.

Finally, Anne's ambition, written predominantly in a serious and realistic mode, is also cloaked in the discourse of romance. Significantly, Anne is not the one using romance here; Montgomery is the negotiator, balancing what she wants Anne to have – ambition – with the extent to which Anne is allowed to have it. The narrator lets the reader know that Anne is "troubled with the stirrings of ambition" like Gilbert.[27] Anne's hard-core ambition to be at the top of her class, to get into Queen's, and to win the Avery scholarship is depicted as displaced and repressed love for Gilbert. She only wants to be at the top of her class to beat him. Throughout the narrative, she attempts to disguise this rivalry by checking herself before finishing Gilbert's name. The following are several examples: "I hate to stay home for Gil– some of the others will get head of the class." "I don't really care whether Gil– whether anybody gets ahead of me in class or not." "And Gil– everybody will get ahead of me in class." "It would be such a disgrace to fail, especially if Gil– if the others passed."[28]

In the discourse of romance this slip of the tongue reveals Anne's emotional feelings towards Gilbert at the same time as it attempts to disguise them in her ambition. Montgomery makes Anne's ambition acceptable, where it might be improper for a young lady to want success so much, by hinting that it is only motivated by love for Gilbert. This use of disguise can be completely reversed. For Montgomery, Anne's repeated slips also disguise, in her feelings towards Gilbert, that very ambition. Anne also simply wants to be the top student in her class. In fact, the passionate sense of rivalry with Gilbert eventually leaves her, yet her ambition remains: "Anne no longer wished to win for the sake of defeating Gilbert; rather, for the proud consciousness of a well-won victory over a worthy foeman."[29] The potential for romance between Anne and Gilbert makes Anne's ambition acceptable. Montgomery is using the discourse of romance to get what she wants for her heroine. However, Anne's ambition clearly needs some kind of disguise in Montgomery's view: it might not be acceptable on its own.

Anne not only shows readers how to embrace contradiction but she operates to teach a new generation of women about the powerful and active position of negotiator. She negotiates with her environment, her needs, her ability to control situations. And she is, in this novel, successful. Instead of critics lamenting the heroines' capitulation to the *status quo* or trumpeting the subversion of girls' stories, critics can isolate the ideological powers at play on the heroine, while locating the girl's agency, through an exploration of her negotiation. Heroines, like Anne, continually negotiate between the ideological forces at work on them. Readers, who potentially identify with the heroine, can learn how and where to negotiate. Ultimately, readers are potentially learning about what they can and cannot get away with, what they need to hide or disguise, and what is acceptable to present to their communities: where they might have to prune down in order to be able to branch out. Montgomery, and writers like her, have, in effect, written survival manuals for the next generation of women readers.

NOTES

I would like to thank Professors Maggie Berg and Tracy Ware from Queen's University for their suggestions for improving the original version of this paper, "Embracing Contradiction: The Subject and the Reader in *Anne of Green Gables.*"

1 *AGG*, 161.
2 MacLulich, "L.M. Montgomery's Portraits"; Epperly, *The Fragrance of Sweet-Grass*; Pike, "The Heroine Who Writes"; Berg, "*Anne of Green Gables*"; Weiss-Townsend, "Sexism Down on the Farm?"
3 Yeast, "Negotiating Friendships"; Drain, "Feminine Convention and Female Identity"; [see also Mary Rubio's "Subverting the Trite," in this volume].
4 *AGG*, 276.
5 Newton and Rosenfelt, "Introduction," xxiii, xxii.
6 Moretti, *The Way of the World*, 6, 15.
7 Althusser, *Lenin and Philosophy*, 153, 146.
8 de Lauretis, *Feminist Studies*, 10.
9 *AGG*, 1; Epperly, *The Fragrance of Sweet-Grass*, 19; *AGG*, 31–32.
10 I am indebted to Barbara Seeber from the Department of English at Queen's University for making this insight in a discussion we had about my paper.
11 Epperly, *The Fragrance of Sweet-Grass*, 37; see also MacLulich, "L.M. Montgomery's Portraits," 466.
12 *AGG*, 254.
13 *AGG*, 208, 269.
14 Segal, "'As the Twig Is Bent,'" 174.
15 Drain, "Community and the Individual," 15, 19.
16 Åhmansson, *A Life and Its Mirrors*, 71.
17 *AGG*, 305, 304.
18 Sheckels, "In Search of Structures"; Santelmann, "Written as Women Write"; Keefer, *Under Eastern Skies*; MacLulich, "L.M. Montgomery's Portraits"; Ross, "Calling Back the Ghost."
19 [See Mary Rubio's "Subverting the Trite" earlier in this volume.]
20 Gay, "'Kindred Spirits' All," 107.
21 *AGG*, 45.
22 *AGG*, 24.
23 *AGG*, 58, 41.
24 *AGG*, 27.
25 Keefer, *Under Eastern Skies*, 196.
26 *AGG*, 73, 74.
27 *AGG*, 277–78.
28 *AGG*, 144, 161, 187, 256.
29 *AGG*, 284.

11

Finding L.M. Montgomery's Short Stories
—— 1995 ——

REA WILMSHURST

In this charming essay, first published as the afterword to *Across the Miles: Tales of Correspondence* (1995), Rea Wilmshurst recounts her discovery of Montgomery's scrapbooks of short stories and poems as well as her tenacity in locating copies of the periodicals in which these items appeared, her efforts to produce several bibliographies of these materials, and finally her work on gathering together eight collections of Montgomery's stories, of which *Across the Miles* was the seventh. The last, *Christmas with Anne and Other Holiday Stories*, would also appear in 1995. Rea Wilmshurst died in 1996.

Great literary finds are not exactly a dime-a-dozen. But even if they were, for the finder they would always be exciting. I had no notion of ever being one of those people who find something interesting in their own or someone else's attic. In fact, I never thought of looking. When a friend and I visited L.M. Montgomery's birthplace in New London, P.E.I., in 1977, we were going simply as interested tourists, tourists interested in the author of the twenty books that began with *Anne of Green Gables*. It was my friend who called me over to a glass-fronted display cabinet to look at a short story pasted in a scrapbook. Did I know it? Silly question. Didn't I know all her twenty novels and four short-story collections almost off by heart by virtue of constant re-reading since the age of eleven? Of course I would know this story. But I didn't.

Luckily, the ladies in charge weren't particularly busy and were pleased to get the scrapbook out of the case for me. It was full of short stories by Montgomery, none of which I had ever seen before. "Well, if you're really interested, there are more upstairs," they told me. Up the stairs, in one of the tiny bedrooms, was a cardboard box, the floor around it sprinkled with Mouse Feast. There were eleven other scrapbooks in the box; all contained clippings of published stories and poems by L.M. Montgomery. A feast indeed, but for mice? Were these collections safe, kept in a cardboard box, in a frame house, surrounded by Mouse Feast? I found out much later that the stories only visited the birthplace in the summer and were carried off to the Confederation Centre archives at the end of the season. But at the time my only concern was that they survive until I could come back with more time and read them all.

That was my original focus. I wanted to read them. Unlike most young women who had read *Anne* and the other novels in their teens and then put them aside as childish things, I never stopped reading them. I read them year in and year out, again and again. I never tired of their apparent simplicity, finding them more complex than they seemed, their emotions true and believable. They were part of my innermost being. But there weren't enough of them. Only twenty novels and forty-eight short stories.

Now here was a collection of hundreds. How many, I had not time on that visit to discover. But I knew that I must make sure they were safe, and that I must get permission from someone to look through and read them all and, if possible, copy them so I could go on re-reading them too. Still, it took me a while to get up my courage to do anything about it. Surely, I thought, it must be just my ignorance that I didn't know about these collections; probably everyone in the field (was there a Montgomery field in 1977?) knew about them. And might I tread on academic toes?

One thing I did know was that Montgomery's younger son, Dr. Stuart Macdonald, lived in Toronto, but I thought that he was probably constantly pestered by Montgomery fans and that I should not intrude on him. Without contacting him, I went back to P.E.I. the next summer and spent a happy couple of days making a list of every story and poem in all twelve collections. Only about half of them, by the way, were bound scrapbooks, into which were pasted the pieces Montgomery had clipped. The other half were sewn gatherings of full pages from magazines. I even read a few of the stories, but again, time was short.

Back home in Toronto I put together a typed pamphlet called "A Listing of Scrapbooks and Gatherings in Montgomery's Birthplace," put a spiral binding on it, and called it a private publication (1978). This seemed rather respectable (it was 27 pages long and contained over 700 entries, half of them poems, the other half stories), so I summoned up the courage to write to Dr. Macdonald. He answered most kindly. He had been unaware of the existence of the stories and, once I had proved my sincere intentions, was willing that I should have access to them. He arranged that his friend Father Francis Bolger, a professor at the University of Prince Edward Island and a trustee of the birthplace, have them photocopied. (Father Bolger was familiar with the collection of scrapbooks because he had used their contents for his book about Montgomery's early publications, *The Years Before "Anne."*) The process of copying took about a year, because only one scrapbook at a time could be removed from the collection. Father Bolger made two copies of the scrapbooks, keeping one for the University of Prince Edward Island archives and sending one to me; on receipt of the second copy I made a set for Dr. Macdonald, which went to the University of Guelph archives on his death.

What a feast of reading I had that year! I revelled in every new story, whether it was good or not so good. Some stories were exceptional; some had obviously been churned out at top speed. Several seemed familiar; they were the originals of vignettes in some of the novels. ("Mrs. Skinner's Story," published in *Westminster Magazine* in 1907, was adapted for Chapter 30 of *Anne of the Island* in 1915; "A House Divided against Itself," published in *Canadian Home Journal* in 1930, became one of the strands in *A Tangled Web* the very next year; *Anne of Windy Poplars* and *Anne of Ingleside* are made up almost wholly of stories that had first seen the light of day previously.) Some stories appeared more than once, having been sold, with few or no alterations, to different magazines. Some had Montgomery's own handwritten corrections of typographical errors and stylistic adjustments. All were interesting to me as showing the range of her talent and her ability to keep at it. Does one today assume that a newspaper writer will produce gems of stylistic brilliance in every column, every day? Of course not. And that is almost the way Montgomery was writing: at that speed and at that volume. But more of the volume later.

There was just enough publication information (magazine names and dates) attached to the stories in the sewn gatherings to make me want to produce a bibliography. The 360 stories of which I now had copies had been published in 134 different magazines and newspapers, running from the *Advocate and Guardian* to *Zion's Herald*, and covering most of the rest of the alphabet in between. Of course I couldn't find all these magazines. Some were tiny affairs, long since deceased. Some were ephemeral Sunday School publications. But in the Library of Congress in Washington, D.C., in the New York Public Library, the Toronto Public

Library, and a few other regional libraries, I tracked down many of them. They had no indexes, of course. No tables of contents. I spent many hours in the stacks of the Library of Congress leafing through enormous bound volumes of *Boys' World* and *Girls' Companion*, freezing my bottom on cold marble floors and covering my top with decaying leather. And every so often, in the midst of keeping track of dates and page numbers, I would find a story not in the scrapbook collections. Eventually my filing cabinet contained over 400 items.

You might think that, with 400 items, I must surely have a complete collection. Not so. Dr. Macdonald let me borrow and copy a ledger Montgomery had kept, in which she listed every dollar she had earned from her publications: stories, poems, and novels. Her list of stories reached No. 517. Reading the list carefully, I discovered that some of those 517 were chapters of books: *Magic for Marigold* and *Emily of New Moon*, for instance, came out serially (the former before, the latter after, publication as a novel), and Montgomery listed those chapters as short stories in her list. To add a little confusion, sometimes Montgomery's numbers got out of order: she would misread a seven as a one and continue with two rather than with eight, thereby repeating numbers already used, or she would do the opposite, jumping from one to eight, having misread the one as a seven. Some of the stories I had were not on her list; others she did list were not in the scrapbooks and I had not found them. Still, when I completed the bibliography in 1985, listing the found and unfound stories, there were 506 titles, and copies of 400 of them were in my collection. I will probably never find the other 106 stories.

All this time, Mary Rubio and Elizabeth Waterston of the University of Guelph had been comforters and sustainers. They had published my first article, a preliminary bibliography of the stories, in *Canadian Children's Literature* in 1983. They had encouraged me, nay, ordered me, to apply for a Canada Council grant to complete the bibliography. Now they leaned on me again: "Get the stories out to the public." Dr. Macdonald had died since my work began, but he had often expressed his hope that I could get some of the stories published. And so I approached McClelland and Stewart in 1985. They accepted my proposal for the first collection of stories, and *Akin to Anne: Tales of Other Orphans* came out three years later. The next three followed year by year: *Along the Shore: Tales by the Sea*, *Among the Shadows: Tales from the Darker Side*, and *After Many Days: Tales of Time Passed*. A fifth, *Against the Odds: Tales of Achievement*, appeared in the spring of 1993; *At the Altar: Matrimonial Tales*, the sixth, in 1994, and now *Across the Miles: Tales of Correspondence* in 1995. I hope there will be at least two more collections.

I have often been asked why the collections have been grouped thematically. As I was reading over the stories to choose those worth publishing they seemed to fall naturally into certain categories, and although it makes for some sameness to have nineteen stories all about orphans, it is also interesting to note the changes Montgomery is able to ring on such a theme. A chronological presentation or a "best of" collection would pose other problems, so the theme decision was adhered to.

I mentioned before that I had been struck, on first reading the scrapbook photocopies through, at finding stories that I recognized from the novels. But even when Montgomery repeats a story or recycles a plot from one story to another she finds ways in her use of character and setting and point of view to vary it. She was, after all, a professional writer; she wrote in order to earn money; and she produced stories in a quantity that is somewhat staggering. Her output of novels is just as amazing, considering that, as she was producing them, she was a minister's wife in a small Ontario community, with all the concomitant duties that position used to entail. And if there is a distinct falling off in the last two *Anne* books, written at her publisher's insistence, when she was sick of Anne, *Jane of Lantern Hill*, her last book, is one of her best.

Montgomery's first poem was published in 1890; her first story in 1895. In 1901, 13 stories and 28 poems appeared; in 1903, the high point for poems, 32; in 1905, the high point for stories, 44. By 1910, when her novel-writing began to take precedence, her output of stories was down to nine (but another 22, previously in print, were re-published); 12 new poems and five re-publications of poems came out that year. An amazing record, and an amazing woman.

Since the publication of her journals, for which we are all eternally grateful to Mary Rubio and Elizabeth Waterston, Montgomery seems much more interesting as a person and worthy of attention as a writer. Is it because we now know of the occasional despair that lay behind the sweetness and light of most of her writing? There are depths to Montgomery, as scholars, critics, and readers are increasingly coming to discover.

12

L.M. Montgomery's Manuscript Revisions

—— 1995 ——

ELIZABETH EPPERLY

In this short article, published in the journal *Atlantis*, Elizabeth Rollins Epperly reveals the results of her research into L.M. Montgomery's handwritten book manuscripts, housed at the Confederation Centre of the Arts in Charlottetown, focusing specifically on the manuscripts of *Anne of Green Gables* and *Emily of New Moon*, both of which imply much about Montgomery's frame of mind during the moments of their composition. Epperly, already co-editor of *My Dear Mr. M: Letters to G.B. MacMillan from L.M. Montgomery* (1980), author of *The Fragrance of Sweet-Grass: L.M. Montgomery's Heroines and the Pursuit of Romance* (1992), and founding chair of the L.M. Montgomery Institute, would become President of the University of Prince Edward Island, also in 1995. Her most recent contributions to the field of Montgomery studies are the book-length studies *Through Lover's Lane: L.M. Montgomery's Photography and Visual Imagination* (2007) and *Imagining Anne: The Island Scrapbooks of L.M. Montgomery* (2008).

Many of the thrills of reading A.S. Byatt's novel *Possession* come from the detective work involved in investigating original manuscripts. On a routine trip to the London Library Roland discovers amid manuscript notes the secret love affair of a famous Nineteenth-Century poet. Anyone who has studied manuscripts knows the excitement of finding out something intimate about the writer in the changes of ink and slant of the words, in the crossings out and the additions, in the marginal notations and in the quality and care of the papers themselves. Thirteen years ago I began to work with Lucy Maud Montgomery's fifteen novel manuscripts owned by the Confederation Centre of the Arts in Charlottetown, Prince Edward Island, and found out things about her methods and choices I would not have suspected. Montgomery's secret affair was with system; she devised a tidy scheme for making additions and changes on the manuscripts and then wrestled with the system as her heroines and personal circumstances became more complicated.

Each of the manuscripts has its own peculiarities and patterns, but we can understand much about the scope and quality of Montgomery's revision scheme by looking at some significant places in the two initial novels of her most successful series – *Anne of Green Gables* and *Emily of New Moon*. The radical differences between Anne and Emily and in Montgomery's circumstances in creating them are reflected in the kinds of changes Montgomery made to the manuscripts and to her system of revision.

The fifteen manuscripts consist of odd-sized and variously shaped bundles of pages – some yellow and brittle and some neatly de-acidified, with Montgomery's rounded hand sometimes plainly legible and other times all but unreadable, with ink in thin and thick flow and the slant as capricious as the waves on a windy day in Cavendish. Montgomery was a careful conserver and reused pages. For only a few of the manuscripts did she use clean sheets of paper and write on front and back. She wrote on the backs of her own typescripts, using, for example, the typescripts for stories that eventually appeared in *Chronicles of Avonlea* (1912) to write *Anne of Green Gables* (1908) or using a carbon of the typescript for *Anne of Green Gables* for her final novel *Anne of Ingleside*, published more than thirty years later in 1939. She also wrote on her husband Ewan's sermons, on fan letters, on her children's school lectures and examination booklets, on advertising and investment letters, on typescripts of poems (some of them signed with her early pen names Maud Eglington and Maud Cavendish), on church circulars, and on Toronto Women's Press Club notices. The manuscripts vary in size – she even used different sizes of sheets within the same bundle. For example, half of *Anne of the Island* was written on the 8 ½ by 11 typescript pages for *The Golden Road* and the other half of *Anne of the Island* is on front to back 6 by 8 letter-sized pages. Few of the sheets of *Jane of Lantern Hill* are exactly the same size since she used letters, circulars, typescripts, and sermons – most of them torn in half – for paper. One spends hours piecing together bits of Montgomery's life from the clues revealed on the backs of these scraps, sometimes more intrigued by the scraps than by the unfolding story on the reverse side.

Early in her career, when writing short stories, Montgomery established the revision technique she was to use with all of her novels. Rather than make long additions on the original pages of the story she was writing, she simply marked a place for the addition with the word "Note" and a letter of the alphabet. Usually she dropped the word "Note" somewhere along in the first run of the alphabet, and then used only a letter and its corresponding sequence number. After completing the alphabet the first time, she would follow with A1 through Z1 and then A2 through Z2 and so on, going through the alphabet as many as twenty-five times for one novel. The additions were written out on separate sheets and were kept at the end of a manuscript. Montgomery worked through a story, making minor local adjustments and additions directly on the page with a crossing through and/or a carat and using the alphabet system for additions and changes she wanted to make after a day's writing or indeed at any time in writing the story. In the early manuscripts the alphabet notations are clear and orderly, but in later manuscripts the alphabet notations for a single page can be staggeringly varied: P23 may be followed by B12 and that followed by Z19. And sometimes, in the later novels, these black ink and pencil alphabet notations are accompanied by new red ink letters and numbers, clearly meant to supersede all other notations, but contradicting themselves with repetitions and reordering.

In theory the system was tidy and effortless. In practice, it became as elaborate and complex as the narratives. The differences between the novels before and after marriage and before and after the First World War suggest the strains of keeping the complicated self-editorial process in Montgomery's increasingly difficult private life from leaking into the apparently effortless and straightforward style she had established as her literary hallmark.

In 1914 Montgomery recalled penning the opening paragraphs of *Anne of Green Gables* almost ten years earlier. She remembered tossing them off easily and happily and then being interrupted by Ewan, who was making the first visit of what was to become a courtship. She knew she had already done what for her was the hardest part of the story – the opening – and she had done so with energy and joy.[1] The manuscript corroborates her recollection. The writing is remarkably free from additions or alterations. The famous opening one hundred and forty-eight word sentence of the printed *Anne of Green Gables* was originally in manuscript two sentences, broken almost exactly half way through. The wording of the original and printed versions are almost identical. Notes A and B appear in this first sentence but they add only two phrases: "fringed with alders and ladies' eardrops and" as well as "from brooks and children up."[2] The local adjustments include a colon in place of the first printed semi-colon and the words "or out of place" added with a carat. The handwriting is clear, cheerfully rounded, and from the uniform slant and quality of the ink, evidently dashed off quickly. In fact, the entire first chapter and much of the manuscript as a whole show the same kinds of ease and speed. She makes small additions of phrases throughout the first chapter, but not one of them changes the narrative line or substantially alters the quality of description or dialogue. The chapter has alphabetic notes A through X, in order, and additions only of phrases or an odd sentence. Montgomery obviously had the story line firmly in mind and made the few local and extra changes while she was composing or shortly afterwards.

The few manuscript changes in this opening chapter – and the consistently minor additions made to dialogue, description, and narrative throughout – confirm what Montgomery herself suggested in describing the process she used for composition. Like Anthony Trollope, who took long walks and rehearsed dialogues and scenes and then produced pages virtually untouched in revision,[3] Montgomery knew exactly where she was going before she wrote. In her journals and letters she talked about "brooding up" a heroine and "blocking out" scenes and chapters. Though we do not have the plans for *Anne of Green Gables* we have a few of them for *Rainbow Valley*[4] and *Mistress Pat*[5] and they suggest what even the most chaotically revised manuscripts show: the main story and the principal scenes were absolutely clear ahead of time. In *Anne of Green Gables* this means that even an exciting chapter such as "An Unfortunate Lily Maid," where Anne plays Elaine, nearly drowns, and is rescued by Gilbert Blythe or the chapter called "Where the Brook and River Meet," that shows the transition from girlhood to young womanhood, are virtually without major changes. Some colourful expressions are added in both cases. In "An Unfortunate Lily Maid" when Anne is lamenting the loss of her play place Idlewild, Montgomery adds these words to a sentence talking about her consolation: "not without an eye to the romance of it."[6] In "Where the Brook and River Meet," after Marilla has asked Anne why she has quieted down and Anne has told her that she now prefers to keep many of her dear thoughts to herself rather than have them laughed at or wondered over, Montgomery adds a longish paragraph with Marilla asking about the fate of the old story club and has Anne explain about it. But in both cases, though the additions enrich the narrative, the main story was already clearly established.

There are, in fact, only two really long additions to the entire manuscript, and they both occur in the famous raspberry scene in the chapter "Diana Is Invited to Tea with Tragic Results," where Anne unwittingly gets Diana drunk by giving her currant wine rather than the brightly coloured and harmless raspberry drink. These two additions come almost immediately together and provide a needed distraction from and sufficient time for Diana's swallowing of three generous tumblers of wine. In the original manuscript version Anne is chattering as Diana drinks, but there is little time for us to focus away from Diana. The manuscript reads: "The last time I made a cake I forgot to put the flour in. Flour is so. essential in cakes, you know. Marilla was very cross and I don't wonder. I'm a great trial to her. Why, Diana, what is the matter?"[7] The appended notes extend the scene considerably and give us a rich helping of Anne's monologue. Between "The last time I made cake and forgot to put the flour in" and "Flour is so essential to cakes, you know" Montgomery added one hundred and eighteen words describing in detail Anne's romantic daydream about Diana dying of smallpox and Anne's rescuing of her that had distracted Anne from putting flour in the cake. And then, right after Anne says of Marilla, "I'm a great trial to her," Montgomery adds four hundred and seventy-four words in which Anne describes her dreadful ordeal with the mouse in the pudding sauce, another important instance – thematically – where Anne's good imagination borrows indiscriminately from romance literature and brings her to grief in the prosaic world around her. The printed version of the scene, containing the 592 words of the two added notes, gives us a wonderful comic byplay that then fits together well with Anne's other trials and ordeals over growing up in staid Avonlea.

Throughout *Anne of Green Gables* the additions offer vividness and humour. But perhaps the most interesting intimate detail the manuscript reveals – for Anne fans – is that Anne's bosom friend was originally Laura and even Gertrude before Montgomery settled on Diana.[8]

In 1920, having just completed *Rilla of Ingleside*, Montgomery made a "dark and deadly vow" in her journal that she was finished with Anne forever. She said that she had been thinking about a new heroine and, sick of Anne, she wanted to do a new kind of writing.[9] At first glance, the manuscript for *Emily of New Moon*, published in 1923, is as different from the manuscript of *Anne of Green Gables* as the Montgomery of her thirties was different from the Montgomery of her forties. Since writing *Green Gables*, Montgomery had married and moved to Ontario, given birth to three children – one of whom only lived a day – written seven more novels, lived through the First World War and the death of her dearest friend and cousin Frederica Campbell MacFarlane, discovered that her husband's mental illness was recurrent and made him abhorrent to her, and embarked on a lengthy and expensive lawsuit with the L.C. Page Company of Boston. The world she had known and loved on Prince Edward Island had disappeared and her life as a minister's wife in rural Ontario was often filled with disappointment and bitterness. In 1920, as she brooded up her new heroine, Emily Byrd Starr, she was also copying into uniform-sized ledgers the journal she had kept since her teens on P.E.I. Emily's story is largely autobiographical; it is important to remember how closely Montgomery was reviewing her own past as she created Emily's attitudes and actions and may explain why there are so many local changes and later additions in the Emily manuscript.

The 716 page *Anne of Green Gables* manuscript is a neat stack of de-acidified sheets of fairly legible script. The chaotically numbered 400 pages of *Emily of New Moon*, on legal-sized and 8 ½ sheets mixed, are yellow and brittle and have not been de-acidified because the porousness of the lined paper would make the ink run. In *Anne of Green Gables*, Montgomery works steadily through the alphabet, making additions in order so that she can follow right through from Note A to S19 in the text as well as on the 137 pages of appended notes; in *Emily of New Moon* the alphabet notations are seldom in order though they do appear in clusters – Notes A, B, C, D, E, and G all appear in the first chapter, but so do G20, N1, K2 and O. The alphabet for any one number is not necessarily complete and later numbers in an alphabet may be superseded by new notations in red ink. The note pages are missing. I had hoped to be able to trace Montgomery's process of revision by pursuing each of the alphabet lists and discovering a pattern to them. But, as in *Green Gables*, here too the additions may be bits of dialogue, description, or narrative. There is no pattern to the kinds of things added except that they are always helpful and colourful details. Clusters of changes that follow roughly the same alphabet order are the most dissimilar in subject and nature. Some of the higher numbers – the late teens and twenties – that are scattered throughout the manuscript may occasionally show some similarity in subject, as though Montgomery may have been thinking about a particular character or scenes relating to him or her and decided to make a series of additions and changes. For example, Q23, R23, S23,

U23, and V23 (there is no T23), which appear on pages 22, 440, 51, 65, and 75 respectively, have to do with cousin Jimmy – he is being described, is speaking or is present conspicuously in the scene involved. But P23, which precedes this cluster, deals with Emily's father and Y23 (there is no W23 or X23) describes Emily's garret retreat.

From first to last the meticulous changes are virtually without pattern. Note A is the first addition to the manuscript, but note T19 appears on the last page, while D25 is the highest notation number and it appears back on page 337 of the printed novel's 351 pages.

Again, as in *Green Gables*, it is obvious that Montgomery had the entire story in mind while she wrote. Nevertheless, there are more long additions in this novel than in *Green Gables* – the additions amounting to more than 23,000 words of the novel's approximately 120,000, whereas in *Green Gables* we find roughly a third of this number of additions.

Some of the highest concentrations of changes and additions occur in Emily's letters to her father; interestingly, these are the parts of the novel that also have much direct autobiography. Chapter IX, "A Special Providence," is filled with facts Montgomery lifted from her own journal account of her childhood in Cavendish, and this chapter has a riot of alphabetical additions. Here Emily begins to write letters to her dead father, addressing them to "Mr. Douglas Starr, On the Road to Heaven" – just as the child Montgomery had addressed letters on precious letter bills to her dead mother. The letter to her father contains nineteen additions; one describing Emily's friendship with Rhoda Stuart is 680 words long, but the others range from seven to seventy-five words, in this bewildering sequence: A21, A24, V4, N4, W3, D4, J5, F21, E5, D21, I5, F4, Y20, J4, E21, R4, Z3, A4, and G21. Whatever pattern Montgomery was following, it is certain that she took great care with the autobiographical additions and went over the additions themselves many times as she polished Emily's story.

The opening paragraphs of *Emily of New Moon* were added later, though the original paragraphs are included immediately after them. Several of the names were changed later in red ink: the Murrays were originally the Cliffords; Blair Water was Allan Water, then Lynn Water; most interesting is that Dean Priest was for some time Dean Temple[10] though the Priest clan and Priest Pond are original names, as though Montgomery may have intended him to be a more distant cousin at first though she retained the suggestion of sacred and mysterious (while perhaps adding the patriarchal) in switching to Priest for Dean's surname. The scenes of most drama and emotion – Emily's rescue by Dean, her battle with Aunt Elizabeth over her letters, her psychic vision of Ilse's mother – all have remarkably few additions and certainly no additions that suggest any shift in focus or theme.

What do we learn from Montgomery as a writer from looking at the manuscripts? We find how conscientiously she planned the novels, how carefully she went over them, how quickly and how slowly she wrote, how readily and how accurately she called to mind lines from her favourite authors, how frequently she tested names for people and places until she found what she wanted. The legibility of her handwriting deteriorates with time and yet when she is describing her own favourite recollections in *Jane of Lantern Hill*, the penultimate completed novel published in 1937, her handwriting can be as legible as the best passages in *Green Gables*. What she chose to preserve for writing stock is itself worth study, as I have suggested, for we can be startled to find her preserving Ewan's caustic remarks about parishioners alongside a carbon copy of her own confidential medical assessment of his mental illness. Montgomery may not have been reliable about page numberings and alphabetical sequences, but I cannot believe this canny woman, who was always looking ahead and writing ahead to her posthumous audience, did not know exactly what trove she was leaving for the A.S. Byatt characters of current academe. Each manuscript reveals something fresh about Montgomery's prolonged affair with system; each story tells us something special about the way this intensely private woman interlaced public and private texts.

NOTES

1 Montgomery, 18 April 1914, in *SJLMM*, 2: 147.
2 Montgomery, "Anne of Green Gables" (manuscript), notes 1.
3 Trollope, "A Walk in the Wood."
4 Montgomery, "Rainbow Valley" (manuscript).
5 Montgomery, "The Girls of Silver Bush" (manuscript of *Mistress Pat*).
6 Montgomery, "Anne of Green Gables" (manuscript), notes 113.
7 Ibid., 273.
8 Ibid., 46.
9 Montgomery, 24 August 1920, in *SJLMM*, 2: 390.
10 Montgomery, "Emily of New Moon" (manuscript), 357. (The page number is rewritten in red ink as 337).

13

"My Secret Garden": Dis/Pleasure in L.M. Montgomery and F.P. Grove

—— 1999 ——

IRENE GAMMEL

This article by Irene Gammel, now a Canada Research Chair in Modern Literature and Culture and a Professor of English at Ryerson University, returns to the topics of sexuality, modernism, and nation-building, but rather than see the work of L.M. Montgomery as in opposition to that of her contemporary Frederick Philip Grove, she argues that both were concerned with eros and sexual health, albeit with differing viewpoints and aims. The publication of Gammel's article coincided with the publication of two collections of essays edited by her: *Confessional Politics*, which "investigates the many different ways in which women are subjected to confessional modalities in life writing and popular media and actively defy traditional confessional readings," and *L.M. Montgomery and Canadian Culture* (with Elizabeth Epperly), which argues that Montgomery's work "strategically inscribes the signifiers of Canadian distinctness, even while appealing to a broad, international readership."[1] It also followed the television series *Emily of New Moon*, which began airing on the Canadian Broadcasting Corporation early in 1998.

"Today I finished *Emily of New Moon*, after six months writing," notes the author of *Anne of Green Gables* in her journal on 15 February 1922. "It is the best book I have ever written – and I have had more intense pleasure in writing it than any of the others – not even excepting *Green Gables*. I have *lived* it."[2] L.M. Montgomery's most autobiographical character follows the author's development as a writer against the backdrop of Prince Edward Island's pastoral landscapes and dramatic seashores. The island garden emerging from Montgomery's pen is a space for girls' and adolescents' emotions and desires, giving expression to girls' raptures, ecstasies, infatuations, longings, and satisfaction, while also detailing the pains arising from the pressures and prohibitions of a repressive society. Yet by the time Montgomery marries off her heroine in *Emily's Quest*, her own pleasure in writing this work has turned into displeasure, and she resorts to what biographers Mary Rubio and Elizabeth Waterston have described as a slapstick closure.[3] Amid journal entries recording her loneliness, unhappy marriage, and "gnawing mental pain" that she is able to obliterate only "by an opiate," Montgomery records her disappointment with *Emily's Quest*: "it is such a relief to feel it is off my mind at last." Sending off the manuscript for typing in November 1926, she pens her final negative verdict in her journal: "It is no good."[4]

Since Elizabeth Waterston's 1966 landmark essay, "Lucy Maud Montgomery 1874–1942," pioneering scholarship has firmly established Montgomery's subversiveness as a writer who covertly undercuts many of the conventions that she overtly upholds. Mary Rubio has reclaimed Montgomery as "a serious, disruptive, political author of adult books,"[5] and has noted Montgomery's social subversiveness, perhaps best illustrated in her religious parodies and satires.[6] In *The Fragrance of Sweet-Grass*, Elizabeth Epperly has argued that Montgomery upholds the value of romance for healthy girls and women, yet systematically subverts the old chivalric romance ideals, as well as "the equally prescriptive romance of love and marriage," to produce a subversively feminist rewriting of the romance genre.[7] Most recently, K.L. Poe has shown that Montgomery constructs a matriarchal view in her novels, yet cleverly masks matriarchal power in the telling of the tale. The message is radical, while the packaging appears reassuringly conventional.[8]

This essay begins by mapping the subversiveness of Montgomery's erotic imaginary, the domain of pleasures, fantasies, dreams, and longing, played out in her fiction. That this domain has remained unexplored is partly due to Montgomery's status as an author of children's fiction and the critics' reluctance to mix childhood with issues of sexuality; yet this gap is also indicative of the extent to which the writing of female eros has been glossed over and silenced in the critical construction of early Canadian literature, a passionate, even fervent, national enterprise during the 1920s. Within the rise of a distinctively Canadian literature, Montgomery's public claiming of female-centred pleasure through her literature and her parallel private narrative of displeasure provide a template for charting the complex debates and negotiations that were underway in the early twentieth-century Canadian literary construction of what Michel Foucault has termed "sexuality."[9] As a writer of best-selling fiction in Canada and the United States, Montgomery silenced the sex act and presented her readers with a version of sexuality that seemed safe and inoffensive for family consumption during a period known for its pushing of the boundaries of sexual representations. At the same time, Montgomery's erotic subversions and sexual disruptions, so powerfully articulated in the journals, can be traced in the subtexts of her fiction, in particular in the *Emily* trilogy, written during a period when Montgomery was recopying her childhood journals. This 1920s girl-series, recently adapted for Canadian prime-time television viewing, presents Montgomery's most unsettling and provocative fiction, and has to be viewed in the context of her journals, as well in the context of the emerging sexual frankness in the Canadian literary tradition, most notably in Frederick Philip Grove's *Settlers of the Marsh* (1925).

"If by sexual behavior, we understand the three poles – acts, pleasure, and desire,"[10] then F.P. Grove privileged the representation of sexual acts, but silenced the realm of pleasure, while L.M. Montgomery privileged the realm of erotic pleasure, but silenced the sex act in her fiction. This comparative approach thus focuses on two "political" interventions in the sexual/textual debates that marked the literature of the twenties as a hotbed of conflicting ideologies. The juxtaposition of these two authors draws attention to Montgomery's gently radical demands for female pleasure, which would change the fabric of social relations from the bottom up, while it also highlights the significance of Grove's frank representation of (hetero)sexual problems, issues directly related to the nation's health. When studied together, Montgomery and Grove present an ideal comparative anchor that powerfully exposes the sexual/textual politics in the construction of a distinctively Canadian "sexuality," one that is deeply concerned with issues of health and well-being, while also revealing the pressures of heteronormative social structures. While referring to the social, legal, and historical issues in the construction of sexuality in early Canadian literature, this essay ultimately contributes to the critical recasting of Montgomery as a deeply subversive Canadian and international writer.

I

In her journals Montgomery uses the tantalizing phrase "my 'secret garden'" to describe her creative realm of imagination and fantasy.[11]

In "Cultivating One's Understanding: The Female Romantic Garden," Jacqueline Labbe writes that women authors are culturally accustomed to being enclosed, and therefore "can actually find more freedom within the garden. Indeed, confinement – whether by garden, parlour, or boudoir walls – is so expected it might prove to be the most open avenue for women to subvert cultural expectations of feminine submission and decorum."[12] Montgomery's imaginary world in her journals is one in which orchards become feminized erotic spaces; trees become responsive lovers; girls are allowed to have passionate love affairs; and cats provide a safe space for sensual caressing. "I myself don't know of many nicer things than to waken up in the night and put out a hand to feel a soft, warm, velvety purring little flank in the darkness," she writes in her journal, while in another scene she erotically anthropomorphizes a tree that she knew since her childhood: "There it was smothered amid that intruding growth. I wonder if it felt my kiss on its gnarled trunk and if its aged sap coursed with a momentary quickening at the step of its lover."[13] These pleasures powerfully spill into Montgomery's fiction, both echoing and transcending the economy of pleasure of the popular Harlequin romance as it has been described by Ann Barr Snitow. The Harlequin romance is a genre that multiplies moments of erotic pleasure for women, yet this pleasure is typically designed to arouse male desires.[14] In contrast to the Harlequin heroine, Montgomery's heroine pursues romance by taking charge of her own pleasure and by creating new and autonomous female subject positions; she thus sidesteps the traditional model of male dominance and female submission. Montgomery experimented with a decidedly autoerotic version of female pleasure when she presented her girl heroines growing into young women delaying marriage, embracing careers, and generating their pleasure through creative work. Eros is projected into nature and played out in passionate girl-girl friendships.

Emily of New Moon presents eroticized girl crushes with great complexity and realistic detail with the result that it critically expands the motif of the bosom friendship such as that between Anne and Diana as presented in *Anne of Green Gables* (1908), Montgomery's template for powerfully emotional female attachments. Emily's crush on the pretty Rhoda Stuart has the emotional intensity of any adult infatuation, such as when she submits to Rhoda's possessive whims and controls: "Rhoda says I mustn't have any chum but her or she will cry her eyes out. Rhoda loves me as much as I love her. We are both going to pray that we may live together all our lives and die the same day." The "Growing Pains" that mark the title of the next chapter announce the end of this affair, which occurs when Emily discovers in Sunday school that "Rhoda was sitting three seats ahead with a strange little girl – a very gay and gorgeous little girl." Publicly displaced and openly scorned, Emily feels the betrayal of her love so deeply that she lacks the words to "write out" her feelings. Montgomery's subtly ironic sympathies give voice to "the violence of emotion that racked her being," but she also encodes a warning about the destructive nature of such infatuations. The novel is propelled forward by the deepening bond between Emily and Ilse Burnley, and even though boys figure in their friendship, they are secondary to the bond connecting the two girls. The pleasure of this bond, in part, is mediated through their bodies, as in the scene when Emily re-awakens to Ilse's physical attractiveness after a period of separation: "Emily discovered she had forgotten how vivid Ilse was – how brilliant her amber eyes, how golden her mane of spun-silk hair, looking more golden than ever under the bright blue silk tam Mrs. Simms had bought her in Shrewsbury."[15]

Montgomery's focus on girl-girl attraction is complemented by erotic fantasies projected into nature and island landscape. The most powerfully erotic fantasy centres on Wind Woman, a figure composed of Emily's idealized dead mother, a mythologized nature goddess and a figure of female Eros. To Emily she is physical and mythological, "tall and misty, with thin, grey, silky clothes blowing all about her – and wings like a bat's – only you can see through them – and shining eyes like stars looking through her long, loose hair."[16] The gale-force winds are a well-known feature of the Canadian Maritime provinces, and Emily's imagining of nature's strength as benevolently female presents an important feminist element in this novel, thoroughly feminizing nature and landscape. Embedded in action verbs, the Wind Woman is an active force, "ruffling" the grass, "tossing the big boughs," "teasing" the pine, and "whispering." Above all, she is a force with seductive allure for Emily, and when forced to share a bed with her tyrannical Aunt Elizabeth, Emily resorts to fantasizing her bond with Wind Woman:

> Her soul suddenly escaped from the bondage of Aunt Elizabeth's stuffy feather-bed and gloomy canopy and sealed windows. She was out in the open with the Wind Woman and the other gipsies of the night – the fireflies, the moths, the brooks, the clouds. Far and wide she wandered in enchanted reverie until she coasted the shore of dreams and fell soundly asleep on the fat, hard pillow, while the Wind Woman sang softly and luringly in the vines that clustered over New Moon.

Wind Woman emerges as a maternal, sensually seductive Calypso figure, whose luring song finally induces sleep in the tortured child. This fantasy is all the more powerful in that the "long and stiff and bony" body of Aunt Elizabeth beside Emily's powerfully signifies the deterrence of physical contact and thus ensures that the child does not indulge in forbidden, masturbatory, pleasures – including the tactile pleasures of her cats that Emily longs for.[17] Yet Emily ultimately does more than escape the disciplinary confines of the bed: her fantasy of Wind Woman actively transcends the solitary focus on the self-contained ego (as represented by Aunt Elizabeth's lonely bed) and inscribes intimately intersubjective motifs of female self-affection.[18]

In Montgomery's garden the forbidden fruit of female independence is intimately connected with writing. Condemned by the world, writing is reclaimed as a sweet, autoerotic secret, as the many references to Emily's "secret documents" imply. Indulging herself "in the delightful throes of literary composition," Emily forgets the duties of the day, just as in *Emily Climbs* an adolescent Emily forgets about being in love with Teddy Kent in the drama of writing a story: "Her cheeks burned, her heart beat, she tingled from head to foot with the keen rapture of creation – a joy that sprang fountain-like from the depths of being and seemed independent of all earthly things."[19] The potential sexual lover is transformed into erotic muse. Montgomery's most powerful evocation of the interweaving of the erotic and the creative is the "flash," what Alice Munro calls Emily's "moment of joy of pure recognition."[20] The flash is a climactic experience: "This moment came rarely – went swiftly, leaving her breathless with the inexpressible delight of it"; unlike Georges Bataille's erotism, it does not lead to "eternity," or to "death," but always to writing.[21] By endowing female creativity with sensual tropes, Montgomery dismantles a cultural norm that associates women's independent work and creativity with lack of attractiveness. Indeed, when we meet Emily as a young adult in *Emily's Quest*, there are "violet shadows under [her eyes] that always seemed darker and more alluring after Emily had sat up to some unholy and un-Elizabethan hour completing a story." In Montgomery's realm, documents, books, and manuscripts are not sexual *ersatz*, as Sigmund Freud's sublimation theory suggests: they are the true sexual rivals in erotic triangles, as when Emily is engaged to be married to Dean Priest. Jealous of her manuscript – "I hated the book. You were more interested in it than in me" – Dean comes close to stifling Emily's life line, her writing. This act is the unpardonable sin in Montgomery's universe, and the relationship is never consummated. Emily continues to adhere to her motto as articulated in *Emily Climbs*: "I shall be *wedded to my art*."[22]

Montgomery's romance presents fantasies that almost systematically thwart or delay male satisfaction, while providing powerful forms of female satisfaction, experienced in the recurring raptures of writing, the ecstasy of the flash, the cooing murmur of the wind, and the delight of spun-silk hair. The lavish multiplying of such moments and the deliberate lack of "restraint and economy" in describing moments of pleasure and joy are Montgomery's trademark and a key to her feminism, for the claiming of women's pleasure is related to heterosexual autonomy in a culture that normalizes heterosexual dependency for women. Montgomery, of course, always returned to conventional reading pleasures to close her novels, as the reader anticipates the inevitable coming together of Teddy and Emily, or of Gilbert and Anne, in the marriage plot. Yet these conventional reading pleasures pale in comparison with the transgressive pleasure provided in feminized nature descriptions, pleasures that leave the female in control and often force the male into a feminized position – the very positioning that will cause a crisis in some of the major literary texts written in English during the 1920s.

II

To contextualize Montgomery's subversive approach, it is important to note that she composed and published her trilogy among a flourishing of landmark texts of modernism, works deliberately pushing against the boundaries of sexual representations. In February 1922 the completion of *Emily of New Moon* coincided with the Paris publication of James Joyce's *Ulysses*, a work of brilliant avant-garde experimentation; first serially published in New York's *Little Review* by the two courageous lesbian editors Margaret Anderson and Jane Heap, it was judged "obscene" in an American court because of the "erotic musings" of Leopold Bloom in the infamous Nausicaa chapter.[23] In 1925 the appearance of *Emily Climbs* coincided with the publication of F.P. Grove's *Settlers of the Marsh* in Canada, a work of scandalous frankness in the realm of sexuality to be discussed in more detail later. The October 1926 completion of *Emily's Quest* coincided with the publication of Ernest Hemingway's *The Sun Also Rises*, a work launching an openly promiscuous heroine in Lady Brett Ashley alongside its emasculated hero Jake Barnes, two literary icons that would preoccupy the decade.

"Some 'sex' novels are interesting and stimulating," Montgomery conceded in a 30 December 1928 journal entry, although she generally dismissed "the arid, sex-obsessed, novels of today," including Morley Callaghan's *Strange Fugitive*, "the deadliest dull thing I ever tried to read."[24] Throughout her long and successful writing career Montgomery remained true to herself in silencing the sex act in her fiction. Swept by a wave of modernist experimentations intent on lifting the veil of Victorian reticence in sexual matters, Montgomery staunchly defended Victorian values through her heroine in *Emily's Quest*: "The whole world to-day seems to be steeped in a scorn for things Victorian. Do they know what they're talking of? But I like sane, decent things – if *that* is Victorian." And Ilse agrees: "After all, the Victorians were right in covering lots of things up. Ugly things should be hidden."[25] Canadian critics took Montgomery at her word and cast her writing in opposition to the new literature. Unaware of the content of her private journals, which would become public only decades later, they aligned the author with the desexualized maiden, and her writing with the sexually innocent realm of childhood – a casting not entirely to Montgomery's liking.[26] Completing *Emily Climbs* in January 1924, she complained in her journals that "the public and the publisher won't allow me to write of a young girl as she really is ... You have to depict a sweet, insipid young thing – really a child grown older – to whom the basic realities of life and reactions to them are quite unknown. *Love* must scarcely be hinted at – yet young girls in their early teens often have some very vivid love affairs. A girl of 'Emily's' type certainly would."[27] And yet Montgomery herself was partly complicitous with the terms of her reception. When she describes Emily's adult sexual awakening for Teddy Kent in *Emily's Quest*, her language undermines the complexities of the teenage girl's emotionality that she had developed in Book I: "But childhood had never known this wild, insurgent sweetness – this unconsidered surrender. Oh, she was his. By a word – a look – an intonation, he was still her master. What matter if, in some calmer mood, she might not quite like it – to be helpless – dominated like this?"[28] The ecstasies, raptures, and infatuations described in *Emily of New Moon* at least partly contradict the narrator's comment in *Emily's Quest*; also, the reader is already familiar with the terms of "sweet surrender," the bondage of infatuation played out in Emily's relations with Rhoda. More importantly still, readers are bound to remember the disturbing appearance of the thirty-six-year-old Dean Priest as quasi-lover for the thirteen-year-old heroine in *New*

Moon, an appearance so disturbing "that the author, after a while, hardly seems to know what to do with him."[29] Given his "magnetic green eyes," his "musical and caressing" voice, and "his ironic tongue,"[30] Emily is scared of this disturbing attraction, as are the author and the reader. Accustomed to news media disclosures of child sexual abuse, the late-twentieth-century reader finds herself startled by this twist into a Lolita plot; Jarback Priest's desires for Emily are sexual, although he is willing to wait. Heightened sensitivity in a mainstream audience prompted the makers of the *Emily of New Moon* CBC television series to rejuvenate Dean Priest by at least ten years, presenting him as in his twenties when he meets Emily on the television screen.[31]

In "The Canon between the Wars," Carole Gerson has shown that the format of early Canadian literature was shaped mainly by publishers, editors, anthologists, and university professors, all of whom had an enormous influence on what was included or excluded in the construction of Canadian culture. For Arthur Phelps and many other supporters, Montgomery presented a welcome escape from the tension and self-conscious craftsmanship and experimental techniques of modernist works like *Ulysses* or T.S. Eliot's *The Waste Land*, novels and poems in which time is out of joint and where language and syntax are fragmented.[32] Terms of escape, however, ultimately reduced the complexity of her enterprise, relegating her work to the apolitical, asexual, and anational. While the realm of serious literature was dominated by sexual and national politics, L.M. Montgomery found herself located in a realm above those terms: located in imperious neutrality, her literature sold well, but ultimately exacted a high price from Montgomery the writer, for she found herself excluded from the canon of serious Canadian literature. For the past two decades feminist scholarship has successfully laboured to reclaim Montgomery as a serious writer, and the recently published journals, with their shocking disclosures of Montgomery's shadowed self, have been an important tool in this enterprise. Given Montgomery's subversive encoding of female pleasures, what ultimately is her positioning within Canada's literature? Or how can we fruitfully position Montgomery's subversive writing of dis/pleasure within our reading and teaching of early Canadian literature?

III

"Rarely have I read a book which gave me so much pleasure," L.M. Montgomery wrote in a 10 March 1923 letter, in which she lavishly thanked her addressee "for the evening of delight when I went with you on those severe dunes and saw that eerie writing world with your eyes." If this language of exulting pleasure is Montgomery's trademark, having already endeared her to a mass readership, the identity of her letter's addressee may come as a surprise to Montgomery scholars. Although she did not "often pester authors with letters after reading their books," Montgomery felt compelled to express her appreciation and gratitude in this letter to Frederick Philip Grove that unstintingly praised his book of travels and nature observations, *Over Prairie Trails* (1922). Tantalizingly brief, consisting of only two extant letters held by the University of Manitoba archives, Montgomery's correspondence to Grove is nonetheless of crucial importance, in that it helps dismantle the commonly held perceptions of these two authors as fierce arch-rivals representing the opposing poles of western realism and eastern sentimentalism.[33]

The nineteen twenties marked a decade of fervent nationalist activity in Canada, as witnessed in the formation of the Group of Seven, the creation of the Canadian Authors Association and the United Church, and the building of the national railways. These formations also gave rise to an unprecedented nationalist interest in Canadian literature, which made it, perhaps, easy to align Montgomery and Grove along classical binaries that opposed prairie and Maritime literature, high and low culture, male and female writing, and national and popular writing. After all, the slow acceptance of immigrant writer F.P. Grove in Canada was enabled on the basis that his works moved beyond Canada's predominantly "sentimental" fiction, associated with popular authors like Mazo de la Roche, Bliss Carman, and L.M. Montgomery. Over the past decade, this opposition has ironically become further entrenched, for the feminist reclamation of L.M. Montgomery has involved an understandable reaction against F.P. Grove. Feminist scholars correctly noted that Grove's focus on the "perennial male discourses of alienation, nation-building and cultural identity"[34] garnered more respect from Canadian critics than Montgomery's focus on girls' and women's issues. The point of my juxtaposition is not to cement further this opposition, however, but to draw attention to the critical nexus of dis/pleasure intimately connecting Montgomery and Grove within the construction of "sexuality" in Canadian literature. Both authors were intimately interested in shaping the nation's sexual health through literature, Montgomery by claiming eros and pleasure as essential for her unconventional heroines' well-being, and Grove by highlighting the sexual problems within the Canadian family. Within the context of nation-building, the readerly and writerly connection cultivated by Montgomery creates an intriguing space of solidarity that reveals the importance of pleasure and support in the construction of Canadian literature.

"I wish every scholar in our Canadian schools could read [your book]," she tells Grove, presenting herself as his ideal, informed Canadian reader, who courts Grove's writing of the western prairie landscape. "Tell us the Story of that 'White-Range Line House.' Do you ever write fiction?" she asks, eliciting more of Grove's writing: "It seems to me you ought to be able to write a novel that would reflect the real atmosphere of the west – not the nauseating west of cowboys etc. etc. etc. but – well in short the west of your 'Prairie trails.' You have caught the spirit of the great Lone Land there. I never sensed it in any other book."[35] Grove followed Montgomery's decidedly seductive call: by the summer of 1923, part one of his first novel, *Settlers of the Marsh*, then tentatively titled "The White-Range Line House," was complete, and part two followed by the fall, with the eventual publication delayed because of publishing difficulties until September 1925.

Following Montgomery's commission with a vengeance, Grove gave voice to the "great Lone Land" in *Settlers of the Marsh*. From Montgomery's erotic garden, with its sensual volubility of words and sounds, the reader enters Grove's Big Marsh, the bush country, with its lone poplars and spruce trees and what Robert Kroetsch has so aptly termed the novel's grammar of silence.[36] Yet if Grove was writing *for* L.M. Montgomery, energized as he must have been by hopes of future expressions of admiration and delight from Canada's most popular author, he was also writing *against* her by superseding her version of eros with his version of sexuality. *Settlers of the Marsh*, a work no less personal and autobiographical than *Emily* was for Montgomery, was replete with the sexual acts that Montgomery eschewed in her fiction. The overdetermined ruler of the "great Lone Land" is the manly Swede Niels Lindstedt, the pioneer immigrant, whose paralysis in dealing with sexual matters uncannily anticipates by one year that of Jake Barnes, Ernest Hemingway's emasculated hero in post-war Paris. Within the Canadian literary tradition, Grove opened the gates to the stammered articulations of male anxieties, including his own and thus revealed conflicting attraction to and fears of female eros.

The historian Karen Dubinsky has highlighted the important link between "moral building and nation building" in Canada's sexual history. She provides a detailed discussion of the curious federal seduction law introduced by John Charlton in 1883 in the House of Commons that regulated consensual sex between unmarried adults well into the first two decades of the twentieth century. "In Charlton's view, young nations, like young women, needed protection lest the strong (speculators, capitalists, or blackguardly men) betray the weak." Many unmarried women resorted to seduction legislation to claim their rights in cases of desertion, with the number of claims increasing during the first two decades of the twentieth century, when "civil prosecutions for seduction were popular and remarkably successful."[37] Yet Dubinsky also highlights the law's deeply anti-feminist implications, for it maintained a paternalistic view of women's sexuality (action always had to be brought by the woman's father) that ultimately curtailed women's sexual autonomy and enshrined the opposing stereotypes of "the maidenly girl" and "the designing woman" in Canada's legal system. These stereotypes would persist well into the first two decades of the twentieth century and are worked into Grove's fiction in the paired characterization of Ellen Amundsen, the maidenly girl, and Clara Vogel, the designing woman.

Niels's wife, Clara Vogel, inhabiting a space of feminine artifice entirely foreign to Niels, powerfully rules the domain of eros: the world of finery, silken clothing, hair, fashion, mirrors, and, most importantly, of books is also the world that Montgomery dwells on and elaborates in lavish detail in her bestselling fiction. Like Emily Byrd Starr in Montgomery's trilogy, and like Montgomery herself, the erotic Clara is an avid and voracious reader of literature: the descriptions of her parcels arriving at the post-office with books inscribed with the names of strangers create a powerful intertext with Montgomery's obsessively reading Island heroines. Moreover, where Montgomery projects female (auto)eroticism into nature descriptions, Grove describes Clara's erotic promiscuity as being in perfect harmony with the prairie landscape, as in the following scene, when Clara and Niels are travelling home through the wilderness: "The sun had set. They passed the point where the trail branched off to the east, angling over the sand-flats. This was wild land, overgrown with low brush which was washed by the almost palpable bluish light of the high half-moon. Every now and then a patch of silvery-grey wolf-willow glistened softly in the dark-green cushions of symphoricarpus." The "bluish light," the "half-moon," and, later in the text, the "snow-white mists" in the prairie fields[38] – all emphasize the veiling effect of Clara's seductive and "artful" powers. The patch of softly glistening, silvery-grey wolf-willow presents an intertextual echo to Montgomery's gently eroticized nature romance. The reference to the multi-syllabic, foreign "symphoricarpus" reinforces Clara's intellectual and verbal

complexity. Nature itself veils itself in artful, feminine rhetoric that en-
tangles the protagonist and makes him yield to Clara's force of eros.

If Montgomery claimed female eros as a powerful source of well-
being and sexual health for her female characters, Grove exposes pleasure's underside, displacing erotic romance with sexual realism. Unlike
Montgomery's heroines (with the exception, perhaps, of Valancy, the
1926 heroine of *Blue Castle*), Clara transgresses from the domain of
erotic fantasy to sexual activity, from female seduction to male sexuality,
not romantically subverting, but aggressively reversing the boundaries
of gender. Clara, not Niels, is in possession of the phallus, which she
usurps as a tool of female sexual satisfaction. Through Niels's unsettled
perspective, Eros is ultimately unmasked as demonic in the reality of the
female-dominated sex-act ironically placed within the bounds of conjugal relations:

> It was [Niels's] duty to make the best of a bad bargain ...
> Distasteful though they were, he satisfied [Clara's] strange, ardent,
> erratic desires. Often she awakened him in the middle of the night, in
> the early morning hours, just before daylight; often she robbed him
> of his sleep in the evening, keeping him up till midnight and later.
> She herself slept much in daytime. He bore up under the additional
> fatigue ... [39]

The language of male sexual revulsion is indicative of the perceived loss
of masculinity, when male "hardness" is reduced to a mere tool of female
satisfaction. Author, narrator, and protagonist take flight into realist plot
structures in order to exorcize the female romance fantasy that thrives
on multiplying moments of female pleasure, without committing itself to
the nation's politics of reproduction. During a period of growing anxiety
about declining birth rates, of intense debates about the nation's health
and sexual morality, the literary scapegoating of Clara as a selfish woman
of pleasure constituted a political gesture. The destruction of Clara assumes ritualistic proportions, when even her belongings are burnt in "purifying" fire, after Niels has served his prison sentence for killing his wife;
this "purifying" process is ritually repeated in the critical reception of the
novel in the male press, and it was not until the 1980s that the scholarly
perception shifted to present a more complex picture of Clara.[40]

While Montgomery claimed subversive eros as essential for the
health and well-being of her heroines, Grove shifted his interest to
the sexual problems in Canada's white settler family, a goal not entirely

incompatible with Montgomery's concerns, as we shall see. In *Settlers*, sexual testimony is strategically placed in the mouth of Ellen Amundsen, whose maidenly conduct functioned as guarantee for her credibility as a witness. Ellen's traumatic sexual history is well documented in scholarship, in particular the seventeen-year-old's witnessing of her father's rape of her mother, a moral offense, yet not a crime according to Canada's legal code, persuading Ellen that married women have little control over their sexuality. Critics have given less attention to the sexual knowledge that Ellen gains as a ten-year-old, when she overhears a neighbour giving advice to her desperate mother on how to abort an unwanted pregnancy: "When I'm just about as far gone as you are now, then I go and lift heavy things; or I take the plow and walk behind it for a day. In less than a week's time the child comes; and it's dead."[41] Ellen's knowledge and testimony gain tremendous power when read within the context of the debates surrounding the health of the nation during the 1920s and 1930s. The sale of birth control was illegal in Canada, and many women were desperate to control their reproduction and sexuality. As Alison Prentice and her colleagues report, many women seeking contraceptive advice would write to Margaret Sanger's *Birth Control Review*, a journal published in New York; women in British Columbia created the first birth control League in 1924; and anarchist Emma Goldman promoted birth control issues during her exile in Canada.[42] As late as 1936, Dorothea Palmer would be charged in Ontario for distributing birth control information, a case attracting national attention in the fight to decriminalize birth control devices.

The nation's sexual health was a highly contested site in Canada's popular press during the twenties, and the debates surrounding sexual morality and organized birth control were conducted within the rhetoric of nation-building. Heated debates abounded in newspapers across the country, and the voice of Mrs. Donald Shaw in an April 1920 column in the Halifax *Herald* was typical in its representation of the conservative side of this debate. A member of the Social and Moral Reform Association in Halifax, she argued against the legalizing of birth control and admonished other women to uphold "the ethics and morals which alone produce real national health and prosperity."[43] Grove's *Settlers* intervened in this debate by showing that the politics regulating Canada's reproduction led to the premature and cruel death of Mrs. Amundsen and seriously affected the health and morality of the nation. Grove's position in making the issue explicit in his novel puts his novel in solidarity with the rhetoric deployed, for instance, in the women's columns of the *Grain*

Growers' Guide in the early twentieth century, which "chastised farmers who took advantage of their wives' good will and self-sacrifice."[44] Grove's concern with the nation's sexual health powerfully exposed Canadian women's lack of sexual well-being, and implicitly argued for a change in legal parameters. This concern proved perhaps too controversial for the Canadian mainstream, for in 1924, McClelland and Stewart, L.M. Montgomery's publisher, as well as Macmillan, had both rejected the novel as too risky, before a carefully orchestrated promotional machinery eventually launched the novel with Ryerson Press in 1925.[45]

IV

Given Grove's focus on the nation's health, where does Montgomery stand with respect to Grove's public voicing of "unspeakable" displeasures? Since her husband's first bout of depression in 1919, diagnosed as religious melancholia, Montgomery herself was wrestling with the expression of unpleasant truths within the bonds of marriage. The writer of subversive romances posthumously shocked readers of her journals by using the realistic rhetoric of bondage, displeasure, and physical repulsion to describe her own marriage, a rhetoric strikingly close to that of sexually frank novels such as *Settlers of the Marsh*. In a typical 11 November 1921 entry, she calls her husband "repulsive and abhorrent," and continues: "And yet to this personality I must be a wife. It is horrible – it is indecent – it should not be. I feel degraded and unclean."[46] Reading these passages several decades later, Montgomery's readers cannot help but look at the gaps left in the writing of the demonic marriage of Leslie to Dick Moore in *Anne's House of Dreams* (1917) in a new light. Montgomery's journals gave voice to reflections about divorce. "I do not approve of lax divorce laws. But I do think our Canadian divorce law errs on the side of over strictness. Adultery is the only ground for divorce. To this I think two others should be added and two only – incurable insanity and desertion for a period extending over three years."[47] The 1925 federal Divorce Law would grant Canadian women equal rights to divorce their husbands. Statistics indicate that Canadian legislation was merely following the trend of a steadily rising divorce rate, a trend beginning with the post-war years, after 1918.[48] While Montgomery theorized and rationalized the legal parameters of divorce, the possibility of a clean, legal exit out of the prison house of her marriage, she remained entrapped in the marital logic advocated by maternal feminists in Canada and encoded as conventional closure in the romance plot.

Like Grove, Montgomery the journal writer advocated a politics of sexual frankness. The author who had refused to add bits of her love life to *The Alpine Path*, her 1917 autobiography, again startled her readers posthumously with disclosures of intensely sexual experiences with Herman Leard in the spring of 1898;[49] she took pleasure in detailing her infatuations and flirtations; and she soberly reported on her masochistic strain during premenstrual depression.[50] Faced with new opportunities for sexual sociability and sexual expression, Montgomery carefully negotiated the realm of "confessional politics": she assumed control of her private disclosures, carefully drawing the boundaries that would allow the writer and the reader to enjoy new pleasures while also remaining protected from new forms of exploitation.[51]

Yet within the realm of fiction, Montgomery, while courageously subverting the genre, carefully refrained from collapsing the genre's boundaries; after all, the romance genre provided her and her readers with the pleasure of female-controlled eros and identity. The girl-series were the ultimate safe space, the last bastion of wholesomeness and well-being, in an increasingly troubled world. An understanding of her fictional boundary-setting is crucial if one is to understand her power as a self-conscious writer and artist. Its personal and psychological importance is revealed in the passionate and panicky language used in the following 17 November 1927 journal entry:

> I was reading *Your Cuckoo Sings by Kind* – a story I had picked up on a Toronto bargain counter. I liked it. It was a simple little story about a child – dear, wholesome, understanding. And then right in the middle of it came the most hideous, loathsome bestial incident – the vilest thing I ever read in any book. Not more than half a page long as far as words go but reaching down to the primeval slime of crawling things. I flung the book from me, as if I had touched a red hot coal. It turned me sick – ruined the whole evening for me … It is *not* sex – it is plain dirt. This was worse than dirt – it was verminous.[52]

Valentine Dobrée's *Your Cuckoo Sings by Kind*, an obscure novel published in 1927 by Alfred Knopf, depicts child sexual abuse through the limited perspective of Christina Maynard. This child character has interesting parallels to Montgomery's Jane Stuart in *Jane of Lantern Hill* (1937), for Christina, like Jane, is labelled plain and stupid by adults. About fifty pages into the text the reader witnesses her brutal sexual assault by a group of adolescents, including her brother Peter: "The world had receded for Christina. Her mind had shrunk and congealed. Her knees pressed together, locked stiff, which prevented her falling; she stood, counting her heart-beats. Slow explosions burst from the very centre of her being, and splintered into a thin procession of little jerks as they reached the resisting surface of her body."[53] Montgomery's shock of reading this rape scene is vivid, as is her response: "I poked [the book] into the fire and held it down with the tongs and watched it burn with delight. Nothing but fire could purify it."[54] Her act is ironically similar to Christina Maynard's desperate act of forgetting: in panic and shame Christina burns her stained overalls after her rape. Montgomery's repression also echoes that of Niels Lindstedt, who burns Clara Vogel's belongings in a purifying fire. In the literary shaping of sexuality, Montgomery insists on relegating some acts into the realm of the unspeakable; Montgomery was adamant that literature needed to express "normal" emotions and acts, yet this insistence entailed that some dark realities confronting her girl and women readers – including her own – had to remain in the dark.

V

At the centre of the dis/pleasure nexus discussed in this essay, then, some of the binaries locating Grove and Montgomery at opposite ends of a spectrum become unravelled. As Karen Dubinsky writes in her influential study of sexual violence in Ontario, "sexual violence has been the subject of surprisingly little historical inquiry";[55] first-wave feminists focused their attention on what was generally termed "white slavery," the problem of prostitution, rather than on issues of heterosexual violence, and Montgomery's feminism follows this tradition. Seen in isolation, Montgomery's fiction could be accused of glossing over social problems such as domestic abuse, rape, and alcoholism, which constituted the reality of many Maritime women.[56] Conversely, seen in isolation, Grove's realism can be accused of perpetuating the image of women enslaved in displeasure. Seen in conjunction, however, Grove's realism fills some of the gaps left by Montgomery's fiction, including her silencing of her own marital displeasure in her fiction, a displeasure neatly compartmentalized into her private journals. This essay ultimately argues for a juxtaposition of the two narratives in the reading and teaching of the two texts. Each one fills the gaps of the other, and reveals biases and cultural blindnesses.

"Montgomery's 'simple yarns,' with their patterns of order, disruption, renegotiation, and a re-established (if a slightly modified) order, provided solace," writes Mary Rubio.[57] On the surface, Montgomery's position coincided with the status quo advocated by conservative feminists in Canada. She advocated a maternal feminism in the tradition of Nellie McClung and Isabel Aberdeen, who assumed that motherhood was a natural desire for every woman. Yet when seen within the context of the sexual/textual debates of the twenties, Montgomery's subtle disruptions and negotiations thoroughly subverted the conservative agenda. Montgomery's literary focus promoted the very subversive moments of female self-satisfaction that Mrs. Donald Shaw of Halifax condemned so thoroughly when she launched out against childless women as being "superlatively supremely and absolutely selfish and self-satisfied."[58] As Prentice and her colleagues report, "after the enactment of the divorce laws in 1925, the popular press constantly reminded women that it was their duty, honour, and privilege to preserve family stability for the benefit not only of the family but also of the nation."[59] While Montgomery clearly advocated the rhetoric of "health," "duty," and "self-sacrifice" in her own adherence to marital and maternal bonds, her relationship to sexuality was deeply subversive on two accounts. She indulged in eros in her *Emily* books, savouring her pleasure of writing pleasure, and she claimed intensive, complex, and even disturbing pleasures for children and adolescents. And while composing *Emily*, Montgomery detailed in her journals the "repulsiveness" of her husband, clearly inscribing sexual distance in the writing of her marriage. During a period when women were admonished to fulfil their marital duties, to study marriage manuals, and to become more sexual in conjugal relations so as to stabilize institutionalized marriage,[60] Montgomery made her fame by writing the "self-satisfying" discourse of female-centred eros, a discourse hardly in line with the moral and sexual traditionalists represented by Mrs. Donald Shaw.

Finally, the comparison between Montgomery and Grove allows us to see the plurality of eros in Montgomery and the constructedness of nationalism in Canadian literature. The comparison allows us to see the complexities in the representations of sexuality in Canadian literature, with both authors claiming unchartered territory, F.P. Grove overtly claiming the sexual realm, Montgomery covertly, and with both articulating sexuality within the context of health and well-being. As post-Victorian writers, both authors, always struggling to draw appropriate boundaries from their respective gender positions, negotiated sexual dangers in new ways. Surrounded by a wave of modernist experimentations, Montgomery assigned new value to old Victorian female rights, including the woman's right to say "no" to male-centred forms of sexuality and the author's right to silence the sexual act; at the same time she strategically carved out a new female erotic by using nature as her canvas, thus paving the way for the eroticizing and feminizing of the Canadian landscape by women writers including Elizabeth Smart, Margaret Laurence, Alice Munro, and Jane Urquhart, all of whom had access to Montgomery's secret garden. Experimenting with erotic pleasures and fantasies for women, she carefully negotiated the sexual dangers implied in such literary ventures. In writing her own girlhood, Montgomery powerfully claimed eros and pleasures, fantasies and ecstasies, while also writing a narrative deeply invested with the power of the real, and producing a text that remains provocative and unsettling even for today's reader, used to the media frenzy of tell-all stories.

NOTES

I would like to thank my two most generous and inspiring readers, Elizabeth R. Epperly and J. Paul Boudreau, as well as the two anonymous *ESC* reviewers, for valuable suggestions and editorial advice. I am grateful to the University of Manitoba Archives for permission to quote L.M. Macdonald [Montgomery]'s correspondence to F.P. Grove, and to Gaby Divay for drawing this correspondence to my attention.

1   [Gammel, Introduction, 2; Gammel and Epperly, "Introduction," 5.]
2   Montgomery, 15 February 1922, in *SJLMM*, 3: 39.
3   Rubio and Waterston, *Writing a Life*, 83.
4   Montgomery, 27 November 1924, in *SJLMM*, 3: 209; Montgomery, 13 October 1926, in *SJLMM*, 3: 310; Montgomery, 20 November 1926, in *SJLMM*, 3: 313. While writing *Emily's Quest*, Montgomery also wrote *The Blue Castle*, a comedy for adults that provided great pleasure for the author. In it she fantasizes a Cinderella-like tale of the belated sexual awakening of twenty-nine-year-old Valancy Stirling.
5   M.H. Rubio, Introduction, 6.
6   M.H. Rubio, "L.M. Montgomery: Scottish-Presbyterian Agency."
7   Epperly, *The Fragrance of Sweet-Grass*, 38.
8   Poe, "The Whole of the Moon."

9 Encompassing much more than sexual acts, desires, pleasures, and fantasies, Foucault's definition of "sexuality" refers to the cultural construction of sexuality, the laws and norms that regulate the articulation of sexual matters, and the play of speech and silence regarding sexual matters. Foucault's influential *History of Sexuality, Volume I* provides a detailed discussion, focusing in particular on the historical changes in the cultural conceptualization of "sexuality" in western society. Thus eros is subsumed in the larger definition of sexuality. My reasons for discussing Montgomery's deployment of sensualized pleasure in terms of eros are three: Eros, the son of the Greek goddess of love, Aphrodite, is a mythological figure and generally appears as a child or youth; as a psychological term, eros is related to the instincts of self-preservation; in the philosophy of art, eros is related to the creative drive. All three domains can be found in Montgomery's fiction.

10 Foucault, "On the Genealogy of Ethics," 242.

11 Montgomery, 30 March 1927, in *SJLMM*, 3: 331.

12 Labbe, "Cultivating One's Understanding," 39.

13 Montgomery, 15 July 1923, in *SJLMM*, 3: 135; Montgomery, 26 July 1927, in *SJLMM*, 3: 347.

14 Snitow, "Mass Market Romance," 252.

15 *ENM*, 96, 102, 105, 279.

16 *ENM*, 5.

17 *ENM*, 5, 60, 57.

18 Emily's fantasy is evocative of Luce Irigaray's discussion of women's "autoeroticism" in *This Sex Which Is Not One*. Even though Emily's fantasy is not a consciously "tactical strike," as is the autoeroticism Irigaray describes, the fantasy enables Emily "to learn to defend [her] desire, especially through speech, to discover the love of other women while sheltered from men's imperious choices" (Irigaray, *The Sex Which Is Not One*, 33).

19 *ENM*, 93–94, 93; *EC*, 271.

20 Munro, Afterword, 359.

21 *ENM*, 7; Bataille, *Erotism*, 25.

22 *EQ*, 4, 97; *EC*, 6; emphasis in original. For a more complete discussion of this issue, see Epperly, *The Fragrance of Sweet-Grass*, 152–56, in particular her discussion of the problematic influence of three male characters (Father Cassidy, Mr. Carpenter, and Dean Priest) who "test" Emily in her development as a writer. Epperly sees the encouragement provided by these characters as deeply suspect. See Marie Campbell's provocative essay, "Wedding Bells and Death Knells: The Writer as Bride in the *Emily*

Trilogy"; Campbell argues that marriage is tantamount to death for Emily the artist. Also noteworthy is the autobiographical intertext in the description of Jarback Priest's jealousy of Emily's writing; Montgomery's husband also "manifested a deep underlying hostility to her success as a writer" (M.H. Rubio, Introduction, 8).

23 Grazia, *Girls Lean Back Everywhere*, 3–19.

24 Montgomery, 30 December 1928, in *SJLMM*, 3: 387; Montgomery, 18 September 1922, in *SJLMM*, 3: 71; Montgomery, 30 December 1928, in *SJLMM*, 3: 387.

25 *EQ*, 205, 206.

26 Mary Rubio notes in the introduction to *Harvesting Thistles* that "between the mid-1920s and the late-1980s Montgomery's novels were increasingly marketed for children." While the original cover of *Anne of Green Gables* showed a sophisticated young woman designed to appeal to adults, Montgomery's publishers had started to market her books differently by the time of the publication of the *Emily* trilogy (M.H. Rubio, Introduction, 2).

27 Montgomery, 20 January 1924, in *SJLMM*, 3: 157.

28 *EQ*, 107.

29 Munro, Afterword, 358.

30 *ENM*, 267, 266, 265.

31 Marlene Matthews, scriptwriter for *Emily* series, in a lecture at the University of Prince Edward Island, Charlottetown, February 1997.

32 Phelps, *Canadian Writers*, 89. For a detailed critical discussion of the reception history of Montgomery's work, see Åhmansson, *A Life and Its Mirrors*, 20–25, in which she details the reductive approaches of Arthur Phelps, Desmond Pacey, and E.K. Brown.

33 L.M. Macdonald to Frederick Philip Grove, 10 March 1923 (unpublished letter). Montgomery's second letter to Grove is dated 3 April 1930 and discusses Grove's *Our Daily Bread* in very supportive terms. The University of Manitoba archives also contain the letters of Arthur Phelps to F.P. Grove (74 letters between 1922 and 1926), which shed light on the publication of *Settlers*.

34 J. Rubio, "'Strewn with Dead Bodies,'" 176.

35 L.M. Macdonald to Frederick Philip Grove, 10 March 1923 (unpublished letter).

36 Kroetsch, *The Lovely Treachery of Words*, 84–94.

37 Dubinsky, *Improper Advances*, 67, 79.

38 Grove, *Settlers of the Marsh*, 103, 104.

39 Ibid., 148; ellipses in original.

40 For early reviews in newspapers and magazines, including *The Montreal Daily Star*, *The Manitoba Free Press*, *The Saskatoon Phoenix*, *The Canadian Author and Bookman*, and *Saturday Night*, see Pacey, *Frederick Philip Grove*, 105–17. Clara was unequivocally associated with the figure of the whore. Scholarship since the 1980s has revised these earlier critical paradigms, drawing attention to Grove's significant subversion of the gender binaries. For detailed studies, see Blodgett, *Configuration*, 125–35; Gammel, *Sexualizing Power in Naturalism*, 226–30; and McGregor, *The Wacousta Syndrome*, 148–49. Most recently, Richard Cavell has criticized the heteronormativity of scholarship on Grove's works and asked for a further opening of the notion of the sexual in the discussions of Grove (Cavell, "Felix Paul Greve").

41 Grove, *Settlers of the Marsh*, 126.

42 Prentice et al., *Canadian Women*, 256–58.

43 D. Shaw, "What Is the World Coming To?" 343.

44 Prentice et al., *Canadian Women*, 154. Theodore Dreiser's most famous novel, *An American Tragedy*, was published in 1925, like *Settlers*, and was banned in Toronto in 1926. Like *Settlers*, it treats the problem of unwanted pregnancy and makes an implicit request for the liberalization of abortion rights. As the novel's title indicates, *An American Tragedy*, like *Settlers*, locates these sexual issues within the context of the national; yet unlike *Settlers*, Dreiser, focussing on premarital sexuality, advocates greater freedom in sexual relations. Grove, in contrast, locates reproductive issues within the marital bonds of the Canadian family and thus highlights the fact that his concern is primarily with health, not with pleasure.

45 For details, see Stobie, *Frederick Philip Grove*, 92–93. The promotional machinery involved Watson Kirkconnell, a professor of classics at Wesley College in Manitoba, Arthur Phelps, a professor of English at McGill University, and Lorne Pierce, editor-in-chief at Ryerson Press; incidentally, the latter two men were also ordained Methodist ministers. Such support may seem strange for a book that, soon after its publication, would be banned for its sexual content by several Canadian libraries. Yet the religiously minded supporters may very well have been drawn to the novel's focus on the nation's sexual health, combined with its moral focus highlighting Niels's innocence, ascetic passion, and ultimate exorcizing of the woman of pleasure who refused her duty to the nation.

46 Montgomery, 1 November 1921, in *SJLMM*, 3: 24.

47 Montgomery, 18 October 1923, in *SJLMM*, 3: 150.

48 The *Canada Year Book 1921* and the Dominion Bureau of Statistics, *Divorces in Canada* (Ottawa, 1923–41), counted 54 divorces in 1917; 114

in 1918; 373 in 1919; 468 in 1920; 558 in 1921; by 1932, the number had risen to 1006.

49 Montgomery, 8 April 1898, in *SJLMM*, 1: 204–21; Montgomery, 10 July 1898, in *SJLMM*, 1: 221–25; Montgomery, 8 October 1898, in *SJLMM*, 1: 225–28.

50 Montgomery, 22 October 1924, in *SJLMM*, 3: 205. The journals also include passing comments on the need for openness in the sexual education of her sons; her rejection of the sense of shame and taboo instilled in her childhood (Montgomery, 11 January 1924, in *SJLMM*, 3: 157); her frank and truthful discussions of sexuality with Captain Smith (Montgomery, 28 February 1922, in *SJLMM*, 3: 39); and discussion of her husband Ewan Macdonald's thyroid condition in relation to his sex life (Montgomery, 19 August 1924, in *SJLMM*, 3: 200).

51 This negotiation is perhaps best illustrated in her response to the Toronto magazine *Everywoman's World*, when its editor asked Montgomery to add bits of her love life to her autobiography *The Alpine Path*, published in the Toronto magazine. "I have snubbed that editor very unmistakably, telling him that I am not one of those who throw open the portals of sacred shrines to the gaze of the crowd," Montgomery writes, and then proceeds to write her love life in her journals – on her own terms: "But for my own amusement I *am* going to write a full and frank – at least as frank as possible – account of all my 'love affairs'" (Montgomery, 5 January 1917, in *SJLMM*, 2: 202).

52 Montgomery, 17 November 1927, in *SJLMM*, 3: 359.

53 Dobrée, *Your Cuckoo Sings by Kind*, 35, 56.

54 Montgomery, 17 November 1927, in *SJLMM*, 3: 359.

55 Dubinsky, *Improper Advances*, 13.

56 Fingard, "The Prevention of Cruelty."

57 M.H. Rubio, Introduction, 6.

58 D. Shaw, "What Is the World Coming To?" 340.

59 Prentice et al., *Canadian Writers*, 255.

60 Ibid., 252.

14

Writing with a "Definite Purpose": L.M. Montgomery, Nellie L. McClung and the Politics of Imperial Motherhood in Fiction for Children

—— 2000 ——

CECILY DEVEREUX

In this article, published in *Canadian Children's Literature / Littérature canadienne pour la jeunesse,* Cecily Devereux argues against scholars who have tracked links between *Anne of Green Gables* and American girls' books such as Wiggin's *Rebecca of Sunnybrook Farm* and Alcott's *Little Women* and argues that *Anne* has much more in common with a Canadian text that was its exact contemporary: Nellie L. McClung's first novel *Sowing Seeds in Danny* (1908). Devereux notes that, although Montgomery and McClung were in many ways polar opposites as far as politics and suffrage were concerned, both authors were heavily implicated in the ideological construction of women as "mothers of the race." Devereux would continue this train of thought in two subsequent book projects: a critical edition of *Anne of Green Gables*, published by Broadview Editions in 2004, and her book-length study *Growing a Race: Nellie L. McClung and the Fiction of Eugenic Feminism* (2006).

> If women could be made to think, they would see that it is woman's
> place to lift high the standard of morality.
> – Nellie L. McClung, *In Times Like These*[1]

In 1924, J.D. Logan and Donald French suggested that what they called the "Second Renaissance" of Canadian literature was heralded by the publication in 1908 of three novels: "*Anne of Green Gables*, by L.M. Montgomery; *Duncan Polite*, by Marian Keith; [and] *Sowing Seeds in Danny*, by Nellie L. McClung."[2] French and Logan's texts are significant, not only because all three novels are written by women, thus reinforcing Carole Gerson's account of the numbers of women who have been eliminated from the national canon in the second half of the century, but because the two which remain well known – *Anne of Green Gables* and *Sowing Seeds in Danny* – both construct an idea of the imperial mother as the empire's "white hope" (McClung's phrase) in Canada, the empire's white dominion and its last best west.[3] Both works, that is, and, ultimately, both of the series of which each is a first instalment, undertake to displace the old new woman of the 1890s with a new "new woman," the woman as "mother of the race," a gesture that is the defining characteristic of first-wave imperialist feminism after the Boer War, especially in the white settler colonies. Both works, moreover, undertake to delineate the nature of the work of the "mother of the race" for an audience which would be composed primarily of children.

Although the idea of women's social work as an extension of what is commonly represented in the nineteenth century as a feminine and specifically maternal domestic function underlies a good deal of mid- to late-Victorian feminism (such as, for instance, women's anti-slavery activism, and the work of Josephine Butler to counter the Contagious Diseases Acts),[4] it is not until after the Boer War that Anglo-Saxon women's perceived function as "mothers of the race" would be regularly articulated in imperialist – or, for that matter, in feminist – rhetoric. The 1899–1902 war had been a disaster for Britain, and it was not so much the loss of the South African territory that had been catastrophic, as the revelation of what was considered to be racial degeneracy amongst young male recruits: "a great many of them," notes Anna Davin, "were found to be physically unfit for service – too small for instance, or too slight, or with heart troubles, weak lungs, rheumatic tendencies, flat feet, or bad teeth."[5] By and large, Davin suggests, the blame for the condition of British youth was foisted upon their mothers, seen to be "ignorant," among the working classes, of "the necessary conditions for the bringing up of healthy children," and to be reluctant, among the middle classes, to forgo the "advancement" won by the "new woman."[6] Frank McDonough has suggested that the Boer War was a "turning point[]" in the history of the Empire, an event which operates as a catalyst for a shift in "British attitudes towards the Empire and imperial defence in the period from 1902 to the outbreak of the First World War in 1914."[7] It had, it might be added, a comparably catalytic effect upon feminism in the British Empire, which, in this same period, struggled to oust the hazardous "new woman" who had come to epitomize women's "advancement." Imperial feminists in the first decade of the twentieth century sought first to demonstrate a commitment to the ideas of progress, civilization, and, ultimately, racial dominance, arguing that these goals could only be achieved through the work of the Anglo-Saxon woman as "mother of the race." By the end of the Boer War, feminism had become a politics of emancipation for the advance of imperial civilization, configuring the womb of the Anglo-Saxon mother as the empire's one inalienable asset and the last best site for the renewal of "the race," and representing mother-women working for social purity as the last hope for imperial regeneration.

The performance of this gesture in fiction written for girls is a compelling sign of the pervasiveness of anxiety about "the race" and the empire in the context of rapid expansion, and a salient reminder of imperial efforts to regulate reproduction through the didactic reinforcement, at an early age, of normative gender roles. The valorizing of this fiction – specifically *Anne of Green Gables* and *Sowing Seeds in Danny* – as the beginning of a nationalist "Renaissance" in English Canada is an indication of a new importance which was accruing to white women as mothers on what were perceived to be the frontiers of empire. In English Canada, which had been constructed in imperialist discourse since the middle of the nineteenth century as "the white man's last opportunity," or the last hope for the westward expansion of the Empire, maternal feminism found a strong foothold – stronger, arguably, than at the imperial centre, primarily because of the perceived need for white women on the frontier.[8] The Anglo-Canadian "mother of the race," it is implicit, was in a better position to push for the vote, since here she was engaged in the work of imperial expansion, and was, moreover, aware of her reproductive worth in the culture of empire-wide race-based anxiety that was exacerbated for white settlers in the last west by the influx of what J.S. Woodsworth in 1909 referred to as "the incoming multitudes" of "foreigners."[9] These factors may help to explain why white female enfranchisement was achieved earlier in the settler colonies than at the centre; they also explain why maternalism became the dominant feminist ideology of the early-twentieth century in English Canada.[10] What remains unexplained are the convergences of maternalism in feminist and apparently non-feminist fiction: this paper begins to address the question of the implications of these convergences for our understanding of the early-twentieth-century feminist movement usually referred to as the first wave, by considering the remarkably similar way in which maternalism is narrativized in and after 1908 by two such politically disparate writers as Montgomery and McClung.

Despite their having been linked by Logan and French, McClung and Montgomery are not usually discussed together, and are rarely presented as "feminist" contemporaries: Erika Rothwell's 1999 essay, "Knitting Up the World: L.M. Montgomery and Maternal Feminism in Canada," is one of very few studies to align the two authors. Part of the reason for this separation is their own positioning in relation to early-twentieth-century feminist discourse: they are not usually regarded as having been political "kindred spirits." McClung is certainly English Canada's best-known and most influential maternal feminist, whose suffrage activism, articulated in her 1915 manifesto, *In Times Like These*, was arguably the driving force in the granting of the vote to women in Manitoba in 1916 and in Canada in 1918. Montgomery, for her part, is almost as well known for her lack of interest in the struggle for female enfranchisement. Mollie Gillen cites an interview in the Boston *Republic* in 1910, two years after the first publication of *Anne of Green Gables*, in which Montgomery is described as "distinctly conservative ... She has no favour for woman suffrage; she believes in the home-loving woman."[11] This stance is re-emphasized in her journals: Montgomery wrote on several occasions of her lack of any "particular interest in politics": "I never," she maintained in 1917, "felt any especial desire to vote. I thought, as a merely academic question, that women certainly should vote. It seemed ridiculous, for example that an educated, intelligent woman should not vote when any illiterate, half or wholly disloyal foreigner could. But it did not worry me in the least."[12]

Montgomery's lack of interest in suffragism at a time when activists like McClung were beginning to make a strong case for the vote for women in Canada suggests that her novels are not engaged with the discourse of early-twentieth-century feminism, such as McClung was producing. However, the many similarities between Montgomery's "Anne" series and McClung's "Pearlie Watson" trilogy demonstrate that the two writers are not quite as far apart on questions of gender and ideology as their different points of view with regard to female enfranchisement seem to indicate. Indeed, it is clear that – in their fiction, at any rate – the two women writers were practising fundamentally the same politics, at least as far as the education and development of young girls and of the English-Canadian nation were concerned. As we can see when we align the "Anne" books with the "Pearlie" stories, both women were reproducing and promoting the culture of imperial motherhood that is the hallmark of feminism in the British Empire in the early twentieth century.

The "Anne" series and the "Pearlie Watson" trilogy have a good deal in common, arguably, indeed, more in common (despite the long-standing rumours of plagiarism) than do Montgomery's novel and American writer Kate Douglas Wiggin's *Rebecca of Sunnybrook Farm*, published five years earlier.[13] *Anne of Green Gables* was Montgomery's first published novel. *Sowing Seeds in Danny* was McClung's. Both were published in 1908. Both turned out to be the first novels of what would become popular serial narratives: Montgomery eventually published eight Anne books; McClung wrote two sequels to the first Pearlie Watson story. Both series – or parts of them – have maintained some currency: as Carrie MacMillan notes, while other English-Canadian women writers of the early twentieth century have disappeared, "L.M. Montgomery and Nellie McClung have always maintained their hold."[14] And, although it is the Anne books that, by the end of the twentieth century, have taken on such immense cultural capital, there are three volumes of McClung's writing still in print, and an increase in academic interest in her work, while not on the scale of the rapidly expanding Anne industry, is certainly evident.[15]

There are some obvious similarities between the Anne and Pearlie narratives: both are stories of young English-Canadian (or, to be more specific, Canadian-born Anglo-Celtic) girls moving from pre-adolescence to mid-teens. Anne Shirley is an orphan, her parents having died of typhoid when she was an infant. Pearl Watson's parents are living, but are absent from home much of the time, working. Both girls have had to take on adult responsibilities: Anne has been caring for other people's children only a little younger than herself; Pearl, we are told, is the "second mother" of the six smaller Watsons, "keeping the house ... six days in the week."[16] Like Anne, Pearl is represented as the best and brightest in her community. Like Anne, she wins scholarships, and is enabled to further her education through a bequest which is represented as a reward for good deeds. Pearl, like Anne, becomes a teacher; subsequently, like Anne, she marries her first love. Indeed, her first love, like Anne's, is a doctor, and, given that the doctor is a figure always invested with especial value in expansionist fiction as an arbiter of social and moral as well as physical hygiene, the union of teacher and doctor in the two stories is worth noting as a sign that the narratives are converging along the lines of race regeneration and, notably, instruction.

But it is the entrenchment of the two narratives in the idea of white woman as "mother of the race" that brings Anne's and Pearlie's stories even more compellingly into alignment within a discourse of imperial maternalism as a reproductive and social politics: this idea is insistently developed throughout each series, and is already readily apparent in the first instalments. In *Anne of Green Gables*, for instance, race and gender are foregrounded as crucial marks of identity for Anne: it matters very much that she is a girl and not a boy; it matters that she is not what Marilla refers to as a "street Arab[]," but is "native born."[17] Pearlie's gender is similarly emphasized, and her Anglo-Celtic identity is comparably performed in the brogue which characterizes her speech before she goes to school. Both *Anne* and *Sowing Seeds in Danny*, moreover, tell stories of older women converted to maternalism by young Anglo-Celtic Canadian girls who are characterized not only by their – more or less – motherlessness, but by their motherliness:[18] Anne, we are told, is "real knacky" with babies: her saving of Minnie May Barry from croup is presented as irrefutable proof of her incipient and already well-developed skill. Pearl, identified at the beginning of the narrative as the alternative "mother" for her brothers and sisters is repeatedly shown to be "instinctively" maternal. They are both thus well-positioned to find what is represented in both works as latent, but untapped, springs of "mother-love," in the Anne stories, in Marilla Cuthbert, and, in McClung's novel, Mrs. J. Burton Francis. These "awakenings" constitute the groundwork upon which both narratives will develop: Anne finds a home where she can grow once she leads Marilla to discover what we are told is "the maternity she had missed, perhaps"; Pearl sets in motion the process of – as we are told in the title of the first novel – sowing seeds in Danny, or the "plant[ing] of the seeds of virtue and honesty in [the] fertile soil" of the eponymous child's character,[19] when she strips away the "encrusted" and, we are to see, impractical theories of motherhood which Mrs. Francis has been reading and attempting to apply to Mrs. Watson, and finds the same "instinctive" maternalism.[20] Marked in its emergence, like Marilla's "throb," with a "strange flush" and a "strange feeling stirring her heart,"[21] "mother-love," we are to see as it wells up in Mrs. Francis, is inherent in all women, and only needs to be revealed and directed by those women for whom it comes naturally, like Anne and Pearlie.

When these two novel series focus so intently on the representation of "mother-love" in childless older women and in adolescent girls, they reproduce and reinforce the early-twentieth-century notions of essential – and, increasingly, in the context of the psychoanalytic discourse of the period, normal – femininity as defined by the desire to have children, and the instinct to care for them.[22] McClung would articulate this notion in her 1915 suffrage manifesto, *In Times Like These*: "Women are naturally the guardians of the race," she wrote, "and every normal woman desires children."[23] This "desire" becomes the focus of both series. Anne's decision to take the "path" that leads to motherhood and not to a career is already implicit in the ending of *Anne of Green Gables*, when she gives up her scholarship to stay at home with Marilla after Matthew's death. She does not diverge from this "path" in the second novel, *Anne of Avonlea* (1909), which begins with a telling epigraph from John Greenleaf Whittier's narrative poem, "Among the Hills":

> Flowers spring to blossom where she walks
> The careful ways of duty;
> Our hard, stiff lines of life with her
> Are flowing curves of beauty.[24]

This second novel, which begins with Anne dreaming of her influence upon male students who will grow up to be "famous personage[s],"[25] gives most of its attention to Anne's growth as a motherly and loving teacher of children; it ends with her about to leave to go to college, but drawn by the sight of Diana's baby to another "path," and to imagine a "home o' dreams" where she and Gilbert Blythe will live. This "home" materializes in the fourth novel, *Anne's House of Dreams* (1917), when it becomes clear that her "ambition," from the beginning, has been to produce, as she puts it, "living epistles," or, of course, children.[26] Anna Davin has pointed out that motherhood in the early twentieth century "was to be given new dignity: it was the duty and destiny of women to be the 'mothers of the race,' but also their great reward."[27] Anne's "choice" of "duty and destiny" leads her to what is suggested is a greater happiness than she could have found if she had chosen not to follow this path.

Pearl's story unfolds along a similar trajectory. She begins the series demonstrating a pronounced love of hygiene and a desire to care for all those in her family and community who need some kind of moral or social "uplift." She thus reaffirms what McClung, like so many first-wave feminists, maintained was white women's superior morality and natural inclination to clean – their societies as well as their homes. Her "mothering" continues as she finds the lost maternalism of the ironically named Mrs. Motherwell, drives drink out of Millford, and helps to cure a child of tuberculosis. Her driving ambition, however, through all three instalments, and, significantly, most emphatically through her push for woman suffrage in the 1921 novel *Purple Springs*, is to marry Horace Clay, and,

it is implicit, to give vent to the maternalism for which she has been finding outlets (and converts, like Mrs. Francis and Mrs. Motherwell) since
the first pages of the first novel. As is the case for Anne, her romance is
not just a love story: rather, it is deliberately embedded in an ideology
of race, gender, nation and empire that directs the young Anglo-Celtic
girl towards motherhood, and the Anglo-Celtic nation towards imperial
regeneration through eugenical reproduction. Gilbert Blythe is not only
a doctor; he is represented as a young man who has come from "fine old
stock"; Horace Clay's sturdy salt-of-the-earth quality is implicit in his
patronym. These are the men who, with these ideal mothers, will bring
the race to the new day which dawns for the "real empire-builders" at the
end of the last Watson novel.[28]

Eve Kornfeld and Susan Jackson have suggested that *Anne of Green
Gables* ought to be regarded, with other "girl" books such as Wiggin's
Rebecca of Sunnybrook Farm (1903) and (more problematically) Louisa
May Alcott's much earlier *Little Women* (1868), as what they call a "female *Bildungsroman*," a genre which they describe as a "synthesis of the
[implicitly male] coming-of-age novel ... and domestic fiction."[29] Given,
however, the extent to which Anne's whole story, from Green Gables orphan to "matron" of Ingleside, is one in which motherhood is insistently
positioned as the culmination of "womanly" ambition, it might be more
to the point to see *Anne of Green Gables* – with McClung's *Sowing Seeds
in Danny* – as what we might call a *Mutterroman*. The *Mutterroman*,
as it emerges in early-twentieth-century English Canada in such novels as
the Anne books, thus may not be explained entirely in terms of what
Kornfeld and Jackson have argued is the "female *Bildungsoman*'s" negotiation of "the constraints of domestic fiction and the need to create a
credible facsimile of life" in a "male world" or what T.D. MacLulich has
described as "Montgomery's acquiescence to the secondary and largely
domestic role her society traditionally assigned women."[30] The *Mutterroman* is, rather, concerned with the promotion of the idea of woman as
"mother of the race." It is a genre which reproduces the ideology of race
regeneration that was being deployed in the first decade of the century
in the wave of imperialist discourse burgeoning in the late-nineteenth-
century expansionist years, and with increasing anxiety in the years
following the crisis of the Boer War. Although it is not concerned primarily with instruction in the science of mothering which Anna Davin
has pointed out appears in the early century under the designation of
"mothercraft,"[31] but with the inculcation of young girls into the culture
of mothering, the *Mutterroman* is a definitively didactic genre. Emerging

in the context of the idea of English Canada's importance as the empire's last best west, it marks a shift in the genres, vocabulary, and narratives of imperial popular fiction for children, from Victorian and late-nineteenth-century stories of mostly male conquest and colonization, to stories of renewal, reform, and reproduction, tasks in which women were to play a crucial role. This shift in genres stages in popular narrative the ideological transition which Davin notes occurring after the turn of the century, from the domestic to the political and social performance of maternalism by women. It also powerfully indicates the cultural pervasiveness of an imperialism which built on the idea of woman as "mother of the race" within the rhetoric of feminism as well as in less overtly political (but no less ideological) constructions of womanhood that were directed at children.

Few readers will object to the categorization of McClung's fiction as explicitly interested in inculcating girl readers into the maternal feminist ideology for which she functioned by 1915 as an influential national representative. McClung's writing has long been regarded as didactic, and we do not have to look far to find McClung herself avowing instruction as the primary motivation for her work. Her declaration of "the position that no one should put pen to paper unless he or she had something to say that would amuse, entertain, instruct, inform, comfort, or guide the reader"[32] is regularly cited by her biographers and critics as what she herself called the "Writer's Creed." It is to make a point of this profession that McClung recounts in her autobiography the story of her response to a "writer in the *Canadian Author*" (it was Wilfrid Eggleston) who, in an October 1943 article called "Nellie McClung – Crusader," argued that McClung's "didactic enthusiasm ... marred her art": "Some of her stories," he wrote, "are sermons in the guise of fiction. There is the flavor of the Sunday School hymn and the Foreign Mission Board in some of her work."[33] McClung, who shows herself to have been (not surprisingly) sensitive to the charge of being unliterary, responded thus: "I hope I have been a crusader, and I would be very proud to think that I had even remotely approached the grandeur of a Sunday School hymn. I have never worried about my art. I have written as clearly as I could, never idly or dishonestly, and if some of my stories are, as Mr. Eggleston says, sermons in disguise, my earnest hope is that the disguise did not obscure the sermon."[34] The sermon, that is, as Randi Warne has demonstrated in her study of the "Christian social activism" of McClung's fiction, is the element which, for McClung, gives art its value.[35]

Montgomery, conversely, disavowed didacticism as deliberately as McClung endorsed it.[36] In *The Alpine Path*, the early story of her career, written in 1917 for the Toronto magazine *Everywoman's World*, and subsequently published in book form under the same title, Montgomery drew attention to her opposition to didacticism in fiction, citing one of her own journal entries from the 1890s:

> I write a great many juvenile stories. I like doing these, but I should like it better if I didn't have to drag a "moral" into most of them. They won't sell without it, as a rule. So in the moral must go, broad or subtle, as suits the fibre of the particular editor I have in view. The kind of juvenile story I like best to write – and read, too, for the matter of that – is a good, jolly one, "art for art's sake," or rather "fun for fun's sake," with no insidious moral hidden away in it like a pill in a spoonful of jam![37]

The implication, of course, is that by 1917 Montgomery was no longer at the mercy of editors, but could write what she liked, "with no insidious moral."

This problematic self-representation raises, however, a number of questions for readers of Montgomery's work: for instance, when it is thus separated between that which necessarily capitulates to editorial constraints and that which promotes this creed of "art for art's sake," how do we distinguish the two categories? Is all her work from what Francis Bolger calls "the years before Anne" to be regarded as didactic, while all subsequent work can be seen to be purely "fun"? Where does *Anne of Green Gables* fit into the scheme within which Montgomery would like her readers to see her writing? And, perhaps most importantly, if *Anne of Green Gables* is not didactic and has "no insidious moral hidden away in it," why does Anne choose home and domestic duty over education? Why does *Anne of Avonlea* begin – and end – with an invocation to womanly duty? Why is Anne directed with such persistence away from a career and towards domesticity in *Anne of the Island*? Why does her path not diverge, through eight novels, from the direction chosen at the end of the first? Why is her story, even into the 1930s, so much like Pearlie's, which is self-consciously and deliberately instructional and profoundly maternalist? And, since it is so much like Pearl's, why is McClung's series seen to be feminist, while Montgomery's is not? Is Montgomery's lack of interest in woman suffrage enough to make her work not-feminist?

It is in fact quite possible to suggest that Montgomery's writing, even after the potentially liberating success of *Anne of Green Gables*, might all be engaged in more than "fun for fun's sake," and to be as much embedded in first-wave feminism's fundamental ideologies of race, gender and empire as McClung's. Indeed, the politics of instruction that can be seen to inform a good deal more of Montgomery's fiction than she is willing to acknowledge are articulated as one of these "insidious moral[s]" in one of her "juvenile stories." In a 1904 story, "At the Bay Shore Farm," Montgomery presents an encounter between a young woman with literary ambitions (like Anne, like Emily) and a woman whom she does not realize is actually her literary idol. The woman, Frances Newbury, and the idol, Sara Beaumont, discuss the hard struggle of a woman writer up what Montgomery would always refer to as "the Alpine path," and end with a new light breaking for Frances on the value and, most significantly, the duty of literature. It was, we are told, "an earnest, helpful talk that went far to inspire Frances's hazy ambition with a definite purpose. She understood that she must not write merely to win fame for herself or even for the higher motive of pure pleasure in her work. She must aim, however humbly, to help her readers to higher planes of thought and endeavour. Then and only then would it be worth while."[38] This is a very McClungian view of the work of fiction, and of the work of the woman writer in particular. McClung spoke frequently throughout her career about what she called "the social responsibilities of women": these responsibilities can be summarized, as the epigraph to this paper suggests, as "see[ing] that it is a woman's place to lift high the standard of morality."[39] Although neither Frances nor Sara Beaumont can function as an unproblematized voice for Montgomery, it is powerfully suggested by this story's moral that these responsibilities cannot be divorced from the work of the woman writer, for either McClung or Montgomery. A woman's fiction, according to both, must "aim ... to help her readers to higher planes of thought and endeavour."

According to the Anne books, as well as the Pearlie Watson trilogy, these "higher planes" – for girl readers at least – have to do with a normativizing of a desire to have children, and a valorizing of the maternal work of women at home and in the community. What is implicit in all of these stories is the objective that Frances imbibes from Sara Beaumont: Montgomery, too, that is, should be seen to want "to help her readers to higher planes of thought and endeavour," specifically with regard to womanly endeavour in the context of imperial expansion and anxiety about the reproduction of "the race." Her imperatives in the "insidious moral" of the 1904 story indicate that her own sense of the work of the woman writer must be understood in the same terms as the work which Anne pursues from the end of the first novel to the end of the series – the idea of womanly and, even at this early stage, a fundamentally maternal duty which closes *Anne of Green Gables* and opens *Anne of Avonlea*, in the Whittier epigraph. The woman writer, that is, is also a "mother of the race," her work necessarily instructional, with the "definite purpose" of presenting girl readers with a maternalist model. It is not simply coincidental that both Anne Shirley and Pearlie Watson become teachers; nor is it a simple indication of one of a very few career options for women in early-twentieth-century English Canada: Anne and Pearlie both function as metonymic representatives of the instructing woman writer herself, and as models of the maternalist ideology which both novel series are so interested in promoting. Both Pearlie and Anne are not only providing instruction to their fictional students, but to their readers as well.

The implication of this didacticism is that Montgomery's writing, like McClung's, should be seen to be embedded in an ideology of maternal feminism and to be reproducing a particular social model which takes up the imperialist position that Anglo-colonial women were especially valuable, as reproductive and moral agents who needed to be able to do their work for the good of "the race." Critics have argued for many years about the feminism of the Anne books: when we situate the novels in relation to the early-twentieth-century idea of white woman as "mother of the race," as texts which reproduce and promote this idea, it is possible to say that the Anne books are feminist because they perform the early-twentieth-century feminist work of valorizing the imperial mother, and, most importantly, of representing the imperial mother as a model for young girls. The Anne books thus work, as McClung's fiction does, to awaken women to their duty and to mobilize them for the work of empire. Anne's story through the eight novels, that is, is feminist precisely because it narrativizes a young Anglo-Celtic Canadian girl's choice of motherhood, as a duty, as a vocation, and as a profession. Anne does not give up writing because she is not good at it, although she does belittle her work in a Jane Austen-esque way in the *House of Dreams*, describing it as "pretty, fanciful little sketches" for children,[40] not to be compared with the muscular and manly work of Owen Ford or even Paul Irving. Anne gives up writing because she sees her work as the production of "living" books. Her path is thus not represented in the series itself as a "decline," although so many readers have, like Gillian Thomas, seen the narrative's trajectory in this light:[41] her path is to be understood as progressive, her taking up of motherhood as a professional decision. Anne actually turns out to be exactly the kind of mother-woman whom McClung would represent for her whole career as the "white hope" for "the race," instinctively maternal, motivated by duty, improving the world as and with their children.

Describing the kind of "trained motherly and tactful women" she imagined working for "the department of social welfare, paid for by the school board," to instruct young girls about pregnancy and birth control, McClung noted that "many mothers are ignorant, foolish, lax, and certainly untrained."[42] The foregrounding of a perceived need for the education of "ignorant" mothers, in part through the institutionalization of mothercraft, is a primary objective of McClung's feminism, which aims to remind women as well as men of the "natural" caregiving qualities of women, the "normal" desire to have children and to care for them, and of the urgent necessity of this – according to McClung, largely untapped – maternal resource for the advancement of "the race." "The woman movement," according to McClung, should be understood to be "a spiritual revival of the best instincts of womanhood – the instinct to serve and save the race."[43] The awakening of this instinct in women is a crucial didactic object of McClung's in the Pearlie Watson trilogy, as in so much of her fiction: it is also a similarly crucial object of Montgomery's in the Anne stories – and well beyond. Indeed, it is possible to see most of Montgomery's fiction undertaking two fundamentally didactic and definitively maternalist projects. First, it repeatedly and consistently constitutes heroines who are characterized by their inherent motherliness. Anne is joined, notably, but not only, by Pat of Silver Bush (1933–35) and Jane of Lantern Hill (1937), who are clearly committed to the values of domesticity and the directing of surplus maternal energy upon the community. Even Emily of New Moon is only offered fulfilment with the return of Teddy Kent: without home and children, as Janet Royal makes clear to Emily, and as Anne comes to see early in her story, success for women is to be seen to be a hollow thing.

Montgomery's second maternalist gesture is as pervasive and ideological, in its almost certainly unavoidable interpellation or identificatory "hailing" of girl readers as maternal subjects-to-be: it is also a crucial point at which her work connects with McClung's.[44] As in McClung's Watson trilogy, there is little in Montgomery's longer work which does not undertake to foreground good mothers – or mother figures – by juxtaposing them with bad ones. McClung deploys this strategy in Sowing Seeds in Danny, first, when she exposes the disjunction between Mrs. J. Burton Francis's ideas of mothering and her application of her "theories," and then when she draws attention to the shortcomings of the unmotherly Mrs. Motherwell. In both of these instances, it is Pearlie's superior mothering skills that make the "bad" mothering so apparent. Montgomery uses a similar methodology. In the first novel, Anne (and the girl reader) negotiate a range of models representing good and bad maternalism: Marilla, who finds her untapped maternalism through Anne's touch, is contrasted with Anne's previous caregivers and with Mrs. Peter Blewett; Marilla is joined by Mrs. Allan and Miss Stacy as mother figures who point Anne in the direction she will follow through the seven subsequent instalments. In *Anne of Ingleside* (1939), the last instalment which Montgomery would write, Anne's own good maternalism is juxtaposed with the lack of mother-love in Christine Stuart who speaks in a "hard" voice: "I'm afraid I'm not the maternal type. I really never thought that it was woman's sole mission to bring children into an already crowded world."[45] Since this has been Anne's "sole mission," we cannot but see her comments as reminding us once again that there is little space in the world Montgomery constructs for women who are not the "maternal type."

The contrasting of good and bad mothers which we see in the Anne books is similarly taken up in other novels: *Jane of Lantern Hill* and the Emily books likewise draw attention to the effects upon the two heroines of their maternal caregivers and their success or failure at nurturing the next generation of mothers. Even in the late 1920s and early '30s, the distinction between good and bad mothers – or between women who follow their maternal "instinct" and those who do not – is arguably the point upon which her fiction pivots. The Pat books and *Jane of Lantern Hill* are both profoundly domestic and maternal. The 1929 novel, *Magic for Marigold*, is a text in which "mothercraft" is actually invoked as a discourse of educated and "scientific" maternalism, represented for Marigold by her aunt Marigold.[46] The 1931 "grown-up" work, *A Tangled Web*, foregrounds the differences between Nan – a "new woman" – and Gay Penhallow as signs of their suitability to reproduce the race. What is clear is that Montgomery, like McClung, was engaged in an ideological work of narrativizing maternal "duty," her own "duty" as a writer closely resembling that of the early story, "to help her readers to higher planes of thought and endeavour." Montgomery's Anne books thus ought to be situated, with the novels which McClung was producing at the same time, in relation to the ideologies of first-wave feminism which they are reproducing. In both the Anne books and the Pearlie Watson series, girls in English Canada are being presented with models of imperial maternalism and, in effect, are being inculcated into imperialism's increasing interest in professionalizing motherhood not only as a "duty," but as a "domestic science" practically applied. In both series what we see is a model mother-woman whose object is to teach young girl readers how, as McClung puts it, to "think."

As is the case elsewhere in the Empire, the increased prominence of the imperial mother in Canada in the first decade of the twentieth century can be traced in a range of ways, all of which can be seen as ideological, working to interpellate white women as imperial subjects whose constructed "duty" to reproduce accorded them a particular value and privilege in the context of the period's expansionism. It is also possible to see the rise of the imperial mother in an increased emphasis upon inculcating children into a gendered culture of empire-building: it is well known that Baden-Powell founded the Boy Scouts and the Girl Guides after the Boer War crisis, in the hope that the Empire could be saved by improving the next generation through physical and moral education. Little boys were to grow up to be better soldiers than the previous generation of young men had proved to be; little girls were to become better mothers than the women who had produced the soldiers of the 1890s. In English Canada, where the ideas of maternalism were finding such purchase in the context of the expansionist west, the ideological work of teaching girls to be good "mothers of the race" is discernible in the formation of numerous organizations, such as the Girl Guides, the Canadian Girls in Training, and the Girls' Friendly Society. It is evident in the new emphasis in the early twentieth century on the teaching in elementary and high schools of "physical culture" and domestic science. It also underpins the emergence of a new imperial genre of fiction which was based, like Montgomery's and McClung's, in a discourse of educated maternalism, and which worked to "sow seeds" of race, gender, empire and duty in the next generation.

NOTES

1 McClung, *In Times Like These*, 43.
2 Logan and French, *Highways of Canadian Literature*, 299.
3 For more on this issue, see Gerson, "Anthologies and the Canon"; Gerson, "The Canon between the Wars."
4 Butler fought for many years for the repeal of the Contagious Diseases Acts, which had been passed 1864, 1868, and 1869 in an effort to regulate prostitution and the spread of sexually transmitted diseases. The Acts made it possible to submit any woman suspected of prostitution to an internal physical examination for signs of disease. See, for instance,

Judith Walkowitz's discussion of Butler and her work against regulation in Walkowitz, *City of Dreadful Delight*.

5 Davin, "Imperialism and Motherhood," 15. McClung, like other feminists of the period, notes the implications of the Boer War, pointing out in *In Times Like These* that "the British War Office had to lower the standard for the army because not enough men could be found to measure up to the previous standard, and an investigation was made into the causes which had led to the physical deterioration of the race" (McClung, *In Times Like These*, 166).

6 Davin, "Imperialism and Motherhood," 15.

7 McDonough, *The British Empire 1815–1914*, 101.

8 The phrase is used by Ernest Thompson Seton in an article published in the immigrationist magazine, *Canada West*. [See Seton, "The White Man's Last Opportunity."]

9 Woodsworth, *Strangers within Our Gates*, 8.

10 See Devereux, "New Woman, New World."

11 Quoted in Gillen, *The Wheel of Things*, 85–86. [See "Miss L.M. Montgomery, Author of *Anne of Green Gables*," in Volume 1 of *The L.M. Montgomery Reader*.]

12 Montgomery, 19 December 1917, in *SJLMM*, 2: 234.

13 See, for instance, a recent report on the front page of the *National Post* which makes reference to work done by David Howes and Constance Classen on similarities between *Rebecca of Sunnybrook Farm* and *Anne of Green Gables* (Lamey, "Is Anne of Green Gables"; Lamey, "Was Our Anne"). See Classen, "Is 'Anne of Green Gables,'" which first noted this theory.

14 MacMillan, McMullen, and Waterston, *Silenced Sextet*, 208. MacMillan also notes that Montgomery and McClung have "maintained their hold [only] as producers of paraliterature in the subgenres of children's fiction and social polemic" (ibid.).

15 Randi R. Warne's *Literature as Pulpit* marks a new academic interest in McClung, as does the University of Toronto reprint edition of *Purple Springs* and the University of Ottawa *Stories Subversive*, edited by one of McClung's most recent biographers, Marilyn Davis. For a review and analysis of recent shifts in the study of McClung, see Janice Fiamengo's extremely useful article, "A Legacy of Ambivalence: Response to Nellie McClung."

16 McClung, *Sowing Seeds in Danny*, 11.

17 *AGG*, 6.

18 For a fuller discussion of the maternal trajectory of the Anne novels, see Devereux, "'Not One of Those Dreadful New Women.'"

19 *AGG*, 76; McClung, *Sowing Seeds in Danny*, 19–20.

20 The theories of Mrs. Francis, we are to see, are not applicable to the real problems of the Watson family: she lectures about "motherhood" to Mrs. Watson, but does not recognize, until she is taught otherwise by Pearlie, that the work of "mothering" as McClung presents it is a practical extension of the work of caring for children at home. Maternalism, as it is presented in *Sowing Seeds in Danny*, situates women as social caregivers, and society (or significant portions of it) as children needing care.

A figure not unlike Mrs. Francis appears in Montgomery's fiction: in *Anne of Ingleside* Mrs. Parker is engaged in similar work, writing an "Institute paper on 'Misunderstood Children,'" while ignoring her own (*AIn*, 42). Her theories are presented as "encrusted" because they are not based on experience or practice. Jennifer Litster has pointed out to me that Montgomery makes a similar suggestion about contemporary theories of motherhood in the short story, "Penelope Struts Her Theories."

21 McClung, *Sowing Seeds in Danny*, 28.

22 For example, Freud's theories of femininity and the Oedipal phase for boys are arguably invested in an ideology of reproduction: women who do not want children are "neurotic."

23 McClung, *In Times Like These*, 25.

24 Whittier, *The Complete Poetical Works*, 88. This poem ends with an image of domestic harmony: on concluding the story of the woman who marries the farmer, the narrator takes the position that,

> ... musing on the tale I heard,
>   'T were well, thought I, if often
> To rugged farm-life came the gift
>   To harmonize and soften;
>
> If more and more we found the troth
>   Of fact and fancy plighted,
> And culture's charm and labor's strength
>   In rural homes united, –
>
> The simple life, the homely hearth,
>   With beauty's sphere surrounding,
> And blessing toil where toil abounds
>   With graces more abounding. (ibid., 89)

25 *AA*, 2.

26 Anne uses this phrase in *Anne of Ingleside*, when Christine Stuart asks if she has given up writing. "Not altogether ... but I'm writing living epistles now" (*AIn*, 265; ellipsis in original).

27 Davin, "Imperialism and Motherhood," 13.

28 *AIn*, 3; McClung, *Purple Springs*, 72.

29 Kornfeld and Jackson, "The Female *Bildungsroman*," 139.

30 Ibid., 151; MacLulich, "L.M. Montgomery's Portraits," 89.

31 Davin, "Imperialism and Motherhood," 39.

32 McClung, *The Stream Runs Fast*, 79.

33 Cited in ibid., 69.

34 Ibid.

35 [See Warne, *Literature as Pulpit*.]

36 Montgomery did not especially like McClung. After attending a dinner held in honour of McClung by the Canadian Authors' Association in 1921, Montgomery wrote disparagingly of McClung in her journal, observing that although "handsome," she was "glib of tongue," making "a speech full of obvious platitudes and amusing little stories which made everyone laugh and deluded us into thinking it was quite a fine thing – until we began to think it over" (Montgomery, 18 November 1921, in *SJLMM*, 3: 25). The two women did not correspond regularly.

37 *AP*, 61–62.

38 Montgomery, *Against the Odds*, 78–79.

39 McClung, *In Times Like These*, 43.

40 *AHD*, 15.

41 [See G. Thomas, "The Decline of Anne."]

42 McClung, *In Times Like These*, 133.

43 Ibid., 100.

44 French Marxist philosopher Louis Althusser uses the term "in order to explain how ideology constitutes and 'centres' subjects in the social world": "the human subject is given back, through ideology, an imaginary construction of his own autonomy, unity and self-preservation. [Althusser] argues that ideology 'recruits' individuals and transforms them, through the 'ideological recognition function,' into subjects. This recognition function is the process of interpellation: ideology 'interpellates' or 'hails' individuals, that is, addresses itself directly to them ... All hailed individuals, recognizing or misrecognizing themselves in the address, are transformed into subjects conceiving of themselves as free and autonomous members of a society that has in fact constructed them" (King, "Interpellation," 566, 567). See Althusser, *Lenin and Philosophy*, 127–86.

45 *AIn*, 263.

46 *MM*, 273.

15

Kinship and Nation in *Amelia* (1848) and *Anne of Green Gables* (1908)

—— 2002 ——

MONIQUE DULL

This essay by Monique Dull, first delivered at a conference hosted by the Association of Canadian Studies in the Netherlands at the University of Leiden in 2000 and published in the conference proceedings *The Rhetoric of Canadian Writing*, traces links between *Anne of Green Gables* and a lesser-known American text, Eliza Leslie's *Amelia; or a Young Lady's Vicissitudes* (1848). Paying particular attention to the use of the term "kindred spirit" as a term that denotes both community and nation, this article is particularly concerned with the ways in which Montgomery's imagined Avonlea, like Leslie's imagined communities, become read and embraced in nationalist terms.

It is a truism of post-colonial Canadian literary criticism that the history of Canadian literature traces an evolving expression of independent nationhood. Homi Bhabha is ritually invoked for his summation of this central post-colonial assumption: "The scraps, patches, and rags of daily life must be repeatedly turned into the signs of a national culture, while the very act of the narrative performance interpellates a growing circle of national subjects."[1] In this view, early colonial literature applies British taste to a colonized land, post-Confederate works shape a dim awakening of a new nation, and postwar narratives establish a nationalist identity forged at least partly on foreign battlefields or in cultural border disputes.[2]

L.M. Montgomery's 1908 novel, *Anne of Green Gables*, has been read by Canadians through a nationalist lens from its first publication.

Popular reviews in Canadian periodicals all emphasized the Canadianness of Anne's setting. One reviewer suggested an organic growth of the story from the red soil of PEI.[3] A reviewer for *The Canadian Magazine* situated Montgomery "in the first rank of our native writers" and stressed that "[Anne's] environment, a picturesque section of Prince Edward Island, is thoroughly Canadian."[4] Robertson Davies eulogized Montgomery with this compliment to her nation-building *oeuvre*: "Nations grow in the eyes of the world less by the work of their statesmen than by their artists. Thousands of people all over the globe are hazy about the exact nature of Canada's government ... but they have clear recollections of *Anne of Green Gables*."[5]

But Montgomery's contract with a Boston publisher suggests that her novel's Canadianness could not have been so inherent as to make it alien to foreign readers. American reviewers, by contrast, saw the author's "deep and wide sympathy" (*Boston Herald*)[6] and in one case even felt that Montgomery "might have made more of her background, for Prince Edward Island has not figured in fiction" (*Boston Budget and Beacon*).[7] Montgomery reportedly resented the American flag flying over the Avonlea schoolhouse in an early Hollywood film. Yet the difference between Canadian and American receptions of the novel from the first implies that there was less nationalism in the novel than in its domestic readers, then and now.

In fact Anne's world of kinship, community, and nation looks more complex than an early nationalist tract. Montgomery's emphasis on "kindred spirits" shifts the structure of the tribe from blood lineage to immaterial qualities. Emphatically, however, Montgomery does not distribute this kinship generously to the people of Anne's village, her metonymic nation. Nor does she rely (as critics imply) on a nation of shared aesthetics. Instead, Montgomery seems to grant "kindred spirit" status as a citizenship outside, or even against, the established Avonlea order, a para-nation mirroring the one that has repeatedly excluded Anne.

Reading Anne alongside an American counterpart bolsters this argument. Tellingly, Constance Classen's attempt to compare Anne with the American *Rebecca of Sunnybrook Farm* (1903) drew sharply worded defensive reactions from Montgomery scholars.[8] But another comparison might work as well, if not better, due to its focus – like Montgomery's – on questions of kinship and community. While Kate Douglas Wiggin's *Rebecca* offers a neatly contemporary talkative heroine, her novel's context in American national development is at odds with Anne's context in a less developed Canada. Rebecca is, in fact, no orphan but the daughter of an overworked mother sent out to her aunts' house; indeed, she almost has an overplus of kin. Moreover, Rebecca and her many relations flourish in Henry Ford's aggressively industrious and isolationist turn-of-the-century America. Anne is a newcomer within turn-of-the-century Canada, whose borders were more osmotic to the force of immigration and migration within.

A closer American counterpoint for Anne's discussion of kinship and nation is found earlier in time. Eliza Leslie's *Amelia; or a Young Lady's Vicissitudes* (1848) also features an orphan heroine with inborn wit, new to an established community. Amelia, like Anne, is the locus of a discussion of kinship and national belonging. More strikingly, Leslie's narrative also uses the phrase so central to Montgomery's world to express Leslie's American reconfiguration of nation: "kindred spirits."

The phrase "kindred spirits" provides a tight focus of comparison. The authors' shared allusion is Thomas Gray's "Elegy Written in a Country Churchyard" (1751). Gray worried about the problem of modern community a century earlier than Leslie, and a century and a half earlier than Montgomery. He hints at a modern break from the blood lineage traditionally defining village kinship, replacing blood kinship with a common aesthetic. Leslie and Montgomery each implicitly play with Gray's famous poem and its kinship revision. Where Leslie's Amelia finds kinship and citizenship in a shared sense of the sublime, Montgomery's Anne chooses kinship in a far more arbitrary and heterogeneous fashion – a fashion either echoing the structure of contemporary Canada, or answering it.

Leslie's *Amelia* opens in a time of high national flux: the 1840s saw a sudden upsurge in immigration to the United States as steamships made oceanic crossings quicker and more plentiful. A concomitant wave of nativism responded to the newcomers. Twenty percent of the American male population joined the nativist political groups which argued for the exclusive enfranchisement of those born on American soil.[9]

The life of the heroine is similarly in flux at the novel's start. Amelia is eighteen, and, though womanly, is not yet an independent twenty-one. She is the American-born daughter of German immigrants, the Helfensteins of Ohio, and the adopted daughter of a New York couple, the otherwise childless Cotterells, who took on Amelia as a toddler in the narrative's prehistory. Compounding Amelia's insecure familial identity is the death, within chapters of the novel's start, of the widow Cotterell. Amelia, "the daughter of [Mrs. Cotterell's] heart"[10] if not of her blood, is defrauded of her inheritance by Mrs. Cotterell's scheming sister. Anglo-American adoptions were not regulated by law until the twentieth century; therefore adoption's kinship by convention was de facto weaker than claims of kinship by blood. Thus Leslie introduces at the core of her story the terms – blood and convention – which occupy Gray, Leslie, and Montgomery.

Amelia's immediate bereavement of her adoptive parents and defraudation reverse the novel's prehistory. That is to say, no sooner does Leslie establish Amelia's adoptive kinship than she undoes it. Leslie affects this change in style by switching from the sentiment of Amelia's and Mrs. Cotterell's familial love to sharply drawn satiric portraits of the New York society which rejects Amelia, and equally satiric portraits of the German biological parents who grudgingly take her back. In plot, no sooner does Leslie have a character comment that Amelia "is, indeed, the most truly American girl that I have ever known"[11] than Leslie tosses Amelia back to her German parents in the backwoods, calling into question both forms of kinship Amelia has known, biological and conventional.

Amelia returns to Ohio and finds her German-born family to be as crude as the nativist stereotype allows. Both parents die in short order, leaving her dependent on her older siblings until the age of twenty-one. Only her younger brother Caspar – born, like Amelia, after the immigration – shows intelligence, endeavour, and elegance. In short, Amelia and Caspar prove the nativist ideal: their very birth within American borders, on American land, sets them apart from their lesser foreign relations. The nativism of Leslie's novel takes the idea of birth on American soil and pushes the metaphor to highlight the Americanness of inhabitants outside the large cities such as New York. Indeed, New Yorkers, removed from their own soil, are almost as unAmerican as the Helfensteins themselves. Both groups receive strong satiric treatment. However, the gentry of small towns still close to the landscape provide suitable company, and future kindred, for civilized native-born Americans such as Amelia and Caspar.

Not just land defines the true American. Leslie's criterion slides from land to landscape, from birthplace to aesthetic appreciation. Amelia's suitor in Ohio is Charles Sedgely, also an orphan, albeit one who has inherited his Philadelphia parents' capital. Leslie describes a courtship mediated by the lovers' passion for the sublime vistas offered by their country:

To-day, he was descanting, in glowing terms, on his own fair land, to an auditress who said, rejoicingly – "I too am an American!" –

for he adverted to the blessings that Heaven has poured upon our country since she broke her chains, and walked forth in the might and majesty of freedom – and to "the visions of glory" too great for imagination to conceive, but which will assuredly become realities in the future destiny of America ... He had gazed as if he could gaze forever, on the cataract of the world, the sublime, the awful, the tremendous, the beautiful Niagara. He had stood under the shadow of the Virginian rock that bridges a ravine two hundred feet below, and ascended the fine old tree that has grown beneath its arch.[12]

Sedgely has physically touched the American sublime, hiking over it and climbing it; Amelia can add her feminine aesthetic appreciation. Leslie joins them in a new kinship springing from a shared aesthetic of the national sublime. They are matched in their sensibility. Together with Sedgely and the local gentry with whom Amelia lives upon reaching independence, she has found her new family: "She was now with such companions as had imbibed knowledge from the same springs, who could catch an allusion at once, who heard everything understandingly, and whose kindred spirits responded to that masonic touch which immediately converts strangers into friends."[13]

Here Leslie relates aesthetic kinship to shared geography. Springs of knowledge are no new figure of speech. But in the context of Leslie's courtship scenes, which dwell on the beautiful physicality of the American landscape, these springs tie even more tightly the true American citizen to the land. Leslie is not only nativist but could be called "geographicist." Leslie's kindred in an immigrant country do not share blood but soil, or, more specifically, landscape.

Leslie challenges her reader to recognize Gray's phrase, "kindred spirits." She places the phrase in a sentence about ideal companions who can "catch an allusion at once," after all. In short, she invites us to revisit Gray's poem. In 1751 Gray published his "Elegy Written in a Country Churchyard," which he had written and privately circulated after the death of his friend Richard West. The "Elegy" considers, among other things, the passing of a much smaller socio-political unit than the nation: Gray concerns himself (more minutely than Leslie) with the English village. The narrator walks through a country churchyard reflecting on the dead, great and lowly. He implies that he knows, or knew of, many people buried here, since he gives us personal and familial details summarized as "The short and simple annals of the poor."[14]

Gray's larger grief – grief for a friend magnified to grief for a passing way of life – lends the poem an already-elegiac tone. The last quarter sees a turn to a second-person interlocutor:

> For thee, who mindful of the unhonored dead,
> Dost in these lines their artless tale relate;
> If chance, by lonely contemplation led,
> Some kindred spirit shall inquire thy fate.[15]

The poem continues with a proposed last memory and epitaph for the second person. Kinship of spirit here is in part affinity of mind: we first read the secondary meaning of "kin," looking for something "akin." The speaker says to the addressee, "Should there be someone with a similarly melancholy turn of mind walking through this graveyard, they might well be told the following about you … " But Gray's powerful nostalgia relies on more than his era's fashionable elective affinity. The strength of the "Elegy" comes from Gray's suggestion of the older meaning of kin, namely, blood relation. Gray's village, on the point of passing, is simple: blood relation and spatial community overlap. Villagers share both ancestry and place.

Gray's poem was wildly popular, going through four editions in two months and seven more in the following few years. It became a staple in the nineteenth century, eminently suited to sentimental poetry albums and, later, school readers and recitals. Leslie's and Montgomery's reliance on the allusion is no surprise: both worked within Gray's wide and long shadow, leaving them able to draw on his phrase for resonant meaning. Leslie's use of "kindred spirits" argues that kinship in America is aesthetic, and that this aesthetic derives with exaggerated emphasis from shared birthplace only, not blood. The two sources of kinship in Gray's community (blood and place) are focused into one (place), since American blood is too diverse. Montgomery's allusion to Gray half a century after Leslie will extend this discussion of community.

Montgomery, too, places her orphan story within a nation – indeed, a nation within a nation. The narrator tells us right away that Green Gables is part of the village Avonlea, which "occupied a little triangular peninsula jutting out into the Gulf of St. Lawrence."[16] At least one critic has concluded that Avonlea's peninsular position leaves it "well-protected."[17] In fact, this position leaves Avonlea flapping on the wind-blown edge of the Atlantic, surveying the main waterway into Lower and Upper Canada, overlooking the very route taken by European immigrants flooding into Canada around the turn of the century.

Thus Avonlea is small, but geographically it is already nationally implicated. Its province of Prince Edward Island was the "cradle of Confederation" due to the political conference held in the capital, Charlottetown, in 1864 to plan the organization of modern Canada. The novel's setting is linked even more strongly with nation and kinship through the phrase – unspoken in the novel but ubiquitous in Canada – for the politicians who had gathered to rock the national cradle: Prime Minister John A. Macdonald and his peers were known as the Fathers of Confederation.[18]

Critical commentary on setting has dwelt on Montgomery's descriptions of Avonlea and Prince Edward Island.[19] Yet Montgomery in fact attends to each of the increasing geographic and civic entities. She roots her province in the precolonial past by referring to it by its aboriginal name, Abegweit. Her translation to a Canadian readership immediately recalls the standard school lesson that the name Canada comes from the Huron-Iroquois word, kanata, or "small village." Avonlea, the small village, is literally Canada in microform. Drain points out that Montgomery also places Avonlea within a comfortable drive of a train station.[20] Trains and tracks, the technology which physically tied together Canada's vast regions, are also associated with national Confederation.

As we saw in *Amelia*, place and landscape provided Leslie, too, with a structure for kinship and nation. Leslie's citizenship for Amelia is ultimately spatial. Amelia has an aesthetic sense granted by the very landscape she was born to and appreciates. It includes Amelia and resolves the plot. Avonlea's nation is also spatial, but it excludes Anne and propels the plot. Anne is born within Canada, but not within Avonlea or within Prince Edward Island. At first Anne's birth on Canadian soil would seem to be her salvation. Marilla's speech to Mrs. Rachel Lynde about the reliability in a xenophobic era of the "born Canadian" has already been examined by Laura M. Robinson for its nativist and racist rhetoric: "At first Matthew suggested getting a Barnado [*sic*] boy. But I said 'no' flat to that. 'They may be all right – I'm not saying they're not – but no London street Arabs for me,' I said. 'Give me a native born at least. There'll be a risk, no matter who we get. But I'll feel easier in my mind and sleep sounder at nights if we get a born Canadian.'"[21] Marilla implicitly rejects those of a foreign culture ("Arabs"); but she equally rejects as foreign the English-born poor, who are modified here with the same root adjective ("London street Arabs"). Even those born in the mother country fall short of the homegrown colonial product.

Anne, however, is born in Nova Scotia, not Prince Edward Island. Montgomery refers to Anne throughout the series as a Bluenoser. This traditional epithet for Nova Scotians refers to the eponymous Nova Scotian sailing ship, and suggests Nova Scotians' seafaring and globe-trotting tendencies. When Marilla announces to Mrs. Lynde that she and her brother Matthew are going to adopt an orphan from Nova Scotia, she shocks Avonlea's policing eye into this comparison with the furthest possible voyage: "If Marilla had said that Matthew had gone to Bright River to meet a kangaroo from Australia Mrs. Rachel could not have been more astonished."[22] In Avonlea's terms Anne is a small-scale immigrant. She is as alien as the immigrants sailing up the Gulf.

Avonlea's miniature nation is no simple entity. As Robinson points out, Montgomery draws several obvious distinctions between peoples: Acadians, who are dismissed as unreliable; European peddlers circulating through small towns; the Scotch-Irish establishment of Avonlea; and among the latter, families of bad nature such as the Pyes versus the rest. We could also add Montgomery's ongoing references to Methodists versus Presbyterians, and the running interfamilial divisions between Tory and Grit.

Thus Anne's personal longing for kin exists within this context of pre-existing divisions within the Avonlea tribe. Kinship must be crucial in Avonlea if Anne wants it in spite of the evidence. Anne is willing to forge kinship by an act of imagination, replacing blood with language:

> "I'd love to call you Aunt Marilla," said Anne wistfully. "I've never had an aunt or any relation at all – not even a grandmother. It would make me feel as if I really belonged to you. Can't I call you Aunt Marilla?"
>
> "No. I'm not your aunt and I don't believe in calling people names that don't belong to them."
>
> "But we could imagine you were my aunt."
>
> "I couldn't," Marilla said grimly.[23]

Perhaps Anne is inspired by the imaginative act of Confederation. It, too, declared a bond, or foedus, into being among disparate entities. And its author, Prime Minister Macdonald, continued to inspire familial and political harmony some forty years later, as Montgomery shows in the novel itself. The inspiration would not be far-fetched. Montgomery links

Anne's fate with Macdonald's at the midpoint of the story. Chapter 18 opens with this observation: "All things great are wound up with all things little. At first glance it might not seem that the decision of a certain Canadian Premier to include Prince Edward Island in a political tour could have much or anything to do with the fortunes of little Anne Shirley of Green Gables. But it had."[24] Certainly Anne's kinship fortunes could use an upturn at the midpoint. Her first friend, Diana Barry, has been forbidden by her mother to consort with Anne. The chapter offers Anne her social redemption.

Redemption comes indirectly through Macdonald. In this literally central episode, the Barrys' youngest child nearly dies of croup. Diana fetches Anne to help; Anne nurses the baby through the night, and wins back Mrs. Barry's acceptance and Diana's sanctioned friendship. But Anne is only allowed into the Barrys' home as a last resort by frantic Diana since nearly all Avonlea adults – including the Barrys, Mrs. Lynde and Marilla – are absent from the village. They are in Charlottetown, visiting the cradle of Confederation where father John A. Macdonald is speaking during an election campaign.[25]

The Charlottetown gathering of Avonlea's adults is a mini-confederation, an act of bonding. Montgomery emphasizes the unusual harmony of admiration shared across entrenched political lines: "Mrs. Rachel Lynde was a red-hot politician and couldn't have believed that the political rally could be carried through without her, although she was on the opposite side of politics."[26] The picture of national kinship over the imaginary federal cradle in Charlottetown frees Avonlea momentarily of its rules, as though the distant concentration in Charlottetown drains away the local protocols of Avonlea. It allows Anne's status to grow. Montgomery chooses the equalizing darkness of night and the abstracted landscape of a snowfall as her background for Anne's sudden freedom and consequent responsibility for a real baby in a real bed.

Yet, while saving the Barrys' baby secures the affection and respect of a crucial family, Montgomery chooses not to have Anne conquer Avonlea, nor to have Avonlea sentimentally declare Anne "kin" in unison. Instead, after the Macdonald episode, Montgomery's use of the phrase "kindred spirits" becomes more frequent, but increasingly unpredictable. The phrase appears to be out of the narrator's hands and transferred to Anne's. She now wields the choice of kinship.

The election of "kindred spirits" in Anne's world is more complex than in Amelia's. The list includes five kindred spirits: Matthew, Diana, Aunt Josephine Barry, Mrs. Allan, and Miss Stacy.[27] It is only after the episode during the Charlottetown gathering that Montgomery shows Anne explicitly rejecting two figures from her list of kindred spirits: a "very nice little girl" she meets at the manse, and school Superintendent Bell, "really a very fine man," who visits her while she convalesces from her broken leg.[28]

Exactly what qualifies or disqualifies a character for kinship with Anne is a perplexing question. Since Anne herself is an outsider, she does not make birthplace a prerequisite. Carol Gay holds that "kindred spirits" here share Anne's "feminine values," which Gay defines as anti-Calvinist romanticism – by which Gay means specifically sentiment – and intuition.[29] Yet upon closer analysis, kinship of spirit here does not appear to depend on a shared aesthetic, as it does in *Amelia* and (to a degree) in Gray's "Elegy." Gay and others may be influenced by the introductory scene for Anne, in which Montgomery says it would take a hypothetical "discerning extraordinary observer" to see Anne's soul in her outwardly bedraggled state.[30] Montgomery proceeds to lead the reader through the extraordinary observations. Montgomery seems to be setting up her reader as a kindred spirit – if kindred spirits are (as in *Amelia*) people, like Anne, blessed with aesthetic sensitivity.

But they are not. The paragraph ends by observing that Matthew – Anne's prime kindred spirit – is "ludicrously afraid" of Anne,[31] something he would not be if he could read her kindred soul. And while Anne says she felt, upon seeing Matthew Cuthbert, that he was a kindred spirit, she admits she could not have predicted the same of elderly Aunt Josephine Barry. Nor do the kindred look alike. Anne's self-chosen kindred are a motley assortment outwardly. More to the point, they have no vision or aesthetic in common. While Miss Stacy is remarkable for her imaginative teaching style, she is also affectionately ironic about Anne. Anne's "kindred" are decidedly prosaic, not "romantic" as Gay suggests: Diana in fact has less wit or fancy in her as the novel progresses; Matthew is sweet but taciturn; Aunt Josephine can be as cutting as Rachel Lynde; Mrs. Allan laughs at Anne's melodramatic pronouncements. The five kindred spirits aesthetically are at best streaks of satire to Anne's sentiment. All that Anne's kindred share is that Anne has chosen them for her own, or not rejected them. They form a confederation by Anne's fiat, much like the nation whose miniature form – Avonlea – has rejected Anne by fiat for the novel's first half. Anne's kindred spirits are an involuntary pseudo-nation constructed under Macdonald's nose.

Anne's assemblage of the satirical with her own sentiment mirrors Montgomery's own narrative streaks, which are blended to a peculiar sweet-sour style. Montgomery's narrative method answers Leslie's earlier blocking of sentiment and satire as positive and negative modes of telling. In *Amelia*, Leslie reserves sentiment for the American landscape, the American sublime, and the appreciative American citizen, who is also a kindred spirit; she reserved satire for the rejected foreigner or the rejected false American, such as New Yorkers.

Montgomery plays with both narrative modes simultaneously in a scene, even about her heroine. In Chapter 8, Marilla is shocked that Anne has not learned the Lord's Prayer. She sends Anne from the kitchen to get the obligatory prayer card from the parlour mantel. Montgomery is thus already working with a sentimental genre within the novel, namely the tableau. Anne, sent to get the prayer card, will herself become a sentimental tableau: a pale young orphan girl reaching up to a mantel in a lonely parlour, striving for her own incipient Christianity which is symbolized by the prayer card – the card itself boasting a tiny tableau in its unavoidable miniature illustration. Montgomery's actual telling of the scene, however, complicates this sentimental trajectory:

> Anne promptly departed for the sitting-room across the hall; she failed to return; after waiting ten minutes Marilla laid down her knitting and marched after her with a grim expression. She found Anne standing motionless before a picture hanging on the wall between the two windows, with her hands clasped behind her, her face uplifted, and her eyes astar with dreams. The white and green light strained through apple trees and clustering vines outside fell over the rapt little figure with a half-unearthly radiance.
>
> "Anne, whatever are you thinking of?" demanded Marilla sharply ...
>
> "That," she said, pointing to the picture – a rather vivid chromo entitled, "Christ Blessing Little Children" – "and I was just imagining I was one of them – that I was the little girl in the blue dress, standing off by herself in the corner as if she didn't belong to anybody, like me."[32]

Montgomery's tableau is both sentimental and satirical, sublime and ridiculous. On one hand, Montgomery states that there really is a half-unearthly radiance illuminating Anne. Her face is "uplifted" to an otherworldly perspective. Her eyes, "astar with dreams," literally reflect the "heaven" to which the prayer more abstractly refers. On the other hand, Anne stands in sanctifying light only because she imitates, and unconsciously mocks, the picture's prescribed pose. Montgomery even mocks Anne's taste for modelling herself on a "vivid chromo" to begin with. Furthermore, Anne imitates the least successful of the converts, the isolated girl at a distance from the sentimentalized Christ.

Montgomery arbitrarily combines the two modes, yoking them in narrative kinship. Her scene itself is a topos to which both sentiment and satire are native. She may indeed pull towards Anne in sentimental passages, much like Anne pulls towards her "kindred," as Gay argues. But she equally withdraws from Anne with her more distant satiric mode, a mode operating simultaneously with Anne's sentimental portrayal. The kinship of the two modes, like Anne's unfathomable bond with her kindred spirits, resembles contemporary Confederation's tense but productive state.

Montgomery's kinship "resembles" Confederation, but in mirror fashion. It is an important distinction that Anne's kin are an answer, a paranation, to the small village, the kanata that has rejected Anne so arbitrarily, up to the story's midpoint, on largely nativist and familial grounds. Far from extending an inclusive enthusiasm throughout Avonlea, or even throughout a mini-circle within Avonlea, kinship of spirit here is almost a parody of community. Anne becomes as arbitrary in her assignments of status as the nation which alternately tolerates, rejects, then accepts her.

This comparative reading of nation, kinship, and mode in *Anne of Green Gables* is admittedly darker than others. Montgomery's elective kinship is subtler than Leslie's in *Amelia*. But where Amelia innocently benefits from the criteria of a nativist narrative, Anne herself by the second half of the novel actively and arbitrarily rejects others with the phrase "kindred spirits." Yet we cannot fairly chastise Montgomery for her own exclusions – of Acadians, peddlars, and the Irish – without considering her heroine's own exclusive, elective kinship, and reasons for it. Little did Gray know that his meditation on place, displacement, and blood would bequeath a phrase central to the self-imagining of a girl and a very distant small village founded on mass migration.

NOTES

1 Bhabha, "DissemiNation," 297.
2 See George Woodcock's collection of Canadianist studies in his *Northern Spring*. Woodcock, founder of *Canadian Literature*, uses his series of essays to tell a national history for nearly all of Canada's discrete literary phenomena. Margaret Atwood's *Survival* also famously reads a Canadian

psyche into landscape and literature. For a recent discussion of national identity in Canadian culture, see Angus, *A Border Within*.

3   " ... she has taken a Canadian countryside, and peopled it, in a manner marvelously natural." *Montreal Daily Herald*, 21 July 1908. Quoted in Montgomery, *The Annotated Anne of Green Gables*, 484. [This review also appears in Volume 3 of *The L.M. Montgomery Reader*.]

4   Quoted in Montgomery, *The Annotated Anne of Green Gables*, 488.

5   Quoted in M.H. Rubio, "*Anne of Green Gables*: The Architect," 65. [See also "The Creator of Anne," in Volume 1 of *The L.M. Montgomery Reader*].

6   Quoted in Montgomery, *The Annotated Anne of Green Gables*, 483.

7   Quoted in Montgomery, *The Annotated Anne of Green Gables*, 486. [This review also appears in Volume 3 of *The L.M. Montgomery Reader*].

8   Lamey, "Was Our Anne Born in Maine?" I would like to thank CBC arts reporter Carmen Klassen and Concordia professor David Howes for helping me find this report. See also Classen, "Is 'Anne of Green Gables,'" which is not listed on the website of the L.M. Montgomery Institute. Also of interest is Howes' and Classen's work in progress, *Framing the Canadian Imaginary*, which puts several iconic Canadian works in context with American parallels.

9   See Curran, *Xenophobia and Immigration 1820–1930*. For a Canadian history of similar hostility, see D. Avery, *Reluctant Host*.

10 Leslie, *Amelia*, 34.

11 Ibid., 17.

12 Ibid., 68–69.

13 Ibid., 67.

14 Gray, "Elegy Written in a Country Churchyard," 2459.

15 Ibid., 2461.

16 *AGG*, 2.

17 Drain, "Community and the Individual," 123.

18 See the reproduction of a political cartoon depicting Macdonald as a father harangued by his whining daughter-provinces of Confederation, in Montgomery, *The Annotated Anne of Green Gables*, 200.

19 See, for instance, Solt, "The Uses of Setting."

20 Drain, "Community and the Individual," 125.

21 [*AGG*, 6]; see also L.M. Robinson, "'A Born Canadian,'" 22.

22 *AGG*, 5.

23 *AGG*, 54–55.

24 *AGG*, 138.

25 Montgomery, *The Annotated Anne of Green Gables*, 199, note 1.

26 *AGG*, 138.
27 *AGG*, 33, 88, 159, 170, 189.
28 *AGG*, 181, 188.
29 Gay, "'Kindred Spirits' All," 105, 107.
30 *AGG*, 11.
31 *AGG*, 11.
32 *AGG*, 55–56.

16

The Maud Squad

—— 2002 ——

CYNTHIA BROUSE

Cynthia Brouse attended L.M. Montgomery and Life Writing, the 2002 international conference hosted by the L.M. Montgomery Institute at the University of Prince Edward Island, as research for this detailed snapshot of the unique community of scholars and readers who continue to be devoted to Montgomery's work at the turn of the twenty-first century. According to the subhead that accompanied the original article in *Saturday Night*, where Brouse was managing editor, "Against all odds, Lucy Maud Montgomery has become the prototypical pop-cult figure of 20th-century literature. Nearly 100 years after writing *Anne of Green Gables*, she brings together the high-brow and the low, the academic and the fan, the virtual and the merely fictional." This article received an honourable mention in the Arts & Entertainment category of the 2002 National Magazine Awards. Cynthia Brouse died in 2010.

It really is just a hole in the ground. The little sandstone-lined cellar is all that remains of the house in Cavendish, Prince Edward Island, where Lucy Maud Montgomery lived more than half her life – and where she wrote *Anne of Green Gables*.

It's not on most tour bus itineraries, even though it's only metres from some of the other Montgomery heritage sites. Hordes of tourists flock to Green Gables (the model for the place where Anne Shirley "lived"), to the author's grave – once located at a lonely country crossroads, now kitty-corner to a wax museum – and to the houses where Maud (as she was known) was born and got married. There might even be time to visit the ersatz "Avonlea Village," the Rainbow Valley Family Fun Park and the Ripley's Believe It or Not! down the road. But most people miss the homestead site altogether.

Not that Jennie and John Macneill would let the big buses stop here anyway. The noise and diesel fumes would spoil the gentleness of the grounds they've maintained for the past 14 years. But they wouldn't mind seeing more small groups drop by. "We're not very good at marketing," admits Jennie, whose husband, now in his early 70s, is Montgomery's first cousin once removed. What you get for the $2 admission fee is the chance to hear the story of Montgomery's life, and then to walk through the yard or sit quietly in the knowledge that the peaceful surroundings are the same ones that inspired the woman Jennie always refers to as "the Author." You can buy a book or a postcard in the tiny bookstore, but, in contrast to the other sites, there are no Anne ashtrays, no "Freckle Frenzy" ice cream, no rides to amuse the kids. Some sightseers refuse to pay the two bucks, and turn back at the door.

I happily fork over my toonie because I'm a bit of a fan, though I like to think I'm not one of those people who'd call the homestead a "sacred site." Nevertheless, like generations of girls, when I read *Anne of Green Gables* at the age of 10, I understood for the first time that a book could make me cry, and I asked for the other seven books in the series at Christmas and birthdays, reading and rereading them well into adulthood. Of course, Montgomery's sweet, humorous novels about feisty young women in P.E.I. have been best-sellers for nearly a century. But since the mid-1980s, when three unrelated factors came together to fan the Montgomery flames, a different spin on the author has emerged: today she's the cornerstone of her own mini-industry, one that goes beyond selling novels, or even souvenirs. The writer who rejected modernity has turned into a postmodern icon in the way her work and her life are commodified and consumed.

In fact, since creating the little red-haired orphan, Montgomery has become one of the few literary figures who bring together both high- and low-brow culture. From Ontario to Sweden, university professors have devoted their life's work to the author, aligning themselves with the little girls who identify with the lonely, loquacious heroine, the thousands of Japanese visitors to P.E.I. who mysteriously seem to have absorbed Anne with their miso soup, and the residents of the Island who make their living selling a version of Montgomery's imagination. (Today, the author gets her own entry in the P.E.I. *Visitors Guide*, along with Beaches, Golf and Dining.)

Montgomery is not the only writer with a cult following, but she may be unique among celebrity authors. Shakespeare attracts sightseers and sells tie pins and dishtowels; Jane Austen draws Janeites from around the globe together on the Internet; Robert Service helped rescue the economy of a small town; Virginia Woolf's letters and journals engender biography after biography; Ernest Hemingway generates academic conferences and countless doctoral theses; Sir Arthur Conan Doyle inspires a weird conflation of the fictional with the real. But Montgomery is the only young people's writer – possibly the only writer of any kind – who does all of these things simultaneously. And while Frodo Baggins, Nancy Drew, Huckleberry Finn and Harry Potter may give Anne a run for her money, only she, like the Mounties, stands in for a nation.

The pleasant June weekend of the biennial conference of the L.M. Montgomery Institute in Charlottetown is a crucible for this mixture of attention, where fans and academics from Tokyo and Texas and Australia rub shoulders, along with tourism workers, filmmakers, and Montgomery's descendants and their lawyers. We all want a piece of her, and though there are as many reasons for being here as there are people – from the loopy to the learned – we're bound together by some kind of glue. Perhaps it's a hangover from our childhood attachment – the book/author as comfort food, to which we turn as we would to Mom's macaroni and cheese.

Whatever it is, if that glue binds the popular to the profound, it also binds reality to illusion – especially when you make the leap from Green Gables to the hole in the ground. In Anne Land, nothing is what it seems.

"Get this," says Karen Macfarlane, an English professor at Mount Saint Vincent University in Halifax and a conference presenter, as she unpacks her things in the University of P.E.I. residence. We attended the last conference together, and have met up again for this one. "They've scheduled a torchlight walk through the homestead site. This is the stuff I hate, but I'll go just so I can regale my academic colleagues with all the kitschy things that go on here. They're *way* more cynical than I am." At her first conference Macfarlane was astonished to find people at the registration desk wearing red braids and straw hats.

On the surface, this is an academic conference – as evidenced by papers that deal with the Bakhtinian dialogic structure of *Anne of Green Gables* or the synecdochic status of Anne's red hair. Some are dry and impenetrable; others provide insight into not only the writer's life and work but also the social history captured in her books, her influence on women's memoir and her impact as a pop culture artifact (a scholarly book arising from the 2000 conference called *Making Avonlea: L.M. Montgomery and Popular Culture*, edited by Irene Gammel, will be published this month). Topics have included everything from the significance of tuberculosis in Montgomery's stories to the way the novels' cover illustrations have reflected attitudes toward women and girls across different eras and cultures.

But the conference also attracts a sizable contingent of "Kindred Spirits" – fans of Montgomery who have Internet handles such as Miriam of the Haunted Spring or Frank of the Big Smoke, who plan tea parties in cyberspace, celebrate Kindred Day and appear to have an intense personal relationship with the author, sometimes even using the novels as precepts for living. Some Kindred Spirits present conference papers, too, often quite thoughtful ones. But the more serious researchers at the conference are occasionally taken aback by the atmosphere of reverence toward the author and by the sentimental or unscholarly quality of a few of the presentations.

Outside the plenary sessions, merchants from Kindred Spirits of P.E.I. sell Anne dolls, Anne stationery and copies of a book called *Anne's World, Maud's World: The Sacred Sites of L.M. Montgomery*. This year, the wackiest presentations include one on Montgomery's astrological chart and a wildly unscientific paper that suggests she died of mercury poisoning from her dental fillings. (What actually caused her death in 1942 at the age of 67 is a little murky, and suicide rumours may or may not be quashed when Mary Rubio of the University of Guelph publishes her long-awaited biography next year. "I know what happened," Rubio tells me cryptically, but won't elaborate.)

If some academics are skeptical of the Kindred Spirits, the feeling can be mutual. There's a minor flap over the presence of Laura Robinson, the English professor whose paper about lesbian desire in the Anne books made national headlines on a slow news day two years ago. Detecting a homoerotic subtext in a literary work is a fairly unremarkable practice in academia, and Robinson wasn't the first to do it with Montgomery's oeuvre. But this year, she's dealing with lesbian desire between real people: in her journals, Montgomery described with vehement abhorrence the unwelcome ardour of a female fan, whom she called a "pervert." The fact that she did not always rebuff the young woman, accepting an invitation to visit and even sleeping in the same bed with her, prompts vigorous discussion.

Someone on the panel refers to a Montgomery character who was "just a secretary." A voice in the audience behind me hisses, "We're not secretaries; we're administrative assistants." Later, I speak to a group of Kindred Spirits, including the slighted administrative assistant, who are all from the Maritimes. They become thin-lipped when I mention Robinson's work. "Oh, come off it," says one of them. But they tell me they find most of the academics' pronouncements at the conference "inspiring."

For example, everybody seems to love Jennifer Litster, a historian who has recently completed her PhD at the University of Edinburgh on the Scottish context of Montgomery and her work, and who can cite endless Montgomery lore off the top of her head, chapter and verse. She attended the inaugural conference, in 1994. "I didn't really fit in at first," she says. "Here I was, this sarcastic 24-year-old whisky-drinking Scot all dressed in black." A self-avowed contrarian when it comes to Montgomery, Litster insists, "I don't know all there is to know about Montgomery because I worship her. I know so much because it's my area of study."

But it's hard to tell the difference on the humid afternoon we spend together in the Cavendish cemetery, where Montgomery and many of her relatives and contemporaries are buried. "I'm going to sound like one of those crazy people, but these are all my friends," says Litster, gesturing at the mossy tombstones. "That guy there? Montgomery used to taunt him in school for having red hair. She called him 'Cavendish Carrots.'" Litster grins. "Which means that Montgomery may not have written herself into Anne, but into [Anne's nemesis] Gilbert Blythe."

Perhaps the conference works because of the blurring between the different types of participant. At times the fan and the academic seem equally peculiar: whether motivated by adoration or by intellectual curiosity, they share an encyclopedic knowledge – and a sense of ownership – of a narrow subject, devote enormous amounts of time to it, practically commit related texts to memory and create their own jargon.

The fuzzy line between fan and scholar has also become easier to accommodate because of recent trends in literary criticism. Before the 1970s, when academia barely took CanLit and women writers seriously, let alone children's books or romance fiction, a graduate student who proposed doing research on Montgomery would have been laughed at. It was only in the 1980s that the rise of reader-response and feminist literary criticism and the serious analysis of both children's books and popular culture, especially "girl culture," built up the author's "scholarly capital." The ivory tower acknowledged what generations of readers had always known: not only was *Anne of Green Gables* an elegantly crafted story, but it was also, at some level, radical. Anne (as well as Montgomery's other heroines, such as the budding writer Emily Byrd Starr) was one of our only intrepid, articulate girl role models, an outsider who subverted the mores of a rigid rural community yet won over its members through the sheer force of her personality – at a time when a personality was the last thing a girl was supposed to have. Add to that the fact that many of Montgomery's characters were matriarchs and single women who adopted children, and suddenly rural Canada of a century ago seemed remarkably of the moment.

Meanwhile, thinkers like Pierre Bourdieu were busily erasing the distinction between high-brow and mass culture, deeming the popular worthy of study for what it tells us about ourselves – and encouraging scholars to admit not only that they study the "social grammars" and "interdiscursive formations" of, say, soap operas, but that they also like to watch them. This influence was apparent at the conference two years ago in a paper by Brenda Weber, now at the University of Kentucky. She confided that she'd received her first Anne books from her grandmother when she was a little girl in Phoenix, Arizona, and that she can't separate her love for the novels from the love she felt for her relative.

It was a risky premise for a scholarly paper; professors who once found it hard to have their Montgomery work taken seriously could be forgiven for wanting to distance themselves from such an approach. But Weber went on to argue persuasively for her right to make a critical study of the texts while publicly acknowledging her emotional attachment to them: "The subject matter we read is less important than the manner in which we read it," she said.[1]

There is the danger, of course, that too much emotional attachment can transform a schoolgirl romance into a hallowed text. "I'd rather teach the bloody Bible," a professor tells me at a dinner party in Halifax; she removed *Anne* from her children's lit syllabus because her students were incapable of looking at it critically. More than once at the conference, I hear people speak of "indoctrinating" children into the world of Anne. I catch myself making the same comment about my niece. At earlier symposiums, even mild criticism of Montgomery was sometimes met with outrage.

Still, this year, some academics I talk to say the atmosphere has matured. I hear more good-natured guffaws, from all participants, over the author's conservatism (at one point she opposed female suffrage) and her sometimes purple prose than I did two years ago. (Even on the Kindred Spirits listserv, fans admit they might not get along with Maud if she showed up for tea, since they belong to ethnic or religious groups to which she apparently felt superior.) Says Janice Fiamengo, an English professor at the University of Saskatchewan, "Obviously you can stifle debate and the furtherance of knowledge if you demand everything be respectful and adoring, and that does happen to a small extent. But there are a lot of people doing very serious work here."

Serious or frivolous, the glue that binds the disparate "Montgomery people" was strengthened not only by an evolution in criticism in the 1980s, but also by two other events that occurred about the same time. Since 1919, numerous *Anne* movies had led to periodic surges in interest, and Kevin Sullivan's 1985 made-for-TV *Anne of Green Gables*, its two sequels and the *Road to Avonlea* series did the trick again. They were some of the most successful Canadian television exports ever made, though they took tremendous liberties with Montgomery's stories. In fact, some of the younger fans and scholars came to Montgomery through the TV shows, not the novels. But what really focused renewed attention on Montgomery, particularly on the part of the middle-aged women at the conference (fewer than 10 per cent of those attending are men) was the publication of her journals, edited by Rubio and Elizabeth Waterston. When the first volume emerged, also in 1985, the startling contrast between Anne's life and Montgomery's made many readers see the novels in a different light – and fired up the academic engines. The New Criticism school, which held that a text should be studied in isolation from its author's life and intentions, was giving way to the notion of intertextuality – where a book's context is the real story. As Fiamengo puts it, Montgomery has become a "text" that is even more interesting than her fiction.

The journals reveal that Montgomery's daily life was to some extent also a fiction; as the wife of a small-town Presbyterian minister, she felt she had to present a facade to the parishioners, never revealing her husband's mental illness, her own exhaustion, boredom, depression, isolation and legal troubles or the follies of her eldest son, lest gossip ensue. Adding another complicating layer is the fact that, like all diarists, Montgomery was an unreliable narrator: she prepared her journals for eventual publication, recopying the earlier versions, excising some passages, and, as Irene Gammel demonstrates at this year's conference, fashioning the events of her life into highly constructed narratives long after they had occurred. When she began the journals, she claimed they were intended to be a secret place to express her anguish: "I would not wish to darken any other life – I want instead to be a messenger of optimism and sunshine."[2] But it's clear that she later decided the world would see a different Maud one day.

That Maud resonates for readers in a different way than Anne. Women like me, who were born in the mid-20th century, identified with the young Anne and Emily when we were kids (Montgomery didn't seem to know what to do with her heroines after she'd married them off; Anne's children keep the plot lines going). But while we boomer readers were turning into adults and then middle-aged women, the first four volumes of the author's journals came out – between 1985 and 1998 (the fifth and final volume is due in 2004) – this time providing us with a maturing woman to relate to. Now we get to have it both ways: for many of us, the novels satisfy a continuing need for escapism and happy endings, while the journals appeal to the adult women we've become, whose romantic ideals have been tarnished, who struggle to reconcile the need for "a room of one's own" with the desire for a conventional family and community life. We are relieved to find that Maud knew what that was like even if Anne never really did. "Maud is closer to the women we now are," writes Margaret Steffler in *Making Avonlea*, "but Anne is closer to the girls we once were."[3]

Kate Macdonald Butler, a 45-year-old mother of two from Toronto, comes to the conference in search of Montgomery, too. But she has a better reason than the rest of us: she's one of the author's granddaughters. "Every one of those researchers and academics knows way more about my grandmother than I do," she says (the author died long before Butler was born). Some academics feel inhibited by the presence at the conference of Montgomery's relatives – they don't want to offend. In fact, a number of scholars also worry about the control that Montgomery's heirs and the University of Guelph exert over her papers and its effect on their ability to conduct research.

Butler's full-time job is to try to manage the commercial uses to which Montgomery's imaginings are put, from Anne key chains to the Kevin Sullivan films (lawsuits stemming from the films continue to volley back and forth). If the Montgomery industry can be likened to those around Jane Austen or Shakespeare, her creation is akin to Mickey Mouse.

Tourists have been coming to the Island in search of Anne since shortly after the first of the novels was published in 1908, especially to Green Gables, though Montgomery never lived in that house. She used the setting of the building and the grounds, which belonged to her elderly cousins, as the basis for the home of Matthew and Marilla Cuthbert (the brother and sister who adopt Anne), and modelled the village of Avonlea after Cavendish, but acknowledged she'd made a loose translation. "It seems of no use to protest that it is not 'Green Gables,'" she wrote in 1929, " – that Green Gables was a purely imaginary place. Tourists by the hundred come here."[4] Myrtle Webb, the cousin who by then had inherited the house, soon began taking in paying guests.

It's hard to blame the people of Cavendish for this conflation of fantasy and reality, since Montgomery's readers would have made their pilgrimages whether or not anybody had invited them. Capitalizing on this phenomenon made good economic sense. Starting in 1936, the Cavendish seashore was expropriated, the gables of the Webb house were painted green and the whole thing was turned into a national park. Today if you amble down the leafy path Montgomery called Lover's Lane, you'll find netting in the trees to prevent you from being pelted by errant golf balls flying off the Green Gables golf course.

Montgomery herself was conflicted about the writer as tourist attraction. Her honeymoon in 1911 had been, in fact, a tour of literary sites in Britain. After seeing the Abbotsford, Scotland, house where Sir Walter Scott had lived, she wrote in her journal, "The rooms were filled by a chattering crowd, harangued by a glib guide. I wondered if Scott would have liked this – to see his home overrun by a horde of curious sight seers. I am sure I would not."[5]

Still, Montgomery co-operated in her transformation into a celebrity. Holly Pike of Newfoundland's Memorial University points out that the author created a congenial media persona and wrote sequel after sequel at the behest of her publisher (even though Anne, she told a friend, had begun to weigh on her "like an incubus").[6] She also made P.E.I. a character in her novels, contributing to *its* celebrity, so that soon people wanted to visit the Land of Anne even though they'd never read the books – "a sure indicator," writes Pike, "of Montgomery's and Anne's entrance into the status of pop culture icon."[7] Both P.E.I. and Anne are now famous for being famous.

The test of that iconic status is its susceptibility to parody. At the tail end of this year's conference program, after the goodbye reception, one item is inserted in small print: a 25-minute film called *Picking Lucy's Brain*. Part of the small but entertaining anti-Anne backlash genre, the film parodies both slasher flicks and Montgomery tourism by raising the author from her grave. Unable to speak in other than grunts, the undead Montgomery is chained to her typewriter at one of the heritage sites by the "Tourism Control Division" ("She wants to write another book, I can see it in her eyes!") with a Japanese tourist having her picture taken in the foreground.

Everyone at the screening laughs hysterically, including Kate Macdonald Butler and one of the legal representatives of the Heirs of L.M. Montgomery Inc., as well as the senior Montgomery scholars. Perhaps it's either laugh or cry – because the joke, after all, is on us.

The French philosopher Jean Baudrillard described what he called "simulacra": copies of things that no longer exist – or never did to start with, as in his example of Disneyland's Main Street U.S.A. – which leave us feeling that nothing is real anymore. In the past few years, the theme-parking of the Green Gables site has pushed it even further in the direction of the unreal. All of the farm's outbuildings have long since disappeared; now there's a big new barn with a farming museum, a theatre, a café, washrooms masquerading as a woodshed, and of course the obligatory gift shop.

Although the short film that all visitors see in the welcome centre explains that Green Gables is based on a fictional location, many tourists – some of whom had never heard of Anne before visiting P.E.I. – think she was a real person, or that Montgomery lived here. Even the diehard fans have been known to cry out when they see "Anne's Room," "There's the slate that Anne broke over Gilbert's head! There's her dress with the puffed sleeves!" despite the fact that Anne and Gilbert weren't real people.

I walk across the narrow hall to "Marilla Cuthbert's Room," where the character's infamous amethyst brooch (or the "*amnesty* brooch," as our young tour guide pronounces it) glitters in the sunlight pouring through the lace curtains onto the old bureau. I find myself musing that the hall wallpaper, a sensual floral print in Georgia O'Keeffe colours, would probably have made the prim Marilla blush. Then I remember that Marilla is a character in a novel, and mentally slap myself. "During your visit to Green Gables," says the narrator of the welcome film, "use your imagination, and perhaps you too can ... catch a glimpse of Anne's spirit." But there's really nothing left for my imagination to conjure up.

This sort of thing irks some academics mightily, but there is a perverse pleasure to be found in the inherent ironies. On a warm Sunday afternoon, I drive the half-hour from Charlottetown to Cavendish with Jennifer Litster and Ben Lefebvre, a puckish young man who has recently finished his master's thesis on Montgomery at the University of Guelph – and who is the only man to give a paper at this year's conference. Just down the road from Green Gables, the privately run "Avonlea: Village of Anne of Green Gables," opened in 1999, is an awkward pastiche of locations from both Montgomery's and Anne's lives. There's a real church that was moved from a nearby town, and a fishing shanty, though the seashore is a kilometre away. In the actual schoolhouse where Montgomery taught, transported from yet another village, an actor playing the writer bores children silly by rambling on about her life story. But in and among Anne of Green Gables Chocolates, the Raspberry Cordial Bottling Co. and the barn are actors playing the characters Montgomery created.

"It's truly bizarre to see Maud *and* Anne running around in a village that never existed in this form, even in the novels," says Lefebvre, shaking his head, though his appreciation for camp has him posing for photos with both actors and purchasing Anne toenail clippers. When we come across a performer playing Avonlea town gossip Mrs. Rachel Lynde, he and Litster take the poor woman to task on a point of authenticity in her portrayal. Minutes later, in the church, Lefebvre sits down at a piano and begins to play the treacly theme from Kevin Sullivan's *Anne* series (which makes me a tad misty-eyed). "Sometimes," admits Lefebvre, "I'm a little embarrassed at how much I'm enjoying myself."

A cynic would say that academics simply justify their love for pop culture by clothing it in a lot of theoretical jargon. I'm not that cynical – some of the academics I meet at the conference are a pretty unsentimental lot. But even they seem to soften their attitudes as the weekend unfolds.

A bus takes us to Park Corner for a reception at Silver Bush, the former home of Montgomery's uncle and aunt John and Annie Campbell, which is now named for another of the novels, *Pat of Silver Bush*, and run as a museum by their great-grandson, George Campbell. Some Japanese tourists choose to get married in the parlour, where Montgomery wed the Rev. Ewan Macdonald. The wedding package includes the hymn that was played at Montgomery's ceremony, reproduced on the original organ, as well as a horse-and-buggy ride with "Matthew Cuthbert" as the driver. ("The Japanese are a little confused," explains Kate Macdonald Butler.)

It certainly seems an inauspicious start for a marriage. At Montgomery's wedding dinner in that house, she later recalled in her journal, she felt that "if I could have torn the wedding ring from my finger and so freed myself I would have done it!"[8] Though she claimed the mood passed, she went on to endure, by her account, an unhappy marriage to a man who barely read a word she wrote.

We reboard the bus and drive to the homestead site for the torchlight walk, pursued not only by mosquitoes but also by a CBC cameraman and reporter. Karen Macfarlane, who was so cynical about this event beforehand, says later, "At first I thought it sounded like some kind of Ku Klux Klan parade," and in fact that's exactly what we will look like on *The National* the next night. But it doesn't feel that way at the moment. John and Jennie Macneill have simply put torches in the ground so that we can see, and they give us a guided tour.

OK – maybe for me there *is* something sacred about the hole in the ground. "Ruins," writes Parks Canada historian James De Jonge in *Making Avonlea*, "can reveal a powerful story."[9] The fact that the house is missing doesn't make the story any less compelling: Montgomery was brought up by her maternal grandparents on this farm after her mother died and her father decamped to the Prairies and started a new family. She cut short her education and teaching career to look after her grandmother, publishing four novels while helping run the local post office out of the kitchen. Because she wasn't a male, the house was willed to her uncle. Before her grandmother's funeral was over, she had arranged to move out and marry, at the age of 36, after a five-year engagement.

The house had been poorly maintained and was never lived in again; after the success of *Anne*, it began to attract sightseers who carted away bits of shingle and old pots. Apparently irritated with both his niece and the tourists, her uncle John Macneill (the current John's grandfather) tore the place down. "It became a myth that the author lived at Green Gables," says Jennie Macneill. "The old folks who remembered she had actually lived on our farm were all dead." Then came the first volume of the journals, which Jennie and John read avidly. "We realized this was our heritage, and we thought it was time folks found out how much she loved her grandfather's place, and how much it influenced her writing," says Jennie.

Nobody seems to know what will happen to this place when Jennie and John are gone. None of their four children could make a living from it. If it were designated a National Historic Site, some funding might be made available, but not for operations. So far nothing has come of the Macneills' application. For one thing, it's rare for a person to have more than one site designated in her honour: Montgomery herself is already officially a "National Historic Person," and the manse at Leaskdale, Ontario, where Montgomery went to live after her marriage, was designated a National Historic Site in 1997. (The "Maud-slept-here" phenomenon has spread in Ontario: the church in Norval where Montgomery's husband also served has been known to prop a stuffed Maud in the front pew. And in Bala, where she once stayed briefly and set the only one of her 20 novels that was not P.E.I.-based, the local museum re-enacts her arrival for a two-week vacation 80 years ago, complete with actors playing the author, her husband and two sons in a vintage car.)

In any case, it's anyone's guess whether others would be able to resist, as the Macneills have, the temptation to recreate the missing house. What makes the site distinctive is exactly what makes it unprofitable. In fact, there's a good chance that if the house had never been torn down, the site would now be the theme park Green Gables has become.

"We didn't rebuild the old house," says John, a slim, gentle man with a soft voice, "because we didn't want to make it commercial." He smiles at us. "This is for special people." Some of us "special people" likely squirm at the characterization, and others probably feel quite chuffed, but we all pay close attention. "We wanted you to be able to use your imagination, because that's what Maud did."

And I believe that's what we all do on this chilly June night. I don't think Karen Macfarlane is just being polite as she hangs on John's every word – he describes how he excavated the cellar, which had all but disappeared in the overgrowth, and struggled to keep alive the one original apple tree in the yard. As for me, I'm imagining the author gazing from the window of her little white room onto her beloved orchard, dreaming of literary success. I picture her drawing water from the well as she created the little girl who became my imaginary friend. And I think of the intense loneliness of the brown-haired orphan Maud, who resigned herself to marrying a man she didn't love because she saw no other option.

That's a lot of scope for the imagination for only two bucks. While Green Gables takes an imaginary creation and fills in the details for us, the homestead presents the literal foundation of something that was real but has succumbed to decay, allowing us to picture it for ourselves. The absence of the house evokes a powerful presence.

Standing in the firelit gloom at the homestead, we swat bugs and try to ignore the TV cameras as Jennie tells the story of Montgomery's life in Cavendish. A slender, white-haired woman with big pale blue eyes and a clear, strong delivery, she manages to seem both regal and girlish. "I don't need to tell you folks this, but I will anyway," she begins, and although we all know the story very well, we don't mind listening to it one more time.

NOTES

1 [Weber, "Confessions of a Kindred Spirit," 55.]
2 [Montgomery, 15 October 1908, in *SJLMM*, 1: 339.]
3 [Steffler, "'This Has Been,'" 82.]
4 [Montgomery, 22 September 1929, in *SJLMM*, 4: 9.]
5 [Montgomery, 6 August 1911, in *SJLMM*, 2: 71.]
6 [Montgomery to Weber, 19 October 1921, in *AfGG*, 88.]
7 [Pike, "Mass Marketing," 248.]
8 [Montgomery, 28 January 1912, in *SJLMM*, 2: 68.]
9 [De Jonge, "Through the Eyes," 262.]

17

"The Golden Road of Youth": L.M. Montgomery and British Children's Books

—— 2004 ——

JENNIFER H. LITSTER

In this article, published in *Canadian Children's Literature / Littérature canadienne pour la jeunesse,* Jennifer H. Litster turns our attention away from *Anne of Green Gables* and toward two lesser-known early Montgomery novels, *The Story Girl* (1911) and its sequel, *The Golden Road* (1913). Litster, who completed her doctoral dissertation at the University of Edinburgh on "The Scottish Context of L.M. Montgomery" (2001), tracks links between Montgomery's fiction and its British counterparts, particularly the work of Kenneth Grahame, drawing on published and unpublished correspondence between her and her Scottish correspondent George Boyd MacMillan. Litster had previously contributed a chapter, co-written with Owen Dudley Edwards, to *L.M. Montgomery and Canadian Culture* (1999) and would go on to contribute to *The Intimate Life of L.M. Montgomery* (2005).

"It's no wonder we can't understand the grown-ups," said the Story Girl indignantly, "because we've never been grown-up ourselves. But *they* have been children, and I don't see why they can't understand us."

– L.M. Montgomery, *The Story Girl*[1]

Every Christmas for almost 40 years, L.M. Montgomery exchanged books with her Scottish correspondent, the Alloa-based journalist George Boyd MacMillan. Naturally enough, they each mailed books that they felt the other would like, but, more often than not, they specifically sought out books that could export a flavour of their own country and culture. Maud Montgomery sent George MacMillan Canadian bestsellers like Martha Ostenso's *Wild Geese* (1925); Canadian poetry by Marjorie Pickthall, Wilson Macdonald, and Ethelwyn Wetherald; books about the Maritime Provinces, like Archibald MacMechan's *Ultima Thule* (1927); and stories of Canadian life, such as Helen Williams's *Spinning Wheels and Homespun* (1923) and F.P. Grove's *Over Prairie Trails* (1922). For his part, MacMillan sent Montgomery material on various Scottish themes, including volumes by a variety of Scottish writers, such as Ian Hay, Janet Beith, and Neil Gunn. He posted books about nature and gardening, books that reminded him of Montgomery's writing (Flora Klickmann's *Flower Patch* series, for example), and British works that were unobtainable or unheard of in Canada.

One such book was Kenneth Grahame's *The Golden Age*, which MacMillan enclosed in his Christmas parcel of 1909. Grahame's landmark idyll of childhood, first published in 1895, was new to Montgomery: she told MacMillan she did not believe that it and its sequel *Dream Days* (1898), which she soon acquired, were "known on this side of the pond at all."[2] The delight she expressed with these British books must have been tangible, for in 1913 MacMillan gave Montgomery the book for which Grahame is best remembered today, *The Wind in the Willows* (1908). Montgomery shared her love of this children's classic with her own sons: she described it as "the most charming fairy tale in the world," which she had read "a score of times and could read ... as many more."[3]

In September 1910, nine months after receiving *The Golden Age* from Scotland, L.M. Montgomery completed work on *The Story Girl* (1911). Some contemporary critics noted the similarities between this novel and its sequel *The Golden Road* (1913) and Grahame's *The Golden Age* and *Dream Days*. In a journal entry of 1 March 1930, Montgomery included Kenneth Grahame's name on the long list of authors to whom she had been compared during her career.[4] Moreover, Maud Montgomery recognized this likeness herself: in 1910, she told MacMillan that her fourth novel – which she considered superior "from a literary point of view" to *Anne of Green Gables* – had something in common with *Dream Days*.[5]

It is important to state from the outset that L.M. Montgomery was not aping Kenneth Grahame's books. Her rudimentary plans for *The Story Girl* took shape several months before she read *The Golden Age*, and she drew her inspiration for the book from her childhood and from her memories of two orphan boys, Wellington and David Nelson, who boarded at her Cavendish home when she was aged seven to ten. Besides, it seems not unlikely that Montgomery's synopsis of The Story Girl's proposed outline – "It is to be about children and will have very little plot"[6] – suggested to MacMillan the idea of sending her The Golden Age in the first place. There are, as will be seen, several important differences between the two sets of books. Nevertheless, there are also interesting parallels between the depictions of a Prince Edward Island childhood in The Story Girl and a Home Counties childhood in The Golden Age: indeed, Montgomery's echo of Grahame's title in The Golden Road seems intentional.

This paper foregrounds a comparison between these two pairs of books about childhood as the foundation of a wider discussion of Montgomery's development as a Canadian writer. While there are clearly valuable critical insights to be made from studying Montgomery's books in conjunction with those that they remind us of, these insights are particularly productive in cases where Montgomery herself noted the comparison. She was always quick to identify parallels with – not to mention borrowings from – previous works. From the early days of her career, which involved writing pot-boilers and poems, sometimes to order, for religious periodicals, farming journals, and children's magazines, Montgomery learned that financial rewards came from studying the form of her colleagues and competitors. She was acutely aware of the demands of genre, of the market, and later of her fans. Therefore, literary connections can potentially reveal self-conscious developments in her literary style and direction.

By way of example, Montgomery's early short stories were often expressly "written to suit the American taste."[7] In the 1890s, Canada had few periodicals with reasonable rates of payment and only a small national book market compared to the United States. To Americanize Canadian material was a sensible tactic for a fledgling author to pursue, especially an author who had to strike a balance between artistic inclination and earning a living. Montgomery did not expand on the practical measures she took to tailor her stories to the "American taste" – using an ambiguous North American setting or subjects peculiar to North America, for example, or perhaps obeying American literary conventions – but these modifications were enough for her to doubt that her stories were "suitable" for British periodicals.[8] In time, she approached only American publishers (in New York, Boston, and Indianapolis) with the manuscript of Anne of Green Gables (1908).[9] Studies that link

Montgomery's first published novel to American classics such as *Little Women, What Katy Did, The Girl of the Limberlost,* and in particular *Rebecca of Sunnybrook Farm* all demonstrate that *Anne of Green Gables* has much in common with a type of children's book produced in the United States.[10] Indeed, as Cecily Devereux points out, the Anne Shirley series is "often accepted as part of the American canon of children's literature, in spite of its Canadian origin."[11]

Montgomery's early stories regularly focus on youngsters with "grown-up" obligations and concerns, such as caring for elderly relatives or working to help pay foreclosed mortgages, features associated with American child-life in literature and at odds with the "English style of family story" where, as Gillian Avery argues, childhood is more usually "sheltered" and "leisurely." American childhood, Avery explains, was rarely secluded from the adult world in literature of the late Victorian and Edwardian period. Additionally, American authors for children were expected to keep "a much closer grip on reality" than were their British counterparts. But, as this paper will demonstrate, *The Story Girl* and *The Golden Road* describe childhood in quite a different way. They share with Booth Tarkington's *Penrod* (1914) something Avery describes as a "rarity" in U.S. children's fiction, "a background in which it is possible to be dreamy and detached."[12] And just as Anne Shirley's Stateside literary cousins can enhance our understanding of the cultural impact of *Anne of Green Gables,* so the special relationship between Britain and Canada witnessed in *The Story Girl* and *The Golden Road* develops our knowledge of Montgomery's place in the history of both Canadian literature and children's literature.

The Path to Arcady

The gods were not all beautiful, you know. And, beautiful or not, nobody ever wanted to meet them face to face.[13]

The Golden Age had its origin in Kenneth Grahame's 1891 essay "The Olympians" and the impact its opening sentence had on poet and editor W.E. Henley. "Looking back to those days of old, ere the gate shut behind me," Grahame's essay begins, "I can see now that to children with the proper equipment of parents these things would have worn a different aspect."[14] Henley suggested to Grahame that his meditation on a childhood spent among indifferent adults (the "Olympians" of the title) would lend itself to a longer, narrative excursion.

The two books that followed – "The Olympians" forms a prologue to the first – chart the adventures of five orphans who are fostered by their aunts and uncles in a large country house. Harold, Selina, Edward, Charlotte, and the anonymous male narrator inhabit their own imaginative world of fairy tales and classical mythology, pets and toys, and the quest for pocket money. More a series of essays than novels, *The Golden Age* and *Dream Days* invoke a rural idyll where children have a special vision and most adults – excepting the odd eccentric bachelor and artist – are unsympathetic, hostile, and, from the child's point of view, hopelessly misinformed. "In my tales about children," Grahame later reflected, "I have tried to show that their simple acceptance of the mood of wonderment, their readiness to welcome a perfect miracle at any hour of the day or night, is a thing more precious than any of the laboured acquisitions of adult mankind."[15]

Montgomery's *The Story Girl* and *The Golden Road* chart the adventures of eight children, five of whom are orphaned in some way,[16] who live and work with a host of aunts and uncles on a Prince Edward Island farm. The children inhabit their own imaginative world of myths and local legends, pets and books, and (as this is a Scots-Presbyterian community in Canada) the quest for church and school funds. Although not unpleasant, the aunts and uncles are all busy farmers who want only limited contact with the small fry. Because these adults lack imagination and have little empathy for their young charges, their child-rearing systems can occasion minor hurts and even induce full-scale panic. As with Grahame's *Dream Days*, *The Golden Road* departs from the idyll, bathed (in the words of male narrator Beverley King) in "the shadow of change."[17] In this book, the boundary between the worlds of child and adult becomes blurred; the golden summer ends.

At a basic level, the parallels between the *Story Girl* books and Grahame's books are clear. Both are adaptations of a formula Humphrey Carpenter describes as prevalent in the golden age of British children's literature, a formula of "a family of children able to conduct their lives with very little adult supervision."[18] Both Montgomery and Grahame envisage two separate worlds of "children and upgrown people,"[19] a distinction that for Grahame was first made in childhood. To describe the world of children, both authors chiefly write from a child's perspective and stylistically combine this journey into childhood – the path to Arcady – with an adult lament for a childhood lost. Both Grahame and Montgomery were ideologically rooted in the Romantic beliefs that children were blessed with uncommon insight, that the incidents of childhood were precious and vital in themselves, and that adults should be guided by remembrance of earlier days. For each author – as for William Wordsworth before them – these sentiments could best be conveyed in writing that was more episodic than plot-driven, writing that captured childhood's formative "spots of time."

For all these parallels, there are important differences between the two pairs of books. Most noticeably, Montgomery's books are more accessible than Grahame's. Although each author uses a reflective voice that is occasionally intrusive and seems designed to speak to adult readers, Montgomery's stories include many more episodes that in action and in tone will entertain younger readers. Grahame's books do not: in the words of the Welsh poet Vernon Watkins, "One cannot for a moment accept *The Golden Age* and *Dream Days* as children's books. Wherever they are found in the juvenile section of a library, they are mistakenly placed there."[20] Secondly, Montgomery's "Olympians" are more rounded and sympathetic characters than Grahame's: although as readers we may sometimes hold their actions in contempt, Beverley King rarely expresses his scorn with quite the incredulity and bitterness that Grahame's narrator does. (Such was the vehemence of Grahame's attack on adult sensibilities that his books met with disapproval from some humourless Victorian reviewers.) Montgomery's aunts and uncles may occupy a separate world – a fact repeatedly emphasized by their segregation as "grown-ups," in the sense of Sara Stanley's comment that "It's really dreadful to have no grown-ups that you can depend on"[21] – but there are more intersections between the grown-up and child worlds than in Grahame's books. This is especially apparent in *The Golden Road*: as its title implies, this sequel leads somewhere. For the older child characters, this journey will involve travelling the road from childhood to adulthood, from summer to the first days of autumn.

These intersections result partly from the practical proscriptions placed on a secluded childhood in Montgomery's Canadian agricultural setting: a character like Peter Craig, who works as a hired boy on the King family farm, cannot afford the luxury of a life spent entirely in play. In addition to this social realism, the class and age backgrounds of the children in *The Story Girl* and *The Golden Road* permit a greater diversity in child experience and character. Whereas Grahame's children, for all their individual passions and preoccupations, share a certain philosophical grace, Montgomery's Sara Ray uses her imagination principally to fuel her hysterical dread of punishment and disaster, and Felicity King's playfulness is always tempered by her awareness of social etiquette. This is increasingly also the case with Grahame's Selina, but a last difference between the two pairs of books would be that, although no ages are given for Grahame's child protagonists, they are markedly younger than the King cousins and their friends in the *Story Girl* books, who are all aged eleven and upward.

There seem to be few parallels between the lives of L.M. Montgomery (1874–1942) and Kenneth Grahame (1859–1932) at the time they wrote these books. Grahame, of upper-middle-class background, worked for the Bank of England and was appointed Secretary of this institution in 1898. Although Grahame, like W.E. Henley, was a mover in London's literary circles – Grahame's cousin Anthony Hope wrote *The Prisoner of Zenda* (1894), a book Maud Montgomery read "every two or three years"[22] – he was principally known only as the author of light essays published in journals such as *The Yellow Book* and the *St. James Gazette*. By 1910, Montgomery had scored international success with *Anne of Green Gables* and its first sequel, *Anne of Avonlea* (1909): her work on *The Story Girl* was punctuated by a three-week trip to Boston, where she was entertained by her publisher and lionized by the American public. Nevertheless, Montgomery was living an increasingly isolated life socially, and her private journal from this period is tinged with depression and a sense of impending loss. With her grandmother Macneill in deteriorating physical and mental health, Montgomery knew that her remaining time in her Cavendish home was limited: on her grandmother's death the farm would pass to a male relative. One similarity that we might find between the two authors at this time – and it is not an unimportant one – is that both, when well into their 30s, were about to depart from the single life: Kenneth Grahame married Elspeth Thomson in 1899; Maud Montgomery married Ewan Macdonald in 1911. Neither marriage was to prove a happy one.

If we look farther back into childhood, however, the similarities between the two writers are more profound. Kenneth Grahame was a Scot by birth, born in Edinburgh in 1859. Like Scots-descended Maud Montgomery, Grahame's mother died when he was a small child (Grahame was five, Montgomery less than two) and, like Montgomery, he (with his siblings) was sent by his father (a lawyer and an alcoholic) to live with an English grandmother. We might compare the observation of Grahame's biographer Peter Green on Grahame's childhood – "There was no cruelty in the positive sense, merely emotional deprivation of a rather subtle kind" – with Montgomery's description of her own childhood: although not "actually unhappy," it "was never as happy as childhood should be and as it easily might have been."[23] In fiction,

Montgomery and Grahame would invoke memories of their powerlessness in the face of an autocratic adult regime (for each, real grandparents would translate into fictional aunts and uncles) and also their memories of the imaginative world – in Montgomery's case "the world of nature and the world of books"[24] – in which they constructed a kind of happiness despite circumstances that might have proved rather more unhappy.

Importantly, literary rewards could come with an authentic return to childhood's imaginative realm. *The Golden Age* and *Dream Days* are often credited with being the first books to take a child's standpoint "as the main theme of a book intended for adult reading."[25] In the words of Roger Lancelyn Green, "*The Golden Age* suddenly presented childhood as a thing in itself: a good thing, a joyous thing – a new world to be explored, a new species to be observed and described. Suddenly children were not being written down to anymore – they were being written up: you were enjoying the Spring for itself, not looking on it anxiously as a prelude to summer."[26] Grahame's books were highly influential on late Victorian and Edwardian children's writers such as Rudyard Kipling, Edith Nesbit, and J.M. Barrie, all of whom were bent on escaping the piety and didacticism of their predecessors and were instrumental in cementing critical respect for children's books.

In this context, it is vital that L.M. Montgomery considered *The Story Girl* to be "the best piece of work I have yet done. It may not be as popular as *Anne* – somehow I don't fancy it will. But from a literary point of view it is far ahead of it."[27] Her confidence in *The Story Girl's* literary credentials raises two important and interrelated questions. If Montgomery believed *The Story Girl* to be a more sophisticated piece of literature than *Anne of Green Gables* – a work she famously if disingenuously referred to as "a simple little tale"[28] – would it appeal to a greater number of discriminating and mature readers? And if it could, was *The Story Girl* (and by implication *The Golden Road*) specifically designed to appeal to this class of readers? In other words, when planning and writing *The Story Girl* and its sequel, did Montgomery consciously effect changes in her style in order to take her work to more adult readers and in turn elevate her literary standing?

The remainder of this paper, in comparing Montgomery's *The Story Girl* and *The Golden Road* to Grahame's *The Golden Age* and *Dream Days*, will explore some of the issues that these questions raise. At this stage, however, it is important to recognize that hand-in-hand with the popular success of *Anne of Green Gables*, particularly with girl readers, came some pitfalls. Montgomery gained a loyal readership and with this the promise of continuing financial returns, but she also faced the prospect of being tied to one character and to a convention that might smother her creativity. As each sequel became a paler imitation of the first success, girls' series frequently descended into spiralling mediocrity, like the "Little Colonel" books of Montgomery's L.C. Page stablemate Annie Fellows Johnstone.[29] In any case, Montgomery was always a somewhat reluctant children's writer. Unlike Grahame, who wrote *The Wind in the Willows* for his son Alistair, Montgomery did not write books for her children, nor did she dedicate any of her novels to them. To enhance her literary standing with the many adult readers and reviewers who had praised *Anne of Green Gables*, it seems conceivable that, in this hiatus from the *Anne* series, Montgomery might experiment with other forms; if so, then as an alternative to catering for the "American taste," it is also conceivable that Montgomery would turn to British models for inspiration, especially where these models had cultivated a track record in earning respect from the literary establishment.

Et in Arcadia Ego

> "What a yarn!" said Dan, drawing a long breath, when we had come to ourselves and discovered that we were really sitting in a dewy Prince Edward Island orchard instead of watching two lovers on a mountain in Thessaly in the Golden Age. "I don't believe a word of it."[30]

In an undated newspaper article titled "How I Became a Writer," Montgomery remarked of her own childhood, "I had, in my imagination, a passport to fairyland. In a twinkling I could whisk myself into regions of wonderful adventure, unhampered by any restrictions of reality."[31] Although a number of Montgomery's child characters, most notably Marigold Lesley in *Magic for Marigold* (1929), would share her passport to fairyland, it is debatable that Anne Shirley truly does. Anne is unquestionably an imaginative child who is ever poised to shake prosaic Avonlea from her feet, but the same capacity for escapism that initially ensures her psychological survival in Nova Scotia is continually thwarted by reality in Prince Edward Island. In imaginative fantasies such as the episode of the Haunted Wood, Anne must learn to be content with the commonplace:[32] the novel is, after all, an exercise in belonging. *Anne of Green Gables* is set in a world where the lives of adults and children are intertwined, where the action stems from intrigues in the schoolhouse or the Presbyterian Church, and where the novel works toward Anne's growing maturity and her acceptance into the adoptive family and community. In a world governed by the Protestant work ethic and a need to keep busy, little allowance is made for the leisure time in which to be a child. Anne's excursions into fairyland are confined to the "odd half hours which she was allowed for play."[33]

By contrast, the King cousins in the *Story Girl* books enjoy the luxury of "long hours for play."[34] Unlike Anne Shirley, these children have few domestic or farming responsibilities and even the winter months in *The Golden Road*, when the exploits might reasonably involve school-based action, have a holiday atmosphere. Whereas Anne's upbringing is a matter of some urgency, to Marilla if not always to Anne herself, the six King cousins are permitted time to grow. Although *The Story Girl* and *The Golden Road* explore some of childhood's spats and spites, these books more often celebrate the companionship between a welter of child characters who find a physical and imaginative shelter in the King family orchard. Within this enclosed and safe haven, the boys and girls are removed from adult concerns and their innocence is protected. Indeed, from the outset of the first book Aunt Olivia King's flower garden is linked with a prelapsarian Eden: "I think I could be always good if I lived in a garden all the time," the Story Girl reflects.[35]

Planted out with fruit trees that mark the birth of family members, the celebration of family festivals, and the visits of beloved friends, the "famous King orchard" unfurls the branches of the King clan and establishes the roots of their history.[36] It is therefore no accident that Felix and Beverley King are taken through the latched gate that separates the farmyard from the orchard by their cousin Sara Stanley, whose flair for storytelling bridges the gap between the mundane present and the hallowed past. This chapter, "Legends of the Old Orchard," welcomes the Toronto visitors into the family circle by locating their birthday trees; it also whisks them into another, more Technicolor world, one that reveals the "tales of wonder," the "glamour of old family traditions" that lend "magic to all sights and sounds around."[37] Moreover, the Story Girl compares the orchard idyll with "a dream of fairyland,"[38] an enchantment that, once discovered, can permeate their daily lives. The fairyland that Montgomery explores in *The Story Girl* and *The Golden Road* lends credibility to ancient superstition, is anchored in history, and is synonymous with childhood perception. In all three areas, there is a marked influence on Montgomery of British children's writers, not only Grahame but also Lewis Carroll, Kipling, Nesbit, George MacDonald, and Robert Louis Stevenson.

It is in the last of these concepts of fairyland that the links between Montgomery and Grahame are clearest. As Beverley King observes, in one of his most syrupy indulgences:

> There is such a place as fairyland – but only children can find the way to it. And they do not know that it is fairyland until they have grown so old that they forget the way. One bitter day, when they seek it and cannot find it, they realize what they have lost; and that is the tragedy of life. On that day the gates of Eden are shut behind them and the age of gold is over. Henceforth they must dwell in the common light of common day. Only a few, who remain children at heart, can ever find that fair, lost path again; and blessed are they above mortals. They, and only they, can bring us tidings from that dear country where we once sojourned and from which we must evermore be exiles. The world calls them its singers and poets and artists and story-tellers; but they are just people who have never forgotten the way to fairyland.[39]

As Montgomery's use of the phrase "age of gold" suggests, the link with Grahame is partly stylistic. Carpenter has remarked of *The Golden Age* that "the prose is sometimes irritatingly ornate,"[40] and the same charge can be levelled at Montgomery. For example, both authors, when their narrators are at their most sentimental, use the biblical phrase "I trow not,"[41] an archaism somewhat incongruous in books for children and a further indication that these books were intended for adult readers. In Montgomery's case, the witty and ironic narrator of *Anne of Green Gables* is ousted by an elegiac and nostalgic voice that echoes Grahame's philosophy that "grown-up people are fairly correct on matters of fact; it is in the higher gift of imagination that they are so sadly to seek"[42] yet also allows certain adults access to this "mood of wonderment." Grahame and Montgomery agree that "children and artists alone are visionaries":[43] we might compare Grahame's "the funny man" (*Dream Days*) with Montgomery's "the Awkward Man" (Jasper Dale), for both characters are marked by an eccentricity that places them in wonderland as honorary children. (Jasper Dale even marries a woman named Alice.) Another point of comparison is "the Artist" who appears in *The Golden Age* – a Grahame self-portrait – and the Story Girl's Bohemian father,

Blair Stanley, who, like Grahame's Artist, possesses all the allure of having lived in Rome.

Toward the end of *The Golden Road*, in a chapter entitled "A Path to Arcady," Blair Stanley rambles in "fairyland" with his daughter and Beverley King: "Hand in hand we wandered through that enchanted place, seeking the folk of elf-land, 'and heard their mystic voices calling, from fairy knoll and haunted hill.'"[44] Here Montgomery slightly misquotes a verse, "The Fairy Minister," by the Scots poet Andrew Lang,[45] that takes for its subject a Scottish minister from Aberfoyle. Legend has it that the Rev. Robert Kirk was taken captive by the fairies in 1692, a year after writing his treatise on supernatural beings, *The Secret Commonwealth*. With this literary allusion, Montgomery not only establishes a lineage of adults who countenance fairy lore, but she also takes a swipe at adults who destroy the wonderment of childhood, for Sara Stanley has been told there are "no such things as fairies" by a *minister* uncle.[46] A similar situation occurs in *The Golden Age* where the governess pompously asserts that fairy tales "had their origin ... in a mistaken anthropomorphism in the interpretation of nature."[47] Each evocation of fairyland privileges the child's reality. To Grahame's narrator, "there are higher things than truth"; to Sara Stanley, "there are two kinds of true things – true things that *are*, and true things that are *not*, but *might* be."[48]

From the child's point of view, then, adults come in two guises. Artistic adults like Blair Stanley remain "pilgrims on the golden road of youth."[49] Other adults can drift briefly into the child world, including those who seem to have grown up into fairy tale archetypes – Grahame's young heroes meet ladies they mistake for princesses; the King cousins forge tentative alliances with ogres like Mr. Campbell and witches like Peg Bowen. These adult characters, invariably from outside the family group, are set apart by their ability to play by the rules of the game, one in which the imagined is as potent as the real. In *The Golden Age*, the narrator's delight in the imagined treasures of a secret drawer is not obliterated by the dreary stuff the "drawer of disillusions" contains;[50] in *The Story Girl*, the mysterious contents of Rachel Ward's hope chest provide more thrills in anticipation than in realization. The magic itself is more important than any possible moral gleaned from its dissolution. At the other end of the adult scale, Olympians, like Montgomery's Uncle Roger King or Grahame's Uncle Thomas, stand fast in the "rooted conviction ... that the reason of a child's existence was to serve as a butt for senseless adult jokes."[51] The "Land of Lost Delight" is therefore vulnerable to the dangers of Olympian intrusions.[52] This is best illustrated by the incident of "The Judgment Sunday" (chapters 19 and 20 of *The Story Girl*), in which the children accept, after reading a newspaper report, that the end of the world is nigh: the Kings believe with the children in Grahame's books that "If a thing's in a book, it *must* be true."[53] Their adult relatives fail to recognize or curb their terror, just as Marilla cannot understand Anne's fear of a self-invented haunted wood, but the lesson is a different one: the King children learn to not trust "grown-ups," either those who write or edit newspapers or the surrounding aunts and uncles who, as Montgomery's blistered chronicler reflects, "considered our terror an exquisite jest."[54] The episode serves to enforce the barriers between child and adult realms, between "simple acceptance" and careworn cynicism.

Furthermore, Montgomery appears to be redefining the scope of a good imagination. Anne Shirley terrifies herself with a set of conventional ghosts, including a white lady, a murdered child, a headless man, and skeletons. Similar spooks – the Family Ghost, the ghostly bell – are handled more lightly in *The Story Girl* and *The Golden Road* and are not attacked as unchristian. In these books, Montgomery draws distinctions between a healthy imagination fueled by legends of old ghosts and a belief in fairies and witches and an unhealthy imagination fueled by the sort of "Last Trump" sensationalism pedaled by the Charlottetown *Daily Enterprise*. And it is not unimportant that the *Enterprise*'s story of the imminent Judgment Day has its origin in "a certain noted sect in the United States," a hint of anti-Americanism that appears also in the story that Peg Bowen's "madness" stems from her experiences in Boston.[55] Montgomery was perhaps passing comment on the increasing proliferation of cheap, sensational literature – the "blood and thunders" – produced for children in the United States and also in Britain, thus advocating the pleasures of more wholesome escapes.

In turning their back on the United States and the real-life sensations its stories had to offer, *The Story Girl* and *The Golden Road* instead promote a timeless idyll. But if it is one that is synonymous with childhood perception and one in which traditional superstition is a healthy pursuit, this idyll is also inextricably linked to the Prince Edward Island setting. The children in *The Golden Age* and *Dream Days* build their magic from English history and the collective English past of Lancelot and Sir Tristram, Roundheads and Cavaliers, Nelson and Grenville. As Jackie Wullschläger writes of Grahame's world and of other British invented wonderlands, "the ideal of a child-centred Arcadian idyll was deeply interwoven into the imaginative life of the country."[56] We can see this theme in Rudyard Kipling's *Puck of Pook's Hill* (1906) and its sequel,

Rewards and Fairies (1910): Dan and Una, the central child characters in this time-slip story, are guided by the fairy Puck through England's past, enabling Kipling to take as his theme "the continuing nature of England, conceived as ever present in its four dimensions of space and time."[57] These books were favourites with Montgomery, who was still singing *Puck of Pook's Hill*'s praises in 1936.[58]

The surname King may acknowledge a British heritage, but when the King cousins substitute "Prince Edward Island" and not "Canada" or "the Empire" for "England" when adapting Nelson's "England expects that every man will do his duty" for the motto of their magazine,[59] Montgomery signals where the patriotism of the children and of these novels lies. Prince Edward Island's history was seldom dramatic or militaristic, but the Story Girl shares the English child's (or Puck's) interest in the past, in myth and legend; in her tales, she substitutes Island folklore and oral family history for the received tales of knights and soldiers and naval commanders. The King cousins, however, are no poorer creatively for their daydreams being homegrown. Although the adults are uninterested in their little dramas, family fascinates the cousins and their friends. They inhabit a world that is out of the ordinary and out of time, because they understand, appreciate, and are energized by the force of the history of their own family and province – they are Kings of the Island.

It is this Island celebration that is witness to the clearest break with the *Anne of Green Gables* model. In *The Story Girl* and *The Golden Road*, Montgomery found a place for her own family stories – many of them told to her by her Aunt Mary Lawson, to whom *The Golden Road* is dedicated – that was wanting in her tale of a rootless orphan from Nova Scotia. By fusing local legends and family folklore with a child's sense of wonder and play, Montgomery created her own Canadian world of fancy, which could compete for charm with the British wonderlands she so enjoyed. In so doing, she seemed to find a new niche as a novelist. The "fairyland" she conjured up in *The Story Girl* and *The Golden Road*, with its emphasis on the magic of memory and on the preciousness of oral history, appears as a stepping stone to her later fiction by enabling her to write about her Canadian world with fewer concessions to American tastes. Her next diversion from Avonlea was, after all, the *Emily* trilogy, the story of an author who eventually defies pressure from a New York literato and elects to stay in Canada.

The Story Girl was to be Montgomery's Island swansong: it was the last book she wrote in Cavendish. In it she tried to distill the essence of Prince Edward Island's charms, not only those of setting which readers of *Anne of Green Gables* were familiar with, but also the delights and imaginative scope of a shared past. It was also her farewell to youth, the last book she wrote about childhood before she was married with children of her own. In retrospect, the publication of *The Golden Road* was also momentous, since all subsequent Montgomery books would bear the imprint of the First World War. Even in the shelter of Rainbow Valley, Anne Blythe's children cannot escape the future conflict's shadow; her boys are the Empire's soldiers in embryo, and Island history walks hand-in-hand with national destiny. For these reasons, the carefree, change-less, and collective childhood in *The Story Girl* and *The Golden Road* remains, in many respects, unique in Montgomery's body of work.

Conclusion: The Island Arcadia

L.M. Montgomery was a great admirer of British children's books: her favourites included stories by Scottish authors such as Kenneth Grahame and J.M. Barrie – the infant Chester Macdonald was nicknamed "Peter Pan" by his mother – as well as George MacDonald, whose *At the Back of the North Wind* (1871) she read a dozen times or more.[60] She read works by a diverse range of British authors to her own children, from the animal stories of Beatrix Potter to the public school stories of Talbot Baines Reed. Her fictional children inherit this love: Dan King reads G.A. Henty's adventure stories; Pat Gardiner reads *The Wind in the Willows*; Jane Stuart knows her *Alice*; both Anne and Emily read *At the Back of the North Wind*, and MacDonald's personification of the north wind is an obvious forerunner for Emily Byrd Starr's "Wind Woman." As this suggests, British children's books inspired L.M. Montgomery. To take E. Nesbit as just one example, *Our Magazine* in *The Golden Road* – although partly a nod to the *Pickwick Portfolio* in Alcott's *Little Women* – is closer in format, style, and humour to the Bastables' *Lewisham Recorder* in Nesbit's *The Story of the Treasure Seekers* (1899). Both the Bastables and Marigold Lesley do not realize that one of their playmates is a real princess and cousin of Queen Victoria; the "Society of the Would-begoods" in Nesbit's *The Wouldbegoods* (1901) predates the Merediths' "Good Conduct Club" in Montgomery's *Rainbow Valley* (1919). Like Montgomery, Nesbit owed a literary debt to Kenneth Grahame's pioneering books; like Nesbit, Montgomery tempered her books "about children" with a comic edge that Grahame's philosophical stories lack.[61]

But on more than one occasion Montgomery lets slip that Canada, being "a new land,"[62] might lack the proper credentials for fairyland that the old world abounded in. (In Susanna Moodie's famous words, Canada was "too new for ghosts."[63]) For Montgomery, this was not only a state of mind but also a literary proscription: she remarked to George MacMillan, with reference to her inability to create books like Flora Klickmann's *Flower Patch* series, "I couldn't have the background here that is ready to the British writer's hand. One has to have ghosts and old gods."[64] In this respect, it is pertinent that Sara Stanley leaves Canada for Europe at the close of *The Golden Road*: only in Europe, we are told, can her imaginative potential be fulfilled. Nevertheless, in reviewing *The Golden Road* on 26 February 1914, *The Scotsman* commented that, although the "American origin of the book is unmistakable ... young people of school age in Charlottetown or Carlisle are pretty much the same in temperament, disposition, inclination, and desire as the young people of Birmingham or Edinburgh."[65] By combining reality and make-believe in the *Story Girl* books, Montgomery created a universal childhood, certainly, but one that was visibly closer to the ideals of an Empire childhood than the American childhood of *Anne of Green Gables*.

Anne of Green Gables may be L.M. Montgomery's finest book and it has certainly had the greatest cultural impact, yet we do her a disservice if we view this book as the model for all her subsequent work. Despite pressure from her publisher and the public, Montgomery did not write more books that were just the same as her first. At several stages in her literary career, Montgomery revealed that she held ambitions beyond writing for young people and that she longed to do "something so much more worthwhile" than "another Anne book."[66] It seems only logical that to fulfil her dreams of literary accomplishment, Montgomery would diversify from the "Anne" type of book and the "Anne" type of heroine. As it would happen, of course, the outbreak of war in 1914 gave new purpose and vigour to the *Anne* series, and Montgomery discovered it was the perfect vehicle for taking the spirit of Canada's war effort to a mass audience.

Yet although Montgomery increasingly resented Anne's grip on the popular imagination, she derived pride from the fact that her depiction of Prince Edward Island was singled out for critical praise. As Janis Dawson writes, "To many critics and general readers, the essence of Anne's Canadianness lies in Montgomery's celebration of the physical landscape of Prince Edward Island."[67] But once *Anne of Green Gables* had proved that there was "scope for imagination" – and scope for book sales – in "a simple P.E.I. farming settlement,"[68] Montgomery's work shows an escalating mandate to describe the *history* and *culture*, as well as the natural beauty, of her native province. Calvin Trillin has made the canny remark that Montgomery's "books are so imbued with the look and feel of Prince Edward Island that the province itself practically qualifies as one of her characters."[69] Before 1911, Montgomery admittedly had little experience of life elsewhere, but the *Story Girl* books demonstrate that there was more than one method for turning this life into fiction.

Four years before the outbreak of the First World War, L.M. Montgomery prophesied that only under "some great crisis of storm and stress" that "fused her varying elements into a harmonious whole" would Canada produce a literary "expression of our national life as a whole."[70] The changes that Montgomery made to her literary output after *Anne of Green Gables* and again after the war mean that for all that they are orphan heroines, Emily Byrd Starr more closely resembles the children of the *Story Girl* books than she does Anne Shirley. Bound to and inspired by the customs of the clan and the province she was born into, Emily also stakes the greater claim as a Canadian heroine. Canadian national identity for Montgomery was rooted in the Canadian past, a past that was preserved in family lore and tradition, and a past that she urged her audiences at literary events in the 1920s and 1930s to preserve. Increasingly in her fiction, Montgomery also preserved the past as a way of articulating Canada and as a way of adding "glamour" and "magic" to the rural farming world. *The Story Girl* and *The Golden Road* are not "British" children's books any more than *Anne of Green Gables* is an "American" one, but British books, with their philosophy of a dreamy, detached childhood and the space they allowed for imaginative journeys into the past, seem curiously enough to have had a critical impact on the way that Montgomery would come to write about Canada.

NOTES

An earlier version of this paper was presented at the L.M. Montgomery and Popular Culture International Conference, University of Prince Edward Island (2000).

1 *SG*, 206.
2 Montgomery to MacMillan, 1 September 1910 (unpublished letter).
3 Montgomery, 7 May 1937 [in *SJLMM*, 5: 163].
4 Montgomery, 1 March 1930, in *SJLMM*, 4: 40.

5 Montgomery to MacMillan, 1 September 1910 (unpublished letter).

6 Montgomery to MacMillan, 24 August 1909 (unpublished letter).

7 Montgomery to MacMillan, 12 January 1905 (unpublished letter).

8 Ibid.

9 The publishers to whom Montgomery claims to have submitted the manuscript of *Anne of Green Gables* are Bobbs–Merrill of Indianapolis; Macmillan Co. of New York; Lothrop, Lee and Shepard of Boston; Henry Holt Co. of New York; and finally L.C. Page & Co. of Boston (Montgomery, 16 August 1907, in *SJLMM*, 1: 330–31).

10 See C. Thomas, "Anne Shirley's American Cousin"; Berke, "'Mother I Can Do It Myself!'"; Kornfeld and Jackson, "The Female *Bildungsroman*"; Classen, "Is 'Anne of Green Gables'"; Dawson, "Literary Relations."

11 Devereux, "'Canadian Classic' and 'Commodity Export,'" 18.

12 G. Avery, *Behold the Child*, 168, 211, 212.

13 *SG*, 136.

14 Grahame, The Golden Age *and* Dream Days, 19.

15 Quoted in P. Green, *Kenneth Grahame 1859–1932*, 356.

16 Sara Stanley's mother is dead and her father is travelling in Europe; Felix and Beverley's mother is dead and their father is absent on business; Sara Ray has no father; Peter's father has deserted his mother.

17 *GR*, 213.

18 Carpenter, *Secret Gardens*, 132.

19 Grahame, The Golden Age *and* Dream Days, 44.

20 Watkins, Foreword, vii.

21 *SG*, 148.

22 Montgomery, 15 July 1933, in *SJLMM*, 4: 226.

23 P. Green, *Kenneth Grahame 1859–1932*, 17; Montgomery, 2 January 1905, in *SJLMM*, 1: 301.

24 Montgomery, 2 January 1905, in *SJLMM*, 1: 301.

25 Lewis, Introduction, ix.

26 R.L. Green, "The Golden Age," 44–45.

27 Montgomery, 29 November 1910, in *SJLMM*, 2: 20.

28 Montgomery, 15 October 1908, in *SJLMM*, 1: 339.

29 For a wider discussion, see Gerson, "'Dragged at Anne's Chariot Wheels.'"

30 *SG*, 137.

31 SR [194]. ["How I Became a Writer" was published in the *Manitoba Free Press* in December 1921. See also "An Autobiographical Sketch," reproduced in Volume 1 of *The L.M. Montgomery Reader*.]

32 *AGG*, 166.

33 *AGG*, 63.

34 *SG*, 25.

35 *SG*, 22.

36 *SG*, 8.

37 *SG*, 23, 5, 6.

38 *SG*, 17.

39 *SG*, 121.

40 Carpenter, *Secret Gardens*, 119.

41 *SG*, 160; Grahame, The Golden Age *and* Dream Days, 22.

42 Grahame, The Golden Age *and* Dream Days, 45.

43 Wullschläger, *Inventing Wonderland*, 153.

44 *GR*, 193.

45 Lang's original line is "And heard your mystic voices calling / From fairy knowe and haunted hill," *knowe* being Scots dialect for *knoll*.

46 *SG*, 39.

47 Grahame, The Golden Age *and* Dream Days, 74.

48 Ibid., 40; *SG*, 137.

49 *GR*, vii.

50 Grahame, The Golden Age *and* Dream Days, 102.

51 Ibid., 31.

52 *GR*, vii.

53 Grahame, The Golden Age *and* Dream Days, 75.

54 *SG*, 150.

55 *SG*, 144, 186. In *Anne of the Island*, Rachel Lynde reads the murder trial reports in a Boston newspaper for excitement, although she advises Anne Shirley that "the States must be an awful place" (*AIs*, 41).

56 Wullschläger, *Inventing Wonderland*, 147.

57 Townsend, *Written for Children*, 107.

58 Montgomery, 18 January 1936 [in *SJLMM*, 5: 55].

59 *GR*, 4.

60 Montgomery to MacMillan, 16 March 1913 (unpublished letter); Montgomery to MacMillan, 31 March 1930 (unpublished letter).

61 L.M. Montgomery, like E. Nesbit and more recently J.K. Rowling, published under her initials and not her first name and could thus be mistaken for a male author. Like Montgomery's *Story Girl* books, Nesbit's trilogy about the Bastable children has a male narrator, Oswald Bastable, who reckons in *The Wouldbegoods* that Grahame's *The Golden Age* is "A1, except where it gets mixed with grown-up nonsense" (Nesbit, *The Wouldbegoods*, 85).

62 *PSB*, 132.

63 Moodie, *Roughing It in the Bush*, 251.

64 Montgomery to MacMillan, 18 February 1923 (unpublished letter).

65 SR [62]. [This review appears in Volume 3 of *The L.M. Montgomery Reader*.]

66 Montgomery, 27 September 1913, in *SJLMM*, 2: 133.

67 Dawson, "Literary Relations," 34.

68 Montgomery, 15 October 1908, in *SJLMM*, 1: 339.

69 Trillin, "Anne of the Red Hair," 217.

70 Quoted in Montgomery, 27 August 1919, in *SJLMM*, 2: 339. [Montgomery quotes from her contribution to "Canadian Writers on Canadian Literature – A Symposium," published in the *Globe* in 1910 and reproduced in Volume 1 of *The L.M. Montgomery Reader*.]

18

Women at War:
L.M. Montgomery, the Great War,
and Canadian Cultural Memory

—— 2008 ——

ANDREA McKENZIE

This chapter, first published in the collection of essays *Storm and Dissonance: L.M. Montgomery and Conflict*, revisits *Rilla of Ingleside* in the context of a more recent reclaiming of women's war literature. Andrea McKenzie, now an Assistant Professor in the Writing Department at York University, has also published chapters on Montgomery's work in *Making Avonlea: L.M. Montgomery and Popular Culture* (2002), *Windows and Words: A Look at Canadian Children's Literature in English* (2003), and *Textual Transformations in Children's Literature: Adaptations, Translations, Considerations* (2013). She also co-edited a restored and annotated edition of *Rilla of Ingleside* (2010).

On 11 November 1918, L.M. Montgomery wrote in her journal:

> Today came the official announcement of the signing of the armistice! The Great War is over – the world's agony has ended. *What has been born*? The next generation may be able to answer that. *We* can never know fully.
>   I picked gum on the old spruces down by the road today while I waited for the mail – and dreamed *young* dreams – just the dreams I dreamed at seventeen.[1]

Montgomery wrote this journal entry at Park Corner, Prince Edward Island, in circumstances that contrast with the hopeful tone of her words. Her cousin George and his son had just died in the 1918 influenza epidemic, and the forty-two-year-old Montgomery had returned to Park Corner to help her cousin, Frederica, nurse the rest of the household. This journal entry demonstrates how strongly Montgomery had internalized the belief that the bloodshed of four-and-a-half years of war would result in some great good or progress for the world; in the midst of the epidemic and family grief, she dreams *"young* dreams," as if she herself has been re-born through hope for the future, her intimate chats with Frede, and the magic of being in Prince Edward Island. Yet Montgomery was not blind to the realities of war, especially as they affected women: the rest of this entry discusses her concerns for Frede, a war bride who may have married in too much haste, and who is not reconciled to giving up her career for marriage.

As her wartime journal reflects, Montgomery agonized over the horrors of the War, and her sensitivity to ugliness caused her "anguish" throughout the War;[2] as a result, she needed to find a correspondingly strong justification for it to balance the horror.[3] In *Rilla of Ingleside*, Montgomery's war novel, the full-fledged form of the myth she internalized and disseminated took shape: Canada as a unified nation born out of the sacrifice and fires of war. In Britain, in its original form, this myth was based on the sacrifice of a generation of young *men* during the war, with women in the secondary role of disseminators of myth, observers, and mourners;[4] the sacrifice, according to wartime propaganda, would purge the British Empire of decadence, lifting its people to a higher plane.[5] Montgomery's Canadian version is based on *female* sacrifice during wartime, the forging of a new nation based on *shared* sacrifice and *shared* suffering,[6] with women as the representatives of the nation-in-the-making. *Rilla of Ingleside* becomes both a reflection of wartime propaganda and a shaping of it into a Canadian-centred, woman-centred form.

Montgomery's transformation of the traditionally European-centred, male-oriented war story into this form has contributed to *Rilla of Ingleside*'s omission from international studies of wartime literature, including those that focus on women's war literature. Yet in writing *Rilla of Ingleside*, her 1919–20 account of the War from a woman's perspective, the Canadian Montgomery succeeded in creating a lasting work where a myriad of British women authors failed. Clare Tylee's *The Great War and Women's Consciousness* provides a long list of women's war books, mostly British, that were published during and after the war, were read, and were largely forgotten until women's war scholarship rescued them. Perhaps only Vera Brittain's *Testament of Youth*, her 1933 autobiographical study of her own experiences and those of her young male companions during the War, has captured and largely retained public readership in the same way as Montgomery's work. Tellingly, Brittain's work upholds the anti-war perspective of a British female participant disillusioned with the War. The postwar attitude of disillusionment was first popularized by male British authors such as Siegfried Sassoon and Robert Graves, with female authors such as Brittain adding a feminist perspective. Unlike Montgomery, many of these British authors wrote after the results of the peace had given time for reflection about the meaning of the War and the personal grief and losses it caused.

Canadian war scholarship, including analyses of Montgomery's *Rilla of Ingleside*, still reflects the struggle between Empire and a new nation – Canada – struggling to assert itself. Jay Winter and Antoine Prost theorize that different nations created their own defining myths about the War. I would further theorize that each nation's defining myth is based on a key battle: in France, Verdun created the myth of the War as saving the nation;[7] in Britain, the Somme fuelled the myth of futility and disillusionment captured in the writings of anti-war authors; in Canada, however, Vimy Ridge created the myth of a young nation unified through the twinned notions of sacrifice and victory.[8] In Canadian cultural memory, Vimy Ridge is the battle that forged a nation, its people bound together by pride in the victory and mourning the men who died. Our greatest monument to the First World War, the Vimy Ridge memorial, epitomizes the Canadian version of the myth that has grown out of the War: the starkly white, immense marble memorial to the dead is juxtaposed with the horror of the still war-torn battlefield. Alone amongst participant nations, Canada has left this cratered landscape largely untouched, its horrific state serving to elevate the heroism of the men who fought their way across (and under) it.[9] Such a myth calls for what Paul Fussell calls the "'raised' ... language" of heroism,[10] a rhetoric that has little place for the shorn language of British disillusionment.

Battle-based myths, however, usually focus on male combatants in the war zone and their sacrifice, loss, or victory. War is a gendering discourse that creates binary modes of thinking: the active, knowledgeable soldier in the trenches versus the inactive, civilian excluded from the war zone.[11] Pierre Bourdieu's theory of a "linguistic marketplace" argues that the "official language" – the language instituted by the state – upholds the dominant power structures.[12] The declaration of war institutionalizes military discourse and its accompanying rites and power structures: during the First World War, gender lines and power structures were heightened because of the need to justify the War.[13] Soldiers became privileged, with women playing supporting roles because of their non-combatant status, despite the collective grief of families throughout the nation at the losses incurred by battles.[14]

Canadian war literature remains a site of struggle, mostly focused on male voices. Most books written during and after the War rapidly went out of print, with the British myth of disillusionment in academically accepted works overshadowing Canada's more positive perspective. Jonathan Vance notes in his exploration of Canadian soldiers' war literature that anti-war books such as Charles Yale Harrison's *Generals Die in Bed*, acclaimed as a Canadian work despite its author's American origins, "has became a staple of undergraduate literature," whereas works by pro-war authors such as Will Bird in their original form are "all but unobtainable."[15] Women's works have suffered much the same fate: Nellie McClung's *The Next of Kin* did not outlast the War, and her more political *In Times Like These* was not reprinted until the recandescence of women's war scholarship in the 1970s. Even eyewitness accounts by female participants are rare. In 1934, Nursing Sister Mabel Clint published her memoir, *Our Bit*, "to fill a gap in the published record in Canada of various phases of the Great War ... the essential and honourable part played by the nursing services." Sixty-five years later, Susan Mann, editor of *The War Diary of Clare Gass*, echoes Clint: "the memory of the [Canadian] war effort, as Jonathan Vance has unintentionally reminded us [in *Death So Noble*], is a profoundly masculine one."[16]

In essence, in the ninety years since the War began, only L.M. Montgomery's *Rilla of Ingleside* and John McCrae's "In Flanders Fields" have been read continuously and maintained their place as part of Canada's cultural memory of the War. Both works support the War, and both have been critiqued, sometimes harshly, for this stance. Montgomery's own words about *Rilla of Ingleside*, now available to scholars through her published journals and letters, are contradictory and may have added to the controversy about this work. Paul Tiessen's study of Montgomery's epistolary exchanges with Ephraim Weber about the War and pacifism shows the contradictions in her stance and her revised attitude towards war in the later years of her life. During the War and into the 1920s, Weber, a pacifist, "argued against her view that war was rooted in questions of honour."[17] This conflict and the negotiations that Tiessen demonstrates in Montgomery's responses show her acute sense of audience. Rather than alienate Weber, she appears to have anticipated his potentially negative response to *Rilla of Ingleside* because of its pro-war stance by providing Weber with "reading instructions": "'Read it,' she tells him, 'from the standpoint of a young girl (if you can!) and not from any sophisticated angle or you will not think much of it.'"18 With this denial of the complexity of her own work and its "purpose," Montgomery reduces *Rilla* to an unsophisticated girls' book and contradicts her own 1930s assessment of it as "the best book [she] ever wrote."19 Weber's anti-war stance, Montgomery's anticipation of his response, and her later evaluation of *Rilla* echo the assessments this work would receive over time, as responses to the War shifted.

When *Rilla* was published, "reviewers shifted *Rilla of Ingleside* from fiction to history: it became a 'true' record of Canada's war, and the fictionalization was merely an artistic device that only served to accentuate the book's authenticity."20 Both McCrae and Montgomery, however, were condemned in the 1970s' reassessment of the War: Fussell's influential work, *The Great War and Modern Memory*, a study of male combatant soldier-authors that largely omits women, states that McCrae's poem was "the most popular poem of the war." Fussell assesses the last six lines as a "propaganda argument – words like *vicious* and *stupid* would not seem to go too far – against a negotiated peace,"21 forgetting that most British and Canadian people were against a negotiated peace in 1916. Montgomery suffered a similar fate: Margery Fee and Ruth Cawker, writing in 1976, state that "*Rilla* degenerates into a chauvinist tract for Canadian support of Britain in World War I."22

Later scholars of Canadian war works have presented more balanced perspectives, but are still influenced by the British anti-war myth as upheld by Fussell. Vance, for instance, while acknowledging Montgomery's impact on Canada's myth of the War, dismisses *Rilla of Ingleside* as "not one of her best works." Vance both celebrates and critiques Fussell's work, a book that other Montgomery scholars have used as the context for their studies of *Rilla of Ingleside*. Tellingly, Vance claims, "No one can deny that [Fussell] drew on the best of Great War literature to reach his conclusions," adding that "Fussell shut himself off from a much larger canon of work, that of the inept novelist, the bad versifier, and the talentless essayist." Vance is aware that Fussell included mostly "white Anglo-American males" but by implication, women war writers, including Montgomery, are relegated to the category of the "inept."23

Similarly, Sandra Gwyn, author of the admirable *Tapestry of War: A Private View of Canadians in the Great War*, describes *Rilla of Ingleside* as "sentimental and jingoistic," but calls it "in some ways [Montgomery's] most interesting book, virtually the only Canadian work of fiction to describe everyday life on the home front from direct experience." Gwyn continues by saying that "Rilla ... is one of Montgomery's less successful heroines," but "through its well-observed detail, the novel takes us under the skin of small town wartime life." Gwyn upholds Montgomery's historical accuracy, but paradoxically condemns her attitude towards the War. (By condemning Montgomery, Gwyn condemns Canadians.) The struggle between British and Canadian, anti-war and war-supporter, is epitomized by Gwyn's comments on Vera Brittain and Montgomery: "Canada," Gwyn states, "sad to say, did not produce a wartime diarist with the intensity and perception of Vera Brittain," the British feminist anti-war author.[24]

These readings omit the growing recognition of a diversity of perspectives about the War, a diversity that includes a continuum of attitudes and participant perspectives. Peter Liddle, for instance, demonstrates that British soldiers' letters show that "enthusiasm waned but war was forging something more enduring in its place, stoic resilience ... the evidence is there of a sustained unity of purpose,"[25] rather than a sense of futility, casting doubt on the postwar school of disillusionment. More recently women's war scholarship has blurred the hitherto firmly drawn lines between combatant soldiers and civilians; Margaret Higonnet, for instance, questions the myth of "civilian propaganda set against soldiers' truth,"[26] a binary opposition premised on soldiers' knowledge of trench warfare versus civilians' ignorance of that experience. In this trope, male soldiers are perceived as active and participatory, while female civilians become passive and excluded, their role to "knit and wait" for the men to return,[27] a perspective that Montgomery contradicts through her depiction of the very busy, active roles women play during the War in *Rilla*. Clare Tylee, Sharon Ouditt, Higonnet and others have shown us the multiplicity of women's voices and perspectives on the War, claiming equal status for women's war experiences and voices;[28] no longer is legitimacy or authenticity of voice measured through combatant status, trench experience, or class. Carol Acton further demonstrates that men's and women's war stories contain multiple sites of connection that balance their separation in and out of the firing zone. Jay Winter and Blaine Baggett have reinforced this work, theorizing that the impact of war legitimates individual experience; civilians and soldiers alike, including marginalized populations, had their lives shaped by the War and influenced postwar culture and society as a result.[29]

Despite these increasingly diversified perspectives and the publication of hitherto marginalized war writers, such as children, Central European diarists, and African participants, for instance,[30] the focus of international studies remains largely European. Winter and Prost, for instance, call for scholars to transcend national perspectives in favour of a broader perspective: a "European war,"[31] a view that leaves out Canada, the United States, African nations, and Japan among the many combatant nations and locations. Women's war scholarship, too, remains Eurocentric: Gail Braybon, arguing against the War as a watershed for women's progress, focuses on Britain, France, and Germany,[32] although many of her claims would apply to Canada and other nations.

When read from these perspectives – a continuum of attitudes and individual experiences, a community in which male and female war stories are shared with equal legitimacy, and a Canadian-focused narrative – *Rilla of Ingleside* is both ahead of its time and of it, a narrative that epitomizes the ongoing struggle to define legitimacy of voice for women and for Canadians. This paper explores Montgomery's transformation of male-oriented war myths, some of them British, into the female-centred Canadian myths that she embedded in *Rilla of Ingleside*. In doing so, it illuminates her unique version of the Great War and suggests why it has remained an ongoing and compelling cultural memory of that War for generations of readers.[33]

The Embedded Myths of War

The myth of bloodshed leading to progress or "good" is not new to war: any government or official institution that involves its nation in a war must persuade the majority of the public that the benefits of that war will outweigh the lives it will cost.[34] Whereas Vera Brittain, writing in the 1930s after time had shown that no lasting good would come from the War, undermined "this glamour, this magic, this incomparable keying up of the spirit in a time of mortal conflict" by saying that "its honour is dishonest and its glory meretricious,"[35] Montgomery, writing in the immediate postwar period, recognized the horror but justified it through the beauty of the sacrifices made and the "great good" to come. In speaking of Vimy Ridge, Montgomery wrote, "Vimy Ridge is a name written in crimson and gold on the Canadian annals of the Great War. 'The British couldn't take it and the French couldn't take it,' said a German prisoner to his captors [in *Rilla of Ingleside*], 'but you Canadians are such fools that you don't know when a place can't be taken!'" Against all odds, and where their more numerous Allies could not succeed, the Canadians did. The heroism of the soldiers fighting the war is reinforced and raised by the horrors they undergo: "Dead men were all around me, lying on the horrible grey, slimy fields," writes Jerry Meredith to Nan, contrasting the battlefield with the beauty of "the old spring in Rainbow Valley under the maples."[36] As Amy Tector notes, "by juxtaposing the pastoral safety of Ingleside with the chaos of war, Montgomery is able to give readers the sense of dislocation and terror that the war evoked, without alienating them from the story."[37] Montgomery brings the war zone into the home through these fictional male voices, foreshadowing Vera Brittain's chorus of actual male voices in *Testament of Youth*. But whereas Brittain mingles male and female voices to condemn the War, Montgomery uses her fictional voices to question the horror, then uphold the sacrifice.[38]

If John McCrae's famous poem "In Flanders Fields" represents the presumed voice of the men who died, then *Rilla of Ingleside* speaks for the Canadian women who survived their absence or loss. In wartime, as Acton notes, grief, especially the image of the mother grieving over a dead son's bloody body, becomes potentially threatening to the aims of the state and the cause of war. The expression of grief, especially on the part of the mother, must be controlled and prescribed so that the mourner "not only uses but also participates in the construction of the dominant discourses of grief and mourning," thus upholding the war effort. "An important part of this regulation," Acton continues, "involves subscribing meaning to wartime death that limits or silences grief and replaces it with abstractions of honour and pride." Notably, postwar, antiwar narratives such as Vera Brittain's *Testament of Youth* captured the public imagination through their frank expression of hitherto repressed grief in an overturning of the convention of heroic silence and endurance. In Canada, the collective "sacrifice" of soldiers at Vimy Ridge became the myth of a new nation forged from loss, yet rejoicing in victory. In essence, this myth was the translation of collective grief into a democratic heroism in which the "meaning" subscribed to loss was "replace[d] with [the] abstractions of honour and pride" in the new nation.[39]

Jonathan F. Vance, analyzing Canadian cultural memories of the First World War, sees "a vision of the war as a nation-building experience of signal importance." The distinctly Canadian war narrative, Vance continues, led to "an idealized image" of the Canadian soldier as possessing two fundamental qualities: "his youth and his attachment to a mother figure. Both of these attributes ... can apply to a country as well."[40] In this construction, the young Canadian soldier parallels the young nation, and, of course, devotion to the mother country – Canada, not Great Britain. Montgomery augments this image in *Rilla of Ingleside* by using both women and men to represent the new Canada, with the role of mother the dominant motif. The sacrificed soldier hero, Walter, becomes the absent body to which Anne, Rilla, and Susan respond, with their roles in the new Canada forged through those responses. The measure of their fitness for this new world is found in their levels of adherence to the discourse of heroic endurance.

Montgomery also embeds British myths that travelled to Canada during the War to create Canadian voices and attitudes, paralleling Canada's presumed movement away from dependence on Great Britain towards full independence. One of the very first myths to appear in print during the War – though in itself, this myth was not new to war literature – was what Samuel Hynes calls "the odd metaphor of decadence and purgation": the belief, as British author Edmund Gosse wrote, that "War ... is the sovereign disinfectant, and its red stream of blood is the Condy's Fluid that cleans out the stagnant pools and clotted channels of the intellect."[41] Rupert Brooke, whose own death created the myth of the beautiful, but sacrificed, soldier-poet-hero, put it more elegantly in his poem "Peace": he sees young soldiers as "swimmers into cleanness leaping / Glad from a world grown old and cold and weary."[42] Both versions of this myth enact Britain as an aging and decadent Empire grown "stagnant" and indifferent, with the sacrifice of its young, eager soldiers the catalyst that will renew its strength and vigour. Montgomery uses the notions of purging and cleansing and turns them into a baptism of fire; young, energetic Canada will forge itself into a dignified nation unified by high, clean values, separating itself from the old (and decadent) mother country. Notably, in Brooke's version, young soldiers will be themselves cleansed by the baptism of fire, and their blood will in turn cleanse the nation (the civilian population). Owen Dudley Edwards and Jennifer H. Litster rightly argue that Montgomery participated in this myth, for she "felt the sacrifices and bloodshed of war would forge real Canadian unity for the first time and produce in their wake great Canadian literature."[43] It is a nice twist, and Montgomery takes it farther: Vance assumes that the young *soldier* represents the nation; Montgomery uses Susan Baker and Rilla Blythe, two civilian women, to represent the nation,[44] with Anne Blythe, the actual mother, representing a failing Britain.[45] Susan Baker represents the nation's broadened perspective and readiness for the world stage, while Rilla represents the nation growing to maturity.[46] In today's context, perhaps this move is not surprising. At the time, although women were an accepted part of the war effort at home, they were considered largely auxiliary. The "legitimate" language of war (in Pierre Bourdieu's terms), was spoken by soldiers, whose experience in the trenches gave them Bourdieu's "symbolic capital," or authority to be heard.[47] Noticeably, in *Rilla*, Montgomery uses male soldier voices to describe the battlefields, thus re-creating Canadian women's experience of the fighting through letters and postwar soldier descriptions, but she avoids having women "appropriate" the seemingly more legitimate male voices of experience. (Brittain uses the same technique more than ten years later to give herself legitimacy in *Testament of Youth*, though her male voices are from actual, not fictional, letters.) For her time, Montgomery's shift is daring, but she mitigates the risk by focusing on the concepts of motherhood and maturity, thus upholding the war-created myth of the valorized mother. In this reading, the war-mother's voice of experience therefore becomes legitimate, equal to, and placed alongside the voices of soldiers to create a community of disparate voices working towards the same end: an independent Canada cleansed and matured by the sacrifices of both women and men.

Anne Blythe: A Mother Sacrificed

Acton distinguishes between private narratives of grief and the discourses that control public expressions of that grief. In *Rilla of Ingleside*, Anne Blythe represents the valorized sacrificial mother, but one whose private grief overcomes her usefulness in supporting the War. Paradoxically, she enacts the actual cost of a mother's sacrifice, yet becomes a hindrance to the younger generation. Symbolically, Anne represents the British Empire from which Canada must gain independence; her fading out from the central story marks the growth to independence of her children and her servant, Susan.

Montgomery inscribes the conventionally allowed responses to absence and loss throughout *Rilla of Ingleside*, with women measured by these responses. Gertrude, for instance, follows the prescribed script when her fiancé, Robert Grant, is reported killed. As Rilla observes,

> At first she was crushed. Then after just a day she pulled herself together and went back to her school. She did not cry – I never saw her shed a tear – but oh, her face and her eyes!
> "I must go on with my work," she said. "That is my duty just now."[48]

Duty and endurance replace the natural response of succumbing to grief, and the public face, with tears unshed, replaces private mourning. But the cost is written on Gertrude's face for the discerning eye, in this case, Rilla's, to see. Gertrude has not just lost Robert Grant, but is touched with the sacrifice of the mother: "I have lost no son," she "bitterly" remarks, "only the sons and daughters who might have been born to me – who will never be born to me now." Her endurance is rewarded when Robert Grant's death is revealed as a mistake, and the depth of her emotion, her public control of private grief, is revealed when "all the tears that she *hadn't* shed all that week came then."[49] Montgomery translates Gertrude into heroine, but illuminates the cost of that heroism – the cost of sacrifice for those who mourn.

Similarly, Rilla's response after Walter's death contrasts public endurance with its private cost, echoing Gertrude's call to duty despite loss: "There was work to be done ... For her mother's sake she had to put on calmness and endurance as a garment in the day; but night after night she lay in her bed, weeping the bitter rebellious tears of youth." Noticeably, Anne and Rilla's roles are reversed. Rilla, the daughter, forces endurance on herself to comfort and sustain her mother, but Anne Blythe collapses under the strain: "For weeks Mrs. Blythe lay ill from grief and shock." Rilla's independence signals Anne's increasing dependence and diminution, a movement that parallels Britain's increasing dependence on its colonies during the War: Rilla sustains the household with "laughter," which "came from her lips only, never from her heart," while Anne's "return to health was slow."[50] Not surprisingly, Walter's last letter is written to his sister, not his mother, as a signal that his courage and sacrifice will be passed to Rilla, who represents his hope for Canada's future.

Yet in Anne Blythe, Montgomery presents us with a realistic picture of a mother's devastating grief. Rilla does translate Walter's death into "abstractions of honour and pride," publicly stating that "he was just one of many fine and splendid boys who have given everything for their country," but her mother is unable to do so.[51] For the rest of the book, she is depicted as the mother who sacrifices all, but who cannot translate personal loss into full public endurance. When Shirley asks permission to enlist, Anne becomes the "pale mother" whose words focus on past and threatened loss: "Two of my sons have gone and one will never return. Must I give you too, Shirley?" Although she does tell him that "he might go," she suffers doubt about her own endurance, "wonder[ing] if she could bear any more. She thought not; surely she had given enough."[52] Anne demonstrates the elasticity of a mother's capacity for suffering, but the effort diminishes her. She becomes of the past, harnessed to the world of buggies and moonlit drives, divorced from the current reality of "machines" such as the war aeroplanes her son Shirley flies. Even Gilbert celebrates not Anne, but Susan, as representative of the "women – courageous, unquailing, patient, heroic – who had made victory possible." "Anne wonders," notes Rothwell, "whether she will really feel wholly at home in the new world."[53] Clearly, she will not; she belongs in the tranquil, pre-war world, and has little place in the new turmoil that is called "peace."

Anne's grief and subsequent health problems after Walter's death and Shirley's enlistment also hinder the younger generation's active participation in the War. Diana Blythe's wish for overseas work as a (volunteer nurse) V.A.D.[54] like Faith Meredith, for instance, is vetoed because of her mother. Diana "had tried to wring from her father consent to her going also but had been told that for her mother's sake it could not be given." Instead of fulfilling the iconic role of volunteer nurse overseas, Di must return to her "Red Cross work in Kingsport," her potential unfulfilled.[55] Anne Blythe's increasing incapacity to adapt to the sacrifices called on by the public discourse of war augurs her diminishing influence in her community.

Anne's connections to the British Empire are indirect, subtly drawn through her ties to her first-born son, Jem Blythe. Jem, the son who goes to war for the "Empire," seeing Canada as one of its "cubs," is the son most closely linked to Anne through the House of Dreams and the imaginative, beautiful pre-war world. Anne is temporarily rejuvenated to youthfulness when Jem is redeemed to her after being reported wounded and missing. Yet Jem, her oldest son, is no longer hers at war's end, instead "belong[ing] to Faith." His independence, like Canada's, comes about by war. Anne loses her influence over Jem and her centrality, just as the British Empire, the "old grey mother," loses Canada as a dependent colony.[56] Anne Blythe thus becomes a complex, paradoxical figure, representing the very real devastation of a mother's sacrifice, but showing how her lack of resilience and inability to translate her grief into the conventional script must signal the end of her influence. Written onto this image of Anne is the image of the waning British Empire and its parallel lack of influence on Canada's destiny. That role of power and influence must be transferred to the deserving younger generation.

Susan Baker: A Unified Canada

If Anne Blythe represents the fading of the British Empire and the devastated mother, then Susan Baker presents the older dynamic woman who broadens her own narrow perspective from the domestic to the world stage, thus representing Canada's similar role in global politics. As Erika Rothwell notes, Susan begins the War with an inward perspective largely circumscribed by Ingleside and its people and ends it with a perspective and character that care about the world: "Traditionally opposed discourses – the domestic and the political – have become deeply and inextricably intertwined. The formerly apolitical Susan becomes intimately acquainted with the politicians of the day and bestows her judgment upon their actions."[57] She steps out of her kitchen and into the fields; she also takes on the public male role of "ordering" the men up to subscribe to the Victory Loan,[58] a scene narrated in Rilla's diary, thus giving it approval and distancing the direct appropriation of men's work.

Susan Baker is also touched with the sacred sacrifice of the mother. Like Rilla, Susan is not a biological mother, but her connection with Shirley and his naming her "Mother Susan" touch her with the pain and sacrifice mothers such as Anne Blythe must make. When Shirley leaves, Susan shows how much her perspective has changed, giving us a measure of her growth: she says, "I did not see once why such things must be but I can see now." The depth of her pain is measured by the possible disruptions to the household's smooth running, but she gallantly accepts the inevitable. In all ways, Susan, the incongruous "heroine," is shown to be fitting of that role: "the spirit that animated her gaunt arms [in the grain fields] was the self-same one that captured Vimy Ridge and held the German legions back from Verdun."[59] Susan is equated with the men of Canada and also with the soldiers of France who save their nation in the greater struggle; Canada is seen as ready to step forward on the world's stage, an independent nation whose gaze is focused outwards instead of inwards.

Susan also helps to purge the community of dissenting voices, creating a unified and peaceful society where doubters, dissenters, and slackers are silenced. Susan vanquishes Mrs. William Reese, the mother of "three stalwart sons, not one of whom had gone to the front," when Mrs. Reese sighs, "Pore, pore Walter," calling Mrs. Reese "poor and naked and mean and small." Although Norman Douglas routs Mr. Pryor at the Union prayer meeting, Susan Baker has the last word, or rather, action, in the hilarious scene when she chases her enemy from her home ground – the kitchen – and off the grounds of Ingleside, as a soldier would rout an enemy. As Epperly notes, "The scene in her kitchen is another of those instances where we see acted out domestically what is happening in Europe on the battlefields."[60] We hear little of Mr. Pryor after this; the pacifist has been silenced. Similarly, Susan vanquishes Cousin Sophia, the war pessimist, driving her from the comfortable kitchen at the worst moment of the War.

But these incidents are troubling; as Edwards comments, they "[suggest] a social sickness beneath the pro-war patriotism."[61] For Canada to be unified, in Montgomery's vision, those who disagree, doubt, or question must be silenced. Dissenting voices, such as those against conscription, are not heard after the Union government wins the election. Mr. Pryor's windows are broken when the Parliament Buildings burn down, and we are left to think that he may deserve it. A small child is so imbued with the notion of sacrifice and suffering that he kills his favourite kitten, and it is deemed "beautiful" and "sad."[62] Women are measured by the number of sons they send to the Front: God is on the Allied side and the Germans are capable of any atrocity. From this aspect, Susan's broadening of outlook towards a global perspective paradoxically inculcates her own small community with the war's biases and prejudices. Canada, to be unified, must undergo the violence of purging dissenting voices.

Rilla Blythe, Canada's Future

Unlike her mother and Susan Baker, Rilla Blythe is the equivalent of the young male soldier of myth, untried and untested until matured by the baptism of war; she also represents the idle "decadence" that requires cleansing. For a Blythe, the Rilla of 1914 is unrepresentative. As she describes herself, "There's bound to be one dunce in every family. I'm quite willing to be a dunce if I can be a pretty, popular, delightful one. I can't be clever. I have no talent at all, and you can't imagine how comfortable it is."[63] In essence, Rilla is vain, immature, and incapable, very unlike her mother at the same age, or any of her siblings – but with the Ingleside charm of laughter and personality. Elizabeth Epperly describes her as a "sunny thoughtless creature who cannot realize the war"; Edwards describes her unwontedly harshly as a "selfish, self-pitying little teenage emptyhead," recognizing her drawbacks but missing her charm. Rilla's unconsciousness of the War and its future significance, of course, represents the many Canadians for whom the declaration of war came, as it did to Montgomery, like a sudden "thundercloud."[64] Suffering, sacrifice, and self-denial temper Rilla's personality: as the War unfolds, she will shed (or purge) herself of her frivolity, like her soldier-brother counterparts. Their maturity stems from their battlefield and trench experiences; her equivalent maturity results from grief, loss, and responsibility.

Her brother Walter's enlistment and death are the catalysts that cause her full adulthood, but it is her (adoptive) motherhood that transforms her into the idealized metaphor representing the future of the young Canada.

The relationship of Rilla and Jims, her adopted war baby, becomes symbolic of Rilla's future status as mother and guardian of the new nation. Jims, an innocent victim of the war, is untouched by the bloodshed that soldiers must commit, and thus becomes a fitting symbol of both the havoc wreaked by war and the generation that will benefit from the great sacrifices of the War. For this future, Rilla gives up the frivolity of the parties she so longs to participate in at the novel's beginning, learning self-sufficiency and self-discipline through caring for this unwanted child, salvaging his at-risk life in a parallel movement to Canada's soldiers saving the world from destruction, creating new hope from the darkness of war. This shift, from soldier's mother to mother of the blessed generation that will benefit from the sacrifices of the war, signals Montgomery's new vision.

Rilla does not come to motherhood easily, and her acceptance of it symbolizes the turning point in her War participation. In the first months of the war, Rilla cares for Jims automatically, but without love; similarly, her participation in the War is unthinking and automatic. One night, however, Rilla returns home to find Jims crying in the dark; she uses her imagination to picture his thoughts: alone, an orphan, in the darkness. She then takes him into her own bed and cuddles him: "Something delightful and yearning and brooding seemed to have taken possession of her ... She realized that – at last – she loved her war baby." Significantly, she is immediately afterwards included as a full participant in the Ingleside community of suffering:

No one at Ingleside ever got up in the morning without a sudden piercing wonder over what the day might bring.
"And I used to welcome the mornings so," thought Rilla.[65]

The wakening of her maternal feelings and her thoughtfulness have brought her into the circle of suffering. Five months before, she was unable to "realize the war";[66] now, she is an adult, a mother, and a war participant.

Epperly notes that because "to Montgomery the war against Germany was sacred, a holy cause, we should not be surprised to find ... Rilla and her war baby depicted as Madonna and child" in the farewell scene with Kenneth Ford, Rilla's fiancé. Epperly continues that "Rilla is certainly meant to be a cultural symbol worth dying for."⁶⁷ Rilla is also worth living for; she represents a future life of desirable (and, at this point, virginal) wife and mother, a cultural symbol of promise and future maturity. Although Jims disrupts the romantic nature of Ken and Rilla's final meeting, it is only when Rilla fulfills her maternal duties, fetching the crying Jims and cuddling him, that Kenneth recognizes his love for her. This domestic disruption parallels the interruption of their romance by the War: responsibility and duty must take precedence over pleasure and romance, and it is Rilla's recognition of her duty towards Jims that leads Kenneth to "[carry] that picture of her in his heart" to the War, a picture that includes the child. Care of Jims and responsibility will change Rilla from Ken's image of a "slim ... schoolgirl" to a "desirable" woman, the equal and equivalent of the battle-scarred veteran he has become.⁶⁸

Jims provides another turning point when Rilla "slump[s]" after Walter's death, breaking her promise to him to "keep faith" and betraying the image of stoicism and endurance of loss prescribed for women mourners. Jims becomes ill with the "real" croup, and Rilla and Susan "cannot save him."⁶⁹ Only the sudden appearance of the capable Mary Vance, who holds Jims over a potentially lethal mixture of sulphur and hot coals, saves Jims's life. Mary Vance literally purges Jims of the germs that are killing him, and so purges Rilla of two last faults: vanity and despondency. Kissing Mary Vance after her daring life-saving action signals Rilla's forgiveness of Mary for both chasing her through the village with a codfish years earlier, and for spreading goose grease over Rilla's romantic dreams after the dance at the opening of the book. We are able, through this reference, to measure Rilla against her former self, a point that Montgomery addresses directly through Betty Mead's comparison of Rilla's pre-war and current selves; Betty's staunch defence of Rilla to Irene Howard validates Rilla's status in the community at large.

Rilla's more important lesson in this episode is to cleanse herself of despondency in private as well as in public. She writes in her diary: "All at once I was tired of keeping up and pretending to be brave and cheerful, and I just gave up for a few days and spent most of the time lying on my face on my bed, crying ... I was cowardly and false to what I promised Walter – and if Jims had died I could never have forgiven myself."⁷⁰ But she does slump, neglects her duty to Jims, and almost loses him; her baby and Canada's metaphorical future are threatened. Never, after this point, will Rilla fail to "hold [the torch] high," even when Susan breaks down at the report that the guns are firing on Paris in the spring of 1918. Walter's enlistment and death bring Rilla to womanhood, but it is the helpless suffering of Jims, her war baby, that brings Rilla to the final, polished maturity. It is no accident that Rilla found herself "thinking that the boys who had been gassed at the front must have looked" like Jims when he is choking to death, or that "gallant little Jims put up a good fight," a phrase that brings the language of battle into Jims's struggle. The War is brought into the home, with Jims representing the soldiers and Rilla the civilian population that must uphold the war effort. Safety, for both Jims and Canada, is due to risky and drastic measures – sulphur on coals and the death of Canadian soldiers – but these risks and sacrifices must be upheld through Walter's principles of being "brave and cheerful," staunch in the face of disaster.[71]

Rilla must make one final sacrifice at War's end: to give up Jims to his father and step-mother. He is still, however, "more [her] baby than any one else's" and has served his purpose. Through Jims, Rilla has become a fitting mother for future sons and daughters of Canada: "a woman with wonderful eyes and a dented lip, and rose-bloom cheek, – a woman altogether beautiful and desirable – the woman of [Ken's] dreams."[72] And a fitting representative of Canada's future, upholding the principles that her brothers have fought for, and in Walter's case, died for. Anne Blythe represents the sacrificial mother; Susan Baker represents the broadening of Canada's influence; and Rilla Blythe represents Canada growing to maturity.

The other crucial player in Rilla's formation of self is her brother Walter. He embodies the mythic soldier-poet (like Britain's Rupert Brooke and Canada's John McCrae) who sacrifices his future for the sake of those at home. Epperly notes that "John Meredith ... preaches Montgomery's own belief about this war, using as a text Hebrews 9:22, 'Without shedding of blood there is no remission of sins,'" another variant on the purging and cleansing myth.[73] Montgomery connects the Bible, the metaphor of the beautiful dead soldier-poet, Canada's epiphany through the sacrifice of the soldiers who died, and women as the responsible nurturers of Canada's future in a network of responsibility, heroism, and sacrifice, with Walter passing on John McCrae's "torch" to Rilla Blythe. The words of his posthumous letter move rhetorically from individual to home, home to nation, nation to the world, thus transforming Canada's role in the Empire to one of independence and nationhood. Rilla becomes both instrument and agent of that change. "You," Walter instructs Rilla, "will tell your children of the *Idea* we fought and died for – [will] teach them it must be *lived for* as well as died for, else the price paid for it will have been given for naught. This will be part of *your* work, Rilla. And if you – all the girls back in the homeland – do it, then we who don't come back will know that you have not 'broken faith' with us."[74] The world lies in the home, with the young women who will mother the coming generations; the future is their responsibility. If each individual does her part, then each home will contribute to Canada, and Canada can contribute to humankind. To not follow Walter's words threatens the individual, Canada, and the world, making his sacrifice of artistry, beauty, and life meaningless.

But this passage is controversial because it seems to lock women into the same role that the dominant wartime discourse and propaganda prescribed for them. According to this discourse, men fight actively overseas; women remain passively at home, their connection to the War made only through the absent male. Montgomery appears to have internalized this ideology in her work, with her use of the authoritative male soldier-poet's voice to express these sentiments being especially troublesome. Walter, the beauty-loving artist with a brilliant future, has sacrificed beauty, his career, and now his life, for the sake of the women at home. It seems as though Rilla and the female reader must believe in the justness of the War and their secondary role in it if Canada's future is to be assured.

And yet women's position as mourners in wartime is itself a trap that is difficult to escape. As Judith Kazantzis explains in the preface to *Scars Upon My Heart*, "the duty of the woman, bereaved and despairing, becomes clear. She will live her life as the dead one bequeathed it to her. She will immortalise him in her obedience to the values for which he died. To question those values is to question the Sacrifice itself – impossible. For then his death must become not only horrible but also meaningless."[75] Montgomery does not question this dominant myth; to do so would be to render the entire anguish of the War, as evidenced in her journal, as futile and purposeless. Idealism and heroic language, as Jay Winter theorizes, are inextricably entwined with mourning. The idealistic vision of a Canada unified by the sacrifice of soldiers such as Walter, couched in heroic language, becomes a compelling means for women to control the chaos of war and mediate their loss. Acton, writing about the complexities of women's position in wartime, points out that the "sacrificial script" provides Vera Brittain with a "form of consolation ... This need for consolation, the need to find some meaning or ideology that would allow her to function on a daily basis ... is crucial to our understanding of the contradictions, paradoxes, and confusions that make up Brittain's war story."[76] Montgomery's consolatory script enables horror to exist beside heroism for both men and women; she attempts to reconcile, as

Brittain does, the conflicting voices. But we are left with a question: does Montgomery's female version of the Canadian war narrative adhere to the dominant ideology or subvert it?

It is too easy to say, as many have done, that the War benefited women or produced, as Montgomery wished, a unified Canada. It is also too easy to condemn Montgomery's version of the War as unrealistic or oversentimentalized. Certainly Canada did, as Vance shows, become a nation with a distinctive voice, politically more independent of Great Britain. But it was neither a unified country nor a Utopia; Montgomery tries to reconcile the voices of dissent, but Vance demonstrates that they were neither silenced nor stilled. What Montgomery shows us is both a dominant ideology and a subversion of it: a nation welded by sacrifice, but a sacrifice made by both the men who fought and the women who mourned them: "'*Our* sacrifice is greater ... ' cried Rilla passionately. 'Our boys give only *themselves. We* give them.'"[77] The reader must believe in Walter's words and Rilla's subsequent actions, or Walter's death *and* Rilla's heroism will become equally meaningless. Montgomery projects this brother-sister sacrifice to affirm a similar equality for the men and women throughout Canada who have won maturity for the new Canada: "Four hundred thousand of our boys gone overseas – fifty thousand of them killed. But – you are worth it!" exclaims Susan Baker, standing beside the flag, representing just "one of the women ... who had made victory possible." Suffering and adoptive motherhood have given Rilla – and by extension, other Canadian women – a primary role in the new Canada. Rilla will not just "tell" her children of the values for which Walter sacrificed his life, and for which she endured his loss: she has become a living example of those values.[78]

Conclusion

By "inscribing the women's private, unofficial story or subtext into the official [war] story," Montgomery "collapse[s] the polarization of men and women, front and home, that has become a conventional trope of war."[79] Although its narrative can be perplexing and problematic, *Rilla of Ingleside* epitomizes this notion of shared war stories, of a community at war, while foregrounding women as active and legitimate participants in the Great War many decades before women's war scholarship would seek to establish them in this very role. Montgomery's text does not need recovering; it has been with us, read, and in print since the War. Montgomery thus holds a unique place in women's war literature and in Canadian war literature: she is perhaps the only English-speaking woman and the only Canadian author, male or female, to have written a contemporary war book that has maintained its place in popular culture since the War. She has also given us a uniquely Canadian version of war myths, focused on women and community, in place of male-combatant, British-based myths.

Montgomery's belief in the good that would come out of the War faltered in the 1930s and 1940s with the threat and then actuality of a world again at war. Benjamin Lefebvre's analysis of Montgomery's as-yet unpublished *The Blythes Are Quoted* demonstrates significant revisions in Montgomery's perspective about war and the First World War. As Lefebvre demonstrates, Montgomery's revisions uniquely intersect with this earlier work through the poetry Montgomery attributes to Walter.[80] Walter's poem "The Piper" garnered him fame and a lasting place in war literature in *Rilla of Ingleside* for its ringing call to "keep faith"; it was a suitably patriotic poem for his sister Rilla to recite at recruiting meetings and thus fulfill her secondary role of inciting male action through discourse. In contrast, "The Aftermath," the poem that Montgomery originally intended to use at the end of *The Blythes Are Quoted* and attribute to Walter Blythe, graphically describes a soldier's (Walter's) "horrid joy" at bayonetting a "stripling boy," the mere thought of which turns him "sick" in *Rilla*. This poem, too, contains echoes of McCrae's "In Flanders Fields," but reverses its sentiments, as it does the attitudes expressed in *Rilla*:

> *We must remember always*; evermore
>   Must spring be hateful and the dawn a shame ...
> We shall not sleep as we have slept before
>   That withering blast of flame.[81]

McCrae's heroically sacrificed dead soldiers "shall not sleep" if readers "break faith" with the cause of war;[82] Montgomery's fictional living soldiers, years after the War, *cannot* sleep because of the memories of the horrors they have perpetrated. It is hardly a poem that Rilla Blythe would recite to recruit more men or to uphold a family's belief in the sacrifice of sons, brothers, and fathers in a just war. The anguish that Montgomery had felt during the War is transformed to the bitterness of disillusionment;[83] her own sons threatened by enlistment in a new war, she recognizes that the First World War's bloodshed and sacrifice cannot be justified. The juxtaposed landscapes of Vimy Ridge, with peace, memorial, and horror side-by-side, would now promise only suffering. Montgomery's attitudes about the War, like her British counterpart Vera Brittain's, were transformed from support to disillusionment after time and the events that followed the War demonstrated that no great benefit would ensue from the "world's agony."[84] Ironically, the future generation, Montgomery's own sons, would inherit not the peace Montgomery dreamed of, but another war.

However much we agree or disagree with Montgomery's immediate postwar "[construction] of reality" through myth,[85] however much we now recognize that many divergent voices inhabit the landscape of the War, she undoubtedly contributed to Canada's cultural memory of that war with a unique Canadian woman's voice that positions women as fighting alongside and connected to their male counterparts, and a continuum of women's private and public responses to the War, its victories, and its griefs. *Rilla of Ingleside* quietly and triumphantly gives us a vision of women in the Great War that is public, yet within the home; heroic, yet realistic; universal, yet uniquely Canadian; women are the backbone of community and nation, the mothers and guardians of the future generations, and of the nation born from the fires of war.

NOTES

[Editor's note: A number of references to other chapters in the collection of essays *Storm and Dissonance*, appearing in the original version of this chapter, have been silently replaced with citations to those chapters.]

1 Montgomery, 11 November 1918, in *SJLMM*, 2: 274.
2 Epperly, *The Fragrance of Sweet-Grass*, 114.
3 For a detailed account of Montgomery's war beliefs and initial justification for Canada going to Britain's aid, and for an account of the influence of the War on her wartime books, see Edwards and Litster, "The End of Canadian Innocence," 118. See also Epperly, *The Fragrance of Sweet-Grass*.
4 The myth of young soldiers' sacrifice runs throughout war literature and private documents of those years. See Vera Brittain's *Testament of Youth* for a British perspective; McKenzie's "Witnesses to War" for an analysis of women's role as discourse disseminators.
5 For an analysis of prevalent British myths during the First World War, including soldiers, sacrifice, and cultural effects, see Hynes, *A War Imagined*.

6 As Epperly notes, Montgomery "focuses on women throughout the novel, but in doing so she also emphasizes the connections between women and men" (Epperly, *The Fragrance of Sweet-Grass*, 127).

7 Winter and Prost, *The Great War in History*, 196. Chapter Nineteen of *Rilla of Ingleside*, "They Shall Not Pass," reflects this belief. Dr. Blythe says, "I have a hunch that the fate of the whole war hangs on the issue of Verdun" (*RI*, 212). Mr. Meredith continues, "in [France] I see the white form of civilization making a determined stand against the black powers of barbarism" (*RI*, 212–13).

8 See Vance, *Death So Noble*; Berton, *Vimy*.

9 Unlike other nations, Canada left the shells, craters, and other detritus of war intact. For a description of the bunkers and tunnels during the war, see *The Letters of Agar Adamson*, a Canadian officer with the Princess Patricias.

10 Fussell, *The Great War*, 21.

11 Higonnet, "All Quiet in No Women's Land," 209.

12 Bourdieu, *Language and Symbolic Power*, 45.

13 McKenzie, "Witnesses to War," 37–38.

14 The Canadian War Museum's website focuses on traditional military history. Its description of the battle of Vimy Ridge focuses on military tactics and the cost of the battle: "more than 10,000 killed and wounded." Omitting the word "men" in this phrase, however, elides the human element of these soldier casualties. "Canada and the First World War" does not mention the home front and refers to women only in the section "Canadians on Other Fronts," with a brief reference to Nursing Sisters. Library and Archives Canada, however, has recently created "The Call to Duty: Canada's Nursing Sisters," which includes diaries and letters written by Canadian Nursing Sisters who served during the War. See Canada War Museum, "Canada and the First World War," http://www.warmuseum.ca/-cwm/exhibitions/chrono/1914first_ww_e.shtml.

15 Vance, "The Soldier as Novelist," 35.

16 Clint, *Our Bit*, 177; Mann, Introduction, xxxviii.

17 P. Tiessen, "Opposing Pacifism," 132.

18 Quoted in ibid., 134.

19 Montgomery, 3 September 1921, in *SJLMM*, 3: 17; Montgomery, 13 July 1936, in *SJLMM*, 5: 80. For an exploration of Montgomery as a "conflicted" woman writer, see Gerson, "L.M. Montgomery."

20 Vance, *Death So Noble*, 176.

21 Fussell, *The Great War*, 248, 250.

22 Quoted in Tector, "A Righteous War?" 72.

23 Vance, *Death So Noble*, 176, 5–6, 5.

24 Gwyn, *Tapestry of War*, 165–66, 164.

25 Liddle, "British Loyalties," 535.

26 Higonnet, "All Quiet in No Women's Land," 209.

27 Rothwell, "Knitting Up the World," 136.

28 Many anthologies and analyses of women's WWI writing, roles, and attitudes are now available. Besides Tylee, see, among others, Goldman, Gledhill, and Hattaway, *Women Writers and the Great War*; Reilly, *Scars Upon My Heart*; Ouditt, *Fighting Forces*; Higonnet, *Lines of Fire*; Potter, *Boys in Khaki*; Acton, *Grief in Wartime*.

29 Acton, "Writing and Waiting," 55; Winter and Baggett, *The Great War*, 10–12.

30 For excerpts from diaries and memoirs of previously marginalized populations, see Palmer and Wallis, *Intimate Voices*.

31 Winter and Prost, *The Great War in History*, 10–12.

32 Braybon, Introduction, 15.

33 Myth both governs Montgomery's version of the War and is transformed by her in *Rilla of Ingleside*. Following Samuel Hynes, I define myth as "not a falsification of reality, but an imaginative version of it, the story of the war that has evolved, and has come to be accepted as true ... a tale that confirms a set of attitudes, an idea of what the war [the First World War] was and what it meant" (Hynes, *A War Imagined*, xi).

34 The discourses of war are grounded in the previous literature, politics, culture, values, and beliefs formulated in peacetime, reaching back to the history of previous wars and forward to the next one. As such, war discourse, like all other discourse, is dialogic, emulating Mikhail Bakhtin's theory that all utterances are "links in the chain" of "speech communion" (Bakhtin, *Speech Genres and Other Late Essays*, 94). The declaration of war becomes a concrete linguistic situation that imposes military discourse, with its corresponding values and assumptions, as the official and, in Pierre Bourdieu's terms, "legitimate language" (Bourdieu, *Language and Symbolic Power*, 45). To accept this event with the enthusiasm displayed in 1914, the people of the country must be, according to Bourdieu's theory, predisposed to accept it (McKenzie, "Witnesses to War," 29).

35 Brittain, *Testament of Youth*, 292. Vera Brittain's life writings are the site of much controversy in war scholarship. Brittain's use of heroic language to describe war participants, including the four young men who died as soldiers, is juxtaposed with her condemnation of war in a seeming paradox that war scholars have critiqued. Carol Acton's analysis of Brittain's wartime correspondence with Roland Leighton explains

the paradox, one common to women in wartime (Acton, "Writing and Waiting"). See also Deborah Gorham's *Vera Brittain: A Feminist Life* and McKenzie's "Witnesses to War" for further discussions and references.

36 *RI*, 266, 136.

37 Tector, "A Righteous War?" 75.

38 See Epperly, *The Fragrance of Sweet-Grass*, 112–30.

39 Acton, *Grief in Wartime*, 2, 5.

40 Vance, *Death So Noble*, 10, 147.

41 Hynes, *A War Imagined*, 12; Edmund Gosse, quoted in ibid.

42 Brooke, *1914 & Other Poems*, 11.

43 Edwards and Litster, "The End of Canadian Innocence," 32.

44 Edwards argues that "Susan is also Canada herself." I agree, but he omits Rilla from the equation. Susan is, as Edwards states, "elderly, maternal ... , unattractive, working-class, resourceful, self-reliant" [see his article "L.M. Montgomery's *Rilla of Ingleside*," in this volume]. As such, she represents only part of the female population, albeit a significant part: the older woman, full of "grit." Rilla, the adoptive mother, is clearly intended to represent the future of the nation, fertile and desirable.

45 I am grateful to Benjamin Lefebvre for suggesting Anne Blythe as representative of the failing influence of the British Empire in his comments on an early draft of this paper (Benjamin Lefebvre, e-mail to the author, 25 March 2007).

46 [See Edwards's "L.M. Montgomery's *Rilla of Ingleside*"]; Rothwell, "Knitting Up the World," 137; Tector, "A Righteous War?" 84.

47 Bourdieu, *Language and Symbolic Power*, 72.

48 *RI*, 216.

49 *RI*, 216, 217, 218.

50 *RI*, 242, 248.

51 Acton, *Grief in Wartime*, 5; *RI*, 248.

52 *RI*, 262, 263.

53 *RI*, 272, 314; Rothwell, "Knitting Up the World," 139.

54 This term was originally used to refer to an entire unit of voluntary aid workers attached to the British Red Cross, but quickly became the common term for an individual aid worker. The best-known role of a V.A.D. was that of volunteer nurse, but other jobs they could do included working as cooks, cleaners, and so on. Accounts of British volunteer nurses can be found in Vera Brittain's *Testament of Youth*; Enid Bagnold's *A Diary without Dates*; and Lyn Macdonald's *The Roses of No Man's Land*. Canada sent relatively few V.A.D.s overseas.

55 *RI*, 266.

56 *RI*, 29, 348, 28

57 Rothwell, "Knitting Up the World," 137.

58 Ibid., 139; Epperly, *The Fragrance of Sweet-Grass*, 125.

59 *RI*, 263, 276.

60 *RI*, 242, 243; Epperly, *The Fragrance of Sweet-Grass*, 126.

61 [See Edwards's "L.M. Montgomery's *Rilla of Ingleside*."]

62 *RI*, 331.

63 *RI*, 23.

64 Epperly, *The Fragrance of Sweet-Grass*, 116; [see Edwards's "L.M. Montgomery's *Rilla of Ingleside*"]; Montgomery, 5 August 1914, in *SJLMM*, 2: 150.

65 *RI*, 124–25.

66 Epperly, *The Fragrance of Sweet-Grass*, 116.

67 Ibid., 118.

68 *RI*, 172, 349, 350.

69 *RI*, 253, 247, 254.

70 *RI*, 253.

71 *RI*, 254, 253.

72 *RI*, 339, 350

73 Epperly, *The Fragrance of Sweet-Grass*, 113.

74 *RI*, 246.

75 Kazantzis, Preface, xix.

76 Acton, "Writing and Waiting," 59.

77 Vance, *Death So Noble*, 10, 260–61; *RI*, 156.

78 *RI*, 314. Montgomery also subverted the imposed script for female authors. Instead of commemorating only the sacrificed soldiers, she has commemorated Canadian girls and women and their sacrifices and struggles. She herself transcends the role prescribed for her, claiming full authority to write about the War.

79 Acton, "Writing and Waiting," 55.

80 Lefebvre, "'That Abominable War!'" [*The Blythes Are Quoted* was subsequently published in 2009.]

81 [*BQ*, 510.]

82 McCrae, "In Flanders Fields."

83 For the impact of the 1930s Depression on Montgomery's writing, see H. MacDonald, "Reflections of the Great Depression."

84 Montgomery, 11 November 1918, in *SJLMM*, 2: 274.

85 Tylee, *The Great War and Women's Consciousness*, 54.

19

Anne of Green Gables / Akage no An: The Flowers of Quiet Happiness

—— 2008 ——

EMILY AOIFE SOMERS

This article in *Canadian Literature*, a journal published out of the University of British Columbia, proposes a new avenue of research for studies of Montgomery's international reach. Rather than rely on generalizations and assumptions about the Japanese fascination with *Anne of Green Gables*, Emily Aoife Somers examines two key Japanese translations of the novel by Hanako Muraoka and Yasuko Kakegawa in order to uncover the pattern of linguistic choices that made the depiction of Prince Edward Island rural life so recognizable and appealing to Japanese readers. Somers, who received her PhD from the University of British Columbia with a dissertation on Irish–Japanese literary networks in the modernist period, has published widely on Japanese, Irish, and Celtic texts, on *manga* and *anime*, and on queer and transgender subjectivities.

Critics often identify the remarkable popularity of *Anne of Green Gables* in Japan by the abundant outcrop of related commercial products that circulate in Japanese pop culture. Anne as emblem, it seems, has enabled romantic infatuations through a fantasy performance of Canadianness. Such investigative perspectives – as from Yoshiko Akamatsu, Douglas Baldwin, and Judy Stoffman – find in *Akage no An* (Red-Haired Anne) forms of Occidentalist nostalgia for a Victorian ideal. The Anne character has become commodified as exotic souvenir, ethnic roleplay, or adventure tourism. But why has Japan, of all nations, so strongly evidenced this tendency to turn Anne into apparatus? Is Anne in Japan only a phenomenon of token appearances? These expressions of *An*, after all, are recent developments of a text that has enjoyed decades of respect. These later social expressions, however understood, derive their effects from initial sympathies previously registered through an imported text. Indeed, the methodology of the translation, intercultural in practice, may hold the clues to the enormous popularity of Anne in Japan. Yuri Lotman and Boris Uspensky have claimed that lexical choices in interlingual renditions are transformative mechanisms. These devices mark the translation as exhibiting interstices of culture and linguistics. The major translations of *Akage no An* are examples of such inflections, exhibiting deliberate usage of classical allusion, substitutive vocabularies, and other Japanese cultural referents. Translation has thus reframed Anne, and her environs, into a blended version of Canadian and Japanese identities. Why do Japanese readers seemingly feel such an attachment to *Anne of Green Gables*? Perhaps it is because Green Gables is not so foreign in expression or environment after all. Muraoka Hanako and Kakegawa Yasuko, the renowned translators of *Akage no An*, both engaged in a purposeful intertwining of Japanese poetic classicism with the characterization of *Anne* as an intertexual *An*. Avonlea thus exists as a Canadian landscape, but one framed by, and interpreted through, such things as traditional *haiku* stylistics. Anne now occupies, and speaks out of, a uniquely hybridized space, a composite of elements from Japanese poetry and Canadian geography.

As I will explain, translators employ various conventions and phrases from Japanese classical literature that institute uncanny resemblances between Anne and Japanese poetic paradigms. Such techniques add layers of *koten* (Japanese classics) as referents that orient the nuances of her personhood with Japanese culture. She becomes, as such, placeable and recognizable to a Japanese reader. Thus, I wish to expand the discussion by investigating how *Akage no An* conjures up an intercultural aesthetic milieu by interpolating conventions from Japanese classical literary heritage. Rather than relying on calque, or loanblends, Muraoka and Kakegawa prefer to insert words derived from an established vocabulary based on Japanese poetic classics. This *wafū* (Japanese-esque) style engages the sensitivity of the reader's background, viewing the original text through a lens pre-established within Japanese classical poetry. To emphasize this approach, Muraoka and Kakegawa use techniques of *shiki no irodori* (seasonal colourings) that derive from the conventions of Japanese poetry. Such a translational strategy exemplifies Hiraga Masako's sense of *iconicity* as a formative practice in the continuous tradition of Japanese poetry. The repetition of conventional words and forms as environmental referents can generate inferred meaning in *haiku* or *waka*. When *haiku* iconicity becomes integrated with Anne, an enormous impact can be made on a Japanese readership. Anne, likewise, is re-constellated according to Japanese poetic sensibilities, conventional moods such as *myô* (wonder), and *shizen to hitotsu* (nature and people in harmony). So, working with these principles, something as everyday as *the flowers of quiet happiness – shizuka-na kôfuku no hana / shizuka-na shiawase no hana –* emerge through tempering translation into a *haiku no sekai* (the *haiku* world, or mindset).[1] The paradigms of *shiki no irodori* as a mechanism for colouring Avonlea with a *haiku* palette thus remind the reader of a shared vision of a poeticized nature, one that resembles Avonlea as well as classical Japanese ambiences (*kotenteki*).

Sonja Arntzen, translator of the poet Ikkyû and the *Kagerô nikki (The Gossamer Years)*, has argued that Japanese-Canadian relationships, based on *Anne of Green Gables (Akage no An)*, must have a deeper correspondence than trivial tokens, such as red-haired wigs:

> We cannot say that the respect for Japanese poetry in Canada now is directly related to the Japanese enthusiasm for *Anne of Green Gables*, but it may be related to qualities in the work itself that resonate with Japanese culture. It suggests the existence of points of common ground between Japanese and Canadian culture (if indeed we take *Anne of Green Gables* as representative of Canadian culture) that may be unconscious to both the Japanese and the Canadians.[2]

Danièle Allard has, in likewise trying to identify a common ground or shared resonance, described the emphasis on natural imagery in the original novel as echoing a quality that "corresponds to the practices of classical Japanese literature."[3] Translators certainly had this echo in mind in terms of Japanese literary heritage. Indeed, they heightened the effect through deliberate uses of allusion, replacement vocabularies based on *kigo* (season words used in *haiku*), and other devices. The *Akage no An* translators thus merge a text in translation according to pre-arranged templates of classical Japanese literature (*koten*). These connotations engage the Japanese reader in a multivalent fashion: their own literary canon is reflected in a Canadian habitation. *Akage no An* thus acts, through intercultural sharing, as an appealing correction to certain entrenched prejudices on both sides of the Pacific. As a hybridized ground between Canada and Japan, this novel, now culturally diversified, challenges prevalent clichés and dichotomies: that *Westerners* are anthropocentric, or that the Japanese have a unique appreciation for nature. *Akage no An* realizes an intermixing of cultural ethos through the allusive procedures of translation, gaining, and sharing cultural ground.

When directly compared, many passages from *Akage no An* read similarly, in spirit and also in phrasing, to some of the Japanese poetic classics. Muraoka and Kakegawa heighten this effect of a dually registered Anne, one seemingly attuned to both Japanese and Canadian environments, by instilling in the text frequent allusions to Japanese classical literature, arts, and culture. Thus, an assessment of Japanese *readings* of this work, as particularly realized patterns, could be informed by identifying those indigenous contexts that influenced the translation and reception of *Anne of Green Gables*. Montgomery most likely did not study *haiku*, although she seems to have had a fondness for the *japonisme* of her time.[4] Likewise, the Japanese reception of Anne evidences a fancy for the trappings of Victorian rurality. *Akage no An* continues to be a striking contrast to the cyborgs, robot *anime*, and video game performances of Tokyo digital virtuality. When translators adopt Anne through a model of classical Japanese poetry and vocabulary, as well as style, they develop a transcultural textual locus in which to characterize the functions of an Anne who speaks both Shakespeare and Issa.

Anne's identity, as a global export, has been hugely popular in the world's imagination. But why her particular appeal has been to the Japanese has been a perennial question.[5] *Akage no An* has been the subject of a diverse range of publications in Japanese: several *manga* – including a multi-volume series published by Kumon, a televised *anime* series directed by Takahata Isao (1979), as well as costume museums and cookbooks. Anne has cachet for tourism: a couple might have a traditional Shintô ceremony in Japan and then travel to Prince Edward Island for a more relaxed, fanciful event. On this account, Okuda Miki has written a sensitive travelogue concerning such an experience, giving her impressions of contemporary Canadian life. During Expo 2005, in Aichi, Japan, the Canada Pavilion prominently enshrined a section dedicated to Anne. That summer, Princess Takamado, who also holds the title of *International Patron of the L.M. Montgomery Institute*, paid a formal visit. Certainly, *Akage no An* has been indexed as a commodity of wide commercial appeal, playing to sentiment and cultural curiosity. As scholars have noted, these tokens and public monuments indicate social popularity. But do these resultant fanfare forms, in fact, explain why such an enduring esteem for Anne had been established in the first place? Why has her appeal, especially so in Japan, persisted increasingly until 2008, the centenary anniversary of the English edition's publication?

In describing the prevalence of *Akage no An*, its position and orientation in Japanese literary and popular imaginations, critics have a responsibility to avoid ethnic generalizations: *Japanese people appreciate Anne because of* ... or other such broad formulae. At the same time, Japan's particular forms of attraction to Anne, the degree and diversity of enthusiasm, is uniquely realized and without comparison when compared to other nations. But identifying what constitutes the experience of the *Japanese reader*, as a social entity, is tricky. Allard hints at ways the text is "Striking Japanese Chords," or becomes a part of the "Japanese psyche."[6] Likewise, Baldwin has a sense of "The Japanese Connection" as an essential claim to Anne-ness.[7] But what are the forces causing these echoes and resonances? Is it something entirely driven by popular psychologies of idealizing the West? Kajihara argues for a social sympathy. Anne shows devotion to the elderly, particularly in her loyalty to Matthew and Marilla as her caretakers. Such a virtue is complementary to the Confucian ethos of ancestral relations and has a sympathetic parallel for the Japanese. Correspondences seem to exist between the ways that gender roles in Victorian Canada and the prescribed femininity defined and encouraged by Japanese society. Certainly, Japanese critics have evaluated *Anne of Green Gables* as an emotionally complex novel, exhibiting the four principal human feelings (*kidoairaku*) of joy, anger, pathos, and humour. In this way, Anne-in-Japan also upholds a defence of *kokoro* – heart, spirit, customs – in the hyper-technological twenty-first century.

Akage no An considered solely as an enactment of Occidentalist fantasy does not justify the depth and complexity of its relationship to Japanese reader-response. The text, rather than the visual apparatus that developed out of it, still receives the most attention. In terms of translations, there have been many, in all kinds of formats, including ones designed for early readers. Two complete renditions of the entire *Anne of Green Gables* series now exist: the first by Muraoka Hanako (Mikasa-shobô, 1952), still the most influential and highly regarded; and more recently by Kakegawa Yasuko (Kôdan-sha, 1999).[8] Academic scholarship includes such examples as Matsumoto Yûko's extensive study of Montgomery's use of Shakespearean references. As a kind of intercultural pedagogy for the classroom, Shimamoto Kaoru has written an ESL workbook, using the English of *Anne of Green Gables* for stylistic examples. Shimamoto analyzes dialogue from the novel as models of elegant

English usage. Documenting the influence of *Anne of Green Gables* on Japanese authors, Kajihara Yuka lists many contemporary writers and artisans in Japan who have described their debt to Montgomery's particular vision. These include a diverse range of authors, such as the children's writer Tachihara Erika and the novelist Takada Hiroshi. What such studies in Japanese begin to indicate is that the *Akage no An* phenomenon owes its origin first to textuality, the process of incorporation in which *Anne* becomes *An*.

When Anne speaks in Japanese as *An*, she sounds antiquated, but not necessarily marked as Western or Victorian. Translators create a voice for Anne by implementing distinctively Japanese stylistics, rather than replicating the Queen's English. Both Muraoka and Kakegawa prefer to use verbal registers associated with old-fashioned modes of Japanese speech. Examples of the archaically feminine (*o-jôhin*) project onto Anne the socio-cultural connotations of *yamato nadeshiko* (old-fashioned femininity). In becoming *An*, Anne takes on the enunciation associated with antiquated Japanese discourse. For example, Muraoka creates qualities of indirectness and archaic in Anne's speech inflections:

> *Atashi ni wa pinku to kiiroga niawanai koto wa wakatteru no.*
> "Oh. I know pink and yellow aren't becoming to me ... "[9]

Such translational choices create a distinctively female register: the use of *atashi* – the feminine first person singular – or, elsewhere, the interjection *ara*, as well as sentence tags such as *no* are used repeatedly by Muraoka. The passage above, taken from the start of chapter 12, depicts a form of *sahô* (education in manners) between Marilla and Anne, the relative status of each speaker defined by the format of language that they use. Although properly humble in this example, *An*'s dialogue also reveals an incongruity between her low social position and the highly elegant diction she employs. This *kihin ga aru* mode of speech demonstrates refinement, regardless of her lack of personal wealth or formal education. Unlike several Japanese versions of *Alice in Wonderland* (*Fushigi no kuni no Arisu*), Muraoka and Kakegawa strive not to modernize Anne's speech in a raucous or trendy manner. *Akage no An* establishes a Canadian backdrop, but one whose citizens are conversant in the etiquette norms of Japan. Thus, based on this situation, *haiku* or other cultural allusions are incorporated into the Japanese narrative without appearing as some poorly done ventriloquism. Anne must dually have a *haiku* voice combined with her original Canadian context. Translational patterns in oral communication thus can establish a cohesive base so that neither Japanese nor Canadian referents seem foreign.

Anne's Canadian context can be maintained, but with an additional layering of Japanese materialia that effect a multicultural common ground. Muraoka will, occasionally, use loanwords for rendering the book's trappings of Western culture. However, she will more likely substitute elements reflective of Japanese lifestyles. Thus, as Lotman and Uspensky describe, culturally specific lexical referents rework the textual space for the reader's imagination. For example, during Anne's first night at Green Gables, Muraoka has her sleep in a *momen no sashiko no futon*,[10] a traditional kind of Japanese bed with indigo handstitching. This culturally specific term replaces the English word, and concept, *bed*. Anne sleeping in such a Japanese manner, of course, is improbable. But Muraoka intentionally positions a Japanese milieu, rather than faithfully replicating the original. This traditional craft of *sashiko*, indicative of Japanese tradition and handicraft (*dentô*), deliberately inspires a more Nipponophilic mood. Likewise, Muraoka can achieve a heightened atmospheric which hearkens to Japaneseness by using ethnically encoded words such as *chôchin*, a paper lantern often associated with *o-bon*, the summer lantern festival and time for ancestral visitations. Matthew, in fact, carries such a lantern – not a *lamp* – when he searches for Anne on a lonely, wintry twilight.[11] Seasonally, *chôchin*, a summer object, does not match this scene. *Chôchin* and snow do not go together, according to cultural conventions. However, the sense of the older generation seeking out the younger, part of the theme of *o-bon*, is produced in Matthew's search for Anne. Such cultural miscegenations deliberately fuse disparate ethnic elements for multicultural effect. Another example of such is the *kinran* cloth, which is available in the Avonlea store while Matthew is dress shopping. *Kinran* refers to a kind of gold brocade whose patterns were imported from China during the Kamakura period, more suitable for a *kimono* or a monk's habit than puffy sleeves. Muraoka also notes the usual Western textiles, but also *kinran*, can be found in the furnishings of Green Gables. Likewise, one would not expect to find in the Maritimes, in that era, Buddhist institutions. None the less, Muraoka uses Japanese architectural terms in place of the original Christian landmarks: *ji'in*, a kind of temple, takes the place of "cathedral."[12]

Another issue for the translator involves the rendering of the extensive plant, flower, and tree names. A translator can preserve imagery as is, but at the expense of taxonomy. For example, in regards to the reoccurring mayflowers, Muraoka uses *sanzashi* (Japanese Hawthorn – *raphiolepis*).[13]

Sanzashi is a *kigo* for early spring. In the same passage, brown is *cha-iro* (tea-coloured). In another passage in which spring arrives with peeping mayflowers, Muraoka inserts the highly classical *harugasumi* (the emergence of spring colour) instead of using *sanzashi*.[14] *Harugasumi* is a key phrase prevalent throughout *koten*, including prominence in such standard texts as the *Kokinwakashû*, and is also the name of a song popular in the *shakuhachi* repertoire. Muraoka links Avonlea to the landscape of classical *waka* in such a way. Noticeably, Kakegawa does tend to prefer contemporary loanwords for flower names – Mayflower is *meifurawâ* – even if generally her characters' diction and syntax remain antiquated.[15] However, like Muraoka, she will use antiquated words such as *hakka* (mint) rather than the currently preferred *minto*. A further issue is the extent that the translation should retain climate-specific botanical terms. Arboreal references are crucial to the atmospheric referents of Montgomery's original. Thus, Muraoka will often find a close approximation to those species which are indigenous to the Canadian ecosystem. Japanese authors could keep a climatologically accurate translation for the Canadian original. For Muraoka, maples are always called *kaede*, the quintessential Canadian maple leaf, a sort which is different from the Japanese variety *momiji* (Acer palmatum). But, on occasion, she will use *botan* (Paeonia suffruticosa), the Japanese tree peony, rather than a loanword (*shaku*), which would be appropriate for the Canadian original. In these ways, nature, in the Japanese text, mixes different species of plants, sometimes faithful to geographic realism, and other times invoking the scenery of Japanese classical literature.

An understanding of climate and nature as primary elements in *haiku* and *Anne of Green Gables* has been a recurring topic for Japanese critics and translators. Their perspective, however, often differs from that of Western counterparts. For example, Margaret Anne Doody's introduction to *The Annotated Anne of Green Gables* allegorizes nature as being a manifestation of the characters' archetypal identities. Anne is a Persephone, a vegetation deity, and an inverted mother to the Madonna figure, Marilla.[16] These mythic equations orient the ecological content of this novel to the abstractions of thematic legend. Canadian folklore, which is one of Anne's scholarly interests, can be expanded through possible Japanese equivalents from folk studies (*minzoku*). The effect is subtle: no *tengu* appear or other goblin creatures appear in Avonlea. However, for Muraoka, the Grecian *dryad* becomes the more authentically Japanese *mori no yôsei*, or forest fairy.[17] Ghosts do not have to be culturally exclusive. Anne and Diana's search for the spectral would also remind a reader of the children's ghost-hunting games of summer (*kimodameshi*). Certainly, that Anne composes *kaidan* (ghost stories), based on her locale, would remind a reader of Lafcadio Hearn's work, or Ueda Akinari's collection, *Ugetsu monogatari* – a film version of which appeared in 1953. Japanese translations maintain Western mythology, when it is obviously apparent, but supplement native poetic practices that situate nature as a kind of experiential performance.

The episodic flow of the narrative follows a calendar of seasonal progression. From this quality, the customs of Japanese poetics find their clearest correspondences in Montgomery. From the moment of Anne's arrival at Avonlea, the novel's rotational energy develops firmly upon the revolving palettes of the seasons. An empowering potential for deep ecological sensitivity must come from a concentration of poetic attitude. Attention to the changes and natural revelations in the elemental world, intermixed with human affairs, constitutes much of the growth and self-development in Anne's poetic imagination:

> Every year
> Thinking of the chrysanthemums,
> Being thought of by them.[18]

> as she talked ...
>   wind and stars and fireflies
> were all tangled up together ... [19]

Spring, independently so, comes to Avonlea regardless of whether Anne is there or not: the floral indicator of a season "blooms as if it meant it."[20] Poetic stylization describes what *sort* of season comes, as filtered through the scopes of literary convention as well as a creative imagination. This is the aforementioned potency of *haiku* iconicity, one that helps to pattern the translation according to established paradigms. Thus, seasonality-in-itself in *Anne of Green Gables* produces many similarities to the panorama of the *haiku* world:

> Every night from now
>   Will dawn
> From the white plum-tree.[21]

> Here and there a wild plum leaned out from the bank like a
> white-clad girl tiptoeing to her own reflection.[22]

Or, consider these shared sympathies, which both describe the common-ality of the organic condition:

> Looking again at the chrysanthemums
> That lost.[23]

> They just looked
> like orphans themselves,
> those trees did.[24]

Anne's emotive identification with natural elements can resemble, in mode and expression, Kobayashi Issa's and the customs of other po-ets. Nature and author share a mutual existence, realized through in-terpersonal interjections, demonstrating the cherished concept of *shinra bansbô* (people and nature in harmony): "I shouldn't shorten their lovely lives by picking them – I wouldn't want to be picked if I were an apple blossom."[25] Anne's short, enthusiastic musings thus are likened to bits of *haiku* verse, producing a poetics of cultural impact.

A Japanese translator can further foster similarities between Anne and *koten* through the supplementation of classical syntax, allusion, stylis-tics, and vocabulary. On this point, Kôno Mariko's book Akage no An *hon'yaku ressun* describes the textual play of nature in the novel as hear-kening back to pre-modern poetry collections. Kôno is also comparing *Anne of Green Gables* to a *saijiki*, or *haiku* almanac, through its customs in using season words. Allard finds that Muraoka's translation often uses phrases developed on the standard syllabic patterns (5–7–5) of *tanka* and *haiku*.[26] The rhythmic quality of short passages thus can beat out along a traditional meter; and the use of specific poetic vocabulary accentuates a *koten* aura for Avonlea. Anne can be seen as having a *haiku*-like voice in how she views nature's charm as immanent and expe-riential. This quality is also apparent by comparing English translations with Montgomery:

> Coming along the mountain path.
> There is something touching
> About these violets.[27]

> a fascination of its own,
> that bend ...
> I wonder how the road beyond it goes[28]

The interpolation of iconic phrases, from *koten*, within Avonlea confirms the supposition of a trans-national milieu, as interstices between culture and linguistics. Muraoka and Kakegawa's writings implement *kigo* conventions into the translation.[29] Avonlea now references specifically Japanese landscape features and their cultural connotations, through the season word. Such additions recast the original English with the nuances of a *koten* poetic palette. Such a pronounced effect immediately draws in the Japanese language reader into an augmented text that strikes a chord with previously known literary examples. The *resonances* of these phrases have power because of their culturally denotative implications, even though here transferred onto the context of a Canadian novel. Japanese and Canadian linguistic and environmental features intermingle, imaginatively, through lexical choices. Thus, *Akage no An*, received as something foreign, can simultaneously be marked as something indigenous. This careful hybridization, revealed as a quality of Anne speaking in the mode of Japanese classics, enhances a process of self-identification for a readership. For example, when Anne sets out to fetch the ipecac bottle, Muraoka describes the cold outdoors with an evocative *kigo*, *yukigeshiki* – *snowy landscape* – instead of "snowy places."[30] *Yukigeshiki* has iconic power because of its repetitious use historically as a poetic idiom. It can correspond with quintessential images of Canada as the snow-country, but the term also summons an established vocabulary for the feelings associated with a frosty climate.[31] In such instances, the *saijiki*, as a common catalogue of such entrenched season words in Japanese poetics, provides Muraoka and Kakegawa with an affective set of phrases that serve as contextualizing feature for translation. Avonlea as an imaginative domain is reoriented through drawn parallels to *haiku* perspectives.

One of the strongest examples of *kigo*, as a replacement for the English original, is Muraoka's substitution of *yamazakura* for "wild cherry tree."[32] At face value, this is perfectly acceptable, as *yamazakura* (mountain cherry) grow uncultivated in raw, natural environs, and thus are "wild cherry trees." However, considered as an extension of Japanese tradition, this spring *kigo* has vivid connotations. Visually, the word calls to mind widely known examples, such as the *Yoshitaka no ôzakura*, in Chiba prefecture, a magnificent specimen that is a national treasure as well as a local landmark. *Yamazakura* is the title of a folk song (*min'yô*), often learned by beginners on folk instruments. *Yamazakura* have extensive allusive value in Japanese poetics. The *Man'yôshû* and *Genji monogatari* both include several references to it and its particular features (untamed prettiness, spontaneity). As a sign of natural regeneration compared to the decay of urban marketplaces, one poet famously wrote in the *Senzaishû*:

> *sazanami ya / shiga no miyako wa arenishi wo*
> *mukashi nagara no / yamazakura kana*

> Shiga, the capital, near the rippling waves, left now to ruins:
> the mountain cherries remain unchanged.

Rather reminiscent of Anne, the following verse by Issa describes the mountain cherries as companion, caregiver, and comforter to the wanderer:

> *yamazakura kami naki hito ni kazasaruru*[33]

> Mountain cherry blossoms: an embellishment of hair to a bald man.

Also, in the *Hyakunin isshu*, a famous poem describes the *yamazakura* as true friendship, realized in the lonely isolation of the hillsides:

> *Morotomo ni ahareto omoe yamazakura hanayori hoka*
> *ni shiruhitomo nashi.*

> Mountain slope cherry tree: solitary and friendless –
> it is you alone who knows me.

Written by Gyoson, a *shugendô* ascetic, the poem above describes the *yamazakura* as possessing the generosity of spirit truly capable of understanding the monk's *kokoro*. And Anne expresses this kind of sentiment on many occasions: "Can I take the apple blossoms with me for company?"[34]

The above examples of *kigo* in Muraoka are embedded patterns within broader frameworks of translation and cross-representation. Muraoka's deliberate placing of such words at critical points in the novel places a subtext of *koten* as an appurtenant dimension to Anne's identity in translation. These references, combined with renderings that draw attention to traditional aesthetic values in Japanese poetry, have an acclimatizing effect on the reader. *Kigo* such as *yamazakura* carry intensive value as a distinct characteristic of Japan, with centuries of poetic embellishment and perspectives. Muraoka has brought forth a kind of *haibun*, passages of prose containing *haiku* interpolations. Even if the atmospheric setting is clearly the geography of PEI, inserting a vocabulary connotative of Japanese *furusato* (hometown) identities connects *An* to an intercultural common space. This translational practice of blending enhances a textual atmosphere of shared heritages, communities, and poetics. The translator superimposes a Japanese poetic vernacular onto the foreign landscape. Japanese topical colourings derive their connotations as iconic tradition. Thus, *kigo* or other cultural allusions act as supplementary referents to the original Avonlea landscape.

Will Ferguson's travelogue about Japan, *Hitching Rides with Buddha*, exposed ·Western audiences to Japan's national obsession for cherry blossoms, as the cascading arrival of spring. Newsreaders announce the expanding *sakura zensen* – the cherry-blossom front – with meteorological precision. *O-hanami*, the festive activity of blossom appreciation, involves socializing and not just passive viewing. Picnics, complete with music and drink, lure entire communities into the outdoors. This enjoyable activity has spread across the Pacific, and now both Vancouver and Washington include *o-hanami* events as part of the public calendar. Contests for composing *haiku* in English, dedicated to these imported trees, feature prominently on these occasions. Canada has imported Japanese festivals and their customs, just as Muraoka and Kakegawa overlaid a thematic of Japanese nature onto Montgomery. *Anne of Green Gables* keenly feels the distinctive presence of the cherry blossom. In a novel that showcases the richness of the local flora, cherry blossoms receive particular consideration. Cherry trees are amongst the first arboreal features identified:

> a glimpse of the bloom white cherry trees in the left orchard …

> *shiroi sakura no hana ga massakari dashi*[35]

Such original references had been expanded and augmented through the more complex poetic argot of Japanese for describing the variety of cherry blossoms. And, to increase this emphasis on something iconically Japanese, Kakegawa will have Anne referring *specifically* to a cherry tree (*sakura*), even if the original reference is generic: "*Ara, sakura no ki no koto dake ittanjanai wa.*" *Sakura* here is substitutive for the nameless tree in the original: "Oh, I don't mean just the tree."[36] The *sakura*, as a predominant feature of both Japan and Prince Edward Island, balances with the nationalist tenor of the emblematic Canadian maple leaf. Asai Ryôi's classic *Ukiyo monogatari* (*Tales of the Floating World*, 1661) affirms that personal delight in the pleasures of maple and cherry trees is a practical form of spirituality. According to Asai, if we give our full attention to the chromatic and emotional changes that accompany the turning of the seasons, then the beauty of nature's evanescence becomes ours to behold. In *Akage no An*, the *yamazakura* of the Japanese classics coexists peacefully with the maple leaf in the landscape.

As another strategy for adding a dimension of *koten*, Muraoka and Kakegawa portray Anne as exhibiting the aesthetic ethos found in those poetic classics. For example, *sabi* – often translated as spareness or simplicity – was a virtue espoused by many poets, including Ikkyû, Ryôkan, Saigyô, Santôka. *Sabi* can amusingly be reflected in Anne's homely flower-arranging habits, rather like *ikebana*, that annoy Marilla:

" ... Look at these maple branches. Don't they give you a thrill – several thrills? I'm going to decorate my room with them."

"Messy things," said Marilla ... "You clutter up your room entirely too much with out-of-doors stuff, Anne. Bedrooms were made to sleep in."

"Oh, and dream in too, Marilla ... "

Ara, sorekara yume o mirutamedemo aru wa.[37]

Dreams, to Marilla, concern themselves with conceit and self-indulgence. Marilla is inclined towards proselytizing rather than poetry. Muraoka replicates Marilla's tendencies by putting didactic proverbs into her mouth, such as *zenrei-zenshin* (all of one's soul and heart).[38]

But, for Anne, poetry and nature must coincide. Thus, overextended intellectual analysis ruins the pleasure of the text: "They had analyzed [a poem] and parsed it and torn it to pieces in general until it was a wonder there was any meaning at all left in it for them." This passage is made to parallel a nearby act of environmental destruction: "Idlewild was a thing of the past, Mr. Bell having ruthlessly cut down the little circle of trees in his back pasture in the spring."[39] Anne delights in the flowers of quiet happiness, the simplicity of everyday beauty as she discovers its expression. Anne appears like the model of the wandering monk-poet Santôka, her red carpet-bag in tow, her clothes patched and well-worn. Anne is fond of elaborate attire and cotillions as well, but a fundamental attribute of her character is the direct appreciation of the sensual, dramatic beauty of nature.

The novel's narrative unfolds according to such observations of seasonal signs, which are temporal indicators and environmental habitats. *Anne of Green Gables*' observations then become augmented through *kigo*. Intentional allusion can be made by choosing translations that echo, for example, a well-known Japanese melody: for example, "Spring had come ... in a succession of sweet, fresh, chilly days, with pink sunsets and miracles of resurrection and growth."[40] Kakegawa renders this phrase, at the start of chapter 20, as *Haru ga yatte kita*,[41] which closely resembles the title of the famous *min'yô* (folk song) *Haru ga kita*. Thus, an original text which had been rather Chaucerian now sings to a Japanese classical melody.

In expression, as well as allusion, poetic interjections in the narrative seem like intimate parallels with *haiku*, in translated versions into English or Japanese:

> Deep autumn;
> My neighbour,
> How does he live?[42]

> Maples are such sociable trees ...
> they're always rustling
> and whispering to you.[43]

Anne understands time's passing in a *saijiki*-like manner by examining a season topic (*kidai*) through its representative natural phenomena: "I'm so glad I live in a world where there are Octobers. It would be terrible if we just skipped from September to November."[44] By using literary templates, as lexical phrases or thematic materials, Anne poetically engages the environment, as a drama of identification:

> Listen to the trees talking in their sleep ...
> What nice dreams they must have!
> *Kigi ga nemurinagara o-hanashishiteiru no o, kiitegorannasai.*[45]

> Have you ever noticed what cheerful things brooks are?
> They're always laughing. Even in wintertime
> I've heard them under the ice.
> *Ogawa no warai koe ga, koko made kikoetekuru wa.*[46]

These passages move beyond personification and into an ecological sensitivity that erases the usual human selfishness. As *haiku* tends to do, psychical barriers between environment and self-consciousness are blurred through poetic cross-identification. Thus, Anne has used poetry, rather than the abstract theology of Marilla's prayerbook, to expose the earthy connotations of *kokoro*:

> And that tea-rose –
> why, it's a song and a hope
> and a prayer all in one.[47]

> Alone tilling the fields,
> a song will come.
> (*Hitori tagayaseba utau nari*)[48]

Although a more dazzling portrait than Bashô's *furu ike* (the old pond), Anne's attention to natural habitats, as a source of poetic instigation, resembles this *haiku* master: "Now I'll look back. Good night, dear Lake of Shining Waters. I always say good night to the things I love, just as I would to people. I think they like it. That water looks as if it was smiling at me."[49] The ripples return the gaze physically, not metaphorically: neither the pond nor Anne confuse or lose one another in the simplicity of experiential moment. This displays the poetic virtue of *myô* (wonder) – the original *kanji* incorporates the radical for *woman* with *small* or *young. Myô* is Anne's endearing impetuousness, her crisp freshness that comes from the quickness of uninhibited inspiration. Bashô's famous *old-pond* poem, according to apocryphal tradition, was a sudden expression of *satori*, or comprehension: "Something just flashes into your mind, so exciting, and you must out with it. If you stop to think it over you spoil it all."[50] *Myô* is, then, not only a quality of the original English, but a mechanism for demonstrating Anne's fundamental ability to absorb the nuances of her surroundings, part Avonlea and part Japanese landscapes. Translators create a *haiku* phraseology for Anne: she acts as an *objet trouvé* of already understood *koten* sensibilities to a Japanese reader.[51]

Anne resembles *haiku* not only in lexical inflections, but also in attitude and perspective. Japanese readers are drawn to the aesthetic of *ninjô* in the novel, a term that describes human kindness, enhanced by the beauty of nature. *Ninjô* is when Anne and Matthew connect to one another through the common ground of the "little white Scotch rosebush," the one that his mother brought out from Scotland long ago: "Matthew always liked those roses the best."[52] *Ninjô* coexists with *shizen* (nature), and this interrelationship has been the sensibility of unity between nature and humanity: known as *shizen to hitotsu*, this has been a prominent feature of the *haiku* poetess Chiyo-ni, whom Anne resembles in spirit and also in letter:

> I was down to the graveyard
> to plant a rosebush on Matthew's grave
> this afternoon.[53]

> In our parting,
> Between boat and shore
> Comes the willow-tree.[54]

As the rosebush's roots had connected Matthew to his mother, now Matthew and Anne coexist through the *kigo* of springtime. This human sharing of *ninjô* proceeds from the novel's first accident, suggesting strongly the concept of *en*, or destined chance, a word readily used in modes of Buddhist thought. This novel's message of a cyclic sense, in phrases similar to Ikkyû's, that "All things great are wound up with all things little."[55] Anne acts like a *haiku* poet, receiving the energy of life, which is made of *ninjô* greetings and goodbyes. The mood of *ichi-go ichi-e* runs throughout Muraoka and Kakegawa. And, importantly, these experiences open up the promissory emergence of "new landscapes" and new relationships.[56] On this theme, Matsumoto finds the most compelling feature of the novel: optimism is empowering to women, in any culture or time.

Anne of Green Gables has a Japanese counterpart in Tsuboi Sakae's *Ni-jû-shi no hitomi* (*Twenty-Four Eyes*), one of the first anti-war novels to appear in the early 1950s, around the same time as Muraoka's translation. Tsuboi's novel depicts how a new, unorthodox teacher – a strange arrival to a rural island – slowly wins over village distrust through persistence and energy. Decidedly pacifist in tone, the pastoral provinciality of the island is torn open by *kamikaze* conscription, as the Pacific War turned villagers into human bombs. In a similar way, the Anne series concludes with Walter's death in the European trenches and the senseless murder of millions. In the post-war situation of Japanese-Canadian relations, *Anne of Green Gables* has been a common ground of reconciliation. Muraoka Mie, granddaughter of the translator, has ardently described Anne as a humanitarian voice: "It is not exaggerating to say that even though Japan and Canada have had over hundred years of contact, the translation of *Anne of Green Gables* lead to a closer understanding and friendship between two countries."[57] Muraoka Mie rightly points out that the *translation*, long before tourism and tokenism, initiated a common ground of intertextuality, one that had led to social good will and understanding. Thus, the literary act deserves most of the credit for introducing Anne's sense of "the beautiful world of blossom and love and friendship" to Japanese readers.[58] Kindred Spirit in Japanese, *fukushin no tomo*, contains the lexical element *kokoro* combined with the word for friendship. This, after all, describes both the translational and multicultural spirit of Kakegawa and Muraoka. They open up, through *Anne of Green Gables*, an emergent space for transnational friendships: "Kindred spirits are not so scarce as I used to think. It's splendid to find out there are so many of them in the world."[59]

In *Akage no An*, the particulars of the Canadian environment have been sympathetically re-configured through iconic terminology, ones that invoke an aesthetic tradition. Comparatively, a recent work entitled *In L.M.'s Garden*, edited by Becky D. Alexander, exhibited a large selection of *haiga* (a painting by a *haiku* author, usually accompanied by a poem) in English, inspired by the L.M. Montgomery gardens in Norval, Ontario, where Montgomery lived with her husband and sons for ten years. Westerners are using *shiki no irodori* to likewise appreciate Montgomery. The forms and patterns of *haiku* and *waka* foreground Anne against a poetic legacy:

> This dewdrop world –
> It may be a dewdrop,
> And yet – and yet – [60]

> "Dear old world," she murmured,
> "you are very lovely, and
> I am glad to be alive in you."[61]

Alexander shows that the sharing of conventions between Japanese and Canadian literature is coming full circle. English-language *haiga* is confirming Muraoka and Kakegawa's fundamental strategy. Classical Japanese poetry, as a stylistic template, enables translators to integrate Anne with the aura of *koten*. *An no kokoro* thus reveals an intercultural space of kindred connections across societies and geographies.

NOTES

All Japanese names are given in their traditional format: surname followed by given name. I am grateful to Danièle Allard and Sonja Arntzen for our conversations and for permission to quote from their works. I would like to thank the anonymous reader, whose suggestions and advice were of great value.

1 AGG, 307; Montgomery, *Akage no An*, translated by Muraoka Hanako, 421; Montgomery, *Akage no An*, translated by Kakegawa Yasuko, 312.

2 Sonja Arntzen, "Exchange? Canada and Japan's *Anne of Green Gables*," *Ex/Change*, Centre for Cultural Studies, City University of Hong Kong, http://www.cityu.edu.hk/ccs/Newsletter/newsletter3/HomePage/Exchange-Canada/ExchangeCanada.html. The City University of Hong Kong invited Arntzen to compose this article, on Anne's relation to multiculturalism in Japan, for its newsletter.

3 Allard, "The Popularity of *Anne of Green Gables*," 148.

4 The website for a Montgomery conference (University of PEI in 2002) featured a self-portrait of the author. In this picture, she has posed herself in chiaroscuro light, a net veil over her face, and a golden Japanese fan displayed on a nearby bookshelf. There is nothing in Montgomery's collected letters or journals that evidences any longstanding interest in Japanese poetry.

5 This phenomenon is well-documented. For PEI as a Japanese tourist destination, see Baldwin, "L.M. Montgomery's"; Trillin, "Anne of Red Hair"; Stoffman, "Anne in Japanese Popular Culture." For a wry description of a Canadian working as a costumed Anne in a Japanese-owned theme park, see Roseanne Harvey, "Between Stops," http://www.writersfest.bc.ca/news/harvey.htm.

6 Allard, "The Popularity of *Anne of Green Gables*," 147, 51.

7 Baldwin, "Anne of Red Hair." Definitions of what or whom might constitute a *Japanese readership*, in relation to this novel, can also be found in Akamatsu, "Japanese Readings," and Katsura, "Red-Haired Anne in Japan." For a compelling discussion of Anne, gender, and Japanese society, see Ogura, "Sengo Nihon to *Akage no An*." She explores how Montgomery's personal life, reflected in Muraoka, had a compelling meaning to Japanese women in the post-war generation.

8 With Muraoka's death, copyright first passed on to her daughter Midori, who has licensed all subsequent printings (which we now read) according to the corrected 1954 edition that appeared with Shinchô-sha, a far larger publisher. This year, Muraoka's granddaughter, Mie, has released a third version of the text, which includes a large number of emendations,

corrections, and additionally translated passages omitted from Muraoka Hanako's original version.

9 Montgomery, *Akage no An*, translated by Muraoka, 121; *AGG*, 84.

10 Montgomery, *Akage no An*, translated by Muraoka, 6.

11 Montgomery, *Akage no An*, translated by Muraoka, 363; *AGG*, 254.

12 *AGG*, 17.

13 Montgomery, *Akage no An*, translated by Muraoka, 234.

14 Ibid., 404.

15 Montgomery, *Akage no An*, translated by Kakegawa, 164.

16 Doody, Introduction, 32, 29, 26.

17 Montgomery, *Akage no An*, translated by Muraoka, 234.

18 Masaoka Shiki, in Blyth, *Haiku*, 4: 1126. Unless otherwise noted as Blyth, translations of Japanese texts are my own.

19 *AGG*, 180.

20 *AGG*, 31.

21 Yosa Buson, in Blyth, *Haiku*, 2: 583.

22 *AGG*, 19.

23 Kobayashi Issa, in Blyth, *Haiku*, 4: 1125.

24 *AGG*, 15.

25 *AGG*, 60.

26 Allard, "The Popularity of *Anne of Green Gables*," 80.

27 Matsuo Bashô, in Blyth, *Haiku*, 2: 638.

28 *AGG*, 303.

29 *Kigo*, or season words, are prominent features of *haiku*. Briefly described, they are set terms, refined through convention and usage, that indicate the seasonal setting of a poem through environmental associations, climate conditions, or cultural allusivity.

30 Montgomery, *Akage no An*, translated by Muraoka, 213; *AGG*, 145.

31 The *Shin Nihon dai-saijiki (fuyu)* lists multiple examples of this *kigo* (71). Further examples can be found in *Haiku saijiki*, including, "*Enpitsu no sende egakishi yukigeshiki* (334) / "I can draw only a pencil's line for the snowy landscape" (Setsuga Kyôryû).

32 Montgomery, *Akage no An*, translated by Muraoka, 23; *AGG*, 12. For comparison, consider Kakegawa, who uses a more generic *sakura no ki* (19). *Sakura* is the umbrella term for many different species of cherry trees. Although a legitimate *kanji* exists, Kakegawa writes *sakura* phonetically in *katakana*, thus giving this Canadian cherry tree a non-Japanese accent. *Katakana* is generally reserved for rendering vocabulary from foreign languages.

33 Kobayashi, *Issa zenshû*, 2: 429.

34 *AGG*, 59.
35 *AGG*, 4; Montgomery, *Akage no An*, translated by Muraoka, 9.
36 Montgomery, *Akage no An*, translated by Kakegawa, 38; *AGG*, 31.
37 *AGG*, 120; Montgomery, *Akage no An*, translated by Muraoka, 175. The modern *Sogetsu* school especially values arrangements culled from windfallen branches and scattered flowers, displayed simply and without contraptions.
38 Montgomery, *Akage no An*, translated by Muraoka, 277.
39 *AGG*, 221.
40 *AGG*, 160.
41 Montgomery, *Akage no An*, translated by Kakegawa, 165.
42 Matsuo Bashô, in Blyth, *Haiku*, 3: 896.
43 *AGG*, 106. Kakegawa uses *katakana* again for *kaede*, but translates this section using poetic onomatopoeia, using the auditory effects found in *haiku*: "*Itsumo sarasara edo o yusutte, sasayakikakete kureru no*" (110).
44 *AGG*, 120.
45 *AGG*, 22; Montgomery, *Akage no An*, translated by Muraoka, 37.
46 *AGG*, 31–32; Montgomery, *Akage no An*, translated by Kakegawa, 38–39. *Haru no ogawa* (The Spring Brook) is an exceptionally famous folk song.
47 *AGG*, 289.
48 Santôka, *Santôka zen kushû*, 76.
49 *AGG*, 20.
50 *AGG*, 156.
51 The English language debate as to what constitutes *haiku* is varied and complex. R.H. Blyth disseminated a notion that *haiku* exhibit realizations and epiphanies expressive of Zen belief. Blyth's views are not without their detractors, but I have used his editions because of their comprehensiveness and dual-language format.
52 *AGG*, 297.
53 *AGG*, 297.
54 Masaoka Shiki, in Blyth, 2: 563.
55 *AGG*, 138.
56 *AGG*, 303.
57 "Mie Muraoka's Speech at the Reception Held by the Dept. of Tourism Parks in PEI in 1989," http://club.pep.ne.jp/~r.miki/speech_e.htm.
58 *AGG*, 296.
59 *AGG*, 159.
60 Kobayashi Issa, in Blyth, 3: 968.
61 *AGG*, 306.

20

Archival Adventures with L.M. Montgomery; or, "As Long as the Leaves Hold Together"

—— 2012 ——

VANESSA BROWN AND BENJAMIN LEFEBVRE

In this final chapter, published in the collection of essays *Basements and Attics, Closets and Cyberspace: Explorations in Canadian Women's Archives*, an antiquarian appraiser and I – both of whom share a long-standing interest in L.M. Montgomery's work and legacy – discuss our respective findings in the Montgomery archives. Each of us interested, albeit for different reasons, in the puzzle surrounding Montgomery's death in 1942, we discuss the ways in which surviving papers end up shaping not only a body of literary work but also an author's cultural legacy.

In her introduction to the collection of essays *Working in Women's Archives* (2001), Helen M. Buss considers how each contributor to the volume has been working at "the tentative beginnings of what we now see as the fortuitous coming together of feminist theory, the breaking of traditional limitations set by the idea of a literary 'canon' of great writers and the increased use of archives to rescue a female tradition in writing."[1] In the case of L.M. Montgomery (1874–1942), the trajectory of her critical reputation in many ways mimics the dominant pattern tracked by the contributors to this current volume:[2] she has long been (and in many ways remains) marginalized by the expanded canon of Canadian literature as a result of her gender, popular appeal, and misrepresentation, generalization, and devaluation as a children's writer. That said, she remains a unique case study as a result of the fact that all her books – including her most popular, *Anne of Green Gables* (1908) and *Emily of New Moon* (1923), and their sequels – remain in print in the twenty-first century; in fact, most of them have never been out of print.[3]

In addition to her continued popularity, the academic field of L.M. Montgomery Studies was significantly stimulated by the simultaneous appearance in late 1985 of the first volume of *The Selected Journals of L.M. Montgomery*, published by Oxford University Press, and Kevin Sullivan's adaptation of *Anne of Green Gables* as a television miniseries. Although the Sullivan production and its sequels renewed Montgomery's popularity by introducing her and her characters to the mass medium of television, the publication of the journals by an established university press had an unprecedented effect on Montgomery's status within and beyond the academy. As Cecily Devereux notes in her review of the fourth volume, published in 1998, "These journals, the handwritten originals of which are held at the McLaughlin Library, University of Guelph, are extraordinary documents, not only in terms of the information they provide about living, writing, and being a woman in English Canada in the first half of the twentieth century, but also because they have radically complicated our understanding of Montgomery."[4]

Although the continued availability of primary Montgomery texts makes her an anomaly in relation to the recovery of women's writing in Canada, what has not been adequately documented is the central role that the archive has played in the recuperation of Montgomery as a subject worthy of study. The detailed work of researchers who have combed the Montgomery archives for crucial new information about the author and her work, and the publication of a number of posthumous Montgomery texts since 1960 – including diaries, letters, photographs, scrapbooks, periodical pieces, and rediscovered typescripts, in addition to the five-volume *Selected Journals* – has led to a series of reconsiderations about her primary work and its significance.[5] Moreover, the "rescue" that Buss mentions above has, at times, been literal: as Mollie Gillen explains in her account of tracking down the nephew of one of Montgomery's correspondents just as he had decided to burn forty years of her letters, "I was just in time."[6]

In what follows, two researchers with vastly different professional backgrounds discuss their respective approaches to and discoveries in the L.M. Montgomery archives, each drawn, personally and professionally, to the puzzle about the end of Montgomery's life in 1942. Vanessa Brown is an antiquarian book cataloguer in London, Ontario, who was a prize winner in the Bibliographical Society of Canada's 2009 National Book Collecting Contest for her collection of rare editions and ephemera related to Montgomery. Benjamin Lefebvre, an academic with a background in Canadian literature and cultural studies, edited Montgomery's rediscovered final book, *The Blythes Are Quoted* (2009), which was reportedly delivered to Montgomery's publishers the very day of her death. Of concern to both are statements made by Montgomery that show the decisions she made about documents and artifacts she wanted to leave behind as the official records of her life. Independently and collaboratively, Brown and Lefebvre discovered that, although the Montgomery archives reveal missing pieces to the overall puzzle, they also point to the impossibility of conclusive answers.

VB: My first exposure to Montgomery was the 1985 miniseries by Kevin Sullivan. I then made quick work of reading all the Anne books and everything else Montgomery wrote. I could closely relate to her heroines then, because I was a bookish child who used big words and lived a lot in my head. As I became an adult, however, I started identifying more with Montgomery than with her characters. I began to grasp the darker elements in her fiction and journals. Whereas as a child I used to look up to Anne, as an adult I look up to Maud and admire her ambition – as she found it in the poem "The Fringed Gentian" – to

> reach that far-off goal
> Of true and honored fame
> And write upon its shining scroll
> A woman's humble name.[7]

BL: I started out with *Road to Avonlea* (1990–1996), which was first on television when I was a teenager, and then with Montgomery's novel *The Story Girl* (1911), which was one of the books used as a foundation for the television series. I've never been the "typical" Montgomery reader – I tend to prefer the realistic social community aspects to Montgomery's work over the romantic parts (which I don't find believable) or the effusive nature descriptions (which I tend to skip). Still, there is something about Montgomery that I have found highly addictive. After reading *Anne of Green Gables* and its sequels in high school, I read and reread all her novels and collections of short stories, continued with journals, letters, and literary criticism, then went to graduate school to learn new ways to study her work. In a way, I've been attracted to the Montgomery archives because they've given me the opportunity to *keep on reading* – to postpone indefinitely the end to Montgomery's work.

VB: For antiquarians, the archives offer a similar never-ending treasure hunt. Although both academics and antiquarians seek buried treasure, antiquarians focus on the materiality of the objects themselves (preferably a first edition with a dust jacket!), rather than solely on the information they convey. Acquiring Montgomery-related items is likewise addictive in this way; despite or perhaps because of her popularity, first editions and the like are scarce. Even more so are letters and other ephemeral objects related to her life. The rarest Montgomery artifacts in several archival collections across Canada make them a reference point both for the uniqueness of the information they contain and for the value of the objects themselves, which are of interest to antiquarians and scholars alike. The archives also secure the availability of these important cultural objects, where in a free market the interests of private collectors can conflict with the needs of those studying Montgomery. In my collection, I have a book that belonged to Montgomery, and I know it should be in an archive along with the rest of her personal library. However, part of me feels that no one deserves to own it like I do, that no one will appreciate it like I will. The problem is that most collectors think this way. If it weren't for archives, all of these great Montgomery-related artifacts would belong to private collectors and would never be part of the public conversation about her work. If her journals and letters had remained in private collections, the field of Montgomery Studies would be very different today.

BL: We owe so much to archival collections at the University of Guelph, the University of Prince Edward Island, McMaster University, Library and Archives Canada, and the Confederation Centre Art Gallery and Museum in Charlottetown, not only for acquiring and preserving these unique documents, but also for making them available to those interested in researching Montgomery's life and legacy. Still, we shouldn't underestimate the combination of timing, good luck, and persistence that led to the acquisition of these materials in the first place. Mary Rubio, who edited Montgomery's journals for publication in collaboration with Elizabeth Waterston, tells the story of her effort to persuade the University of Guelph in the early 1980s to purchase Montgomery's journals from her son, Stuart Macdonald. Dr. Macdonald had inherited not only the ten ledgers of handwritten entries covering the period 1889 to 1942 but also the responsibility of having their contents published after a sufficient amount of time had elapsed. Guelph was the logical place for these items, primarily because it was the academic home of Rubio, Waterston, and the journal *Canadian Children's Literature*, which had published a special issue on Montgomery in 1975; it was also a logical place for the deposition of her papers because of Montgomery's connection to the archive's existing Scottish Studies collection (since she was a Canadian woman of Scottish ancestry). It was this connection that convinced the then-chief librarian – who also had fond memories of reading *Anne of Green Gables* as a child – to advocate for their purchase.[8] Countless additional items were donated to Guelph after Stuart Macdonald's death in 1982, and today, Guelph's L.M. Montgomery Collection is a must-see for anyone looking for archival documents related to Montgomery.

VB: In spite of such extensive archives, researchers are often frustrated in their archival work because they are restricted to working with photocopies or digital images, even if they want to see the original object. My experience as an appraiser in handling valuable documents has often helped me get around these barriers. Someone studying Montgomery from an academic viewpoint could also benefit from this access. As Elizabeth Rollins Epperly noted in "Revisiting Archives," a lecture she gave at a conference devoted to Montgomery held at the University of Guelph in 2008, "Most of us who visit archives and work with original materials do get to find things that no one else may have noticed." This desire to examine original artifacts is counterbalanced by the absolute necessity of preserving them for future generations. Every time someone handles a piece of paper, its integrity is weakened, which is why Guelph's plans to digitize archival documents related to Montgomery is vital for preservation.[9] Still, I have to agree with Epperly that "copies, no matter how useful for one level of study, cannot definitively solve puzzles or subtly suggest intimate feelings."[10]

BL: Montgomery was conscious enough of the value of these important documents that she left detailed instructions concerning their use after her death, not only in her will but also in the items themselves. Beginning in the winter of 1919, Montgomery began to transcribe her journals into uniform ledgers, each one five hundred pages. She claimed to "be careful to copy it exactly as it is written,"[11] although scholars find it hard to believe that she did so without making any alterations based on her growing awareness of their cultural value. Once this was done in 1922, she made an explicit declaration about her intentions for them beyond her lifetime:

> But today I finished copying my journal into uniform volumes. It has been a long piece of work but an interesting one ...
>
> This journal is a faithful record of one human being's life and so should have a certain literary value. My heirs might publish an *abridged volume* after my death, if I do not myself do it before ...
>
> I *desire that these journals never be destroyed but kept as long as the leaves hold together.* I leave this to my descendants or my literary heirs as a sacred charge and invoke a Shakespearean curse on them if they disregard it. There is so much of myself in these volumes that I cannot bear the thought of their ever being destroyed. It would seem to me like a sort of murder ... [12]

Montgomery's caveat about the possibility of an "abridged volume" would return in the 1930s, when she began a typescript of selected entries for precisely this purpose.[13] Rubio and Waterston would then use the handwritten ledgers as the basis for the five published volumes of *Selected Journals*. What I find fascinating here is the sheer effort to which Montgomery goes: even while acknowledging that only selections of their contents could (or should) be published, she also intended the ten uniform ledgers to stand on their own as the "official" record of her life. The process of the recovery of Montgomery's work is thus begun by Montgomery herself, in anticipation of future reconsideration.

The eventual publication of these journals certainly opened up the field of Montgomery Studies, because they reveal a woman who, even under the guise of absolute frankness, is surprisingly cryptic and elusive about several aspects of her life, particularly in the later journals concerning some of the dynamics in her own family. In many ways, her gifts as a natural storyteller might have impeded her commitment to writing a "faithful" record of her life, since the journals contain her version of how she wished to be remembered. In a retrospective diary entry dated January 9, 1938, but pertaining to events from January 1937, she revealed that although she had not written in her journal in over a year, she had nevertheless kept a daily record of events: "But such records were little else than shrieks of anguish. I knew they must not be preserved as they were. They were too dreadful – too bitter. I shall copy some of them in a condensed form here, so that this account of a most unhappy life will be complete. But there are many things I cannot write – for this journal will be read by others when I am dead and there are some things it would not be good for anyone but myself to know. It is bitter enough that I know them – and can never forget them – and cannot tell them – to anyone."[14] Bearing this kind of entry in mind, it is perhaps less surprising that her journals end abruptly almost three years before her death, save for two final entries – the first in July 1941, the second in March 1942 – that show Montgomery's despair with life. "Oh God, forgive me," she wrote in an entry dated a month before her death. This was revealed to the public with the publication of the last volume of her journals in 2004. "Nobody dreams what my awful position is."[15] The carefully vague phrasing of the annotation for this entry by Rubio and Waterston – "The 'primary cause' of death on her death certificate was 'Coronary Thrombosis'"[16] – clearly indicates that there is much more to this story.

VB: The first clues concerning the mystery that is Montgomery's death were revealed only a few years later, during the centenary of the publication of *Anne of Green Gables*. On September 27, 2008, Kate Macdonald Butler (Montgomery's granddaughter through her son Stuart) published an article in *The Globe and Mail* entitled "The Heartbreaking Truth about Anne's Creator," revealing her family's secret, that Montgomery "took her own life at the age of 67 through a drug overdose." Butler added, "I wasn't told the details of what happened, and I never saw the note she left, but I do know that it asked for forgiveness."[17] At a conference held at the University of Guelph less than a month later, Mary Rubio revealed that she had the suicide note in her possession, and presented an overhead copy to a room of very interested scholars and enthusiasts. This conference was where we both saw the document for the first time. Rubio addressed several interesting discrepancies at that presentation as well as in her biography, *Lucy Maud Montgomery: The Gift of Wings* (2008), published shortly after the publication of Butler's article. As Rubio notes, "there was a very specific page number – 176 – at the top of it. The note, which was dated April 22 (two days before her death), was not, as they believed, and as Stuart believed all his life, specifically a suicide note." In fact, in Rubio's view, the note was actually "the final page of Maud's journal, her 'life-book.'" Rubio speculates that 176 pages of loose sheets of paper contained notes for journal entries that Montgomery had not yet transcribed into her tenth ledger, which she had begun in 1936. The absence of these pages would account for the abrupt end to her journal entries in 1939, although it does not account for the two brief entries made in July 1941 and March 1942. As Rubio notes, "The question is: *where did the other 175 pages go?*"[18] To me, Rubio's question meant only one thing: there was an important, undiscovered Montgomery document out there, which I had to be the one to find. To the antiquarian, Rubio's supposition pointed to the best achievement a treasure hunter could possibly hope for. Of course, this mystery is just another example of how the truth about Montgomery always seems to be hidden behind a curtain, like her character Emily Starr's "flash."

I worked on the appraisal of Montgomery's suicide note for the University of Guelph a year after these puzzle pieces first came to light. One of the important factors I had to take into account when determining a value for the document was whether or not it was an actual suicide note. Having to make such a decision forced me to examine every option. In her biography, Rubio notes that Montgomery used a piece of scrap paper – the back of a Frederick A. Stokes Company royalty statement from 1939, to be exact – to write the note that would be found on her bedside table after her death. "This was not a recent scrap of paper on which she had scribbled out a suicide note, but part of the advance jottings that she did before copying her entries into a journal ledger later on." However, as Rubio points out, Montgomery "had only twenty free legal-sized pages left in Volume Ten" – hardly enough space to transcribe 176 handwritten pages – "but the handwritten letter-sized pages could have been greatly condensed ... I doubt she would have [started another volume] because ten was a round number to end off a life."[19] Rubio later questions whether Montgomery or her eldest son Chester destroyed the missing 175 pages, and if it was Chester's act, whether they were destroyed before or after Montgomery's death. This single piece of paper, a decisive document in a woman's literary life, raises more questions than it answers.

BL: Figuring out where *The Blythes Are Quoted* fit into the puzzle of Montgomery's death was equally challenging, especially since my work on the book began long before any of these clues were revealed. Despite the fact that only sixteen of Montgomery's twenty novels survive in the form of handwritten manuscripts (typescripts and proofs being stages in the production process that were not preserved by her publishers), the University of Guelph has in its Montgomery collection three different typescript versions of this final book. These include one typed draft with numerous handwritten corrections and two seemingly complete versions that were not typed on the same typewriter, and that contain numerous textual variations. No handwritten version survives, and none of the three typescripts is dated. The book's contents are also an anomaly: instead of writing a new Anne novel, Montgomery rewrote several of her most recent short stories (some of which had been published in periodicals as early as 1931, and some of which have never been found in published form) to include Anne and her family, and added vignettes of poems (most of which had already been published) and dialogue between the stories. It is impossible to ascertain when Montgomery actually worked on this book, just as figuring out which typescript is the final copy is also a matter of conjecture. The typed draft and one of the "final" typescripts came from the files of Dr. Stuart Macdonald; his final typescript was used as the basis for an abridged version, *The Road to Yesterday*, which was published in 1974. The remaining typescript was part of a group of files that belonged to Chester Macdonald and were donated to Guelph by his son, David Macdonald. I was surprised to find that both typescripts appeared to be complete, since most scholars and reviewers who had commented on the final book had assumed that it remained unfinished when Montgomery died. After reading the two finished typescripts side by side and considering the variations between them, I eventually concluded that the version in the Stuart Macdonald files was the final one.

I was hired as a research assistant for the final volume of Montgomery's journals, so I had the opportunity to read the last journal entries long before the public did, but it was only when I started researching Montgomery's obituaries that I discovered another clue: namely, according to the *Globe and Mail*, that the typescript had been "placed in the hands of a publishing firm" the day of her death.[20] The use of the passive voice made it impossible to confirm that Montgomery herself had dropped it off, but the article seemed to imply that it had been delivered in person, rather than mailed. It was only several months later when I discovered the copies of the typescript that had been donated by David Macdonald were also in the McClelland & Stewart archives at McMaster University. This detail revealed that it was this version – which Stuart Macdonald had apparently not known about – that Montgomery had intended to be published.[21] In this case, new findings in the archives radically altered the claims made by earlier scholars.

VB: Likewise, the holdings at the McLaughlin Library at the University of Guelph led to a new understanding of the context of Montgomery's "suicide note." I examined a range of additional documents in the archives to help in my appraisal, including the typescript of her journals, which she had made for her son Stuart. The typescript for the tenth volume, which contains entries from 1936 onward, ends mid-sentence after eleven pages. This fact struck me as odd: why did she stop so abruptly if she intended this typescript to serve as the basis for a posthumous publication? Intrigued, I proceeded backward to the typescript of the ninth volume, which ends at page 175. That was when it hit me: I had found the missing 175 pages that preceded the suicide note – page 176 – that was found next to Montgomery's deathbed. Montgomery had started to include the contents of the tenth handwritten ledger in her typescript for future publication, but changed her mind and decided to end with the ninth ledger. Suddenly, the wording of the suicide note on page 176 made sense:

> This copy is unfinished and never will be. It is in a terrible state because I made it when I had begun to suffer my terrible breakdown of 1940. It must end here. If any publishers wish to publish extracts from it under the terms of my will they must stop here. The tenth volume can never be copied and must not be made public during my lifetime. Parts of it are too terrible and would hurt people. I have lost my mind by spells and I do not dare to think what I may do in those spells. May God forgive me and I hope everyone else will forgive me even if they cannot understand. My position is too awful to endure and nobody realizes it. What an end to a life in which I tried always to do my best in spite of many mistakes.[22]

Montgomery had begun typing this abridged version of her handwritten journals as early as 1937.[23] This note confirms that the project was completed under excruciating circumstances sometime after 1940. She had fallen and hurt her right arm that year, and this typescript would have been a good fallback project for her, since she wrote journal entries and the drafts of her novels in longhand, and typing would have presumably been less painful. Depending on when she began *The Blythes Are Quoted*, her injury could explain why there are three typescripts for that book but no handwritten manuscript. The year 1940 was also difficult for her emotionally, as Rubio outlines in her biography: Montgomery endured her husband's ongoing mental illness, the dissolution of her eldest son's marriage, her own increased reliance on prescription drugs, the beginning of the Second World War, and her frustration with a literary community that had begun to marginalize her as a children's writer.[24]

The typescript version of her journals shows several passes of revision in different pens and in pencil. She could very well have worked on it in revision until just before her death, even though the typing was completed long before – after all, Rubio and Waterston note that a handwritten interpolation dated 1942 was added to the typescript version of a journal entry dated 1921.[25] The "suicide note" was a final handwritten note to accompany the typescript. As a postscript to the typed version of the ninth ledger, the single sheet found at Montgomery's death would indicate that, rather than offering missing notes for further journal entries, it contains her final instructions to her son with respect to this important record of her life.

Additionally, Montgomery used considerable scrap paper in finalizing the presentation of her typescript for Stuart. She wrote her original instructions on the paper boxes in which the typescript was stored; she outlined that the journals and their publishing rights should be given to Chester, and then his daughter Luella on her twenty-first birthday. Then she scratched these out, possibly as a result of the falling out she had with Chester in 1940, when his marriage dissolved, and glued new ones to the front of the paper boxes on scrap paper, on which she gave full rights to Stuart and his heirs. Montgomery was so distressed by Chester's separation that she added provisions in her will that disinherited him if he were not living with his wife at the time of her death.[26] It is entirely in keeping with these measures that page 176 was written on scrap paper. The date on the note – April 22, 1942, two days before her death – is also significant; this day could have been when she made her final revisions to the typescript and the final preparations to *The Blythes Are Quoted*. One possible scenario is that Montgomery met with Stuart on April 23, 1942, to give him the typescript of the journals, and perhaps even asked him to drop off her manuscript at the publishers the next day. Unbeknownst to him, this would have been her final farewell. If so, then these two documents made up her final act as a writer and mother. The puzzle can only be put together using pieces preserved by the archives: the suicide note, the typescript, and the original box covers.

BL: Montgomery's ambivalence about which of her sons should inherit the journals had concerned her for several decades, from the time they were children. When I started research for this article, I was intrigued by the number of ellipses in the published version of the 1922 entry, quoted earlier, in which Montgomery outlined her wish that the ten ledgers be preserved and their contents published. Curious as to what had been cut by Rubio and Waterston in the process of preparing these journals for publication, I discovered that both the handwritten original and Montgomery's own typescript contained further sets of instructions that are entirely in keeping with the preoccupations revealed in the note found by her deathbed:

> But to-day I finished copying my journal into uniform volumes. It has been a long piece of work but an interesting one. Perhaps a hundred years from now my descendants may read over this diary and regard it as an interesting heirloom. By that time they can give it to the world if they like. Everyone would be dead whom its publication could hurt and I would like it to be published in full *without omission*, save for this very paragraph I have just written. Cut it out, descendants!
>
> This journal is a faithful record of one human being's life and so should have a certain literary value. My heirs might publish an *abridged volume* after my death, if I do not myself do it before. It might be a good financial proposition for them. They should not include anything that would hurt or annoy anyone living.
>
> I *desire that these journals never be destroyed but kept as long as the leaves hold together*. I leave this to my descendants or my literary heirs as a sacred charge and invoke a Shakespearean curse on them if they disregard it. There is so much of myself in these volumes that I cannot bear the thought of their ever being destroyed. It would seem to me like a sort of murder.
>
> I do not yet know to which of my boys I shall finally bequeath this journal. Time must show which is the fitter to receive and guard it. Perhaps as yet unborn grandchildren and great-grandchildren will pore over these pages, with curious interest in a life lived so long before, in a world that will have so wholly passed away. Will some great-great-granddaughter of mine ever bend her pretty young head over this page? If so – I salute you, dear! Here and now, across the gulf of generations, I put out my hand and say to you,
>
> "I lived a hundred years before you did; but my blood runs in your veins and I lived and loved and suffered and enjoyed and toiled and struggled just as you do. I found life good, in spite of everything. May you find it so. I found that courage and kindness are the two essential things. They are just as essential in your century as they were in mine. Here's to you, little great-great-granddaughter,

not to be born for a hundred years! I hope you'll be merry and witty and brave and wise; and I hope you'll say to yourself, 'If Great-great-grandmother were alive to-day I think I'd like her in spite of her faults.'"[27]

In the unabridged entry, we see more of the ambivalences and contradictions that are implied in the published version: on the one hand, Montgomery adamantly wants the journals published, but on the other hand, she leaves it up to her descendants to decide whether or not to do so. Moreover, she contradicts herself about whether to have the journals published with or without omissions. She ultimately left them to Stuart Macdonald, who then entrusted them to Rubio and Waterston and left it to their editorial discretion to select and edit them.

VB: No matter how much we learn about Montgomery's death, a great deal will always be left to speculation. I believe that either she kept back the final handwritten instructions for the typescript, her suicide note, because it betrayed her intentions to kill herself, or perhaps she wrote it as a definitive suicide note, using the typescript as a frame for her approach. It was poetic timing to have her final and most subversive text, *The Blythes Are Quoted*, dropped off at the publishers as she lay dying in her bed.

The original suicide note, owing another debt to the archives, shows that she crossed out the word "would" ("I hope everyone else would forgive me") and replaced it with "will," outlining a moment of decisiveness to end her life. She was also concerned with leaving final instructions about the publication of her journals, confirming the open question posed in 1922 about which son would inherit them. According to Alix Strauss, whose book *Death Becomes Them* (2009) traces the suicides of public figures, "for some, there is planning – which brings momentary relief. It's the well-crafted, highly-organized strategy that allows a suicide to write the notes and divide up her belongings, that gives her time to say her proper farewells."[28] In my view, the note found at Montgomery's deathbed was partly a letter of formal instruction to her son and lawyers, and partly a final note of farewell. In a way, one part of her wanted to express what she planned to do, but another part wanted to preserve the secrecy of those plans. Such ambivalence between disclosure and subterfuge is not only the dominant pattern of her journals but also characteristic of suicide. According to Edwin Shneidman, a world authority on suicide, "the prototypical suicide state is one in which an individual cuts his throat and cries for help at the same time, and is genuine in both of these acts."[29] Further, the note would make sense only to Stuart Macdonald, who had been given the typescript of her journal and who she could have presumed to be among the first contacted when her body was found, because of his profession. As Strauss notes, "In many cases the letters are a puzzle, decipherable only to the people they're intended for."[30] What gives this story a kind of happy ending is that Stuart Macdonald understood the message. When he made a facsimile of the typescript to edit for publication sometime in the 1970s, he did not copy the tenth volume of her journals, respecting his mother's instructions. Moreover, in a 1974 interview in the *Globe and Mail* about his plans to edit the journals himself, he is reported to have said that the published journals would end at 1933 "because mother says some unkind things about people who are still living."[31] The typescript becomes an intimate message to her son, but also a final offering to her readers. We can read Montgomery as having set up her journals and *The Blythes Are Quoted* as her suicide notes, the lengthy farewell of a prolific writer. After all, as Strauss remarks, "Some suicide notes are meant for a single pair of eyes; others reach out to the masses."[32]

BL: In Montgomery's case, the note found on her deathbed is both intimate and public, as are the journals and final typescript that she confided to her son. And although *The Blythes Are Quoted* isn't mentioned explicitly in the note, the fact that she had apparently arranged for it to be dropped off on the day of her death indicates that she saw it as publishable, unlike the final ledger of her journals. Ultimately, what this all shows is both the rewards and challenges of using archival documents in an attempt to solve a puzzle about a well-known author. Although such discoveries make this kind of sleuthing so rewarding, researchers can never predict what clues will be unearthed next to modify earlier claims.

VB: It would be superficial to say simply that the archives make these discoveries possible. Rather, there is an interconnected and ongoing relationship between archives, antiquarians, and scholars that creates a dynamic of discovery and learning that is akin to a breathing organism. The strength of this community is what rescues the stories of Canadian women, preserving them *and* renewing them for the future – the force that holds all the leaves together.

NOTES

1 Buss, Introduction, 1.
2 [Editor's note: the authors refer here to the chapters throughout Linda M. Morra and Jessica Schagerl's collection *Basements and Attics, Closets and Cyberspace*, in which this essay originally appears.]
3 The two exceptions to this generalization are *The Watchman and Other Poems* (1916) and *Courageous Women* (1934), a book of essays co-authored with Marian Keith and Mabel Burns McKinley, both of which went out of print soon after their publication. Even the unauthorized collection of short stories *Further Chronicles of Avonlea* (1920), which Montgomery fought in court for eight years to be removed from circulation, remains in print today. [Editor's note: Montgomery's three chapters in *Courageous Women* appear in Volume 1 of *The L.M. Montgomery Reader*.]
4 Devereux, "The Continuing Story," 180.
5 In addition to the *Selected Journals*, the posthumous texts attributed to Montgomery have included three volumes of letters (*The Green Gables Letters* in 1960, *My Dear Mr. M* in 1980, and *After Green Gables* in 2006), diaries (including a joint diary kept by Montgomery and close friend Nora Lefurgey, published in *The Intimate Life of L.M. Montgomery* in 2005), short stories, essays, and poems culled from periodicals (*The Alpine Path* in 1974, *The Doctor's Sweetheart* in 1979, *The Poetry of Lucy Maud Montgomery* in 1987, and *Akin to Anne*, the first of eight collections edited by Rea Wilmshurst, in 1988), and a book-length work not published in Montgomery's lifetime (*The Blythes Are Quoted* in 2009, which had been published in significantly abridged form as *The Road to Yesterday* in 1974). Archival documents and artifacts, including photographs, have also been a major focus of recent academic studies (Epperly's *Through Lover's Lane* in 2007 and Gammel's *Looking for Anne* in 2008).
6 Gillen, "The Rescue of the Montgomery–MacMillan Letters," 484. Gillen used Montgomery's letters to G.B. MacMillan as a major basis for her 1975 biography, *The Wheel of Things*. Although a fraction of the letter collection was published as *My Dear Mr. M* in 1980, the originals are available to researchers at Library and Archives Canada, as are Montgomery's letters to Ephraim Weber.
7 *AP*, 10.
8 M.H. Rubio, "Why L.M. Montgomery's Journals," 476–77.
9 Bruce, Johnston, and Salmon, "The L.M. Montgomery Collection," 128.
10 Epperly, "Revisiting Archives."

11 Montgomery, 2 September 1919, in *SJLMM*, 2: 341.
12 Montgomery, 16 April 1922, in *SJLMM*, 3: 51; ellipses in original.
13 Montgomery, "Edited Version."
14 Montgomery, 9 January 1938, in *SJLMM*, 5: 120.
15 Montgomery, 23 March 1942, in *SJLMM*, 5: 350.
16 Montgomery, *SJLMM*, 5: 399.
17 Butler, "The Heartbreaking Truth about Anne's Creator," F1.
18 M.H. Rubio, *Lucy Maud Montgomery*, 575, 576, emphasis in original.
19 Ibid., 640n104, 641n105.
20 Quoted in Lefebvre, Afterword, 513. [See "Noted Author Dies Suddenly at Home Here," in Volume 1 of *The L.M. Montgomery Reader*.]
21 See Benjamin Lefebvre, "L.M. Montgomery and Her Publishers," Historical Perspectives on Canadian Publishing, McMaster University / Queen's University / University of Toronto Thomas Fisher Rare Books Library, 2009. http://hpcanpub.mcmaster.ca/case-study/lm-montgomery-and-her-publishers.
22 Montgomery, "'Suicide' Note Written by L.M. Montgomery."
23 Montgomery, 7 July 1937, in *SJLMM*, 5: 185.
24 M.H. Rubio, *Lucy Maud Montgomery*, 566.
25 Montgomery, *SJLMM*, 2: 434.
26 Devereux, "'See My Journal,'" 242.
27 Montgomery, 16 April 1922, in UJ, 5: 266–67. This extract appears in near identical form in Montgomery, "Edited Version," 5: 85.
28 Strauss, *Death Becomes Them*, 11.
29 Shneidman, *Definition of Suicide*, 135.
30 Strauss, *Death Becomes Them*, 17.
31 Carson, "Million Words in 10-Volume Diary," W4.
32 Strauss, *Death Becomes Them*, 19.

Sources

The items included in this volume were originally published as follows:

"Lucy Maud Montgomery 1874–1942," by Elizabeth Waterston, in *The Clear Spirit: Twenty Canadian Women and Their Times*, edited by Mary Quayle Innis (Toronto: University of Toronto Press, 1966), 198–220; reproduced by permission of the publisher.

"The Fair World of L.M. Montgomery," by Helen Porter, as a review of new editions of L.M. Montgomery's *The Blue Castle* and *A Tangled Web*, *Journal of Canadian Fiction* 2, no. 4 (1973): 102–4; reprinted by permission of the author.

"*Anne of Green Gables* and the Regional Idyll," by T.D. MacLulich, in *The Dalhousie Review* 63, no. 3 (Autumn 1983): 488–502; reprinted by permission of the journal.

"Little Orphan Mary: Anne's Hoydenish Double," by Rosamond Bailey, in *Canadian Children's Literature / Littérature canadienne pour la jeunesse* 55 (1989): 10–17; reprinted by permission of *Jeunesse: Young People, Texts, Cultures* (formerly *Canadian Children's Literature / Littérature canadienne pour la jeunesse*), published by the Centre for Research in Young People's Texts and Cultures (CRYTC) at the University of Winnipeg.

"Subverting the Trite: L.M. Montgomery's 'Room of Her Own,'" by Mary Rubio, in *Canadian Children's Literature / Littérature canadienne pour la jeunesse* 65 (1992): 6–39; reprinted by permission of the author.

"Women's Oral Narrative Traditions as Depicted in Lucy Maud Montgomery's Fiction, 1918–1939," by Diane Tye, in *Myth and Milieu: Atlantic Literature and Culture 1918–1939*, edited by Gwendolyn Davies (Fredericton: Acadiensis Press, 1993), 123–35; reprinted by permission of the publisher.

"L.M. Montgomery's *Rilla of Ingleside*: Intention, Inclusion, Implosion," by Owen Dudley Edwards, in *Harvesting Thistles: The Textual Garden of L.M. Montgomery; Essays on Her Novels and Journals*, edited by Mary Henley Rubio (Guelph: Canadian Children's Press, 1994), 126–36; reprinted by permission of *Jeunesse: Young People, Texts, Cultures* (formerly *Canadian Children's Literature / Littérature canadienne pour la jeunesse*), published by the Centre for Research in Young People's Texts and Cultures (CRYTC) at the University of Winnipeg.

"Decoding L.M. Montgomery's Journals / Encoding a Critical Practice for Women's Private Literature," by Helen M. Buss, in *Essays on Canadian Writing* 54 (Winter 1994): 80–100; reprinted by permission of the journal.

"'Fitted to Earn Her Own Living': Figures of the New Woman in the Writing of L.M. Montgomery," by Carole Gerson, in *Children's Voices in Atlantic Literature and Culture: Essays on Childhood*, edited by Hilary Thompson (Guelph: Canadian Children's Press, 1995), 24–34; reprinted by permission of the author.

"'Pruned Down and Branched Out': Embracing Contradiction in *Anne of Green Gables*," by Laura M. Robinson, in *Children's Voices in Atlantic Literature and Culture: Essays on Childhood*, edited by Hilary Thompson (Guelph: Canadian Children's Press, 1995), 35–43; reprinted by permission of the author.

"Finding L.M. Montgomery's Short Stories," by Rea Wilmshurst, as the afterword to *Across the Miles: Tales of Correspondence*, by L.M. Montgomery, edited by Rea Wilmshurst (Toronto: McClelland and Stewart, 1995), 255–60; reprinted by permission of C. Anderson Silber.

"L.M. Montgomery's Manuscript Revisions," by Elizabeth Epperly, in *Atlantis* 20, no. 1 (Fall–Winter 1995): 149–55; reprinted by permission of the author.

"'My Secret Garden': Dis/Pleasure in L.M. Montgomery and F.P. Grove," by Irene Gammel, in *English Studies in Canada* 25, no. 1 (March 1999): 39–65; reprinted by permission of the journal.

"Writing with a 'Definite Purpose': L.M. Montgomery, Nellie L. McClung and the Politics of Imperial Motherhood in Fiction for Children," by Cecily Devereux, in *Canadian Children's Literature / Littérature canadienne pour la jeunesse* 99 (Fall 2000): 6–22; reprinted by permission of the author.

"Kinship and Nation in *Amelia* (1848) and *Anne of Green Gables* (1908)," by Monique Dull, first appeared in *The Rhetoric of Canadian Writing*, edited by Conny Steenman-Marcusse (Amsterdam: Rodopi, 2002), 161–78; reprinted by permission of the publisher.

"The Maud Squad," by Cynthia Brouse, in *Saturday Night* (Toronto, ON), September 2002, 32–34, 36, 39–40; reprinted by permission of Jean Brouse.

"'The Golden Road of Youth': L.M. Montgomery and British Children's Books," by Jennifer H. Litster, in "Reassessments of L.M. Montgomery,"

edited by Benjamin Lefebvre, a special issue of *Canadian Children's Literature /
Littérature canadienne pour la jeunesse* 113–14 (Spring–Summer 2004): 56–72;
reprinted by permission of the author.

"Women and War: L.M. Montgomery, the Great War, and Canadian Cultural
Memory," by Andrea McKenzie, in *Storm and Dissonance: L.M. Montgomery
and Conflict*, edited by Jean Mitchell (Newcastle, UK: Cambridge Scholars Publishing, 2008), 85–108; reprinted by permission of the author.

"*Anne of Green Gables / Akage no An*: The Flowers of Quiet Happiness," by
Emily Aoife Somers (formerly Sean Somers), first appeared in *Canadian Literature* 197 (Summer 2008): 42–60; reprinted by permission of the journal.

"Archival Adventures with L.M. Montgomery; or, 'As Long as the Leaves
Hold Together,'" by Vanessa Brown and Benjamin Lefebvre, in *Basements and
Attics, Closets and Cyberspace: Explorations in Canadian Women's Archives*,
edited by Linda Morra and Jessica Schagerl (Waterloo: Wilfrid Laurier University
Press, 2012), 229–44; reprinted by permission of the publisher.

Bibliography

Abate, Michelle Ann. Introduction. *The Lion and the Unicorn* 34, no. 2 (April 2010): v–ix.

Abley, Mark. "The Girl She Never Was." *Saturday Night* (Toronto, ON), November 1987, 52, 54, 56, 58–59.

Abrahams, Roger D. "A Performance-Centred Approach to Gossip." *Man* n.s. 5, no. 2 (June 1970): 290–301.

Acton, Carol. *Grief in Wartime: Private Pain, Public Discourse*. Basingstoke, Hampshire: Palgrave Macmillan, 2007.

———. "Writing and Waiting: The First World War Correspondence between Vera Brittain and Roland Leighton." *Gender and History* 11, no. 1 (April 1998): 54–93.

Adair, Dennis, and Janet Rosenstock. *The Journey Begins*. Toronto: HarperCollins Publishers, 1991. New York: Bantam Skylark, 1992. Road to Avonlea 1.

Adamson, Agar. *Letters of Agar Adamson, 1914 to 1919: Lieutenant Colonel, Princess Patricia's Canadian Light Infantry*. Edited by N.M. Christie. Nepean, ON: CEF Books, 1997.

Adderley, Nanci. *Kate Charms Avonlea*. N.p.: n.p., 2011. Kate Series 2.

———. *Kate's Castle*. N.p.: n.p., 2013. Kate Series 4.

———. *Kate's Prince Charming*. N.p.: n.p., 2013. Kate Series 3.

———. *Kate Visits Green Gables*. N.p.: n.p., 2011. Kate Series 1.

Åhmansson, Gabriella. *A Life and Its Mirrors: A Feminist Reading of L.M. Montgomery's Fiction*, Volume 1: *An Introduction to Lucy Maud Montgomery, Anne Shirley*. Uppsala: University of Uppsala, 1991.

———. "'Mayflowers Grow in Sweden Too': L.M. Montgomery, Astrid Lindgren, and the Swedish Literary Consciousness." In M.H. Rubio, *Harvesting Thistles*, 14–22.

———. "The Survival of the Artist: L.M. Montgomery and the Attempted Murder of Emily Byrd Starr." In *Literary Responses to Arctic Canada: Proceedings from the Third International Conference of the Nordic Association for Canadian Studies, University of Oslo, 1990*, edited by Jørn Carlsen, 185–92. Lund: Nordic Association for Canadian Studies / L'Association nordique d'études canadiennes, 1993. The Nordic Association for Canadian Studies Text Series 7.

Akage no An. 50 episodes. Nippon Animation, 1979.

Akamatsu, Yoshiko. "Japanese Readings of *Anne of Green Gables*." In Gammel and Epperly, *L.M. Montgomery and Canadian Culture*, 201–12.

———. "Japanese Translations of *Anne of Green Gables*: Their Historical and Metaphorical Meanings." *The Canadian Literary Society of Japan* 10 (2002): 77–92.

Alexander, Becky D. *In L.M.'s Garden.* Cambridge, ON: Craigleigh, 2002.

Allard, Danièle. "The Popularity of *Anne of Green Gables* in Japan – A Study of Hanako Muroaka's Translation of L.M. Montgomery's Novel and Its Reception." PhD dissertation, Université de Sherbrooke, 2002.

———. "Reader Reception of *Anne of Green Gables* in Japan." *CREArTA* 5 (2005): 97–111.

———. "*Taishu Bunka* and Anne Clubs in Japan." In Gammel, *Making Avonlea*, 295–309.

Allen, Antonia. "Not for Grandmas: 20 Canadian Juveniles." *Saturday Night* (Toronto, ON), January 1973, 33–34.

Althusser, Louis. *Lenin and Philosophy and Other Essays.* Translated by Ben Brewster. London: New Left Books, 1977.

Andronik, Catherine M. *Kindred Spirit: A Biography of L.M. Montgomery, Creator of Anne of Green Gables.* New York: Atheneum; Don Mills, ON: Maxwell MacMillan, 1993.

Angus, Ian. *A Border Within: National Identity, Cultural Plurality, and Wilderness.* Montreal: McGill–Queen's University Press, 1997.

Anne of Avonlea. Directed by Joan Craft. Dramatized by Elaine Morgan. 6 episodes. BBC, 1975.

Anne of Green Gables. Directed by Joan Craft. Dramatized by Julia Jones. 5 episodes. BBC, 1972.

Anne of Green Gables. Directed by Kevin Sullivan. Screen adaptation by Kevin Sullivan and Joe Wiesenfeld. Sullivan Films, 1985.

Bibliography

Anne of Green Gables: A New Beginning. Written and directed by Kevin Sullivan. Sullivan Entertainment, 2008.

Anne of Green Gables: The Animated Series. 26 episodes. Sullivan Animation, 2000–1.

Anne of Green Gables: The Continuing Story. Directed by Stefan Scaini. Written by Kevin Sullivan and Laurie Pearson. Sullivan Entertainment, 2000.

Anne of Green Gables: The Sequel. Written and directed by Kevin Sullivan. Sullivan Films, 1987.

Anthony, Edward. *Thy Rod and Staff: New Light on the Flagellatory Impulse*. London: Virago Press, 1996.

Ardis, Ann. *New Women, New Novels: Feminism and Early Modernism*. New Brunswick, NJ: Rutgers University Press, 1990.

Atwood, Margaret. Afterword to *Anne of Green Gables*, by L.M. Montgomery, 331–36. Toronto: McClelland and Stewart, 1992. New Canadian Library. Also as "Reflection Piece: Revisiting Anne" in Gammel and Epperly, *L.M. Montgomery and Canadian Culture*, 222–26.

———. Radio interview. With Lil Världen. Götenberg, Sweden, 13–16 August 1990.

———. *Survival: A Thematic Guide to Canadian Literature*. Toronto: Anansi, 1972.

Avery, Donald. *Reluctant Host: Canada's Response to Immigrant Workers, 1896–1994*. Toronto: McClelland and Stewart, 1995.

Avery, Gillian. *Behold the Child: American Children and Their Books*. London: Bodley Head, 1994.

———. "'Remarkable and Winning': A Hundred Years of American Heroines." *The Lion and the Unicorn* 13, no. 1 (June 1989): 7–20.

The Avonlea Traditions Chronicle. Newmarket, ON: Avonlea Traditions, 1991–99.

Bagnold, Enid. *A Diary without Dates*. London: Virago, 1978.

Bailey, Thomas A. *Woodrow Wilson and the Great Betrayal*. Chicago: Quadrangle Books, 1963.

Baker, Janet E. "Archibald MacMechan: Canadian Man of Letters." PhD dissertation, Dalhousie University, 1977.

Bakhtin, Mikhail. *Speech Genres and Other Late Essays*. Translated by Vern W. McGee. Austin: University of Texas Press, 1986.

Baldwin, Douglas. "L.M. Montgomery's *Anne of Green Gables*: The Japanese Connection." *Journal of Canadian Studies / Revue d'études canadiennes* 28, no. 3 (Fall 1993): 123–33.

Bibliography

Bataille, Georges. *Erotism: Death and Sensuality*. San Francisco: City Lights, 1986.

Bauman, Richard. *Verbal Art as Performance*. 1977. Prospect Heights, IL: Waveland Press, 1984.

Belsey, Catherine. *Critical Practice*. London: Methuen, 1980. New Accents.

Berg, Temma F. "*Anne of Green Gables*: A Girl's Reading." In Reimer, *Such a Simple Little Tale*, 153–64.

Berke, Jacqueline. "'Mother I Can Do It Myself!': The Self-Sufficient Heroine in Popular Girls' Fiction." *Women's Studies* 6, no. 2 (1979): 187–203.

Berton, Pierre. *Vimy*. 1986. N.p.: Anchor Canada, 2001.

Bhabha, Homi K. "DissemiNation: Time, Narrative, and the Margins of the Modern Nation." In *Nation and Narration*, edited by Homi K. Bhabha, 291–322. London: Routledge, 1990.

Bhadury, Poushali. "Fictional Spaces, Contested Images: *Anne*'s 'Authentic' Afterlife." *Children's Literature Association Quarterly* 36, no. 2 (Summer 2011): 214–37.

Bishop, Edward. *A Virginia Woolf Chronology*. Boston: G.K. Hall, 1989.

Blackford, Holly, ed. *100 Years of Anne with an "e": The Centennial Study of Anne of Green Gables*. Calgary: University of Calgary Press, 2009.

Blakemore, Erin. *The Heroine's Bookshelf: Life Lessons, from Jane Austen to Laura Ingalls Wilder*. New York: HarperCollins, 2010.

Blodgett, E.D. *Configuration: Essays on Canadian Literatures*. Toronto: ECW Press, 1982.

Blyth, R.H. *Haiku*, Volume 1: *Eastern Culture*; Volume 2: *Spring*; Volume 3: *Summer–Autumn*; Volume 4: *Autumn–Winter*. Tokyo: The Hokuseido Press, 1949–52.

Bolger, Francis W.P. "Lucy Maud's Island." *The Island Magazine* 2, no. 1 (Spring–Summer 1977): 4–10.

———, ed. *Spirit of Place: Lucy Maud Montgomery and Prince Edward Island*. Photography by Wayne Barrett and Anne MacKay. Toronto: Oxford University Press, 1982.

———. *The Years Before "Anne."* N.p.: The Prince Edward Island Heritage Foundation, 1974. Halifax: Nimbus Publishing, 1991.

Borker, Ruth. "Anthropology: Social and Cultural Perspectives." In *Women and Language in Literature and Society*, edited by Sally McConnell-Ginet, Ruth Borker, and Nelly Furman, 25–46. New York: Praeger, 1980.

Bourdieu, Pierre. *Language and Symbolic Power*. Edited by John B. Thompson. Translated by Gino Raymond and Matthew Adamson. Cambridge, MA: Harvard University Press, 1991.

Braybon, Gail. Introduction to *Evidence, History and the Great War: Historians and the Impact of 1914–18*, edited by Gail Braybon, 1–29. New York: Berghahn Books, 2003.

Brinklow, Laurie, Frank Ledwell, and Jane Ledwell, eds. *Message in a Bottle: The Literature of Small Islands*. Charlottetown: Institute of Island Studies, 2000.

Brittain, Vera. *Testament of Youth: An Autobiographical Study of the Years 1900–1925*. London: Gollancz, 1933. New York: The Macmillan Company, 1934.

Brooke, Rupert. *1914 & Other Poems*. London: Sidgwick and Jackson, 1915.

Brown, E.K. *On Canadian Poetry*. Rev. ed. 1944. Ottawa: The Tecumseh Press, 1973.

———. "The Problem of a Canadian Literature." In *Masks of Fiction: Canadian Critics on Canadian Prose*, edited by A.J.M. Smith, 40–52. Toronto: McClelland and Stewart, 1961.

Browning, Robert. *Robert Browning's Poetry*. Edited by James F. Loucks. New York: W.W. Norton Company, 1979. A Norton Critical Edition.

Bruce, Harry. *Maud: La Vie de Lucy Maud Montgomery*. Translated by Michèle Marineau. Montreal: Éditions Québec–Amérique, 1997.

———. *Maud: The Early Years of L.M. Montgomery*. Halifax: Nimbus Publishing, 2003.

———. *Maud: The Life of L.M. Montgomery*. New York: Seal Bantam Books, 1992.

Bruce, Lorne, Wayne Johnston, and Helen Salmon. "The L.M. Montgomery Collection at the University of Guelph." *Canadian Children's Literature / Littérature canadienne pour la jeunesse* 34, no. 2 (Fall 2008): 124–29.

Buitenhuis, Peter. *The Great War of Words: Literature as Propaganda, 1914–1918 and After*. London: B.T. Batsford, 1989.

Bumsted, J.M. "'The Only Island There Is': The Writing of Prince Edward Island History." In *The Garden Transformed: Prince Edward Island, 1945–1980*, edited by Verner Smitheram, David Milne, and Satadal Dasgupta, 11–38. Charlottetown: Ragweed Press, 1982.

Bunkers, Suzanne L. "Midwestern Diaries and Journals: What Women Were (Not) Saying in the Late 1800s." In Olney, *Studies in Autobiography*, 190–210.

Burns, Jane. "Anne and Emily: L.M. Montgomery's Children." *Room of One's Own* 3, no. 3 (1977): 37–48.

Buss, Helen M. Introduction to Buss and Kadar, *Working in Women's Archives*, 1–5.

———. *Mapping Our Selves: Canadian Women's Autobiography in English*. Montreal: McGill–Queen's University Press, 1993.

———. *Repossessing the World: Reading Memoirs by Contemporary Women*. Waterloo: Wilfrid Laurier University Press, 2002.

Buss, Helen M., and Marlene Kadar, eds. *Working in Women's Archives: Researching Women's Private Literature and Archival Documents*. Waterloo: Wilfrid Laurier University Press, 2001.

Butler, Kate Macdonald. "The Heartbreaking Truth about Anne's Creator." *The Globe and Mail* (Toronto, ON), 20 September 2008, F1, F6.

Cadogan, Mary. "Montgomery, L(ucy) M(aud)." In *Twentieth-Century Romance and Gothic Writers*, edited by James Vinson, 503–5. Detroit: Gale Research Company, 1982.

Cadogan, Mary, and Patricia Craig. *Women and Children First: The Fiction of Two World Wars*. London: Victor Gollancz, 1978.

———. *You're a Brick, Angela! The Girls' Story 1839–1985*. London: Victor Gollancz, 1986.

Campbell, Marie. "Wedding Bells and Death Knells: The Writer as Bride in the *Emily* Trilogy." In M.H. Rubio, *Harvesting Thistles*, 137–45.

Campbell, Norman, and Don Harron. "*Anne of Green Gables* the Musical." In McCabe, *The Lucy Maud Montgomery Album*, 336–44.

Careless, Virginia. "The Hijacking of 'Anne.'" *Canadian Children's Literature / Littérature canadienne pour la jeunesse* 67 (1992): 48–55.

Carpenter, Humphrey. *Secret Gardens: A Study of the Golden Age of Children's Literature*. London: George Allen and Unwin, 1985.

Carpenter, Humphrey, and Mari Prichard. *The Oxford Companion to Children's Literature*. Oxford: Oxford University Press, 1984.

Carson, Jo. "Million Words in 10-Volume Diary Tell Lucy Maud Montgomery's Own Tale." *The Globe and Mail* (Toronto, ON), 3 October 1974, W4.

Cavell, Richard. "Felix Paul Greve, the Eulenburg Scandal, and Frederick Philip Grove." *Essays on Canadian Writing* 62 (Fall 1997): 12–45.

Cavert, Mary Beth. "Nora, Maud, and Isabel: Summoning Voices in Diaries and Memories." In Gammel, *The Intimate Life of L.M. Montgomery*, 106–25.

Ceraldi, Gabrielle. "Utopia Awry: L.M. Montgomery's Emily Series and the Aftermath of the Great War." In Brinklow, Ledwell, and Ledwell, *Message in a Bottle*, 247–63.

Chambers, Debbie (Nash). "Kids' Stuff." *Guelph Alumnus* 13, no. 4 (Fall 1980): 28–29.

Christian-Smith, Linda K. *Becoming a Woman through Romance*. New York: Routledge, 1990.

Classen, Constance. "Is 'Anne of Green Gables' an American Import?" *Canadian Children's Literature / Littérature canadienne pour la jeunesse* 55 (1989): 42–50.

Clint, Mabel. *Our Bit: Memories of War Service by a Canadian Nursing Sister.* Montreal: Barwick, 1934.

Coady, Mary Frances. *Lucy Maud and Me.* Vancouver: Beach Holme Publishing, 1999.

Coates, Donna. "The Best Soldiers of All: Unsung Heroines in Canadian Women's Great War Fictions." *Canadian Literature* 151 (Winter 1996): 66–99.

Coffey, M. Carol. *Zoe Lucky and the Green Gables' Mystery.* Denver: Outskirts Press, 2009.

Cohen, Joseph. *Journey to the Trenches: A Life of Isaac Rosenberg (1890–1918).* London: Robson Books, 1975.

Coldwell, Joyce-Ione Harrington. "Folklore as Fiction: The Writings of Lucy Maud Montgomery." In *Folklore Studies in Honor of Herbert Halpert: A Festschrift,* edited by Kenneth Goldstein and Neil V. Rosenberg, 125–36. St. John's: Memorial University of Newfoundland, 1980.

Cole, Stephen. *Here's Looking at Us: Celebrating Fifty Years of CBC-TV.* Toronto: McClelland and Stewart, 2002.

Collins, Carolyn Strom, and Christina Wyss Eriksson. *The Anne of Green Gables Christmas Treasury.* Toronto: Viking, 1997.

———. *The Anne of Green Gables Treasury.* 1991. Toronto: Penguin Books Canada, 1997.

———. *The Anne of Green Gables Treasury of Days.* Toronto: Viking, 1994.

Colombo, John Robert. *Colombo's Canadian Quotations.* Edmonton: Hurtig Publishers, 1974.

———. *Colombo's Canadian References.* Toronto: Oxford University Press, 1976.

Conkie, Heather. *Dreamer of Dreams.* Toronto: HarperCollins Publishers, 1992. New York: Bantam Skylark, 1993. Road to Avonlea 18.

———. *Felix and Blackie.* Toronto: HarperCollins Publishers, 1994. New York: Bantam Skylark, 1994. Road to Avonlea 22.

———. *Friends and Relations.* Toronto: HarperCollins Publishers, 1995. New York: Bantam Skylark, 1995. Road to Avonlea 26.

———. *Malcolm and the Baby.* Toronto: HarperCollins Publishers, 1991. New York: Bantam Skylark, 1992. Road to Avonlea 8.

———. *The Materializing of Duncan McTavish.* Toronto: HarperCollins Publishers, 1991. New York: Bantam Skylark, 1992. Road to Avonlea 4.

——. *Old Quarrels, Old Love*. Toronto: HarperCollins Publishers, 1992. New York: Bantam Skylark, 1993. Road to Avonlea 15.

——. *Sara's Homecoming*. Toronto: HarperCollins Publishers, 1992. New York: Bantam Skylark, 1993. Road to Avonlea 12.

——. *The Ties That Bind*. Toronto: HarperCollins Publishers, 1994. New York: Bantam Skylark, 1994. Road to Avonlea 21.

Cooper, Amy Jo. *Aunt Abigail's Beau*. Toronto: HarperCollins Publishers, 1991. New York: Bantam Skylark, 1992. Road to Avonlea 7.

——. *It's Just a Stage*. Toronto: HarperCollins Publishers, 1992. New York: Bantam Skylark, 1993. Road to Avonlea 19.

Cott, Jonathan. "The Astonishment of Being." *The New Yorker* (New York, NY), 28 February 1983, 46–63.

Cowan, Ann S. "Canadian Writers: Lucy Maud and Emily Byrd." *Canadian Children's Literature* 1, no. 3 (Autumn 1975): 42–49.

——. Review of *The Wheel of Things: A Biography of L.M. Montgomery, Author of* Anne of Green Gables, by Mollie Gillen. *The Canadian Historical Review* 58, no. 4 (December 1977): 512–13.

Cowger, Ashley. "From 'Pretty Nearly Perfectly Happy' to 'the Depths of Despair': Mania and Depression in L.M. Montgomery's Anne Series." *The Lion and the Unicorn* 34, no. 2 (April 2010): 188–99.

Crawford, Elaine, and Kelly Crawford. *Aunt Maud's Recipe Book: From the Kitchen of L.M. Montgomery*. Norval, ON: Crawford's, 1996.

Culley, Margo. Introduction to *A Day at a Time: The Diary Literature of American Women from 1764 to the Present*, edited by Margo Culley, 3–36. New York: Feminist Press at the City University of New York, 1985.

Curran, Thomas. *Xenophobia and Immigration, 1820–1930*. Boston: Twayne Publishers, 1975.

David, Alison Matthews, and Kimberly Wahl. "'Matthew Insists on Puffed Sleeves': Ambivalence towards Fashion in *Anne of Green Gables*." In Gammel and Lefebvre, *Anne's World*, 35–49.

Davin, Anna. "Imperialism and Motherhood." *History Workshop Journal* 5 (1978): 9–65.

Dawson, Janis. "Literary Relations: Anne Shirley and Her American Cousins." *Children's Literature in Education* 33, no. 1 (March 2002): 29–51.

Daymond, Douglas, and Leslie Monkman, eds. *Canadian Novelists and the Novel*. Ottawa: Borealis Press, 1981.

De Jonge, James. "Through the Eyes of Memory: L.M. Montgomery's Cavendish." In Gammel, *Making Avonlea*, 252–67.

de Lauretis, Teresa. *Feminist Studies/Critical Studies*. Bloomington: Indiana University Press, 1986.

Bibliography

DeSalvo, Louise. *Virginia Woolf: The Impact of Childhood Sexual Abuse on Her Life and Work*. Boston: Beacon Press, 1989.

Devereux, Cecily. "Anatomy of a 'National Icon': *Anne of Green Gables* and the 'Bosom Friends' Affair." In Gammel, *Making Avonlea*, 32–42.

———. "'Canadian Classic' and 'Commodity Export': The Nationalism of 'Our' *Anne of Green Gables*." *Journal of Canadian Studies / Revue d'études canadiennes* 36, no. 1 (Spring 2001): 11–28.

———. "The Continuing Story." Review of *The Selected Journals of L.M. Montgomery, Volume 4: 1929–1935*, edited by Mary Rubio and Elizabeth Waterston. *Canadian Literature* 177 (Summer 2003): 180–81.

———. *Growing a Race: Nellie L. McClung and the Fiction of Eugenic Feminism*. Montreal: McGill–Queen's University Press, 2006.

———. "New Woman, New World: Maternal Feminism and the New Imperialism in the White Settler Colonies." *Women's Studies International Forum* 22, no. 2 (March–April 1999): 175–84.

———. "'Not a "Usual" Property': A Hundred Years of Protecting *Anne of Green Gables*." *Law, Culture, and the Humanities* 7, no. 1 (February 2011): 121–41.

———. "'Not One of Those Dreadful New Women': Anne Shirley and the Culture of Imperial Motherhood." In Hudson and Cooper, *Windows and Words*, 119–30.

———. "'See My Journal for the Full Story': Fictions of Truth in *Anne of Green Gables* and L.M. Montgomery's Journals." In Gammel, *The Intimate Life of L.M. Montgomery*, 241–57.

Dobrée, Valentine. *Your Cuckoo Sings by Kind*. London: A.A. Knopf, 1927.

Doody, Margaret Anne. Introduction to Montgomery, *The Annotated Anne of Green Gables*, 9–34.

Drain, Susan. "Community and the Individual in *Anne of Green Gables*: The Meaning of Belonging." *Children's Literature Association Quarterly* 11, no. 1 (Spring 1986): 15–19.

———. "Feminine Convention and Female Identity: The Persistent Challenge of *Anne of Green Gables*." *Canadian Children's Literature / Littérature canadienne pour la jeunesse* 65 (1992): 40–47.

———. "'Too Much Love-Making': *Anne of Green Gables* on Television." *The Lion and the Unicorn* 11, no. 2 (October 1987): 63–72.

Drew, Lorna. "The Emily Connection: Ann Radcliffe, L.M. Montgomery and 'The Female Gothic.'" *Canadian Children's Literature / Littérature canadienne pour la jeunesse* 77 (Spring 1995): 19–32.

Dubinsky, Karen. *Improper Advances: Rape and Heterosexual Conflict in Ontario, 1880–1929*. Chicago: The University of Chicago Press, 1993.

Dublin, Anne. *Lucy Maud Montgomery: A Writer's Life*. Don Mills, ON: Pearson Education Canada, 2005.

Duncan, Sara Jeannette. *A Daughter of Today*. 1894. Ottawa: The Tecumseh Press, 1988.

DuPlessis, Rachel Blau. *Writing beyond the Ending: Narrative Strategies of Twentieth-Century Women Writers*. Bloomington: Indiana University Press, 1985.

DuVernet, Sylvia. *L.M. Montgomery and the Mystique of Muskoka*. N.p.: DuVernet, 1988.

———. *L.M. Montgomery on the Red Road to Reconstruction: A Survey of Her Novels*. N.p.: n.p., 1993.

———. *The Meaning of the Men and the Boys in the Anne Books*. N.p.: n.p., 1998.

———. *Theosophic Thoughts Concerning L.M. Montgomery: Including a "Conference" Concerning* The Ladies of Missalonghi *and* The Blue Castle. N.p.: DuVernet, 1988.

Edwards, Owen Dudley. *British Children's Fiction in the Second World War*. 2008. Edinburgh: Edinburgh University Press, 2009.

Edwards, Owen Dudley, and Jennifer H. Litster. "The End of Canadian Innocence: L.M. Montgomery and the First World War." In Gammel and Epperly, *L.M. Montgomery and Canadian Culture*, 31–46.

Eggleston, Wilfrid. "General Introduction." In Montgomery, *The Green Gables Letters*, 1–22.

Egoff, Sheila. "Children's Literature in English." In Toye, *The Oxford Companion to Canadian Literature*, 117–23.

———. *The Republic of Childhood: A Critical Guide to Canadian Children's Literature in English*. Toronto: Oxford University Press, 1967.

Egoff, Sheila, with Wendy K. Sutton. *Once upon a Time: My Life with Children's Books*. Victoria: Orca Book Publishers, 2005.

Emmett, Hilary. "'Mute Misery': Speaking the Unspeakable in L.M. Montgomery's Anne Books." In Blackford, *100 Years of Anne with an "e,"* 81–104.

Emily of New Moon. 46 episodes. Salter Street Films/CINAR Productions, 1998–99, 2002–3.

Encyclopedia Canadiana. 1957. Volume 7. Toronto: Grolier of Canada, 1972.

Epperly, Elizabeth Rollins. "Approaching the Montgomery Manuscripts." In M.H. Rubio, *Harvesting Thistles*, 74–83.

———. *The Fragrance of Sweet-Grass: L.M. Montgomery's Heroines and the Pursuit of Romance*. 1992. Toronto: University of Toronto Press, 1993.

————. *Imagining Anne: The Island Scrapbooks of L.M. Montgomery.* Toronto: Penguin Canada, 2008. 100 Years of Anne.

————. "L.M. Montgomery and the Changing Times." *Acadiensis* 17, no. 2 (Spring 1988): 177–85.

————. "L.M. Montgomery's *Anne's House of Dreams*: Reworking Poetry." *Canadian Children's Literature / Littérature canadienne pour la jeunesse* 37 (1985): 40–46.

————. "Revisiting Archives." Paper delivered at From Canada to the World: The Cultural Influence of Lucy Maud Montgomery, University of Guelph, 25 October 2008.

————. "A Successful Montgomery." Review of *L.M. Montgomery*, by Genevieve Wiggins. *Canadian Children's Literature / Littérature canadienne pour la jeunesse* 69 (Spring 1993): 38–39.

————. *Through Lover's Lane: L.M. Montgomery's Photography and Visual Imagination.* Toronto: University of Toronto Press, 2007.

Epperly, Elizabeth Rollins, Deirdre Kessler, and Anne-Louise Brookes. *The Bend in the Road: An Invitation to the World and Work of L.M. Montgomery.* CD-ROM. Charlottetown: L.M. Montgomery Institute, 2000.

Fawcett, Clare, and Patricia Cormack. "Guarding Authenticity at Literary Tourism Sites." *Annals of Tourism Research* 28, no. 3 (2001): 686–704.

Fenwick, Julie. "The Silence of the Mermaid: *Lady Oracle* and *Anne of Green Gables*." *Essays on Canadian Writing* 47 (Fall 1992): 51–64.

Ferguson, Will. *Hitching Rides with Buddha.* Toronto: Alfred A. Knopf Canada, 2005.

Ferns, John. "'Rainbow Dreams': The Poetry of Lucy Maud Montgomery." *Canadian Children's Literature / Littérature canadienne pour la jeunesse* 42 (1986): 29–40.

Fiamengo, Janice. "A Legacy of Ambivalence: Response to Nellie McClung." *Journal of Canadian Studies / Revue d'études canadiennes* 34, no. 4 (Winter 1999–2000): 70–87.

————. " ' … The Refuge of My Sick Spirit … ': L.M. Montgomery and the Shadows of Depression." In Gammel, *The Intimate Life of L.M. Montgomery*, 170–86.

Fingard, Judith. "College, Career, and Community: Dalhousie Coeds, 1881–1921." In *Youth, University, and Canadian Society: Essays in the Social History of Higher Education*, edited by Paul Axelrod and John G. Reid, 26–50. Montreal: McGill–Queen's University Press, 1989.

————. "The Prevention of Cruelty, Marriage Breakdown, and the Rights of Wives in Nova Scotia, 1880–1900." In *Separate Spheres: Women's Worlds in the 19th-Century Maritimes*, edited by Janet Guildford and Suzanne Morton, 211–31. Fredericton: Acadiensis Press, 1994.

FitzPatrick, Helen. "Anne's First Sixty Years." *Canadian Author & Bookman and Canadian Poetry* 44, no. 3 (Spring 1969): 5–7, 13.

Foster, D.J. *Lucy Maud Montgomery's* Anne of Green Gables *for the 21st Century: A Modern Revision*. Pelham, AL: Sycamore Books, 2009.

Foster, Shirley, and Judy Simons. *What Katy Read: Feminist Re-readings of "Classic" Stories for Girls*. Iowa City: University of Iowa Press, 1995.

Foucault, Michel. *The History of Sexuality*, Volume 1: *An Introduction*. Translated by Robert Hurley. New York: Vintage Books, 1980.

———. "On the Genealogy of Ethics: An Overview of Work in Progress." In *Michel Foucault: Beyond Structuralism and Hermeneutics*, by Hubert L. Dreyfus and Paul Rabinow, 229–52. Chicago: The University of Chicago Press, 1983.

Frazer, Frances M. "Island Writers." *Canadian Literature* 68–69 (Spring–Summer 1976): 76–87.

———. "Lucy Maud Montgomery (30 November 1974–24 April 1942)." In *Canadian Writers, 1890–1920*, edited by W.H. New, 246–53. Detroit: Gale Research, 1990.

———. "Not the Whole Story." Review of *The Wheel of Things: A Biography of L.M. Montgomery, Author of* Anne of Green Gables, by Mollie Gillen. *Canadian Literature* 74 (Autumn 1977): 105–7.

———. "Scarcely an End." Review of *The Road to Yesterday*, by L.M. Montgomery. *Canadian Literature* 63 (Winter 1975): 89–92.

Fredeman, Jane Cowan. "The Land of Lost Content: The Use of Fantasy in L.M. Montgomery's Novels." *Canadian Children's Literature* 1, no. 3 (Autumn 1975): 60–70.

Frederick, Heather Vogel. *Much Ado about Anne: The Mother–Daughter Book Club*. New York: Simon and Schuster Books for Young Readers, 2008.

Fredericks, Carrie. Review of *The Wheel of Things: A Biography of L.M. Montgomery, Author of* Anne of Green Gables, by Mollie Gillen. *Atlantis: A Women's Studies Journal* 2, no. 1 (Fall 1976): 129–32.

Frever, Trinna S. "Vaguely Familiar: Cinematic Intertextuality in Kevin Sullivan's *Anne of Avonlea*." *Canadian Children's Literature / Littérature canadienne pour la jeunesse* 91–92 (Fall–Winter 1998): 36–52.

Frye, Northrop. Conclusion to Klinck, *Literary History of Canada*, 821–49.

———. *The Educated Imagination*. 1963. Toronto: House of Anansi Press, 2002.

Fussell, Paul. *The Bloody Game: An Anthology of Modern War*. London: Scribner's and Sons, 1991.

——. *The Great War and Modern Memory*. London: Oxford University Press, 1975.

Gagnon, André, and Ann Gagnon, eds. *Canadian Books for Young People / Livres canadiens pour la jeunesse*. 4th ed. Toronto: University of Toronto Press, 1988.

Gammel, Irene. "Embodied Landscape Aesthetics in *Anne of Green Gables*." *The Lion and the Unicorn* 34, no. 2 (April 2010): 228–47.

——, ed. *The Intimate Life of L.M. Montgomery*. Toronto: University of Toronto Press, 2005.

——. "Introduction: Reconsidering Anne's World." In Gammel and Lefebvre, *Anne's World*, 3–16.

——. Introduction to *Confessional Politics: Women's Sexual Self-Representations in Life Writing and Popular Media*, edited by Irene Gammel, 1–10. Carbondale: Southern Illinois University Press, 1999.

——. *Looking for Anne: How Lucy Maud Montgomery Dreamed Up a Literary Classic*. 2008. Toronto: Key Porter Books, 2009.

——, ed. *Making Avonlea: L.M. Montgomery and Popular Culture*. Toronto: University of Toronto Press, 2002.

——. "Mirror Looks: The Visual and Performative Diaries of L.M. Montgomery, Baroness Elsa von Freytag-Loringhoven, and Elvira Bach." In *Interfaces: Women, Autobiography, Image, Performance*, edited by Sidonie Smith and Julia Watson, 289–313. Ann Arbor: The University of Michigan Press, 2002.

——. *Sexualizing Power in Naturalism: Theodore Dreiser and Frederick Philip Grove*. Calgary: University of Calgary Press, 1994.

Gammel, Irene, and Elizabeth Epperly. "Introduction: L.M. Montgomery and the Shaping of Canadian Culture." In Gammel and Epperly, *L.M. Montgomery and Canadian Culture*, 3–13.

——, eds. *L.M. Montgomery and Canadian Culture*. Toronto: University of Toronto Press, 1999.

Gammel, Irene, and Benjamin Lefebvre, eds. *Anne's World: A New Century of Anne of Green Gables*. Toronto: University of Toronto Press, 2010.

Garvie, Maureen. "A Tale of Two Books." *The Kingston Whig–Standard Magazine* (Kingston, ON), 26 December 1987, 20–21.

Gates, Charlene E. "Image, Imagination, and Initiation: Teaching as a Rite of Passage in the Novels of L.M. Montgomery and Laura Ingalls Wilder." *Children's Literature in Education* 20, no. 3 (September 1989): 165–73.

Gates, Philippa, and Stacy Gillis. "Screening L.M. Montgomery: Heritage, Nostalgia, and National Identity." *British Journal of Canadian Studies* 17, no. 2 (2004): 186–96.

Gay, Carol. "'Kindred Spirits' All: Green Gables Revisited." In Reimer, *Such a Simple Little Tale*, 101–8.

The Gazette (Montreal, QC). "Is McCullough Novel Based on Story by Green Gables' Author?" 16 January 1988, B9.

Gerson, Carole. "*Anne of Green Gables* Goes to University: L.M. Montgomery and Academic Culture." In Gammel, *Making Avonlea*, 17–31.

–––––. "Anthologies and the Canon of Early Canadian Women Writers." In *Rediscovering Our Foremothers: Nineteenth-Century Canadian Women Writers*, edited by Lorraine McMullen, 55–76. Ottawa: University of Ottawa Press, 1990.

–––––. *Canadian Women in Print 1750–1918*. Waterloo: Wilfrid Laurier University Press, 2010.

–––––. "Canadian Women Writers and American Markets, 1880–1940." In *Context North America: Canadian/US Literary Relations*, edited by Camille R. LaBossière, 107–18. Ottawa: University of Ottawa Press, 1994.

–––––. "The Canon between the Wars: Field-Notes of a Feminist Literary Archaeologist." In *Canadian Canons: Essays in Literary Value*, edited by Robert Lecker, 46–56. Toronto: University of Toronto Press, 1991.

–––––. "'Dragged at Anne's Chariot Wheels': The Triangle of Author, Publisher, and Fictional Character." In Gammel and Epperly, *L.M. Montgomery and Canadian Culture*, 49–63.

–––––. "L.M. Montgomery and the Conflictedness of a Woman Writer." In Mitchell, *Storm and Dissonance*, 67–80.

–––––. "Seven Milestones: How *Anne of Green Gables* Became a Canadian Icon." In Gammel and Lefebvre, *Anne's World*, 17–34.

Gillen, Mollie. *Lucy Maud Montgomery*. Toronto: Fitzhenry and Whiteside, 1978. The Canadians Series.

–––––. "Maud Montgomery: The Girl Who Wrote Green Gables." *Chatelaine* (Toronto, ON), July 1973, 40–41, 52–55, 58.

–––––. "The Rescue of the Montgomery–MacMillan Letters." In K. McCabe, *The Lucy Maud Montgomery Album*, 484–85.

–––––. *The Wheel of Things: A Biography of L.M. Montgomery, Author of Anne of Green Gables*. Don Mills, ON: Fitzhenry and Whiteside, 1975. London: Harrap, 1976. Halifax: Goodread Biographies/Formac Publishing Company, 1983.

Gittings, Christopher. "Re-visioning *Emily of New Moon*: Family Melodrama for the Nation." *Canadian Children's Literature / Littérature canadienne pour la jeunesse* 91–92 (Fall–Winter 1998): 22–35. Also as "Melodrama for the Nation: *Emily of New Moon*" in Gammel, *Making Avonlea*, 186–200.

Bibliography

The Globe and Mail (Toronto, ON). "The Power to Enchant." Review of *The Story of L.M. Montgomery*, by Hilda M. Ridley. 3 March 1956, 8.

———. "The Ten Most Influential Canadians in the Arts." 1 July 1999, C1.

Goffman, Erving. *The Presentation of Self in Everyday Life*. New York: Doubleday Anchor, 1959.

Golden, Anne. "The Extraction/Fusion Apparatus: Dayna McLeod's Engaged Mash-Up Art Practice." *Canadian Theatre Review* 149 (Winter 2012): 36–39.

Goldman, Dorothy, Jane Gledhill, and Judith Hattaway. *Women Writers and the Great War*. New York: Twayne Publishers, 1995.

Gorham, Deborah. *Vera Brittain: A Feminist Life*. Oxford: Blackwell, 1996.

Gould, Allan. *Anne of Green Gables vs. G.I. Joe: Friendly Fire between Canada and the U.S*. Toronto: ECW Press, 2003.

Grahame, Kenneth. The Golden Age *and* Dream Days. 1895/1898. New York: Signet, 1964.

Gray, Thomas. "Elegy Written in a Country Churchyard." In *The Norton Anthology of English Literature*, 6th ed., edited by M.H. Abrams, 1: 2458–61. New York: W.W. Norton and Company, 1993.

Grazia, Edward de. *Girls Lean Back Everywhere: The Law of Obscenity and the Assault on Genius*. New York: Vintage, 1993.

Green, Peter. *Kenneth Grahame 1859–1932: A Study of His Life, Work, and Times*. London: John Murray, 1959.

Green, Roger Lancelyn. "The Golden Age of Children's Books." In *Children's Literature: The Development of Criticism*, edited by Peter Hunt, 36–48. London: Routledge, 1990.

Greene, Michael. "Criticism and Theory." In *Encyclopedia of Literature in Canada*, edited by William H. New, 248–63. Toronto: University of Toronto Press, 2002.

Grove, Frederick Philip. *Settlers of the Marsh*. 1925. Toronto: McClelland and Stewart, 1992.

Gubar, Marah. "'Where Is the Boy?': The Pleasures of Postponement in the *Anne of Green Gables* Series." *The Lion and the Unicorn* 25, no. 1 (January 2001): 47–69.

Gwyn, Sandra. *Tapestry of War: A Private View of Canadians in the Great War*. Toronto: HarperCollins Publishers, 1992.

———. *Women in the Arts in Canada*. Ottawa: Information Canada, 1971. Studies of the Royal Commission on the Status of Women in Canada.

Hackett, Alice Payne. *70 Years of Best Sellers 1895–1965*. New York: R.R. Bowker Company, 1967.

Haire-Sargeant, Lin. "American Girl to New Woman: Themes of Transformation in Books for Girls, 1850–1925." PhD dissertation, Tufts University, 2004.

Hamilton, Gail. *Aunt Hetty's Ordeal.* Toronto: HarperCollins Publishers, 1992. New York: Bantam Skylark, 1993. Road to Avonlea 13.

———. *Conversions.* Toronto: HarperCollins Publishers, 1991. New York: Bantam Skylark, 1992. Road to Avonlea 6.

———. *A Dark and Stormy Night.* Toronto: HarperCollins Publishers, 1994. New York: Bantam Skylark, 1994. Road to Avonlea 25.

———. *Family Rivalry.* Toronto: HarperCollins Publishers, 1992. New York: Bantam Skylark, 1993. Road to Avonlea 16.

———. *Felicity's Challenge.* Toronto: HarperCollins Publishers, 1991. New York: Bantam Skylark, 1992. Road to Avonlea 9.

———. *May the Best Man Win.* Toronto: HarperCollins Publishers, 1992. New York: Bantam Skylark, 1993. Road to Avonlea 17.

———. *Nothing Endures but Change.* Toronto: HarperCollins Publishers, 1991. New York: Bantam Skylark, 1993. Road to Avonlea 11.

———. *Old Friends, Old Wounds.* New York: Bantam Skylark, 1995. Road to Avonlea 29.

———. *The Story Girl Earns Her Name.* Toronto: HarperCollins Publishers, 1991. New York: Bantam Skylark, 1992. Road to Avonlea 2.

———. *Vows of Silence.* New York: Bantam Skylark, 1995. Road to Avonlea 27.

Hammill, Faye. *Women, Celebrity, and Literary Culture between the Wars.* Austin: University of Texas Press, 2007.

Hancock, Emily. *The Girl Within: A Radical Approach to Female Identity.* New York: Random House, 1989.

Handler, Richard, and Daniel Segal. *Jane Austen and the Fiction of Culture: An Essay on the Narration of Social Realities.* Tucson: University of Arizona Press, 1990.

Hannah, Don. *The Wooden Hill.* Toronto: Playwrights Guild of Canada, 1994.

Harding, Susan. "Women and Words in a Spanish Village." In *Toward an Anthropology of Women,* edited by Rayna R. Reiter, 297–305. New York: Monthly Review Press, 1975.

Harron, Don. *Anne of Green Gables the Musical: 101 Things You Didn't Know.* Toronto: White Knight Books, 2008.

Heilbron, Alexandra. "Canada's Commemorative Stamps." In K. McCabe, *The Lucy Maud Montgomery Album,* 463.

———. *Remembering Lucy Maud Montgomery.* Toronto: The Dundurn Group, 2001.

Henderson, Jennifer. "At Normal School: Seton, Montgomery, and the New Education." In *Home-Work: Postcolonialism, Pedagogy, and Canadian Literature*, edited by Cynthia Sugars, 461–85. Ottawa: University of Ottawa Press, 2004. Reappraisals: Canadian Writers 28.

Hendrickson, Linnea. *Children's Literature: A Guide to the Criticism*. Boston: G.K. Hall and Company, 1987.

Hersey, Eleanor. "'Tennyson Would Never Approve': Reading and Performance in Kevin Sullivan's *Anne of Green Gables*." *Canadian Children's Literature / Littérature canadienne pour la jeunesse* 105–6 (Spring–Summer 2002): 48–67.

Higonnet, Margaret R. "All Quiet in No Women's Land." In *Gendering War Talk*, edited by Miriam Cook and Angela Woollacott, 205–26. Princeton: Princeton University Press, 1993.

———, ed. *Lines of Fire: Women Writers of World War I*. New York: Plume, 1999.

Hilder, Monika B. "The Ethos of Nurture: Revisiting Domesticity in L.M. Montgomery's *Anne of Green Gables*." In Blackford, *100 Years of Anne with an "e,"* 211–27.

———. "Imagining the Ultimate Kindred Spirit: The Feminist Theological Vision in L.M. Montgomery." In *Feminist Theology with a Canadian Accent: Canadian Perspectives on Contextual Feminist Theology*, edited by Mary Ann Beavis with Elaine Guillemin and Barbara Pell, 307–30, 431–34. Ottawa: Novalis, 2008.

———. "'That Unholy Tendency to Laughter': L.M. Montgomery's Iconoclastic Affirmation of Faith in *Anne of Green Gables*." In Lefebvre, "Reassessments of L.M. Montgomery," 34–55.

Hill, Colin. "Generic Experiment and Confusion in Early Canadian Novels of the Great War." *Studies in Canadian Literature / Études en littérature canadienne* 34, no. 2 (2009): 58–76.

Hills, Ben. "Thorn Birds Colleen in Book Plot Row." *Melbourne Herald* (Melbourne, Australia), 19 January 1988, 1+.

Hingston, Kylee-Anne. "Montgomery's 'Imp': Conflicting Representations of Illness in L.M. Montgomery's *The Blue Castle*." In Mitchell, *Storm and Dissonance*, 194–208.

Hiraga, Masako. *Metaphor and Iconicity: A Cognitive Approach to Analysing Texts*. London: Palgrave Macmillan, 2005.

Hoffmann, Marion. *Anne of Green Gables Puzzle Book*. Illustrated by Muriel Wood. Markham, ON: Fitzhenry and Whiteside, 2007.

Holmes, Nancy. "How Green Is *Green Gables*? An Ecofeminist Perspective on L.M. Montgomery." In Mitchell, *Storm and Dissonance*, 373–90.

Holmlund, Mona, and Gail Youngsberg. *Inspiring Women: A Celebration of Herstory*. Regina: Coteau Books, 2003.

Holtz, Patricia. "Lucy Maud's Album." *The Canadian Magazine*, 6 September 1975, n.pag.

Howey, Ann F. "Secular or Spiritual: Rereading *Anne of Green Gables*." *Christianity and Literature* 62, no. 3 (Spring 2013): 395–416.

Hoy, Helen. *Modern English-Canadian Prose: A Guide to Information Sources*. Detroit: Gale Research Company, 1983.

———. "'Too Heedless and Impulsive': Re-reading *Anne of Green Gables* through a Clinical Approach." In Gammel and Lefebvre, *Anne's World*, 65–81.

Hubler, Angela E. "Can Anne Shirley Help 'Revive Ophelia'? Listening to Girl Readers." In *Deliquents and Debutantes: Twentieth-Century American Girls' Cultures*, edited by Sherrie A. Inness, 261–84. New York: New York University Press, 1998.

Hudson, Aïda, and Susan-Ann Cooper, eds. *Windows and Words: A Look at Canadian Children's Literature in English*. Ottawa: University of Ottawa Press, 2003. Reappraisals: Canadian Writers 25.

Humez, Jean M. "'We Got Our History Lesson': Oral Historical Autobiography and Women's Narrative Arts Traditions." In *Traditions and the Talents of Women*, edited by Florence Howe, 125–44. Urbana: University of Illinois Press, 1991.

Huse, Nancy. "Journeys of the Mother in the World of Green Gables." In Reimer, *Such a Simple Little Tale*, 131–38.

Hutton, Jack, and Linda Jackson-Hutton. *Lucy Maud Montgomery and Bala: A Love Story of the North Woods*. Bala, ON: Bala's Museum with Memories of Lucy Maud Montgomery, 1998.

Hynes, Samuel. *A War Imagined: The First World War and English Culture*. New York: Atheneum, 1991.

Innis, Mary Quayle, ed. *The Clear Spirit: Twenty Canadian Women and Their Times*. Toronto: University of Toronto Press, 1966.

———. Introduction to Innis, *The Clear Spirit*, ix–xii.

Irigaray, Luce. *The Sex Which Is Not One*. Translated by Catherine Porter with Carolyn Burke. Ithaca: Cornell University Press, 1985.

Izawa, Yuko. "*Anne of Green Gables* in Japanese Landscapes." *CREArTA* 5 (2005): 177–85.

Jack, Christine Trimingham. "Education and Ambition in *Anne of Avonlea*." *History of Education Review* 38, no. 2 (2009): 109–20.

Jacquot, Martine. "Anne of Green Gables in Translation." Review of *Anne …
La Maison aux pignons verts*, by Lucy Maud Montgomery, translated by

Henri-Dominique Paratte. *The Atlantic Provinces Book Review* 14, no. 1 (February–March 1987): 13.

Jansen, William Hugh. "Classifying Performance in the Study of Verbal Folklore." In *Studies in Folklore: In Honour of Distinguished Service Professor Stith Thompson*, edited by W. Edson Richmond, 110–18. Bloomington: Indiana University Press, 1957.

Johnston, Rosemary Ross. "Landscape as Palimpsest, Pentimento, Epiphany: Lucy Maud Montgomery's Interiorisation of the Exterior, Exteriorisation of the Interior." *CREArTA* 5 (2005): 13–31.

–––––. "'Reaching beyond the Word': Religious Themes as 'Deep Structure' in the 'Anne' Books of L.M. Montgomery." *Canadian Children's Literature / Littérature canadienne pour la jeunesse* 88 (Winter 1997): 7–18.

Jones, Caroline E. "'Nice Folks': L.M. Montgomery's Classic and Subversive Inscriptions and Transgressions of Class." In Ledwell and Mitchell, *Anne Around the World*, 133–46.

Jones, Joseph, and Johanna Jones. *Canadian Fiction*. Boston: Twayne Publishers, 1981. Twayne's World Authors Series 630.

Jones, Susan Elizabeth. "Recurring Patterns in the Novels of L.M. Montgomery." MA thesis, University of Windsor, 1977.

Kajihara, Yuka. Akage no An o *kakitakunakatta Mongomeri*. Tokyo: Aoyama, 2000.

–––––. "An Influential Anne in Japan." In McCabe, *The Lucy Maud Montgomery Album*, 432–39.

Kalčik, Susan J. "' ... Like Ann's Gynecologist or the Time I Was Almost Raped': Personal Narratives in Women's Rap Groups." *The Journal of American Folklore* 88, no. 347 (January–March 1979): 3–11.

Karr, Clarence. "Addicted to Reading: L.M. Montgomery and the Value of Reading." In Lefebvre, "Reassessments of L.M. Montgomery," 17–33.

–––––. *Authors and Audiences: Popular Canadian Fiction in the Early Twentieth Century*. Montreal: McGill–Queen's University Press, 2000.

Katsura, Yuko. "Red-Haired Anne in Japan." *Canadian Children's Literature / Littérature canadienne pour la jeunesse* 34 (1984): 57–60.

Kazantzis, Judith. Preface to *Scars Upon My Heart: An Anthology of Women's War Poetry*, edited by Catherine W. Reilly, xv–xxiv. London: Virago, 1981.

Keefer, Janice Kulyk. *Under Eastern Eyes: A Critical Reading of Maritime Fiction*. Toronto: University of Toronto Press, 1987.

Kennard, Jean E. *Victims of Convention*. Hamden, CT: Archon Books, 1978.

Kessler, Deirdre. *Green Gables: Lucy Maud Montgomery's Favourite Places*. Photographs by Martin Caird. Halifax: Formac Publishing Company, 2001.

————. *Green Gables: Lucy Maud Montgomery's Favourite Places.* [Revised ed.] Photography by Alanna Jankov. Halifax: Formac Publishing Company, 2010.

Kindred Spirits. Avonlea, PE: Anne of Green Gables Museum, 1990–2012.

King, Ross. "Interpellation." In *Encyclopedia of Contemporary Literary Theory: Approaches, Scholars, Terms,* edited by Irena R. Makaryk, 566–68. Toronto: University of Toronto Press, 1993.

Kirchhoff, H.J. "Echoes of Montgomery in McCullough Novel?" *The Globe and Mail* (Toronto, ON), 15 January 1988, D8.

Klinck, Carl F., ed. *Literary History of Canada: Canadian Literature in English.* 1965. Toronto: University of Toronto Press, 1966.

Kjelle, Marylou Morano. *L.M. Montgomery.* Philadelphia: Chelsea House, 2005. Who Wrote That?

Kobayashi, Shin'ichirô, et al., eds. *Issa zenshû.* Tokyo: Shinano mainichi shinbun-sha, 1978.

Kodish, Debora. "Moving towards the Everyday: Some Thoughts on Gossip and Visiting as Secular Procession." *Folklore Papers of the University Folklore Association Centre for Intercultural Studies in Folklore and Ethnomusicology* 9 (1980): 93–104.

Kon'nichiwa Anne: Before Green Gables. 39 episodes. Nippon Animation, 2009.

Kornfeld, Eve, and Susan Jackson. "The Female *Bildungsroman* in Nineteenth-Century America: Parameters of a Vision." In Reimer, *Such a Simple Little Tale,* 139–52.

Kotsopoulos, Patsy Aspasia. "Avonlea as Main Street USA? Genre, Adaptation, and the Making of a Borderless Romance." *Essays on Canadian Writing* 76 (Spring 2002): 170–94.

————. "Romance and Industry on the Road to Avonlea." PhD dissertation, Simon Fraser University, 2004.

Kouno, Mariko. Akage no An *no hon'yaku ressun.* Tokyo: Babel, 1997.

Kristeva, Julia. *Desire in Language: A Semiotic Approach to Literature and Art.* Translated by Thomas Gora, Alice Jardine, and Leon S. Roudiez. Edited by Leon S. Roudiez. New York: Columbia University Press, 1980.

Kroetsch, Robert. *The Lovely Treachery of Words: Essays Selected and New.* Toronto: Oxford University Press, 1989.

Labbe, Jacqueline M. "Cultivating One's Understanding: The Female Romantic Garden." *Women's Writing* 4, no. 1 (1997): 39–56.

Lamey, Andy. "Is Anne of Green Gables Really from Sunnybrook Farm? New Book Points Out Many Similarities to American Classic." *National Post* (Toronto, ON), 10 April 1999, A1.

———. "Was Our Anne Born in Maine? Authors Claim Canada's Famous Book Owes More Than a Little to an American Classic." *National Post* (Toronto, ON), 10 April 1999, B12.

Lane, Richard J. *The Routledge Concise History of Canadian Literature.* London: Routledge, 2011.

Langille, Jacqueline. *Lucy Maud Montgomery.* Tantallon: Four East Publications, 1992. Famous Canadians.

Laurence, Margaret. *Dance on the Earth: A Memoir.* Toronto: McClelland and Stewart, 1989.

Lawson, Kate. "Adolescence and the Trauma of Maternal Inheritance in L.M. Montgomery's *Emily of New Moon.*" *Canadian Children's Literature / Littérature canadienne pour la jeunesse* 94 (Summer 1999): 21–41.

———. "The Victorian Sickroom in L.M. Montgomery's *The Blue Castle* and *Emily's Quest*: Sentimental Fiction and the Selling of Dreams." *The Lion and the Unicorn* 31, no. 3 (September 2007): 232–49.

Lecker, Robert, and Jack David, eds. *The Annotated Bibliography of Canada's Major Authors.* 8 volumes. Toronto: ECW Press, 1979–94.

Lecker, Robert, Jack David, and Ellen Quigley, eds. *Canadian Writers and Their Works: Fiction Series.* 12 volumes. Toronto: ECW Press, 1983–95.

———. *Canadian Writers and Their Works: Poetry Series.* 12 volumes. Toronto: ECW Press, 1988–96.

Ledwell, Jane, and Jean Mitchell, eds. *Anne Around the World: L.M. Montgomery and Her Classic.* Montreal: McGill–Queen's University Press, 2013.

Lefebvre, Benjamin. Afterword to Montgomery, *The Blythes Are Quoted,* 511–20.

———. "Editorial: Assessments and Reassessments." In Lefebvre, "Reassessments of L.M. Montgomery," 6–13.

———. "Pigsties and Sunsets: L.M. Montgomery, *A Tangled Web,* and a Modernism of Her Own." *English Studies in Canada* 31, no. 4 (December 2005): 123–46.

———. "Présentation: Méthodes d'évaluation." In Lefebvre, "Reassessments of L.M. Montgomery," 14–16.

———, ed. "Reassessments of L.M. Montgomery." Special issue, *Canadian Children's Literature / Littérature canadienne pour la jeunesse* 113–14 (Spring–Summer 2004).

———. "*Road to Avonlea*: A Co-production of the Disney Corporation." In Gammel, *Making Avonlea,* 174–85.

———. "Stand by Your Man: Adapting L.M. Montgomery's *Anne of Green Gables.*" *Essays on Canadian Writing* 76 (Spring 2002): 149–69.

————, ed. *Textual Transformations in Children's Literature: Adaptations, Translations, Reconsiderations.* New York: Routledge, 2013.

————. "'That Abominable War!' *The Blythes Are Quoted* and Thoughts on L.M. Montgomery's Late Style." In Mitchell, *Storm and Dissonance*, 83–108.

————. "Walter's Closet." *Canadian Children's Literature / Littérature canadienne pour la jeunesse* 94 (Summer 1999): 7–20.

————. "What's in a Name? Towards a Theory of the Anne Brand." In Gammel and Lefebvre, *Anne's World*, 192–211.

Lefebvre, Benjamin, and Andrea McKenzie. "A Note on the Text." In Montgomery, *Rilla of Ingleside*, edited by Lefebvre and McKenzie, xx.

Leslie, Eliza. *Amelia; or, a Young Lady's Vicissitudes.* Philadelphia: Carey and Hart, 1848.

Lewis, Naomi. Introduction to *The Penguin Kenneth Grahame:* The Golden Age, Dream Days, The Wind in the Willows, vii–xiv. Harmondsworth, UK: Penguin, 1983.

Liddle, Peter. "British Loyalties: The Evidence of an Archive." In *Facing Armageddon: The First World War Experienced*, edited by Hugh Cecil and Peter H. Liddle, 523–38. London: Leo Cooper, 1996.

Life and Times: The Many Mauds. Directed by Barbara Doran. Morag Productions/Canadian Broadcasting Corporation, 1996.

Litster, Jennifer H. "The Scottish Context of L.M. Montgomery." PhD dissertation, University of Edinburgh, 2001.

————. "The 'Secret' Diary of Maud Montgomery, Aged 28 1/4." In Gammel, *The Intimate Life of L.M. Montgomery*, 88–105.

Little, Jean. "But What about Jane?" *Canadian Children's Literature* 1, no. 3 (Autumn 1975): 71–81.

————. "A Long-Distance Friendship." *Canadian Children's Literature / Littérature canadienne pour la jeunesse* 34 (1984): 23–30.

"L.M. Montgomery and Popular Culture." Special issue, *Canadian Children's Literature / Littérature canadienne pour la jeunesse* 91–92 (Fall–Winter 1998).

"L.M. Montgomery and Popular Culture II." Special issue, *Canadian Children's Literature / Littérature canadienne pour la jeunesse* 99 (Fall 2000).

"L.M. Montgomery's Interior/Exterior Landscapes." Special issue, *CREArTA* 5 (2005).

Logan, J.D., and Donald G. French. *Highways of Canadian Literature: A Synoptic Introduction to the Literary History of Canada (English) from 1760 to 1924.* Toronto: McClelland and Stewart, 1924.

Lönnroth, Ami. "Halva himlens frihetshjaltinna." *Svenska Dagbladet* (Stockholm, Sweden), 8 March 1991, D2, D16.

Lucy Maud Montgomery: The Road to Green Gables. Directed by Terence Macartney-Filgate. Canadian Broadcasting Corporation, 1975.

Lunn, Janet. *Maud's House of Dreams: The Life of Lucy Maud Montgomery.* N.p.: Doubleday Canada, 2002.

Lynes, Jeanette. "Consumable Avonlea: The Commodification of the Green Gables Mythlogy." *Canadian Children's Literature / Littérature canadienne pour la jeunesse* 91–92 (Fall–Winter 1998): 7–21. Also in Gammel, *Making Avonlea*, 268–79.

MacDonald, Heidi. "Reflections of the Great Depression in L.M. Montgomery's Life and Her *Pat* Books." In Mitchell, *Storm and Dissonance*, 142–58.

Macdonald, Kate. *The Anne of Green Gables Cookbook.* Illustrated by Barbara Di Lella. Toronto: Oxford University Press, 1985. Toronto: Seal Books, 1988. Don Mills, ON: Oxford University Press, 2003.

Macdonald, Lyn. *The Roses of No Man's Land.* 1980. London: Penguin Books, 1993.

Macdonald, Rae M. "The Regional Novel in Canada, 1880–1925." PhD dissertation, Dalhousie University, 1975.

MacEachern, Alan. *Natural Selections: National Parks in Atlantic Canada, 1935–1970.* Montreal: McGill–Queen's University Press, 2001.

Mackey, Margaret. "Inhabiting *Anne*'s World: The Performance of a Story Space." In *Turning the Page: Children's Literature in Performance and the Media*, edited by Fiona M. Collins and Jeremy Ridgman, 61–82. Bern: Peter Lang, 2006.

MacLeod, Anne Scott. "The *Caddie Woodlawn* Syndrome: American Girlhood in the Nineteenth Century." In *A Century of Childhood 1820–1920*, by Mary Lynn Stevens Heininger et al., 97–119. Rochester: The Margaret Woodbury Strong Museum, 1984.

MacLeod, Elizabeth. *The Kids Book of Great Canadians.* Illustrated by John Mantha. Toronto: Kids Can Press, 2004.

———. *Lucy Maud Montgomery.* Illustrated by John Mantha. Toronto: Kids Can Press, 2008. Kids Can Read.

———. *Lucy Maud Montgomery: A Writer's Life.* Toronto: Kids Can Press, 2001.

MacLulich, T.D. *Between Europe and America: The Canadian Tradition in Fiction.* N.p.: ECW Press, 1988.

———. *Hugh MacLennan.* Boston: Twayne Publishers, 1983. Twayne's World Authors Series 708.

————. "L.M. Montgomery and the Literary Heroine: Jo, Rebecca, Anne and Emily." *Canadian Children's Literature / Littérature canadienne pour la jeunesse* 37 (1985): 5–17.

————. "L.M. Montgomery's Portraits of the Artist: Realism, Idealism, and the Domestic Imagination." In Reimer, *Such a Simple Little Tale*, 83–100.

MacMillan, Carrie, Lorraine McMullen, and Elizabeth Waterston. *Silenced Sextet: Six Nineteenth-Century Canadian Women Novelists*. Montreal: McGill–Queen's University Press, 1992.

Macquarrie, Jenn. "Growing Up in Nature: Health and Adolescent Dance in L.M. Montgomery's Emily Series." *Studies in Canadian Literature / Études en littérature canadienne* 36, no. 1 (2011): 34–50.

Mann, Susan. Introduction to *The War Diary of Clare Gass, 1915–1918*, edited by Susan Mann, xiii–xlvii. Montreal: McGill–Queen's University Press, 2000.

Manuel, Lynn. *Lucy Maud and the Cavendish Cat*. Illustrated by Janet Wilson. Toronto: Tundra Books, 1997.

Marchildon, Leo, and Adam-Michael James. *The Nine Lives of L.M. Montgomery*. Unpublished play, 2008.

Marks, Patricia. *Bicycles, Bangs and Bloomers: The Image of the New Woman in the Popular Press*. Lexington: University Press of Kentucky, 1990.

Matsumoto, Yûko. Akage no An *ni kakusareta Sheikusupia*. Tokyo: Shûei-sha, 2001.

————. *Dare mo shiranai* Akage no An. Tokyo: Shûei-sha, 2000.

Matthews, Marlene. *But When She Was Bad ...* Toronto: HarperCollins Publishers, 1994. New York: Bantam Skylark, 1994. Road to Avonlea 23.

————. *Double Trouble*. Toronto: HarperCollins Publishers, 1994. New York: Bantam Skylark, 1994. Road to Avonlea 24.

McAnn, Aida B. "Life and Works of L.M. Montgomery." *The Maritime Advocate and Busy East* (Sackville, NB), June–July 1942, 19–22.

McCabe, Kevin, comp. *The Lucy Maud Montgomery Album*. Edited by Alexandra Heilbron. Toronto: Fitzhenry and Whiteside, 1999.

————. "Lucy Maud Montgomery: The Person and the Poet." *Canadian Children's Literature / Littérature canadienne pour la jeunesse* 38 (1985): 68–80.

McCabe, Shauna Joanne. "Representing Islandness: Myth, Memory, and Modernisation in Prince Edward Island." PhD dissertation, The University of British Columbia, 2001.

McClung, Nellie L. *In Times Like These*. Toronto: McLeod and Allen, 1915.

————. *Purple Springs*. 1921. Toronto: University of Toronto Press, 1992.

————. *Sowing Seeds in Danny*. Toronto: William Briggs, 1908.

————. *Stories Subversive: Through the Field with Gloves Off*. Edited by Marilyn I. Davis. Ottawa: University of Ottawa Press, 1996.

————. *The Stream Runs Fast: My Own Story*. Toronto: Thomas Allen and Son, 1945.

McCrae, John. "In Flanders Fields." *Punch, or the London Charivari* (London, UK), 8 December 1915, 468.

————. *"In Flanders Fields" and Other Poems*. Edited by Andrew Macphail. Toronto: William Briggs, 1919.

McCullough, Colleen. *The Ladies of Missalonghi*. London: Century–Hutchinson, 1987.

McDonald-Rissanen, Mary. *In the Interval of the Wave: Prince Edward Island Women's Nineteenth- and Twentieth-Century Life Writing*. Montreal: McGill–Queen's University Press, 2013.

McDonough, Frank. *The British Empire 1815–1914*. London: Hodder and Stoughton, 1994.

McDowell, Marjorie. "Children's Books." In Klinck, *Literary History of Canada*, 624–32.

McGrath, Robin. "Alice of New Moon: The Influence of Lewis Carroll on L.M. Montgomery's Emily Bird [*sic*] Starr." *Canadian Children's Literature / Littérature canadienne pour la jeunesse* 65 (1992): 62–67.

McGregor, Gaile. *The Wacousta Syndrome: Explorations in the Canadian Langscape*. Toronto: University of Toronto Press, 1985.

McHugh, Fiona, adapt. *The Anne of Green Gables Storybook*. Based on the Kevin Sullivan Film of Lucy Maud Montgomery's Classic Novel. 1987. Richmond Hill, ON: Firefly Books, 2002.

————, ed. *The Avonlea Album*. From the Sullivan Films Television Series Based on the Novels of L.M. Montgomery. Willowdale, ON: Firefly Books, 1991.

————. *The Calamitous Courting of Hetty King*. New York: Bantam Skylark, 1995. Road to Avonlea 28.

————. *Of Corsets and Secrets and True True Love*. Toronto: HarperCollins Publishers, 1992. New York: Bantam Skylark, 1993. Road to Avonlea 14.

————. *Quarantine at Alexander Abraham's*. Toronto: HarperCollins Publishers, 1991. New York: Bantam Skylark, 1992. Road to Avonlea 5.

————. *Song of the Night*. Toronto: HarperCollins Publishers, 1991. New York: Bantam Skylark, 1992. Road to Avonlea 3.

McKenna, Isobel. "Women in Canadian Literature." *Canadian Literature* 62 (Autumn 1974): 69–78.

McKenzie, Andrea. "The Changing Faces of Canadian Children: Pictures, Power, and Pedagogy." In Hudson and Cooper, *Windows and Words*, 201–18.

———. "Patterns, Power, and Paradox: International Book Covers of *Anne of Green Gables* across a Century." In Lefebvre, *Textual Transformations in Children's Literature*, 127–53.

———. "Witnesses to War: Discourse and Community in the Correspondence of Vera Brittain, Roland Leighton, Edward Brittain, Geoffrey Thurlow and Victor Richardson, 1914–1918." PhD dissertation, University of Waterloo, 2000.

———. "Writing in Pictures: International Images of Emily." In Gammel, *Making Avonlea*, 99–113.

McKenzie, Catherine. *Arranged*. Toronto: HarperCollins Publishers, 2011.

McLaughlin, Anne Kathleen. *Maud of Cavendish*. Unpublished play, 2004.

McLaughlin, Gertrude (Sister M. Joanne of Christ). "The Literary Art of L.M. Montgomery." MA thesis, Université de Montréal, 1961.

McQuillan, Julia, and Julie Pfeiffer. "Why Anne Makes Us Dizzy: Reading *Anne of Green Gables* from a Gender Perspective." *Mosaic* 34, no. 2 (June 2001): 17–32.

Mehlinger, Laura Li-Jing. *Anne of Green Gables; L.M. Montgomery*. New York: Spark Publishing, 2002. SparkNotes: Today's Most Popular Study Guides.

Menzies, Ian. "The Moral of the Rose: L.M. Montgomery's Emily." *Canadian Children's Literature / Littérature canadienne pour la jeunesse* 65 (1992): 48–61.

Miller, Kathleen A. "Weaving a Tapestry of Beauty: Anne Shirley as Domestic Artist." *Canadian Children's Literature / Littérature canadienne pour la jeunesse* 34, no. 2 (Fall 2008): 30–49.

Miller, Nancy K. *Subject to Change: Reading Feminist Writing*. New York: Columbia University Press, 1988.

Mitchell, Jean, ed. *Storm and Dissonance: L.M. Montgomery and Conflict*. Newcastle, UK: Cambridge Scholars Publishing, 2008.

Montgomery, L.M. *Across the Miles: Tales of Correspondence*. Edited by Rea Wilmshurst. Toronto: McClelland and Stewart, 1995.

———. *After Green Gables: L.M. Montgomery's Letters to Ephraim Weber, 1916–1941*. Edited by Hildi Froese Tiessen and Paul Gerard Tiessen. Toronto: University of Toronto Press, 2006.

———. *After Many Days: Tales of Time Passed*. Edited by Rea Wilmshurst. Toronto: McClelland and Stewart, 1991.

———. *Against the Odds: Tales of Achievement*. Edited by Rea Wilmshurst. Toronto: McClelland and Stewart, 1993.

———. *Akage no An*. Translated by Yasuko Kakegawa. Tokyo: Kôdan-sha, 1999. Japanese translation of *Anne of Green Gables*.

———. *Akage no An*. Translated by Hanako Muraoka. 1954. Tokyo: Shinchô-sha, 1993. Japanese translation of *Anne of Green Gables*.

———. *Akin to Anne: Tales of Other Orphans*. Edited by Rea Wilmshurst. Toronto: McClelland and Stewart, 1988.

———. *Along the Shore: Tales by the Sea*. Edited by Rea Wilmshurst. Toronto: McClelland and Stewart, 1989.

———. "The Alpine Path: The Story of My Career." *Everywoman's World* (Toronto, ON), June 1917, 38–39, 41; July 1917, 16, 32–33, 35; August 1917, 16, 32–33; September 1917, 8, 49; October 1917, 8, 58; November 1917, 25, 38, 40.

———. *The Alpine Path: The Story of My Career*. 1917. Toronto: Fitzhenry and Whiteside, n.d.

———. *Among the Shadows: Tales from the Darker Side*. Edited by Rea Wilmshurst. Toronto: McClelland and Stewart, 1990.

———. *Anne et le bonheur*. Translated by Suzanne Pairault. Illustrated by Jacques Fromont. Paris: Hachette, 1964. French translation of *Anne of Green Gables*.

——— [Lucy Maud Montgomery]. *Anne ... La Maison aux pignons verts*. Translated by Henri-Dominique Paratte. Montreal: Éditions Québec–Amérique; Charlottetown: Ragweed Press, 1986. French translation of *Anne of Green Gables*.

———. *Anne of Avonlea*. 1909. Toronto: Seal Books, 1996.

———. *Anne of Green Gables*. 1908. Toronto: Seal Books, 1996.

———. *Anne of Green Gables*. 1908. New York: The Modern Library, 2008.

———. *Anne of Green Gables*. 1908. Toronto: Penguin Canada, 2008. 100 Years of Anne.

———. "Anne of Green Gables" (manuscript). CM 67.5.1, Confederation Centre Art Gallery and Museum, Charlottetown.

———. *Anne of Green Gables*. Condensed and abridged by Mary W. Cushing and D.C. Williams. Illustrated by Robert Patterson. New York: Grosset and Dunlap, 1961.

———. *Anne of Green Gables*. 1908. Edited by Cecily Devereux. Peterborough, ON: Broadview Editions, 2004.

———. *Anne of Green Gables*. 1908. Edited by Mary Henley Rubio and Elizabeth Waterston. New York: W.W. Norton and Company, 2007. A Norton Critical Edition.

———. *Anne of Green Gables*. 1908. Introduction and Afterword by Joe Wheeler. Wheaton, IL: Tyndale House Publishers, 1999. Focus on the Family: Great Stories.

———. *Anne of Ingleside*. 1939. Toronto: Seal Books, 1996.

———. *Anne of the Island*. 1915. Toronto: Seal Books, 1996.

———. *Anne of Windy Poplars*. 1936. Toronto: Seal Books, 1996.

———. *Anne ou les illusions heureuses*. Translated by S. Maerky-Richard. Illustrated by W.F. Burger. Geneva: J.-H. Jeheber, 1925. French translation of *Anne of Green Gables*.

———. "Anne Says Her Prayers." In *A Century of Canadian Literature / Un siècle de littérature canadienne*, edited by Gordon Greene and Guy Sylvestre, 83–86. Toronto: The Ryerson Press; Montreal: Éditions HMH, 1967.

———. "Anne's Company Gets Drunk." In *Atlantic Anthology*, edited by Will R. Bird, 204–11. Toronto: McClelland and Stewart, 1959.

———. *Anne's House of Dreams*. 1917. Toronto: Seal Books, 1996.

———. *The Annotated Anne of Green Gables*. Edited by Wendy E. Barry, Margaret Anne Doody, and Mary E. Doody Jones. New York: Oxford University Press, 1997.

———. *At the Altar: Matrimonial Tales*. Edited by Rea Wilmshurst. Toronto: McClelland and Stewart, 1994.

———. *The Blue Castle*. 1926. Toronto: Seal Books, 1988.

———. *The Blythes Are Quoted*. Edited by Benjamin Lefebvre. Toronto: Viking Canada, 2009.

———. "The Blythes Are Quoted" (typescript). File 10–11, Box 31, Jack McClelland fonds, William Ready Division of Archives and Research Collections, McMaster University Library.

———. "The Blythes Are Quoted" (typescript). Box 328, Series X, McClelland and Stewart fonds, Manuscript Bundles, William Ready Division of Archives and Research Collections, McMaster University Library.

———. "The Blythes Are Quoted – Original MS. with annotations by E. Stuart Macdonald" (typescript). XZ1 MS A098001, L.M. Montgomery Collection, Archival and Special Collections, University of Guelph Library.

———. "The Blythes Are Quoted – Typescript" (typescript). XZ1 MS A098002, L.M. Montgomery Collection, Archival and Special Collections, University of Guelph Library.

———. Book Price Record Book, 1908–1942. XZ1 MS A098043, L.M. Montgomery Collection, Archival and Special Collections, University of Guelph Library.

———. "Calling a Minister." In *A Book of Canada*, edited by William Toye, 359–66. London: Collins, 1962.

———. *Christmas with Anne and Other Holiday Stories*. Edited by Rea Wilmshurst. Toronto: McClelland and Stewart, 1995.

———. *Chronicles of Avonlea*. 1912. Toronto: Seal Books, 1993.

Bibliography

————. *The Complete Journals of L.M. Montgomery: The PEI Years, 1889–1900*. Edited by Mary Henley Rubio and Elizabeth Hillman Waterston. Don Mills, ON: Oxford University Press, 2012.

————. *The Complete Journals of L.M. Montgomery: The PEI Years, 1901–1911*. Edited by Mary Henley Rubio and Elizabeth Hillman Waterston. Don Mills, ON: Oxford University Press, 2013.

————. "Contracts, Picture of S.K. Woolner, MS. of 'The Blythes Are Quoted,' Journal and Literary MSS. of C.C. Macdonald, 1916–1945." XZ1 MS A100, L.M. Montgomery Collection, Archival and Special Collections, University of Guelph Library.

————. *The Doctor's Sweetheart and Other Stories*. Selected by Catherine McLay. Toronto: McGraw–Hill Ryerson, 1979. Toronto: Seal Books, 1993.

————. "Edited Version of L.M. Montgomery Journals" (typescript). XZ5 MS A021, L.M. Montgomery Collection, Archival and Special Collections, University of Guelph Library.

———— [Lucy Maud Montgomery]. *Émilie de la Nouvelle Lune*. 4 volumes. Translated by Paule Daveluy. Montreal: Pierre Tisseyre, 1983. French translation of *Emily of New Moon* (in two volumes), *Emily Climbs*, and *Emily's Quest*.

————. *Emily Climbs*. 1925. Toronto: Seal Books, 1998.

————. *Emily of New Moon*. 1923. Leicester, UK: F.A. Thorpe Publishing, 1980. Ulverscroft Large Print.

————. *Emily of New Moon*. 1923. Toronto: Seal Books, 1998.

————. "Emily of New Moon" (manuscript). CM 67.5.8, Confederation Centre Art Gallery and Museum, Charlottetown.

————. *Emily's Quest*. 1927. Toronto: Seal Books, 1998.

————. *Further Chronicles of Avonlea*. 1920. Toronto: Seal Books, 1987.

————. "The Girls of Silver Bush" (manuscript of *Mistress Pat*). CM 78.5.6, Confederation Centre Art Gallery and Museum, Charlottetown.

————. "A Girl's Place at Dalhousie College." *Atlantis: A Women's Studies Journal* 5 (Fall 1979): 146–53.

————. *The Green Gables Letters from L.M. Montgomery to Ephraim Weber, 1905–1909*. Edited by Wilfrid Eggleston. 1960. Ottawa: Borealis Press, 1981.

————. "How I Became a Writer." *Manitoba Free Press* (Winnipeg, MB), 3 December 1921, Christmas Book Section, 3.

————. *Jane of Lantern Hill*. 1937. Toronto: Seal Books, 1993.

————. "Journals of L.M. Montgomery; September 21, 1889 to March 23, 1942." XZ5 MS A001, L.M. Montgomery Collection, Archival and Special Collections, University of Guelph Library.

———. *Kilmeny of the Orchard*. 1910. Toronto: Seal Books, 1987.

———. Letters to Frederick Philip Grove. Collection MSS2, Box 3, Folder 10, University of Manitoba Archives.

———. Letters to G.B. MacMillan. George Boyd MacMillan fonds, Library and Archives Canada.

———. Letters to Ephraim Weber. Ephraim Weber fonds, Library and Archives Canada.

———. *Magic for Marigold*. 1929. Toronto: Seal Books, 1988.

———. *Mistress Pat*. 1935. Toronto: Seal Books, 1988.

———. *My Dear Mr. M: Letters to G.B. MacMillan from L.M. Montgomery*. Edited by Francis W.P. Bolger and Elizabeth R. Epperly. 1980. Toronto: Oxford University Press, 1992.

———. *Pat of Silver Bush*. 1935. Toronto: Seal Books, 1988.

———. *The Poetry of Lucy Maud Montgomery*. Selected by John Ferns and Kevin McCabe. Toronto: Fitzhenry and Whiteside, 1987.

———. *Rainbow Valley*. 1919. Toronto: Seal Books, 1996.

———. "Rainbow Valley" (manuscript). CM 78.5.2, Confederation Centre Art Gallery and Museum, Charlottetown.

———, comp. Red Scrapbook 1. Scrapbooks of Clippings, Programs, and Other Memorabilia. XZ5 MS A002, L.M. Montgomery Collection, Archival and Special Collections, University of Guelph Library.

———. *Rilla of Ingleside*. 1921. Edited by Benjamin Lefebvre and Andrea McKenzie. Toronto: Viking Canada, 2010.

———. *The Road to Yesterday*. Toronto: McGraw–Hill Ryerson, 1974. London: Angus and Robertson, 1975. Toronto: Seal Books, 1993.

———, comp. "Scrapbook of Reviews from Around the World Which L.M. Montgomery's Clipping Service Sent to Her, 1910–1935." XZ5 MS A003, L.M. Montgomery Collection, Archival and Special Collections, University of Guelph Library.

———. *The Selected Journals of L.M. Montgomery*, Volume 1: *1889–1910*; Volume 2: *1910–1921*; Volume 3: *1921–1929*; Volume 4: *1929–1935*; Volume 5: *1935–1942*. Edited by Mary Rubio and Elizabeth Waterston. Toronto: Oxford University Press, 1985, 1987, 1992, 1998, 2004.

———. *The Story Girl*. 1911. Toronto: Seal Books, 1987.

———. "'Suicide' Note Written by L.M. Montgomery, April 22, 1942." XZ1 MS A098197, L.M. Montgomery Collection, Archival and Special Collections, University of Guelph Library.

———. *A Tangled Web*. 1931. Toronto: Seal Books, 1989.

———. *Una of the Garden*. 1908–9. Edited by Donna J. Campbell and Simon Lloyd. N.p.: L.M. Montgomery Institute, 2010.

———. *The Watchman and Other Poems*. Toronto: McClelland, Goodchild, and Stewart, 1916.

———. *The Way to Slumbertown*. Illustrated by Rachel Bédard. Montreal: Lobster Press, 2005.

———. "Will, Codicil, and Estate Papers of L.M. Montgomery [1939]." XZ1 MS A098008, L.M. Montgomery Collection, Archival and Special Collections, University of Guelph Library.

———. "The Wood Pool." *Christian Endeavor World* (Boston, MA), 11 September 1913, 987. Also in Montgomery, *The Watchman and Other Poems*, 54. Also in Montgomery, *The Poetry of Lucy Maud Montgomery*, 43.

Montgomery, L.M., Marian Keith, and Mabel Burns McKinley. *Courageous Women*. Toronto: McClelland and Stewart, 1934.

Montgomery, L.M., and Nora Lefurgey. "' ... Where Has My Yellow Garter Gone?' The Diary of L.M. Montgomery and Nora Lefurgey." Edited by Irene Gammel. In Gammel, *The Intimate Life of L.M. Montgomery*, 19–87.

"Montgomery, Lucy Maud." In *Twentieth-Century Authors: A Biographical Dictionary of Modern Literature*, edited by Stanley J. Kunitz and Howard Haycraft, 974–75. New York: The H.W. Wilson Company, 1942.

Moodie, Susanna. *Roughing It in the Bush*. 1852. London: Virago, 1986.

Moretti, Franco. *The Way of the World: The Bildungsroman in European Culture*. London: Verso Press, 1987.

Moritz, Albert, and Theresa Moritz. *The Oxford Illustrated Literary Guide to Canada*. Toronto: Oxford University Press, 1987.

Moss, Anita, and Jon C. Stott. *The Family of Stories: An Anthology of Children's Literature*. New York: Holt, Rinehart, and Winston, 1986.

Moss, John. *A Reader's Guide to the Canadian Novel*. Toronto: McClelland and Stewart, 1981.

Munro, Alice. Afterword to *Emily of New Moon*, by L.M. Montgomery, 357–61. Toronto: McClelland and Stewart, 1989. New Canadian Library.

———. "An Interview with Alice Munro." With Catherine Ross. *Canadian Children's Literature / Littérature canadienne pour la jeunesse* 53 (1989): 14–24.

———. "The Real Material: An Interview with Alice Munro." With J.R. (Tim) Struthers. In *Probable Fictions: Alice Munro's Narrative Acts*, edited by Louis K. MacKendrick, 5–36. Toronto: ECW Press, 1983.

Muuss, Rolf E. *Theories of Adolescence*. New York: Random House, 1962.

Narbonne, Andre. "The Order of Good Cheer: Carlylean Idealism and the Confederation Humorists Sara Jeannette Duncan, Lucy Maud

Montgomery, Stephen Leacock." PhD dissertation, University of Western Ontario, 2004.

Nesbit, E. *The Wouldbegoods*. 1901. Harmondsworth, UK: Puffin, 1987.

Neutze, Christine Dorothy. "Colonial Children: The Fictional Worlds of L.M. Montgomery, Isabel Maud Peacocke, and Ethel Turner." PhD dissertation, University of Auckland, 1981.

Newton, Judith, and Deborah Rosenfelt. "Introduction: Toward a Materialist-Feminist Criticism." In *Feminist Criticism and Social Change: Sex, Class, and Race in Literature and Culture*, edited by Judith Newton and Deborah Rosenfelt, xv–xxxix. New York: Methuen, 1985.

Niall, Brenda. "Writing from Home: The Literary Careers of Ethel Turner and L.M. Montgomery." *Children's Literature Association Quarterly* 15, no. 4 (Winter 1990): 175–80.

Nikolajeva, Maria. "Beyond Happily Ever After: The Aesthetic Dilemma of Multivolume Fiction for Children." In Lefebvre, *Textual Transformations in Children's Literature*, 197–213.

Nodelman, Perry. "Editorial: Goodnight, Sweet Prints." *Canadian Children's Literature / Littérature canadienne pour la jeunesse* 34, no. 2 (Fall 2008): 1–4.

———. "Progressive Utopia: Or, How to Grow Up without Growing Up." In Reimer, *Such a Simple Little Tale*, 29–38.

———. "Rereading *Anne of Green Gables* in *Anne of Ingleside*: L.M. Montgomery's Variations." *Canadian Children's Literature / Littérature canadienne pour la jeunesse* 34, no. 2 (Fall 2008): 75–97.

Nolan, D. Jason, Jeff Lawrence, and Yuka Kajihara. "Montgomery's Island in the Net: Metaphor and Community on the Kindred Spirits E-mail List." *Canadian Children's Literature / Littérature canadienne pour la jeunesse* 91–92 (Fall–Winter 1998): 64–77.

Nolan, D. Jason, and Joel Weiss. "Learning in Cyberspace: An Educational View of Virtual Community." In *Building Virtual Communities: Learning and Change in Cyberspace*, edited by K. Ann Renninger and Wesley Shumar, 293–320. Cambridge: Cambridge University Press, 2002.

Norcross, E. Blanche. *Pioneers Every One: Canadian Women of Achievement*. N.p.: Burns and MacEachern, 1979.

Nussbaum, Felicity A. *The Autobiographical Subject: Gender and Ideology in Eighteenth-Century England*. Baltimore, MD: The Johns Hopkins University Press, 1989.

Ogura, Chikako. "Sengo Nihon to *Akage no An*." In *Danjo toiu seido*, edited by Saitô Minako, 137–59. Toyko: Iwanami shoten, 2001.

Okuda, Miki. *Kikô* Akage no An. Tokyo: Shoubun-sha, 1997.

Olney, James, ed. *Studies in Autobiography*. New York: Oxford University Press, 1988.

Oppel, Kenneth. "The Best Canadian Kids Book of All Time." *Quill and Quire* (Toronto, ON), October 1997, 1, 15–16.

Orwen, Patricia. "Kindred Spirits." *The Toronto Star* (Toronto, ON), 18 August 1991, C1, C3.

Ouditt, Sharon. *Fighting Forces, Writing Women: Identity and Ideology in the First World War*. New York: Routledge, 1994.

Owen, Wilfrid. *Collected Poems of Wilfrid Owen*. London: Chatto and Windus, 1974.

Pacey, Desmond. *Creative Writing in Canada: A Short History of English-Canadian Literature*. Toronto: The Ryerson Press, 1952.

——. *Creative Writing in Canada*. Rev. ed. Toronto: The Ryerson Press, 1967.

——. *Essays in Canadian Criticism 1938–1968*. Toronto: The Ryerson Press, 1969.

——. *Frederick Philip Grove*. 1945. Toronto: The Ryerson Press, 1970.

——. *Ten Canadian Poets: A Group of Biographical and Critical Essays*. Toronto: The Ryerson Press, 1958.

Page, P.K. Afterword to *Emily's Quest*, by L.M. Montgomery, 237–42. Toronto: McClelland and Stewart, 1989. New Canadian Library.

Paine, Robert. "What Is Gossip About? An Alternative Hypothesis." *Man* n.s. 2, no. 2 (June 1967): 278–85.

Palk, Helen. *The Book of Canadian Achievement*. Toronto: J.M. Dent and Sons, 1951.

Palmer, Svetlana, and Sarah Wallis. *Intimate Voices from the First World War*. New York: William Morrow and Company, 2003.

Parker, George L. "*Anne of Green Gables* (1908)." In Toye, *The Oxford Companion to Canadian Literature*, 14–15.

——. "Montgomery, L.M. (1874–1942)." In Toye, *The Oxford Companion to Canadian Literature*, 528–29. Also in *The Oxford Companion to Canadian Literature*, edited by Eugene Benson and William Toye, 2nd ed., 760–62. Toronto: Oxford University Press, 1997.

Parsons, I.M., ed. *Men Who March Away: Poems of the First World War; An Anthology*. London: Chatto and Windus, 1965.

Patchell, Kathleen. "Faith, Fiction, and Fame: *Sowing Seeds in Danny* and *Anne of Green Gables*." PhD dissertation, University of Ottawa, 2011.

Peene, Vida. Foreword to Innis, *The Clear Spirit*, v.

Peters, Sara. *1996*. Toronto: House of Anansi Press, 2013.

Petrey, Sandy. *Speech Acts and Literary Theory*. New York: Routledge, 1990.

Pevere, Geoff, and Greig Dymond. *Mondo Canuck: A Canadian Pop Culture Odyssey*. Scarborough, ON: Prentice Hall Canada, 1996.

Phelps, Arthur L. *Canadian Writers*. Toronto: McClelland and Stewart, 1951.

Pierpont, Claudia Roth. "A Woman's Place." *The New Yorker* (New York, NY), 27 January 1992, 69–83.

Pike, E. Holly. "The Heroine Who Writes and Her Creator." In M.H. Rubio, *Harvesting Thistles*, 50–57.

———. "Mass Marketing, Popular Culture, and the Canadian Celebrity Author." In Gammel, *Making Avonlea*, 238–51.

———. "'Tempest in a Teapot': Domestic Service and Class Conflict in L.M. Montgomery's Journals and Fiction." In Mitchell, *Storm and Dissonance*, 161–77.

Poe, K.L. "The Whole of the Moon: L.M. Montgomery's Anne of Green Gables Series." In *Nancy Drew and Company: Culture, Gender, and Girls' Series*, edited by Sherrie A. Inness, 15–35. Bowling Green: Bowling Green State University Popular Press, 1997.

Posey, Catherine. "Ethereal Etchings: Connecting with the Natural World in Lucy Maud Montgomery's *Anne of Green Gables* (1908), *Emily of New Moon* (1923), and *Magic for Marigold* (1929)." In *Knowing Their Place? Identity and Space in Children's Literature*, edited by Terri Doughty and Dawn Thompson, 95–108. Newcastle upon Tyne, UK: Cambridge Scholars Publishing, 2011.

Potter, Jane. *Boys in Khaki, Girls in Print: Women's Literary Responses to the Great War 1914–1918*. Oxford: Oxford University Press, 2005.

Pratt, Annis. *Archetypal Patterns in Women's Fiction*. Bloomington: Indiana University Press, 1981.

Pratt, Mary Louise. *Toward a Speech Act Theory of Literary Discourse*. Bloomington: Indiana University Press, 1977.

Preface to Montgomery, *The Alpine Path*, 5–6.

Prentice, Alison, et al. *Canadian Women: A History*. Toronto: Harcourt Brace, 1988.

Pykett, Lyn. *The "Improper" Feminine: The Women's Sensation Novel and the New Woman Writing*. London: Routledge, 1992.

Quaile, Deborah. *L.M. Montgomery: The Norval Years, 1926–1935*. N.p.: Wordbird Press, 2006.

Rae, Arlene Perly. *Everybody's Favourites: Canadians Talk about Books That Changed Their Lives*. 1997. Toronto: Penguin Books, 1998.

Read, Robert W. "Writing for Children in Canada." *Canadian Author & Bookman*, Summer 1975, 9–10.

Redekop, Magdalene. "Canadian Literary Criticism and the Idea of a National Literature." In *The Cambridge Companion to Canadian Literature*, edited by Eva-Marie Kröller, 269–95. Cambridge: Cambridge University Press, 2004.

Reid, Verna. "From Anne of G.G. to Jacob Two-Two: A Response to Canadian Children's Fiction." *The English Quarterly* 9, no. 4 (Winter 1976–1977): 11–23.

Reimer, Mavis. "The Child of Nature and the Home Child." *Jeunesse: Young People, Texts, Cultures* 5, no. 2 (Winter 2013): 1–16.

——. "A Daughter of the House: Discourses of Adoption in L.M. Montgomery's *Anne of Green Gables*." In *The Oxford Handbook of Children's Literature*, edited by Julia L. Mickenberg and Lynne Vallone, 329–50. New York: Oxford University Press, 2011.

——, ed. *Such a Simple Little Tale: Critical Responses to L.M. Montgomery's Anne of Green Gables*. Metuchen, NJ: Children's Literature Association and Scarecrow Press, 1992.

Rhodenizer, Vernon Blair. *Canadian Literature in English*. Montreal: Quality Press, 1965.

——. *A Handbook of Canadian Literature*. Ottawa: Graphic Publishers, 1930.

Ridley, Hilda M. *The Story of L.M. Montgomery*. Toronto: The Ryerson Press, 1956. London: George G. Harrap and Co., 1956. Toronto: McGraw–Hill Ryerson, n.d.

Road to Avonlea. 91 episodes. Sullivan Entertainment, 1990–96.

Robinson, John A. "Personal Narratives Reconsidered." *Journal of American Folklore* 94, no. 371 (January–March 1981): 58–85.

Robinson, Laura M. "'Big Gay Anne': Queering Anne of Green Gables and Canadian Culture." In *Canadian Studies: An Introductory Reader*, edited by Donald Wright, 377–85. Dubuque, IO: Kendall/Hunt, 2004.

——. "'A Born Canadian': The Bonds of Communal Identity in *Anne of Green Gables* and *A Tangled Web*." In Gammel and Epperly, *L.M. Montgomery and Canadian Culture*, 19–30.

——. "Bosom Friends: Lesbian Desire in L.M. Montgomery's Anne Books." *Canadian Literature* 180 (Spring 2004): 12–28.

——. "Educating the Reader: Negotiation in Nineteenth-Century Popular Girls' Stories." PhD dissertation, Queen's University, 1998.

——. "'"Outrageously Sexual" Anne': The Media and Montgomery." In Mitchell, *Storm and Dissonance*, 311–27.

——. "'Sex Matters': L.M. Montgomery, Friendship, and Sexuality." *Children's Literature* 40 (2012): 167–90.

Ronish, Donna Yavorsky. "Sweet Girl Graduates: The Admission of Women to English-Speaking Universities in Canada in the Nineteenth Century." PhD dissertation, Université de Montréal, 1985.

Rootland, Nancy. *Anne's World, Maud's World: The Sacred Sites of L.M. Montgomery*. Halifax: Nimbus, 1996.

Roper, Gordon, S. Ross Beharriell, and Rupert Schieder. "Writers of Fiction 1880–1920." In Klinck, *Literary History of Canada*, 313–39.

Ross, Catherine Sheldrick. "Calling Back the Ghost of the Old-Time Heroine: Duncan, Montgomery, Atwood, Laurence, and Munro." In Reimer, *Such a Simple Little Tale*, 39–55.

———. "Readers Reading L.M. Montgomery." In M.H. Rubio, *Harvesting Thistles*, 23–35.

Rothwell, Erika. "Knitting Up the World: L.M. Montgomery and Maternal Feminism in Canada." In Gammel and Epperly, *L.M. Montgomery and Canadian Culture*, 133–44.

Rowe, Rosemary. "*Anne Made Me Gay*: When Kindred Spirits Get Naked." *Canadian Theatre Review* 149 (Winter 2012): 6–11.

Roy, Wendy. "Home as Middle Ground in Adaptations of *Anne of Green Gables* and *Jalna*." *International Journal of Canadian Studies / Revue internationale d'études canadiennes* 48 (2014): 9–31.

Rubio, Jennie. "'Strewn with Dead Bodies': Women and Gossip in *Anne of Ingleside*." In M.H. Rubio, *Harvesting Thistles*, 167–77.

Rubio, Mary Henley. "*Anne of Green Gables*." In *The Oxford Companion to Canadian Theatre*, edited by Eugene Benson and L.W. Conolly, 24–25. Toronto: Oxford University Press, 1989.

———. "*Anne of Green Gables*: The Architect of Adolescence." In Reimer, *Such a Simple Little Tale*, 65–82.

———. "'A Dusting Off': An Anecdotal Account of Editing the L.M. Montgomery Journals." In Buss and Kadar, *Working in Women's Archives*, 51–78.

———, ed. *Harvesting Thistles: The Textual Garden of L.M. Montgomery; Essays on Her Novels and Journals*. Guelph: Canadian Children's Press, 1994.

———. Introduction to M.H. Rubio, *Harvesting Thistles*, 1–13.

———. "L.M. Montgomery: Scottish-Presbyterian Agency in Canadian Culture." In Gammel and Epperly, *L.M. Montgomery and Canadian Culture*, 89–105.

———. "L.M. Montgomery: Where Does the Voice Come From?" In *Canadiana: Studies in Canadian Literature / Études de littérature canadienne*, edited by Jørn Carlsen and Knud Larsen, 109–19. Aarhus, Denmark: Canadian Studies Conference / Conférence d'études canadiennes, 1984.

———. "Lucy Maud Montgomery." In *Profiles in Canadian Literature* 7, edited by Jeffrey Heath, 37–45. Toronto: Dundurn Press, 1991.

———. *Lucy Maud Montgomery: The Gift of Wings*. 2008. N.p.: Anchor Canada, 2010.

———. "Satire, Realism, and Imagination in *Anne of Green Gables*." *Canadian Children's Literature* 1, no. 3 (Autumn 1975): 27–36.

———. "Uncertainties Surrounding the Death of L.M. Montgomery." In Ledwell and Mitchell, *Anne Around the World*, 45–62.

———. Untitled paper given at From Canada to the World: The Cultural Influence of Lucy Maud Montgomery, University of Guelph, 25 October 2008.

———. "Why L.M. Montgomery's Journals Came to Guelph." In K. McCabe, *The Lucy Maud Montgomery Album*, 473–78.

Rubio, Mary, and Elizabeth Waterston. Afterword to *Chronicles of Avonlea*, by L.M. Montgomery, 238–48. New York: New American Library, 1988. A Signet Classic.

———. Afterword to *The Story Girl*, by L.M. Montgomery, 277–86. New York: New American Library, 1991. A Signet Classic.

———. *Writing a Life: L.M. Montgomery*. Toronto: ECW Press, 1995. Canadian Biography Series.

Russell, Danielle. "A New 'Bend in the Road': Navigating Nationhood through L.M. Montgomery's *Anne of Green Gables*." In *The Nation in Children's Literature: Nations of Childhood*, edited by Christopher (Kit) Kelen and Björn Sundmark, 11–22. New York: Routledge, 2013. Children's Literature and Culture.

Russell, D.W. "L.M. Montgomery: La vie et l'œuvre d'un écrivain populaire." *Études canadiennes / Canadian Studies* 20 (1986): 101–13.

Russell, Ruth Weber, D.W. Russell, and Rea Wilmshurst. *Lucy Maud Montgomery: A Preliminary Bibliography*. Waterloo: University of Waterloo Library, 1986.

Saltman, Judith. *Modern Canadian Children's Books*. Toronto: Oxford University Press, 1987.

Santelmann, Patricia Kelly. "Written as Women Write: *Anne of Green Gables* within the Female Literary Tradition." In M.H. Rubio, *Harvesting Thistles*, 64–73.

Santôka, Taneda. *Santôka zen kushû*. Tokyo: Shun'yôdô, 2002.

Sardella-Ayres, Dawn. "Under the Umbrella: The Author-Heroine's Love Triangle." *Canadian Children's Literature / Littérature canadienne pour la jeunesse* 105–6 (Spring–Summer 2002): 100–13.

Sauerwein, Stan. *Lucy Maud Montgomery: The Incredible Life of the Creator of Anne of Green Gables.* Canmore, AB: Altitude Publishing Canada, 2004. True Canadian Amazing Stories.

Saunders, Tom. "Anne's Author." *Winnipeg Free Press* (Winnipeg, MB), 30 November 1974, 25.

Scanlon, Leslie Goddard. "Alternatives: The Search for a Heroine in the Novels of Lucy Maud Montgomery." MA thesis, Carleton University, 1977.

Schwartz, Lynne Sharon. Introduction to *The Yellow Wallpaper and Other Writings*, by Charlotte Perkins Gilman, vii–xxvii. New York: Bantam, 1989.

Schwarz-Eisler, Hanna. *L.M. Montgomery: A Popular Canadian Writer for Children.* Pfaffenweiler, Germany: Centaurus–Verlagsgesellschaft, 1991.

Schweickart, Patrocinio. "Reading Ourselves: Toward a Feminist Theory of Reading." In *Contemporary Literary Criticism: Literary and Cultural Studies*, edited by Robert Con Davis and Ronald Schleifer, 118–41. 2nd ed. New York: Longman, 1989.

Sclanders, Ian. "Lucy of Green Gables." *Maclean's Magazine* (Toronto, ON), 15 December 1951, 12–13, 33–36.

Seelye, John. *Jane Eyre's American Daughters: From* The Wide, Wide World *to* Anne of Green Gables; *A Study of Marginalized Maidens and What They Mean.* Newark: University of Delaware Press, 2005.

Segal, Elizabeth. "'As the Twig Is Bent ... ': Gender and Childhood Reading." In *Gender and Reading: Essays on Readers, Texts, and Contexts*, edited by Elizabeth A. Flynn and Patrocinio P. Schweickart, 165–87. Baltimore, MD: The Johns Hopkins University Press, 1986.

Senick, Gerard J., ed. *Children's Literature Review 8: Excerpts from Reviews, Criticism, and Commentary on Books for Children.* Detroit: Gale Research Company, 1985.

Seton, Ernest Thompson. "The White Man's Last Opportunity." *Canada West* 3, no. 6 (April 1908): 525–32.

Shaw, Mrs. [Donald]. "What Is the World Coming To?" *Halifax Herald* (Halifax, NS), 5 April 1920. Also in *The Challenge of Modernity: A Reader on Post-Confederation Canada*, by Ian McKay, 336–43. Toronto: McGraw–Hill Ryerson, 1992.

Sheckels, Theodore F., Jr. "In Search of Structures for the Stories of Girls and Women: L.M. Montgomery's Life-Long Struggle." *The American Review of Canadian Studies* 23, no. 4 (Winter 1993): 523–38.

Bibliography

———. *The Island Motif in the Fiction of L.M. Montgomery, Margaret Laurence, Margaret Atwood, and Other Canadian Women Novelists.* New York: Peter Lang, 2003. Studies on Themes and Motifs in Literature 68.

Shields, Carol. "Interview with Carol Shields." With Eleanor Wachtel. *Room of One's Own* 13, no. 1–2 (July 1989): 5–45.

Shimamoto, Kaoru. *Akage no An no o-shaberi eigo ressun.* Tokyo: Asa shupan, 2006.

Shin Nihon dai-saijiki. Tokyo: Kôdan-sha, 1991–92.

Shneidman, Edwin. *Definition of Suicide.* New York: John Wiley and Sons, 1985.

Showalter, Elaine. *A Literature of Their Own: British Women Novelists from Brontë to Lessing.* Princeton: Princeton University Press, 1977.

———. *Sexual Anarchy: Gender and Culture at the Fin de Siècle.* New York: Viking, 1990.

Slane, Andrea. "Guarding a Cultural Icon: Concurrent Intellectual Property Regimes and the Perpetual Protection of *Anne of Green Gables* in Canada." *McGill Law Journal / Revue de droit de McGill* 56, no. 4 (June 2011): 1011–55.

Slater, Katharine. "'The Other Was Whole': *Anne of Green Gables*, Trauma and Mirroring." *The Lion and the Unicorn* 34, no. 2 (April 2010): 167–87.

Smith, Sidonie. *A Poetics of Women's Autobiography: Marginality and the Fictions of Self-Representation.* Bloomington: Indiana University Press, 1987.

Smith-Rosenberg, Carroll. *Disorderly Conduct: Visions of Gender in Victorian America.* New York: Alfred A. Knopf, 1985.

———. "The Female World of Love and Ritual: Relations between Women in Nineteenth-Century America." *Signs: Journal of Women in Culture and Society* 1, no. 1 (Autumn 1975): 1–29.

Snitow, Ann Barr. "Mass Market Romance: Pornography for Women Is Different." In *Powers of Desire: The Politics of Sexuality*, edited by Ann Snitow, Christine Stansell, and Sharon Thompson, 245–63. New York: Monthly Review Press, 1983.

Sobkowska, Krystyna. "The Reception of the 'Anne of Green Gables' Series by Lucy Maud Montgomery in Poland." MA thesis, University of Lodz, 1982–83.

Solt, Marilyn. "The Uses of Setting in *Anne of Green Gables*." In Reimer, *Such a Simple Little Tale*, 57–64.

Somers, Emily. "*An no shinjô* [Anne's Feelings]: Politeness and Passion as *Anime* Paradox in Takahata's *Akage no An*." In Lefebvre, *Textual Transformations in Children's Literature*, 155–73.

Bibliography

Sorfleet, John Robert. "Introduction: L.M. Montgomery: Canadian Authoress."
    Canadian Children's Literature 1, no. 3 (Autumn 1975): 4–7.
———, ed. *L.M. Montgomery: An Assessment*. Guelph: Canadian Children's
    Press, 1976.
———. "Montgomery, L(ucy) M(aud)." In *Twentieth-Century Children's Writ-
    ers*, edited by D.L. Kirkpatrick, 905–8. New York: St. Martin's Press, 1978.
Spacks, Patricia Meyer. *Gossip*. Chicago: The University of Chicago Press, 1985.
———. "In Praise of Gossip." *The Hudson Review* 35, no. 1 (Spring 1982):
    19–38.
Squire, Shelagh J. "Ways of Seeing, Ways of Being: Literature, Place, and
    Tourism in L.M. Montgomery's Prince Edward Island." In *A Few Acres
    of Snow: Literary and Artistic Images of Canada*, edited by Paul Simpson-
    Housley and Glen Norcliffe, 137–47. Toronto: Dundurn Press, 1992.
Stallcup, Jackie E. "'She Knew She Wanted to Kiss Him': Expert Advice and
    Women's Authority in L.M. Montgomery's Works." *Children's Literature
    Association Quarterly* 26, no. 3 (Fall 2001): 121–32.
Stanton, Domna C. "Autogynography: Is the Subject Different?" In *The Female
    Autograph: Theory and Practice of Autobiography from the Tenth to the
    Twentieth Century*, edited by Domna C. Stanton, 3–20. Chicago: The
    University of Chicago Press, 1987.
Steffler, Margaret. "Anne in a 'Globalized' World: Nation, Nostalgia, and
    Postcolonial Perspectives of Home." In Gammel and Lefebvre, *Anne's
    World*, 150–65.
———. "'This Has Been a Day in Hell': Montgomery, Popular Literature, Life
    Writing." In Gammel, *Making Avonlea*, 72–83.
Stellings, Caroline. *The Contest*. Toronto: Second Story Press, 2009. A Gutsy
    Girl Book.
Stobie, Margaret. *Frederick Philip Grove*. New York: Twayne Publishers, 1973.
    Twayne's World Authors Series.
Stoffman, Judy. "Anne in Japanese Popular Culture." *Canadian Children's
    Literature / Littérature canadienne pour la jeunesse* 91–92 (Fall–Winter
    1998): 53–63.
Story, Norah. *The Oxford Companion to Canadian History and Literature*.
    Toronto: Oxford University Press, 1967.
Stott, Jon C. "L.M. Montgomery (1874–1942)." In *Writers for Children:
    Critical Studies of Major Authors since the Seventeenth Century*, edited by
    Jane M. Bingham, 415–22. New York: Charles Scribner's Sons, 1988.
Stott, Jon C., and Raymond E. Jones. *Canadian Books for Children: A Guide
    to Authors and Illustrators*. Toronto: Harcourt Brace Jovanovich Canada,
    1988.

Stouck, David. *Major Canadian Authors: A Critical Introduction.* Lincoln: University of Nebraska Press, 1984.

Strauss, Alix. *Death Becomes Them: Unearthing the Suicides of the Brilliant, the Famous and the Notorious.* New York: HarperCollins, 2009.

Stuart, Jed. "'Nearer to God in Lover's Lane.'" *Winnipeg Free Press* (Winnipeg, MB), 6 September 1975, 44.

Sullivan, Kevin. *Anne of Green Gables: A New Beginning.* Adapted from His Screenplay. Toronto: Key Porter Books, 2008. Toronto: Davenport Press, 2009.

Sullivan, Kevin, and Elizabeth Morgan. *Anne's New Home.* Adapted from *Anne of Green Gables: The Animated Series.* Toronto: Davenport Press, 2010.

Swart, L.A. *Anne of Green Gremlins: Pixie Slayer.* N.p.: n.p., 2010.

Sylvestre, Guy, Brandon Conron, and Carl F. Klinck, eds. *Canadian Writers / Écrivains canadiens: A Biographical Dictionary / Un dictionnaire biographique.* 1964. Rev. ed. Toronto: The Ryerson Press, 1967.

Szwed, John. "Gossip, Drinking and Social Control: Consensus and Communication in a Newfoundland Parish." *Ethnology* 5, no. 4 (October 1966): 434–41.

Tanaka, Shelley, comp. *The Anne of Green Gables Diary.* Illustrated by Wes Lowe. Toronto: Seal Books; New York: Bantam Books, 1987.

Tausky, Thomas E. "L.M. Montgomery and 'The Alpine Path, So Hard, So Steep.'" *Canadian Children's Literature / Littérature canadienne pour la jeunesse* 30 (1983): 5–20.

Taylor, Kate. "Anne of Hokkaido." *The Globe and Mail* (Toronto, ON), 6 July 1991, C1, C3.

Tector, Amy. "A Righteous War? L.M. Montgomery's Depiction of the First World War in *Rilla of Ingleside.*" *Canadian Literature* 179 (Winter 2003): 72–86.

Thomas, Christa Zeller. "The Sweetness of Saying 'Mother'? Maternity and Narrativity in L.M. Montgomery's *Anne of Green Gables.*" *Studies in Canadian Literature / Études en littérature canadienne* 34, no. 2 (2009): 40–57.

Thomas, Clara. "Anne Shirley's American Cousin: *The Girl of the Limberlost.*" In M.H. Rubio, *Harvesting Thistles,* 58–63. Also in *All My Sisters: Essays on the Work of Canadian Women Writers,* by Clara Thomas, 213–22. Ottawa: The Tecumseh Press, 1994.

———. *Canadian Novelists 1920–1945.* Volume 1. Toronto: Longmans, Green and Company, 1946.

———. *Our Nature – Our Voices: A Guidebook to English-Canadian Literature.* Toronto: New Press, 1972.

Thomas, Elizabeth Ebony. "The Pleasures of Dreaming: How L.M. Montgomery Shaped My Lifeworlds." In *A Narrative Compass: Stories That Guide Women's Lives*, edited by Betsy Hearne and Roberta Seelinger Trites, 80–95. Urbana: University of Illinois Press, 2009.

Thomas, Gillian. "The Decline of Anne: Matron vs. Child." In Reimer, *Such a Simple Little Tale*, 23–28.

Thompson, Kent. Introduction to *Stories from Atlantic Canada*, selected by Kent Thompson, ix–xv. Toronto: Macmillan of Canada, 1973.

Thomson, Denise. "National Sorrow, National Pride: Commemoration of War in Canada, 1918–1945." *Journal of Canadian Studies / Revue d'études canadiennes* 30, no. 4 (Winter 1995–1996): 5–27.

Tiessen, Hildi Froese, and Paul Gerard Tiessen. Introduction to Montgomery, *After Green Gables*, 3–52.

Tiessen, Paul. "Opposing Pacifism: L.M. Montgomery and the Trouble with Ephraim Weber." In Mitchell, *Storm and Dissonance*, 131–41.

Tiessen, Paul, and Hildi Froese Tiessen. "Lucy Maud Montgomery's Ephraim Weber (1870–1956): 'A Slight Degree of Literary Recognition.'" *Journal of Mennonite Studies* 11 (1993): 43–54.

The Times Literary Supplement (London, UK). "Lives That Led to Fame." 23 November 1956, xi.

Townsend, John Rowe. *Written for Children*. Harmondsworth, UK: Penguin, 1975.

Toye, William, ed. *The Oxford Companion to Canadian Literature*. Toronto: Oxford University Press, 1983.

Trillin, Calvin. "Anne of Red Hair: What Do the Japanese See in *Anne of Green Gables*?" In Gammel and Epperly, *L.M. Montgomery and Canadian Culture*, 213–21.

Trollope, Anthony. "A Walk in the Wood." *Good Words* (London, UK), September 1879, 595–600.

Turner, Gordon Philip. "The Protagonists' Initiatory Experiences in the Canadian Bildungsroman: 1908–1971." PhD dissertation, University of British Columbia, 1979.

Turner, Margaret. "'I Mean to Try, As Far As in Me Lies, to Paint My Life and Deeds Truthfully': Autobiographical Process in the L.M. Montgomery Journals." In M.H. Rubio, *Harvesting Thistles*, 93–100.

Tye, Diane. *Baking as Biography: A Life Story in Recipes*. Montreal: McGill–Queen's University Press, 2010.

———. "Multiple Meanings Called Cavendish: The Interaction of Tourism with Traditional Culture." *Journal of Canadian Studies / Revue d'études canadiennes* 29, no. 1 (Spring 1994): 122–34.

Bibliography

Tylee, Clare. *The Great War and Women's Consciousness: Images of Militarism and Womanhood in Women's Writings, 1914–64.* Iowa City: University of Iowa Press, 1990.

Vance, Jonathan F. *Death So Noble: Memory, Meaning and the First World War.* Vancouver: UBC Press, 1997.

———. "The Soldier as Novelist: Literature, History and the Great War." *Canadian Literature* 179 (Winter 2003): 22–37.

Vipond, Mary. "Best Sellers in English Canada, 1899–1918: An Overview." *Journal of Canadian Fiction* 24 (1979): 96–119.

———. "Best Sellers in English Canada: 1919–1928." *Journal of Canadian Fiction* 35–36 (1986): 73–105.

Urquhart, Jane. Afterword to *Emily Climbs*, by L.M. Montgomery, 330–34. Toronto: McClelland and Stewart, 1989. New Canadian Library.

———. *L.M. Montgomery.* Toronto: Penguin Canada, 2009. Extraordinary Canadians.

Wachowicz, Barbara. "L.M. Montgomery: At Home in Poland." *Canadian Children's Literature / Littérature canadienne pour la jeunesse* 46 (1987): 7–36.

Wales, Julia Grace. Review of *The Story of L.M. Montgomery*, by Hilda M. Ridley. *Canadian Author & Bookman* 32, no. 1 (Spring 1956): 20.

Walker, Elspeth. Review of *The Wheel of Things: A Biography of L.M. Montgomery, Author of* Anne of Green Gables, by Mollie Gillen. *The Lethbridge Herald* (Lethbridge, AB), 12 February 1976, 5.

Walkowitz, Judith R. *City of Dreadful Delight: Narratives of Sexual Danger in Late-Victorian London.* Chicago: The University of Chicago Press, 1992.

Waller, Adrian. "Lucy Maud of Green Gables." *Reader's Digest* (Canadian edition), December 1975, 38–43.

Wallner, Alexandra. *Lucy Maud Montgomery: The Author of* Anne of Green Gables. New York: Holiday House, 2006.

Warne, Randi R. *Literature as Pulpit: The Christian Social Activism of Nellie L. McClung.* Waterloo: Wilfrid Laurier University Press, 1993.

Waterston, Elizabeth. *Kindling Spirit: L.M. Montgomery's* Anne of Green Gables. Toronto: ECW Press, 1993. Canadian Fiction Studies 19.

———. "L.M. Montgomery (1884 [*sic*]–1942): Witness and Wife." In *Called to Witness: Profiles of Canadian Presbyterians; A Supplement to Enduring Witness*, Volume 4, edited by John S. Moir, 61–73. Hamilton: Committee on History, The Presbyterian Church of Canada, 1999.

———. *Magic Island: The Fictions of L.M. Montgomery.* Don Mills, ON: Oxford University Press, 2008.

———. "Orphans, Twins, and L.M. Montgomery." In *Family Fictions in Canadian Literature*, edited by Peter Hinchcliffe, 68–76. Waterloo: University of Waterloo Press, 1988.

———. *Survey: A Short History of Canadian Literature*. Toronto: Methuen, 1973.

Waterston, Elizabeth, and Mary Henley Rubio. Afterword to *Anne of Avonlea*, by L.M. Montgomery, 274–82. New York: New American Library, 1987. A Signet Classic.

———. Afterword to *Anne of Green Gables*, by L.M. Montgomery, 307–14. New York: New American Library, 1987. A Signet Classic.

———. Afterword to *Anne of the Island*, by L.M. Montgomery, 239–46. New York: New American Library, 1991. A Signet Classic.

———. Afterword to *Anne's House of Dreams*, by L.M. Montgomery, 277–86. New York: New American Library, 1989. A Signet Classic.

Watkins, Vernon. Foreword to Grahame, The Golden Age *and* Dream Days, vii–xv.

Watson, Julia. "Shadowed Presence: Modern Women Writers' Autobiographies and the Other." In Olney, *Studies in Autobiography*, 180–89.

Weale, David. "'No Scope for Imagination': Another Side of Anne of Green Gables." *The Island Magazine* 20 (Fall–Winter 1986): 3–8.

Weaver, Robyn. "Terminal (Mis)diagnosis and the Physician-Patient Relationship in L.M. Montgomery's *The Blue Castle*." *Journal of General Internal Medicine* 25, no. 10 (October 2010): 1129–31.

Weber, Brenda R. "Confessions of a Kindred Spirit with an Academic Bent." In Gammel, *Making Avonlea*, 43–57.

Weigle, Marta. "Women as Verbal Artists: Reclaiming the Sisters of Enheduanna." *Frontiers: A Journal of Women Studies* 3, no. 3 (Autumn 1978): 1–9.

Weiss-Townsend, Janet. "Sexism Down on the Farm? *Anne of Green Gables*." In Reimer, *Such a Simple Little Tale*, 109–17.

Whitaker, Muriel A. "'Queer Children': L.M. Montgomery's Heroines." *Canadian Children's Literature* 1, no. 3 (Autumn 1975): 50–59.

White, Gavin. "Falling Out of the Haystack: L.M. Montgomery and Lesbian Desire." *Canadian Children's Literature / Littérature canadienne pour la jeunesse* 102 (Summer 2001): 43–59.

———. "L.M. Montgomery and the French." *Canadian Children's Literature / Littérature canadienne pour la jeunesse* 78 (Summer 1995): 65–68.

———. "The Religious Thought of L.M. Montgomery." In M.H. Rubio, *Harvesting Thistles*, 84–88.

Whittier, John Greenleaf. *The Complete Poetical Works of Whittier*. Boston: Houghton Mifflin, 1894.

Wiggins, Genevieve. *L.M. Montgomery*. New York: Twayne Publishers, 1992. Twayne's World Authors Series 834.

———. Review of *The Fragrance of Sweet-Grass: L.M. Montgomery's Heroines and the Pursuit of Romance*, by Elizabeth Rollins Epperly. *The American Review of Canadian Studies* 23, no. 3 (Autumn 1993): 460–62.

Willis, Lesley. "The Bogus Ugly Duckling: Anne Shirley Unmasked." *The Dalhousie Review* 56, no. 2 (Summer 1976): 246–51.

Wilmshurst, Rea. "L.M. Montgomery's Use of Quotations and Allusions in the 'Anne' Books." *Canadian Children's Literature / Littérature canadienne pour la jeunesse* 56 (1989): 15–45.

———. "Quotations and Allusions in L.M. Montgomery's Other Novels." Unpublished study, 1990.

Wilson, Budge. *Before Green Gables*. Toronto: Penguin Canada; New York: G.P. Putnam's Sons; London: Puffin Books, 2008.

Wilson, Eric. *The Green Gables Detectives: A Liz Austen Mystery*. Don Mills, ON: Collins Publishers, 1987.

Wilson, Jane. *The Strike at Putney Church*. Toronto: Playwright's Co-op, 1990.

Wilson, Lady (Mrs. Harold Wilson). Foreword to *Emily of New Moon*, by L.M. Montgomery, vi–x. London: Harrap Books, 1977.

Winter, Jay. *Sites of Memory, Sites of Mourning*. Cambridge: Cambridge University Press, 1995.

Winter, Jay, and Blaine Baggett. *The Great War and the Shaping of the Twentieth Century*. New York: Penguin Studio, 1996.

Winter, Jay, and Antoine Prost. *The Great War in History: Debates and Controversies, 1914 to the Present*. Cambridge: Cambridge University Press, 2005.

Wood, Kate. "In the News: *Anne of Green Gables* and PEI's Turn-of-the-Century Press." *Canadian Children's Literature / Littérature canadienne pour la jeunesse* 99 (Fall 2000): 23–42.

Woodcock, George. *Northern Spring: The Flowering of Canadian Literature*. Vancouver: Douglas and McIntyre, 1987.

———. "Possessing the Land: Notes on Canadian Fiction." In *The Canadian Imagination: Dimension of a Literary Culture*, edited by David Staines, 69–96. Cambridge, MA: Harvard University Press, 1977.

———. *The World of Canadian Writing: Critiques and Recollections*. Vancouver: Douglas and McIntyre; Seattle: University of Washington Press, 1980.

Woods, G.A. "The (W)rite of Passage: From Childhood to Womanhood in Lucy Maud Montgomery's Emily Novels." In *Gender and Narrativity*, edited by Barry Rutland, 147–58. Ottawa: Carleton University Press, 1997.

Woodsworth, James S. *Strangers within Our Gates, or Coming Canadians.* 1909. Edited by Marilyn Barber. Toronto: University of Toronto Press, 1972.

Woolf, Virginia. *A Room of One's Own/Three Guineas.* Edited by Michèle Barrett. London: Penguin Books, 1993.

Woster, Emily S. "Intertextuality and Life Writing: The Reading Autobiography of L.M. Montgomery." PhD dissertation, Illinois State University, 2013.

Wright, Shirley. "Images of Canada in English Canadian Landscape for Children: Or, After *Anne of Green Gables.*" In *Sharing: A Challenge for All*, edited by John G. Wright, 179–94. Kalamazoo: Western Michigan University, 1982.

Wullschläger, Jackie. *Inventing Wonderland: The Lives and Fantasies of Lewis Carroll, Edward Lear, J.M. Barrie, Kenneth Grahame, and A.A. Milne.* New York: Free Press, 1995.

Wyile, Herb. *Anne of Tim Hortons: Globalization and the Reshaping of Atlantic-Canadian Literature.* Waterloo: Wilfrid Laurier University Press, 2011.

Yeast, Denyse. "Negotiating Friendships: The Reading and Writing of L.M. Montgomery." In M.H. Rubio, *Harvesting Thistles*, 113–25.

York, Lorraine. *Literary Celebrity in Canada.* Toronto: University of Toronto Press, 2007.

Young, Alan R. "L.M. Montgomery's *Rilla of Ingleside* (1920): Romance and the Experience of War." In *Myth and Milieu: Atlantic Literature and Culture 1918–1939*, edited by Gwendolyn Davies, 95–122. Fredericton: Acadiensis Press, 1993.

———. "'We Throw the Torch': Canadian Memorials of the Great War and the Mythology of Heroic Sacrifice." *Journal of Canadian Studies / Revue d'études canadiennes* 24, no. 4 (Winter 1989–1990): 5–28.

Zipes, Jack. "Introduction: The Anne-Girl: She Is What We're Not." In *Anne of Green Gables*, by L.M. Montgomery, ix–xxi. New York: The Modern Library, 2008.

Zwicker, Linda. *The Hope Chest of Arabella King.* Toronto: HarperCollins Publishers, 1991. New York: Bantam Skylark, 1992. Road to Avonlea 10.

———. *Misfits and Miracles.* Toronto: HarperCollins Publishers, 1992. New York: Bantam Skylark, 1993. Road to Avonlea 20.

Index

Index

Index

Index

Index

Index

Index